DATE DUE

MAY 1 1 2006					

DEMCO, INC. 38-3012

The
PSYCHOLOGY
of
PERSONALITY

VIEWPOINTS, RESEARCH, AND APPLICATIONS

About the Cover

"The Kiss" was painted by Gustav Klimt (1862–1918), a turn-of-the-century Viennese painter noted for his use of vibrant colors and striking and sensual images. I personally selected this painting for the cover of the book because it is my favorite work of art. In this painting, you get a sense of Klimt's passionate personality for art, for love, and for life. I have tried to emulate some of Klimt's passion in the writing of this book.

B.J.C.

The *PSYCHOLOGY* *of* *PERSONALITY*

VIEWPOINTS, RESEARCH, AND APPLICATIONS

Bernardo J. Carducci

Indiana University Southeast

Brooks/Cole Publishing Company

I(T)P® An International Thomson Publishing Company

Pacific Grove • Albany • Belmont • Bonn • Boston • Cincinnati • Detroit • Johannesburg • London • Madrid
Melbourne • Mexico City • New York • Paris • Singapore • Tokyo • Toronto • Washington

Sponsoring Editor: Marianne Taflinger
Marketing Team: Marcy Perman, Deborah Petit, Alicia Barelli
Editorial Assistant: Scott Brearton
Production Coordinator: Karen Ralling
Production Service: Hespenheide Design
Manuscript Editor: Christine Thillen
Permissions Editor: Lillian Campobasso
Interior Design: Hespenheide Design
Interior Illustration: Hespenheide Design

Cover Design: Vernon T. Boes
Cover Illustration: *The Kiss*, Gustav Klimt.
   Erich Lessing/Art Resource, NY
Art Coordinator: Hespenheide Design
Photo Editor: Loredana Carson/Hespenheide Design
Indexer: Sonsie Carbonara Conroy
Typesetting: Hespenheide Design
Cover Printing: West Publishing Company
Printing and Binding: West Publishing Company

WEST PUBLISHING
Acquiring Editor: Robert Jucha
Production Coordinator: Sharon Kavanagh

COPYRIGHT © 1998 by Brooks/Cole Publishing Company
A division of International Thomson Publishing Inc.
I(T)P The ITP logo is a registered trademark under license.

For more information, contact:

BROOKS/COLE PUBLISHING COMPANY
511 Forest Lodge Road
Pacific Grove, CA 93950
USA

International Thomson Publishing Europe
Berkshire House 168-173
High Holborn
London WC1V 7AA
England

Thomas Nelson Australia
102 Dodds Street
South Melbourne, 3205
Victoria, Australia

Nelson Canada
1120 Birchmount Road
Scarborough, Ontario
Canada M1K 5G4

International Thomson Editores
Seneca 53
Col. Polanco
México, D. F., México
C.P. 11560

International Thomson Publishing GmbH
Königswinterer Strasse 418
53227 Bonn
Germany

International Thomson Publishing Asia
221 Henderson Road
#05-10 Henderson Building
Singapore 0315

International Thomson Publishing Japan
Hirakawacho Kyowa Building, 3F
2-2-1 Hirakawacho
Chiyoda-ku, Tokyo 102
Japan

Printed in the United States of America

10 9 8 7 6 5 4 3 2 1

Library of Congress Cataloging-in-Publication Data

Carducci, Bernardo J.
   The psychology of personality : viewpoints, research, and applications / Bernardo J. Carducci.
     p. cm.
   Includes bibliographical references and index.
   ISBN 0-534-35019-4
   1. Personality.   I. Title.
BF698.C177   1998   97-25802
155.2—dc21   CIP

For Rozana,
a loving daughter who always made me
feel like a dad, even when the many miles
between us made me just a father.

ABOUT THE AUTHOR

Bernardo J. Carducci (Ph.D., Kansas State University, 1981) is professor of psychology at Indiana University Southeast, where he has taught classes on personality psychology, psychology of adjustment, and introductory psychology for the past 18 years. He is a fellow of Division 1: General Psychology and Division 2: Teaching of Psychology of the American Psychological Association, past national president of the Council of Teachers of Undergraduate Psychology, member of the *Journal of Business and Psychology* editorial board, and the director of the Indiana University Southeast Shyness Research Institute. In addition to his research interest in the study of shyness, Bernie's professional writings related to such topics as teaching activities to enhance classroom instruction, student development, and career opportunities for psychology majors have appeared in *Teaching of Psychology, Teaching Psychology: A Handbook,* and many American Psychological Association–sponsored publications on teaching. For the past ten years, eight of those as treasurer, Bernie has served on the Board of Directors of the Southern Indiana Transitional Shelter, which provides independent-living housing to abused women and their children. A lover of all types of music, Bernie finally decided to try his hand at becoming a musician and, against the advice of family and friends, started accordion lessons fours years ago at the age of 41. On starting to play the accordion at his age, Bernie said, "Trying to learn something totally different, like playing the accordion, has given me a greater appreciation for students who are taking a course in personality psychology for the first time. It has helped me to become a more sensitive teacher and writer, but has done nothing to improve the quality of my playing of the accordion."

Contents

CHAPTER 14
ANXIETY: AN ALL-ENCOMPASSING INTRAPERSONAL PROCESS OF PERSONALITY   411

Features

APPLICATIONS IN PERSONALITY PSYCHOLOGY

YOU CAN DO IT

The "Personality" of this Personality Textbook: Special Features of this Book

When I initially began to consider writing a personality text, one of the first things I had to do was to think about the type of text I wanted to write. I began working on this book by looking at the personality textbooks I had used in my classes in the past and other books already available. When examining these books, I discovered that personality textbooks, like the personalities of various people, are very different from one another. Again, like people, it was as if each textbook had its own "personality," or characteristic way in which the material was presented. While each of these books did a good job in its own way, they did not provide the balance of personality theory, research, and the application of personality psychology in a manner consistent with what I wanted to present to the students in my classes. Because I could not find a book with the right "personality," I decided to write this book.

After deciding to write this book, I then had to think about the personality of this text. Thus, I not only had to think about what I wanted to say in the book but how I was going to say it. Following much consideration, I decided that I wanted to write a book that would have a style, or personality, that would be different from the other personality textbooks. More specifically, I wanted to write a textbook that would provide a balanced coverage of personality theory, research, and applications in a manner that would be interesting to read, easy to learn from, and convey the enthusiasm I have for the field of personality psychology. In developing the type of book I

had in mind, I decided to include a number of special features. A brief description of these features is presented in the following paragraphs. In a sense, these special features are the characteristics of this book's personality.

Special Learning Aids: To Ease Your Efforts and Maximize Your Success

This textbook has a number of built-in learning aids that are specifically designed to make it interesting to read, as well as to maximize your understanding of the material presented. For example, each chapter starts with a chapter overview, which is designed to provide a quick synopsis of the material to be covered in the chapter. Throughout the book, the important terms are in **bold print**, like this, and are defined at the end of each chapter. Providing you with these definitions at the end of the chapter will make it possible for you to get the meaning of important terms without having to interrupt your reading to turn to the glossary at the end of the book. At the end of each chapter, a summary of the chapter will be presented. A review of this summary after reading the chapter will serve to remind you of the major points discussed.

The Use of Examples: Variety is the Spice of Life. When reading this book, you will notice a few things about my writing style. One of the first things you will notice is that I have tried to supplement the material with a number of examples. Some of the examples will occur in parentheses within the sentence you are reading while others will be much more elaborate. Providing you with these examples will help make the material more concrete and, therefore, more meaningful and easier to learn. I have tried to select examples that not only illustrate the point being made or the concept being presented but also have some relevance to the type of "everyday living experiences" most of us have probably encountered. As you will see, these examples involve family, friends, and lovers; work, school, and leisure activities; and psychology, sociology, biology, criminology, medicine, business, marketing, nursing, education, and human resources, to name just a few. Through the extensive use of examples, I wanted to show you how this book is not only a textbook about personality psychology but about life in general.

The Use of Tables and Figures: A Picture is Worth a Thousand Words. You will also notice that I have included a number of pictorial and other visual aids in the form of photographs, tables, and figures. All of the photographs in this book have been selected by me to help illustrate in a more dramatic way a particular point being made in the book when words alone would not do (see the photograph on page 111). Some of the tables will contain material summarizing the important points of particular sections of each chapter (see Figure 3.5 on page 75). When reading this book, it is possible for you to make sure you have mastered all the major points in a specific section by reviewing the material presented in these summary tables before going on to the next section. Some of the figures you will see will be used to illustrate certain concepts that are better understood when presented visually than simply reading about them (see Figure 1.1 on page 6). Other tables, figures, and graphs will be used to summarize the statistical results of research being discussed (see Figure 1.3 on page 18).

The Use of Box Inserts: Boxing Your Ears Off. Another special learning aid of this book is the material presented in the "boxes." These boxes are designed to highlight and extend the presentation of specific material that I believe you will find of special interest. You will notice three distinctively different types of boxes. One type of box insert is entitled "Applications in Personality Psychology" (see Application box on page 8). These Application boxes will present examples of how personality psychology has been applied to a variety of interesting and important areas, as well as demonstrating the relevance and implications of personality psychology in our lives.

A second type of box insert is entitled "You Can Do It" (see page 45). In these boxes, you will have the opportunity to complete a variety of exercises and projects designed to illustrate specific concepts discussed in the text. All of these exercises and projects are safe, ethical, and do not require any elaborate apparatus. Completing the exercises in these boxes will give you a feel for what it is like to do your own personality research.

The third type of box insert is entitled "A Closer Look" (see page 33). These boxes will include in-depth examples and illustrative material of certain concepts and topics being presented. In addition to providing you with a better understanding of the material, these boxes will make it possible to take "a closer look" at a selected number of special topics by developing them in more detail without disturbing the overall depth of coverage of other topics.

Thus, the special features of this book are designed to give it its own personality. These features are also designed to make this book interesting and informative to read and a book from which it is easy to learn. Finally, These features are designed to make this book fun and to convey the enjoyment I have when I teach, write, and talk about personality psychology.

Beyond The Psychology of Personality: Getting Your Money's Worth

One of the most frequent comments I hear students make about their textbooks is the high price they must pay. Such comments are not only common but also very familiar; I can remember making those same comments. While the pricing of this textbook is beyond my control, I have decided that I would deal with the price of textbooks by writing a book that would allow you to maximize your return on your initial investment. More specifically, I have tried to write a book that is not only about personality psychology but many other aspects of life as well. As such, I have tried to present you with information that will not only be of benefit to you for this course in personality psychology but other courses you will take throughout your college career. I believe you will find this book to be a valuable source of ideas as well as a reference book to help you write speeches and term papers in your other classes both inside and outside of psychology. I hope you will get your money's worth out of this book by using it again and again. I also hope that you will talk to friends, co-workers, family members, and acquaintances about what you are reading and learning from this book. Sharing what you are learning from this book will not only help you to learn the material better, but it will also help you to get more value for what you paid. The more people who benefit from what is written in this book, the greater the return on your initial investment. More specifically, you can share this book and the knowledge you have gained from studying it with others to help them see how personality psychology can be applied to their college career and beyond. In my view, keeping this book to use in your other classes and sharing it with others is the highest compliment you could pay to an author of a textbook. I hope my efforts are worthy of such a compliment from you.

The Pervasiveness of Personality Psychology: On Knowing How and Where to Look

By reading this book, I hope to make it possible for you to realize that personality psychology is all around you. All you have to do is know how and where to look for it. With the help of this book and your instructor, you should be able to start viewing the world through the eyes of a personality psychologist. Is such a view better than others? All I can say is that my life is much more interesting and exciting since I have become involved in the study of personality psychology. I hope my sense of excitement and enthusiasm is contagious.

While I realize that personality textbooks, unlike people, really do not have personalities, after spending so much time and energy, after all of the good times and bad times, after all of the pleasant and unpleasant memories I have associated with writing this book, I have almost come to view it as a unique person with a unique personality for whom I care a great deal and want other people to like, as well. With this in mind, let me say that I have made every attempt to write a textbook that will give you a thorough coverage of the field of personality psychology in a manner that you will find interesting and with special features that will make it possible for you to get the most out of this book in the time you spend reading it. I hope that this book meets with your approval.

A Request For Help: Let's Keep In Touch

I would like to hear from you. Do you have examples, ideas for topics, or constructive criticism? If you care to contact me, here is how I can be reached:

Bernardo J. Carducci
Department of Psychology
Indiana University Southeast
New Albany, IN 47150
e-mail: bcarducc@IUS.Indiana.edu
fax: 812-941-2591

I look forward to hearing from you soon. And, I wish you continued success. Let's keep in touch.

Best regards,
Bernardo J. Carducci

ACKNOWLEDGMENTS

Some Words of Thanks

While the many hours I spent alone at my computer might suggest that writing this book was an individual effort, nothing could be further from the truth. I would like to acknowledge those individuals who had a hand in making this book possible, whether they were aware of their contribution or not.

Madora Manson was a high school art teacher who always saw artistic greatness and a creative personality in the efforts of all of her students, even those without any artistic talent, like me. Chris Cozby was the person who sparked my initial interest in the study of psychology when I was an aimless undergraduate seeking a college major after my dismal attempt to play college-level football led me to reject physical education as a major. Stanley Woll taught an undergraduate course in personality theories that excited my interest in the study of personality and served to solidify my career choice—to be a personality psychologist. Bill Griffitt taught me how to be a personality psychologist during those many informal discussions in his office. Whenever I asked, David G. Myers shared his advice about the behind-the-scenes process of writing a textbook so that I could take his vast experience and turn it into my experience.

I would like to acknowledge the support of Indiana University Southeast for creating the type of environment that makes writing a book possible. Within the university, there are several people whose efforts I must acknowledge. I want to thank Thomas P. Wolf, my "boss," who understood when I

seemed to be preoccupied with other concerns but never stopped asking "How's the book?" Brigette Colligan and Lesley Schulz provided clerical and editorial assistance that kept many versions of the manuscript flowing. A special debt of gratitude goes to Gabrielle Carr, Jacqueline Johnson, Dennis Kreps, Marty Rosen, Kevin Peers, and especially Nancy Totten, who are all reference librarians that, I am convinced, searched from here to the moon to obtain many of the reference sources I needed to write this book. To them, I owe a tremendous debt of gratitude.

Bob Jucha was the acquisition editor of the book and guided me through the initial rough spots. Marianne Taflinger welcomed my book to Brooks/Cole with generous warmth and support that made me realize right away that she was someone who really understood what I was trying to do with my book. Marianne did everything you would expect an editor to do and more. Karen Ralling served as production editor and made sure all of the important tasks were done on time with a sense of calm and decisiveness that seemed to override my tendency to procrastinate. Vernon Boes designed a magnificent book cover based on my favorite work of art. Gary Hespenheide and his staff at Hespenheide Design created a very "reader friendly" page format throughout the book. Lillian Campobasso managed all of the details required to secure the necessary permissions for the copyrighted material used in the book. Faith Stoddard managed the production of the *Student Study Guide* and *Instructor's Manual* that supplement this textbook and serve to complete the "total package" for *The Psychology of Personality*.

I would also like to acknowledge those individuals who served as manuscript reviewers and provided me with a variety of insightful comments that helped to make my words into a book. These individuals are: Dr. Joel Aronoff, Michigan State University; Dr. Michael D. Dwyer, Baldwin Wallace College; Dr. Jon B. Ellis, East Tennessee State University; Dr. Anthony Fazio, University of Wisconsin–Milwaukee; Dr. Colleen Gift, Highland Community College; Dr. William Griffitt, Kansas State University; Dr. W. Bruce Haslam, Weber State University; Dr. Thomas Holtgraves, Ball State University; Dr. Gale F. Hicks, Eastern Washington University; Dr. Scott Huebner, Georgia State University; Dr. Trina Nahm-Mijo, Hawaii Community College; Dr. Ronald E. Riggio, Claremont McKenna College; Dr. Thomas Schoeneman, Lewis and Clark College; Dr. Jane Spain, High Point University; Dr. John Stabler, Georgia State University; Dr. David B. Sugarman, Rhode Island College; Dr. Alvin Y. Wang, University of Central Florida; Dr. John D. York, McAllen Independent School District.

Finally, many very special words of acknowledgment are expressed to Jan Carducci, my wife, who served as a source of encouragement, comfort, support, and inspiration in a way that can come only from a loving heart. To our dogs, Vinny, Bub, Foley, Solomon, Sadie, and in memory of Maddie, I want to say thanks for reminding me what it really means to live a dog's life, which at times I wanted to believe was the life of a textbook writer.

Like I said, this book is the product of many individuals. The personality of each of these individuals has found its way into this book about personality psychology, and this book is much better as a result of their efforts. To all, once again, I say, "Thanks."

Bernardo J. Carducci

The Scope and Methods of Personality: An Introduction to the Psychology of Personality

Welcome to the study of the psychology of personality. Part One serves as a general introduction to the study of personality. As part of this introduction, you will be exposed to information that will help you understand the scope of personality psychology by illustrating how personality is defined and what constitutes the study of personality psychology. You will also be exposed to the methods of personality psychology by considering the research strategies and assessment techniques personality psychologists use to gather information while studying the underlying nature, operation, and development of personality, as well as how this information can be used in applications to our everyday living experiences. The information you gain in Part One will lay the foundation for all of the viewpoints, research, and applications of personality psychology you will be exposed to in the remainder of this book.

CHAPTER 1

The Psychology of Personality: An Overview to the Study of the Person

CHAPTER OVERVIEW: A PREVIEW OF COMING ATTRACTIONS

*P*eople use the word personality *every day. They say, "He has such a dynamic personality" or "She gets her personality from her mother's side of the family." But most people do not really understand what the study of* **personality** *is all about. In this chapter, you will learn what* **personality psychologists** *mean by personality, as well as the types of questions they ask and the research methods they use.*

Defining Personality: Putting the Word Personality into Words

Think for a moment about the word *personality* and how it is used. Now compare your definition with those of some experts in the field (see "A Closer Look" below).

A Closer Look:

How Personality Psychologists Define Personality: Words from the Wise

The way personality psychologists define **personality** has changed over the years (Pervin, 1990). Here is how some prominent personality psychologists have defined personality:

▲ "The dynamic organization within the individual of those psychophysical systems that determine his characteristic behavior and thought"—Gordon W. Allport (1961, p. 28)

▲ "The distinctive patterns of behavior (including thoughts and emotions) that characterize each individual's adaptation to the situations of his or her life"—Walter Mischel (1986, p. 4)

▲ "Those characteristics of the person or of people generally that account for consistent patterns of behavior"—Lawrence A. Pervin (1989, p. 4)

▲ "A person's unique pattern of traits"—J. P. Guilford (1959, p. 5)

▲ "The most adequate conceptualization of a person's behavior in all its detail"—David McClelland (1951, p. 69)

▲ "That which permits a prediction of what a person will do in a given situation"—Raymond B. Cattell (1950, p. 2)

Upon reading the preceding quotations, you might conclude that there are almost as many definitions of personality as there are authors (Pervin, 1990). But all the definitions express a common concern for using personality to help predict and explain people's behavior. The major lesson to be learned is that like so many other complex (e.g., origin of the universe) and interesting (e.g., why people fall in love) things in life, the human personality is not easily defined. Ideally, students studying the psychology

of personality will develop a healthy tolerance for diversity and an appreciation that most of the important things in life do not come packaged in simple, concise categories.

Common Features of Definitions of Personality: Uniqueness, Consistency, and Content and Process

Developing a definition of personality that is accepted by everyone studying personality does seem difficult. But it is useful to identify certain features common to most of these definitions.

Uniqueness of the Individual

Most definitions of personality include some statement about the uniqueness of an individual's personality. This uniqueness can be explained from various theoretical viewpoints held by different personality psychologists. A biological viewpoint might consider differences in bodily processes (e.g., hormonal levels). A learning viewpoint might consider distinctive reinforcement patterns (e.g., aggressiveness being rewarded). And a Freudian viewpoint might emphasize early childhood experiences (e.g., parent-child interactions). But no matter which theoretical viewpoint a personality psychologist holds, any definition of personality *must* take into account that each person is unique.

Consistency of Behavior

Personality psychologists generally assume some degree of continuity in an individual's personality. As a result, another feature common to most definitions of personality is a concern for the consistency of behavior across time and situations. By assuming consistency across time, personality psychologists can link high-risk behavior in high school (e.g., riding a motorcycle) with a decision in adulthood to enter a high-risk occupation (e.g., police officer). By assuming consistency across situations, they can link the competitive nature displayed by an individual while playing tennis with the desire to be the top sales representative in the company. If behavioral consistency did not exist, studying personality would make little sense.

Emphasizing behavioral consistency does not mean an individual's personality never changes. Concerns with the consistency of behavior are at the heart of some of the most controversial debates in personality psychology. The degree of behavioral consistency is influenced by the extent to which situational factors, as well as one's personality, determine thoughts, feelings, and behavior.

Content and Process of Personality

In the words of highly regarded personality psychologist Gordon W. Allport, "Personality is something that does something" (1937, p. 48). By "is something," Allport refers to the content of personality. Each major personality theory discussed in this book offers a somewhat different explanation of the basic content of the human personality. By "does something," Allport refers to the process of personality, the dynamic nature by which the contents of the personality influence the individual's thoughts, feelings, and behavior.

The content and process features of personality are interrelated. The basic makeup of the human personality directly influences—across time and situations—how the personality operates. For example, some personality psychologists assume that various traits make up the basic content of the human personality and also influence behavior. They would explain the aggressive style of the office tyrant across a variety of situations as resulting from a personality that contains a combination of the traits of aggressiveness and hostility. They would attribute variations in the uniqueness and behavioral consistency of other office workers to other numerous combinations of personality traits.

Combining common features such as those noted to formulate a definition of personality is significant, because it determines how a personality psychologist views the development, measurement, and modification of the human personality. Thus, a definition of personality is far more than simply a series of words.

The Scope of Personality Psychology: What Personality Psychologists Do

The scope of personality psychology goes far beyond simply defining terms. Some general areas of study are presented in this section.

Theory Development: Viewpoints of Personality

Theory development is one of the most important areas of study within personality psychology. A **theory** serves many important purposes in the study of personality. A particular theoretical viewpoint determines the research questions that are asked about personality, the methodology used to answer these questions, what is done to influence personality development, and the treatment used to modify an individual's personality, if a change is necessary.

There are many different theoretical viewpoints of the human personality, each of them explaining personality from a different perspective. Figure 1.1 illustrates how the same behavior is interpreted differently from various theoretical viewpoints. None of the different viewpoints is right or wrong; they simply vary in how useful they are in helping personality psychologists to understand behavior.

Personality psychologists use certain criteria to assess how much better one theory is than another (Hall & Lindzey, 1978; Levy, 1970). The criterion of internal consistency requires that assumptions, principles, and dynamics of a particular theory of personality fit with one another. The more logically the various pieces of the theory fit together, the more favorably the theory is evaluated. The criterion of comprehensiveness focuses on how many aspects of personality (e.g., morality, aggression, and anxiety) are covered by the theory. The more comprehensive a theory, the more favorably it is evaluated. The criterion of **parsimony** suggests, all other things being equal, that the more simple a theory is (e.g., fewer assumptions and principles), the more adequate it is. The criterion of utility has to do with how useful the theory is in stimulating additional research, predicting various outcomes, or being applied to different problems (e.g., personnel selection, reducing shyness, and treating

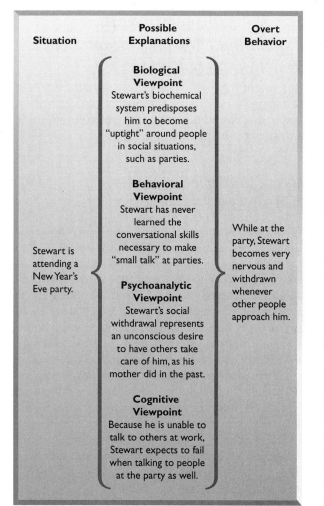

Situation	Possible Explanations	Overt Behavior

Biological Viewpoint
Stewart's biochemical system predisposes him to become "uptight" around people in social situations, such as parties.

Behavioral Viewpoint
Stewart has never learned the conversational skills necessary to make "small talk" at parties.

Psychoanalytic Viewpoint
Stewart's social withdrawal represents an unconscious desire to have others take care of him, as his mother did in the past.

Cognitive Viewpoint
Because he is unable to talk to others at work, Stewart expects to fail when talking to people at the party as well.

Stewart is attending a New Year's Eve party.

While at the party, Stewart becomes very nervous and withdrawn whenever other people approach him.

Figure 1.1
Explaining the same overt behavior from four theoretical viewpoints

depression). Thus, a good theory is internally consistent, comprehensive, simple, and useful.

Personality Research: The Testing of Theory

Personality psychologists must test the theories they develop through systematic research involving hypothesis testing. A **hypothesis** is a statement made about the relationship between at least two variables in a manner consistent with a particular theory. For example, a learning theory of aggression might propose the following hypothesis: Viewers who see others rewarded for aggressive behavior will act more aggressively than viewers who observe others being punished for aggressive behavior. To test the hypothesized effect of observed outcome for aggressiveness on viewer aggressive behavior, a psychologist might have one group of children watch a videotape showing an adult being rewarded for behaving aggressively. At the same time, an equal number of other children would watch a videotape showing the adult being scolded for the aggressive behavior. After watching the videotapes, the children would be allowed to engage in a free-play period while the psychologist monitored the amount of aggressive play through a one-way mirror. Documenting more aggressive behavior in the children who observed the adult rewarded rather than scolded for aggressiveness would confirm the hypothesis and support this learning theory of personality.

Confirming a hypothesis does not mean the research on the learning theory of aggression is complete. Subsequent research would need to be done to determine if such variables as the sex or age of the aggressive adult model or the nature of the reward (e.g., candy vs. verbal praise) make a difference in the children's tendency to imitate the aggressive behavior. Such additional research more completely tests the theory and allows for better understanding of the relationship between observed rewards and imitative aggressive behavior.

Based on additional research, a particular theory of personality is modified and refined to account for the observed results. If the theory cannot be modified to be consistent with the research results, it is usually abandoned and another one proposed and tested in its place.

Personality Development: The Emergence of Personality

Researchers studying **personality development** examine those factors contributing to the emergence of an individual's personality. Examining factors from the past can offer insight into the current state of an individual's personality. For example, examining such childhood factors as birth order, family size, parenting practices, and early trauma might provide insight into experiences of shyness in adulthood.

Personality development is an interactive process involving other aspects of human development. For example, research indicates that the rate of physical development (e.g., being big or small for one's age) influences personality development during adolescence (Papalia & Olds, 1992), and these influences on personality development can remain into adulthood (Gross & Duke, 1980). The gradual effect of various physical changes—slowing down of motor responses—and social changes—retirement or death of a spouse—on the process of personality adjustment in the later years is also studied by psychologists in the area of personality development (Papalia & Olds, 1992).

As researchers in the field of personality psychology acquire more knowledge about the factors contributing to the development of certain aspects of personality, they can use the information to help individuals make decisions about changing and/or developing certain aspects of their own personality or the personality of others. For example, if certain parenting styles are known to foster high self-esteem (Coopersmith, 1967) or a heightened sense of independence and achievement (Baumrind, 1971) in children, then creating these types of family atmospheres will maximize the likelihood of children developing these personality characteristics.

Personality Assessment: The Measurement of Personality

Personality assessment refers to the development and use of techniques to accurately and consistently measure different aspects of personality. Personality assessment is a vital link to the other major aspects of personality psychology. Following are some ways researchers use personality assessment techniques:

▲ Testing various personality theories (e.g., shyness vs. introversion)
▲ Measuring developmental changes in personality (e.g., moral reasoning) from childhood to adulthood

▲ Evaluating the effectiveness of various psychotherapies (e.g., a stress reduction workshop)

Personality psychologists and other professionals also use personality assessment in a variety of important applications to everyday situations, ranging from screening potential job applicants to assisting in the diagnosis of heart problems.

Applications in Personality Psychology: Putting Personality Psychology to Use

The application of personality psychology involves utilizing what is known about personality theories, research, development, and assessment to help individuals lead more happy, healthy, and productive lives. Effective applications of personality psychology have a solid theoretical framework and are based on systematic research. A long-standing application of personality psychology is to the area of **psychotherapy** (Phares, 1984). **Psychotherapists** rely on theories of personality to help guide their thinking about what factors may have caused a client's emotional and behavior difficulties and what should be done to modify the client's problem behavior. In fact, many major theories of personality and techniques of personality assessment were developed and refined in the context of the personality theorist's clinical experience and research.

Outside of psychotherapy, personality psychology is applied in many other aspects of life. Personality psychologists are contributing valuable information to help understand how certain personality factors contribute to such medical disorders as coronary heart disease and cancer (Matthews & Glass, 1981; Taylor, 1991). In the military, personality research is being conducted in an attempt to investigate the relationship between personality test scores and pilot error in aviation (Collister & Straatmeyer, 1983). In law enforcement, personality tests are used to help in the selection of police officers, to determine the competency of criminals to stand trial, and to evaluate potential jurors (Wrightsman, 1991). Information about the personality of nurses is being used to assess reactions to occupational stress and nursing burnout (Carducci & Applegeet, 1984) and examine the theft of drugs and hospital supplies among nursing personnel (Jones, 1981). In an attempt to help minimize the loss of employees due to on-the-job injuries, research in the area of occupational safety is concerned with identifying the personality of "accident prone" employees and job applicants (Hansen, 1991; Jones & Wuebker, 1984; Jones, Wuebker, & Dubois, 1984).

Information about the personality of people working in such areas as supermarkets, department stores, and home improvement centers has also been used to help predict employee theft (Jones & Terris, 1982, 1991; Terris & Jones, 1980, 1982). Personality research is also being conducted to investigate how effectively people interact with computers (Derby & Cozby, 1983). You can read about an application of personality psychology to the area of small-business ownership, in the feature "Applications in Personality Psychology" below.

APPLICATION

APPLICATIONS IN PERSONALITY PSYCHOLOGY

A Money-Making Personality: Personality Correlates of Successful Small-Business Owners

In his research, Alan Carsrud of the University of Texas Department of Management investigates the relationship between the personality of small-business owners and the success and productivity of their firms. The measure of personality Carsrud uses in this research is the Work and Family Orientation Inventory, or the WOFO for short (Helmreich & Spence, 1978). The WOFO is a 23-item scale measuring three aspects of an individual's motivation to achieve success: mastery, work orientation, and competitiveness. The mastery subscale of the WOFO assesses an individual's preference for challenging tasks: "If I am not good at something, I would rather keep struggling to master it than move on to something at which I may be good." The work orientation subscale assesses positive attitudes toward work: "Once I undertake a task, I is like goofing up and not doing the best I can." The

competitiveness subscale assesses an individual's desire to succeed in interpersonal situations: "I enjoy working in situations involving competition with others."

In one study, Carsrud and his colleagues (Carsrud, Olm, & Thomas, 1984) asked 96 owners of retail building supply firms in the South and Southwest United States, having gross annual sales between $500,000 and $28,000,000, to complete the WOFO. The results of this study indicate that the greater the owner's sense of mastery, work orientation, and competitiveness, the more financially successful the business, as measured by annual sales and worker productivity (total annual sales divided by the total number of employees). Thus, these results do seem to suggest that the personality of the owner may play a role in the success of the business.

If these results continue to be validated by future research, it is possible that in addition to asking loan applicants for a financial statement listing their assets and credit ratings, a bank's business loan officer might also ask them to complete a measure of achievement motivation in order to assess the chances of their business succeeding and paying back the loan. Such a possibility suggests that personality research has some very interesting implications for the business and finance community (Wong & Carducci, 1991).

Research Methods in Personality Psychology: Three Approaches to Studying Personality

Personality psychologists use various research methods in studying personality. Three major approaches are the clinical, correlational, and experimental. As you will discover in this section, each approach contributes a unique perspective to our knowledge about personality.

The Clinical Approach: Probing the Depths of the Individual

The characteristic feature of the clinical approach is the attention given to the in-depth study of the individual or a small group of individuals. Three methods illustrating the clinical approach are the case study, the individual interview, and the analysis of personal documents.

The Case Study: An Individual Analysis

The **case study method** involves a rather detailed investigation and description of an individual's history and present status. Information about the individual's past and present family history, educational background, previous history of emotional or adjustment problems, employment record, and medical history is part of a comprehensive case history. Researchers can obtain this valuable information about the individual's past and present behavior by talking directly to the individual or to others familiar with the person (e.g., family members, coworkers), or by gaining access to certain records (e.g., college or employment records). See "A Closer Look" below for an example of the kind of information gathered as part of a case study.

A Closer Look

Piecing Together the Picture of a Mass Murderer

Consider the case of James Huberty. In the late afternoon on July 19, 1984, Huberty, after casually telling his wife he was "going hunting for humans," walked into a McDonald's family restaurant, where he shot and killed 21 people and wounded 15 others, including children.

What kind of person would do such a thing? Information about past and present circumstances of James Huberty's life, as obtained from acquaintances and assorted records, indicated that:

The killer, said neighbors, was "a sour man" who regularly exploded in towering rages against his wife Etna and their two daughters, 14 and 10. Even the bumper sticker on his car was testy: "I'M NOT DEAF, I'M IGNORING YOU. (*Time*, July 30, 1984, p. 91)

Acquaintances in Ohio were not altogether surprised.

One said, "I knew there was something wrong with him."

Another recalled that when Huberty lost his job at the Babcock & Wilcox plant in nearby Canton, "He said

While the smiling face of James Huberty in this photograph provides little information about his personality, the case study method can help us to understand why this mass murderer killed 21 people and wounded 15 others.

that if this was the end of his making a living for his family, he was going to take everyone with him. He was always talking about shooting somebody."

A portrait of Huberty, drawn from law enforcement officials and those who knew him, reveals an uncertain man who shifted directions several times in his life. One personality trait was consistent, however. Huberty struck others as a loner who did not much like people.

In Canton, Ohio, Brother Dave Lombardl, minister of the Trinity Gospel Temple, said he believed Huberty's problems went back to childhood, when the boy's mother deserted the family to become a religious missionary to an Indian reservation. Huberty grew up in Ohio, raised mainly by his father, Lombardl said.

"He had real inner conflicts," said Lombardl, who performed the marriage ceremony for Huberty and his wife in 1965. "He was pent-up; he was a loner, and he had kind of an explosive personality. When you talked to him, you knew he had nervous anxiety and was wound up inside."

In 1964 and 1965, while attending Malone College in Canton part-time, Huberty became an apprentice mortician at Don Williams Funeral Home.

"He was a very clean-cut chap and he was more or less of a loner type," Williams recalled yesterday. "He would rather just be off by himself."

Williams said Huberty was better at embalming bodies than dealing with clients. "I told him that I thought he was pursuing the wrong profession. He didn't seem to have the personality for it," Williams said.

Huberty married the former Etna Markland during this period, Williams said, and the couple had two children.

In the 1970s, Huberty appeared to achieve some success. He graduated from Malone with a bachelor's degree in sociology after on-again, off-again study there. He went to work as a welder for Babcock & Wilcox, reportedly making $25,000 to $30,000 a year.

He moved to Massillon eight years ago and bought a home and a six-unit apartment building next door, according to James Aslanes, a coworker at Babcock & Wilcox.

Aslanes got to know Huberty there but, before very long, he became wary of him.

"We first became friendly when he found out I was studying kung fu," Aslanes recalled. "He was inquiring about how to 'put his daughter into the program' for some kind of self-defense."

The two men visited each other's homes. Aslanes, a gun owner himself, noticed that Huberty's house was filled with guns: shotguns, rifles, handguns and an Israeli-made Uzi machine gun. While Aslanes said their mutual interest reinforced their friendship, one incident caused him concern.

"We went shooting one time with the Uzi," he said, "and he began shooting at a rock. It was dangerous. The bullets might come back to us. It shocked me that anybody that knowledgeable about guns would do that."

When Huberty was laid off in October 1982 after 10 years' employment, Aslanes said he became concerned about making his house payments.

"He became despondent," Aslanes said. "He worried. He blamed the whole country for his misfortune. He said that Ronald Reagan and the government were conniving against him. The working class were going to have to pay for this inflation. . . . He became so discouraged that he wrote the Mexican government and applied for residence. . . .

"He bought a lot of food, survival foods. He had tons and tons of ammunition, and when he left Massillon,

I was under the impression that he was going to Mexico, a couple of miles south of Tijuana."

Huberty was well-known to Massillon police, although he was never charged with a violent crime. Sgt. Don Adams recalled that Huberty's two German shepherds repeatedly harassed motorcycle police.

When calls came in on minor matters, Adams recalled, officers often joked that it was "the Hubertys again" because of the numerous complaints that Huberty filed against others and the complaints filed against him. Adams said Huberty once was accused of shooting a dog with an airgun.

In October, 1980, Massillon police charged Huberty with disorderly conduct after a neighborhood quarrel. In September 1981, neighbors accused Mrs. Huberty of threatening them with a 9mm pistol; she later pleaded guilty to a disorderly conduct charge, Massillon police said.

Huberty took his family to Southern California seven months ago. San Diego neighbors described Huberty as an angry, unsmiling man.

Although he had recently lost his job, Huberty did not fit the profile of the classically unemployed, according to neighbors. They described the family as well-clothed and Huberty as a clean-cut dresser, "like an executive."

Police officials said Huberty showed up at the restaurant wearing camouflage trousers. According to those who spoke of him yesterday, he had never been seen in such garb before.

Although Huberty's wife was quoted as saying he liked children, some neighbors said he hated them and people of Mexican descent. The massacre at the restaurant, a neighborhood gathering spot, took a heavy toll of both groups. (*The Courier Journal*, July 20, 1984, p. A–12)

From Huberty's father and widow, we get some additional information:

SAN DIEGO—Adding depth to the portrait of mass murderer James Oliver Huberty, his father and widow have described him as a troubled, hot-tempered man who was often abusive to his family and once tried to kill himself.

Earl V. Huberty said Friday that a combination of medical problems and an unsuccessful career left his son "angry at the whole world." A clinical psychologist who sat in on an interview Thursday with Huberty's widow described the slayer's actions on his final day as a "grandiose last stand."

In an interview with the San Diego Union published Friday, Mrs. Huberty, 41, recalled that last year, when the family still lived in Ohio, her husband tried to kill himself.

She wrested the gun away and hid it, she said, adding, "When I came back, he was sitting on the sofa crying."

She told the newspaper that a couple of months ago, Huberty said, "You should have let me kill myself." (*The Courier-Journal,* July 22, 1984, p. A–10)

Mrs. Huberty said in the interview that her husband "would never have done this . . . if he had been in his right mind."

"If he . . . hadn't been hearing voices . . . I know definitely he would never have killed a child," she said. "He was very fond of children, extremely fond of children, and he always talked very vehemently about what should happen to people that hurt children." (*The Courier-Journal,* July 20, 1984, p. A–1)

While obtaining information from these various sources does give some understanding of what past and present social and emotional factors may have contributed to this incident, they make possible only "educated guesses":

Lt. Paul Ybarrondo, commander of the San Diego Police Department's homicide squad, said investigators had not determined a motive for the killings.

"I don't expect that we will," Ybarrondo said. "You're talking about getting into a deceased person's thought process. We might be able to come up with something in his background. . . . But as far as why he went over the brink at this very moment, I can't answer that, and I don't think we'll ever be able to." (*The Courier-Journal,* July 20, 1984, p. A–1)

Under such conditions, educated guesses seem to be better than nothing. But for more concrete answers, additional systematic research involving in-depth analyses of the case studies of other mass murderers is required.

Documenting rare phenomena and helping to test theory are other important functions of the case study. Presenting a detailed case study of the success-ful treatment of a person with a rare form of multiple-personality disorder not only demonstrates the disorder's existence but also gives support for testing the theory upon which the treatment is based. Such results would then encourage additional research, with a larger number of other individuals suffering from multiple-personality disorder being treated at different hospitals to test this theory.

The Individual Interview: Information for the Asking

The general format of the **individual interview** involves more than just asking and answering questions. Conducting a successful interview involves establishing rapport and considering both verbal and nonverbal communication.

▲ *Establishing rapport.* **Rapport** refers to the positive, warm relationship established between the individuals participating in the interview. Establishing rapport makes the expression of intimate and oftentimes very painful information much easier. Refraining from expressing disapproval or appearing judgmental of the individual's responses and offering confidentiality are just a few ways to establish rapport.

▲ *Nonverbal behavior.* In addition to the verbal message and variety of verbal cues, a skillful interviewer is also sensitive to the individual's nonverbal messages (e.g., posture, gestures, and facial expressions). Subtle changes in the individual's nonverbal messages can help provide more information about the true meaning of the verbal message. "A Closer Look," on this page, examines the dynamics involved in an individual interview.

A Closer Look:

Interview with a College Student: Sometimes Talking About It Can Help

The following excerpt illustrates many basic features of the individual interview, such as establishing rapport and the progressive "opening up" of the individual to the interviewer. The comments presented opposite the dialogue are included to make clear what objectives the interviewer is trying to achieve and/or what significant topic is being explored.

This sample illustrates an initial interview that might occur at a university psychological clinic.

Interview Dialogue	Comments
INTERVIEWER (I): Beautiful day isn't it?	Initial nonstressful conversation can help to reduce some of the client's anxiety.
CLIENT (C): Yeah. (Sighs) Not that nice.	Note the nonverbal sign of gloomy feelings.
I: Could you tell me why you decided to come to our clinic today.	Interviewer highlights significance of client's choice to come to the clinic at this particular time.
C: Well, I'm having real difficulties in school.	
I: Am I correct in assuming that you came on your own.	Interviewer checks to see if client has been referred or is under pressure.
C: Yes.	
I: O.K. I'd like to briefly explain what I hope we can accomplish in the next hour, to give you a clear idea of what to expect and how this interview can be of help to you.	Interviewer provides basic goals and guidelines to reduce the client's uncertainty and to promote positive expectations.
This hour is a chance for us to talk openly about you as a person and the concerns that have brought you here.	
I'll ask questions to help us explore all the important areas for you, but I'll rely on you to fill me in as completely as you can. Of course, everything we talk about will be completely confidential, so you can talk freely. At the end, we'll discuss what steps to take next so that your needs can be fully taken care of.	General orientation to the roles and responsibilities of client and interviewer. Emphasis on teamwork between client and interviewer.
Maybe we could start by talking about how you decided to come to the clinic at this particular point in your life.	Open-ended question, but with a focus on "why now?"
C: I can't have my way. My parents won't let me.	
I: Your parents have a powerful and hurtful impact on you, I hear you very clearly. I'm just wondering what you'd do if you could magically have control of your own future?	Acknowledges client's belief, but challenges the hopelessness. Facilitates exploration of alternatives.
C: Well, I guess I'd change my major to theatre, that's where my real interests and talents are.	
I: How are you stopping yourself from doing that now?	Focus on the client's responsibility.
C: I'm not. It's my parents.	
I: Your parents certainly make it hard, but I wonder if you aren't concerned that bad things will happen if you change your major. What would happen, do you think?	Exploring the client's fears.
C: Well, I'd enjoy school, finally. But my parents might stop paying my tuition. And, they'd be mean as hell.	
I: I'd like to explore that, but first, let's get a picture of what it's like to be in your family. Could you describe your family, and how you fit it?	Holds off on specific issues, to get a general background.

(10 minutes later)

I: Could you tell me about your experience in school as you've grown	Exploring school issues.

up—how have you been doing academically over the years? And how have you handled your feelings about tests until now?

(10 minutes later)

I: Tell me about your relationships with friends, including both casual and close friends of both sexes.

Exploring social relationships.

C: Well, I'm afraid I'll flunk out of the university if I don't get over feeling anxious about tests (begins to clasp hands nervously and blushes while looking at the ground, some light laughter also).

Nonverbal cues reflecting anxiety.

I: I notice that you seem to be worried. Troubles at school can really be painful.

Gentle acknowledgment of client's nonverbal cues and distress.

C: Especially when your parents are pressuring you to get into law school.

An important tie-in: the family plays a role as well as school problems.

I: Are you feeling that kind of pressure?

An open-ended encouragement to continue.

C: My parents just won't let up (voice is tight and cracks).

I: Mm-hmm.

Brief encouragement to continue.

C: What can I do?

I: If you had your way, what would you choose to do?

Interviewer emphasizes the client's capability and responsibility for resolving problems.

(10 minutes later)

I: Well, you've given an excellent sketch of several important areas in your life.

Relying on client to fill in gaps.

Have we missed some important sides of you or your situation?

C: I don't know if it's relevant, but I'm concerned about how much I've been drinking lately.

Another important life concern.

I: Why don't you tell me more about it.

(10 minutes later)

I: We may not have covered everything, but I'd like to use our remaining time to summarize my understanding of you and your situation, and then to have us both discuss what you might do next.

Acknowledges that more information may still be needed, but makes sure to provide a summary and a discussion of the client's alternatives.

(From Kendall & Norton-Ford, 1982, pp. 209–211)

As these comments illustrate, a considerable amount of personal information about the nature of the individual's problems at school was obtained by asking the right question at the right time. If performed appropriately, the individual interview is a very useful tool.

Analysis of Personal Documents: A Look at Personal Statements

A third research method characteristic of the clinical approach is the analysis of personal documents. According to Allport (1961), a **personal document** may be defined as "any freely written or spoken record that intentionally or unintentionally yields information regarding the structure and dynamics of the author's life" (p. 401). Personal documents include diaries, letters, autobiographies, and verbatim recordings. For a closer look at some excerpts taken from personal documents, consider the feature "A Closer Look" on page 14.

A Closer Look:

Words from the Heart: Excerpts from the Personal Documents of President Nixon's Public and Private Farewell Speeches

In his book *Personality in Politics*, Alan Elms (1976) illustrates how psychobiographies have been used to study the personality of famous politicians. A **psychobiography** is a detailed psychological case study of an individual (Elms, 1976, 1994).

In a discussion of the psychobiographies of President Nixon, Elms (1976) notes that

> Nixon's formal statement of resignation from the Presidency was a calm and controlled performance. . . . It could almost have been the retirement speech by a respected President turning over the reins to his elected successor, or perhaps a State of the Union oration designed to comfort more than inform. It certainly informed the audience very little about Nixon's internal state. (p. 103)

In sharp contrast to his public appearance, when alone, Nixon's private appearance was very somber and projected a sense of weakness and defeat.

In contrast, in his farewell speech to his staff, "with sweat and tears streaming down his face" (Elms, 1976, p. 103), Nixon seems to have been speaking words from the heart. During a more emotional part of his speech, Nixon remembers his mother:

> Nobody will ever write a book about my mother. Well, I guess all of you would say this about your mother: my mother was a saint. And I think of her two boys dying of tuberculosis, nursing four others in order that she could take care of my older brother for three years in Arizona and seeing each of them die. And when they died it was like one of her own. Yes, she will have no books written about her. But she was a saint. (p. 103)

In his closing remarks, Nixon becomes philosophical:

> Because the greatness comes not only when things go always good for you, but the greatness comes when you're really tested, when you take some knocks and some disappointments, when sadness comes. . . . Always give your best. Never get discouraged. Never be petty. Always remember, others may hate you, but those who hate you don't win unless you hate them. And then you destroy yourself. (p. 104)

Bruce Mazlish (1973), in his rather detailed psychobiography of Nixon, emphasized many of the themes noted in his speeches as a means of identifying some of the major influences on the characteris-

At the time of his resignation of the presidency, Nixon's public appearance was animated and projected a sense of strength.

tics of Nixon's personality. For example, according to Mazlish, Nixon's "Protestant ethics" traits—emphasizing planning, hard work, and persistence—were influenced by his mother and maternal grandmother.

Information from such personal documents made possible some insights into the Nixon's private personality not seen in public.

Achieving an in-depth understanding of an individual's feelings and behavior involves much more than simply reading personal documents. As Allport (1961) notes, "Anyone, of course, can read these documents and form interpretations in a common-sense way" (p. 406). To go beyond common sense, researchers in personality psychology might conduct a content analysis of the document. A **content analysis** is a systematic assessment of the themes, ideas, and expressions presented in a document. In one form of content analysis, a researcher can identify the major overlapping themes by asking different raters to read the document and indicate what themes they observe. The feature "Applications in Personality Psychology" below illustrates how the content analysis of personal documents is used to help increase our understanding of one of the most tragic examples of human suffering—suicide.

APPLICATION

APPLICATIONS IN PERSONALITY PSYCHOLOGY

Closing Statements: Content Analysis of Suicide Notes

Psychologists and other mental health professionals cannot currently explain why people commit suicide. But researchers continue to analyze the contents of suicide notes in an attempt to better understand the motives and feelings of those individuals who committed suicide (Leenaars, 1989). In a very early and important study, Tuckman, Kleiner, and Lavell (1959) investigated 724 suicides and found that 24% left notes. Analyzing the content of these notes revealed four general emotional categories: positive, negative, neutral, and mixed affect.

▲ *Positive emotional content.* Fifty-one percent of the notes express what might be defined as positive affect, such as expressing affection, gratitude, and concern for others:

> Please forgive me and please forget me. I'll always love you. All I have was yours. No one ever did more for me than you, oh please pray for me please. (p. 60)

▲ *Negative (hostile) emotional content.* Only 6% of the notes were classified as expressing primarily hostile or negative affect:

> I hate all of you and all of your family and I hope you never have peace of mind. I hope I haunt this house as long as you live here and I wish you all the bad luck in the world. (p. 60)

▲ *Neutral emotional content.* Twenty-five percent of the notes contained a generally neutral affective tone. As you read the following note, notice it conveys neither a sense of anger nor a sense of relief, just a sense of order:

> To Whom It May Concern,
>
> I, Mary Smith, being of sound mind, do this day, make my last will as follows—I bequeath my rings, Diamond and Black Opal to my daughter-in-law, Doris Jones and any other personal belongings she might wish. What money I have in my savings account and my checking account goes to my dear father, as he won't have me to help him. To my husband, Ed Smith, I leave my furniture and car.
>
> I would like to be buried as close to the grave of John Jones as possible. (Darbonne, 1969, p. 50)

▲ Mixed emotional content. Eighteen percent of the notes were classified as having a mixed emotional content, containing a combination of both positive and negative affect:

> I am sorry I have to take this way out. But you can see there's no other way. She would just give me and the kids a hard time for the rest of our lives, also the club deal is away out of my hands contact.

S——— about the Girls and the M———s about
B———. All the money I have in the world is here.
May God Bless you and your family and may he look
after mine.
    May she rot in hell after me. (Tuckman et al., 1959,
p. 60)

Information gained from such content analysis is
used to test theories of suicide, assess others' reactions to it, and help individuals working with suicidal
persons in such places as mental hospitals, counseling
centers, and suicide intervention telephone centers
(Comer, 1992, 1995).

Evaluating the Clinical Approach: Characteristic Strengths and Limitations

Being aware of the characteristic strengths and limitations of the clinical approach will make evaluating
its use easier.

Here are some strengths of the clinical
approach:

▲ *In-depth understanding of the individual.* A major
strength of the clinical approach is that it offers
several ways of studying a particular individual
or small group of individuals in considerable
detail. An example would be studying the personality development of female state governors.

▲ *Studying development and adjustment processes
over time.* Taking an in-depth look at an individual over time makes it possible to observe developmental changes and their presumed effects
(Funder, Parke, Tomlinson-Keasey, & Widaman,
1993). An example is a therapist examining
changes in a client's self-esteem and job satisfaction over a two-year period.

▲ *Investigating extreme and rare events.* Studying
extreme and rare events is made possible with
the clinical approach. As an example, investigating the coping skills of survivors of a mur-
derous prisoner-of-war camp makes studying
the extremes of personality adaptability possible. Because they are so rare, such events must
be studied when they can be found, and in as
much depth as possible.

The following are some limitations of the clinical
approach:

▲ *Limited generalizability.* The issue of **generalizability** involves extending the findings about
one group of individuals to another group.
Findings based on the clinical approach typically use a small number of individuals, which
limits their extension to other groups. For
example, it is unclear how information about
the coping skills of a handful of prisoner-of-war
camp survivors may be generalized to the development of a survival training program taught
to thousands of other soldiers.

▲ *Personal biases.* The rather personal nature of
the clinical approach introduces subject and
researcher biases. **Subject biases** are systematic
alterations in the recall of an individual when
reporting information to a researcher. Subjects
may withhold information out of embarrassment or "fill in the gaps" of distant events.
Researcher biases are tendencies to gather and
interpret information in a manner consistent
with the researcher's point of view. For example, a researcher testing a theory of sibling
rivalry may overemphasize the role of siblings
when studying the personality development of
U.S. presidents.

The Correlational Approach: Knowledge by Association

The clinical approach provides insights into the personality of an individual or a very small number of
individuals by identifying important personality
variables. The major purpose of **correlational
research** is to investigate the extent to which any two
variables are associated with one another. For example, a researcher might be interested in studying the
relationship between shyness and loneliness or the
need for achievement and worker productivity.

The Scatter Plot: The Illustrating of Relationships

A **scatter plot** is a graph summarizing the scores
obtained by many individuals on two different variables. Figure 1.2a is a scatter plot showing the relationship between scores on a measure of shyness and
a measure of loneliness. Each point on the scatter plot
represents an individual's score for the two different
variables. For example, the point on the scatter plot

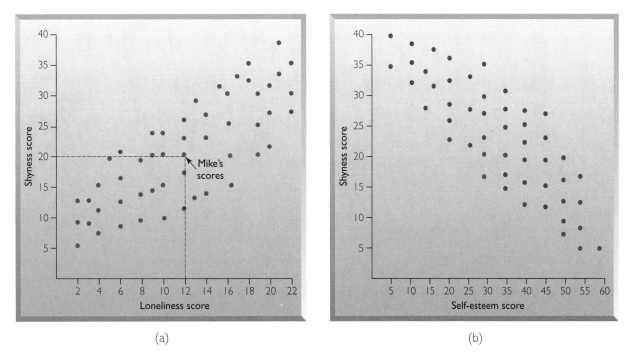

(a)   (b)

Figure 1.2
Scatter plots illustrating a positive and negative correlational relationship

corresponding to Mike's scores indicates a score of 12 on the measure of loneliness and 20 on the measure of shyness. Interpreting correlational relationships involves identifying the direction and strength of the relationship between the two variables.

Correlational Relationships: Identifying Associations

The direction of a correlational relationship reveals how the two variables are related. The two basic patterns indicating direction are the positive and negative correlational relationships. The general pattern of association of a **positive correlational relationship** reveals that as the scores on one variable increase, the corresponding scores on the other variable also tend to show an increase. Figure 1.2a shows that as the loneliness scores increase, the corresponding shyness scores also tend to increase. The general pattern of association of a **negative correlational relationship** reveals that as the scores on one variable increase, the corresponding scores on the other variable tend to decrease. Figure 1.2b shows that as the shyness scores increase, the corresponding self-esteem scores tend to decrease.

The Correlational Coefficient: Assessing the Strength of the Correlational Relationship

After determining the direction, the next step is to assess the strength of the correlational relationship by determining the extent to which scores on the two variables are related. The index used to indicate the strength of association between two variables is called the **correlation coefficient** and is symbolized by the letter r. The strength of the association between two variables is reflected in a value ranging from $r = +1.00$ to 0.00 to -1.00 and is determined by a specific statistical formula. The closer to $+1.00$ or -1.00 the value for r, the stronger the association between the two variables. In a similar manner, the closer to zero the value of r, the weaker the association between the two variables.

The strongest relationship possible between two variables is $r = +1.00$ or -1.00. Figure 1.3a indicates that there is a perfect positive correlational relationship ($r = +1.00$) between the scores on a measure of aggressiveness and hostility. Figure 1.3e indicates that there is a perfect negative correlational relationship ($r = -1.00$) between a measure of shyness and popularity ratings. In a perfect positive correlation,

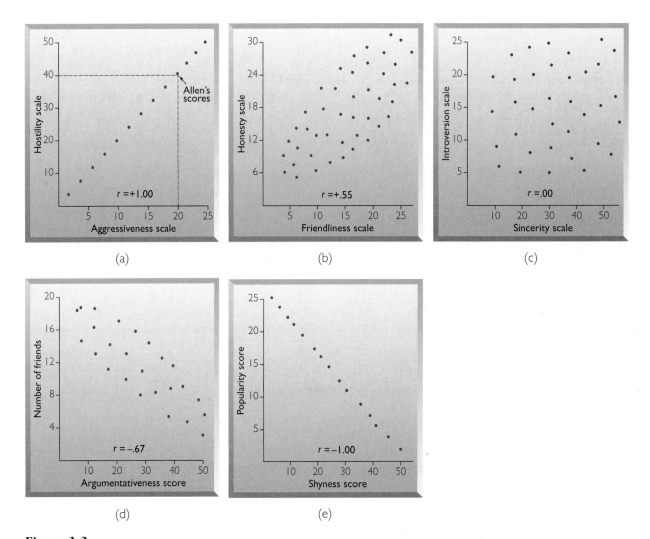

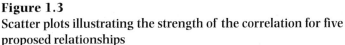

Figure 1.3
Scatter plots illustrating the strength of the correlation for five
proposed relationships

the value for one variable is associated with one and only one value of the second variable, creating a straight line on the graph.

Perfect correlational relationships in personality research are extremely rare. A less-than-perfect correlational relationship indicates that a particular score on one variable is not necessarily associated with one and only one value on the second variable, creating some spread in the scores in the scatter plot. Figure 1.3b is an example of a moderately strong positive correlational relationship ($r = +.55$) between guilt and honesty. Figure 1.3d is an example of a

moderately strong negative correlational relationship ($r = -67$) between argumentativeness and number of friends.

The scatter plot in Figure 1.3c illustrates an uncorrelated relationship ($r = 0.00$) between scores on measures of sincerity and introversion. In uncorrelated relationships, the association between the two variables is extremely weak or nonexistent. In assessing the strength of a correlational relationship through visual inspection, a general rule of thumb is the less spread in the scores on the scatter plot, the stronger the relationship.

The Third-Variable Problem:
Looking Beyond the Observed Relationship

Interpreting correlational relationships is made difficult by the potential presence of third variables. The **third-variable problem** exists when the observed relationship between two variables is actually produced by their relationship with another unobserved, or third, variable. Figure 1.4a illustrates a relationship between shyness and test anxiety. Figure 1.4b illustrates how this relationship is explained by considering the relationship of these two variables to a third variable, self-consciousness.

Interpreting correlational relationships involves considering the direction and strength of the relationship and the third-variable problem.

Evaluating the Correlational Approach:
Characteristic Strengths and Limitations

An understanding of the correlational approach also involves considering its characteristic strengths and limitations. The following are some characteristic strengths of this approach:

▲   *Exploring and identifying relationships.* An important use of the correlational approach is in searching for relationships among variables during early stages of research. A personality psychologist might first explore the relationship of shyness with such variables as self-esteem, social anxiety, self-consciousness, and loneliness to determine the strongest correlations and the

Figure 1.4
An illustration of the third-variable problem

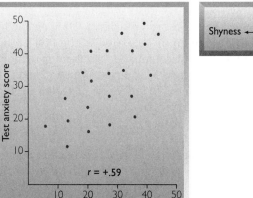

(a) A proposed relationship between shyness and test anxiety

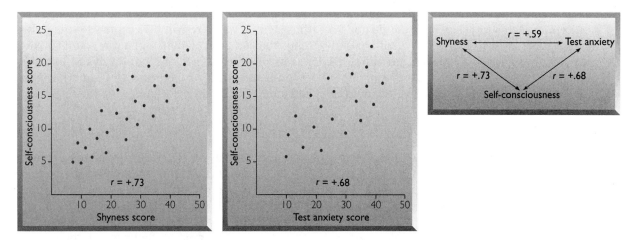

(b) A proposed relationship between shyness, test anxiety, and the third variable of self-conciousness

to determine the strongest correlations and the best research potential.

▲ *Ethical considerations.* Using the correlational approach, researchers can investigate some important problems that they could not ordinarily study because of ethical restrictions. For example, it is not ethically permissible for a researcher to separate children from their parents in order to study personality development in single-parent families. But it is possible to correlate information about personality variables by studying children who are already in single-parent families.

Here are some characteristic limitations of the correlational approach:

▲ *The third-variable problem.* The possibility of third variables going unidentified by the researcher decreases a thorough understanding of the relationship between two variables. But being aware of potential third variables and taking them into consideration can minimize their negative impact.

▲ *Undetermined causal relationships.* While the correlational approach can identify the nature and strength of the relationship between two variables, this does not mean that one variable causes the change in the other to occur. For example, in the relationship between shyness and self-esteem (see Figure 1.2b), it is not known whether shyness causes people to have low self-esteem or having low self-esteem causes people to be shy. Unfortunately, the results from such a correlational study do not tell researchers which explanation, if either, is correct. This is a serious limitation, since the goal of most personality research is to explain why the human personality operates as it does.

The Experimental Approach: Knowledge by Systematic Intervention

The correlational approach can determine the degree to which two variables are associated, but not the causal nature of the relationship. Personality psychologists searching for causal relationships use the experimental approach in studying personality.

Basic Principles of the Experimental Approach: Intervention, Observation, and Control

The **experimental research** approach requires three elements: intervention, observation, and control. The logic of the experimental approach involves investigating how the systematic intervention of one variable creates changes that can be observed in a second variable. At the same time, researchers attempt to control for outside factors that might also produce changes in the second variable.

Systematic Intervention   Establishing a causal relationship involves determining that varying the level of one variable produces corresponding changes in a second variable. The **independent variable** is what you believe causes the change in the second variable. For example, psychotherapists might wish to investigate how receiving positive comments causes changes in the self-esteem of clients. They divide 30 clients into three groups of 10 with the first group receiving five positive comments per 1-hour session, the second receiving 20 positive comments, and the third receiving none. The independent variable is the number of positive comments.

Observation   The behavior affected by the independent variable and being observed is called the **dependent variable**. The dependent variable in this example is the change in the clients' self-esteem. Figure 1.5 summarizes the changes in the clients' self-esteem by plotting the **group mean** (i.e., average) of the self-esteem scores for each of the three feedback groups.

Experimental Control   **Experimental control** refers to the extent to which researchers control for the possibility that other explanations may account for the results observed. There are many ways to increase experimental control; here are three of the most common:

▲ *Randomly assigning subjects.* Decreases in experimental control occur whenever there is the possibility of biases in the way researchers assign individuals to different conditions of the experiment. Random assignment is a procedure designed to help control for biases in selection. According to the principle of **random assignment**, all individuals participating in the research have an equal chance of being exposed

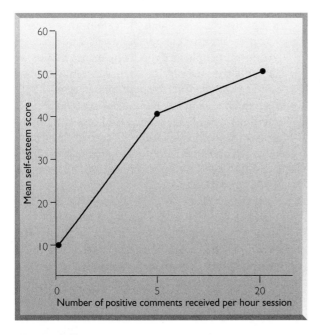

Figure 1.5
The hypothetical results in a study of the effects of positive feedback on self-esteem

to the different levels of the independent variable. For example, because individuals who have morning appointments may be somewhat different in age or employment status, assigning all clients with morning appointments to the no-feedback condition creates a bias. To avoid this bias, the group to which a client is assigned could be based on the order in which their names are drawn out of a box. This procedure increases the likelihood that the outcome of the study is due to the treatment itself rather than to the composition of the groups.

▲ *Standardizing procedures.* **Standardization of procedures** involves treating all of the subjects in a similar manner. In this way, the only difference among individuals in each group is the treatment produced by variations in the independent variable. Standardization of procedures might include such things as testing subjects in rooms with similar lighting and temperature and at around the same time of day, or presenting the instructions with a tape recorder. As an example, to control for the possibility of acting friendlier when giving feedback than when not giving

feedback, researchers must maintain a neutral facial expression and speak in a similar manner and tone of voice to all individuals.

▲ *Using a control group.* The **control group** contains individuals who are treated the same as other groups but are not exposed to the treatment conditions of the independent variable. The control group serves as a basis of comparison for the treatment groups. In the self-esteem example, (Figure 1.5), the group receiving no positive feedback is the control group.

Experimental control is not an either-or situation; it varies in degree. Experimental control is increased through careful planning of the research. Careful planning helps to control for or eliminate other factors that can serve as erroneous explanations of the results.

Meta-Analysis: A Tool for the Comparison of Experimental Research

Meta-analysis is an important development in interpreting the results of experimental research. Although the actual statistical computations for performing a meta-analysis are complex and well beyond the scope of this discussion, the underlying logic of this technique is very simple.

Meta-analysis is a statistical technique used in determining the consistency and magnitude of results from different studies that address a similar issue. An outstanding example is the work by Alice H. Eagly of Purdue University on sex differences in aggression. In one meta-analytic study on sex differences in aggression, Eagly and Steffen (1986) compared the results from 63 different studies. Using meta-analysis, these researchers could assess the direction of the results and the size of these differences by making gender comparisons across the various forms of aggression (e.g., hitting, verbal and written forms of aggression, and making noxious noise) used in the different studies. In their meta-analysis, Eagly and Steffen also looked at the sex of the individual who was the target of the aggression, the setting in which the aggression was observed (e.g., natural vs. laboratory setting), the sex of the participants in the different studies, and the sex of the researcher conducting the study.

Because it would not be possible to examine so many different factors in a single study, the ability to make comparisons across a number of different studies contributes significantly to our understanding of sex differences in aggression. Another rather extensive meta-analysis of 133 studies drawn from 17 countries assessed the extent to which conformity was related to certain general cultural characteristics (Bond & Smith, 1996). You can explore additional examples and more information about meta-analysis in *Meta-analysis for Explanation: A Casebook* (Cook et al., 1992) and *Reading and Understanding Multivariate Statistics* (Grimm & Yarnold, 1995).

Evaluating the Experimental Approach: Strengths and Limitations

The experimental approach is one of the most powerful research tools personality psychologists have at their disposal. But it also has its characteristic strengths and limitations.

Here are some of the strengths of the experimental approach:

▲ *Controlled observations.* Much of the research employing the experimental approach is **laboratory research**, conducted in a very structured and controlled setting. The major advantage of laboratory research is that it gives the researcher control over how and when the independent variable is introduced, what the surrounding conditions are like, and how the dependent variable is assessed. Such experimental control greatly increases the ability to eliminate alternative explanations of the results.

▲ *Causal explanations.* Conclusions about the independent variable causing observable changes in the dependent variable increase when the experimental approach is used correctly. The ability to make causal statements creates a level of understanding that allows a researcher to know "why" something happens. Knowing why personality operates the way it does is a principal objective of the systematic study of personality.

Following are some characteristic limitations of the experimental approach:

▲ *Group means vs. the individual.* Statements made about causal relationships are based on reporting group means, which indicate how the average person in that group behaved. Studying groups of people and reporting group means indicate the "average" response but may or may not accurately describe how each person responds. This heavy emphasis on the experimental study of personality and reporting of group means has led some personality psychologists to question "whatever happened to the person in personality psychology?" (Carlson, 1971, 1984).

▲ *Generalizability of results from the lab to the real world.* A concern with research conducted under well-controlled laboratory conditions is how fully the results can be generalized to the real world. For example, how much can studying frustration and aggression in college students for 45 minutes in a laboratory help researchers in understanding the reactions of workers being laid off after many years on a job? A partial solution to this issue is to conduct field research whenever possible. **Field research** includes investigations done outside the controlled conditions of the laboratory in such places as counseling centers, personnel offices, nursing homes, and shopping malls. Although it is somewhat more difficult when doing field research, the researcher still attempts to achieve experimental control over as many external factors as possible.

▲ *Experimenter bias.* **Experimenter bias** refers to any intentional or unintentional influences the experimenter exerts on the participants of the experiment to behave in a manner consistent with his or her hypothesis (Rosenthal, 1966, 1969). In the example investigating the effects of positive feedback on self-esteem (Figure 1.5), the experimenter might intentionally have been very friendly and nice to those individuals while giving them positive feedback and quite unfriendly to those not receiving any feedback in an attempt to find support for the hypothesis. Such behavior is dishonest, inexcusable, and rare. Much more likely are unintentional influences involving the researcher unwittingly communicating to the participants (e.g., smiling, nodding one's head) when they behave in a way that supports the hypothesis. Employing research assistants who are not aware of the hypothesis to carry out the experimental procedures helps to control for such unintentional but damaging communication; it is difficult to communicate unintentionally what participants are expected to do if the assistant is unaware of the hypothesis.

Research Ethics: Protecting the Individual's Rights in the Study of Personality Psychology

The participants in personality research have contributed greatly to our knowledge of personality. To maintain a favorable relationship with them, personality researchers must follow certain ethical standards of behavior. This section presents a discussion of the ethical issues associated with doing personality research and considers some potential solutions.

Some Ethical Concerns: Hurting, Lying, and Justifying

Some of the ethical concerns associated with conducting research in personality psychology include inducing stress, using deception, and justifying research procedures.

Inducing Stress
Minimizing any emotional harm experienced by participating in personality research is an important ethical concern. But in certain cases, inducing some harm is a byproduct of the type of research. Such is the case when the researcher studying the effects of failure on self-esteem or need for achievement gives participants false feedback by telling some of them they did very poorly on a task and others they did very well.

Deception
Sometimes participants in research attempt to guess what the researcher is trying to find out and modify their behavior accordingly. Such modifications can alter the research results. To help minimize this threat to experimental control, researchers may disguise the true purpose of the study by employing a certain amount of deception. **Deception** involves the researcher deliberately misleading the individual as to the true nature of the experiment. The degree of deception can range from modifying the title of the survey to staging fake injuries, arguments, and property destruction. As an example, a researcher may have a coworker fake an epileptic seizure to study the effect of situational uncertainty on helping behavior.

Justifying Research Procedure
Deception is not the rule in personality research; it is justified only as a last resort, when the researcher believes that results from such research will contribute to a greater understanding of the human personality. For example, faking injuries may be justified if the results of the study increase our understanding of how to make people more responsive to the needs of others. Allowing researchers to make decisions justifying their own research introduces the potential of biased judgments. Problems may occur when personal biases about the importance of one's research begin to overshadow concerns for the protection of research participants.

Some Solutions to Ethical Issues: Trying to Make Things Right

The ethical issues just described illustrate some of the special considerations personality psychologists must address when planning the procedures of their research. Some solutions for dealing with these and other ethical considerations include informed consent, debriefing, establishing ethical guidelines, and ethics review boards.

Informed Consent
Informed consent involves giving individuals the chance to decide whether they wish to participate before the actual start of the research. The decision to participate should be based on a reasonable description of the procedures being given to the individuals. Informed consent also involves informing individuals of their right to terminate their participation in the research project at any time they wish for *any* reason. Finally, assuring individuals that their

responses will be kept confidential is also an important element of informed consent.

Debriefing

Debriefing participants after their participation is designed to help deal with the issue of deception. During a **debriefing session**, the researcher explains to the individual what the purpose of the project was, why it was necessary to use the deception, and how their participation contributed to the project. The purpose of the debriefing session is to minimize any harm or ill feelings the individual might have experienced during his or her participation in the research project. In the debriefing session, explaining what is being studied and why can help to make the individual's participation a more educational and rewarding experience. In the example of the research investigating helping behavior, the researcher would explain that the coworker's injury was fake, say that no one outside the study will know how individual participants behaved, and describe how their participation contributes to our understanding of why people help others. Are such debriefing sessions effective? Research on the effectiveness of debriefing seems to indicate that most participants perceive such temporary uses of deception as acceptable (Rogers, 1980) and express more positive feelings about psychological research when such deception is followed by a thorough debriefing session (Smith & Richardson, 1983).

Ethical Guidelines

In addition to informed consent and debriefing, many other ethical considerations are involved when designing and implementing a research project (Blanck, Bellack, Rosnow, Rotheram-Borus, & Schooler, 1992). To help researchers identify and resolve potential ethical issues, the **American Psychological Association** (APA) has formulated a set of ethical principles to be used as guidelines when planning and conducting research (APA, 1981a, 1982, 1992a, 1992b). Psychologists who conduct research involving humans are obligated to conform to this set of ethical guidelines. The APA has also developed a set of guidelines for research conducted with animal subjects (APA, 1981a) and for many of the other activities engaged in by professional psychologists, such as testing, teaching, and counseling (APA, 1977, 1981b, 1990). Finally, any student of psychology

who assumes the role of a researcher is also expected to adhere to the ethical standards of professional psychologists (APA, 1977, 1981a, 1982). For example, any student assisting with the research of a professor must behave in a manner consistent with these ethical principles.

Ethics Review Boards

Preventing researchers from exaggerating the importance of their research as a means of justifying deception or the presence of stress is the major function of an **ethics review board**. The review board evaluates research proposals with respect to their adherence to certain ethical standards. Board members include psychologists and nonpsychologists. Because the board members are not connected directly with the proposals being considered, they can take a much more objective stand on evaluating the ethical nature of the procedures.

Chapter Summary: Reexamining the Highlights

▲ *Defining Personality*. Although personality psychologists define personality in many different ways, the definitions share the three common features of uniqueness of the individual, consistency of behavior, and explanations of the content and process of personality.

▲ *The Scope of Personality Psychology*. The study of personality psychology covers such areas as theory development, personality research, personality development, personality assessment, and applications of personality psychology.

▲ *Research Methods in Personality Psychology*
—The clinical approach involves in-depth study of the individual or a small group of individuals through such techniques as case study, individual interview, and analysis of personal documents. Strengths of this approach are its usefulness in gaining a deeper understanding of the individual, studying development and adjustment processes over time, and investigating extreme and rare cases. Limitations include decreased generalizability of results and the potential for personal biases.
—The correlational approach identifies the relationship between two variables. The relationships can

be positive or negative and vary in the strength of association between the two variables. Strengths of this approach include the ability to explore and identify relationships between variables and overcome certain ethical considerations. Limitations include the potential presence of the third-variable problem and undetermined causal relationships.

—The experimental approach helps to establish causal relationships among variables. This approach involves systematic intervention of the independent variable to observe any changes it produces in the dependent variable while maintaining experimental control over outside influences. Three techniques for increasing experimental control are random assignment of subjects, standardization of procedures, and use of a control group. Meta-analysis compares the results across different experimental studies. Strengths of this approach include making controlled observations and providing causal explanations. Limitations include an emphasis of the group mean over the individual, limited generalizability of results from the controlled laboratory to the real world, and the potential for experimenter biases.

▲ *Research Ethics.* Some ethical issues and concerns associated with doing research in personality psychology involve inducing stress, using deception, and justifying research procedures. Possible solutions for dealing with these ethical issues include using informed consent, debriefing, following APA ethics guidelines, and consulting ethics review boards.

Glossary

American Psychological Association   The largest national professional organization of psychologists in the United States.

case study method   An extensive investigation of an individual.

content analysis   The identification of recurring themes and ideas through the systematic analysis of a specific set of documents.

control group   The comparison group in experimental research that does not receive any level of the independent variable.

correlation coefficient   A numerical value indicating the strength of the association between two variables.

correlational research   An approach to research designed to identify the relationship between two variables.

debriefing session   A period at the end of the experimental session when a complete explanation of the research is given to the participants.

deception   The partial withholding of information about the experiment from the participants.

dependent variable   That variable in experimental research for which observed changes are attributed to the independent variable.

ethics review board   A panel of judges made up of individuals from different disciplines who independently evaluate the ethical standards of proposed research procedures.

experimenter bias   Any attempt by the researcher to influence the behavior of the subjects in order to achieve support for the hypothesis.

experimental control   The elimination of outside influences on the changes observed in the dependent variable.

experimental research   A method of research designed to identify causal relationships.

field research   Research conducted in locations other than the controlled conditions of the laboratory.

generalizability   The extent to which the information obtained from one situation can be extended to new and different situations.

group mean   The arithmetic average of set of scores from a particular group.

hypothesis   A statement expressing the predicted outcome of the relationships between variables.

independent variable   That variable in experimental research believed to be the causal factor.

individual interview   A one-to-one verbal exchange designed to yield critical information about the interviewee.

informed consent   Individuals making their decision to participate based on receiving information about the procedures of the research before their actual participation.

laboratory research   Research done in the controlled conditions of a laboratory.

meta-analysis   A statistical technique used to compare the results from different studies addressing a similar issue.

negative correlational relationship   A correlational relationship between two variables characterized by a downward trend in the points in the scatter plot.

parsimony   A condition of being simple or economical.

personal document   Any document a person uses to reveal personal thoughts, feelings, or ideas.

personality   The characteristics of the individual that create a unique expression of thoughts, feelings, and behavior.

personality assessment   An area of study emphasizing the development of techniques designed to measure different aspects and dimensions of personality.

personality development   The study of the factors and processes associated with the development of personality across the life span and in conjunction with other aspects of individual development.

personality psychologist   A psychologist whose professional training and research interests are in studying the different aspects and dimensions of personality.

positive correlational relationship   A correlational relationship between two variables characterized by an upward trend in the points in the scatter plot.

psychobiography   A case study of an individual for the purpose of formulating statements about the individual's psychological characteristics.

psychotherapy   The systematic application of principles of psychology in modifying the thoughts, feelings, and behavior of individuals experiencing difficulty coping with life.

psychotherapist   A psychologist specially trained to provide psychotherapy.

random assignment   A procedure guaranteeing that all individuals have an equal chance of being assigned to any of the treatment groups.

rapport   The sense of warmth and trust the interviewer creates with the interviewee.

researcher biases   The systematic distortion of information by researchers in support of their position.

scatter plot   A graph illustrating the relationship between two variables.

standardization of procedures   Treating of all subjects in all treatment groups in a similar manner.

subject biases   The systematic distortion of information when reported by individuals to the researcher.

third-variable problem   The mediating influence of an outside variable on the observed correlation between two other variables.

theory   A systematic collection of ideas and explanations designed to account for a set of observations and predict future observations.

CHAPTER 2

Personality Assessment: An Introduction to the Measurement of Personality

CHAPTER OVERVIEW: A PREVIEW OF COMING ATTRACTIONS

*P*ersonality assessment involves the development, evaluation, and utilization of personality tests in diverse settings (Ozer & Reise, 1994). This chapter explains the nature of personality assessment, describes the procedures for evaluating measures of personality, gives examples of some types of personality tests, and discusses some of the ethical and legal issues associated with personality assessment.

Personality Assessment: What, Why, and Where

Personality Assessment Defined: What Is It?

Personality assessment is the systematic measurement of various aspects of personality. Among the many aspects of personality measured by personality tests are motivation (e.g., achievement striving), personality pathology (e.g., depression), various personality traits (e.g., aggression, self-esteem, and introversion), personality dynamics (e.g., reactions to anxiety), and personality development (e.g., styles of aging). Personality tests are characterized by a variety of techniques, including paper-and-pencil inventories, direct observation of behavior, physiological recordings (e.g., heart rate), and verbal responses (e.g., comments about inkblots).

The Function of Personality Assessment: Why Do It?

Personality assessment has two major functions:

▲   To help obtain information about people in a meaningful and precise manner
▲   To help communicate this information more effectively among personality psychologists and other professionals (e.g., psychiatrists and personnel managers) using personality tests.

Promoting Purpose and Precision in Assessment

Personality assessment uses many specialized techniques, each designed to perform a particular function. Personality tests are used by mental health workers in assigning clients to specific treatment programs, by businesses to select sales representatives, and by the FBI in screening potential agents.

Before putting a personality test into use, researchers systematically evaluate it to make sure it measures precisely what it says it is measuring. For example, research in the development of a personality test designed to select sales representatives might involve administering the test to existing sales representatives and correlating their test scores with their total dollars-in-sales performance records for each of the last four years. Only if the test score is highly and consistently related to sales performance would the test be used in the actual hiring of future sales representatives.

Promoting Effective Communication

Important decisions may be based on the ability to communicate precise descriptions of personality. In deciding to admit an individual to the police academy, members of the selection committee might depend on a description of the applicant's personality provided by a personality psychologist. Since personality factors and job stress have been linked with indices of lower mental health in police personnel (Girodo, 1991), effective communication of this information has some serious consequences for the future safety and protection of many citizens.

To provide a more effective means of communicating information about the personality of individuals, personality psychologists typically compare an individual's test scores with some type of **group norm**. For example, an applicant's score on a test measuring adjustment to stress is compared to that of the group norm of successful police officers. If the individual's score is above the norm, the application may go forward. If the score is below, the application process is stopped. Because group norms for many personality tests are readily available to those individuals qualified to interpret the test results, it becomes very easy to communicate with others in different locations a rather precise description of a person's personality based on test scores.

The Use of Personality Assessment: Where Is It Done?

Personality assessment is done in many different settings, by many different people. The assessment of psychological attributes, including personality, is used by clinical psychologists, psychiatrists, personnel managers, social workers, and guidance counselors (Matarazzo, 1990). Anthropologists, criminologists, and sociologists also use personality assessment, although to a lesser extent. Personality assessment is mainly done in clinical, counseling, legal, educational and vocational guidance, personnel, and research settings.

Clinical Settings

Clinical settings include mental hospitals, community mental health centers, and the private offices of **psychometricians** and some psychotherapists. The principal purpose of psychological assessment in clinical settings is to help diagnose and classify the emotional or behavioral problems of the individual. This information is very useful in determining the most effective treatment plan for individuals experiencing an emotional problem.

Counseling Settings

Counseling settings include colleges, rehabilitation centers, and a variety of industrial settings (Phares, 1984). In counseling settings, **counseling psychologists** work to help individuals cope with and adjust more effectively to problems in their daily life (e.g., job dissatisfaction, loneliness). A counseling psychologist implementing a two-month stress management treatment program for the employees of an auto manufacturing plant might use a personality test measuring stress reactions to assess the effectiveness of the program.

Legal Settings

Personality tests are also used in legal settings such as the courtroom, prisons, and law enforcement agencies (Meyer, 1992). Information from personality tests is used as evidence in court to help determine if a person is sane and can be held responsible for criminal actions (Matarazzo, 1990; Meyer, 1992). Based on psychiatric interviews and various personality tests, John W. Hinckley, Jr. was found not guilty by reason of insanity in the shooting of President Reagan and three other individuals. Personality tests given to prospective jurors are used by lawyers to help in selecting jury members (Wrightsman, 1991).

Law enforcement agencies use personality assessment to help solve crimes. They might create a **personality profile** based on clinical interviews with and personality tests taken by incarcerated criminals who have committed a certain type of crime (e.g., serial killings). Information in the profile about the motives and behavior patterns of this type of criminal is used to help solve the crime by identifying potential suspects or potential victims.

Educational and Vocational Guidance Settings

High schools, colleges, and vocational guidance centers employ personality assessment in helping individuals to make educational and vocational decisions. For example, should group norms indicate that most successful forest rangers are independent-minded and enjoy physical exercise, then an individual whose test scores do not reflect these basic characteristics probably should not be a forestry major in college or plan a career as a forest ranger. Personality assessment techniques have also been used to investigate the pre- and post-examination strategies of college students (Drumheller, Eicke, & Scherer, 1991).

Personnel Settings

In personnel settings, information obtained from personality tests is used to help in selecting and placing personnel to promote employee satisfaction and organizational productivity. To minimize corporate loss, assessments of personality and other related factors are used to eliminate prospective job applicants most likely to engage in counterproductive behavior, such as employee theft, property damage and waste, employee violence, and the use of drugs or alcohol on the job (Terris & Jones, 1985; Slora, Joy, & Terris, 1991).

In personnel placement, personality assessment techniques are used in determining what job within a group of jobs seems most appropriate for an individual (Riggio, 1990) and in gauging the effectiveness of different personality styles on management performance (Gable & Topol, 1991). For example, in a construction company, systematic placement might involve giving all new employees a test of accident proneness (Hansen, 1991; Jones & Weubker, 1984). New employees with high accident proneness scores might be placed in low-risk jobs. In the commercial fishing industry, personality tests are used to assess the coping styles of individuals in response to the stress and dangers associated with being at sea for long periods of time (Riordan, Johnson, & Thomas, 1991). Thus, the use of personality assessment for both personnel selection and placement in an organization helps to maximize the probability of placing the right person in the right job.

Research Settings

Almost anyplace where personality assessment is used has the potential to be a research setting: university research laboratories, counseling centers, mental hospitals, community mental health centers, the military, and industry.

Personality assessment is used in research settings in three basic ways: to evaluate treatment outcome, develop new assessment techniques, and test theories. Personality research conducted in a mental hospital might use a test of anxiety to assess changes in patients before and after receiving a new type of group therapy. In military and industrial settings, research on personality assessment might be done to develop new personality tests to help in selecting and placing individuals as new jobs are created due to changes in technology. In a university setting, a psychologist developing a theory of body image might use personality assessment techniques to test hypotheses linking body image with various personality dimensions, such as loneliness and depression (Cash & Pruzinsky, 1990).

Standards for Evaluating Personality Assessment Techniques: Assessing Personality Assessment

Regardless why or where they are done, certain standards of quality are used in evaluating techniques of personality assessment (Anastasi, 1988; Briggs, 1991; Groth-Marnat, 1990; Kaplan & Sacuzzo, 1989). Two of the most important standards are reliability and validity.

Standards of Reliability: Looking for Consistency

The basic issue of **reliability** is how consistent the test is in what it is measuring. For example, a personnel manager might use a test of achievement striving when selecting potential employees for a management training program. For the selection process to be effective, the personnel manager has to assume that if an individual took the test of achievement striving today or three weeks from today, the scores on the test would be similar. If the test does not produce reliable scores, the wrong individuals may be selected for the training program.

Although there are several types of reliability, the standard used to evaluate the consistency of a particular technique of personality assessment is referred to as the **reliability coefficient** (Anastasi, 1988; Sherman, 1979). The logic and evaluation of the reliability coefficient are very similar to those of the correlation coefficient discussed in Chapter 1 (pages 17–18). The major difference is that the pairs of scores used to calculate the reliability coefficient are based on the *same* measure instead of two different measures. To measure the reliability of a new test of extraversion, a researcher might have a group of 60 students take the test and then take it again three weeks later. If the test is a reliable measure of extraversion, the correlation between the two scores should be high. As a general rule, a desirable value for a reliability coefficient is $r = .80$s or greater (Anastasi, 1988).

Types of Reliability: Different Standards of Consistency

There are several types of reliability, depending on the way consistency is measured. Two of the most important are test-retest and examiner reliability.

Test-Retest Reliability: Consistency Across Time

Test-retest reliability examines the consistency of assessment over time. A common method for assessing the degree of test-retest reliability is to give the same group of individuals a personality test on two separate occasions and calculate the reliability coefficient (r) between the two sets of scores. For example, researchers developing a measure of self-consciousness might give their test to a group of individuals on one day and then give them the same test 30 days later.

Test-retest reliability can be affected by the length of time between each administration of the test. If the interval is very short (i.e., two days), the similarity in the scores may simply be due to the individuals' memory of how they responded just two days ago. If the interval is too long (e.g., 10 months), the dissimilarity in the scores may be due to actual changes that have occurred in the individual over time (e.g., development of acne increasing one's self-consciousness). Although there is no hard-and-fast rule, the recommended interval between the two occasions of testing is at least one week but no more than two or three months for personality tests (Kleinmuntz, 1982).

Examiner Reliability: Consistency Across Raters

The principal rationale of **examiner reliability** is to establish the extent to which different individuals administering and scoring a particular test will come to similar conclusions about the results. A personality test assessing depression for the purpose of developing a plan of therapy is of little value if the test is scored differently by different clinical psychologists. Another issue related to examiner reliability is how consistently an individual administering and scoring the test does so over time. It is extremely unfair if the answers to a standard set of questions given by applicants during a job interview are evaluated not on the basis of their content but on the mood of the personnel manager during the interview.

Several precautions can be taken to increase the examiner reliability of a test. One is to give detailed training or clear instructions on how to interpret the results of the test. This is why distributors of personality tests go to great lengths to develop and produce scoring manuals to accompany their tests. These manuals include detailed explanations and examples of how to interpret the results obtained from the tests. Another precaution is to standardize the procedures for scoring the tests as much as possible in order to eliminate personal biases in the interpretations. The logic underlying standardization is to make the procedures for scoring the test as consistent and straightforward as possible, so that everybody scores the test in the same manner. The standardization of scoring procedures might involve providing a standard set of scoring keys or requiring that the test be scored by a computer (Groth-Marnat, 1990; Matarazzo, 1986). Both of these precautions are designed to minimize human error entering into the scoring and interpretation of the test results.

Standards of Validity: Measuring What You Say You're Measuring

Measures of personality must be valid as well as reliable. The **validity** of assessment is how completely a test measures what it says it is measuring. Validity of assessment is considered to be the most critical issue in the development of tests (Groth-Marnat, 1990; Messick, 1995).

Types of Validity: Establishing the True Meaning of Your Test

Four types of validity are face validity, content validity, criterion validity, and construct validity. Each considers a different aspect in measuring personality.

Face Validity: Judging a Book by Its Cover

Face validity refers to how appropriate a test looks, considering what it is supposed to measure. One of the most important reasons for having a high degree of face validity is to help maintain the interest and involvement of individuals taking the test. For example, a test for selecting potential executives should include some questions about making financial and personnel decisions, as well as questions about personal goals. Just having face validity, however, does not really offer any valuable information concerning whether a test is really measuring what it says it is measuring. That information is provided by the other three types of validity.

Content Validity: It's What's Inside that Counts

Content validity refers to how well the items (i.e., content) making up the test represent the personality dimension supposedly being measured by the test. A test for measuring shyness should contain items reflecting aspects of shyness, such as the personal (Is your shyness a major source of personal unhappiness?), social (Do you find it difficult to talk in small groups of people?), cognitive (Do you believe that people are always evaluating you?), and physiological (Do you experience sweaty palms when talking to members of the opposite sex?). Because shyness involves all of these components (Zimbardo, 1977), a valid test of shyness must measure all of them. To enhance content validity of a test, researchers must make sure that all aspects of the dimension supposedly being measured are included in the test.

Another issue related to content validity addresses how clearly the dimension of personality being measured by the test is defined. When developing a test to measure anxiety, researchers must consider many types of anxiety, such as social anxiety, trait anxiety, state anxiety, moral anxiety, neurotic anxiety, and test anxiety, to name just a few. Defining a specific dimension of anxiety determines which items are contained in the test. Because personality psychologists from different theoretical viewpoints do not necessarily agree on how a certain dimension of personality might be specified or defined, establishing content validity relies heavily on the definition of the concept used by the individuals developing the test.

Criterion Validity: Making Predictions

Criterion validity addresses how thoroughly the scores of a test can predict the behavior of an individual in specific situations. The behavior predicted from the test score is called the **criterion measure.** The extent to which the criterion measured is predicted from the test score is indicated by the **validity coefficient** and involves correlating the test scores with some agreed-upon criterion measure. Two types of criterion validity are predictive validity and concurrent validity.

Predictive validity involves assessing how accurately the test scores can predict some specific criterion behavior in the future. In the area of industrial security, scores on personality tests are used to help predict employee thefts in a chain of home improvement centers (Jones & Terris, 1983, 1991) and in convenience stores (Terris & Jones, 1985). In these studies, the criterion measure was the amount of unexplained missing merchandise. In the large commercial rail industry, test scores were able to predict who would and would not have a work-related injury within a 12-month period (Sherry, 1991).

Concurrent validity refers to how closely the test scores are related to other currently existing criterion measures. In a mental hospital, a clinical psychologist trying to establish the concurrent validity of a personality test measuring paranoia might correlate patients' test scores with the ratings of paranoid tendencies made by other clinical psychologists who interviewed these same individuals. A high degree of correlation between the scores on the paranoia test and the paranoia ratings made by the clinicians is evidence to support the concurrent validity of this test.

Establishing predictive validity is not without its difficulties; among them is getting individuals to agree on an appropriate criterion measure. When developing a test designed to measure happiness, researchers might have real problems in agreeing on what *happiness* means (Myers, 1992). Another issue is **criterion contamination**, referring to a situation in which the researcher's knowledge about a person's score on one test influences the score given to that person on the second test. In the earlier example involving the test of paranoid tendencies, a potential problem arises when the person scoring the test also knows the interview scores. Fortunately, this situation can be easily rectified by making sure that the same person is not making both ratings.

Construct Validity

In their classic article on construct validity, Lee J. Cronbach & Paul E. Meehl (1955) state, "A construct is some postulated attribute of people, assumed to be reflected in test performance" (p. 283). The phrase "postulated attribute" simply means a characteristic assumed to be possessed by the individual, such as cheerfulness, intelligence, aggressiveness, or being in love, that can be measured (i.e., reflected in test performance) and used to help us describe, explain, and predict behavior in various situations. Although they cannot actually be seen—that is, have no physical embodiment—the concepts of intelligence and friendliness are constructs used to explain a variety of behaviors. Thus, constructs are attributes assumed to exist in the individual, measured by personality tests even though they cannot necessarily be seen, whose existence can be used to help explain and predict behavior.

Construct validity represents how effectively the evidence documents the presence of the construct as defined by the researcher. For example, if a researcher defines shyness as involving social withdrawal, the construct of shyness is supported when individuals scoring high on a measure of shyness are found to stand at a greater distance from others (Carducci & Webber, 1979) and to speak less in groups (Pilkonis, 1977) than individuals scoring low.

Establishing construct validity is a continuing process involving three basic steps:

1. Define the construct, making sure to include as many behavior references as possible.
2. Develop a test designed to measure the construct, making sure items in the test reflect the definition of the construct (i.e., content validity).
3. Conduct research designed to provide evidence that scores on the test can predict behaviors in a manner consistent with the definition of the construct.

Read "A Closer Look" below for a systematic illustration of an actual series of construct validation studies.

A CLOSER LOOK

Developing and Validating the Situational Humor Response Questionnaire: Documenting a Sense of Humor

Probably one of the things we value most in other people, besides honesty, is a sense of humor. You might hear people saying such things as, "I met the most interesting person at a party last week; what a great sense of humor!" or "I'm sure you'll have a great time; your blind date has such a wonderful sense of humor!" Although we may frequently talk about having a sense of humor, what do we really mean? How would you spot someone with a sense of humor? What do you look for in a sense of humor? In other words, how would you go about defining and then assessing a sense of humor?

An excellent and rather interesting example of the step-by-step process of construct validation is the research by Rod Martin and Herbert Lefcourt, who have developed and validated a measure of personality for assessing a person's sense of humor.

Step One: Defining the Construct

In developing the Situational Humor Response Questionnaire (SHRQ), Martin and Lefcourt (1984) defined *sense of humor* as "the frequency with which the individual smiles, laughs, or otherwise displays amusement in a variety of situations" (p. 147). As emphasized previously, a major advantage of this definition is that it is based on behavioral references (e.g., smiling, laughing, and other displays of amusement) that can be easily and reliably measured. Thus, this rather behavioral

A sense of humor is something we seem to desire in others, from celebrities to friends of all ages. Because of its importance, some personality psychologists are trying to develop personality tests to assess a sense of humor.

definition of a sense of humor focuses on how frequently individuals experience humor and joyful amusement rather than on a preference for a particular type of humor (e.g., political, sexual).

Step Two: Developing a Test to Measure the Construct

The SHRQ contains 21 items (see the following excerpt). To ensure content validity, the items included in the SHRQ represent a wide variety of both pleasant and unpleasant situations in which most individuals would probably have experienced and had the opportunity to demonstrate the extent of their sense of humor (e.g., items 1–7). In addition to measuring situational humor responses, the SHRQ also includes three items designed to measure the person's self-report sense of humor (items 8–10). According to Martin and Lefcourt, they included item 8 because they assumed that people who laugh and smile a great deal would most likely have friends who do the same. They included item 9 because people are probably pretty good judges of whether they would laugh in various situations. Finally, the researchers included item 10 on the assumption that people who demonstrate consistency in their level of laughter or humor would probably score high on the SHRQ. Thus, they are careful to include items representing many different dimensions contributing to what they define as a sense of humor.

Assessing Sense of Humor by Questionnaire: Do You Have a Sense of Humor?

In this questionnaire, you will find descriptions of a number of situations in which you may have found yourself from time to time. For each question, please take a moment to recall a time when you were actually in such a situation. If you cannot remember such an experience, try to *imagine* yourself in such a situation, filling in the details in ways that reflect your own experience. Then circle the letter (*a, b, c, d,* or *e*) beside the phrase that best describes the way you have responded or would respond in such a situation.

1. You accidentally hurt yourself and had to spend a few days in bed. During that time in bed, how would you have responded?
   a. I would not have found anything particularly amusing.
   b. I would have smiled occasionally.
   c. I would have smiled a lot and laughed from time to time.
   d. I would have found quite a lot to laugh about.
   e. I would have laughed heartily much of the time.

2. If you arrived at a party and found that someone else was wearing a piece of clothing identical to yours . . .
   a. I wouldn't have found it particularly amusing.
   b. I would have been amused but wouldn't have shown it outwardly.
   c. I would have smiled.
   d. I would have laughed.
   e. I would have laughed heartily.

3. You were traveling in a car in the winter and suddenly the car spun around on an ice patch and came to rest facing the wrong way on the opposite side of the highway. You were relieved to find that no one was hurt and no damage had been done to the car . . .
   a. I wouldn't have found it particularly amusing.
   b. I would have been amused but wouldn't have shown it outwardly.
   c. I would have smiled.
   d. I would have laughed.
   e. I would have laughed heartily.

4. If you were watching a movie or TV program with some friends and you found one scene particularly funny, but no one else appeared to find it humorous, how would you have reacted most commonly?
   a. I would have concluded that I must have misunderstood something or that it wasn't really funny.
   b. I would have "smiled to myself," but wouldn't have shown my amusement outwardly.
   c. I would have smiled visibly.
   d. I would have laughed aloud.
   e. I would have laughed heartily.

5. If you got an unexpectedly low mark on an exam and later that evening you were telling a friend about it . . .
   a. I would not have been amused.
   b. I would have been amused but wouldn't have shown it outwardly.
   c. I would have smiled.
   d. I would have laughed.
   e. I would have laughed heartily.

6. If you were eating in a restaurant with some friends and the waiter accidentally spilled a drink on you . . .

a. I would not have been particularly amused.

b. I would have been amused but wouldn't have shown it outwardly.

c. I would have smiled.

d. I would have laughed.

e. I would have laughed heartily.

7. If there had been a computer error and you had spent all morning standing in line-ups at various offices trying to get the problem sorted out . . .

a. I wouldn't have found it particularly amusing.

b. I would have been able to experience some amusement, but wouldn't have shown it.

c. I would have smiled a lot.

d. I would have laughed a lot.

e. I would have laughed heartily.

8. In choosing your friends, how desirable do you feel it is for them to be easily amused and able to laugh in a wide variety of situations?

a. the most important characteristic I look for in a friend.

b. very desirable, but not the most important characteristic.

c. quite desirable.

d. neither desirable nor undesirable.

e. not very desirable.

9. How would you rate yourself in terms of your likelihood of being amused and of laughing in a wide variety of situations?

a. my most outstanding characteristic.

b. above average.

c. about average

d. less than average.

e. very little.

10. How much do you vary from one situation to another in the extent to which you laugh or otherwise respond with humor? For example, how much does it depend on who you are with, where you are, how you feel, etc.?

a. not at all.

b. not very much.

c. to some extent.

d. quite a lot.

e. very much so.

Scoring instructions: The scoring key for the sense of humor questionnaire is $a = 1$, $b = 2$, $c = 3$, $d = 4$, and $e = 5$. Each time you circled a particular letter in response to an item on the questionnaire, give yourself the point value correspond-

ing to that letter. To get your sense of humor score, add together all of the points; possible total scores range from 10 to 50.

When interpreting your score, you should realize that this questionnaire is an incomplete version of the SHRQ and, therefore, not a true measure of your sense of humor.

Situational Humor Response Questionnaire: Quantitative measure of sense of humor.

Note. From *Journal of Personality and Social Psychology,* by R. H. Martin and H. M. Lefcourt, 1984, Vol. 47, pp.145–155.

Step Three: Validating the Construct through Systematic Research

As the third step in the validation process, Martin and Lefcourt (1984) conducted three validation studies in an attempt to relate scores on the SHRQ to various external behaviors that indicate a sense of humor.

▲ *Validation study 1.* In the first study, 19 male and 19 female undergraduates were asked to describe some of the most outstanding positive and negative events they could recall in their lives. The interviews were videotaped and later rated for the percentage of total interview time the individual spent smiling or laughing. Each participant was also asked to provide the name and telephone number of a friend who knew them well. The friend was contacted by the researchers and asked to rate how much time this person spends smiling and laughing, with ratings ranging from 1 (never smiles or laughs) to 10 (is always smiling or laughing). Finally, in addition to completing the SHRQ, the 38 subjects were asked to complete a personality test measuring their overall level of positive mood and total mood disturbance for the past year. In support of the validity of the sense of humor construct, scores on the SHRQ correlated positively with the percentage of time laughing and smiling during the interview, peer humor ratings, and overall positive mood and lack of overall mood disturbance.

▲ *Validation study 2.* The second validation investigated how closely the scores on the SHRQ were related to humor production. Twenty-nine males and 33 females were asked to sit at a table with 12 miscellaneous objects on it (e.g., shoe, broken toys, wrist watch, etc.). After completing the

SHRQ, the subjects were instructed to make up a 3-minute humorous monologue involving the items on the table. The monologues were recorded and later rated for their humor level by two judges. As in the first validation study, peer ratings of the person's sense of humor were also obtained. In support of the validity of the humor questionnaire, scores on the SHRQ were positively correlated with the number of witty comments made in the monologue, the humorous rating of the monologue, and peer humor ratings.

▲ *Validation study 3.* The third validation study was designed to investigate the role of humor in reducing stress. In this study, after completing the SHRQ, 14 males and 11 females were asked to watch a rather stressful silent film about the male initiation rites among a tribe of aborigines in Australia. While watching the silent film, the individuals were instructed to make up a humorous narrative describing what they were seeing in the film. These narratives were recorded and later rated for their overall level of humor. In support of the SHRQ as a valid measure of sense of humor, humorousness ratings of the narratives were positively correlated with SHRQ scores.

Although these three validation studies provide supportive evidence for the SHRQ as a measure of sense of humor, construct validation research is an ongoing process. To further establish the validity of the SHRQ, additional validation studies will have to be done using individuals other than college-age students and people from different cultures. Also, because the three validation studies involved individuals being observed in isolation, future research should be conducted that attempts to relate scores on the SHRQ to laughing, smiling, and producing humor in more realistic settings, such as informal groups at parties, work, or school.

If you have not already done so, try answering the items in the modified version of the SHRQ presented here. The instructions for scoring the test are at the bottom of the table.

Although the different types of reliability and validity are discussed separately here, personality psychologists consider all of them when developing and evaluating techniques to assess personality.

Methods of Personality Measurement: A Survey of Personality Assessment Techniques

There are several different methods of measuring personality, including objective self-report, projective, behavioral, and psychophysiological assessment techniques. This section examines the characteristic features and examples of these techniques.

Objective Self-Report Techniques: Treating Everybody the Same

Objective self-report techniques are characterized by individuals providing information about their thoughts, feelings, and behaviors in response to questions asked in personality tests. The response alternatives available to the items in these tests and the procedures for scoring the responses are standardized; they are the same for anyone completing the test. By treating everybody taking the test the same, researchers can minimize potential biases and subjective influences on interpreting the results that might affect the person's test score. The standardization of test items and procedures for scoring the responses adds to the speed and ease of administering the tests. It also increases the level of reliability that characterizes objective self-report techniques of personality assessment and makes them attractive to many personality psychologists and other individuals who use them.

Types of Objective Self-Report Techniques: Single- vs. Multiple-Dimension Personality Tests

Single-dimension personality tests attempt to measure only one dimension of personality (e.g., shyness, creativity, or aggressiveness) at a time. An excellent example of a single-dimension objective self-report personality test is the **California F Scale** (Adorno, Frenkel-Brunswik, Levinson, & Sanford, 1950). The F scale is designed to measure the personality dimension called **authoritarianism**. Authoritarianism is characterized by rather conventional attitudes and beliefs, submissiveness to authority, and intolerance of others perceived as different (e.g., members of racial minorities). The F scale consists of 29 items, each having a standardized 6-point agreement-disagreement response option. Here is a sample F-scale item:

Obedience and respect for authority are the most important virtues children should learn.

___ Strong Support, Agreement

___ Moderate Support, Agreement

___ Slight Support, Agreement

___ Slight Opposition, Disagreement

___ Moderate Opposition, Disagreement

___ Strong Opposition, Disagreement

Multiple-dimension personality tests attempt to measure more than one dimension of personality at a time and usually contain a much larger number of items than single-dimension tests. The **California Psychological Inventory (CPI)** (Gough, 1957, 1987) is a multiple-dimension personality test that contains 462 true-false questions and measures 20 different personality dimensions such as dominance, self-control, flexibility, socialization, self-acceptance, and a sense of well-being, to name just a few.

Another widely used objective self-report personality test is the **Edwards Personal Preference Schedule (EPPS)** (Edwards, 1954, 1959). The EPPS contains 210 forced-choice pairs of items assessing 15 separate personality dimensions, expressed as need preferences in such domains as achievement, autonomy, affiliation, dominance, endurance, heterosexuality, and aggression. A unique feature of the EPPS is that items associated with each specific need preference are paired with items from the remaining 14 need preferences. Here is an example of an item similar to those in the EPPS:

a. I find it very satisfying to achieve success on my own.
b. The most enjoyable times I have involve being with other people.

By demonstrating a tendency to select items like the first one, an achievement-type item, over items like the second, an affiliation-type item, an individual is assessed as having a high need for achievement and a low need for affiliation. The EPPS assesses how certain needs are more characteristic of the individual's personality than others. Similarly, intelligence tests, like the Wechsler Adult Intelligence Scale-Revised, are objective tests assessing many different aspects of intelligence (Groth-Marnat, 1990).

The Minnesota Multiphasic Personality Inventory

The most widely used and extensively researched clinical personality inventory is the Minnesota Multiphasic Personality Inventory (Groth-Marnat, 1990). The **Minnesota Multiphasic Personality Inventory-2 (MMPI-2)** (Butcher, Dahlstrom, Graham, Tellegen, & Kaemmer, 1989), as well as the original MMPI (Hathaway & McKinley, 1940, 1943), is a multiple-dimension personality test.

The MMPI-2 contains 567 true-false questions. The 10 dimensions of personality measured by the principal clinical scales appearing in the original MMPI and the revised MMPI-2 are presented in the upper portion of Table 2.1. The table also contains a sample item from each of the clinical scales and a brief interpretation of the characteristics of someone scoring high on the scale. The labels of the clinical scales reflect the fact that the MMPI was principally designed to help in diagnosing and classifying individuals experiencing various psychopathologies. Although it was developed originally to help classify mental patients into a variety of psychiatric disorders, the MMPI is used as a screening and diagnostic device in industrial, military, and educational settings.

In addition to the 10 principal clinical scales appearing in the original MMPI and the MMPI-2, the MMPI-2 also contains 12 supplementary scales (Butcher et al., 1989). These scales were developed using items from the existing MMPI and MMPI-2 item pool and recombining them using factor analytic and other item-grouping techniques. Each supplementary scale was then validated against various clinical and nonclinical populations (Butcher et al., 1989; Graham, 1990). The lower portion of Table 2.1 contains a listing of five of the supplementary scales, a sample item, and a brief interpretation of the characteristic features of someone scoring high on the scale. The other supplementary scales and a brief interpretation of someone scoring high on the scales include:

Table 2.1
Sample Items from and Interpretations of the Clinical and Supplementary Scales of the MMPI-2

Scale Name (Symbol)	Sample Item*	Interpretation†
THE CLINICAL SCALES		
Hypochondriasis (HS)	I am almost never bothered by pains over my heart or in my chest. (False)	Tendency to have excessive bodily concerns and complain of chronic weakness, lack of energy, and sleep disturbances
Depression (D)	I usually feel like life is worth living. (False)	Tendency to feel unhappy and depressed and be pessimistic about the future
Hysteria (Hy)	I have periods of such great restlessness that I cannot sit still. (True)	Tendency to react to stress by developing physical symptoms that appear and disappear suddenly
Psychopathic Deviate (Pd)	I have had very peculiar and strange experiences. (True)	Tendency to be rebellious, impulsive, and lacking in warm attachments with others
Masculinity-Femininity (Mf)	I wish I were not bothered by thoughts about sex (True for males; False for females)	Tendency to lack appropriate sex-role behavior for one's gender
Paranoia (Pa)	If people had not had it in for me, I would have been much more successful.	Tendency to feel mistreated and picked on and to have delusions of persecution or grandeur
Psychasthenia (Pt)	I have had periods of days, weeks, or months when I couldn't take care of things because I couldn't "get going." (True)	Tendency to be worried, fearful, apprehensive, high-strung, and jumpy
Schizophrenia (Sc)	At one or more times in my life I felt that someone was making me do things by hypnotizing me. (True)	Tendency to report unusual thoughts or attitudes or hallucinations and may be confused, disorganized, and disoriented
Hypomania (Ma)	My speech is the same as always (not faster or slower, slurring or hoarseness). (False)	Tendency to be energetic and talkative and prefer action to thought
Social Introversion (Si)	I find it hard to keep my mind on a task or job. (True)	Tendency to be shy, reserved, timid, and retiring
THE SUPPLEMENTARY SCALES		
Anxiety (A)	I sometimes feel that I am about to go to pieces. (True)	Tendency to be anxious, uncomfortable, shy, and retiring
Repression (R)	I am about as able to work as I ever was. (False)	Tendency to be careful and cautious
Ego Strength (Es)	I get mad easily and then get over it soon. (True)	Tendency to be stable, reliable, and self-confident
MacAndrew Alcoholism Revised Scale (MAC-R)	I have had periods in which I carried on activities without knowing later what I had been doing. (True)	Tendency to abuse alcohol and other substances and to be socially extraverted, exhibitionistic, and possibly experience blackouts
Overcontrolled-Hostility Scale (O-H)	I work under a great deal of tension. (False)	Tendency not to respond to provocation and to report few angry feelings, but may experience occasional exaggerated aggressive responses

*The "true" or "false" responses within parentheses indicate how each item is scored.
†Adapted from Graham, 1990.

Note: From *Minnesota Multiphasic Personality Inventory-2 (MMPI-2): Manual for administration and scoring,* by J. N. Butcher, W. G. Dahlstrom, J. R. Graham, A. Tellegen, and B. Kaemmer, 1989. Minneapolis, The University of Minnesota Press.

▲ *Dominance Scale (DO)*—Tendency to feel confident and cope with life's stresses
▲ *Social Responsibility Scale (RE)*—Tendency to incorporate societal and cultural values and behave accordingly
▲ *College Maladjustment Scale (MT)*—Tendency to show general maladjustment, to procrastinate, and be ineffectual
▲ *Masculine Gender Role Scale (GM)*—Tendency to be self-confident and free from fears and worries
▲ *Feminine Gender Role Scale (GF)*—Tendency toward religiosity and to abuse alcohol and nonprescription drugs
▲ *Post-Traumatic Stress Disorder Scale (PK)*—Tendency among veterans to report intense emotional distress and guilt
▲ *Subtle-Obvious Subscales*—Tendency to endorse items on the clinical scales that indicate obvious emotional disturbances (e.g., trying to appear emotionally disturbed)

The labeling used in these supplementary scales reflects their tendency to assess other aspects of personality that might be helpful in the diagnostic process. But note that the supplementary scales are not designed to replace the clinical scales; they are to be used in conjunction with them (Graham, 1990).

The MMPI-2 Validity Scales   As one of its most important features, the MMPI-2 contains four **validity scales** designed to assess the validity of the responses given by individuals taking the test:

▲ *The Cannot Say Scale (?)* counts the number of items the individual leaves blank and is believed to reflect a desire to be evasive.
▲ *The Lie Scale (L)* contains 15 items (e.g., I get angry sometimes. [False]) and assesses how much the individuals taking the test are trying to present themselves in a favorable or extremely positive manner.
▲ *The Frequency Scale (F)* contains 60 items (e.g., I have nightmares every few nights. [True]) and assesses carelessness on the part of the individual taking the test, such as giving different answers for the same question asked two separate times in the test.
▲ *The Correction Scale (K)* contains 30 items assessing the extent to which the person's

responses demonstrate a tendency to guard against admitting to psychopathology (e.g., I have very few fears compared to my friends. [False]).

These validity scales increase the likelihood of detecting individuals whose responses to the items lack trustworthiness. They also help to strengthen the test givers' confidence in the results obtained and the interpretation based on these results.

The MMPI-2 Personality Profile   Another distinctive feature of the MMPI-2 is that the subscales can be used to construct a personality profile. A **profile analysis** involves plotting the scores of each subscale on an MMPI-2 profile chart and then connecting these points to reveal a particular response pattern. Through extensive, systematic analysis of many MMPI and MMPI-2 profiles, researchers discovered that certain profiles are associated with particular psychiatric disorders and personality characteristics (Hathaway & Meehl, 1951; Dahlstrom, Welsh, & Dahlstrom, 1972, 1975; Graham, 1990; Groth-Marnat, 1990).

The profile pattern in Figure 2.1 has been identified as the "paranoid valley" (Dahlstrom & Welsh, 1960; Groth-Marnat, 1990) because patients suffering from paranoid schizophrenia tend to have this profile pattern. The valley is created by high scores on the Paranoia (Pa) and Schizophrenia (Sc) scales (numbers 6 and 8 on the profile chart) and relatively lower scores on the Psychasthenia (Pt) and Hypomania (Ma) scales (numbers 7 and 9 on the profile chart). Because patients with certain psychiatric disorders produce certain profiles, the MMPI-2 is an extremely valuable tool to many mental health professionals when diagnosing psychiatric disorders and establishing treatment plans (Butcher, 1990; Graham, 1990).

The Problem of Response Sets: Subjective Influences on Objective Tests

Although being objective in nature helps to minimize any subjective influences in the scoring and interpretations, certain response sets can influence the nature of the results obtained from objective self-report tests. A **response set** refers to a tendency to answer test items in a particular way regardless of how the person taking the test really feels about the content of the item.

Figure 2.1
A sample MMPI profile: the "paranoid valley"

Note. From *Personality and Psychological Assessment,* by B. Kleinmuntz, 1982. New York: St. Martin's Press, p. 228 and *Handbook of Psychological Assessment* (2nd ed.), by G. Groth-Marnat, 1990. New York: John Wiley & Sons p. 226.

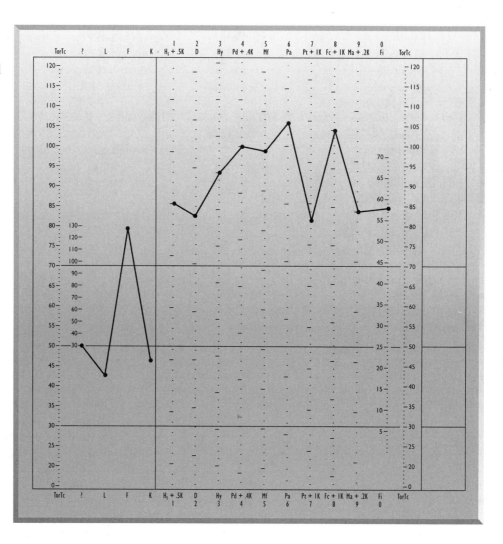

The **acquiescence response set** refers to the tendency for the person to respond with agreement to test items for which there is some uncertainty. A person may obtain a very high need-for-achievement score only because of a tendency to answer "true" to the many items on the test for which there was some uncertainty about the meaning of the items.

The **social desirability response set** is characterized by a tendency to select those response alternatives appearing the most socially acceptable. The individual might agree consistently with such statements as "I am very loyal to all of my friends" and disagree consistently with such statements as "I tell lies to cover my mistakes." Although such response sets can be problematic, they can be minimized by developing and including validity scales in the tests

(i.e., MMPI-2 and EPPS) to identify and correct the test scores for such tendencies. They can also be minimized by carefully considering the wording of the test items and the scoring procedures. For example, wording the test items so half of the alternatives appearing most socially acceptable are scored as "true" and half as "false" can also help to control for both the acquiescence and social desirability response sets.

Evaluating Objective Self-Report Techniques:
Characteristic Strengths and Limitations
A summary of the characteristic strengths and limitations of the objective self-report techniques is presented below.

Characteristic Strengths   The major strength of objective self-report personality tests is their objective and rather standardized nature. The objective nature makes it possible for these tests to be administered quite easily in individual as well as group settings. Their standardized procedures make it possible for every person taking the test to be treated the same. Besides contributing to how easily the tests can be scored, standard scoring procedures have the major advantage of minimizing any bias on the part of the person scoring the test, which helps to increase test reliability. For multiple-dimension tests, a major advantage is that many different aspects of the individual's personality can be assessed at the same time.

Characteristic Limitations   A major limitation of objective self-report tests is their heavy reliance on the person taking the test to provide honest and un-biased answers. But research on response sets makes it clear that test takers may not always give answers that accurately describe themselves. Such response sets make interpretation difficult and decrease the test validity. Another limitation is that the rather standardized and limited response options available in objective self-report tests do not allow the persons taking the test to elaborate or clarify their answers. Still another limitation is the somewhat restricted ability of the test score, based on a specific set of items, to predict more general and complex behavioral patterns, such as might be the case when selecting personnel, determining educational placement, and classifying mental patients for psychotherapy.

Projective Techniques: Assessing Personality Indirectly

Protective techniques of personality assessment involve asking individuals to respond to rather ambiguous test stimuli with no apparent meaning. For projective techniques, researchers assume that the meaning a person projects into the ambiguous stimuli indicates his or her unconscious feelings, needs, desires, attitudes, motives, and other core aspects of personality (Frank, 1939). Thus, the individual reveals information about her or his personality without realizing it. From this perspective, the major advantage of projective techniques is that the abstract nature of the stimuli minimizes the likeli-

hood of the individual's guessing what the test is all about and trying to respond in a socially desirable manner.

Although there are a variety of projective techniques, they seem to share the following characteristics:

▲ *Ambiguous test stimuli*. In projective techniques, the testing stimuli are relatively ambiguous. For example, the test stimuli might include responding to a series of inkblots or completing a series of sentences (e.g., If I were president, . . .).

▲ *An indirect method*. Instead of responding directly to items on objective self-report techniques (e.g., Are you anxious in public places?), projective techniques take a much more indirect approach to personality assessment by requiring the individual to respond to the ambiguous test stimuli. This rather indirect method makes individuals less certain of the actual purpose of the test and makes it more difficult to modify their responses accordingly.

▲ *Freedom of response*. Projective techniques allow for more freedom in responding to the test stimuli. Because the stimuli are ambiguous, there are no right or wrong responses. As an example, the ink blot presented in Figure 2.2 could be perceived as almost anything.

Figure 2.2
An inkblot used in projective personality assessment

▲ *Subjective nature of scoring procedures.* Although attempts have been made to standardize their scoring, a considerable amount of subjective interpretation of the responses by those scoring the tests is a common characteristic of projective techniques. For example, depending on the theoretical viewpoint of the individual scoring the test, a response of "If I were president, I would get rid of all the rules for paying taxes" could be interpreted by some as expressing an individual's sense of freedom or by others as indicating a lack of responsibility.

Types of Projective Techniques:
Many Methods of Indirect Assessment
Researchers can assess and interpret the individual's personality through projective techniques by analyzing the themes and patterns of responses generated in reaction to the ambiguous stimuli contained in the test. One of the most interesting aspects of projective techniques is the diversity of the stimuli employed. According to Lindzey (1961), projective techniques can be classified into the following five general categories:

▲ With **association techniques**, the individual is given a test stimulus and then asked to respond with the first word, thought, or feeling that comes to mind. The most famous example of this technique is the Rorschach Inkblot Test (Rorschach, 1942) discussed in more detail in Chapter 3.
▲ **Completion techniques** require individuals to complete a test stimulus that is presented to them unfinished. An example of this technique is the Rotter Incomplete Sentences Test (Rotter & Rafferty, 1950), for which the individual completes a series of sentences such as "Men seem to be anxious . . ." and "My secret desire is . . ."
▲ **Choice or ordering projective techniques** require the individual to select from, or arrange in some preferred order, a set of test stimuli. For example, the Szondi Test (Szondi, 1944) requires the person to select from a set of pictures the individuals they like the most and those they like the least.
▲ **Expressive projective techniques** require individual expression through such activities as taking

the role of another person or drawing a picture. For example, in the Kinetic House-Tree-Person Test (Burns, 1987), the individual is asked to draw a picture of a person "doing something."
▲ **Constructive projective techniques** require the individual to create something, such as a story based on the test stimuli. For a closer look at a famous constructive projective technique written about in over 1800 articles (Groth-Marnat, 1990), consider the material in "A Closer Look" below.

A CLOSER LOOK

The Thematic Apperception Test: Of Pictures and Personality

The **Thematic Apperception Test (TAT)** (Morgan & Murray, 1935; Murray, 1938, 1943) was developed by the famous American personality psychologist Henry Murray and his colleagues at the Harvard Psychological Clinic. The TAT is based on Murray's (1938) theory of needs.

Administering the TAT
The TAT consists of 20 cards, 19 cards containing black-and-white pictures of one or more people in rather ambiguous situations and one blank white card. Figure 2.3 is a sample TAT card. When administering the test, the examiner gives the individual each picture separately, and asks him or her to make up a story about what is going on in the picture by telling what has led up to this moment in the story, what is happening now, what will happen next, and what the individuals may be feeling, thinking, or saying to each other. The logic underlying the TAT is that important aspects of the individual's personality will be revealed by the nature of the stories created from these ambiguous pictures.

Scoring and Interpreting the TAT
According to Murray's procedures (1943; Groth-Marnat, 1990), scoring the TAT involves evaluating the following five aspects of the stories:

▲ *The hero.* Scoring for the **hero** involves identifying who is the central character(s) in the story. In

Subject's Story

Why . . . the young woman doesn't know what to do about the old crone. They've just had an argument. The old lady is feeling very smug and satisfied. She's got the younger one just where she wants her . . . in her control. The young woman is very angry; this always happens to her. People manipulate her . . . make her do things. She hates it. She's going to get rid of the old woman. I mean . . . get away from her. But it won't work. Someone else will come along to try to control her. She can't escape from it.

Interpretation

The subject (a 32-year-old woman) feels controlled by others, and resents their influence. She feels powerless and helpless in avoiding the control of others. She perceives others as purposely manipulating her and tries to deal with her anger by escape, but recognizes the futility of her attempts. Her sense of being controlled, the helplessness she experiences, and her anger are consistent with paranoid-like behavior and with the major themes in her other stories.

Figure 2.3.

An example of a TAT card, sample story, and clinical interpretation

Note. From *Abnormal Psychology,* by J. Mehr, 1983. New York: Holt, Rinehart and Winston, p. 83. TAT Card © : Harvard University Press.

reading the response to the TAT picture in Figure 2.3, it is clear that the younger woman is the hero, since all of the action seems to revolve around her.

▲ *Needs of the hero.* For Murray, it was also critical to identify the **needs**, motives, and desires of the hero. In Figure 2.3, the hero seems to be expressing a rather intensive need for regaining control of her life and a desire to be independent.

▲ *Identifying the presses.* A **press** refers to any important environmental factor that may influence or interfere with the needs of the hero. For our female hero in Figure 2.3, a very important press is the older woman. Other presses might involve particular authority figures (e.g., parents or a boss), external obstacles (e.g., the lock on the door is broken), or physical disabilities (e.g., being sick or injured).

▲ *Scoring for themes.* Scoring for themes in TAT stories involves noting the nature of the interplay and conflict between the needs and presses, what emotions are elicited by this conflict, and how the conflict is resolved. A clear theme found in the response in Figure 2.3 is the struggle between the need of the younger woman to be free and the press created by the manipulative tendencies of the older woman.

▲ *Scoring for outcome.* Scoring for the outcome of the story involves analyzing how the stories end by noting a happy versus unhappy ending and assessing the extent to which the ending is controlled by the strengths of the hero or forces (i.e., presses) in the environment. The outcome of the story in Figure 2.3 is unhappy, and environmental forces determine what eventually happens.

Interpreting the TAT involves the overall interpretation of the individual's personality based on the general pattern of responses to the TAT cards in expressing needs, motives, and modes of interacting with other people. The female hero's responses in Figure 2.3 and the other TAT cards stress the person's need for control over her life and her feelings of being manipulated in her interactions with others.

Evaluating Projective Techniques: Characteristic Strengths and Limitations

Here is a summary of the characteristic strengths and limitations of the projective techniques.

Characteristic Strengths   The major strength of projective techniques is the freedom of response they allow. Their indirect method and the ambiguous nature of the stimuli make it possible to minimize any attempts by individuals to modify their responses in accordance with what they think the test is measuring and what the examiner wants to hear. Finally, because projective techniques attempt to measure many deep-seated core aspects of personality at once, the assumption is that a much more global and meaningful picture of the individual's personality results.

Characteristic Limitations   Because of the tremendous freedom of response made available, the scoring procedures of projective techniques are often extremely complex. This complexity introduces many subjective decisions made by the examiner and contributes to the characteristically low reliability coefficients of these techniques. The rather global nature of projective techniques also creates problems of validity in what is actually being measured by these tests. If they supposedly measure different core aspects and dimensions of personality, which ones are they, and what criterion measures should be used to assess their validity? Finally, there is a fundamental question about the validity of the projection process as an indirect means of assessing personality. More specifically, how accurately can examiners interpret what the individual "really means" when responding to ambiguous stimuli?

Behavioral Techniques: Assessing Personality by Direct Observation

In sharp contrast to assessing constructs (e.g., traits, needs) that characterize the objective self-report and projective techniques, the most salient feature of **behavioral techniques of assessment** is their emphasis on the systematic observation of behavior in assessing the personality of individuals. Because behavior can be determined by many factors, personality psychologists employing behavioral assessment techniques to study personality (e.g., shyness) also focus on what cues in the environment elicit the behavior (e.g., being approached by a stranger), what thoughts and feelings influence behavior (e.g., anxiety about being evaluated by that person), and what the consequences are for engaging in such behavior (e.g., reducing anxiety by being a "wallflower"). Thus, behavioral techniques of personality assessment attempt to assess directly the more observable (e.g., actions) and less observable (e.g., thoughts and feelings) dimensions influencing personality.

Types of Behavioral Assessment Techniques: Looking at What People Are Doing

Although behavioral techniques may vary, they all share a characteristic emphasis on assessing behavior and the factors influencing it. Four types of behavioral techniques include direct observations, self-monitoring, behavior inventories, and cognitive assessment.

Direct Observation Techniques   As the name implies, **direct observation techniques** involve obtaining actual samples of the individual's behavior. Such observations can be obtained in various formats. **Naturalistic observations** involve viewing the individual's behavior in real-life settings (e.g., mental hospitals, work settings, and classrooms). **Controlled observations** involve the assessment of behavior in more structured situations (i.e., a laboratory room). To study gender differences in aggression in children, a psychologist might observe the aggressive play of boys and girls on the playground, or watch through a one-way mirror while they play with toys in a laboratory room. **Role playing** combines both the naturalistic and controlled observational methods and involves a person playing certain assigned roles (e.g., having to terminate an employee) for the purpose of assessing the individual's behavior in various situations (e.g., assessing compassion in office managers).

Self-monitoring Techniques   In contrast to direct observation techniques, which typically involve others (e.g., therapists, researchers, teachers, or nursing staff) recording the observations, **self-monitoring techniques** require individuals to maintain observational records of their own behavior (e.g., noting when and where feelings of anxiety occur). An advantage of self-monitoring techniques is that they can be applied to many kinds of behavior (e.g., eating, sleeping, arguing, feeling anxious, talking on the phone). They are also very convenient and flexible; they can be done almost anywhere and anytime. This is in contrast to direct observation techniques that require the presence of an outside observer.

The validity of self-monitoring techniques is threatened when observing their own behavior causes individuals to act differently because of it. But a rather interesting side benefit of self-monitoring is that simply monitoring a behavior is often enough to modify the behavior constructively. For example, a person using a self-report technique requiring them to document all food consumed (e.g., noting what is eaten and when) will probably eat less food. To illustrate this side benefit of self-monitoring, try the exercise outlined in the feature "You Can Do It" below.

Self-report Behavioral Inventories   Self-report behavioral inventories typically require individuals to indicate the extent to which they have engaged in a series of specific behaviors in different situations. A good example of a self-report behavioral inventory is known as a fear survey schedule (Geer, 1965; Wolpe & Lang, 1964). In general, **fear survey schedules** include a list of common situations or objects for which individuals are asked to indicate their level of fear. See "A Closer Look" below for an example of a fear survey schedule.

Self-report behavioral inventories assess a wide variety of behaviors such as depression, assertiveness, and ability to resolve conflicts, to name just a few (Groth-Marnat, 1990). Possible threats to the

YOU CAN DO IT

Looking Over Your Own Shoulder: An Exercise in Self-Monitoring

If you are interested in gaining some information about your personality and why you do some of the things you do, try your hand at this rather simple self-monitoring exercise. Select some behavior that is important to you. Eating, drinking, smoking, studying, watching TV, or interacting with friends are all behaviors that will work just fine. For the next several days, note very carefully when you engage in each of these behaviors and what the surrounding conditions were (e.g., what was happening at that time or just before you started doing the target behavior?). Also note what happened when you engaged in this behavior. For example, did you stop studying, feel better, avoid some unpleasant task, or have fun? You should write down all of this information. After about a week of self-monitoring, go back over your written records to gain some possible insight into why you do some of the things you do. What you find may surprise even you!

A CLOSER LOOK

What Are You Afraid Of?
A Look at a Fear Survey Schedule

On a scale of 1 (not at all afraid) to 5 (very afraid), indicate the level of fear you feel toward the 20 objects and situations listed here.

_____ 1. Sharp objects
_____ 2. Dead bodies
_____ 3. Being self-conscious
_____ 4. Mental illness
_____ 5. Being in an airplane
_____ 6. Worms
_____ 7. Rats and mice
_____ 8. Being alone
_____ 9. Giving a speech
_____ 10. Roller coasters
_____ 11. Being with drunks
_____ 12. Heights
_____ 13. Failing a test
_____ 14. Death
_____ 15. Meeting strangers
_____ 16. Snakes
_____ 17. Dark places
_____ 18. Thunderstorms
_____ 19. Blood
_____ 20. Crowded places

The development of a scale to measure fear.

Note. From *Behavior Research and Therapy,* by J. H. Geer, 1965, Vol. *3,* pp. 45–53.

reliability and validity of self-report behavior inventories arise because they tend to rely heavily on the person's memory and willingness to admit to such behaviors.

Cognitive Behavioral Assessment   **Cognitive events** are activities occurring in the person's head that serve to influence behavior. Techniques of **cognitive behavioral assessment** attempt to measure such events as the thoughts or feelings an individual is experiencing while in a particular situation. The technique of **thought sampling** requires the individual to monitor the thoughts (e.g., all those people are evaluating me) experienced in certain situations (e.g., giving a speech) that can be used to explain the observed behavior (e.g., fumbling over words). **Self-statement inventories** require individuals to read a series of statements describing the types of thoughts people may have about themselves and to indicate how fully they might endorse these statements for themselves. Here is a sample of items from the Automatic Thoughts Questionnaire (Hollon & Kendall, 1980):

1. I feel like I'm up against the world.
2. I wish I were a better person.

Being able to assess the extent to which a person endorses such statements might help explain why that person exhibits a behavior pattern characteristic of depression.

Evaluating Behavioral Assessment Techniques: Characteristic Strengths and Limitations

A summary of the characteristic strengths and limitations of the behavior assessment techniques is presented next.

Strengths   Behavioral assessment techniques, with their emphasis on both overt (e.g., actions) and covert (e.g., thoughts) forms of behaviors, make clear the importance of environmental and cognitive variables in the study of personality. Behavioral techniques also represent a diverse collection of methods having the flexibility to be employed almost anywhere (e.g., home, work, school) and by individuals with minimal training in personality assessment (e.g., truck drivers, office managers, high school students).

Limitations   Some behavioral assessment techniques lack standards or guidelines to indicate what behaviors are worthy of observation. In studying depression or conflict resolution, for example, what are the critical environmental, situational, and cognitive variables that should be viewed by the therapist or monitored by the client? Another limitation is the variety of potential biases associated with direct observations of behaviors made by an observer, or self-observations made by the individual. Merely knowing that you are being observed can change the way you act. In addition, different observers may view the same behavior (e.g., avoiding eye contact) differently (e.g., shyness vs. boredom). Finally, potential biases hampering the ability of individuals to reliably—and validly—assess their own thoughts and behavior limit the effectiveness of certain behavioral assessment techniques. For example, individuals may be too embarrassed to indicate all of the situations that actually make them fearful, or to reveal the rather illogical nature of many of their thoughts.

Psychophysiological Techniques of Personality Assessment: The Measurement of Bodily Processes

The essential logic of psychophysiological techniques of personality assessment is that certain aspects of the individual's personality (e.g., aggression, anxiety, or risk taking) are related to various bodily processes (e.g., blood chemistry, hormonal levels, heart rate). **Psychophysiological assessment techniques** are characterized by their ability to measure a variety of physiological changes occurring "underneath the skin" and link them with various interpersonal (Cacioppo & Berntson, 1992), cognitive (Matarazzo, 1992), and emotional (Comer, 1992) aspects of behavior and personality differences (Eysenck, 1990).

Types of Psychophysiological Assessment Techniques: *Looking from the Inside Out*

In this section, we will consider some of the more frequently used psychophysiological assessment techniques in the study of personality.

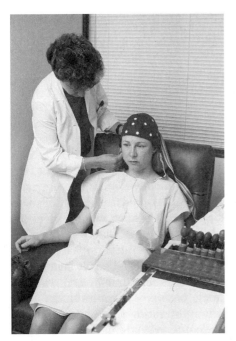

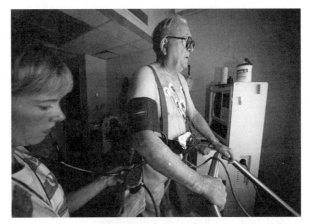

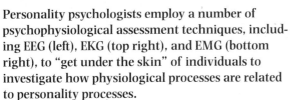

Personality psychologists employ a number of psychophysiological assessment techniques, including EEG (left), EKG (top right), and EMG (bottom right), to "get under the skin" of individuals to investigate how physiological processes are related to personality processes.

Electrophysiological Measures: Assessment That "Gets Under Your Skin"   Although there are a variety of psychophysiological assessment techniques, they all measure some aspect of an underlying bodily process. Here are four common psychophysiological assessment techniques used in the study of personality:

▲ The **electroencephalograph (EEG)** assesses the electrical activity of the brain occurring in the form of various "brain waves" (wavelengths displayed on a visual monitor). Different wavelength patterns have been found to be associated with different states of arousal (e.g., sleeping, excited) and certain disorders involving personality (e.g., antisocial personality disorder, also known as psychopathy, and schizophrenia).

▲ The **electrocardiogram (EKG)** assesses changes in electrical activity of the heart and makes it

possible to assess heart rate. Changes in heart rate are associated with different levels of arousal and excitement, as well as indicating heart disorders. Personality researchers have used EKG measures extensively to study the relationship between coronary heart disease and personality factors.

▲ The **electromyograph (EMG)** measures muscular activity associated with muscle tension and relaxation. The EMG is used extensively as a therapeutic technique to help individuals suffering from excessive stress and anxiety learn to relax by receiving muscle relaxation training (see Chapter 10).

▲ Techniques assessing **electrodermal activity (EDA)** note changes occurring on the skin's surface in response to different emotional states. A frequently assessed EDA is **galvanic skin response (GSR)**. GSR measures the skin's level of moisture (i.e., sweat) in response to various physical and emotional states and is assessed using a **galvanometer**. A somewhat controversial application of the GSR is its accuracy when used in a polygraph (lie detector) test (Bashore & Rapp, 1993; Jones & Terris, 1991).

Biochemical Assessment: The Measurement of the Biological Bases of Personality   In addition to electrophysiological measures, psychophysiological assessment of personality involves measuring an assortment of biochemical processes (Zuckerman, 1995). These biochemical measures include

▲   Assessing various neurotransmitters, such as monoamine oxidase (MAO), dopamine, and catecholamine, to name just a few (Depue, Luciana, Arbisi, Collins, & Leon, 1994; Zuckerman, 1994).

▲   Measuring hormones, such as testosterone and cortisol. Biochemical assessment of neurotransmitters and hormones can be obtained by analyzing cerebrospinal fluid (CSF), blood, or urine samples.

▲   Analyzing the individual's genetic makeup. Genetic assessment has been an important tool in determining the inherited dimensions of personality (Bronfenbrenner & Ceci, 1994; Heath, Cloninger, & Martin, 1994).

Evaluating Psychophysiological Assessment Techniques: Characteristic Strengths and Limitations
Presented in this section is a summary of the characteristic strengths and limitations of the psychophysiological assessment techniques.

Characteristic Strengths   Psychophysiological techniques provide different methods of assessing bodily reactions, many of which can be obtained at the same time. Researchers investigating aggressive adolescents can simultaneously assess EEG and GSR recordings (Gilbert, Gilbert, Johnson, & McColloch, 1991). These techniques can also be employed in conjunction with other types of assessment techniques. A researcher can monitor the heart rate of an individual in response to the stories being constructed from TAT pictures to assess the level of stress

produced. Psychophysiological techniques have enabled personality psychologists to more systematically examine the possible biological bases of personality (see Chapter 9).

Characteristic Limitations   A frequent criticism of psychophysiological assessment techniques is that any given bodily reaction can have several meanings. For example, increased heart rate can indicate fear, love, happiness, and pain. Another limitation is that it is relatively easy to modify bodily processes and invalidate the readings obtained from many of these psychophysiological techniques. Being nervous about taking a polygraph test can increase the muscle tension of a person telling the truth. Finally, variation in the ways individuals respond physiologically to the same stimuli can contaminate the research results. For example, because some individuals might respond primarily by sweating when anxious while others may respond with muscle tension, a researcher using only a GSR measure when studying anxiety might mistakenly assume that an individual is very calm even though the person may have a great deal of muscle tension.

Which Personality Assessment Technique to Use? Some General Guidelines and Closing Remarks

After surveying the various techniques of personality assessment, you may be wondering which one is the best. But there is no such thing as the best technique; each has its characteristic strengths and limitations. In determining which assessment technique to use, personality psychologists consider the nature of the question being asked and the dimension of personality being assessed. In studying the effectiveness of a treatment program designed to increase an individual's assertive behavior, researchers would use one of the behavioral techniques. In studying the interrelationship between various traits, a multiple-dimension objective self-report technique might be most useful. An even better approach might be to combine more than one of the techniques. For example, when studying anxiety reactions to certain environmental stimuli, a projective test combined with a measure of muscle tension and responses to an objective self-report test of anxiety would give researchers a global picture of this aspect of the individual's personality.

Ethical Issues in Personality Assessment: Personal, Legal, and Social Concerns

As personality and other psychological tests become more and more widely used, their potential for misuse and abuse increases (Jones, Ash, & Soto, 1990). The closing section of this chapter presents a discussion of some personal, legal, and social issues associated with the ethics of personality assessment.

Personal Concerns: Protecting the Individual's Rights

Protecting the rights of those individuals who take personality tests is an important ethical concern for personality psychologists. Presented next is a summary of these concerns and the efforts taken by personality psychologists to protect the rights of these individuals.

Invasion of Privacy

A major concern for many individuals taking personality tests is that they will be unknowingly revealing things about themselves. Examples might be when a researcher is studying aggressive tendencies, or a personnel manager is screening potential applicants for a propensity to steal. Whenever possible, individuals taking the test should be given a complete description of the purpose of the test and testing procedures, in language that they can understand, without contaminating the results of the test. Under no circumstances should the individual be deliberately lied to or coerced into taking the test under false pretenses. To deal with such ethical concerns, responsible individuals using personality assessment techniques practice the procedure of informed consent. Finally, all items on the test should be directly relevant to the specific testing purposes. Questions concerning religious and/or sexual attitudes, for example, should not be asked unless they directly relate to the job or task for which the testing is being conducted (Jones & Terris, 1991).

Confidentiality

The issue of **confidentiality** has to do with who will have access to the information obtained from the tests. To help ensure confidentiality, individuals should be told beforehand how the results will be used, that only those persons for whom the results have direct relevance will have access to them, and that permission from individuals must be granted before the results can be released to any outside sources. Finally, it is the responsibility of the organization doing the testing to eliminate dated or obsolete information. For example, information located at the university counseling center about a student's level of depression during the freshman year should be eliminated after graduation.

Legal Concerns: Assessment and the Law

Whether they are used in clinics, universities, the military, or industry, personality assessment techniques cannot be used if the items in or procedures of the test tend to discriminate against certain groups of individuals. On a management selection test given by a company, certain minority and ethnic groups may tend to score lower than white individuals taking the test. The ethnic and minority individuals' lower scores may reflect a lack of familiarity with the information on the test due to cultural differences. The situation described is considered discrimination against these minority and ethnic individuals because only those scoring high on the test are selected into the company's management training program.

Equal Rights Legislation

The Equal Employment Opportunity Act of 1972, as well as guidelines published by the **Equal Employment Opportunity Commission (EEOC)** and other court decisions, have done much to reduce discrimination. With respect to testing, these laws state that institutions and organizations must be able to prove that (1) the tests they are using do predict success and failure on the specific tasks for which they are being used, and (2) the tests do not unfairly discriminate against any minority or ethnic subgroups. In short, examiners must establish or prove that the tests they use are valid and fair.

A recent controversy involving personality tests addressed by the EEOC is whether screening potential employees with personality tests that use separate gender norms violates civil rights law (Adler, 1993). At the heart of this issue is the tendency of women to be more willing than men to reveal negative aspects of themselves when taking personality tests. For example, if women on the average endorse 10 items on an anxiety scale while men endorse an average of only six, a female applicant who endorses eight items might still be considered highly anxious and a less desirable job candidate. A potential solution to this problem is to eliminate separate gender norms, using norms that combine the responses of both men and women. As reasonable as this solution seems, it still may discriminate against women because of their tendency to be more likely to report negative aspects of themselves on tests.

Impact of Equal Rights Legislation on Testing

Probably the biggest impact of equal rights legislation is that it requires people who employ tests in the process of selection and placement to examine the tests more closely. It also requires that

▲ People involved in the business of developing and marketing such tests spend more time and money on research in their attempts to establish the validity of their tests.
▲ More attention be paid to the nature of the individuals and groups included in research designed to establish the validity of these tests.
▲ Greater care be taken to ensure that test items are culturally fair.

As a result of this legislation, users of tests must take greater care to use the tests only for the purposes for which they are specifically designed. Greater knowledge of reliability and validity issues and more advanced training in test selection and administration are now required of those involved in testing others for selection and placement (e.g., admissions counselors, personnel managers). All of these efforts not only make possible more sophisticated and legally sound decisions about what and how tests are being used but also ensure more fair and equal treatment of people taking the test.

Social Concerns: Assessment and Society

One of the biggest social concerns of the large-scale usage of assessment techniques is that of labeling. Labeling concerns what can happen when a label is attached to an individual, based on the use of assessment techniques. Consider what can happen to Roberto who has been labeled as emotionally disturbed on the basis of a set of personality tests. Other people may react to him differently, perhaps treating him rather impersonally. Because people are now treating him differently, Roberto may eventually come to internalize the label of being emotionally disturbed and start behaving in a more bizarre way. Such bizarre behavior will then serve to reinforce the placement of the label and the differential treatment he is now receiving. In short, the label becomes the beginning of a **self-fulfilling prophecy**. Keep in mind that such problems are not created by the tests and labels themselves, but by the way people begin to react to and believe in the labels.

Ethical Guidelines: Rules for Using Assessment

The ethical issues associated with the assessment of personality are numerous, complex, and have some serious legal and social implications. To help address and resolve these issues, the American Psychological Association (1981, 1990, 1992) has developed a set of ethical principles to be followed by psychologists and others when developing and administering psychological assessment techniques, interpreting and explaining test results, maintaining test security, and dealing with obsolete tests and outdated test results. Many professional organizations also publish guidelines for the use of tests. For example, the Association of Test Publishers (1989) publishes the *Model Guidelines for Preemployment Integrity Testing Programs*. These guidelines are published to

ensure that both test publishers and test users adhere to effective ethical and legal integrity testing practices in the following areas: (1) test development and selection, (2) test administration, (3) scoring, (4) test fairness and confidentiality, and (5) public statements and test marketing practices. (Jones & Terris, 1991, p. 857)

Such ethical guidelines are primarily concerned with protecting the rights of people taking the tests.

Chapter Summary: Reexamining the Highlights

▲ *Personality Assessment*   Personality assessment is the systematic measurement of various aspects of personality designed to increase precision and effectiveness in communicating about the personality of individuals. Personality assessment techniques are used in industrial, clinical, legal, military, and educational settings.

▲ *Standards for Evaluating Personality Assessment Techniques*   Standards of reliability include test-retest reliability and examiner reliability. Standards of validity include face validity, content validity, criterion validity (including predictive and concurrent validity), and the process of construct validity.

▲ *Methods of Personality Assessment*   Objective self-report techniques assess personality through single-dimension and multiple-dimension tests containing a standardized set of responses and scoring procedures. Acquiescence and social desirability response sets may influence the results of objective self-report techniques. A principal strength of objective self-report techniques is their standardization; a principal limitation is the lack of freedom of response they allow.

Projective techniques of assessment interpret personality based on responses to ambiguous stimuli. Characteristic features of projective techniques include ambiguous stimuli, indirect method of assessment, freedom of response, and increased possibility of subjective scoring procedures. Types of projective techniques include association techniques, completion techniques, choice or ordering techniques, expressive techniques, and constructive techniques. A major strength of projective techniques is the freedom of response allowed to the individual taking the tests; limitations are the subjective nature of the scoring procedures and the uncertainty about what dimensions of personality they assess.

Behavior techniques of assessment focus on observable behavior, environmental cues, and cognitive processes. Types of behavioral assessment include direct observation, self-monitoring, self-report behavioral interviews, and cognitive assessment techniques. A principal strength of behavioral assessment techniques is the emphasis on various kinds of behavior; limitations include the uncertainty of what should be observed and biases in the recording and recalling of information.

Psychophysiological assessment techniques measure bodily responses associated with personality processes. Electrophysiological measurements include the electroencephalograph (EEG), the electrocardiogram (EKG), the electromyograph (EMG), and techniques assessing electrodermal activity (EDA). Biochemical measurements include the assessment of neurotransmitters, hormones, and genetic material. A principal strength of psychophysiological assessment techniques is the linking of bodily and personality processes; limitations include the unclear meaning of measures of bodily processes and how much they can be modified.

The nature of the question being asked about personality determines the type of assessment technique to be used.

▲ *Ethical Issues in Personality Assessment*   Preventing invasions of privacy and ensuring confidentiality are personal concerns associated with the ethics of personality assessment. Preventing discrimination, regulating who has access to the results of tests, and focusing more attention on the use of assessment techniques are legal concerns associated with personality assessment. The process of labeling and the consequences of such labeling are social concerns associated with personality assessment.

Glossary

acquiescence response set   A tendency to respond with agreement to the items on a test for which the person is uncertain.

association techniques   A projective technique that assesses personality based on the individual's associations to test stimuli.

authoritarianism   A personality dimension characterized by conservative attitudes and submission to authority.

behavioral techniques of assessment   A type of assessment that emphasizes observable behaviors and the environmental factors, cognitive processes, and consequences that affect them.

California F Scale   A single-dimension objective self-report technique assessing authoritarianism.

California Psychological Inventory (CPI)   A multiple-dimension test assessing 20 different aspects of personality.

choice or ordering projective techniques   A projective technique that assesses personality based on the individual's expressed preferences in choosing or ranking test stimuli.

confidentiality   A condition of testing in which access to the results of the test are restricted to ensure the privacy rights of those taking the test.

cognitive behavior assessment   The measure of cognitive events that serve to influence behavior.

cognitive events   Any number of mental activities (e.g., reasoning and expectations).

completion techniques   A projective technique that assesses personality based on the individual's completed responses to incomplete test stimuli.

concurrent validity   The ability of a test score to predict a currently existing criterion measure.

content validity   The extent to which a test contains items reflecting the dimension of personality being measured.

construct validity   Establishing the relationship between a test score and a set of behaviors consistent with a particular theory.

constructive projective techniques   A projective technique that assesses personality based on stories created in response to test stimuli.

controlled observations   The recording of behavior in environments with highly regulated environmental conditions.

counseling psychologists   Psychologists who are trained professionally to help individuals cope more effectively with problems of everyday adjustment.

criterion contamination   Biases introduced in the assessment of reliability and validity when the same person makes all of the observations.

criterion measure   A specific behavior to be predicted by the score on a test.

criterion validity   The ability of a test to predict a behavior in a particular situation.

direct observation techniques   A behavioral assessment technique that emphasizes the recording of overt behaviors occurring in different situations.

Edwards Personal Preference Schedule (EPPS)   A multiple-dimension objective self-report technique assessing 15 aspects of personality as expressed by need preferences.

electrocardiogram (EKG)   An electrical device for assessing the muscular activity of the heart.

electrodermal activity (EDA)   The activity associated with changes in the skin's surface in response to various environmental and emotional stimuli.

electroencephalograph (EEG)   A tool for assessing electrical activity in the brain in the form of electrical wavelengths.

electromyograph (EMG)   An electrical recording device for assessing muscular activity.

Equal Employment Opportunity Commission (EEOC)   A legislative body designed to protect individuals from discrimination in employment practices.

examiner reliability   The extent to which different examiners scoring a test arrive at the same score.

expressive projective techniques   A projective technique that assesses personality based on an individual's creative actions, such as drawing and role playing.

face validity   The degree to which a test looks like what it says it is supposedly measuring.

fear survey schedule   A self-report technique in which individuals indicate from many different alternatives those objects or situations eliciting fear in them.

galvanic skin response (GSR)   An activity of the skin's surface associated with changes in moisture level (e.g., perspiration).

galvanometer   An electrical device for assessing galvanic skin response (GSR).

group norm   A numerical index of how a specific group of individuals scored on a particular measure of personality.

hero   The central figure in a story generated in response to a picture from the Thematic Appreciation Test.

Minnesota Multiphasic Personality Inventory-2 (MMPI-2)   A multiple-dimension objective self-report technique assessing 10 different aspects of personality and containing four separate validity scales.

naturalistic observations   The recording of behavior in real-life settings.

need   A state of deprivation that creates a desire or motivation for a particular object or state of affairs.

objective self-report techniques   Techniques of personality assessment characterized by standardized administration and scoring procedures.

personality assessment   The systematic measurement of different aspects of personality.

personality profile   A summarized interpretation of a collection of personality characteristics in written and graphic form.

predictive validity   The ability of a test score to predict a criterion measure in the future.

press   An environmental factor that affects needs as measured by the Thematic Apperception Test.

profile analysis   The identification of a specific personality pattern based on the scores of several dimensions of personality.

projective techniques   Techniques of personality assessment based on an interpretation of the subject's responses to ambiguous stimuli.

psychometricians   Individuals who have specialized professional training in administering, scoring, and interpreting the results of personality and other techniques of psychological assessment.

psychophysiological assessment techniques   Procedures for measuring bodily processes.

reliability   The assessment consistency of a personality test.

reliability coefficient   A numerical index of the consistency of a test score.

response set   Answering test questions in a biased manner.

role playing   The acting out of an assigned role for the purpose of assessing behavioral and emotional reactions.

self-fulfilling prophecy   A tendency of individuals to begin to behave in a manner consistent with a diagnostic label attributed to them, thus providing after-the-fact support of the label.

self-monitoring techniques   A form of behavioral assessment in which the recording of behavior is done by the individual.

self-statement inventories   A self-report technique in which individuals choose from many alternatives the thoughts that occur to them in certain situations.

social desirability response set   A tendency to endorse items on a test in a pattern that creates a favorable impression.

test-retest reliability   The consistency of a test score obtained on two separate occasions.

Thematic Apperception Test (TAT)   A constructive projective technique that assesses personality by identifying the needs expressed in the stories generated by individuals in response to pictures with ambiguous themes.

thought sampling   The assessment of the various thoughts occurring to an individual in certain situations.

validity   The extent to which a test measures what it says it measures.

validity coefficient   A numerical index of the ability of a test score to predict a criterion measure.

validity scale   A set of items within a test designed specifically to detect certain biases in response patterns that can negatively affect the test results.

The Viewpoints of Personality: Different Perspectives of the Person

In Part One, the general principles for studying the psychology of personality were presented. Part Two applies those principles to an examination of several viewpoints of the person as proposed by different personality theorists. Each chapter explores the basic assumptions, principal processes, assessment techniques, and practical applications associated with each viewpoint. As you read those chapters, do not feel compelled to find the "right" or "best" viewpoint; there is none. Instead, try to understand each viewpoint, evaluate it based on the standards discussed in Part One and select those aspects that are most applicable to your own view of personality.

CHAPTER 3

The Psychodynamic Viewpoint: Forging Personality Out of Conflict Resolution

CHAPTER OVERVIEW: A PREVIEW OF COMING ATTRACTIONS

If you ask anyone from a professional personality psychologist to the average person in the street, Sigmund Freud is without a doubt the most famous personality theorist. It was Freud who postulated, in a staggering 23 volumes, the first comprehensive modern-day viewpoint of personality. This chapter gives you an overview of Freud's work and contributions to the study of personality psychology. First is a discussion of the basic assumptions, principles, and processes associated with the psychodynamic viewpoint. Next comes a discussion of personality development, followed by the applications of the psychodynamic viewpoint to personality change, personality assessment, and advertising. The chapter ends with a discussion of the characteristic strengths and limitations of the psychodynamic viewpoint. To learn more about the personal life of the man who forever changed the study of personality, consider the material "A Closer Look" on page 58.

A CLOSER LOOK

Biographical Background: The Life of Sigmund Freud

Sigmund Freud was born on May 6, 1856, in the small town of Freidberg, Moravia (now called Pribor, Czechoslovakia). He was the oldest of seven children. In 1860, his father moved the family to Vienna, where Sigmund Freud would live for almost eighty years. Freud was an extremely good student. He began reading Shakespeare at the age of 8 and excelled in science. He exhibited an unusual talent for writing and languages, mastering Latin, Greek, French, English, Italian, and Spanish, and graduated at the head of his class.

Freud dreamed of becoming a great military general or minister of state, but in 1873—at the age of 17—he began studying medicine at the University of Vienna. Freud had aspirations of becoming a medical researcher and did some rather exceptional research on the nervous system and other work that earned him a minor reputation in the scientific community. But limited employment opportunities and concerns over financial matters resulted in Freud experiencing episodes of anxiety and depression, for which he began using cocaine. Although Freud used and researched the analgesic possibilities of cocaine, there is no evidence to suggest that he was ever addicted to the drug.

Freud's aspirations for a career as a medical researcher were cut short because of the limited opportunities for Jews in such areas, and because he fell in love with and became engaged to Martha Bernays. In preparation to support a family, Freud established a private practice specializing in the treatment of the nervous system in 1881 and married Martha in 1886. They had six children, three girls and three boys. The youngest child, Anna, would eventually become a world-famous psychoanalyst herself.

Freud's career was enhanced greatly by his collaboration with the highly successful Viennese neurologist Joseph Breuer. In his practice, Breuer had considerable success treating many patients suffering from physical disabilities (e.g., muscle twitching or paralysis) that seemed to be related to emotional problems by having them simply talk about their thoughts and feelings. In 1895, Breuer and Freud (1895/1955) published a book titled *Studies in Hysteria*. Although the book sold

Although Sigmund Freud's conservative appearance was similar to that of most other intellectuals at the time in Vienna, his ideas were certainly not conservative and helped change forever the study of personality.

only 626 copies in 13 years, it is now considered a classic and is regarded as marking the beginning of the psychoanalytic movement. But shortly after the book was published, Freud and Breuer had a major falling out due to Freud's emphasis on the importance of sexual conflicts as a cause of **hysteria**. The disagreement completely ended their personal and professional relationship and resulted in Freud's dismissal from the Vienna Medical Society in 1896.

After the death of his father, also in 1896, Freud began to experience intense feelings of depression and anxiety, including an unnatural fear of traveling by train. To help overcome these emotional difficulties, Freud began his historical self-analysis, from which he eventually formed many of the founding principles of the psychodynamic viewpoint (e.g., emphasizing the unconscious and dreams). One of the most significant outcomes of this analysis was a book called *The Interpretation of Dreams*, which was published in 1900 and is considered Freud's greatest work.

As the 20th century began, the fame of Freud (1901/1960) increased, with the publication of *The Psychopathology of Everyday Life* in 1901 and the founding in 1902 of the Vienna Psychoanalytical Society. The society boasted of members from all over Europe, including Alfred Adler and Carl Jung—both of whom would eventually disagree with Freud and go on to develop their own schools of thought and theories of personality (see Chapter 4). In 1909, G. Stanley Hall, a famous American psychologist, asked Freud to give a series of lectures at Clark University in Worcester, Massachusetts. Hall's invitation established Freud as an international figure, but it was to be his first and only visit to America.

For the most part, in the 1920s Freud's fame rose to new heights, through the establishment of the International Psychoanalytic Association and a supporting journal to help spread the information throughout the world. Freud was offered lucrative contracts to write popular articles for *Cosmopolitan* magazine and to work for a movie studio as a consultant in making films of famous love stories. Although he was not a wealthy man, Freud turned down these offers, fearing they would compromise his scientific credibility. In 1923, Freud was diagnosed with cancer of the jaw. The cancer was linked to his lifelong habit of smoking 20 cigars a day, but he refused to give them up. Over the next 16 years, he would endure some 33 operations on his mouth and jaw, continuing to write and develop his ideas despite great physical pain.

As a Jew living in Europe in the 1930s, Freud found that his increased fame brought with it a considerable amount of harassment from the Nazis, who burned his books, attacked his character, and raided his house. Although he was in great danger, Freud refused to leave his beloved city of Vienna, even after the Nazis invaded and occupied Austria in 1938. But shortly afterward, when his daughter Anna was arrested, detained, and subsequently released by the Gestapo, Freud consented to leave Austria for England. There, he was accepted with all the warmth and honor deserving of a man of his stature. In London, on September 23, 1939, Freud died of cancer.

You can learn more about the life of Sigmund Freud by reading *The Life and Work of Sigmund Freud* by Ernest Jones (1953, 1955, 1957), who was Freud's biographer, fellow psychoanalyst, and lifelong friend. For a much shorter account, read Hall and Lindzey's (1978) *Theories of Personality*.

An Introduction to the Pyschodynamic Viewpoint: Laying the Foundation for Building a Comprehensive Theory of Personality

The four basic theoretical assumptions discussed in this section served as the mortar Freud used in forming the foundation for the rest of his views on such aspects of personality as the nature and dynamics of personality, personality development and psychopathology, and psychotherapy.

▲ *Psychic determinism: Leaving nothing to chance.* **Psychic determinism** refers to Freud's belief that behavior does not just happen by chance, but is governed by some purpose or meaning. He theorized that such everyday occurrences as slips of the tongue, jokes, and dreams are expressions of psychic determinism (Freud, 1900/1953, 1901/1960, 1905/1960). For example, according to Freud, the content of dreams is determined by an individual's unconscious wishes and desires. Thus, according to the assumption of psychic determinism, nothing about behavior is left to chance.

▲ *The influence of the unconscious mind: Powers of the unknown.* Freud also assumed that behavior is governed by powerful forces in the unconscious region of the mind (Freud, 1900/1953; Kihlstrom, 1990). Freud said these forces are unconscious because they contain thoughts, ideas, desires, and impulses that individuals find threatening, shameful, or unacceptable; but these forces are still part of the personality. For example, the telling of dirty jokes is a relatively safe expression of an individual's sexual desires and impulses.

▲ *The dynamic nature of personality: The give and take of personality.* A dynamic nature of personality assumes that several different elements work together in a **homeostatic** fashion, maintaining balance within the personality. You can experience homeostasis yourself by taking a break after studying for a couple of hours, walking to a local coffee shop to chat with friends, and then going back to studying. In balancing the studious and social aspects of your personality, you achieve homeostasis.

▲ *Personality as a closed system: Operating on a limited amount of energy.* Freud also viewed personality as a **closed system** that operates on a fixed amount of psychic energy, or **libido**. In such a closed system, the energy is shifted continuously from one part of the system to the other in a dynamic and interactive manner in an attempt to maintain a sense of internal balance. In the preceding example, you shifted some of the energy away from studying to the activity of talking to friends, and then shifted back to studying. By taking a break, you can actually save psychic energy by relaxing a bit and not wasting lots of energy trying to concentrate while tired.

Although they are not the only theoretical assumptions of the psychodynamic approach to personality (Westen, 1990), these four assumptions helped to guide many of Freud's most important ideas about the nature and operation of personality. A basic understanding of these four theoretical assumptions should help you see more clearly how and why Freud viewed personality the way he did.

Basic Concepts and Processes: The Building Blocks of a Comprehensive Theory of Personality

This section examines some of the concepts that serve as fundamental building blocks of the psychodynamic viewpoint.

The Regions of the Mind: Mapping the Levels of Consciousness

Very early in his career, in about 1900, Freud (1900/1953) began to describe his view of how the mind was organized. As Figure 3.1 shows, Freud's map of the mind had three sections: the conscious, preconscious, and unconscious regions. He believed that each of these regions had unique features and special functions.

The Conscious Mind: The Tip of the Iceberg

The **conscious mind** is characterized by sensory awareness and limited only to what people are capable of hearing, seeing, smelling, touching, tasting, or thinking at any particular time. For example, while reading a book, you might find it difficult to hear the words of a favorite song on the radio. With its limited capacity, Freud believed the conscious mind had very little to do with determining behavior.

The Preconscious Mind: What You Need to Play Trivial Pursuit

As shown in Figure 3.1, the **preconscious mind** is just below the level of conscious awareness. It contains pieces of information that can be brought

into conscious awareness when needed (e.g., a word rhyming with *red).* Because he viewed it as simply a storage bin for information, Freud did not believe the preconscious mind had much influence on behavior. But it was the location of the **secondary censorship point** for keeping threatening information out of our conscious awareness. Forgetting an appointment with the dentist until the day after is an example of the censorship function of the preconscious mind preventing the recall of threatening information until it is no longer a source of unpleasantness.

The Unconscious Mind: The Land Down Under   Figure 3.1 shows that the largest and most influential region of the mind postulated by Freud was the **unconscious mind**. A characteristic feature of the unconscious mind is its supposedly unlimited capacity for storing information for an unlimited amount of time. The unconscious mind holds all of an individual's unacceptable memories, urges, desires, and impulses that could seriously threaten the person's sense of self if they were expressed directly, at the conscious level of awareness.

Freud proposed that unconscious information can also be expressed at the conscious level in ways that are not directly understood by the individual. For example, stored in the unconscious mind of an executive may be the tragic memory of being locked accidentally in a dark room as an infant. This experience is manifested consciously in adulthood by the individual's little-understood extreme fear of flying in the confined space of airplanes. This threatening information is kept out of the preconscious mind and prevented from eventually being expressed at the conscious level of the mind by the **primary censorship point**. which Freud said is located between the unconscious and preconscious regions (Freud, 1900/1953). While research into the operation of the unconscious is still a topic of much discussion today (Anooshian & Seibert, 1996), nobody has clearly explained how the censorship mechanism operates (Silverman, 1982). However, evidence supporting its operation continues to mount (Dixion, 1981; Kihlstrom, 1990; Silverman, 1976, 1980; Silverman, Ross, Adler, & Lustig, 1978; Westen, 1990).

Instincts and Psychic Energy: The Fuel of Personality

Freud believed that the operation of personality was powered by a force of psychic energy that was fueled

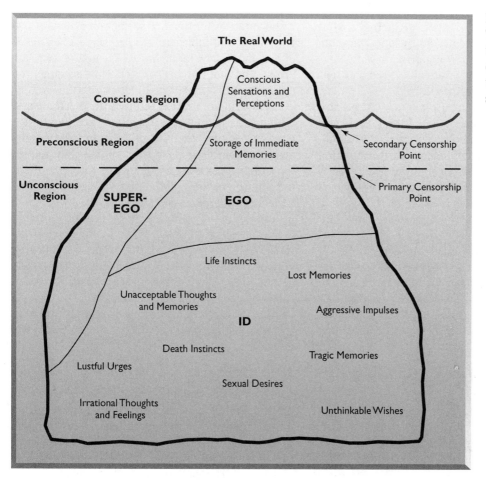

Figure 3.1
The three regions of the mind, with their corresponding features and psychic structures

by **instincts** (Westen, 1990). As defined by Freud, "an instinct is a mental representation of a physical or bodily need" (Freud, 1915/1957, p. 122). Physical or bodily needs include such things as the need for food, water, sleep, and mental and sexual stimulation. Mental representations of bodily needs manifest themselves in the form of a wish or desire. The mental representation of your state of hunger might involve wishing for pizza. However, because simply wishing for something does not make it so, a major function of instincts is to motivate you to do something to satisfy these desires, reduce the tension, and maintain a state of homeostasis.

Characteristics of Instincts: What Are They Like?
Freud (1915/1957) postulated that instincts have four basic characteristics: aim, pressure, object, and source. The **aim** of the instinct is to reduce an inter-

nal state of tension (e.g., reduce boredom). The **pressure** of an instinct is the amount of motivating influence it has on the individual (e.g., degree of boredom). To achieve the aim of tension reduction, the individual must seek out some instinctual **object** (e.g., the company of others or a movie). The **source** of the instinct refers to the area of the body from which the state of tension originates (e.g., the brain for boredom). Psychic instincts are rather variable and are expressed in a unique combination of these four characteristics for each person.

The Nature of Instincts: To Live and Die   Freud subdivided psychic instincts into two categories, defined as life and death instincts (Freud, 1914/1957a). **Life instincts** use psychic energy for preserving the organism and achieving pleasure through such activities as reducing a state of hunger or thirst, taking action to avoid danger, reducing sexual arousal, resting when sleepy, and seeking company when bored or lonely. Satisfying all of these instinctual desires with an appropriate object reduces tension and contributes to a satisfying life.

In sharp contrast to the life instincts, Freud also postulated death instincts. According to Freud (1920/1955), **death instincts** represented the individual's desire to complete the life cycle by returning to an earlier inactive and tension-free state. Freud spoke of death not literally, but symbolically, by postulating a set of instincts that could be used to explain the rather destructive, aggressive, and dark side of human nature (e.g., war). But because the life instincts exert too much pressure and generally make it difficult for people to express their death instincts inwardly against themselves, we have a tendency to express them outwardly toward other people (e.g., arguing, fighting, and murder). In this manner, we can express the death instincts while still preserving the aim of the life instincts.

The Structural Nature of Personality: Introducing the Id, Ego, and Superego

In a later theoretical modification, Freud (1923/1961) introduced the id, ego, and superego, and characterized them as having their own special set of features and processes of operation. These new concepts were introduced as structures operating within the three regions of the mind (see Figure 3.1) and categorized by their function (Jahoda, 1977).

The Id: The Core of Personality   The **id** is seen as the core of personality, because it is believed to be present and operating completely at birth. The id is characterized as being located completely in the unconscious region of the mind, and therefore has no actual contact with the external world, operating within its own sense of reality. Because of its proposed location, the id also reflects those characteristics associated with the unacceptable urges, desires, memories, and impulses found in the unconscious region. It is the expression of the contents of the unconscious in the form of instincts that serves as the source of psychic energy of the individual's personality.

The expression of these impulses and desires is based on the pleasure principle. The **pleasure principle** is the tendency for the id to seek immediate gratification of any unfulfilled impulse or desire when a state of tension in the individual is created (e.g., sexual arousal) without any regard for what is going on in the real world (e.g., sitting in a business meeting).

The **primary process action** is the mechanism by which this state of immediate gratification is achieved. It involves a set of behaviors and mental activities the id can use that immediately reduces tension, such as reflexive behaviors (e.g., an infant's automatic sucking) and fantasy (e.g., dreaming). Other primary process actions might be daydreaming of a loved one to immediately reduce the tension of being lonely, or thinking about food when you are hungry. A major limitation of primary process actions is that while they provide immediate gratification, the need or wish is not really satisfied; it eventually returns with even greater force. For example, thinking about food when you are hungry helps for the moment, but you typically become even hungrier afterward.

The Ego: The Master of Reality   To deal more effectively with the demands created by impulses and desires, the id then channels some psychic energy into forming and developing the ego. The major function of the **ego** is to help meet the needs and wishes of the id by serving as a buffer between the id and the real world. The ego spans all three regions of the mind (Figure 3.1); as a result, it has contact with the id at the unconscious level and with the external world at the conscious level. This characteristic enables the ego to be aware of the unconscious needs and wishes of the id and the external conditions under which it must operate to meet them.

The ego meets the needs and desires of the id by operating on the reality principle. The **reality principle** dictates that while trying to meet the unconscious and often irrational needs and wishes of the id, the ego must follow the rules of reality, one of which is delaying gratification. In its simplest sense, the **delay of gratification** involves postponing the satisfaction of the id's needs and wishes until a realistic object or method can be achieved.

The reality principle and delay of gratification operate through secondary process actions. **Secondary process actions** are a set of behaviors and mental activities that the ego can utilize to meet realistically the needs of the id. Included in secondary process actions are such things as learning and memorizing strategies, planning alternatives, and modifying behavior based on feedback. For example, rather than coping with loneliness by fantasizing about being with others, enrolling in a course titled "How to Meet People" at the local community center is a much more realistic solution. By foregoing the immediate gratification based on fantasy and delaying the gratification by having the ego develop a more realistic solution to satisfying the id's needs, a greater degree of tension reduction and much more pleasure are achieved in the long run.

The Superego: The Supreme Court of Personality   The **superego** is conceptualized as the center of moral standards for the individual. Like a court of law, the superego's task is to make sure the individual's thoughts, feelings, and behaviors stay within the moral standards of society when the ego is dealing with the demands of the id. By dealing with the demands of the superego while trying to meet the needs of the id, the ego must consider not only what is realistic and unrealistic but also what is right and wrong. For example, while approaching others to chat is a realistic and immediate solution to reducing boredom and loneliness, bothering or harassing these individuals is morally wrong.

Characteristics of the superego include the ego ideal and conscience. The **ego ideal** is the part of the superego that rewards all behavior that is considered right, appropriate, and morally acceptable. On the other hand, the **conscience** is the part that punishes all behavior that is considered wrong, inappropriate, and morally unacceptable. These two parts of the superego are used to help maintain a morally acceptable level of behavior. Whenever you behave in a way that is considered socially acceptable (e.g., returning lost money to its owner), your ego is rewarded by the superego in the form of pride or an increase in self-esteem. On the other hand, when the ego produces a set of actions the conscience considers unacceptable (e.g., failing to return the money), the superego punishes the ego in the form of guilt feelings, embarrassment, shame, or loss of self-respect. Because the superego cuts across all three regions of the mind (see Figure 3.1), much of the control the superego exerts over the ego to behave in an acceptable man-

ner occurs outside of awareness. Using the example, this helps to explain why even when you need the money, you do not think twice about keeping it; the conflict concerning stealing between the ego and superego has already been resolved at an unconscious level.

The Dynamic Interaction of the Id, Ego, and Superego: Maintaining a Balance of Psychic Power   Figure 3.2 is a graphic representation of the dynamic relationship among the id, ego, and superego. With the ego placed in the middle, and if all demands are met, the system maintains its balance and the outcome is an adjusted personality. If there is imbalance, the outcome is a maladaptive personality. For example, with a dominant id, the outcome could be a rather impulsive and uncontrollable individual (e.g., a criminal). With an overactive superego, the outcome might be an extremely moralistic individual (e.g., a television evangelist). An overpowering ego could create an individual who is caught up in reality, is unable to be spontaneous (e.g., express id impulses), or lacks a

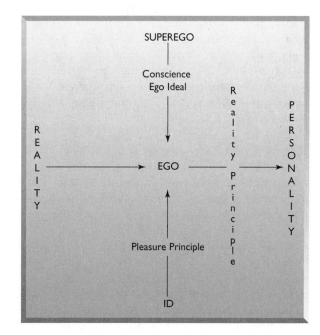

Figure 3.2
The nature of each personality is the outcome of the dynamic relationship involving the interaction of the id, ego, and superego.

personal sense of what is right and wrong (e.g., somebody who always goes by the book). Thus, even with temporary states of imbalance (e.g., screaming and yelling when the id is out of control), most people are able to maintain psychic balance and exhibit a rather healthy personality.

The Nature and Role of Anxiety: That "Alarming" Feeling

Although serving as a mediator between the id and superego, the ego does not have to work alone. Assistance to the ego comes in the form of anxiety. According to Freud (1926/1959), **anxiety** serves as a psychic warning sign to the ego that it is near danger. With some warning of impending danger, the ego is in a much better position to protect itself by developing an appropriate strategy. Because the ego can experience many kinds of dangers, Freud postulated three types of anxiety: reality, neurotic, and moral anxiety.

Reality Anxiety: A Signal for Danger in the Real World
Reality anxiety is the signal the ego receives when a source of danger exists in the real world. You might experience reality anxiety if you were caught in a smoke-filled room, saw a mean-looking dog approaching quickly, or felt uneasy when walking down a dark street in a high-crime area. By having this sense of real danger being signaled by feelings of reality anxiety, the ego is in a much better position to plan a strategy for coping with and minimizing this level of anxiety.

Neurotic Anxiety: The Feeling of Losing Control   **Neurotic anxiety** is a feeling that signals the possible conscious expression of id impulses that have reached conscious awareness. Although no actual physical danger exists, neurotic anxiety is triggered by the superego when it believes the ego is losing control over the ability to inhibit these impulses. For example, even though they are very safe, many people experience anxiety when looking over the edge of a very tall building because of the impulse they feel to jump off. The anxiety they feel is a result of the possibility of losing control over the impulse and jumping. As a result, the ego makes the individual step back. As a more extreme form of self-protection against the impulse to jump, the individual might develop a case of **acrophobia** (i.e., an irrational fear of heights).

Moral Anxiety: The Security Officer within Us   **Moral anxiety** is a signal by the superego given when the ego is contemplating doing something that violates the superego's moral standards. This signal often appears in the form of guilt feelings or shame, which are designed to prevent the ego from carrying out these unacceptable thoughts or behaviors.

While on a date, two people might become sexually aroused and desire to have sexual intercourse. But, because such casual sex is considered socially unacceptable and physically dangerous, the superego of one or both people generates feelings of guilt that force their ego to engage in more restrictive and socially acceptable sexual behavior, such as intense kissing and fondling. Thus, moral anxiety is a signal of internal conflict between the ego and the superego.

The ego generally tries to respond to the different types of anxiety by proposing and executing a course of action designed to minimize the unpleasant feelings. In some situations, it is overwhelmed by the anxiety and takes actions that are more irrational and less effective as long-term solutions. These actions are referred to as ego defense mechanisms.

Ego Defense Mechanisms: A Psychic System of Defense against Anxiety

Ego defense mechanisms are a series of unconscious and somewhat irrational reactions taken by the ego, designed to produce the immediate reduction of anxiety (e.g., forgetting a dentist appointment). By using defense mechanisms to immediately reduce this unpleasant state, the ego can supposedly concentrate more on developing a long-term solution to the problem (e.g., thinking of the benefits of having good teeth). Some common ego defense mechanisms are discussed in the following sections.

Repression: Out of Sight, Out of Mind   According to Freud (1914/1957b), the most basic defense mechanism is repression. **Repression** involves the ego unconsciously removing threatening impulses, desires, and memories from conscious awareness. The logic of repression is that those things that people are not aware of cannot cause them any problems. In addition, because the process of repression occurs at an unconscious level, the individual is not even aware that it is happening. But a problem develops with repression; because the repressed material is not resolved, it reappears more intensely when psychic defenses are lowered (e.g., when sleeping, under hypnosis, or while intoxicated). For example, a rape victim might have a difficult time telling police the details of the assault, because thinking about it triggers the entire episode again. At the same time, she may have trouble sleeping because she cannot stop dreaming about the assault.

Denial: That Can't Be True   The defense mechanism of **denial** involves the ego distorting reality to make dealing with threatening impulses and information easier. People engaging in unsafe sexual practices cope with the unpleasant possibility of getting AIDS by employing denial when reasoning, "It won't happen to me."

Reaction Formation: Expressing the Opposite Reaction The defense mechanism of **reaction formation** involves dealing with unacceptable impulses by expressing just the opposite feeling. People who are unable to accept their own strong sexual desires may devote much of their time and considerable psychic energy waging strong protests against pornography and birth control clinics.

Projection: Pointing the Finger at Others   The defense mechanism of **projection** is characterized by an individual attributing his or her own negative characteristics to others. To help justify his or her own angry feelings, a person arguing with a spouse might say, "Why is it that you are so angry with me?"

Displacement: Finding a Safe and Easy Target **Displacement** is a defense mechanism the ego uses to shift the expression of an impulse from an unacceptable or threatening target (e.g., person or object) to a more acceptable or less threatening one. The classic example of displacement is the woman who, after being "chewed out" by her boss, comes home and begins to express the anger toward the boss by yelling at her husband who yells at their child, who then strikes the cat. Thus, each person selects a safe target at which to express anger and frustration.

Rationalization: Saving Face by Using Logic   The defense mechanism of **rationalization** involves making up what are supposed to be rational or logical explanations to justify unacceptable behavior. For example, a man might justify "cheating" on his income taxes by saying, "Well, everybody else is doing it, and besides, I don't want my money to buy bombs." Such explanations are seen by the individual as being rational.

Regression: Acting Like a Baby **Regression** is a defense mechanism by which the individual attempts to cope with a threatening situation by retreating to earlier, less mature behavior patterns. The screaming and yelling of a surgeon at the surgical staff each time she begins to have difficulties during an operation may represent the regression to an early childhood tendency to get her way by throwing a tantrum.

Undoing: Atoning for Sins **Undoing** as a defense mechanism involves an individual engaging in some sort of behavior (e.g., saying "I'm sorry") designed to compensate or make amends for other unacceptable feelings or actions expressed. For example, after having lustful feelings about a fellow coworker, an office supervisor may go home with a gift for his spouse to atone for these feelings.

Sublimation: Turning Bad into Good The defense mechanism of **sublimation** involves converting unacceptable impulses into actions serving a more socially acceptable purpose. Becoming a sex therapist and teaching courses in human sexuality might be an acceptable way of expressing unconscious sexual desires while helping others with their sexual problems. The major advantage of sublimation is that it makes possible the best of both worlds; both the individual and society benefit by the expression of unconscious impulses through the process of sublimation. For this reason, Freud considered sublimation the only completely successful defense mechanism.

Evaluating Ego Defense Mechanisms: A Good-News/ Bad-News Scenario When used appropriately, ego defense mechanisms can provide an immediate sense of relief. But in the long term, they are not effective for coping with the actual source of anxiety: yelling at your spouse might make you feel better after being chewed out by your boss, but you still have not resolved the long-term problem of why your boss yelled at you in the first place. And now, you have the added problem of having hurt your spouse's feelings. As this example illustrates, defense mechanisms can create more problems than they solve.

Another problem with defense mechanisms is that since they do not actually solve the problem, it typically returns in a more intense form. The bigger the problem gets, the more psychic energy required to cope with it, which results in less energy available for coping with other aspects of a person's life. For example, denying that she has a drinking problem helps Marie to cope with the problem in the short run. But as it gets worse, she spends more energy trying to cover up the drinking problem through denial and has less energy for coping with other more important tasks in life, such as doing her job and caring for loved ones. Thus, another major problem with defense mechanisms is that they avoid coping directly with the real problem.

Health vs. Unhealthy Use of Defense Mechanisms: Caution and Clarification   Although everybody uses defense mechanisms in one form or another, they can be used in an unhealthy manner. Most people who use them are generally aware of what they are doing (e.g., seeking temporary relief), but those who engage in maladaptive use of defense mechanisms are not aware of the defensive nature of their actions. In contrast to using many defense mechanisms to a modest degree, maladaptive use of defense mechanisms involves the exclusive use of one or two of them to an extreme degree. For example, it is the emotionally unhealthy individual who deals with all problems by always denying reality and does not seem to be aware of this denial. In support of Freud's view on the use of defense mechanisms, recent research has documented a relationship between the use of defense mechanisms and levels of anxiety (Hedegard, 1969) and personality maladjustment (Perry & Cooper, 1986, 1989; Vaillant, 1977, 1986; Vaillant & Drake, 1985).

At this point, you have gained a basic understanding of how Freud conceptualized the nature and operation of personality. The focus of this chapter shifts next to how he believed personality developed.

Psychodynamic Personality Development: Building for the Future

In addition to conceptualizing the structure and operation of personality, Freud also described the process by which personality develops (Freud,

1905/9153; Arlow, 1995). This section presents a discussion of the psychodynamic viewpoint of personality development.

Psychodynamic Personality Development: Characteristic Features and Processes

For Freud, the basic purpose of personality development was to help prepare the individual to cope with the psychic conflicts and crises of life (Westen, 1990). This was done, supposedly, by the individual resolving a series of conflicts during early childhood. The skills developed in resolving these conflicts during childhood would serve as the basis for resolving conflicts that would occur later in life.

Psychosexual Stages: The Milestones of Personality Development   At the center of Freud's theory of personality development was his idea of individuals resolving a series of conflicts associated with a sequence of **psychosexual stages**. **Psychosexual conflicts** involve the release of psychic energy (e.g., tension reduction), concentrated at different regions of the body, and external constraints against doing so (e.g., parents, social customs). **Erogenous zones** are those regions of the body containing this concentrated source of psychic energy. At each psychosexual stage, a different erogenous zone was the center of the psychosexual conflict.

The Importance of Early Experience: Getting It Right the First Time   The heavy emphasis on early childhood experiences in his theory was based on Freud's view that the way individuals learn to resolve the conflicts associated with each of the psychosexual stages in childhood determines, to some extent, the way they will cope with conflicts as adults. Failing to pass through these stages successfully meant an individual may have trouble expressing and satisfying instinctual needs and desires as an adult. Thus, Freud viewed childhood as the time for individuals to acquire and practice those coping skills that would be of some value later in life (Westen, 1990).

Fixation and Regression: Barriers to Successful Personality Development   Failure to resolve satisfactorily the conflicts at any of the psychosexual stages would result in fixation and regression. **Fixation** involves the individual investing a considerable amount of psychic energy trying to resolve a particular psycho-

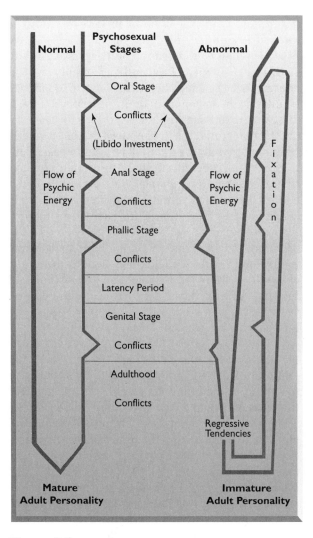

Figure 3.3

The fixation-regression relationship as illustrated by the normal and abnormal flow of psychic energy

Note: Based on *Introduction to Personality and Psychotherapy: A Theory-Construction Approach* (2nd ed.), by J. F. Rychlak, 1981. Boston: Houghton Mifflin Company.

sexual conflict. Because Freud viewed personality as a closed system, the more energy invested at one sexual conflict, the less energy there would be left for successfully solving later conflicts. Balanced and imbalanced distribution of psychic energy as part of personality development are illustrated in Figure 3.3.

, Fixation is believed to occur for two basic reasons: overgratification and undergratification of instinctual desires. With the overgratification of

instinctual desires, the individual might find the pleasure associated with one erogenous zone so powerful that she or he remains at that stage of development by investing an excess amount of psychic energy trying to continuously achieve this source of pleasure. With the undergratification of instinctual desires, the individual may invest an excessive amount of energy trying to satisfy an unfulfilled or denied source of pleasure associated with a particular erogenous zone.

Regardless of the reason, fixation at one psychosexual stage increases the likelihood of regression. In psychosexual development, **regression** refers to the tendency for an individual to return to an earlier, more immature behavior pattern that is associated with a specific psychosexual stage for the purpose of coping with a psychic conflict. For example, eating, drinking, and smoking cigarettes are all activities associated with the oral region as the erogenous zone in the first psychosexual stage of personality development. The relationship between fixation and regression is that the more a person has fixated at a particular psychosexual stage, the more likely he or she is to regress to a form of behavior associated with that stage later in life; see right side of Figure 3.3. Since returning to immature forms of coping prevents the learning of more mature and effective coping methods, both fixation and regression are major barriers to successful personality development.

The Psychosexual Stages:
The Road to Personality Development
Probably one of the most controversial aspects of Freud's theory was his notion of the psychosexual stages occurring during childhood. While the term *sexual* is used to describe the stages, it would be an extreme oversimplification of Freud's view to assume that he used this term literally. Instead, he was referring primarily to the expression of libido and pleasure associated with reducing bodily tension. The basic characteristics and dynamics of the psychosexual stages are discussed in this section.

The Oral Stage: Learning to Cope with Significant Losses
Infants tend to put everything in their mouths, mainly because most of the pleasure they receive in life comes from eating and reducing the tension associated with hunger. During the **oral stage**, an excessive amount of libido was believed to be concentrated

A characteristic feature of the oral incorporative personality is to engage in oral activities, such as drinking, to cope with stress and personal conflicts.

around the oral region. Thus, activities such as sucking, biting, chewing, licking, and swallowing were all associated with eating and the seeking of pleasure from activities involving the mouth. The oral stage was believed to occur during the first 18 to 24 months of the infant's life.

During the oral stage, nursing on the mother's breast is a primary source of pleasure (e.g., reduction of hunger tension) for the infant. But about halfway through the oral stage, the infant is confronted with its first major psychosexual conflict. When the child is 8 to 10 months old, the mother begins to wean it from breast feeding. Since the breast becomes an object of tension reduction and pleasure for the child, Freud believed that the manner in which the weaning process was resolved had important implications for subsequent personality development and the resolution of future psychosexual conflicts. For example, weaning that is too abrupt creates the undergratification of needs and frustration, while weaning that is prolonged creates overgratification of needs and dependency. In both cases, fixating at the early part of the oral stage might result in the individual developing an **oral incorporative personality**, characterized by the tendency to cope with the conflicts of adult life in an oral manner (e.g., eating or drinking). Toward the end of the oral stage (around 18 to 24 months of age), the infant also begins to develop teeth that can be used to express anger or

frustration during the weaning process by biting the mother. Fixating at this later part of the oral stage produces what is known as an **oral aggressive or oral sadistic personality**. This oral personality type is characterized in adults by the tendency to cope with conflicts by behaving in an orally aggressive manner (e.g., yelling or swearing).

If the conflict associated with the weaning process goes well, the infant develops the basic skills necessary to cope effectively with certain conflicts that may arise later in life. This person is better equipped to handle situations involving the loss of a significant source of pleasure, such as giving up a security blanket at age 5 or losing a love interest to a romantic rival at age 26. In addition, by learning to distinguish between objects of significance in the external environment (e.g., mother's breast) and an internal sense of his or her own needs and desires, the infant begins to show the first signs of an emerging ego—an independent sense of the self.

The Anal Stage: Learning When and Where   At the second year of life, the primary erogenous zone begins to shift from the oral region to the anal region. For this reason, Freud referred to the second psychosexual stage as the **anal stage**. The principal source of pleasure associated with the anal stage is the reduction of tension that accompanies reducing bodily tension by urinating and defecating. The conflict arises when parents begin to make demands on the infant to regulate this source of pleasure during the process of toilet training. The basic task of toilet training is teaching the child to delay this source of gratification until proper toilet facilities are available.

Freud believed that difficulties in the course of toilet training also had implications for future personality development. Some infants may cope with the rather strict and harsh demands of neatness and cleanliness during toilet training by resisting or holding back and not defecating. Overextending psychic energy during the process of toilet training by holding back can result in fixating at the anal stage, creating an anal retentive personality as an adult. The **anal retentive personality** is characterized by the tendency to cope with conflicts later in life by demonstrating an extreme sense of cleanliness and orderliness, such as ironing clothes or waxing the car when troubled. The child may also respond to the challenge of toilet training with anger and aggression and fixate at the anal stage by developing an anal sadistic personality. The **anal sadistic personality** is characterized by the tendency to deal with stress in a rather explosive and unexpected manner, such as getting very angry over the slightest disturbance.

So the basic lessons the child is being taught through toilet training involve the need to consider external constraints and the process of delaying gratification—the expression of pleasures must be done at the proper time and place. This concern for what is acceptable and proper is the beginning of a sense of social conscience (i.e., superego).

The Phallic Stage: Laying the Foundation for Morality and Sex-Role Behavior   Around the fourth or fifth year of life, the individual enters what Freud called the **phallic stage**. The erogenous zone for the phallic stage is the genital region. With an increased sense of bodily awareness and the exploration of various body parts, the child discovers the sense of pleasure that can be achieved by touching the genitals. Because of the central role the mother has played in the previous

THE FAMILY CIRCUS.   By Bil Keane

11-23
Copyright 1979
The Register and Tribune
Syndicate, Inc.

"Know what, Daddy? I love your wife."

Figure 3.4
During the phallic stage, the child expresses intense emotional affection for the opposite-sex parent while viewing the same-sex parent as a source of competition.
Reprinted with special permission of King Features Syndicate.

Successful resolution of the Oedipus complex and the Electra complex during the phallic stage produces culturally appropriate sex-role identification. Children demonstrate this process of identification during play by engaging in activities that are consistent with their respective genders, such as the little girl wearing a dress and necklace and the little boy wearing a shirt and tie.

stages in helping the child to achieve pleasure (e.g., breastfeeding and teaching the child how to use the toilet), she is seen as the person most likely to maximize the child's pleasure during this stage as well. While both boys and girls show similar interests in their genitals as a source of pleasure, Freud believed the course of personality development taken by each during the phallic stage was quite different.

For little boys, the principal conflict involves the father as a source of competition for the gratification provided by the mother (see Figure 3.4). More specifically, the boy supposedly realizes that because his father's penis is much bigger than his own, the father has a greater need for the mother's attention. With this realization, Freud believed boys begin to experience feelings of castration anxiety. **Castration anxiety** involves the little boy believing that the father is going to cut off the boy's penis so that he will not be in competition for the mother's attention. The psychosexual conflict this creates is between the little boy's desires to maximize his sense of pleasure via the mother versus the possibility of losing the entire source of pleasure if he tries to compete against the father. Freud called this "love triangle" involving the little boy and his parents the **Oedipus complex**, after the mythical Greek character King Oedipus, who unknowingly killed his father and married his mother.

Freud proposed that in successfully resolving this conflict, the boy engages in the process of **identification with the aggressor**; that is, the boy acts like his father by adopting his values, attitudes, and characteristic behaviors. By acting like his father, he then becomes "mama's little man" and can experience a vicarious sense of genital pleasure by observing the pleasure his father receives from his mother. Resolving the Oedipus complex in this way serves two important functions of socialization. First, because the father's values and attitudes generally reflect the moral standards of society, the internalization of the father's values through the process of identification fosters the development of the superego (i.e., a conscience). Second, internalizing his father's behavior also helps the boy to learn how men are supposed to act in society (e.g., sex-typed behavior). At the end of a successfully resolved phallic stage, the boy has formed the basis of his superego and sex-role behavior patterns. On the other hand, unsuccessful resolution of the Oedipus complex can result in the formation of a weak superego that can be expressed in impulsive, criminal behavior or the development of more feminine sex-role values.

The phallic stage for a young girl begins when she notices that little boys have a penis and little girls do not. This realization results in what Freud referred to as **penis envy**. The little girl feels that she is being denied the extra genital pleasure that a penis would allow her. As in the past, the girl turns to her mother as a means of achieving this additional pleasure. But her mother also lacks a penis, so the girl turns her affection toward her father. Knowing that the mother has no penis, the girl begins to feel that the mother also desires the father's penis. The psychosexual conflict this creates is between the little girl's desires to maximize her sense of pleasure via the father versus the possibility of losing other sources of considerable pleasure by having the mother as a rival. The girl's mixed feelings for her parents form the basis of what Freud referred to as

the **Electra complex**, so named after the mythical Greek character Electra, who persuaded her brother to kill their father.

The resolution of the Electra complex involves the little girl identifying with her mother and incorporating all of her characteristic behaviors, attitudes, and values. By acting like her mother, the little girl is then able to experience a vicarious sense of pleasure by observing the pleasure her mother receives from the father. As with the little boy, the process of identification results in the appearance of a superego that reflects society's moral standards and feminine sex-role behavior patterns. Freud proposed that to completely resolve the issue of penis envy, the woman will marry and have a baby boy of her own. Her son's penis then serves as a symbol of the penis she never had. Failure to completely resolve the Electra complex can result in an ever-active sense of penis envy and the development of a phallic personality as an adult. The **phallic personality** is characterized by a woman who deals with her penis envy by behaving in a very dominating or aggressive manner toward men (e.g., publicly or privately humiliating them), symbolically castrating them and decreasing their masculinity. Another manifestation of the phallic personality might involve the female having sexual relations with many men as a means of symbolically obtaining a penis. Such views of female personality development are not shared by all personality theorists, but seem to reflect the beliefs Freud developed while working in the primarily male-dominated Viennese society in the early 1900s.

The Latency Period: A Time of Peace for Practicing Sex Roles Freud believed that after dealing with the extremely traumatic experiences of the phallic stages, children enter into the latency period, from around 5 to 7 years of age until about 13. The **latency period** is characterized by a reduction in the overall activity level of psychic energy. During this time, boys and girls begin to form closely knit same-sex peer groups. Boys typically form clubs "for boys only," playing games and other group activities considered socially appropriate for them. Little girls spend most of their time playing with dolls or other socially approved activities. This rather exclusive same-sex interaction allows these children to begin experimenting with the new roles and modes of behaviors that society says should be reflected in

During the genital stage of psychosexual development, there is an awakening of interest in the opposite sex as a source of emotional pleasure. Such emotional attachments during adolescence lay the foundation for the more mature and intimate relationships to be experienced in adulthood.

their superego as young adults. Because of the newness of these behaviors, it just seems easier for children to begin practicing them in the company of others sharing similar experiences.

The Genital Stage: Learning to Love   The onset of puberty initiates the **genital stage**, the final psychosexual stage. During adolescence, hormonal shifts produce changes in the individual's body that are manifested in the development of **secondary sex characteristics**: the development of breasts in females, further development of the genitals for both sexes, appearance of pubic hair, start of nocturnal emissions (e.g., "wet dreams") for boys, and onset of menstruation for girls. All of these events reintroduce the genital region as a source of interest, tension, and pleasure, as was the case during the phallic stage. But instead of turning to the opposite-sex parent as an agent of gratification and tension reduction, adolescents turn to their opposite-sex peers. It is during this time that adolescents begin to experience their first strong emotional feelings for someone outside of their parents (e.g., a "crush" or puppy love). In coping with these new feelings, adolescents begin to use those sex-role behaviors first acquired and

rehearsed during the phallic and latency stages. These early romantic relationships help to prepare individuals for the more significant emotional relationships that will develop as adults.

It is during these relationships that adolescents first become aware of meeting not only their own sense of pleasure but also the needs and pleasures of others. They display this consideration by giving things (romantic cards, class rings, and other gifts) to the person they have feelings for, and ideally these expressions of affection are reciprocated. The lesson learned from this type of activity is that by giving pleasure to others, it is possible to receive pleasure. Freud believed that such selflessness formed the basis for what is needed in the mature emotional relationships of adulthood. Thus Freud believed the genital stage continued from adolescence well into adulthood.

In adulthood, the major psychosexual conflict to be resolved involves expressing and releasing psychic energy in a socially acceptable manner. For Freud, successful resolution of this conflict involved the development of **genital sexuality** in romantic relationships, in which both partners gain pleasure by helping to reduce their partner's sexual tension while also meeting their own emotional needs. Freud believed that the most acceptable means of sexual release as adults is through the institution of marriage. Although starting out as very lustful in nature, successful marriages develop a sense of affection and emotional commitment that involves considering the needs, desires, and pleasures of one's spouse. The nature of genital sexuality comes very close to what we might define as love. To take this process one step further, marriages based on genital sexuality also serve as models for children to incorporate during the development of the superego in the phallic stage. Thus, children learn that one of the things adults do is to treat others in a manner involving respect, commitment, and consideration.

Individuals who fail to establish a sense of genital sexuality run the risk of becoming involved with others for the purpose of satisfying their own sexual needs and desires while being unable to commit themselves to others in any emotional sense other than lust.

Psychosexual Stages: Some Closing Remarks   It should be made clear that the conflicts at each stage are symbolic, and not literal in their nature (Westen,

1990). The conflicts encountered at each of these stages represent a "dress rehearsal" for events that are to come as adults. Thus, successfully passing through the psychosexual stages is the foundation for developing a healthy personality. Although Freud developed his ideas about personality development at the turn of the century, and did so without the benefit of much of what we know today about personality development, more recent research supports his views concerning the relationship between early childhood experiences—particularly with primary caregivers—and subsequent adjustment and interpersonal relationships (Ainsworth, 1979; Ainsworth, Blehar, Waters, & Wall, 1978; Bowlby, 1982; Bretherton, 1985; Ricks, 1985; Sroufe & Fleeson, 1986; Zeanah & Zeanah, 1989). To read about some other psychoanalytical thinkers who used Freud's views on the importance of early childhood in personality development, see "A Closer Look" below.

A CLOSER LOOK

Object Relations Theory: Recent Developments in Psychoanalytic Thinking on Development

One of the most recent and significant developments in psychodynamic thinking has been **object relations theory** (Westen, 1990, 1991). Like Freud, most object relations theorists place great emphasis on the importance of early childhood experience as critical elements in the formation of the adult personality. But in contrast to Freud's emphasis on intrapsychic conflict and tension reduction, object relations theorists tend to place more emphasis on the interpersonal nature of relationships with significant objects (i.e., parents) and the development of a personal identity during early childhood.

Early Thinking in Object Relations Theory: Good and Bad Objects in the Development of a Sense of Self

One of the earliest object relations theorists was the English psychoanalyst Melanie Klein, who was a contemporary of Freud's. In her work, Klein (1937, 1948) focused on how infants, during the first few years of life, developed a sense of self based on their perceptions of significant objects (e.g., parents or primary caretakers) in their lives. Klein proposed that during the first year of life, the infant classifies significant pieces of the object into "good" and "bad" categories based on its experiences with each piece of the object (Cashdan, 1988). For example, the child perceives the mother's breast as "good" because it is a source of pleasure and her hand as "bad" because it is the object that takes the breast away from the infant's mouth. However, toward the end of the first year of life, the child begins to combine the pieces to formulate an image of the object as a whole unit.

The child's ability to form a sense of attachment to the object and use its image as a source of comfort is indicated by the extent to which the object is perceived as good, can be related to by the child to deal with discomfort, and is incorporated into the child's establishment of an independent sense of identity. Bad objects contribute to the infant's sense of discomfort and make identity formation difficult. Problems of adjustment in later life are related to the individual's relationship with these significant objects in infancy and those that are developed later on (e.g., teachers, coaches, and bosses).

In a similar manner, Otto Kernberg (1984), a contemporary object relations theorist, has proposed that these early object relationships set the stage for how subsequent relations are internalized. For example, a young man's feelings about seeking psychotherapy are, in part, related to the extent to which he was able to find comfort from significant others in his early childhood.

In a close approximation to Freud's psychosexual stages, Margaret Mahler (1968; Mahler, Pine, & Bergman, 1975) has also proposed a theory of object relations. Mahler believes that the infant passes through a series of stages during the first three years of life. During this time, the infant attempts to establish supportive object relationships that enable it to explore and take risks in order to establish its own sense of self. Like Klein and Kernberg, Mahler believes that the object relations developed very early in life are critical to establishing healthy and meaningful object relationships in adulthood.

Contemporary Thinking in Object Relations Theory: In Reaction to Narcissism

Perhaps the most influential object relations theorist is Heinz Kohut (1971, 1977, 1984). Like Freud, Kohut

Object relations theorists, such as Margaret Mahler and Otto Kernberg, sought to expand Freud's ideas by taking an interpersonal viewpoint that emphasized the individual's relationships with significant others.

(1913–1981) received his medical training at the University of Vienna; but he was trained in psycho-analysis at the University of Chicago. Also like Freud, Kohut developed his theory based on the observa-tions of individuals he saw in his clinical practice.

More specifically, while Freud's observations were based primarily on those clients whose experiences of anxiety produced symptoms of hysteria, Kohut noticed that many of his clients were individuals whose principal complaint seemed to be feelings of depression, a sense of emptiness, and a general dissatisfaction with life. These symptoms were said to be characteristic of **narcissistic personality disorder**. Narcissistic individuals are characterized by a very shallow sense of self, for which they require constant reassurance from others (Morf & Rhode-walt, 1993). They are likely to spend a considerable amount of time in self-absorbed, attention-seeking activities trying to figure out who they are as a means of avoiding the feelings of depression and emptiness that accompany not having a sense of self or personal identity.

At the core of Kohut's view of personality is the bipolar self. The **bipolar self** is characterized by a desire for power and success on one hand and individual goals and personal values on the other. These two aspects of the self are linked by the individual's talents and skills. Personality development is the process by which the individual establishes a sense of self by using his or her talents and skills to achieve success and reach goals that are of personal value. For example, you are most likely using your intellectual skills and ability to pursue a college education because it will maximize the likelihood of your reaching the career goal you have set for yourself. Achieving career goals is important because what we do for a living is a significant aspect of our sense of self. Individuals who fail to establish a sense of self are likely to develop a sense of narcissism.

According to Kohut (1977), narcissism can be traced back to early childhood when children are searching for objects in their lives that they can use to help define their sense of self. In this regard, parents are considered self-objects. **Self-objects** are primary objects with which children are most likely to identify in trying to establish their sense of identity. They are also objects that are so important to the children's lives that they are likely to view them as being part of their own sense of self. But, for some children, such identification with their parents does not occur, usually because the parents fail to give the child a sense of empathic mirroring. **Empathic mirroring** is the process by which parents provide attention and praise when the child tries to establish a sense of self by taking a risk or expressing an interest in a particular activity. For example, a parent who stays home to watch baseball on the television instead of going to his child's softball games would be demonstrating a very low level of empathic mirroring. On the other hand, a parent who serves as a coach on the child's team or works at the ball park's concession stand is showing a very high degree of empathic mirroring. A lack of empathetic mirroring can also exist when parents display behaviors that their children would not want to model or incorporate as part of their own identity. A parent who sits around watching television is not very likely to be a model for a child who wants to attend college to become a doctor.

The development of a healthy personality is most likely to occur when individuals unite their talents, goals, and desire for success with the support of significant self-objects who provide empathic mirroring. For example, an adolescent who wants to be a rock star starts a band. His efforts are encouraged by his parents who show their approval and support by taking him to music lessons and helping to pay for his equipment.

For Kohut, the healthy personality is defined as the **autonomous self**. The autonomous self is characterized by high self-esteem and self-assuredness. It includes an appreciation for the importance of social support provided by significant others in reaching one's goals, as well as the necessity of such support in the establishment of meaningful relationships. Individuals whose self-objects provide too little empathic mirroring are likely to seek attention by engaging in self-indulgent and adventurous life-styles, such as drug abuse, promiscuous sexual behaviors, or gang activities. Individuals whose self-objects provide too much attention are likely to develop an unrealistic sense of their abilities, which creates a greater likelihood of failure.

Object relations theories extended Freud's ideas about the importance of early childhood and the process of identifying with significant others as critical dynamics in establishing a sense of identity. You will also see that many of the ideas proposed by object relations theorists are reflected in the neo-Freudian (see Chapter 5), phenomenological (Chapter 6), humanistic (Chapter 7), and social-cognitive (Chapter 11) viewpoints of personality.

Because there is so much information associated with Freud's view of personality development, the basic processes and dynamics of the psychosexual stages are summarized in Figure 3.5.

Maladaptive Personality Development: When Things Do Not Go According to the Plan

Failure to resolve conflicts and pass successfully through the psychosexual stages can result in an individual who is ill prepared to cope with the more complex conflicts that arise throughout adult life. In some extreme cases, such individuals may be prone to the development of more serious emotional and interpersonal problems (Arlow, 1995).

Oral Stage Disorders   Probably the most serious type of emotional disorder is **schizophrenia**, in which the individual loses touch with reality (e.g., the belief of being chased by FBI agents constantly). According to the psychodynamic perspective, schizophrenia is due to an individual failing to develop a clear distinction between a sense of self and reality that is accomplished while passing successfully through the oral stage. Alcoholism is believed to have its root causes in the oral stage, because alcoholics are individuals who have fixated at and regress back to the oral stage (e.g., drinking to reduce stress). A similar line of reasoning might also be applied to individuals who are compulsive overeaters or smokers.

Anal Stage Disorders   **Obsessive-compulsive disorders** involve the presence of uncontrollable thoughts (e.g., sensing germs all over the house) and/or recurring behavior patterns (e.g., washing the same dish 25 times to kill all the germs). As explained by psychodynamic theory, such rigid forms of actions are believed to be caused by strict and excessive toilet training during the anal stage (e.g., parents giving praise only when no mess is made in the diapers or toilet).

Phallic Stage Disorders   **Multiple-personality disorder** is characterized by the individual developing at least two completely different identities. Each identity might be characterized by a different way of speaking and behaving, a separate memory set, and a different style of dress; it might also include being a different age, race, or sex from the other identities. From the psychodynamic perspective, multiple-personality disorder represents a rather extensive repression of sexual urges that have their origin in the phallic stage. Because the individual is not able to accept and express these urges within the existing personality, a series of other unconscious identities are formulated and surface only when such urges are present. For example, an individual who feels guilty about her sexuality might develop one personality that is very moralistic and one that is very sensual, but keep them separate through the process of repression.

Conversion disorder is characterized by the presence of some physical paralysis (e.g., loss of movement in the arm) with no corresponding organic or physiological explanation (e.g., no muscle or nerve damage). One psychodynamic explanation

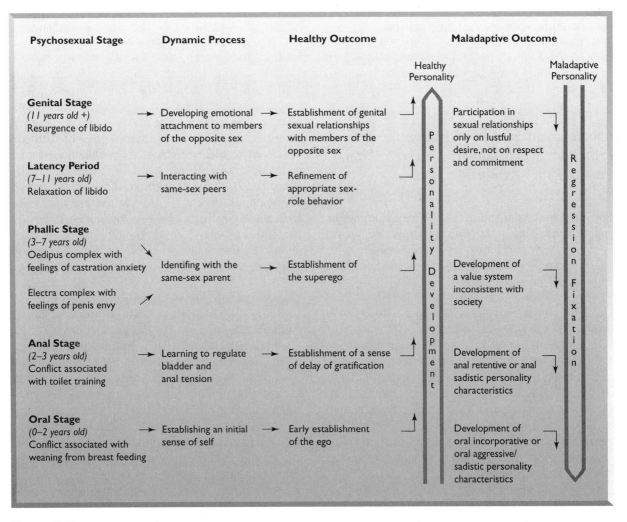

Figure 3.5
The psychosexual stages of development: A summary

of conversion disorders is that they represent unacceptable sexual and aggressive feelings, repressed by the superego during the phallic stage and kept repressed by developing the paralysis. For example, when conflicts with authority figures at work represent earlier unresolved conflicts with parents, a person may develop a conversion disorder of paralysis in the legs that makes going to work impossible.

Failing to successfully resolve the psychosexual stages can result in individuals developing personality patterns that reflect serious emotional and behavioral problems (Arlow, 1995). To help people recover from such emotional disturbances,

Freud developed a method of treatment known as psychoanalysis.

Applications of the Psychodynamic Viewpoint: Using What Is Known

Few people have had a greater impact on Western civilization than Freud. His work has influenced such areas as psychiatry, literature, education, psychology, cultural anthropology, sociology, advertising, and philosophy, to name just a few. This section discusses the specific applications of psychodynamic principals to psychotherapy, personality assessment, and advertising.

The Application of Psychodynamic Principles to Psychotherapy: The Talking Cure of Psychoanalysis

The principal application of the psychodynamic approach has been in the clinical setting, as a form of psychotherapy referred to as psychoanalysis. This section examines the basic objectives, methods, and dynamics of psychoanalysis.

The Basic Objectives of Psychoanalysis: To Provide Insight and Conflict Resolution

Because Freud believed that personality pathology was a result of unresolved unconscious conflict, **psychoanalysis** is a therapeutic technique that made it possible to gain access to the operation of the individual's unconscious mind. The primary objectives of psychoanalysis are to allow the individual to become aware of the unconscious motives and conflicts that seem to be negatively affecting his or her behavior and to resolve these conflicts.

The knowledge into the operation of an individual's unconscious mind gained during psychoanalysis is referred to as **insight**. Insight is achieved by having the individual relate information to the **psychoanalyst**, who then gives the client an interpretation of the information as it relates to the client's unconscious conflicts. So important is insight through interpretation that Bibring (1954) referred to it as the "supreme agent in the hierarchy of therapeutic principles" (p. 763).

After insight is achieved, psychoanalysis is also designed to help the individual resolve the conflicts creating his or her existing emotional problems. For example, during psychoanalysis, a psychoanalyst explains to an office supervisor that his tendency to direct excessive criticism toward his coworkers is actually a manifestation of his own unconscious sense of uncertainty, fostered by the extensive criticism he received from parents during childhood. With this insight, the individual can then begin to

resolve his childhood conflicts with his parents, which will then create less of a need for him to take his hostility out on his coworkers.

By dealing with the underlying unconscious conflict, instead of only the surface problem (i.e., giving negative feedback to coworkers), the psychoanalyst helps the client to minimize the problem of symptom substitution. **Symptom substitution** occurs when the symptoms of a problem occur in a different manner than they appeared originally (Kazdin, 1982). In the example, if the office supervisor is simply taught to provide more constructive feedback to coworkers, the psychic tension reflecting the still-unresolved conflict might manifest itself again, in the form of chest pains and tension headaches.

The Methods of Psychoanalysis: How Is It Done?

Although psychoanalysis involves many different methods, they all involve the process of catharsis. The logic behind **catharsis** is that when an individual expresses the feelings associated with an impulse or emotion, the pressure exerted by them is reduced. By discussing the extensive parental criticism received during childhood, the individual repressing these feelings can release the tension they create. In addition to verbal expressions of catharsis (e.g., crying or yelling), there are also physical (e.g., hitting a pillow or writing in a diary) and mental (e.g., dreaming or fantasizing) forms of cathartic expression.

The Psychoanalytic Situation: The Therapeutic Setting

The process of psychoanalysis is conducted in a therapeutic environment referred to as the **psychoanalytical situation** (Arlow, 1995). The stereotypical view of a psychoanalytic situation is that of a client reclining on a couch while the psychoanalyst sits in the background with a notebook (see Figure 3.6). The creation of the psychoanalytical situation was no accident. Freud believed that having the client in a comfortable position, with the psychoanalyst out of view, would help the individual feel less threatened about the situation and more willing to discuss topics of some emotional significance. During the session, the psychoanalyst makes notes but does not express emotion or pass judgment on what the client says. This method was also designed by Freud to help the individual feel less self-conscious.

Figure 3.6
This somewhat amusing situation illustrates the "classic" psychoanalytic environment, with the client in a relaxed position and the psychoanalyst out of view. ZIGGY copyright Tom Wilson. Reprinted with permission of UNIVERSAL PRESS SYNDICATE. All rights reserved.

The Technique of Free Association: Saying What's on Your Mind   As a technique of psychoanalysis, **free association** involves the client simply telling the psychoanalyst anything and everything that comes to mind, no matter how foolish or unimportant it sounds. Based on psychic determinism, the logic of free association is that everything said during the analytic session has some value because Freud believed that the uncensored pieces of information would offer insights into the unconscious mind and root causes of the emotional problems experienced by the client. To find out what the method of free association is all about, try the exercise described in "You Can Do It" on this page.

Dream Analysis: On Things That Go Bump in the Night
One of Freud's most famous statements is that "The interpretation of dreams is the royal road to a knowledge of the unconscious activities of the mind" (1900/1953, p. 608). What he meant by this was that during sleep, the ego's censorship mechanisms weaken and unconscious wishes, desires, and impulses are allowed to surface to a conscious level in the individual's dreams. In **dream analysis**, the analyst uses the information about the dreams provided by the

client during psychoanalysis to interpret their actual unconscious meaning and psychic relationship to the individual's past and present experiences and conflicts. The **manifest content** of the dream is what the dreamer is able to recall about the dream, such as who was in it, where it took place, and the nature of the action. The **latent content**, supposedly the true meaning of the dream, is believed to reflect the dreamer's unconscious motives and desires. By carefully analyzing the manifest content, the analyst is then able to get some insight into the client's unconscious wishes, desires, and motives. For an example of Freud's dream analysis under some unique circumstances, consider the material in "A Closer Look" on page 78.

YOU CAN DO IT

Free Association: An Exercise in Free Thinking

To get a feel for how free association works, simply sit back in a comfortable chair, close your eyes, and start to think about anything that comes into your mind. Try hard not to filter out or censor anything that appears. If possible, try to do this for about 20 minutes. For the first few minutes, you will probably be thinking about how ridiculous this is making you feel. But after a few more minutes, you will notice your thoughts are becoming a bit clearer. At first, you may try to block out certain thoughts. If that happens, try to recall their nature or meaning. If you continue the exercise for the entire 20 minutes, you may begin to notice certain themes or topics that keep occurring again and again.

According to Freud, the key to analyzing the information obtained from free association is a considerable amount of training in psychoanalysis and an extensive amount of information about the individual's patterns of associations. So do not despair if you do not completely understand the nature of your patterns of association. After all, the purpose of this exercise is not for you to psychoanalyze yourself—something Freud said could not be done anyway—but to demonstrate what can surface from your unconscious mind when you just let your thoughts run free.

A CLOSER LOOK

Freud's Mail-Order Dream Analysis

On the morning of October 18, 1927, 20-year-old Mary Fields* awoke early from a dream that had been troubling her for weeks. To seek some relief from this dream, she decided to get a professional's opinion. So, on November 11th, she described in a typed three-page letter the details of this dream and mailed it from her family's country home in the midwestern United States to Sigmund Freud in Vienna.

November 11th, 1927.

Professor Sigmund Freud,
Bertggasse 19,
Vienna, Austria.

Dear Professor Freud:

I am writing you because I have read a great many of your books and admire you immensely and also because I hope you can help me. In the event that you find yourself too busy to do so I hope that you can tell me who I can go to that will be able to overcome the difficulty.

My desired information is concerning dreams, or rather a dream. First I should like to know the meaning of the dream and secondly whether it will have any direct meaning or reference on my future. I must sound as if I wanted you to be a fortune teller or the like but this is not so because I realize that a man of your fame certainly would be anything but. You see among your books I have read your views on dreams and because of my great respect for you and because of my interest in your work I thought you might be able to help me. Now to go on with the dream and the series of events connected with it. I mention the events previously connected with the dream because if I remember your text on Dream Psychology rightly, you spoke many times of previous occurrences often times having a great deal of influence on dreams. Now for the basis of this letter.

But a short two months ago I met a young man who since has held a great fascination for me. Not being of age as yet of course my parents tyranize over me in many respects and one of them happens to be the choosing of my friends. Possibly you may think me an ungrateful child but still it is only a few short months

until I reach the age of independence. Perhaps also I ought to mention the fact that I am the only child in our family. In the case of this young gentleman there have been some very hard words spoken. The reason for this is that the young man in question is an Italian and of course is Catholic. My parents are thorough bred Americans and also are of a Protestant Religion and although they are not snobbish they feel that in going around with an Italian I am going around with some one who is not my equal. Of course the religious part of it comes in pretty strong as neither father or mother have a very strong love for the Catholic Religion. As for my self it does not bother me at all for I feel that because a person happened to be born into a family of the Catholic or Jewish Religion is nothing against them. In fact if I want to marry either a Jewish or Catholic fellow you may rest assured that I shall do so. But how well I shall accept that religion is another question.

The fascination which this young man has for me has twice transported us into a forbidden paradise, it is also a fool's paradise, leaving us forgetful of every day morals and conventions. Before I met the young man in question he had been going steady with a girl of his own station in life and was going steadily enough with her so that she was wearing his ring, but since he has practically given her up entirely and devoted his time to me. Those are the circumstances leading up to the dream. Now for the dream.

I saw myself sitting in a place that was unfamiliar to me still I seemed to be very much at home. It seemed to be a place poorly furnished so it could not have been home for our place is very beautifully furnished. My uncle, rather my mother's brother, and my father were sitting on the front porch talking and as it was a very hot day I was seated inside by an open window fanning my self, and while I was dreaming as I sat there the door bell rang. Upon answering the ring I found the brother of my yourn Italian friend. He was dressed very pecularily wearing the modern civilian clothes of the average American but with a large gaudy colored Mexican Sombrero on his head. We passed the time of day and for several minutes conversed politely on daily news topics of interest, the both of us standing up he on the porch and [me] in the house. He did not disclose the object of his visit until he was ready to depart when he handed me a letter saying that it was from his brother. As a parting remark he told me that he was coming into the city to see me next week and probably there would be four or five other fellows along with him. To which I replied that I would be glad to see them. Upon that he left. In the meantime my father and uncle seemed to have disappeared when they went I have no recolection of but when I answered the door bell they were not upon the porch. The young man who called upon me lives in a small town not far from my summer home and that is why he told me he was coming in to see me.

Well I opened the letter and I can still see the expression of horror, dismay, and dispair which was shown on my face. The letter told me that this young Italian boy had been married on the afternoon of October 17th to a Miss Mildred Dowl. I cannot account for the girl's name because it is not the name of the girl to whom he was formerly engaged or even her initials. The name I cannot account for as I have never known any one by the whole name given above or even the last name.

Well in my dispair I happened to look down on a small table standing near me and saw a large brass paper knife with a sharp edge. Grabbing the thing up I struck myself a hard blow around the region of the heart (I must sound quite dramatic, but I assure that I was and am far from feeling that way). I remember the sensation distinctly of the knife passing into my body. The first was the somewhat like the eternal thrill and it passed into something more powerful, lasting and serious, which cannot possibly be explained. I distinctly remember dropping to the floor without the slightest cry or shudder. I saw myself laying on the floor on my right side with my legs drawn up and my left hand outstretched and my right hand still clutching the paser knif. At this time I awoke and I was somewhat startled to find myself lying in the same position in bed as I was when I last saw myself lying on the floor presumably dead. Upon awakening I found the tears coursing down my face and it took me some little time before I could control myself. The next day I found myself thrown into the worst case of blues or dejection or whatever you want to call it and it was an impossibility to pull myself out of it. This comes back to me after I have been thinking about the dream and trying to find a solution of it myself.

This dream occurred during the early morning of the 18th of October. I hope that you will not think me bold for telling you the things I have and also for writing you and asking the favour that I have. If I have annoyed you with my troubles please dear Professor Freud forgive me I really did not intend to. Please believe me when I say that. And also please won't you help me for there seems to have been nothing on my mind but this confounded dream and as I am a stenographer it does not pay to have your mind occupied with anything other than business during business hours. I feel perhaps that just writing you and waiting a reply will relieve the sense of something formidable hanging over me which was caused by the dream.

Awaiting your reply, I am thanking you now for whatever help you can be to me, and begging you to pardon me for bothering you with my troubles.

Sincerely Yours,
Mary Fields

At the time he received this letter, Freud was 71 years old and at the height of this career, but he was also in failing health. Despite his poor health and an enormous work schedule, Freud took the time to answer Mary Field's letter in a one-and-a-half-page typed letter on his personal stationery. As you can see, Freud's response was polite and gracious but guarded in the amount of analysis he was able to do with such limited contact with Mary.

PROF. DR. FREUD
WIEN IX. BERGGASSE 19

Dec. 2nd 1927.

Dear Miss Fields,

I found your letter charming and I am willing to give you as much help as I can. Unhappily it does not reach very far. Dream interpretation is a difficult affair. As long as you cannot explain the name Mildred Dowl in your dream, find out what the source of these two names is, where you got it, a trustworthy explanation of the dream is not possible. You must have heard or read this name somewhere, a dream never creates, it only repeats or puts together. If you were here in Vienna and could talk to me in my study, we could detect where these names come from. But you are not here and the fact is, you have forgotten it and not yet remembered.

Now for the little I can grasp of the hidden meaning of your dream. I see your emotions towards the young Italian are not undivided, not free from conflict. Besides the love you feel for him there is a trend of perhaps distrust, perhaps remorse. This antagonistic feeling is covered up during your wake life by the love-attraction you undergo and by another motive, your resistance against your parents. Perhaps if your parents did not dislike the boy, it would be much easier for you to become aware of the splitting in your feelings. So you are in a conflict about him and the dream is a way out of the maze. To be sure, you will not leave him and fulfill your parents' request. But if he drops you this is a solution. I guess that is the meaning of the dream and your emotional reaction is produced by the intensity of your love while the content of the dream is the result of the repressed antagonism which yet is active in your soul.

Please write me another letter if after receipt of mine you are able to explain the origin of the two names. With best wishes

Yours sincerely
Freud

Mary Fields never married and was employed as a secretary her entire life. A carbon copy of her letter to Freud and a copy of his reply to her were found among her papers following her death in 1984. It is unclear if Freud's words helped her to lessen the pain of her dream. Perhaps it was relief enough to know that such a world-famous individual would take the time to reply to her request for help (Benjamin & Dixon, 1996).

*Mary Fields is a pseudonym, used at the request of the writer's surviving family. The writer's letter is reprinted with permission from her estate. Freud's letter is reprinted with permission from Mark Peterson & Associates.

Some Additional Remarks about the Methods of Psychoanalysis   Although it may seem that the processes by which free associations are interpreted and dreams are analyzed are pretty straightforward, they are, in fact, extremely complex. According to Freud and other psychoanalysts, such interpretation and analysis can only be done when the analyst has a thorough knowledge of the individual's past and the way these past events relate to current unconscious forces. It takes a considerable amount of training, time, and effort on the analyst's part to progress through all the notes and other pieces of information obtained during the many years of psychoanalyzing an individual to achieve this level of knowledge.

The Dynamics of Psychoanalysis: What Happens in Analysis?

During psychoanalysis, a number of processes occur. Some of these processes facilitate therapeutic progress; some of them hinder it.

Transference: The Therapist as a Symbol of a Significant Other   **Transference** occurs when the client begins to express feelings and actions toward the analyst as if he or she were some other significant individual in the client's life (e.g., spouse, parents, supervisor). The thoughts, feelings, and actions revealed through the process of transference can be extremely helpful in facilitating the process of analysis, because they give clients another opportunity to face their unresolved unconscious conflicts.

For example, a woman arguing with her analyst may be symbolically expressing the anger she feels toward the restrictive actions of her parents during childhood. In this case, the hostile feelings toward the parent would then be analyzed and a more acceptable resolution to the conflict achieved. While transference has been found to be a useful tool during psychoanalysis (Henry, Strupp, Schacht, & Gaston, 1994), research into the process of transference indicates that it can result in clients feeling criticized (Piper, Azim, Joyce, & McCallum, 1991) and responding defensively (McCullough et al., 1991; Porter, 1987).

Countertransference: The Client as a Significant Other   **Countertransference** is when the psychoanalyst begins to express feelings and actions toward the client as if the latter were a child or significant person from the past. The analyst might express affection or make sexual advances toward the client as a reflection of an unresolved Oedipus complex. In such a situation, the analyst runs the risk of undermining the process of analysis by introducing his or her own personal problems. As part of their training, analysts themselves are required to undergo psychoanalysis with a certified analyst to make sure they have no unresolved conflicts that might interfere with their ability to analyze others.

Resistance: Dragging One's Psychic Heels   **Resistance**, the process by which the client avoids facing difficult information during analysis, makes it very hard for further progress to take place. Resistance can take many forms. Clients may begin to "forget" or show up late for their appointments, engage the analyst in conversation about current events to delay the start of the session, or abruptly stop a train of thought during free association. The underlying dynamics of resistance involve the ego trying to protect the individual against unpleasant information.

The Dynamics of Insight: Meeting and Resolving Unconscious Conflict In addition to making the client aware of the unsuccessful resolution of unconscious conflicts, the dynamics of insight also involve giving the client other chances to resolve them in a more satisfactory manner under the guidance of the psychoanalyst. For example, it is not enough to discover that a client's feelings of resentment toward authority figures are a result of a failure to identify completely with the same-sex parent during the phallic stage. In this case, the client must now reexperience, confront, and resolve these intense feelings in order to deal effectively with other authority figures in life, such as supervisors or police officers.

The Effectiveness of Psychoanalysis: How Good Is It? One of the biggest problems in determining the effectiveness of psychoanalysis is coming to some agreement about what is meant by treatment effectiveness, and with whom it is effective. As a subjective measure of effectiveness, research suggests that many people who have gone through analysis report that they benefited from the experience (Strupp, Fox, & Lessler, 1969). A more objective measure of effectiveness is the research comparing clients in psychoanalysis with clients receiving other types of therapy, and with those waiting but not yet receiving any other form of treatment. This research suggests that psychoanalytical or "insight-oriented therapy" is similar in effectiveness to other forms of therapy and more effective than no treatment at all (Critis-Christoph, 1992; Cross, Sheehan, & Khan, 1982; Slone, Staples, Cristol, Yorkston, & Whipple, 1975; Smith & Glass, 1977; Smith, Glass, & Miller, 1980; Svartberg & Stiles, 1991). But such research is not without critics (Eysenck, 1978; Gallo, 1978; Strahan, 1978).

Certain characteristics of the client have also been associated with increasing the effectiveness of psychoanalysis (Arlow, 1995, Luborsky & Spence, 1978; Svartberg & Stiles, 1991). Given the highly verbal nature of psychoanalysis, bright, articulate individuals are very good candidates for psycho-

analysis, while severely mentally disturbed individuals with thought and communication deficits (e.g., schizophrenics) would not generally benefit significantly from traditional psychoanalysis (Klein, 1980; Mosher & Keith, 1979).

The methods, processes, and dynamics of psychoanalysis are rather complex but highly intriguing. As you read about other forms of therapy, you will see the extent to which they have been influenced by psychoanalysis. For a unique use of psychoanalysis, consider the material in "Applications in Personality Psychology" below.

APPLICATION

APPLICATIONS IN PERSONALITY PSYCHOLOGY

Military Applications of Psychoanalysis: Freud's Contribution to World War I

Because of his emphasis on sexual matters, Freud and his ideas were, for the most part, initially ignored by his German and Austrian colleagues. They viewed his "excessive concern" with such sexual matters as both distasteful and depraved. It is very likely that Freud and his ideas might have remained of interest to only a relatively small group of individuals, had it not been for World War I.

During the war, in reaction to the horrendous conditions experienced when fighting in the trenches, many soldiers developed a variety of hysterical symptoms—including blindness, deafness, tremors, and paralysis—for which no medical basis could be determined. These unexplained symptoms rendered the soldiers unfit for combat duty (Stone, 1985). Because no medical basis for the symptoms could be determined, these soldiers were viewed as "fakers," and treated as disciplinary problems, and punished for their dishonorable behavior. But the punishment did not work; the symptoms continued. The incidence of these hysterical symptoms became so great that combat effectiveness was threatened.

In response to this crisis, British psychoanalysts offered their assistance. They first pointed out that these soldiers were not fakers or cowards; they were suffering from a mental condition the analysts called "shellshock." Shellshock was defined as a nervous condition resulting from the cumulative emotional, physical, and psychological strains of prolonged warfare, which could be treated by psychoanalysis. Because they had a label and an explanation for this condition, as well as a method for treating it, psychoanalysts were soon in great demand in Great Britain and subsequently the United States.

Following the war, psychoanalysis became influential in both countries. Freud's name and ideas began to spread. Although he had initially been shunned, Freud's fame continued to increase. He was awarded honorary degrees, and his ideas and works were studied more extensively (Schwartz, in press).

The Application of Psychodynamic Principles to Personality Assessment: The Assessment of the Unconscious Mind

Because the principal information related to personality is believed to be located in the unconscious mind, personality assessment based on psychodynamic principles relies primarily on the use of projective techniques. The logic underlying psychodynamic assessment is that the meaning given to the ambiguous test stimuli contained in projective techniques represents unconscious processes. The **Blacky Pictures** (Blum, 1949, 1950, 1968) are a projective

Figure 3.7
The Blacky Picture (I) representing oral eroticism

Note: From A Study of the Psychoanalytic Theory of Psychosexual Development. *Genetic Psychology Monograph,* by G. S. Blum, 1949, pp. *39,* 3–99.

technique consisting of 12 cartoon-like drawings featuring a dog named Blacky. The pictures are designed to elicit stories directly relevant to a specific psychosexual stage. For example, the test stimuli from the Blacky Picture in Figure 3.7 depicts Blacky nursing intensely on Mama. This picture is designed to trigger themes of oral eroticism, which—as would be predicted from psychodynamic theory—has been more closely linked to heavy smokers than to nonsmokers (Kimeldorf & Geiwitz, 1966).

The Thematic Apperception Test (TAT) is another projective technique used in assessing the manifestation of unconscious needs (see pages 42–44). But probably the best-known and most widely used projective technique for assessing unconscious processes is the Rorschach Inkblot Test (Erdberg & Exner, 1984; Gray-Little, 1995). To learn more about this famous test, see "A Closer Look" below.

A CLOSER LOOK

The Rorschach Inkblot Test: The Most Famous Projective Technique

The **Rorschach Inkblot Test** (Rorschach, 1921/1942) consists of 10 inkblots on a white background. Five of the cards are black (with shades of gray) and five are colored. A sample inkblot card is presented in Figure 3.8. The individual is shown each card separately and asked to indicate what the card looks like (e.g., two people dancing) and what factors seem to influence the response (e.g., the middle part with their hands touching).

Scoring the Rorschach: Five Characteristics of a Rorschach Response

Several different systems have been developed for scoring the almost unlimited number of responses to the Rorschach cards (Exner, 1978, 1986; Exner & Weiner, 1982). One system, developed by Klopfer and Davidson (1962), scores each response using five major characteristics:

▲ *Location.* Scoring involves noting what part of the card seems to trigger the response (e.g., the entire card, only the upper right corner).
▲ *Content.* Scoring involves noting the extent to which the responses fall into three general cate-

gories: human figures (e.g., an Indian dancing), animal figures (e.g., looks like a bat), and abstract figures (e.g., looks like a spaceship).

▲ *Determinants.* Scoring involves noting what aspects of the card seem to trigger the response, such as colors (e.g., emphasizing the red in the card), forms (e.g., the hole in the middle), shading (e.g., comparing the gray in the card with the green and red), and movement (e.g., the reflection of a dog jumping over water).

▲ *Popularity.* Scoring involves noting how common (e.g., a bat) or original (e.g., the antenna of a spaceship) the response is in comparison to those of others who have taken the test.

▲ *Form level.* Scoring involves assessing the extent to which various components of the inkblot are tied together (e.g., the tips at the top and grayish color make it look like an antenna).

Interpreting Responses to the Rorschach: Forming Conclusions about the Unconscious

After scoring the individual's responses, the examiner must then interpret the responses and come to some conclusion about the nature of the individual's personality. Assessment of the individual's personality is based on the analyst's interpretation of the responses within the following categories:

▲ *Number of responses.* The greater the number of responses made, the more intelligent the person is assumed to be. On the average, normal adults typically can generate between 20 to 45 responses to the 10 inkblot cards.

▲ *Content interpretation.* People who demonstrate a wide degree of diversity (e.g., see humans, animals, and physical structures) in the content of their responses are presumed to be highly intelligent. Sexual problems are supposedly interpreted based on content responses that demonstrate some confusion regarding human figures.

▲ *Determinant interpretation.* The person's emotionality is believed to be interpreted from determinant scores. For example, a high degree of human movement in the person's responses is said to indicate an ability to empathize with other people, while a strong sense of external control is expressed when the responses are determined largely by the inkblot's shape.

▲ *Popularity interpretation.* Making a large number of popular (i.e., similar to others) responses is said to reflect a strong desire to think like other people, but too many original responses reflects erratic thinking. According to Klopfer and Davidson (1962), a superior person exhibits about twice as many original responses as popular responses, provided there are at least five popular responses.

Scoring and interpreting the Rorschach is no simple matter; it takes many hours of training and supervision. But the sheer number of possible responses and the many subjective interpretative judgments made by the examiners contribute to the rather low level of reliability coefficients. In an effort to establish more consistency in the scoring of the Rorschach, a number of testing services now offer computerized scoring of the inkblot test. In addition, as with other types of projection techniques discussed previously (see pp. 41–44), the Rorschach's validity is being questioned—including its ability to predict behavior and assess specific dimensions of personality. Despite its limitations of reliability and validity, the Rorschach is still used widely by clinicians as a diagnostic tool (Murphy & Davidshofer, 1994) and as a means of gathering information similar to what might be obtained in a clinical interview (Anastasi, 1988). Because of the different ways it is used, a more specific evaluation of the quality of the Rorschach would be difficult.

Figure 3.8
A sample inkblot card

The Application of Psychodynamic Principles to Buying Behavior: Freud Meets Madison Avenue

Whether we realize it or not, our decision to purchase a particular product is influenced by many psychodynamic factors (e.g., fantasies and psychic needs and desires) as well as the more common features of the product itself (e.g., price or ease of operation). For example, although its use and effectiveness are controversial, subliminal advertising is a related example of applying Freud's notion of the important influence of the unconscious mind on overt behavior (e.g., the purchase of products).

Motivation Research and Lifestyle Analysis: Classic and Contemporary Freudian Contributions to Marketing

One of the earliest and most influential applications of psychodynamic principles to consumer behavior was in the area of motivational research, a major force in marketing from the late 1940s to the early 1960s. At its peak of popularity, **motivational research** was attempting to uncover the deep-seated reasons and unconscious influences for purchasing particular products. To overcome the ego's defenses, motivation researchers used many projective techniques (e.g., word association and picture-completion tests) and in-depth, psychoanalytically based interviews to get at these unconscious determinants of buying behavior (Dichter, 1949, 1964).

Motivational researchers also relied heavily on psychodynamic concepts and processes in explaining and interpreting their findings. Study results included these ideas: wearing suspenders reflects unresolved castration complexes, making cakes symbolizes giving birth, and people do not like to buy prunes because their wrinkled shape brings back memories of parental authority figures (Dichter, 1960). The use of motivation research principles became so popular that in 1957, Vance Packard published *The Hidden Persuaders* as a means of trying to cast "a penetrating light into the murky world of the motivational researchers. It tells how these shock troops of the advertising world are subtly charting your inner thoughts, fears, and dreams so that they can influence your daily living" (p. i).

Although its influence as the driving force in marketing has long since waned, the significance of motivation research is that it focused the attention of marketing researchers on the underlying reasons *why* people buy. It also demonstrated the usefulness of psychological theories and assessment techniques in identifying and interpreting consumer behavior patterns (Foxall & Goldsmith, 1988).

The emphasis on personality dynamics (e.g., needs and desires) is still a major force in contemporary marketing research (Kotler & Armstrong, 1994). **Psychographics**, also known as **life-style analysis**, is a technique that uses people's attitudes, interests, and behavior patterns to help those in marketing and advertising promote products in a manner that fits with the social (e.g., leisure activities) and psychological (e.g., status seeking) profile of a particular segment of the buying public (e.g., young adults) for which the products are being targeted (Schiffman & Kanuk, 1987; Schoell & Guiltinan, 1995). To boost ticket sales at a local amusement park, marketing researchers might promote it as a quick and simple way to meet certain needs of busy working parents (e.g., guilt about not spending enough time with their children). In a somewhat indirect manner, traditional Freudian concepts like tension reduction and defense mechanisms are major considerations in consumer decisions (Schiffman & Kanuk, 1987). For example, to overcome feelings of loneliness, a person rationalizes the extra cost and responds to an advertisement showing an increase in popularity for those who use the advertised toothpaste.

One of the latest trends in advertising is the use of dream themes by such major companies as Toyota, the Gap, Avon, Citibank, and British Airways (Garchik, 1996). The logic seems to be to promote dream themes as a form of wish fulfillment for the consumer (e.g., I can be sexier with a new car, or slimmer with this exercise machine). Such reasoning is consistent with primary process thought and the pleasure principle, but only at a more conscious level. As the real world becomes a harsher place, with massive employee downsizing and increases in violent crime, advertisers using dream themes hope to incorporate the less critical and more fluid thinking characteristic of the dream state. Of course, even though the individual fantasizes that having the car will

An early application of the psychodynamic viewpoint was to explain the influence of unconscious forces on buying behavior. For example, baking breads and cakes symbolizes an unconscious desire of women to give birth, like their mothers, as an expression of identification as part of the Electra complex. For men, wearing suspenders reflects unresolved castration complexes carried into adulthood from the Oedipus complex.

make him sexier, the reality of the situation is that the car comes with a large monthly car payment. Such reality-based details are typically not part of the dream themes used in the advertisement. Thus, the Freudian influence is still very much alive on Madison Avenue.

Subliminal Advertising: Where the Message Supposedly Meets the Unconscious Mind

As a rather interesting application of the psychodynamic contention that our unconscious mind influences our behavior, some marketing researchers began exploring the possibility of using **subliminal advertising** to influence consumer behavior. Essential to the logic of subliminal advertising is subliminal perception. **Subliminal perception** refers to a person's ability to perceive and respond to stimuli that are below the **limen**. The word *limen* means "threshold," and in this instance refers to the threshold of consciousness. In a very strict sense, a stimulus that is below the limen (i.e., subliminal) is presented in such a weak fashion that you would be conscious of it much less than 50% of the time but still strong enough so that it would, on *some occasions*, reach your conscious level of awareness. But before discussing subliminal advertising, it is necessary to determine if subliminal perception is possible.

Is Subliminal Perception Possible? Perceiving When You Are Not Aware   There is considerable evidence that perception without awareness is possible. Research conducted by Robert Zajonc, of the University of Michigan, supports the contention that some stimuli that are not recognized can influence the affective reactions of individuals (i.e., like/dislike ratings of stimuli) (Kunst-Wilson & Zajonc, 1980; Zajonc, 1980). Thus, there does seem to be sufficient evidence that people are capable of subliminal perception.

Does Subliminal Advertising Work? Purchasing without Awareness   In 1956, James M. Vicary, a public relations executive used a special projector to flash the messages "Drink Coca-Cola" or "Eat Popcorn" on the screen every five seconds, for less than 1/1000 of a second, while an audience was watching a movie. This subtle manipulation resulted in an increase in the sale of popcorn by 57.7 percent and Coca-Cola by 18.8 percent over the sales for the previous six weeks (Wilhelm, 1956).

At a glance, these results seem impressive. They might make you concerned about advertisers being able to control your mind without your knowledge. But you need not worry; to date, the general consensus seems to be that evidence supporting the existence of the persuasive power of subliminal advertising is extremely weak (Dixion, 1971;

Greenwald, Spangenberg, Pratkanis, & Eskenasi, 1991; Heart & McDaniel, 1982; Kotler & Armstrong, 1995; McConnell, Cutler, & McNeil, 1958; Moore, 1982; Schoell & Guiltinan, 1995; Vivian, 1993). There seem to be several reasons for this inconclusive evidence:

▲ There is a considerable amount of variation in what is subliminal from person to person. As a result, it would be impossible to establish a "standard subliminal stimulus" that would be effective for a large enough group of people to make it cost effective (Moore, 1982).

▲ Studies that have found subliminal message effects have been done in very controlled laboratory settings, where the participants were given strict instructions to concentrate on the screen (Moore, 1982). In more realistic settings, such as movie theaters with many distractions going on, it is very likely that people might not even attend to the message or possibly misinterpret it (Runyon, 1980). Research on subliminal advertising conducted in "real life settings," such as on television, has failed to demonstrate its effectiveness (DeFleur & Petranoff, 1959).

▲ A recent variation of subliminal advertising is the promotion of audiotapes with subliminal messages on them. The tapes supposedly help individuals with an assortment of problems, including losing weight, increasing motivation, raising self-esteem, improving memory, quitting smoking, and learning a foreign language. But, like subliminal advertising, subliminal audiotapes have not been found to be effective. Any improvement noted seems to be based on believing what is on the label of the tape (e.g., "Increase Your Self-Esteem") and not on being affected by the actual messages on the tape (Greenwald, Spangenberg, Pratkanis, & Eskenasi, 1991).

In conclusion, people do have the ability to be affectively or physiologically influenced slightly by stimuli they may not be able to recognize. But their recall of and/or preference for certain product brands—or the modification of their behavior—seems to be unaffected by subliminal messages (Greenwald, Spangenberg, Pratkanis, & Eskenasi, 1991; Heart & McDaniel, 1982; Vivian, 1993).

Finally, as a side note, you should know that the firm that supposedly helped to conduct the original subliminal advertising study in 1956 also happened to be in the business of selling subliminal projectors (Runyon, 1980). This alone should make you question the validity of those results. Thus, while Freud stated that we are controlled by our unconscious mind, you can rest assured that you are probably safe from subliminal messages targeted at your unconscious mind by advertisers and marketing researchers.

Evaluation of the Psychodynamic Viewpoint: Strengths and Limitations

Sigmund Freud is probably one of the most famous people of the 20th century because of the impact his work has had on so many aspects of our lives. This discussion of the psychodynamic viewpoint that grew out of Freud's work concludes by evaluating its strengths and limitations.

Characteristic Strengths

Here are some strengths of the psychodynamic viewpoint:

▲ *Comprehensiveness of theory: Freud said it all.* Probably one of the most significant strengths of the psychodynamic viewpoint developed by Freud was its comprehensiveness in the nature of behaviors it sought to explain. His viewpoint attempted to explain the overall nature and dynamics of personality, personality development, and personality pathology and its treatment (psychoanalysis).

▲ *Internal consistency of the psychodynamic viewpoint: Fitting the pieces together.* Freud went to great lengths to establish a high degree of internal consistency within his viewpoint by trying to explain how all the different aspects of personality (e.g., structure of the mind; id, ego, superego; and personality development) fit together theoretically. Given the comprehensiveness and complexity of his theory, this was not an easy task.

▲ *Attention to complex behavior: Creating a new point of view*. The development of the psychodynamic viewpoint brought to the world's attention a new appreciation for the complexity of personality (e.g., unconscious dynamics, psychosexual stages). The psychodynamic approach also produced innovative techniques (e.g., dream analysis) for studying the complex nature of personality.

▲ *Functional utility: Getting the ball rolling*. The theoretical utility of Freud's psychodynamic viewpoint is unparalleled. Because Freud's was the first real modern psychological theory of personality, almost everything presented in this book is a direct extension of or reaction to his work. The impact his work had on disciplines outside of personality (e.g., literature, marketing) is also extensive and impressive.

▲ *Freud as an observer: Making sense out of the senseless*. Probably the greatest strength of the psychodynamic approach is that it had Freud as its founder and principal investigator. Freud was an extremely skilled observer who used his abilities to extract from the seemingly meaningless statements, fantasies, and dreams of his clients the concepts that formed the foundation of the psychodynamic viewpoint.

Characteristic Limitations

Here are limitations of the psychodynamic viewpoint:

▲ *The psychodynamic view of the individual: People aren't all that bad*. One major criticism of the psychodynamic viewpoint is that it generally portrays human nature in somewhat negative terms. It assumes that for the most part, people are pleasure seekers, and we are simply at the mercy of an assortment of unconscious demands. In addition, too little attention is given to situational or social factors residing outside the individual as determinants of behavior.

▲ *Ambiguous terms and explanations: Definition difficulties*. The ambiguity of the psychodynamic viewpoint is reflected in the rather loose manner in which the terms used to explain the concepts and processes are defined. For example, how do you objectively measure penis envy or the superego? Although the evidence supports many of Freud's concepts and processes (Blum, 1968; Erdelyi, 1985; Holmes, 1974; Silverman, 1976; Westen, 1991), ambiguity makes testing them and communicating the results difficult.

▲ *Observational biases: Can you really believe what you are hearing?* Serious criticism has also focused on the observational nature in which Freud collected information from his clients and the information they provided him. For example, a serious consideration is the extent to which Freud might have attended to in a biased manner and recalled only those details from his clients that were consistent with his theory. Although Freud tried very hard to make his clients feel less self-conscious, the validity of what they told him and their ability to perceive and recall it in an unbiased manner is also worthy of consideration (see Figure 3.9)

▲ *Methodological problems: Shortcomings in the tools used to build the theory*. Critics of the psychodynamic viewpoint have argued that many of the

Figure 3.9

A criticism of information provided by clients is its accuracy. ZIGGY copyright Tom Wilson. Reprinted with permission of UNIVERSAL PRESS SYNDICATE. All rights reserved.

methods employed by those developing the psychodynamic viewpoint have some serious limitations. Placing a heavy emphasis on using case studies, relying significantly on self-report information from clients, and using dream analysis and projective techniques as ways of tapping into the unconscious all have serious methodological concerns.

▲ *Freud vs. feminism: Was Freud a sexist?* The psychodynamic viewpoint has been criticized because of the rather unflattering picture it paints of women. This less-than-equal view of men and women is best exemplified by some of the ideas proposed during the phallic stage. The idea of penis envy seems to suggest that what all women really want is to be just like men. Without question, Freud's views about men and women were shaped by the culture and times in which he lived. But why is it that a man who—with his astute insights and powers of observation—almost single-handedly challenged many of the prevailing ideas about sexuality was not able to demonstrate more of this wonderful insight into his views concerning women? Long before the rise of contemporary feminism, Karen Horney, another famous psychoanalyst practicing in the 1930s and 1940s (see Chapter 5), was already busy questioning the assumptions underlying the notion of penis envy.

This presentation of the characteristic strengths and limitations completes the coverage of Freud's psychodynamic viewpoint. If you want to read more about Freud and his ideas, *A Primer of Freudian Psychology* (Hall, 1954) and *An Elementary Textbook on Psychoanalysis* (Brenner, 1955) are two excellent sources. Vance Packard's (1957) *The Hidden Persuaders* is a very short paperback containing several interesting and amusing illustrations of how psychodynamic ideas were applied to marketing and advertising. Additional information on empirical research investigating many psychodynamic principles and processes is summarized in a well-written book chapter by Drew Westen (1990) titled "Psychoanalytical Approaches to Personality." A book chapter by William Henry, Hans Strupp, Thomas Schact, and Louise Gaston (1994) provides a very comprehensive summary of recent research on psychodynamic

approaches to therapy. In the next chapter, you will learn about some of the reactions to Freud's ideas.

Chapter Summary: Reexamining the Highlights

▲ *An Introduction to the Psychodynamic Viewpoint*   The basic assumptions of the psychodynamic viewpoint include the role of psychic determinism, the significant influence of the unconscious mind, and the dynamic nature of personality operating within a closed system.

—*Basic Concepts and Processes of the Psychodynamic Viewpoint*. The structural subdivision of the regions of the mind includes the conscious mind, the preconscious mind and the primary censorship point.

The energy source of personality comes in the form of instincts. Instincts are characterized by an aim to reduce tension, the amount of pressure exerted, their object of gratification, and their source of origin in the body. Life instincts involve the preservation of the organism and achievement of pleasure; death instincts involve the reduction of tension.

The structural nature of personality consists of the id, ego, and superego. The id, the core of personality, operates on the pleasure principle and primary process actions. The ego, the mediator of personality, operates on the reality principle, delay of gratification, and secondary process actions. The superego, the moral center of personality, operates on rewards offered by the ego ideal and punishment triggered by the conscience. Balance is maintained within the personality by the ego meeting the demands of the id within the constraints of reality and morality.

The role of anxiety is to signal the presence of potential danger to the ego; it comes in the form of reality, neurotic, and moral anxiety. A series of ego defense mechanisms can be employed by the ego to achieve temporary relief from anxiety.

—*Psychodynamic Personality Development*. Personality development is the process by which the individual passes through a series of stages associated with resolving a set of conflicts designed to help develop coping skills for the future. The source of the conflicts is the external constraints placed on the expression of pleasure versus tension reduction. Unsatisfactory resolution to these conflicts can result in fixation and regressions.

Each psychosexual stage corresponds to resolving a conflict involving the tension of a specific erogenous zone. Successful resolution of the conflict at the oral stage results in learning to cope with the loss of sources of pleasure and the emergence of the ego. Successful resolution of the phallic stage results in the emergence of the superego and the onset of sex-role behavior. The latency period is used to practice in same-sex groups the newly acquired sex-role behaviors. Successful resolution of the genital stage results in learning to consider first the needs of others. Failure to pass through the psychosexual stages successfully can result in maladaptive forms of personality development.

▲ *Applications of the Psychodynamic Viewpoint*
—*Psychodynamic Principles in Psychoanalysis.* Psychoanalysis is a form of psychotherapy designed to help bring into awareness unresolved unconscious conflicts. The structure of psychoanalysis involves creating a nonthreatening environment and employing free association and dream analysis to facilitate insight. Transference, countertransference, and resistance are dynamic processes that can serve as barriers to successful treatment.
—*Psychodynamic Principles in Personality Assessment.* Projective techniques have been utilized to assess unconscious processes and form the basis of personality assessment from the psychodynamic perspective. The Rorschach Inkblot Test assesses personality by interpreting the meaning individuals project onto ambiguous test stimuli, presented in the form of inkblots.
—*Psychodynamic Principles in Buying Behaviors.* Motivation research, a marketing approach made popular in the 1940s through 1960s, applied psychodynamic principles to the process of determining and explaining purchasing decisions. More recent variations on the logic of motivational research include psychographics and life-style analysis.

Subliminal advertising attempts to influence consumer decisions by presenting messages into the unconscious mind. Perception without awareness has been demonstrated in the controlled conditions of the laboratory, but its effectiveness has not been demonstrated in real-life settings.

▲ *Evaluation of Psychodynamic Viewpoint*
—*Characteristic Strengths.* The characteristic strengths of the psychodynamic viewpoint include its comprehensive nature, internal theoretical consistency, the attention it gives to studying complex personality processes, its functional utility in helping to develop the field of personality psychology, and the observational skills of Freud.
—*Characteristic Limitations.* The characteristic limitations of the psychodynamic viewpoint include its rather unfavorable view of human nature, the ambiguous nature of some of its principal elements, the potential for observational biases on the part of Freud and his clients, and the methodological problems associated with some of the techniques used in its development and validation, and its unequal treatment of the personality development of women.

Glossary

acrophobia   An emotionally unrealistic fear of being in high places.

aim   The tension-reduction purpose of an instinct.

anal retentive personality   A maladaptive personality style characterized by withholding information and objects from others.

anal sadistic personality   A maladaptive personality style characterized by explosive tendencies during times of crisis.

anal stage   The second psychosexual stage, during which the erogenous zone is the anal region.

anxiety   A sense of unpleasantness produced to signal a possible threat to the ego.

autonomous self   According to Kohut, the expression of a healthy personality characterized by an independent sense of self and an appreciation for the social support of others.

bipolar self   Kohut's core of personality, consisting of opposing dimensions of ambition and personal goals, which are linked by the individual's abilities and expressed in personality development.

Blacky Pictures   A projective technique designed specifically to assess information relevant to psychosexual stages.

castration anxiety   The symbolic loss of his penis, expressed as the fear a boy has for his father as a rival for the affection of his mother.

catharsis   Removing the symptoms of a disorder by discussing the thoughts and feelings underlying the disorder.

closed system   A limited amount of energy operating within a system.

conscience   The source of guilt when performing actions inconsistent with the standards of the superego.

conscious mind   The region of the mind in direct contact with sensory awareness.

conversion disorder   Formerly called hysteria; the presence of physical paralysis with no underlying neurological disturbances, triggered as a reaction to emotional crises.

countertransference   The therapist's expression of emotions toward the client in a manner reflecting feelings toward significant others.

death instinct   The driving force motivating the organism into achieving a tension-free state.

delay of gratification   The ego postponing the satisfaction of the needs of the id until a realistic solution is achieved.

denial   A defense mechanism by which information is altered to make it less threatening.

displacement   A defense mechanism by which feelings of hostility are expressed toward a safe target instead of the original, more threatening source.

dream analysis   The interpretation of information obtained from dreams recalled, designed to reveal significant information from the unconscious.

ego   A mediating psychic structure serving to meet the needs of the id.

ego defense mechanisms   A set of actions designed to immediately reduce feelings of anxiety.

ego ideal   The source of esteem for performing actions consistent with the standards of the superego.

Electra complex   The expressed affection a girl has for her father while perceiving her mother as a rival for the father; named after the mythical Greek character Electra.

empathic mirroring   The attention provided by parents and significant others to children as they engage in activities designed to help establish a personal identity.

erogenous zones   Regions of the body associated with a high concentration of psychic energy within each psychosexual stage.

fixation   The excessive attachment to a psychosexual stage as a result of the inability to resolve it successfully.

free association   Unrestrained thinking and verbal expressions designed to reveal significant information from the unconscious.

genital sexuality   The expression of affection through which pleasure is received by satisfying the needs of others first.

genital stage   The fourth psychosexual stage, during which the genital region is once again the erogenous zone.

homeostasis   The tendency of a system or organism to maintain a certain level of stability based on an internal system of feedback.

hysteria   A psychiatric disorder characterized by a loss of physical abilities or paralysis with no corresponding physiological or neurological damage.

id   The core and energy source of personality operating completely in the unconscious mind.

identification with the aggressor   The process by which a boy internalizes the characteristics of his father as a means of successfully resolving the Oedipus complex.

insight   The gaining of knowledge about unresolved unconscious conflicts achieved through psychoanalysis.

instincts   Psychic forces that motivate the individual.

latent content   The unconscious meaning of dreams determined through dream analysis.

latency period   The third psychosexual stage, in which adolescents form same-sex groups for the purpose of practicing sex-role behaviors.

libido   A form of psychic energy responsible for helping to promote the preservation of the organism.

life instinct   The driving force behind the preservation of the organism.

life-style analysis   The use of psychographics to direct marketing strategies at social and psychological needs of consumers.

limen   The point of awareness between conscious and unconscious perception.

manifest content   The information about dreams recalled at the conscious level of awareness.

moral anxiety   A signal to indicate that actions are being considered or performed that violate the superego's standards.

motivational research   An approach to marketing using psychodynamic processes, techniques, and explanations to understand purchasing decisions and behaviors.

multiple-personality disorder   A psychological disorder characterized by the formation of two or more complete identities as a means of coping with threatening situations.

narcissistic personality disorder   A form of psychopathology characterized by patterns of grandiosity, a chronic need for admiration, and a lack of empathy.

neurotic anxiety   A signal for the existence of danger, created by the possible expression of unconscious impulses.

object   Any item serving to satisfy the aim of an instinct.

object relations theory   A variation of psychoanalytical thought emphasizing the infant's emotional attachment to individuals and the symbolic representation of these attachments in developing subsequent interpersonal relationships.

obsessive-compulsive disorder   A psychological disorder characterized by recurring intrusive thoughts and behaviors.

Oedipus complex   The expressed affection a boy feels for his mother while perceiving his father as a rival for the mother; named after Oedipus, the mythical Greek character.

oral aggressive or oral sadistic personality   A maladaptive personality style characterized by expressions of verbal hostility to cope with stress.

oral incorporative personality   A maladaptive personality style characterized by taking in substances by the mouth to cope with crises.

oral stage   The first psychosexual stage, in which the erogenous zone is the mouth.

penis envy   The symbolic desire for a penis, expressed by little girls as the genital region becomes the focus of attention during the phallic stage.

phallic stage   The third psychosexual stage in which the erogenous zone is the genital region.

phallic personality   A maladaptive personality style of females, characterized by expressions of hostility toward men or of sexual promiscuity as a means of symbolically resolving penis envy.

pleasure principle   The seeking of immediate gratification by the id.

preconscious mind   The region of the mind that serves as a storage center for access of retrievable information by the conscious mind.

pressure   The degree of force exerted by an instinct.

primary censorship   A process that helps to keep threatening information in the unconscious mind from entering the preconscious mind.

primary process actions   A set of responses designed to produce immediate gratification.

projection   A defense mechanism by which one's unacceptable impulses are seen as existing in others.

psychic determinism   The assumption that all forms of behavior have some reason for occurring.

psychographics   The assessment of attitudes, interests, and behavior patterns to determine and develop marketing plans.

psychosexual conflicts   A set of dilemmas involving the expression of psychic impulses at different psychosexual stages.

psychoanalysis   A form of psychotherapy designed to uncover unconscious emotional conflicts.

psychoanalyst   A mental health professional trained to perform psychoanalysis.

psychoanalytical situation   The specific physical arrangement of the client and the analyst, and the nonjudgmental demeanor of the analyst during psychoanalysis, designed to facilitate insight.

psychosexual stages   A sequence of psychological milestones individuals pass through in the process of personality development.

rationalization   A defense mechanism by which unacceptable actions are given explanations to make them seem reasonable.

reaction formation   A defense mechanism by which just the opposite reaction to a threatening impulse is expressed.

reality anxiety   A signal for the existence of an objective source of danger.

reality principle   The process by which the ego seeks to satisfy the needs of the id within the constraints of reality.

regression   A defense mechanism that involves using less mature forms of behavior to deal with threatening situations.

regression   The increased tendency to return in times of crisis to a course of action characteristic of a fixated psychosexual stage.

repression   A defense mechanism by which threatening information is removed from conscious awareness.

resistance   Responses made by a client to avoid confrontation with threatening information during psychoanalysis.

Rorschach Inkblot Test   A projective technique designed to assess information from the unconscious by analyzing the meaning given to a set of ambiguous inkblots.

schizophrenia   A serious psychological disturbance characterized by a separation from reality through the expression of inappropriate affect, bizarre behavior, and incoherent speech.

secondary censorship   A process that helps to keep threatening information in the preconscious mind from entering the conscious mind.

secondary process actions   A set of behaviors and mental processes designed to produce a realistic solution to meeting the needs of the id.

secondary sex characteristics   Physical features appearing during puberty that distinguish the masculine and feminine physiques.

self-objects   Individuals with whom infants form a deep emotional attachment and incorporate as part of their own sense of personal identity.

source   The location of origin of an instinct within the body.

sublimation   A defense mechanism by which unacceptable impulses are channeled into socially acceptable actions.

subliminal advertising   An advertising technique by which the consumer message is presented into the unconscious mind.

superego   The psychic structure serving as the moral center of personality.

symptom substitution   The resurfacing of an emotional disorder in a different form from the original symptoms.

transference   The client's expression of emotions toward the therapist in a manner reflecting feelings toward significant others.

unconscious mind   A region of the mind not in contact with conscious awareness, having an unlimited storage capacity, and containing unacceptable and threatening information.

undoing   A defense mechanism that involves engaging in one form of action to compensate for another, less acceptable action.

CHAPTER 4

The Viewpoints of Jung and Adler: Early Reactions to Freud

CHAPTER OVERVIEW: A PREVIEW OF COMING ATTRACTIONS

A significant aspect of Freud's work was the role he played in stimulating the thinking of other personality theorists. Carl Jung and Alfred Adler are two of the earliest theorists whose thinking was influenced by their professional and personal associations with Freud. Initially, both Jung and Adler were very strong supporters of Freud's ideas. But they would both develop considerable theoretical differences with Freud. Each theorist formulated his own viewpoint of personality, and both viewpoints were considerably different from Freud's views and from each other. This chapter presents the unique viewpoints of personality proposed by Jung and Adler.

Jung's Analytical Viewpoint: Probing Deeper into the Unconscious Mind

Jung's viewpoint was termed **analytical psychology**. In reaction to Freud, Jung probed deeper into the unconscious mind and expanded the role it played in maintaining balance among the different aspects of personality. For a glimpse into the life of one of personality psychology's most original thinkers, read "A Closer Look" below.

A CLOSER LOOK

Biographical Background: The Life of Carl G. Jung

Carl Gustav Jung was born in the small Swiss country village of Kesswyl on July 26, 1875. He was later to describe his mother as having emotional problems. His father was a poor country pastor and an extremely well read man who introduced his son to the study of Latin at age 6. Jung describes his childhood as rather lonely and isolated.

Jung originally wanted to be an archaeologist. Because of limited financial resources, he was forced to attend the University of Basel, which did not offer courses in that area. Jung decided to study medicine because of the greater career alternatives it would afford him. He intended to be a surgeon, but switched to psychiatry because he felt that it would allow him to pursue his interests in dreams, fantasies, the occult, theology, and archaeology. Upon graduation, he

Carl Jung reacted to his disagreements with Freud by developing a viewpoint of personality that expanded the nature and role of the unconscious mind.

received an appointment to the Burgholzli Mental Hospital in Zurich where, from 1900 to 1909, he studied the nature of schizophrenia, established an extensive clinical practice, and developed into a world authority on abnormal behavior.

Jung was an early supporter of Freud because of their shared interest in the unconscious. In 1907, Jung traveled to Vienna to have his first meeting with Freud, and the two talked for 13 straight hours. In 1909, Jung traveled with Freud to America, where they were to give a series of lectures at Clark University. It was on this trip that a split in their relationship first occurred. During the trip to America, the two men were analyzing each other's dreams. In one of their interactions, Jung noticed that Freud reacted to him very condescendingly, giving the impression of being the greater authority. This stunned Jung. To completely understand and appreciate Jung's reaction, realize that Jung came to Freud with a world-class reputation, not as some intellectual neophyte.

When the International Psychoanalytic Association was formed in 1910, Jung became its first president at the request of Freud. Jung was being groomed to be Freud's heir to the psychoanalytic movement. But the two men's growing theoretical differences, especially over the importance of sexual energy, resulted in Jung's resignation from the group only four years later. The split was bitter and clean. The two men never met or spoke to each other again.

From 1913 to 1917, while experiencing some serious emotional difficulties in his own life and even contemplating suicide, Jung engaged in a monumental effort of self-analysis. The outcome was some of Jung's most original theoretical concepts. After recovering from his emotional disturbances, Jung continued his work for over 60 years, eventually establishing himself as one of the most noted psychological thinkers of the 20th century. He studied schizophrenics in Switzerland, Navajo Indians in America, native tribes in Africa, and African American patients in Washington, D.C. He participated in archaeological and anthropological expeditions in such places as Egypt, the Sudan, and India, all in an attempt to verify his theory of personality. He was extremely well read in theology, anthropology, archaeology, psychology, ancient texts, the occult, and mythology, as well as psychiatry. He incorporated this diverse knowledge in his theory of personality.

Jung died in Zurich on June 6, 1961, at the age of 85. He was an active and productive researcher and writer his entire life, with a collection of works (20 volumes) second only in size to Freud's.

More information on Jung's life can be found in *Memories, Dreams, Reflections*, written in part by Jung (1961) during the last year of his life and with edited additions by his confidential secretary of many years, Aniela Jaffe. In addition, the motion picture "A Matter of Heart," which was released in 1983, highlights the life and work of Jung.

Basic Assumptions of the Analytical Viewpoint: Jung Reacts to Freud

Most of the basic assumptions of Jung's analytical psychology reflect his major theoretical differences with Freud. The following subsections examine those differences in detail.

The Nature and Purpose of Libido

A major point of theoretical disagreement was the central focus Freud gave to sexual energy, or libido. For Jung (1948b/1960), libido is a much more generalized source of life energy that motivates the individual in various ways, including spiritually, intellectually, and creatively. Libido is also the individual's motivational source for seeking pleasure and reducing conflict. Thus, in reaction to Freud, Jung attempted to expand the nature of libido.

The Nature of the Unconscious

Jung also felt that Freud's views on the unconscious (i.e., a storehouse for unacceptable desires) were rather limited. Jung viewed the unconscious as being a **phylogenetic** structure that has developed over the generations. It contains certain elements—shared by all people from all times—that have been passed along from one generation to the next. For example, the idea that all people believe in some sort of supreme being is a concept that has been passed from one generation to another.

The Retrospective and Teleological Nature of Behavioral Causality

While Freud took a rather **retrospective** view of personality (i.e., emphasizing early childhood experiences), Jung combined this retrospective view with a **teleological** perspective as a means of explaining the causes of behavior. For Jung, personality is pushed from the past, but is also pulled along by hope, goals, and future aims and aspirations. For example, both grade school experiences and career goals can act as important sources of motivation for college success. Thus, by considering both past and present influences on behavior, Jung felt that people could better understand how and why the personality operates.

Seeking Balance as the Motivational Nature of Personality

Freud viewed the various aspects of personality (e.g., id, ego, and superego) as operating in opposition to each other; Jung assumed more of a balanced relationship. For Jung, the primary mode of interaction among the various elements of personality is a tendency to achieve a state of balance. This involves each element being fully developed and then integrated with the other elements into a well-developed sense of the self. For example, during college it is important to develop equally the intellectual and social aspects of the self by going to the library as well as to various social events.

Although Jung and Freud began with very similar assumptions about the nature of personality, their differences became clear.

The Structure of Personality: Redefining the Unconscious Mind

In comparison to Freud, Jung's view of the structural nature of personality clearly reflected an expanded view of the unconscious mind (Jung, 1934/1960). Figure 4.1 is a graphic representation of Jung's structural view of personality. The following subsections examine this viewpoint in greater detail.

The Conscious Ego as the Center of Conscious Awareness

The **conscious ego** is the center of conscious awareness of the self (Kaufmann, 1989). The major functions of the conscious ego are to make the individual aware of his or her internal processes (e.g., thoughts or feelings of pain) and the external world (e.g., surrounding noises) through sensations and perceptions at a level of awareness necessary for day-to-day functioning. For example, being consciously aware of the

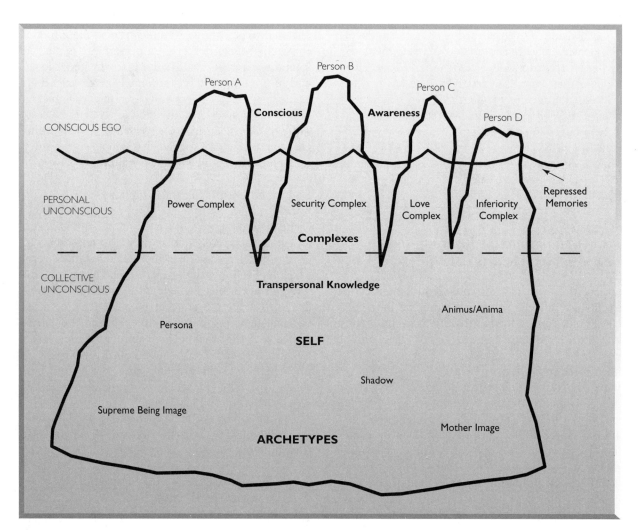

Figure 4.1
No one is an island. According to Jung's structural view of the mind, each person's separate conscious ego and personal unconscious are connected to a shared collective unconscious.

traffic problems ahead, a motorist would recall the alternate route for driving into town.

The Personal Unconscious
Directly next to the conscious ego and completely below conscious awareness, Jung proposed the **personal unconscious** region of the mind. He held that the personal unconscious included all those thoughts, memories, and experiences that are momentarily not being thought about and/or are repressed because they are too emotionally threatening.

Probably the most important elements in the personal unconscious are what Jung described as complexes (Jung, 1934/1960), 1954a/1959). A **complex** is a collection of thoughts, feelings, attitudes, and memories that center around a particular concept. The more elements attached to the complex, the greater its influence on the individual. The many elements associated with a rather strong power complex might include a desire to dominate the discussion in a study group, decide what's for dinner at home, and order around one's coworkers. If the complex becomes too strong, it can also become pathological, as was the case with the power complex often attributed to Hitler.

Jung also expanded the influence of the personal unconscious beyond simply being a storehouse of unconscious memories to include prospective and compensatory functions. Its **prospective function** helps the individual look into the future (Jung, 1916/1969). Dreaming about what might happen in a job interview two days from now helps a person to prepare for it. The **compensatory function** (Jung, 1916/1969) of the personal unconscious helps people to balance out at an unconscious level the conscious aspects of personality being ignored. For example, a rather shy person may dream of being the life of the party.

The Collective Unconscious

While the personal unconscious is unique to each of us, the **collective unconscious** is conceptualized as being **transpersonal** in nature (Jung, 1917/1966, 1936b/1959, 1943/1953). The transpersonal nature of the collective unconscious reflected Jung's view that there is a region of the unconscious mind containing a collection of general wisdom that is shared by all people, has developed over time, and is passed along from generation to generation across the ages.

The principal function of this wisdom is to *predispose* individuals to respond to certain external situations in a given manner. This maximizes the development of the individual. For example, any time a group of individuals gets together, there is a natural tendency or predisposition for them to establish some sort of social order (e.g., a democracy, a division of labor by skill performed, or by sheer size and strength). Such organizations seem to help in maximizing the possibility of survival of the individuals. Thus, because these predispositions, or hereditary wisdom, are passed along from generation to generation, we do not need to start all over again with each new generation, making the task of survival that much easier.

Archetypes

The most significant of these predispositions or images in the collective unconscious are referred to as archetypes. **Archetypes** (Jung, 1936a/1959, 1943/1953) are universal thoughts, symbols, or images having a large amount of emotion attached to them. Their special status comes from the importance they have gained across the many generations and the significant role they play in day-to-day living. For example, the archetype of "mother" is an image of a nurturing and compassionate individual that can take many forms (e.g., mother nature, mother earth, a mother's love). Table 4.1 provides some additional examples of archetypes. While there are a variety of archetypes, the persona, animus/anima, shadow, and self are four archetypes that play a significant role in establishing a balanced personality.

The Persona   The persona is an archetype that develops over time as a result of the tendency of people to adopt the social roles and norms that go along with living with other people. From the Latin word meaning "mask," the persona reflects what might be defined as our public personality (Jung, 1917/1966, 1945/1953). For example, when interacting with potential business clients, a sales representative might behave in a very friendly and outgoing manner through the use of compliments, praise, and amusing remarks. But attaching too much emotion and importance to the persona can result in the individual losing contact with his or her true feelings and identity, which then can become dictated by others (e.g., an individual with a very shallow and conforming personality) (Kaufmann, 1989).

The Animus and Anima   Jung believed that people are psychologically bisexual in nature, in that each person has characteristics and tendencies of the opposite sex (Kaufmann, 1989). Along these lines, Jung (1917/1966, 1945/1953, 1954b/1959) formulated the archetypes of the animus and anima. The **animus** is the masculine aspect of females, such as being aggressive. The **anima** is the feminine aspect of males, such as being nurturant. The well-developed personality contains both masculine and feminine characteristics. Failing to recognize and integrate the alternate sexual aspects of one's personality can result in a person who is sexist and chauvinistic regarding members of the opposite sex.

The Shadow   The **shadow** represents the dark and more primitive side of personality (Jung, 1948a/1959). Like the id, the shadow represents all the instinctive and impulsive aspects of personality

Table 4.1
Some Archetypes with Their Meanings, Images, and Manifestations

Archetype	Transpersonal Meaning	Symbolic Image	Contemporary Manifestation
Child	The potentiality of adults; the future; goodness to come.	The Christ child	The New Year's Eve baby wrapped in the banner of the coming year; E.T. in the movie "E.T.: The Extraterrestrial"
Supreme Being	A power beyond that on earth that can be used to explain phenomena outside of our control.	God; the sun	"The Force" in the "Star Wars" films
Mother	*Positive:* The image of a compassionate caretaker.	Virgin Mary	The Statue of Liberty
	Negative: The image of a wicked individual or object causing harm.	A witch	The Wicked Witch in "The Wizard of Oz"
Hero	*Positive:* An individual or object to fight evil and suffer punishment for others.	Christ on the cross; any martyr	The characters Rambo and Rocky from the "Rambo" and "Rocky" films
	Negative: An individual or object that opposes goodness.	The devil	Darth Vader in the "Star Wars" films
Wise Old Man	To learn from the past; to receive help from those older and stronger; to value the past.	A religious prophet; a witch doctor or medicine man	The Wizard in "The Wizard of Oz"; Obi Wan Kenobi in "Star Wars" films
Trickster or Magician	A mythical figure fond of playing jokes and pranks.	The clown; the court jester	Trapper John and Hawkeye Pierce of "M*A*S*H"; cartoon characters such as Bugs Bunny and the Roadrunner
Anima	The female side of males; males expressing feminine characteristics.	Woman	Media personalities Tom Selleck and Alan Alda
Animus	The male side of females; females expressing masculine characteristics.	Man	Sigourney Weaver appearing as the alien-fighting "Rippley" in the "Alien" films
Shadow	The dark side of personality; our base and instinctive tendencies.	Various demons, such as snakes, dragons, and monsters	Norman Bates in the classic film "Psycho"
Persona	The public side of our personality; a positive image we create for the purpose of pleasing others.	The actor and actress	The ingratiating character of Eddie Haskell in the TV series "Leave It to Beaver"
Self	The desire for unity, harmony, and balance within the individual.	The circle; the principle of Yin and Yang in Chinese philosophy	The tremendous growth in psychotherapies designed to help people "get in touch with themselves"

typically kept out of the public personality and repressed in the unconscious regions of the mind. But to deny the shadow would be like trying to assume that everyone is perfect, without any sense of base desires (e.g., sexual needs) and impulses (e.g., wanting to hit your boss for yelling at you).

Jung proposed that well-adjusted people learn to incorporate these private aspects of their personality into the persona and to express them consciously: an employee can file a complaint instead of hitting the supervisor when feelings of hostility arise out of a sense of perceived injustice.

The Self The most important archetype is that of the self. The **self** is that element of the personality predisposing the individual to unite all the other aspects of the personality (Kaufmann, 1989). The development of the self as an archetype reflects the desire by people across the generations to seek unity and harmony (Wilhelm & Jung, 1931). In the individual, the self is the motivating force seeking unity and harmony between all the private and public, masculine and feminine, and conscious and unconscious aspects of the individual. Failure on the part of the self to achieve this sense of unity and balance can result in the overdevelopment of one aspect of the personality at the expense of all others. An example would be a workaholic who becomes depressed after becoming alienated from family and friends. As illustrated in Figure 4.2, a major function of the self is to sit at the center and attempt to balance all the different aspects of personality.

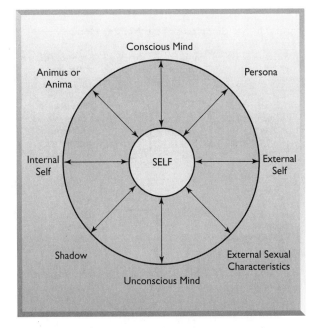

Figure 4.2
At the center of the personality is the self. The bidirectional nature of the arrows represents the self's attempt to seek unity and harmony among the various aspects of the personality. The circle represents a balanced expression of all aspects of the personality.

The Dynamics of Personality: The Ebb and Flow of Psychic Energy

Jung (1948b/1960) viewed psychic energy as a generalized motivational source designed to help the self achieve a sense of balance. The self achieves a sense of balance within the personality by shifting psychic energy among the self's various aspects. The principles of opposites, equivalence, and entropy are three processes by which energy is shifted and balance is achieved.

▲ *The principle of opposites.* According to the **principle of opposites**, for each conscious or unconscious reaction within the personality there is an opposite reaction to it somewhere else within the system. For example, a person's conscious desire to develop the more analytical side of their personality while at work is offset when they seek more creative pursuits by visiting art museums while on vacation.

▲ *The principles of equivalence and entropy.* The flow of psychic energy is based on the principle of opposites and is regulated by the principles of equivalence and entropy (Jung, 1948b/1960). According to the **principle of equivalence**, any psychic energy taken from one psychic structure is found somewhere else in the system. On the other hand, the **principle of entropy** states that when one aspect of the personality has a

greater amount of psychic energy, the energy flows back to the weaker aspect to create a sense of balance.

Figure 4.3 presents a graphic summary of these two principles.

The Nature and Processes of Personality Development: A Lifetime Attempt to Achieve Balance

Jung conceptualized the development of personality as an ongoing process continuing throughout life (Jung, 1931a/1960). The principal objective of personality development is the balanced development of each separate aspect of personality and their harmonious integration as a single entity.

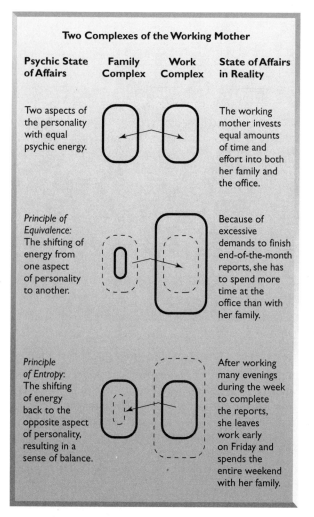

Figure 4.3
As psychic energy is shifted away from one aspect of the personality, it then flows back to the opposite aspect.

Developmental Processes:
The Basics of Personality Development
To explain the development of personality, Jung proposed the following developmental processes: individuation, the transcendent function, and self-realization.

Individuation   In the process of **individuation**, the individual becomes aware of the different aspects of personality at both the conscious and unconscious level and expends psychic energy to develop them

(Jung, 1931b/1971, 1939/1959). An environmentally conscious young executive might try to invest psychic energy in career efforts that will demonstrate the greatest potential for developing both the conscious persona (e.g., potential for promotion to vice-president) and unconscious persona (e.g., opportunities for creative expression) when seeking employment with an environmental engineering company. Thus, by exploring both public and private forms of personal growth, the young executive can make career decisions that promote the development of all aspects of personality.

The Transcendent Function   Once the components of personality have developed separately through the processes of individuation, the transcendent function can occur. The **transcendent function** is an operation of the self that blends all aspects of the personality into a unified system with a meaningful purpose in life (Jung, 1916/1960), 1936a/1959). Extending the preceding example, the young executive might start to invest psychic energy in efforts to be a vice-president in the visual arts division of the company's marketing department. Thus, the self must rise above (i.e., transcend) the task (i.e., function) of simply supervising the separate expression and development of the various aspects of personality and work to blend them into a unifying purpose (i.e., preserving the environment).

Self-Realization   The unifying purpose of the self takes the form of each person trying to establish or determine the true meaning of life through the process of self-realization. **Self-realization** refers to the tendency of the self to continue to explore and expand all the elements of personality in a never-ending attempt to gain a better understanding of the total personality and its purpose. For example, even while not at work, the environmentally conscious young executive continues to think about ways to help recycle products, or organizes letter-writing campaigns for local recycling legislation.

Figure 4.4 is a graphic summary of the processes associated with healthy personality development.

Maladaptive Personality Development:
The Unbalanced Personality
Since the objective of healthy personality development is the balanced evolution and subsequent inte-

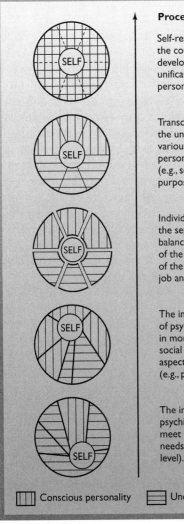

Processes

Self-realization: the continued development and unification of the personality.

Transcendent function: the unification of the various elements of personality by the self (e.g., seeking one's purpose in life).

Individuation: the separate but balanced development of the various aspects of the personality (e.g., job and home).

The investment of psychic energy in more public and social (conscious level) aspects of personality (e.g., persona).

The investment of psychic energy to meet basic survival needs (unconscious level).

▦ Conscious personality ▦ Unconscious personality

Figure 4.4
A summary of Jung's developmental processes. For Jung, the major objective of personality development is the continuous integration of all aspects of personality at both the conscious and unconscious levels.

gration of the various elements of personality, maladaptive development is defined by the extent to which this process is not achieved. Investing too much psychic energy in the persona might result in an individual becoming extremely self-conscious and conforming. The anxiety and depression associated with retirement for some people reflect the loss of a significant and overly developed aspect of the self—

what they did for a living. More serious forms of mental disorders occur when the pressure to express the severely neglected aspects of the unconscious become so great that something analogous to the breaking of a dam of psychic energy occurs. In this situation, like the breaking of a dam, the explosion produces an overwhelming rush of psychic energy from the unconscious into the individual's conscious awareness. For example, a person may become extremely depressed and immobile as a means of blocking out and completely avoiding the extreme shift of psychic energy.

Applications of Jung's Analytical Viewpoint: Using What Is Known

From Jung's viewpoint, failure to achieve a satisfactory balance within the personality can have some serious consequences. To help cope with such psychic imbalances, Jung developed what he referred to as **analytical psychotherapy** (Kaufmann, 1989).

Analytical Psychotherapy: Confronting the Unconscious
Jung believed that much of personality pathology results from an imbalance between the development of the conscious aspects of personality and the unconscious aspects. He proposed that the principal aim of psychotherapy should be to weaken the stronghold of the conscious on the imbalanced development of the self, and to help people use their unconscious as a guiding force in reestablishing a sense of psychic balance.

The Stages of Analytical Psychotherapy: A Step-by-Step Progression into the Unconscious
In his systematic attempt to help the client more effectively utilize unconscious psychic energy, Jung divided the process of analytical psychotherapy into four separate stages.

1. *The confession stage.* The **confession stage** includes those early therapy sessions characterized by uncertainty within the client. During this stage, clients talk about their problems and the feelings associated with them with a certain degree of confusion (e.g., unexplained feelings of anxiety).

2. *The elucidation stage*. After expressing their feelings, clients begin to enter into the **elucidation stage**. During this stage, clients now desire to seek answers and explanations for their problems by exploring how past events may have caused the current problem. As this stage progresses, a deeper exploration into the personal and collective unconscious begins with the aid of the therapist. This stage often includes dream analysis.

3. *The education stage*. Further exploration into the unconscious characterizes the **education stage**. In this stage, the therapist and the client begin to explore the variety of alternatives available to achieve a greater sense of balance. Jung was not very specific about formulating a standard approach to what clients should do to achieve psychic balance (Kaufmann, 1989). Instead, he approached each person as a unique case, exploring various psychological, spiritual, and behavioral alternatives in the treatment process.

4. *The transformation stage*. The final step in the therapeutic process is the **transformation stage**, which requires the client to go beyond a state of psychic balance to achieve self-realization by establishing a sense of meaning in life. Establishing this sense of meaning was a task Jung typically found many of his middle-aged clients were engaged in; it involves a much deeper and more intense search of the unconscious. Such a search might involve switching careers to one that is more meaningful to the client (e.g., opening a restaurant or teaching the disadvantaged in a foreign country). One of Jung's most significant contributions was the attention and importance he gave to such mid-life crises.

The Methods of Analytical Psychotherapy: How Is It Done?

For Jung, the therapeutic environment consisted of the client and analyst engaging in a free and reciprocal discussion. In some cases, Jung might share one of his dreams with a client. By making the nature of the communication mutual and egalitarian, Jung gave the client the impression that the journey into the unconscious is a joint venture with the analyst. Two common techniques developed by Jung to explore the unconsciousness included the word association test and the method of amplification.

The Word Association Test   In a **word association test**, the client is given a word and asked to report the first word that comes to mind. Jung (1905/1973, 1909/1973, 1907; Peterson & Jung, 1907; Rickscher & Jung, 1908) was the first to systematically employ the word association test in the clinical setting. His principal purpose was to help identify the client's problematic complexes. By examining which words produced various kinds of nervous behavior (e.g., stammering or changes in respiration rate) in the client, as well as the associations themselves, Jung was able to assess the degree of emotionality of the word associations and uncover their attachment to problematic complexes. For example, a client with a problematic family complex might respond to the words *house, father*, and *vacations* with an increasing heart rate, by leaning back in the chair, and by verbally stumbling over the associations produced. With the problematic complex identified, the client and analyst would start to explore the root causes of the problem by probing deeper into the specific complexes and archetypes in the unconscious.

Method of Amplification   Going beyond the identification of problematic complexes, Jung used dream analysis to explore the archetypes of clients. For Jung, the dream was to be studied in great detail by elaborating, expanding, and reanalyzing the images in it (Kaufmann, 1989). To do this, Jung developed the method of amplification. In the **method of amplification**, the client not only reports what is going on in the dream but expands on the details as if they are actually a part of the dream. For example, an overly self-conscious client is asked to take the role of a sports car appearing in the dream by describing how it feels to be free and very powerful. This active participation of the client in the dream reflected Jung's view that each archetype (e.g., the self as a car) could take many different forms.

To facilitate this process, Jung also used the **dream series method**. This technique involves amplifying and analyzing a series of dreams for the repeated occurrence of particular archetype symbols (e.g., the self appearing as the sun or a tall building). Jung also used the **method of active imagination** in which the client is asked to imagine having an interaction with the significant archetypes identified during treatment (e.g., talking to a "mechanic/therapist" about making the "car/self" perform more effectively). In many cases, Jung felt that these methods could be used to help clients prepare for solving problems in the future (e.g., preparing for questions to be asked by the therapist).

In summary, Jung used the word association test and the method of amplification to bring into better focus the contents of the unconscious as a means of enhancing the client's ability to achieve a sense of psychic balance.

Personality Assessment from Jung's Viewpoint: The Identification of Personality Types

In this section, we will examine personality assessment from Jung's viewpoint, with particular emphasis on the identification of personality types.

Jung's Personality Types: Personality Attitudes and Functions

Personality assessment in Jung's viewpoint focuses on identifying particular types of personality. According to Jung (1921/1971), there are two general types of personality attitudes by which people orient themselves toward their environment: extraversion and introversion.

The Extraversion and Introversion Attitudes   The **extraverted attitude** is an outward orientation by which psychic energy is invested in events and objects in the external environment (e.g., prefers group activities). The **introverted attitude** reflects an inward orientation by which psychic energy is invested in internal and more personal experiences (e.g., prefers to spend time alone). While Jung believed that both types of attitudes are present within each personality, he also thought that in each person one attitude is expressed more consciously than the other (Ellenberger, 1970).

The Functions of Personality   Besides the two basic attitudes of personality, Jung (1921/1971; Ellen-

berger, 1970) also proposed the existence of four functions of personality. Each **function** is characterized by a specific orientation for understanding the events and experiences in the environment:

▲   The **sensation function** involves relating to the world through the senses (e.g., To know something, you must be able to hear, smell, see, or feel it.).

▲   The **thinking function** refers to the tendency to relate to the world through ideas and intellect (e.g., If something is out there, what is its relation to other things?).

▲   The **feeling function** concerns reacting to the world on the basis of the affective quality of the person's experiences with it (e.g., Is that something good, valuable, acceptable, harmful, or unpleasant?).

▲   The **intuition function** goes beyond all the other conscious functions and relies on a deeper, more internal sense of understanding (e.g., Although knowing what something is and how it feels, it still does not seem quite right for some strange reason.).

As with the two attitude types, Jung assumed that each personality possesses all four functions, but one is often expressed at a more conscious level and is more predominant at the expense of the others (Ellenberger, 1970). Thus, while a feeling-type person will have to "see it to believe it," an intuitive-type person will know by just having a "gut feeling about it."

A rather interesting application of Jung's four personality functions is how they are manifested in varying styles of literary criticism (Helson, 1978, 1982). According to Helson, sensation-dominant critics tend to stress the meaning of the material, while intuition-dominant critics tend to go beyond the surface meaning and try to identify symbolism and hidden meaning by reading between the lines. Thinking-dominant critics tend to take a more analytical and logical approach to their reviews, while feeling-dominant critics try to establish a sense of intimacy with the reader. The significance of this research is that it demonstrates a systematic link between differences in personality and specific styles of cognitive functioning.

Table 4.2 summarizes the eight personality types created when combining the two attitudes with the four functions.

The Myers-Briggs Type Indicator: The Assessment of Jungian Types

An instrument designed to assess the two attitude types and four functions defined by Jung is the Myers-Briggs Type Indicator (Myers, 1962, 1980; Myers & McCaulley, 1985). The **Myers-Briggs Type Indicator** (MBTI) is based on Jung's (1921/1971) type theory concerning differences in the way individuals use perception and judgment as general orientations to their experiences.

Testing with the MBTI The MBTI is an objective self-report inventory designed to measure four dimensions of Jung's typology: Extraversion-Introversion (E-I), Sensation--Intuition (S-N), Thinking-Feeling (T-F), and Judgment-Perception (J-P). Because the E-I, S-N, and T-F dimensions were described previously, only the J-P dimension remains to be defined. **Judging types** tend to be orderly, systematic, and try to regulate and control their life. On the other hand, **perceiving types** tend to be curious, open-minded, spontaneous, and try to understand life and adapt to it.

The MBTI contains 126 pairs of items, each containing two statements that reflect opposing orientations on the four separate dimensions. Scoring and interpreting the MBTI involves assessing the extent to which a person's choices for the items characterize one or the other orientation on the four separate dimensions. Based on the choices made, scores on each of the four dimensions are calculated for that person. These four scores are then used to classify the person into one of 16 possible types (e.g., ISTJ, ISTP, ENFJ, ENTJ, etc.) To determine your own possible Jungian typology, try completing the exercise outlined in "You Can Do It" on page 105.

Table 4.2
Jungian Types and Their Characteristics: A Summary Table

Type	Characteristics	Example
Extravert/Sensation	Constantly searches for novel sensory experiences; may develop sensory skills by becoming an art critic, wine-tasting expert, masseuse, or marksman.	Indiana Jones in "Raiders of the Lost Ark"
Extravert/Thinking	Heavily emphasizes external objects and ideas; ruled by logic and intellect—objective and rigid.	Judge Wapner of "The People's Court"
Extravert/Feeling	Publicly expresses feelings and emotions; makes friends easily but is highly influenced by the mood of the situation—intense and sociable.	The stereotype of the "used car salesperson"
Extravert/Intuition	Experiences sudden changes in interests; when interested, the level reflects enthusiasm; a leader of causes when interested in them.	The politician who jumps from one bandwagon to another
Introvert/Sensation	Dominated by internal feelings to external events in rather dichotomous ways (e.g., good or evil); may become disassociated from the external world in response to their feelings.	Political or religious extremists for whom you are either for or against.
Introvert/Thinking	Overly concerned with ideas for their own sake; tends to dwell on abstractions and ignore practical considerations—very theoretical.	The stereotypical scientist working alone in the laboratory.
Introvert/Feeling	Tendency to keep their feelings to themselves makes them appear cold, aloof, and indifferent.	Dr. Spock of "Star Trek" or the character "Dirty Harry"
Introvert/Intuition	Generally unconcerned with the external world and its events; more concerned with finding meaning in reality satisfying to them—a dreamer.	The "starving artist"

Note: From *The Discovery of the Unconscious: The History and Evolution of Dynamic Psychiatry,* by H. F. Ellenberger, 1970, New York: Basic Books and *Beneath the Mask: An Introduction to Personality* (3rd ed.), by C. F. Monte, 1987. New York: Holt, Rinehart, and Winston.

YOU CAN DO IT

What's Your Type? Personal and Vocational Correlates of Jungian Types

For each of the 12 items below, indicate "true" (T) if the statement reflects a belief you have about yourself and "false" (F) if the opposite of the statement reflects a belief you have about yourself.

1. While attending a party, I prefer interacting with a lot of different people than with just a few individuals.
   T or F
2. I prefer movies with a clear-cut story line over movies with a lot of flashbacks.
   T or F
3. I would consider myself to be more rational than emotional.
   T or F
4. I prefer to follow a set schedule than to cope with things as they occur.
   T or F
5. I would rather play games with people, like Pictionary than read a book.
   T or F
6. I would describe my thoughts as being more conventional than novel.
   T or F
7. To me. my thoughts are more important than my feelings.
   T or F
8. I am considered by those who know me to be more orderly than easygoing.
   T or F
9. I am someone who is generally able to express my feelings.
   T or F
10. I would rather take college classes that emphasize facts than theoretical information.
    T or F
11. I would rather people think of me as a reasonable person than a compassionate person.
    T or F
12. I would rather be decisive than impulsive.
    T or F

Scoring

Items 1, 5, and 9: If you selected "T" more often than "F," then you indicated what might be described as an extraverted type; if you selected "F" more often for these items, then you might be described as an introverted type.

Items 2, 6, and 10: If you selected "T" more often than "F," then you indicated what might be considered a sensing type. More "F" responses to these items might be described as an intuitive type.

Items 3, 7, and 11: If you selected "T" more than "F," then you indicated what might be called a thinking type; if you had more "F's" than "T's," your response pattern reflected what might be called a feeling type.

Items 4, 8, and 12: More "T's" reflect what might be called a judging type, while more "F's" reflect what might be considered a perceptive type.

What's your type?

Based on the scoring procedures just described, check those type categories that seem to reflect your response patterns.

Extravert type (E) _____ or Introvert type (I) _____
Sensing type (S) _____ or Intuitive type (N) _____
Thinking type (T) _____ or Feeling type (F) _____
Judging type (J) _____ or Perceptive type (P) _____

Interpretation Personal and Vocational Correlates of Jungian Types

Although it is not possible to assess actual Jungian types from the limited number of items presented in this test, the following are brief descriptions of some personal characteristics and possible vocational preferences of the eight types based on other research.

▲ *Extraverted types* desire novel situations and tend to be talkative and impulsive. Their vocational interests tend to be in careers such as sales, public administration, and personnel director.
▲ *Introverted types* tend to be reflective, self-sufficient, and like privacy. Their vocational interests tend to draw them to technical-scientific professions where they can work alone, such as being an engineer, mathematician, dentist, farmer, writer, or carpenter.

▲ *Sensing types* emphasize reality and authority and tend to be cooperative and pragmatic. They tend to be attracted to practical vocations, including banking, medicine, office management, business administration, and police work.

▲ *Intuitive types* evidence a high tolerance for complexity, enjoy mental activities (e.g., reading and reasoning) and desire independence. They tend to prefer professional vocations involving autonomy, such as being a psychologist, minister, musician, chemist, or architect.

▲ *Thinking types* are objective and analytical. They desire order and demonstrate endurance. Their vocational preferences tend to include scientific, technical, and business professions that require logical thinking.

▲ *Feeling types* are interested in human values and interpersonal relationships and tend to be nurturing. Their vocational interests tend to be in the helping professions, such as social work, counseling, nursing, customer relations, and preaching.

▲ *Judging types* tend to be responsible, industrious, steady workers, and like to have things decided and settled. Their vocational interests are directed at business-oriented professions emphasizing administrative skills.

▲ *Perceptive types* tend to be spontaneous, flexible, and open-minded. Their vocational choices tend to include writing, art, music, advertising, psychology, and architecture.

Note: Scale items adapted from Myers, I. B. (1962). *The Myers-Briggs Type Indicator Manual*. Palo Alto, CA: Consulting Psychologist Press. Interpretations from Carlyn, M. (1977). An Assessment of the Myers-Briggs Type Indicator. *Journal of Personality Assessment, 41*, 461–473; Stricker, L. J., & Ross, J. (1964b). Some Correlates of a Jungian Personality Inventory. *Psychological Reports, 14*, 623–643.

Research with the MBTI　　The research of Rae Carlson and her colleagues links Jungian personality types with various cognitive and interpersonal processes. Carlson et al. noted that introvert-thinking types were better able to memorize information of an objective nature (e.g., numbers) than extravert-feeling types, while just the opposite was true for information of a social nature (e.g., faces) (Carlson & Levy, 1973). In addition, when asked to search their memories for their most vivid experience, extravert types reported more memories of a social nature than introvert types, while feeling types reported more memories of an affective tone (e.g., joy, fear) than thinking types (Carlson, 1980). These differences in cognitive ability seem to be due to the tendency of introvert-thinking types to pay more attention to internal personal events and extravert-feeling types to pay more attention to external social events (Carlson & Levy, 1973; Carlson, 1980).

The tendency for extravert-intuitive types to be oriented toward others was demonstrated by identifying a greater percentage of them in a group of volunteers at a halfway house for disturbed children than in a comparison group of nonvolunteers (Carlson & Levy, 1973).

Although considerable research supports these Jungian concepts (Cann & Donderi, 1986; Maddi, 1989), Carlson's work is particularly important because it attempts to validate the unique Jungian contribution of combining different personality dimensions and linking them systematically with other cognitive and social indices of behavior (Maddi, 1989).

Evaluation of Jung's Analytical Viewpoint: Strengths and Limitations

We will conclude our discussion of Jung's viewpoint by considering the characteristic strengths and limitations of his analytical viewpoint.

Characteristic Strengths
This section focuses on strengths of the analytical viewpoint.

Richness of Ideas　　Jung's viewpoint produced many rich and novel ideas. Concepts such as the collective unconscious and archetypes demonstrate the novelty in his viewpoint, while his emphasis on life-long personality development through self-realization illustrates its richness.

An Expanded View of Personality　　Jung did much to expand the way personality is viewed. He made it clear that future expectations, as well as past events, are critical to understanding personality. His increased emphasis on the self as a major component of personality did much to broaden the role of the self in defining the uniqueness of the person. That view is reflected in recent theoretical formulations of the self (Pervin, 1992). Interest in Jungian psychotherapy has grown considerably in the United States since the early 1960s (Kaufmann, 1989). Jung's theoretical influence has also attracted the attention of people working in diverse areas, from sociology, religion, economics, and political science (Ellenberger, 1970) to interior design and apparel merchandising (Bonner, 1989).

Methodological Impact on the Study of Personality
Jung's most significant contribution to how personality is studied is the word association test (Ellenberger, 1970). From a methodological perspective, the real significance of the word association test is the importance Jung placed on using it as an objective measure (e.g., obtaining physiological reactions to the words) of subjective psychological constructs (e.g., complexes). His introduction of the psychological types, including those of introversion and extraversion, has also stimulated the work of many other researchers (Morris, 1979; Eysenck, 1990).

A More Optimistic View of Human Nature   Unlike Freud, Jung proposed a view of human nature that was somewhat optimistic. The essence of this optimism is expressed in his concept of self-realization and the emphasis it places on the individual striving for a greater sense of self-awareness.

Characteristic Limitations
The analytical viewpoint put forth by Jung has the following limitations.

Concepts Difficult to Test   As a major limitation, the novelty of many of Jung's principal concepts (e.g., archetypes, the collective unconscious) makes them very difficult to test empirically. But in all fairness, a very limited number of Jungian concepts, such as the psychological types, are supported by much evidence (Cann & Donderi, 1986).

Limited Acceptance   A major problem Jung has had in achieving a wider level of acceptance is that many

of his original writings are very hard to understand. Jung was an extremely well read man who used many obscure references to archeology, theology, and mythology in his writings. Further, because he studied and made many references to the occult sciences, Jung has not been well received by the scientific community.

More information on Jung is available in Hall and Nordby's (1973) *A Primer of Jungian Psychology* and Anthony Storr's (1991) *Jung*. Each of these books presents a very readable synthesis and presentation of Jung's viewpoint and ideas.

Adler's Individual Psychology: A Viewpoint for the Promotion of Social Interest

While Jung reacted to Freud by looking inward and probing deeper into the unconscious mind, Alfred Adler was looking outward and examining interpersonal relationships. Adler's viewpoint of personality emphasized the individual's interpersonal actions with others at a very conscious level of awareness as critical factors in the operation and development of personality. For a glimpse into the life of Alfred Adler, read "A Closer Look" on page 108.

Basic Assumptions of Adler's Individual Psychology: Adler Reacts to Freud

Adler was a prolific writer (he wrote more than a hundred books and articles in his lifetime) and lecturer. Much of his lecturing was to—and in a style geared directly for—the general public. Almost as a reflection of his own personality, Adler developed a viewpoint of personality that was rather straightforward, easily understood by nonprofessionals, and emphasized a social concern for others (Ellenberger, 1970). He referred to this approach as individual psychology. The basis of **individual psychology** was Adler's view of each person being *unique* in the way that he or she elects to help promote the social well-being of others and the betterment of the society.

A CLOSER LOOK

Biographical Background: The Life of Alfred Adler

Alfred Adler was born in a suburb of Vienna on February 17, 1870. While his family was rather secure financially, Adler describes his childhood in less than pleasant terms. He perceived himself as being rather ugly and too small. Being second of six children, he was constantly trying to compete with his older brother, who was a very good athlete. Adler's problems as a child were further complicated by his health; he suffered from rickets. This disease, which affects the bones, made it very difficult for him to walk or move about.

Adler recalls that his mother pampered him as a small child—until the birth of his younger brother. At that time, he sensed that his mother was shifting her attention more and more fully to the new baby. Feeling dethroned, Adler turned his affection toward his father, who seemed to have had high expectations for him.

During his childhood, Adler was run over twice in the streets. At the age of 3, he saw his younger brother die in the bed next to him, and he almost died from pneumonia at age 4. It was these brushes with death that Adler recalls as having triggered his interest in becoming a doctor.

Through all of these traumatic experiences, Adler remained a friendly and socially active child. In school, he was not a very good student. One of his teachers recommended that he be taken out of school and trained as a shoemaker, since he was not going to be able to do much else. But with a tremendous display of sustained hard work, Adler became an excellent student. He attended the University of Vienna and received a medical degree in 1895. He began by studying ophthalmology, but then settled into psychiatry.

Adler's association with Freud began when he wrote a paper publicly defending Freud's position. As a result, in 1902 Freud invited Adler to attend weekly meetings where psychoanalysis was being discussed. This discussion group would later become the Vienna Psychoanalytic Society, with Adler serving as its first president. But at these meetings, and in Freud's presence, Adler began expressing ideas and attitudes about such significant topics as sexuality, childhood

Alfred Adler reacted to his disagreement with Freud by developing a viewpoint of personality that focused on interpersonal relationships that promoted the welfare of others.

experiences, repression, and the unconscious mind that were increasingly at odds with the views of Freud. In 1911, after a nine-year association as one of Freud's earliest colleagues, Adler resigned from the society and took about one-third of the society's members with him. After this separation, Freud and Adler, although living in the same city, never met again. Adler and his followers subsequently formed the Society of Free Psychoanalytic Research, an obvious bit of sarcasm aimed at Freud's domineering tendencies.

After serving as a physician in the Austrian Army during World War I, Adler was asked by the government to help open a number of child guidance clinics in Vienna. Through his work with the clinics, Adler spent a great deal of time lecturing to, writing for, and interacting with parents, teachers, and other members of the general public. Such efforts made him extremely popular in Vienna. This display of public concern, especially for children, was to be expressed in many different aspects of Adler's theory.

In 1926, Adler made the first of many frequent and extensive trips to the United States and was well received by U.S. educators. As a result of the Nazi takeover in Europe, Adler settled permanently in the United States in 1935. Adler died on May 28, 1937, while on a lecture tour in Aberdeen, Scotland.

More information about the life of Alfred Adler can be found in "Alfred Adler: A Biographical Essay" by Carl Furtmuller (1964), who has been described as Adler's best lifelong friend (Bottome, 1957), and a chapter titled "Alfred Adler and Individual Psychology" in a book by Henri F. Ellenberger (1970) titled *The Discovery of the Unconscious: The History and Evolution of Dynamic Psychiatry.*

The Social Nature of Motivation

For Freud, the primary motivational source of personality was the reduction of individual tension, especially psychosexual urges. In sharp contrast, Adler assumed that the principal motivating force in personality took the form of the individual being motivated to behave in ways that serve the interests of the group over those of the individual.

Conscious Control of Personality and an Awareness of Helping Others

To a greater extent than Freud and Jung, Adler gave increased emphasis to the operation of personality at the conscious level (Mosak, 1989). More specifically, he believed that behavior was governed by conscious processes related to the individual's desire to work with and for others.

A Teleological Perspective on Personality

Like Jung, Adler also greatly emphasized teleological explanations of behavior. He assumed that behavior is governed by the goals individuals set for themselves (e.g., a student's selection of a major while in college reflects future career goals). But Adler also looked into the past during psychotherapy to help identify the early childhood experiences that might have shaped the goal in its present form (e.g., more parental attention given to other siblings during childhood, creating a desire to be a success).

Intrapersonal vs. Interpersonal Nature of Personality

While Freud stressed **intrapersonal** forces as the primary cause of behavior, Adler tended to stress **interpersonal** forces operating within the external social environment. The nature of a person's relationships with siblings and how teachers reacted to that person at school were two social environments Adler considered important in determining present and future goals and behavior.

The Role of the Self

Adler believed that the self is more than just a mediator of intrapsychic conflict (e.g., the ego); it is the component of personality that gives each person a sense of uniqueness. The self helps to determine a person's view of the world, the goals set based on that view, and the strategy developed to achieve those goals.

Basic Concepts of Individual Psychology: Essential Elements for Developing a Basic Concern for Others

The concepts comprised by Adler's viewpoint of personality had at their basis the goal of helping the individual to develop a sense of social concern for others.

Inferiority Feelings and Compensation

While operating a clinic near a famous amusement park early in his career and treating many of the circus performers, Adler noted that these people developed great skills as a reaction to their physical weaknesses or handicaps. A performer with a deformed leg might display considerable skill as a trapeze artist and develop tremendous strength in the upper body and arms.

On the basis of such observations, Adler proposed the concept of organ inferiority (Adler, 1907/1956). The idea behind **organ inferiority** is that each person is born with some type of physical limitation, such as having weak eyes, a weak stomach, or being a slow runner. In response to this limitation, the person is motivated to either overcome it or develop another aspect of the self (Ellenberger, 1970). For example, a weak, frail young person might develop the ability to be an effective speaker and become captain of the debate team.

Inferiority Feelings However, Adler (1910/1956) soon realized that just as important as actual physical inferiorities were perceived inferiorities. Adler used the more general phrase "inferiority feelings" to reflect this belief. **Inferiority feelings** involve the response to the real or imagined inferiorities people perceive themselves as having. For example, in downplaying the potential quality of his or her contribution to a discussion in class, a shy student may be reluctant to make any comments.

Compensation Adler assumed that people would be motivated to overcome their inferiority feelings through some form of compensation (Ellenberger, 1970). **Compensation** consists of the individual taking positive steps to deal with and overcome inferiority feelings. To help overcome a sense of shyness, the shy student might start by trying to speak with classmates before class. Next, the student might try asking just one question in class. But there is also the possibility of overcompensating for inferiority feelings.

Overcompensation was viewed by Adler as an excessive reaction to inferiority feelings. For example, in an effort to lose weight, a person might become so involved with an exercise and diet routine that he or she ignores friends and family and begins showing symptoms of anorexia nervosa (e.g., self-induced vomiting after eating). To avoid such overcompensation, Adler (1931) recommended altering personal goals or seeking alternative methods of compensation. The dieter might try setting a goal of losing just 20 pounds in six months—instead of 60 pounds. The person might also decide to incorporate a moderate exercise program along with the diet. Thus, people can develop their strengths by being motivated to overcome feelings of inferiority.

Striving for Superiority

Striving for superiority was the concept Adler developed to explain the desire to go beyond simple compensation in an attempt to achieve a superior level of competence (Adler, 1930). He used the term *superiority* to express his view that people should strive to be perfect by developing all aspects of their personality to their fullest potential. For example, dieting and exercise will help a person improve the physical aspect of the self. But by helping others to lose weight and offering advice and moral support, a person can also strengthen the development of the social aspect of the self. From Adler's perspective, being in great physical shape is of little value if you are very self-centered and lonely.

While Adler assumed that striving for superiority was a fundamental part of human nature, he knew that it did not happen in isolation. Striving for superiority must be fostered by others (e.g., parents, friends, teachers, and employers) in supportive social environments (e.g., at home, school, work, and in the community). As an illustration of the role a supportive environment plays in helping others who are striving for superiority, read "Applications in Personality Psychology" on page 111.

On the positive side, striving for superiority can motivate people to achieve their fullest potential. On the negative side, Adler also noted the possibility of this desire taking a turn for the worse and manifesting itself in the form of a superiority complex. A person suffering from a **superiority complex** seeks to abuse, exploit, and dominate others in an attempt to achieve superiority. Examples of people with superiority complexes would be the playground bully or adults who practice a dog-eat-dog philosophy so they can advance their career.

Social Interest

The ultimate expression of striving for superiority occurs with the development of social interest (Adler, 1939). **Social interest** is the tendency for individuals to put the needs of others over their own needs when striving for superiority. It reflects the feeling and commitment that people have to others and to the society in which they live. When expressing social interest, the primary goal of self-improvement is, in reality, the betterment of society. By making themselves better through striving for superiority, people are sometimes able to make society better, which in turn makes it possible for others to better themselves. This in turn can improve society and start the cycle again. For example, an individual might compensate for poor athletic ability by becoming an outstanding teacher and helping others to strive for superiority.

Style of Life

Adler's (1929a, 1931) concept of a **style of life** refers to the unique way that each person seeks to express the universal desire to strive for superiority through social interest. For example, one person may seek superiority by becoming a political activist, while another might decide to write children's books designed to reduce prejudice.

The unique style of life a person develops reflects both personal and environmental factors. Personal factors include inferiority feelings based on objective (e.g., not being very tall) and subjective (e.g., seeing oneself as being stupid) perceptions and a desire to strive for superiority in order to overcome these shortcomings. Environmental factors include the structural and emotional nature of the family. Structural factors include the family size, presence of both parents, or birth order. Emotional factors within the

APPLICATION

APPLICATIONS IN PERSONALITY PSYCHOLOGY

A Conversation with Trina Nahm-Mijo: Helping Others Strive for Superiority

In addition to teaching courses in personality psychology at Hawaii Community College in Hilo, Hawaii, Professor Trina Nahm-Mijo is an accomplished ballet dancer (on the left in the photo) and professional choreographer. She has combined her interests in ballet and personality psychology when teaching ballet to and choreographing ballets for wheelchair-bound individuals.

Professor Nahm-Mijo talked about how this work relates to many of Adler's notions:

My wheelchair ballets have been inspired by the wheelchair performers themselves. They are a striking example of Adler's concept of how organ inferiority can lead to a striving for superiority or perfection. In these individuals, I discovered a wealth of personal victories as I learned how each dealt with their particular reality of physical limitations. The creativity and courage exhibited by these individuals willing to face their physical disabilities as a challenge rather than a burden

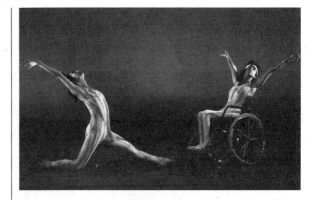

This wheelchair ballet dancer exemplifies, in a very graceful manner, Adler's concept of striving for superiority. The dedication and skill necessary to perform the wheelchair ballet illustrate a desire to go beyond using the wheelchair only as a means to compensate for a lack of physical mobility.

underscores Adler's belief in the creative power of the self—the notion that an individual's attitude towards his or her circumstances has greater power than childhood events in shaping one's adult personality. In essence, these wheelchair ballets have taught me that the human universal handicap is not physical limitations but limited vision or perspective. They serve as a clear example of Adler's premise that all individual progress, growth, and development result from one's attempt to compensate for one's inferiorities.

family involve the nature of the emotional relationships between the family members (e.g., the basic sense of mistrust in abusive families). Environmental factors might also include relationships outside the family (e.g., a compassionate teacher). Adler felt that a person's style of life is determined by the age of 5 years.

Adler proposed that the major function of a style of life was as a unifying force for all aspects of the individual's personality. So important is the style of life, Adler believed, that it determines everything a person does. For example, an individual with an artistic style of life might elect to enroll in art courses as electives instead of science or writing courses in high school, decide to major in art while in college, donate money to community art organizations, and

want to marry someone with a similar commitment to the arts. Thus, the style of life a person develops can have some important consequences.

The Creative Self

While a variety of factors can influence the style of life, Adler believed that in the end, the individual must take personal responsibility for the style selected and its outcomes. The central concept Adler (1935) used to assume all of this responsibility is the creative self. The **creative self** perceives, analyzes, interprets, and gives meaning to life's experiences. Further, the interpretation of and subjective meaning given to a situation determines a person's reaction to it. One person from an abusive family might elect to major in social work in order to help other abuse victims, while another might view his or her family experiences as justification for expressing anger and abusing others. The creative self of the first person produces a style of life high in social interest, and for the second person, it produces one low in social interest. Because it so profoundly influences the unique and characteristic way each person responds to the world around them, Adler considered the creative self the crown jewel in his viewpoint of personality.

As a final point, be aware that although the concepts comprised in Adler's viewpoint were discussed separately, Adler viewed them as operating in an interrelated manner. Figure 4.5 summarizes the relationships among the major concepts discussed in this section.

The Nature of Personality Development: Development and Expression of Social Interest throughout Life

The process of personality development was to prepare the individual to meet the challenges in what Adler (1931, 1933/1956) believed to be life's three major tasks: social, occupational, and love. Successful personality development required the individual to resolve problems in each of these three areas in the direction of fostering greater social interest. Although he assumed that personality development is a lifelong process, Adler also believed that early childhood experiences play an important role in preparing the individual to confront life's challenges.

Childhood and Adolescence: Developing the Initial Sense of Cooperation with Others in Social Relationships

During childhood and adolescence, each person starts to develop an initial sense of social relationships. The first life task is a social one that involves learning to cooperate and consider the needs of others. Two of the most significant social relationships to occur during this period are those with parents and siblings.

Parent-Child Interactions as the First Social Relationship

A child's early interactions with its parents can sig-

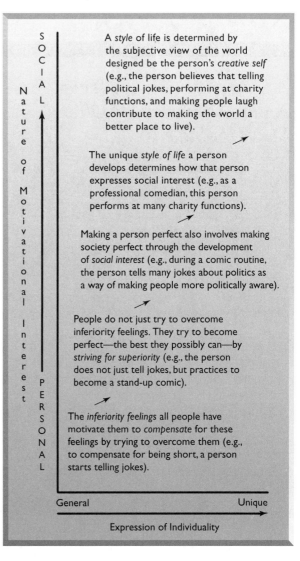

Figure 4.5
The basic concepts of Adler's individual viewpoint

nificantly affect the child's personality development and degree of social interest. Adler described two personality types that were a result of specific parent-child relationships: the pampered child and the rejected child.

The personality of the **pampered child** develops out of a parent-child relationship characterized by overprotection, overindulgence, and/or domination over the child. As adults, pampered children tend to rely on others, be rather unsure, and display a low level of social interest by placing their needs above those of others. On the other hand, children who are not pampered, allowed to take small risks, and taught to take responsibility feel more confident and display a healthy need for cooperation and social interest. These characteristics tend to be carried over into adulthood.

The personality of the **rejected child** develops out of parent-child relationships characterized by rejection and neglect that might be due to the presence of too many other children. Such children may develop a style of life that reflects a lack of trust and withdrawal from social participation. As adults, rejected children may become rather independent of others but feel socially isolated, display a low level of social interest, and possibly become criminals. Children who are not rejected grow up in an environment of warmth, acceptance, and trust. As adults, they are not afraid to get involved with others, both socially (e.g., join clubs) and emotionally (e.g., fall in love). Such individuals tend to display a high degree of social interest.

Sibling Relationships and Birth Order as Determinants of Personality   Part of what constitutes the family environment is the **birth-order** relationship with one's brothers and sisters (Adler, 1931; Hoffman, 1991). Adler believed that a child's birth order exposes him or her to particular types of family environments that have systematic effects on the child's personality development. Although there are various birth-order combinations, Adler (1931) emphasized these four: firstborn (eldest), second-born, the youngest child, and the only child.

▲ *The firstborn child.* The firstborn child is, for a time, given special attention as the only child. But with the arrival of the second child, the eldest child is dethroned from this favored position. Adler believed that as adults, firstborns tend to be more independent of others and try to solve their problems on their own, supposedly as a result of being abandoned by their parents. But these feelings of dethronement in the first-born child can be minimized by parents encouraging the oldest child to be their "helper" with the newborn. Caring for younger siblings fosters the development of an initial sense of social interest for helping others who are less able.

▲ *The second-born child.* Because the second-born child lives in the shadow of the older sibling, feelings of inferiority are intensified and expressed by a heightened level of motivation to achieve and get ahead of the older sibling. In a healthy sense, this high degree of achievement motivation is channeled into the direction of helping others (e.g., becoming a superior community activist). It is interesting to note that Adler was a second-born child. In a negative sense, this high need for achievement can be expressed in a desire to dominate others (e.g., a cutthroat politician).

▲ *The youngest child.* Being the baby of the family can create a rather perplexing situation in that there are older siblings to contribute to feelings of inferiority. But there are also more people around to care for and pamper the youngest child. In a healthy sense, the youngest child has many models from which to learn how to strive for superiority. In a negative sense, the youngest child can become discouraged by all of this competition, develop excessive feelings of inferiority, and lack social interest. Adler believed that next to the oldest child, the youngest child has the greatest potential to be a problem child and develop neurotic tendencies as an adult.

▲ *The only child.* The only child is the most likely to be pampered by the parents and to spend a considerable amount of time around adults. In a healthy sense, spending a lot of time around adults as a child without siblings can contribute to a higher level of intellectual ability and academic success than one having lots of other siblings (Zajonc, 1976). In a negative sense, when no longer the center of attention, the only child as an adult may become timid, passive, and withdrawn and still feel the need to be pampered by others.

Although Adler first introduced the notion of birth order as a determinant of personality development over fifty years ago, the idea is still receiving considerable research attention today. See "A Closer Look" (page 114) for more about the topic of birth order.

A CLOSER LOOK

Birth Order and Personality: Knowing Your Place in the Family

Does knowing a person's place in the family birth order reveal something about their personality? Some evidence does support the relationship between birth order and various personality and interpersonal characteristics, such as achievement striving, intelligence, affiliation, and popularity.

Achievement Striving

Extensive research suggests that firstborns have a higher need for achievement than later-born individuals (Howarth, 1980). Firstborn children tend to score higher than later-born children on personality tests measuring the need for achievement (Glass, Neulinger, & Brim, 1974) and on tests measuring English, mathematical, and verbal achievement (Eysenck & Cookson, 1969; Breland, 1974; Glass et al., 1974).

Going beyond simple test scores, a larger representation of firstborns than later-borns has been found among the ranks of eminent people and college students (Schachter, 1963; Warren, 1966). Firstborns have also been found to be overrepresented among those listed in *Who's Who* (Altus, 1966), individuals involved in American politics (Zweigenhaft, 1975), those who were U.S. astronauts (Harris, 1964), and women who were business executives (Hoyenga & Hoyenga, 1984).

One explanation for the high achievement of firstborns seems to be that parents tend to give the firstborn child more attention and stimulation, and have higher expectations for them than they do for their later-born children (Belsky, Gilstrap, & Rovine, 1984; Boroson, 1973; Rothbart, 1971). These early expectations of achievement for firstborns may result in their becoming higher achievers than later-born children as adults.

Intelligence

Firstborns, as well as only children (Falbo & Polit, 1986), were found to have IQ scores that, on the average, were higher than those of later-born children (Belmont & Marolla, 1973; Falbo & Polit, 1986; Zajonc,

1975; Zajonc & Markus, 1975). To explain this relationship, Zajonc (1975; Zajonc & Markus, 1975) proposed that while they are alone, firstborn children receive a large amount of attention and verbal stimulation. As other children are added to the family, the amount of attention and stimulation the parents can give each child decreases, resulting in subsequently lower IQ scores. This relationship could also be due to socioeconomic status. More specifically, families with high socioeconomic status tend to be small; consequently, there are fewer later-born children (Blake, 1989). Birth-order differences in IQ among siblings are not that great, however; they average only about 10 points and may disappear by the age of 17 (McCall, 1984).

Affiliation

Under conditions of stress, firstborns display a greater desire to be with others than later-born children (cf. Darley & Aronson, 1966; Schachter, 1959; Zimbardo & Formica, 1963). This seems to be caused by the increased anxiety created in and excessive comforting given to the child by inexperienced parents (Hilton, 1967; Ring, Lipinski, & Braginsky, 1965; Schachter, 1959). As a result, firstborn children may become more anxious and, as both children and adults, dependent on others to reduce this anxiety and provide some emotional comfort.

Popularity

Later-born children, youngest children in particular, have been found to be more extraverted (Thompson, 1974) and popular among their peers than their firstborn siblings or only children (Miller & Maruyama, 1976). This increased popularity may be a consequence of their having developed social skills (e.g., negotiation, cooperation) to compensate for their lack of physical size when resolving power struggles with older siblings (Miller & Maruyama, 1976; Ickes & Turner, 1983).

Table 4.3 gives brief samples of additional relationships between birth order and other personality characteristics and social behaviors. More information on the subject of birth order and personality can be found in *Birth Order: Its Influence on Personality* (Ernst & Angst, 1983).

Table 4.3

More Illustrations of the Relationship between Birth Order and Personality Characteristics and Social Behaviors

Nature of Relationship	Reference
Cigarette consumption: Youngest children of both sexes have the highest percentage of smokers.	Ernst & Angst, 1983
Alcohol consumption: Youngest male children with three or more siblings have the highest rate of alcohol consumption; no relationship found for females.	Ernst & Angst, 1983
Self-esteem: Firstborns tend to have a lower sense of self-esteem than later-born children.	Forer, 1976
Mate selection: Firstborns and later-borns tend to select as their mates others with a similar birth-order rank.	Ward, Castro, & Wilcox, 1974
Self-disclosure: Later-borns tend to reveal more about themselves than firstborns.	Dimond & Munz, 1968
Cheating at school: Among college students, more cheating was observed in firstborns than in later-born children.	Hetherington & Feldman, 1964
Alcoholism: No relationship between birth order and alcoholism has been established.	Ernst & Angst, 1983
Shyness: As children, firstborns tend to be more shy than later-born children.	Zimbardo, 1977
Criminal behavior: No relationship between birth order and criminal behavior has been established.	Ernst & Angst, 1983
Creativity: Firstborns have been found to be more creative than later-born individuals.	Corneau, 1980
Aggressiveness: No relationship between birth order and aggressiveness has been established.	Owang, 1971
Risk-taking behavior: Later-borns seem to take more risks than firstborn individuals.	Nisbett, 1968
Handedness: No relationship between birth order and being left- or right-handed.	Searleman, Porac, & Coren, 1989
Acceptance of new ideas: Laterborn scientists, and religious and political leaders, tend to be more accepting and supportive of new ideas than firstborns.	Sulloway, 1990

Young Adulthood: Developing a Sense of Society through Work

Adler viewed the major developmental task during young adulthood as one of selecting an occupation that enables a person to express style of life in a manner reflecting social interest (1933/1956). By striving for occupational superiority, the person would develop a purpose in life and make a positive contribution to the development of society. Adler believed that the fear of failure was a reason that some young adults avoid making career choices. Because he placed so much importance on selecting an occupation as a means of overcoming feelings of inferiority and expressing social interest, Adler firmly believed that schools must provide career counseling for young adults.

Adulthood and Old Age: Demonstrating Social Interest through Love

In Adler's view, the major developmental task in adulthood involves expressing social interest in the form of love, within an intimate relationship characterized by each person being more concerned about the needs and happiness of their partner than about their own needs. The expression of love in adulthood also involves raising children in a family environment that supports their efforts to strive for superiority and promotes a sense of social interest. Thus, teaching children to respect and care about the needs of others starts when the adults in the family demonstrate a sense of concern and respect for each other's needs.

In old age, the elderly can express their love by stepping aside and letting young people have their opportunity to exhibit social interest and strive for superiority. Continued involvement in society by the elderly (e.g., serving on advisory boards) demonstrates a sense of hope for the future and in the life hereafter. Without such a hope for the future, the only thing elderly individuals will have to look forward to is death.

In summary, Adler's perspective on personality development emphasizes developing a sense of social interest that focuses on cooperation and helping to satisfy the needs of others.

The Well-Adjusted vs. Maladjusted Personality: Differences in Degree of Social Interest

In addition to describing the process of personality development, Adler was very clear about what he considered to be the nature of well-adjusted individuals. To illustrate his views, we will compare the characteristic features of the well-adjusted and maladjusted individual.

The Well-Adjusted Individual   Adler believed that the well-adjusted individual approaches the problems of life in a realistic way, displaying courage, common sense, and social interest (Rotter & Hochreich, 1975). Courage involves not being afraid to take risks or to fail, as well as confronting difficult situations directly. Common sense involves seeing things as they exist in reality, not as you wish they were in life. Finally, the well-adjusted person displays a high degree of social interest by considering the needs of others and wanting to make a meaningful contribution to society. Thus, like the lion, scarecrow, and tin man in "The Wizard of Oz," the well-adjusted individual shows courage, brains, and heart when coping with problems in life.

The Maladjusted Individual   At their core, people with maladaptive personalities tend to have excessive feelings of inferiority. In response to these feelings, they tend to develop styles of life that are self-defeating and display little social interest. Thus, rather than simply attempting to compensate for these feelings of inferiority, they tend to overcompensate and behave in an excessive manner. For example, in an attempt to show up an older sibling, a college student might become obsessed with studying to the point of mental and psychological exhaustion. Maladjusted people tend to think in rather simplistic, absolute, and opposing terms (e.g., a for-me-or-against-me perspective). They also tend to engage in the process of **distancing**, in which they place the blame for their problems elsewhere (e.g., the supervisor dislikes me).

While overcompensating, simplistic thinking, and distancing demonstrate maladaptive behavioral tendencies, it is living a life lie that truly represents the self-defeating style of life characteristic of the maladaptive individual. A **life lie** involves the person living "as if" things were a particular way. An example of a life lie is the alcoholic who says he or she could stop drinking "if only" the kids or boss would stop making so many demands. Maladjusted people live in a make-believe world. They pretend to be in a life situation that really does not exist, and they interact with others accordingly. The severity of maladjustment is gauged by its effects on the person's ability to express social interest and to deal competently with the social, occupational, and love tasks of life. Some of the more severe psychological disorders and their possible causes, based on Adler's viewpoint, are presented in Table 4.4.

The Application of Adler's Individual Viewpoint: Using What Is Known

Our discussion of the applications of Adler's viewpoint will focus on psychotherapy and personality assessment.

Adlerian Psychotherapy: Straightening Out a Maladaptive Style of Life

The major goal of Adlerian psychotherapy is to help people correct their maladaptive style of life. The therapist proposes a healthy style of life that includes more constructive ways of compensating for inferiority and a greater emphasis on social interest. For example, a therapist might give vocational counseling and training to youth gang members to help them achieve a sense of superiority through a career instead of through antisocial behavior.

Table 4.4

Some Severe Psychological Disorders as Explained from Adler's Viewpoint

Psychological Disorder	Adlerian Explanation
Depression	Depressed people are characterized by a distrusting and critical view of life. Rather than participate in social interactions, they withdraw into their depression. For example, depressed individuals find it too tiresome to interact with others.
Alcoholism	By developing a drinking problem and becoming helpless, the alcoholic can have others do things for him or her and can use drinking as an excuse for not succeeding in life. For example, the alcoholic is not expected to be able to keep a job.
Sexual perversion	In general, sexual perversions are attempts to avoid the challenges of love. Sexual perverts are generally selfish people seeking to satisfy their own sexual needs. For example, the exhibitionist seeks sexual gratification from a distance rather than dealing directly with others.
Obsessive-Compulsive	People with this disorder reflect an excessive need to be perfect, and they may also use it to avoid others. For example, if a woman is always cleaning the house in an attempt to keep it spotless, she will not have time to be with others.
Schizophrenia	In this most severe form of psychological disorder, the individual gives up all hope of being able to live in the real world and retreats into a make-believe world having little contact with reality. For example, by speaking in some make-believe language, the schizophrenic can avoid communicating with others.

Note: From *The Individual Psychology of Alfred Adler*, by H. L. Ansbacher and Ansbacher, 1956. New York: Harper, pp. 299–325 and *Introduction to Personality and Psychotherapy* (2nd ed.), by J. F. Rychlak, 1981. Boston: Houghton Mifflin, pp. 155–158.

The Progression of Adlerian Psychotherapy: The Systematic Reconstruction of a Life-Style High in Social Interest

Adler divided his individual psychotherapy into three steps, described in the following subsections.

Step One: Establishing a Therapeutic Relationship Based on Confidence and Trust The first step in Adlerian therapy involves the therapist gaining the client's confidence and trust (Adler, 1929b). The therapist begins by outlining, clearly and optimistically, the nature of the therapeutic procedures and processes. This approach presumably inspires the client and increases the client's confidence in the therapist's ability to provide help. Adler (1927) felt that to help gain the client's trust, the therapist must establish a level of mutual respect by demonstrating a willingness to take the client's perspective. The therapist can do so by offering explanations that reflect the client's point of view (e.g., social norms of gang members) and are in language the client can easily understand

(e.g., avoid overly complicated psychological terminology). Such actions demonstrate a direct attempt by the therapist to create a therapeutic relationship based on mutual respect and involvement.

Step Two: Tracing the Development of a Mistaken Style of Life The second step in the therapeutic process involves modifying the self-defeating strategies being employed by the client to achieve superiority. This step requires making clear to the client the dangers of leading such a mistaken style of life (e.g., compensating for feelings of inferiority and alienation through gang violence will lead to a criminal life-style). The therapist must also try to make the client understand how this maladaptive style of life developed initially and what functions it currently serves (e.g., gang violence bring social status).

Step Three: Developing Social Interest Rather than simply replacing the mistaken style of life with one that is less self-defeating, the final step in the therapeutic process is an attempt to foster social interest as part of the client's newly developed style of life. For example, in addition to a gang member dropping out of the gang and being successful in school, the individual could also help others succeed by serving as a volunteer at a day-care center helping young children learn to read.

In summary, the major objective of Adlerian therapy is to foster a pattern of action that is consistent with both the needs of the individual and society through a pattern of action high in social interest.

Some Techniques of Adlerian Psychotherapy: Trying to Understand from Where You Came

Because each person's style of life develops during childhood, Adler used several therapeutic techniques in an attempt to trace the development of the mistaken style of life back to its source in youth.

Identifying Early Recollections   With the technique of **early recollections**, the client is asked to report the earliest memories he or she can recall. Adler believed that since our style of life was formed in childhood, such early memories could offer hints about its origin and development (Adler, 1931; Parrott, 1992) An early childhood recollection of the youth gang member might include images of the older boys in gangs receiving considerable attention and respect from other children in the neighborhood.

Investigating Early Childhood Experiences   An investigation into childhood experiences involves getting information from the client about the nature of early family experiences. By becoming aware of such things as how the client was treated by the parents and the nature of sibling relationships, the therapist can develop a more effective treatment plan to offset the negative consequences of these experiences. For example, the client might have turned to gang activity to compensate for an emotionally distant relationship with parents during childhood. In the course of treatment, the therapist might tell the client that emotional support can also be obtained by doing volunteer work at the local community center. These childhood experiences can also give the therapist insights into the motivation behind the client's current behavior patterns.

Analyzing Dreams   Adler viewed dreams as a means of providing information in the *present* about those feelings and aspirations the client wants to have in the *future* (Mosak, 1989). By investigating dreams, the therapist can begin to see how the client would like the world to be. For example, in his dream, the youth gang member dreams of being a powerful leader and commanding the respect of many people. The therapist might point out that instead of participating in gang activity, the youth could realize such desires more constructively and gain some valuable experience by serving as an aide to a local politician.

Focusing on the Family   Because Adler placed so much emphasis on the early childhood family environment, he was one of the first to practice family therapy. **Family therapy** is a form of psychotherapy that focuses on the interpersonal relationships among members of a family. The logic of family therapy is that some disturbances are caused and/or maintained by faulty family relationships. The goal of family therapy is to help create a more psychologically healthy environment by pointing out self-defeating relationships and providing instruction for rectifying the situation (e.g., parenting skills, group communication skills).

By employing these therapeutic techniques, the therapist is in a much better position to begin understanding the origins of the client's mistaken style of life and the underlying motivational forces that serve to maintain it into adulthood.

Personality Assessment from Adler's Viewpoint: The Measurement of Social Interest

In the tradition of the Adlerian viewpoint, Dr. James E. Crandall (1975) has developed the **Social Interest Scale** (SIS). The SIS is a 15-item scale containing a series of personal characteristics or traits arranged in pairs (e.g., respectable vs. original). A person's SIS score, ranging from 0 to 15, reflects the extent to which that person would like to possess personal characteristics indicative of social interest. To examine your own level of social interest, complete the SIS in "You Can Do It" on page 119.

James Crandall's work on the development and systematic research of the Social Interest Scale has helped to validate one of Adler's most significant theoretical concepts.

YOU CAN DO IT

The Social Interest Scale: Measuring the Desire to Care for Others

For each of the item pairs in the following list, select the one you would rather possess as one of your own personal characteristics. Indicate your choice by writing a *1* or *2* on the line next to each pair. The scoring directions are listed at the end of this feature.

The Social Interest Scale

_____ 1. respectful
2. original
_____ 1. generous
2. individualistic
_____ 1. trustworthy
2. wise
_____ 1. forgiving
2. gentle
_____ 1. considerate
2. wise

_____ 1. neat
2. sympathetic
_____ 1. alert
2. cooperative
_____ 1. imaginative
2. helpful
_____ 1. realistic
2. moral
_____ 1. ambitious
2. patient

Scoring

For the five items on the left, count the number of times you selected the first trait in the pair. Add that number to the number of times you selected the second trait in the pair for the five items on the right. The higher the score, the greater degree of expressed social interest. Since only 10 items were included, however, you should not consider this to be an absolute measure of your social interest.

Note: From *A Scale for Social Interest: Journal of Individual Psychology,* by J. E. Crandall, 1975, pp. *31,* 187–195.

Behavioral Correlates of Social Interest

In support of its validity, scores on the SIS have been found to be related to a variety of other personal attributes and social behaviors in a manner consistent with Adler's conceptualization of social interest. Table 4.5 illustrates that consistent with Adler's

Table 4.5
Mean Scores for Different Groups on the Social Interest Scale

Group	Mean Score
Ursuline sisters (6)*	13.33
Adult church members (147)	11.21
Charity volunteers (9)	10.78
High social interest high school students† (23)	10.22
High social interest college students† (21)	9.48
University employees (165)	9.24
University students (1784)	8.17
Mental hospital patients (25)	7.56
Low social interest college students† (35)	7.40
Female professional models (54)	7.06
Low social interest high school students† (22)	6.86
Adult atheists (30)	6.70
Convicted felons (30)	6.37

*Group size given in parentheses.
†Based on peer ratings.

views on social interest and personality adjustment, criminals and mental patients displayed a lower level of social interest when compared to other groups, such as church members and charity volunteers (Crandall, 1980). SIS scores were also found to be positively correlated with measures of cooperation, helping, empathy, liking of others, being liked by others, and responsibility. On the other hand, SIS scores have been found to be negatively correlated with hostility and self-centeredness (Crandall, 1980, 1981).

Attitudinal Correlates of Social Interest

Do people with varying degrees of social interest view the world differently? There is some evidence to support this contention. SIS scores have been found to be positively correlated with a personal value system emphasizing the importance of peace, equality, and family security (Crandall, 1975) and a positive view of others as being altruistic and trustworthy (Crandall, 1980). In a more global sense, SIS scores have also been positively correlated with how interesting individuals perceive their day-to-day life to be and how much beauty and attractiveness they find in the world (Crandall & Putman, 1980).

It is possible that such an optimistic view of the world may lie at the foundation of social interest. In a very simple sense, it could be that when people are in a good mood, they are more likely to help others (Baron & Byrne, 1991). Another benefit of maintaining a high level of social interest is that people with high SIS scores report fewer stressful life experiences and fewer symptoms of stress than those with low SIS scores (Crandall, 1984). It seems that having a more positive outlook on life and taking a more active role in life and in the lives of others can help reduce the stress in everyday life.

Evaluation of Adler's Viewpoint: Strengths and Limitations

We will conclude our discussion of Adler by considering some of the characteristic strengths and limitations of his viewpoint.

Characteristic Strengths

Adler's individual viewpoint has the following strengths:

▲ *Impact on contemporary psychology.* Although not as visible as Freud's, Adler's influence on contemporary psychology is reflected in a number of ways. His emphasis on striving for superiority is consistent with the humanistic viewpoints of personality discussed in Chapter 7. His concept of the creative self as an interpreter of information is consistent with some of the more cognitive and social learning viewpoints of personality discussed in Chapter 11.

The research on birth order is clearly rooted in the Adlerian tradition.

▲ *Adler the optimist.* Adler offered a view of human nature that stressed compassion for others as the major motivating force of personality. Nothing illustrates this better than the tremendous significance Adler gave to social interest throughout his theory and the many applications of Adlerian theory based on social interest. For Adler, people are striving not only for self-perfection, but for perfection of the society and the world in which they live.

▲ *Adler the pragmatist.* In trying to help individuals strive for superiority, Adler turned to those places most likely to have the greatest impact—the school and family (Mosak, 1989). Practicing what he preached, Adler lectured widely to groups of parents and teachers and helped to develop family therapy and community intervention programs (Ellenberger, 1970; Mosak, 1989).

Characteristic Limitations

Adler's viewpoint has the following limitations:

▲ *Less systematic theorizing.* Adler developed a theory of personality consisting of a relatively few number of concepts that were loosely related to each other. Adler's approach to therapy was not very well defined or linked systematically with his views on personality development.

▲ *Limited empirical investigations.* To some extent, Adler devoted more effort to the clinical and social applications of his theory than to its empirical validation. Part of the problem may be that the relative looseness of his theory made formulating specific hypotheses difficult. But, Crandall's work does provide supporting evidence for one of Adler's most important concepts—assessing social interest.

Additional information on Adler's views of personality can be obtained by reading *Social Interest* (Adler, 1939) and *Alfred Adler: His Influence on Psychology Today* (Mosak, 1973).

A final comment on the Freud-Jung-Adler relationship is in order at this point. Jung and Adler were among the first to propose alternatives to Freud's psychology of personality. Jung reacted to Freud by going deeper into the individual unconscious (e.g., collective unconscious). Adler did just the opposite, focusing on conscious motives (e.g., striving for superiority) and social factors (e.g., family and school) as the principal determinants of personality. The next chapter presents still other reactions to Freud's viewpoint.

Chapter Summary: Reexamining the Highlights

▲ JUNG'S ANALYTICAL VIEWPOINT
—*Basic Assumptions of the Analytical Viewpoint*. The basic assumptions of Jung's viewpoint include an expanded view of libido, extending the structure and nature of the unconscious, studying both the past and future as critical determinants of behavior, and seeking psychic balance as a principal motivator of personality.
—*The Structure of Personality*. Jung viewed the structure of personality as consisting of the conscious ego, the personal unconscious, and the collective unconscious, and containing complexes in the personal unconscious and archetypes in the collective unconscious. Significant archetypes include the persona, animus and anima, the shadow, and the self.
—*The Dynamics of Personality*. The dynamics of personality consist of the flow of psychic energy based on the principle of opposites and the principles of equivalence and entropy.
—*The Nature and Processes of Personality Development*. Personality development is a lifelong process involving individuation, transcendence, and self-realization. Maladaptive personality development is characterized by a lack of balance among the various aspects of personality.
—*Analytical Psychotherapy*. The aim of analytical psychotherapy is to reestablish a balance among the various aspects of personality. The process of analytical psychotherapy includes the confession, elucidation, education, and transformation stages. Analytical psychotherapy involves creating a primarily egalitarian relationship between the client and analyst, using the word association test to identify significant complexes, and applying the method of amplification to analyze dreams and explore archetypes.
—*Personality Assessment from Jung's Viewpoint*. The extraverted attitude and introverted attitude are two personality types identified by Jung. The four functions of personality include the sensation, thinking, feeling, and the intuition functions. The Myers-Briggs Type Indicator is an objective self-report technique designed to assess these personality types and functions.
—*Evaluation of Jung's Analytical Viewpoints*. Some characteristic strengths associated with Jung's viewpoint are its rich and novel ideas, an expanded view of the nature of personality, the methodological developments it produced and stimulated, and an optimistic view of human nature. Some limitations include proposing concepts that are difficult to test and a limited acceptance due to Jung's sometimes rather esoteric writing style.

▲ ADLER'S INDIVIDUAL PSYCHOLOGY
—*Basic Assumptions of Adler's Individual Psychology*. The basic assumptions of Adler's viewpoint include an emphasis on helping others as a primary motivational force, the conscious control of personality, an emphasis on the future and the importance of interpersonal relationships as principal determinants of behavior, and an expanded role of the self.
—*Basic Concepts of Individual Psychology*. Adler's viewpoint includes the concepts of organ inferiority, inferiority feelings, and compensation and overcompensation for inferiority feelings by striving for superiority and the expression of social interest. The development of a style of life under the influence of the creative self helps to produce a pattern of behavior high in social interest.
—*The Nature of Personality Development*. The goal of personality development is to learn to solve life's tasks with a high degree of social interest. During childhood and adolescence, learning to get along with parents and siblings establishes an initial sense of cooperation. Such factors as parent-child relationships and birth order can influence this aspect of development. In young adulthood, the developmental tasks are learning to express social interest and striving for superiority through work and community involvement. In adulthood and old age, the developmental task involves providing love

and support for those who are younger. The degree of personality adjustment is reflected in the amount of social interest demonstrated by the individual.

—*Adlerian Psychotherapy.* The goal of Adlerian psychotherapy is to establish a style of life high in social interest. The process requires that the client establish confidence and trust in the therapist, identify the origins of the maladaptive style of life, and develop an alternative style of life high in social interest. Some of the therapeutic methods include exploring early recollections, examining childhood experiences, analyzing dreams for goals and aspirations, and providing family therapy.

—*Personality Assessment and Adler's Viewpoint.* The Social Interest Scale (SIS) measures the tendency of an individual to desire characteristics indicative of social interest. SIS scores are associated with helping others and a more positive world view.

—*Evaluation of Adler's Viewpoint.* The characteristic strengths associated with Adler's viewpoint include the somewhat pervasive but subtle impact he has had on contemporary personality psychology, his rather optimistic view of human nature, and his rather pragmatic approach to promoting changes in social interest. Some characteristic limitations of Adler's viewpoint include the somewhat unsystematic nature of his theory and his limited attempts to gather empirical evidence in support of his viewpoint.

Glossary

analytical psychology   The name given to Jung's viewpoint of personality.

analytical psychotherapy   The process of treating emotional disorders, as practiced from the Jungian viewpoint.

anima   The archetype for expressing the feminine characteristics within males.

animus   The archetype for expressing the masculine characteristics within females.

archetypes   Generalized or universal ideas and concepts.

birth order   The order in which persons are born into a family.

collective unconscious   The region of the unconscious mind Jung believed was shared by all people.

compensatory function   An activity of the personal unconscious that could be used to help a person achieve psychic balance.

complex   A collection of emotions or information centering around a particular concept.

conscious ego   The structure used by Jung to account for conscious awareness.

collective unconscious   The region of the unconscious mind Jung believed was shared by all people.

compensation   Attempts made by people to overcome actual or perceived limitations and weaknesses.

confession stage   The initial stage of Jungian psychotherapy, in which the client begins to express troubled feelings and ideas.

creative self   That aspect of personality responsible for processing information in a manner that promotes the development of each person's full potential.

distancing   A strategy used by people for shifting the blame for their problems to sources other than themselves.

dream series method   The analysis of several dreams for consistency of contents and symbolism.

early recollections   A technique in Adlerian psychotherapy in which clients are asked to identify the earliest memories they can recall.

education stage   The third stage of Jungian psychotherapy in which the therapist helps the client to explore more adaptive forms of behavior.

elucidation stage   The second stage of Jungian psychotherapy in which the client and therapist discuss explanations for problematic feelings.

extraverted attitude   A personality style geared toward objects and events in the external or social environment.

feeling function   Using affective reactions as the dominant means of experiencing the environment.

function   A systematic approach to experiencing the environment.

family therapy   A systematic attempt to modify the maladaptive behavioral patterns operating within families.

individuation   The systematic development of separate aspects of personality.

individual psychology   The name given to Adler's viewpoint of personality.

inferiority feelings   Subjective limitations and weaknesses that people perceive they possess.

intrapersonal   Dynamics operating within the individual.

interpersonal   Dynamics operating between two or more people.

introverted attitude   A personality style geared toward objects and events in the internal or personal environment.

intuition function   Using an internal sense of judgment as the dominant means of experiencing the environment.

judging types   People who are orderly and systematic.

life lie   A strategy for responding to the world in a way that a person perceives it instead of the way it actually is.

method of active imagination   A technique of Jungian psychotherapy in which the client is asked to interact with the objects and symbols appearing in dreams.

method of amplification   A technique in Jungian psychotherapy used to elaborate on and explore the contents of dreams.

Myers-Briggs Type Indicator   A personality test designed to assess Jungian personality types and functions.

organ inferiority   Objective physical limitations and weakness possessed by people.

overcompensation   Excessive attempts made by people to overcome actual or perceived limitations and weaknesses.

pampered child   A style of personality characterized by overindulgence and self-centeredness.

perceiving types   People who are rather open-minded.

persona   The archetype predisposing people to conform to social norms.

personal unconscious   The region of the mind described by Jung as the storehouse of information that was not in awareness or was too emotionally threatening.

phylogenetic   A process of systematic development or evolution.

principle of entropy   The compensatory flow of psychic energy from a high-concentration area to a low-concentration area.

principle of equivalence   The displacement of psychic energy from one aspect of personality to another.

principle of opposites   The corresponding flow of psychic energy in an opposing direction within two aspects of personality.

prospective function   An activity of the personal unconscious that could be used to help a person think about future events.

rejected child   A style of personality characterized by emotional isolation and social withdrawal.

retrospective   The influence of the past on current behavior.

shadow   The archetype representing the impulsive and instinctive characteristics of personality.

self   The archetype that seeks balance and harmony.

self-realization   The continuous development and integration of the separate aspects of personality to express their full potential.

sensation function   Using the senses as the dominant means of experiencing the environment.

social interest   Considering the needs of others while attempting to develop your own potential to the fullest.

Social Interest Scale   A personality test designed to assess a client's tendency to express concern for the needs of others and to help them.

striving for superiority   Attempts made by people to develop themselves to their fullest potential.

style of life   The general approach taken when people are developing their potential to the fullest.

superiority complex   Excessive attempts by people to develop their own potential at the expense of others.

teleological   The influence of the future on current behavior.

thinking function   Using intellect and reasoning as the dominant means of experiencing the environment.

transcendent function   The systematic reintegration of the developed aspects of the self.

transformation stage   The final stage of Jungian psychotherapy in which the client explores and develops a sense of meaning in life.

transpersonal   Term used by Jung to describe the process of sharing or passing along information across people, cultures, and generations.

word association test   A projective test designed to assess unconscious content and problematic complexes.

CHAPTER 5

The Viewpoints of Horney, Erikson, Sullivan, and Fromm: The Neo-Freudians

CHAPTER OVERVIEW: A PREVIEW OF COMING ATTRACTIONS

*The viewpoints of Carl Jung and Alfred Adler were two of the most significant early reactions to Freud. However, they were followed by others. The **neo-Freudians** represent a group of theorists who proposed viewpoints of personality that also reacted to and extended many of Freud's ideas. A characteristic of the neo-Freudians is their shift away from Freud's intrapsychic emphasis (i.e., conflict within the individual) to a more interpersonal emphasis (i.e., relationships between people). They also tend to place more emphasis on the conscious-level operation of personality. Four of the most prominent of the neo-Freudians are Karen Horney, Erik Erikson, Harry Stack Sullivan, and Erich Fromm. This chapter introduces you to the viewpoints of these four personality theorists.*

Karen Horney's Social Psychological Viewpoint: The Search for Social Security

Although Karen Horney was not a contemporary of Freud in the sense of Jung and Adler, much of her theoretical development was in response to what she perceived as major limitations in traditional Freudian thinking so dominant at the time. Her theoretical focus was to place more importance on interpersonal relationships as a determinant of personality development and to reformulate the dynamics of the female personality. For a glimpse into the life of Karen Horney, read "A Closer Look" below.

A Closer Look:

Biographical Background: The Life of Karen Horney

Karen Danielson Horney was born on September 16, 1885, near Hamburg, Germany, into an upper-middle-class family. While the economic climate of Horney's childhood was rather secure, the emotional nature of her early years was less than tranquil. Horney's father, Berndt Wackels Danielson, was a sea captain. He was described as being rather stern and morose in temperament, and he was an extreme fundamentalist in his religious beliefs. In sharp contrast to his rather gruff and authoritarian personality was the personality of Captain Danielson's second wife—and Karen's mother. Clothilde Danielson was a youthful (18 years younger than her husband), attractive, sophisticated, dynamic, spirited, and free-thinking woman.

The emotional climate of Horney's childhood could probably best be described as rather ambivalent. Her father conveyed the feelings of being critical of his daughter's appearance, interests, and intellectual desires, including discouraging her from the idea of pursuing a career as a physician. On the other hand, her mother encouraged her to pursue her intellectual interests. Even so, Horney always felt that her mother loved her brother more than her, which made her feel unwanted. Horney supposedly dealt with these feelings of insecurity by immersing herself in her studies, reasoning that "If I couldn't be beautiful, I decided I would be smart" (Rubins, 1978, p. 14).

Karen Horney pioneered the role of women in the psychology of personality with her astute observations on the role of cultural circumstances in the study of personality and a reformulation of the dynamics of the female personality.

The result of this mixed emotional climate was that Horney developed a very warm and close relationship with her mother. But for a while during her thirties, Karen took to wearing a captain's-style cap, implying some positive identification with her father. In 1904—when Karen was 19—Clothilde, not being able to take any more of her husband's authoritarian ways, took her two children and separated from him. Growing up in an environment of such emotional turmoil created in Horney feelings of anxiety and insecurity she knew she would have to overcome if she was to be successful in life.

In 1906, Karen began to pursue her medical career in Freiburg, Germany, where she enrolled in one of the few medical schools accepting women at that time. In 1909, she married Oskar Horney, a Berlin lawyer. In 1913, Horney received her masters degree from the University of Berlin. From 1914 to 1918, she received psychoanalytic training at the Berlin Psychoanalytic Institute, where she was psychoanalyzed by Karl Abraham and Hanns Sachs, two of the most noted training analysts in Europe at that time. From 1918 to 1932, she taught at the Berlin Psychoanalytic Institute, maintained a private clinical practice, and wrote many professional articles, some expressing her disagreement with the very dominant Freudian views of the time.

In 1923, the investment firm for which Oskar was working collapsed, making his salary worth almost nothing. As a result, he began to borrow heavily. Partly because of Oskar's personal and financial problems and partly because of her own very demanding schedule, Horney's marriage began to deteriorate. In addition, shortly after, her brother, Berndt, died at the age of 40. Because of all of this emotional turmoil,

Horney began to experience severe feelings of depression and contemplated suicide. In 1926, Horney and her three children separated from Oskar by moving into their own small apartment. The termination of the Horneys' marriage became final in 1939, because she waited more than 10 years before actually filing for the divorce.

In 1932, Horney was invited to come to the United States and assume the associate directorship of the Chicago Institute for Psychoanalysis. Two years later, she left Chicago for a position at the New York Psychoanalytic Institute. But she was becoming more and more dissatisfied with traditional psychoanalysis and expressed her views openly. As a result, the more traditional supporters of Freud's ideas at the New York Psychoanalytic Institute voted in April 1941 to demote Horney from her roles of teacher and clinical supervisor to the position of "instructor" (Quinn, 1988).

In quick response, Horney and some of her followers left the institute and within three weeks had formed a new organization called the Association for the Advancement of Psychoanalysis. Shortly afterward, they published the first issue of the association's journal, the *American Journal of Psychoanalysis*. Before 1941 ended, they also established the American Institute of Psychoanalysis. The purpose of the new association, journal, and institute was to promote the study of psychoanalysis in a more democratic and open manner than was practiced by the more traditional Freudian approach so dominant at the time. Horney remained as dean of the institute until her death on December 4, 1952.

Karen Horney's life was filled with the pressures of being a professional woman and single parent in a male-dominated profession. Her experience is not unlike the experiences many professional women have today. You can read about the life of Karen Horney in *A Mind of Her Own: The Life of Karen Horney* (Quinn, 1988), or *Karen Horney: Gentle Rebel of Psychoanalysis*, a book-length biography written by Jack Rubins (1978), a psychoanalyst trained in the tradition of Karen Horney.

Basic Assumptions: Horney Reacts to Freud

The principal theoretical differences Horney had with the dominant Freudian thinking of the time are best expressed in the basic assumptions of her viewpoint on the motivational, social, and cultural nature of personality.

Motivational Nature of Personality

While Freud viewed personality as being motivated by a tendency to reduce psychic tension, Horney emphasized the individual's search for a sense of security in the world as the primary motivational force in personality. In attempting to establish a sense of security, Horney said, each person develops a particular personality style for coping with the world. For example, an insecure adult might develop a very domineering personality as a means of establishing security and predictability at work and home.

Social Nature of Early Childhood

Horney agreed with Freud that many of the emotional problems people experience as adults can be traced back to early childhood. But she did not assume that these problems resulted from the unsuccessful resolution of a particular developmental stage, nor by psychological regression. Like Freud and Adler, she assumed that the nature of the early social relationship between parent and child was extremely important in determining personality maladjustment in adulthood. For example, if a boy is raised in a household with very little expression of love, as an adult he may develop a personality style that involves agreeing with everybody in the hopes of gaining their approval and affection.

Cultural Nature of Personality

Horney was in considerable disagreement with Freud's view that the development of the female personality has as its basis the desire of women to be like men (i.e., penis envy). Taking a more cultural perspective, Horney proposed that both men and women are motivated by the same desire to seek security. And since the culture in which Freud was working gave men a much more active role in determining their security, Horney stated that it only made sense to assume that women wanted to be like men. Had the cultural circumstances been reversed, it is doubtful that women would still have wanted to be like men. Thus, Horney emphasized specific cultural differences to account for personality development, not unconscious desires.

Basic Concepts: The Causes and Consequences of Seeking Security

Like Adler, Horney emphasized the influence of social interactions on the nature of personality adjustment. But her emphasis was on the causes and consequences of feeling insecure in the social environment.

Basic Hostility

Horney (1937) noted that the two most powerful needs that children demonstrate are for safety and satisfaction. Being completely dependent on others for these needs creates feelings of insecurity in children. If the parents respond with genuine love and affection, the child perceives the environment as safe, anticipates that all needs will be met, and develops a sense of security. If the parents respond with a lack of affection or emotional concern, the child perceives the environment as threatening and unfriendly, acquires a sense of increased insecurity, and develops feelings of basic hostility toward the parents. **Basic hostility** is the sense of anger and betrayal the child feels for the parents who are not helping to create a secure environment. Since no parents can be entirely consistent and satisfying, basic hostility is an inevitable experience for the child.

In dealing with such feelings of insecurity and basic hostility, children may repress them and express overtly false feelings of affection toward the parents so they will not make the situation worse. An example of this is the child who says "I love you" at bedtime to a physically abusive parent. In a sense, the child is really saying, "I will act like I love you because I am afraid that if I don't, you will make my world even worse." When the child turns these feelings of hostility inward, the feelings of insecurity, helplessness, and basic hostility only increase (Horney, 1937).

Basic Anxiety

Basic anxiety refers to feelings of insecurity, insignificance, powerlessness, inferiority, and hopelessness in a social environment that an individual feels is full of hostility, betrayal, and unfaithfulness (Horney, 1945). Thus, basic anxiety involves an expanded sense of basic hostility being generalized from the parents to other people in the individual's personal and social environment. As a result of these feelings of basic anxiety, the individual behaves in a manner reflecting this view of the world. For example, believing that people cannot be trusted, a person may become very reluctant to fall in love or become very abusive as a means of maintaining emotional distance.

Neurotic Trends

Neurotic trends are irrational needs and desires developed by the individual in trying to achieve a sense of security. They are created by intense feelings of basic anxiety (Horney, 1942). The logic is that if the specific need is fulfilled, then the individual will feel safe and secure. The trends are described as neurotic because they represent unrealistic or irrational solutions to the problem of achieving psychological security. Table 5.1 presents the 10 neurotic trends noted by Horney. For a very specific example of a neurotic tendency, read "A Closer Look" on page 130.

Moving Toward, Against, and Away from People: Three Strategies for Achieving Social Security

In fulfilling the neurotic trends noted in Table 5.1, people use various interpersonal coping strategies in an attempt to achieve a sense of security and minimize feelings of basic anxiety. In a general sense, these interpersonal coping strategies are characterized by their inflexibility and limited effectiveness. Horney (1945) identified three broad interpersonal coping strategies for seeking social security: moving toward people, moving against people, and moving away from people.

Moving Toward People

As an interpersonal coping strategy, **moving toward people** involves believing that if you go along with people and give them what they want, they will give you love and a sense of affection, approval, and admiration (see Table 5.1, neurotic needs 1 and 2). For example, by going along with and catering to the needs of her abusive husband, the wife hopes he will not abuse her in the future and will continue to take care of her and the children. Thus, the salient belief here is "if I love you, you won't hurt me." In a more normal sense, each of us to some extent might be

Table 5.1
Neurotic Trends Defined by Horney

Neurotic Trends	Illustrations of the Trends
1. The neurotic need for affection and approval	The adolescent who will do or say anything to gain the acceptance of his or her peers.
2. The neurotic need for a "partner" who will take over one's life	The "clinging vine" lover whose partner is expected to meet all of his or her emotional needs.
3. The neurotic need to restrict one's life within narrow borders	The rather meek person who does not want to be a bother to anyone and settles for very little in life.
4. The neurotic need for power	The military dictator who uses unscrupulous tactics to gain control over the people in that country.
5. The neurotic need to exploit others	The thief or rapist who commits such acts for the sake of taking advantage of others.
6. The neurotic need for prestige	The middle-aged person who defines his or her sense of self-worth by the size of the house owned or status of the car driven.
7. The neurotic need for personal admiration	The politician who wishes to be seen based on his or her own exaggerated sense of importance, not on what has actually been accomplished.
8. The neurotic ambition for personal achievement	The student who spends so much time studying as a means of gaining recognition that it begins to affect his or her health.
9. The neurotic need for self-sufficiency and independence	To avoid any more ridicule from his or her peers, the adolescent who becomes a "social loner," proclaiming not to need anyone.
10. The neurotic need for perfection and unassailability	The compulsive student with low self-esteem who, because he or she spends so much time worrying about every little detail, never completes an assignment.

Note. Based on *Self-Analysis,* by K. Horney, 1942, New York, NY: Norton.

willing to be the butt of many jokes from our friends or "go along" with what the group decides to do because we really do like them and want their approval.

Moving Against People

Moving against people involves a style of interaction characterized by aggressiveness, hostility, and exploitation. This coping strategy is founded on the belief that the world is full of people who are only looking out for themselves and, as a result, will attempt to exploit others if given the chance. By taking advantage of others first, an individual is able to achieve the exaggerated need for power, exploitation of others, social recognition and prestige, personal admiration, and personal achievement reflected in neurotic needs 4 through 8 of Table 5.1. Examples of people using this strategy are the ruthless criminal, the corrupt government official, and the unscrupu-

lous business owner who continue to take from others for their personal gain. The salient belief here is "if I have power, people can't hurt me." This extremely pessimistic view of others allows such individuals to justify their self-centered and exploitative behavioral pattern. In a more normal sense, most students would be more than willing to borrow someone's class notes if they really needed to do so. On the other hand, most students would probably be less willing to lend their notes to someone else, because that person might boost the grading curve in the class.

Moving Away from People

Moving away from people is a coping strategy characterized by withdrawing or detaching oneself from others. By retreating into his or her own world, the individual achieves a sense of self-sufficiency, independence, and perfection while gaining protection

A Closer Look:

Morbid Dependency: A Precursor to Adult Codependency

Morbid dependency is the neurotic tendency to seek and maintain affection through involvement in exploitative or manipulative relationships (Horney, 1942). Such a tendency can have its origin in dysfunctional families where children must sacrifice their own needs, desires, and expectations to obtain esteem and affection from parents (Horney, 1942). Morbid dependency is reflected in the dynamics associated with codependency (Lyon & Greenberg, 1991).

The phenomenon of **codependency** describes the tendency of adults who were the children or spouses of alcoholics to find themselves in other dysfunctional relationships, in which they make personal sacrifices in order to maintain these relationships (Cocores, 1987; Schaef, 1986). Having learned to establish a sense of self-worth by conforming to the desires and expectations of dependent and exploitative alcoholic parents or spouses, codependent adults demonstrate a specific tendency to be interested in and want to help others who possess these same characteristics of being dependent and exploitative.

A rather interesting attempt to assess this specific tendency of codependent adults was performed by Deborah Lyon and Jeff Greenberg of the University of Arizona. In their research, Lyon and Greenberg had people described as codependent (i.e., indicated that at least one of their parents has or had trouble with alcohol) and non-codependent (i.e., indicated that neither of their parents has or had trouble with alcohol) interact with another person who was described as either nurturant (e.g., helped a friend with everything from homework to laundry) or exploitative (e.g., had a friend do everything for them, from homework to laundry). After a short time, the codependent and non-codependent people were asked by the other person if they would be willing to volunteer additional time, ranging from zero to three hours, to help him with another project.

Figure 5.1 shows the amount of time volunteered by the codependent and non-codependent people. The results indicated that the codependent people were willing to spend significantly more time helping

the exploitative person than the nurturant person. But the non-codependent people were significantly more willing to help the nurturant person than the exploitative one. In fact, the non-codependent people indicated that they would not offer the exploitative person *any* free time. The codependent people also perceived as more intelligent and indicated more liking for the exploitative person than the nurturant one. In just the opposite pattern, non-codependent people perceived the nurturant person more favorably than the exploitative one.

The results of this investigation support Horney's (1942) concept of morbid dependency as a possible explanation for the origins of codependency. The codependency observed in adults may have as its roots the dysfunctional tendency for children of alcoholics to sacrifice their own needs to gain the affection of parents who come to depend on these sacrifices. Such dysfunctional dynamics are characteristic of morbid dependency.

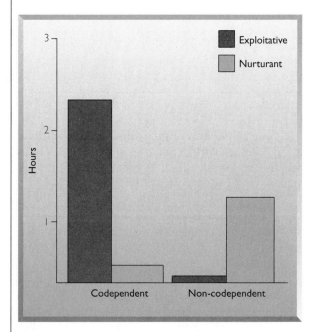

Figure 5.1
The amount of free time being volunteered to help an exploitative ■ or nurturant ▨ individual by people with codependent and non-codependent personalities

against attacks from others (see neurotic needs 3, 9, and 10 of Table 5.1). As an example, some adults can gain a sense of emotional self-sufficiency and safety by terminating a relationship each time they feel they are falling in love, but the price they may pay for their emotional independence and protection is loneliness. Thus, the salient belief here is that "if I withdraw, I can't be hurt." In a more normal sense, a person might elect to stand in the corner at a party rather than ask someone to dance and run the risk of being rejected.

Healthy vs. Maladaptive Strategies

Horney believed that some feelings of basic anxiety exist within all of us. As a result, she assumed that everyone would need to use interpersonal coping strategies at some time or another. She also made the distinction between healthy and maladaptive uses of the coping strategies and neurotic tendencies.

In general, the major differences have to do with the degree, flexibility, and emotionality of their use. The healthy person uses all three coping strategies to some extent, depending on the nature of the relationship (e.g., child, boss, spouse), type of situation (e.g., physically dangerous, emotionally threatening), and type of interaction (e.g., business, social, family). As an example of the healthy use of all three strategies, a person may go along (i.e., move with) with the boss, take a firm stand (i.e., move against) when dealing with the demand for a later curfew of a teenager, and withdraw (i.e., move away) from a potentially physical argument.

Maladaptive use of the three coping strategies involves the exclusive use of one strategy regardless of the nature and type of the relationship and an excessive emotional reaction when its use does not succeed. For example, a middle-aged man trying to please his spouse might become even more accommodating in an attempt to "save the marriage" when he discovers that his spouse is having an affair. When trying to be even more accommodating does not work, the man becomes extremely depressed. In this case, a more appropriate strategy might involve moving against and moving away from the unfaithful spouse with the aid of a good attorney and supportive psychotherapist. Thus, neurotic tendencies are classified as such because they are irrational, unreal-

istic solutions for overcoming basic anxiety and have little regard for their consequence (e.g., the development of codependency). "Applications in Personality Psychology" (below) examines a rather interesting application of Horney's three interpersonal coping styles to the maladaptive coping strategies used by some diabetics.

APPLICATION

APPLICATIONS IN PERSONALITY PSYCHOLOGY

The Coping Strategies of Diabetics: Some Insights from a Horneyan Perspective

In their work with diabetics, physicians Michael Bergam, Saim Akin, and Philip Felig (1990) noted that although many patients do well in adjusting to the physical and psychological challenges of diabetes, certain people find such adjustments more difficult. They suspected that these difficulties had something to do with the nature of the interpersonal relationships between the diabetic and significant others in the diabetic's life (e.g., medical personnel and family members).

In examining the interpersonal dynamics of diabetes management, the doctors noted three distinct patterns corresponding very closely to the three interpersonal coping styles described by Horney (1945). They labeled the three coping styles as self-effacement, need for mastery, and resignation.

Self-effacement: Moving Toward People by Becoming Dependent

Bergam et al. characterized patients in the self-effacement group by their dependency on the care of others for the control of their diabetes. These patients may actually sabotage their control over diabetes when they feel ignored or despondent. They do so unknowingly (e.g., accidentally forget to take the insulin) and sometimes knowingly (e.g., deliberately eat sweets). This sabotage typically results in additional hospital visits and more attention from medical personnel.

By gaining increased medical attention, those in the self-effacement group can remind family members of their inability to take care of themselves and of their "need" to have others care for them. Those family members, who are then expected to take more responsibility for controlling the individual's diabetes, often begin to feel anger and hostility toward the diabetic. But patients in this group are often successful in using the family's expressed anger and hostility to create a sense of guilt (e.g., "Don't you feel awful yelling at someone who is as sick as me?"). The patient then uses guilt feelings created in the family members to gain even more help from them, which in turn fosters even more dependency on others. Thus, becoming dependent on others to control their diabetes illustrates how patients in this group move toward people. In treating patients in this group, medical personnel need to help them realize how their actions are creating emotional difficulties for themselves and others around them. They also need to discuss how the patient can become more independent in controlling diabetes and in handling interpersonal relationships.

Need for Mastery: Moving Against People by Ignoring Their Assistance

Patients in the need for mastery group are characterized by the need to take control of their diabetes. They typically try to be masters of their own fate by moving against the medical personnel attempting to work with them. These patients often express a higher level of medical insight, knowledge, experience, and awareness of their condition than they actually possess. They also have rather high and unrealistic expectations concerning their own ability to cope effectively with diabetes.

With such an attitude, these patients typically ignore the true limitations of their life situation (e.g., what they can eat and how often they need to take insulin). No matter what is recommended, such patients tend to impose or substitute their own perceived solutions and remedies to their medical condition. They become angry and frustrated with their inability to meet the high expectations they have set for themselves and express this frustration through hostility toward and criticism of people who are trying to help them. Thus, attempting to take direct control of their own treatment program illustrates how individuals in this group move against people trying to help them. In helping these patients, medical personnel should focus on encouraging greater compliance with recommended procedures and on establishing more realistic expectations about the support these patients need from others.

Resignation: Moving Away from People by Withdrawing into the Treatment Program

Patients in the resignation group are characterized by a tendency to use their diabetes for isolating themselves from others. These patients, who often perceive themselves as being victimized by their condition, demonstrate a sense of martyrdom in trying to deal with and overcome diabetes. They tend to cope with their diabetes by becoming extremely regimented in their treatment program, to the point of removing themselves from more meaningful contacts with the health care system. Developing a sense of "perfectionism" is their way of avoiding dependency on the health care system and creating a sense of independence, which reinforces the tendency to move away from medical personnel.

The tendency of patients in the resignation group to be overly regimented in their treatment program also restricts their opportunities for social interactions (e.g., dating) and for establishing meaningful relationships with others. This form of social isolation is another manifestation of trying to move away from others by withdrawing. Praising these patients for their excessive efforts to cope with the diabetes only increases their sense of victimization and martyrdom and strengthens their efforts to withdraw from others. To help patients in the resignation group, health care personnel must try to make them realize the dangers of such overly regimented treatment efforts (e.g., administering too much insulin and producing hypoglycemia), especially when they have already established a tendency for withdrawing from medical support.

Using Horney's three interpersonal coping styles to classify diabetics who have some difficulty in controlling the disease is helpful in several ways:

▲ It helps to illustrate the diversity of the interpersonal needs of diabetics and the strategies they use to meet these needs.
▲ It provides a framework for understanding the underlying psychological dynamics of these patients' interpersonal difficulties.

▲ It establishes specific objectives of psychological counseling in an effort to help these patients more successfully meet their interpersonal needs.

▲ It demonstrates how knowledge of personality psychology can be applied to important issues of medicine and health maintenance.

The Nature of Personality Adjustment: The Overlapping of the Real and Ideal Self

Horney (1950) made a distinction between the real and the idealized self. The **real self** is what a person believes is true and unique about himself or herself. Information contained about the real self might involve personal likes and dislikes, strengths and weaknesses, and needs and desires. It is also involved in the process of motivating the individual toward healthy personal growth and achievement.

The **idealized self** is the individual's perception of how he or she would like to be. Information contained in the idealized self might include wanting to be more independent, powerful, outgoing, honest, emotionally involved with someone, or responsible. The idealized self is a yardstick by which people assess the extent of their personal growth and the realization of their true potential. The idealized self is also used to develop strategies for overcoming basic anxiety and achieving a greater sense of security. For example, in an attempt to "move toward others," a lonely person might reason: "If I were 15 pounds lighter and more talkative and self-confident, I would have plenty of friends."

For Horney, the nature and extent of personality adjustment is determined by looking at the degree of overlap between the real self (e.g., a person's degree of emotional independence) and the idealized self (e.g., the desire to be more emotionally independent). The greater the degree of overlap, the greater the degree of personality adjustment. Figure 5.2 illustrates this relationship between the real self, idealized self, and the degree of personality adjustment.

Successful Personality Adjustment
As shown in the top portion of Figure 5.2, successful personality development involves a considerable degree of overlap between the real and idealized self. This overlap creates a sense of satisfaction and secu-

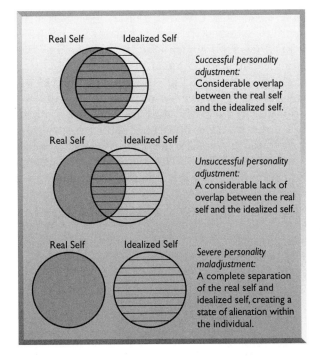

Figure 5.2
Horney's conceptualization of personality adjustment as indicated by the degree of overlap between the real self and the idealized self

rity in the individual, who knows that he or she is capable of coping with and mastering events in the real world. For example, feeling that you have the necessary study skills (i.e., real self) to complete your education and attain your career goals (i.e., idealized self) should give you a pretty secure feeling about your present and future life situation.

Unsuccessful Personality Adjustment
The middle and bottom portions of Figure 5.2 indicate that moderate and more severe forms of personality maladjustment are characterized by the greater separation of the real self from ideal self. These conditions are often brought on by what Horney called the **tyranny of the should**—an excessive emphasis by the individual on what "should" be in life. It is an overemphasis on the idealized self to the point of ignoring the real self. For example, neurotic feelings and personality maladjustment are likely to be experienced by a man who expects never to show professional jealousy toward coworkers, express public

disagreements with close friends, or experience amorous thoughts for anyone but his spouse. The point is that creating such a "state of shoulds" clearly ignores what are real human characteristics.

Horney believed that the neurotic individual employs the excessive tyranny of the should to escape reality. To extend the earlier example, rather than trying to resolve his feelings of professional jealousy toward coworkers, the man tries to deny them by assuming that such feelings should never happen. But the more separated he becomes from reality, the more insecure the man is going to feel. This is due to a perceived lack of competence to cope effectively with the life events occurring in the real world. When alienation from the real self becomes too excessive, Horney believed, the only hope for the individual is psychotherapy.

The Application of Horney's Social Psychological Viewpoint: Using What Is Known

For Horney, the basic goal of psychotherapy was to increase the client's sense of security and minimize the maladaptive use of interpersonal coping styles. Achieving a sense of security helps the individual to gain a more accurate perception of the real self and makes possible more realistic interactions with others. To help people with maladjusted personalities achieve this sense of realism in their lives, Horney (1942) proposed her own form of psychotherapy, referred to as self-analysis.

Horney's Self-Analysis Approach to Psychotherapy: Bridging the Gap between the Real and Ideal Self

Self-analysis is a process by which the person can gain (either alone or with the aid of a psychotherapist) a greater understanding and acceptance of the real self, while reducing the influence of the tyranny of the should that prevents them from gaining a sense of security. The process of self-analysis involves three basic stages: (1) achieving freedom of expression, (2) learning from this freedom of expression, and (3) using this freedom of expression to improve interpersonal relationships.

Achieving Freedom of Expression   Self-analysis employs the technique of free association to help clients think more openly about problematic interpersonal relationships. Because there are no actual consequences for the thoughts and feelings experienced during free association, clients can be more open to a wider range of possible alternatives. More specifically, free association allows clients to consider more realistic and personally rewarding responses to interpersonal problems instead of how they *should* have felt, thought, or acted. An example would be using free association to help an unhappy student realize that the decision to go to college has as its basis a desire to conform to her parents' expectations rather than any desire of her own.

Learning from Freedom of Expression   The next step in the process of self-analysis involves learning from these free associations. To learn from these associations, Horney recommended that clients review them repeatedly, in great detail. A review might include starting to examine what neurotic needs are being met by engaging in a particular type of self-defeating coping strategy and the consequences for such actions. For the student in the example, review might include realizing that being depressed and getting poor grades are two consequences of her neurotic tendency to stay in school to obtain parental respect.

Using Freedom of Expression to Improve Interpersonal Relationships   As the final step in the process of self-analysis, clients use their new-found knowledge to develop more realistic perceptions of the self and relationships with other people. With a more realistic view of their strengths and limitations, clients are in a much better position to develop goals that will bring personal satisfaction. This satisfaction brings the real and the ideal self closer together. In the example, the unhappy student can work with the therapist to develop the sense of security necessary to tell her parents what would be more personally satisfying academic and career goals.

In summary, the process of self-analysis creates the opportunity to become more free in thinking. With this freedom, clients can more closely examine the true nature of their beliefs and relationships and formulate more realistic and beneficial alternatives for interacting with others.

Personality Assessment from Horney's Viewpoint: The Measurement of Interpersonal Coping Styles

The CAD (Cohen, 1967) is a self-report inventory designed to measure the three interpersonal coping styles described by Horney (1945). The CAD contains 35 items measuring three separate subscales: compliant, aggressive, and detached. The compliant subscale (C) measures the interpersonal style of moving toward others; the aggressive subscale (A) measures the interpersonal style of moving against people; and the detached subscale (D) measures the interpersonal style of moving away from people. Each item is measured on a six-point scale, from "extremely undesirable" to "extremely desirable." The compliant and detached subscales contain 10 items each, while the aggressive subscale contains 15 items. A separate score is calculated for each of the three subscales. Here are some examples of items from the CAD:

Complaint Scale Items

To have something good to say about everybody seems:
Putting myself out to be considerate of others' feelings is:

Aggressive Scale Items

To be able to spot and exploit weakness in others is:
Having to compete with others for various rewards is:

Detached Scale Items

Being free of emotional ties with others is:
If I could live all alone in a cabin in the woods or mountains it would be:

To support the validity of the CAD, the CAD subscale scores for students with educational and career preferences in helping professions (e.g., social welfare, nursing), competitive professions (e.g., business), and scientific professions (e.g., geology) were compared (Cohen, 1967; Rendon, 1987). The results indicated that students in the helping professions group scored higher on the compliant subscale than students in the competitive and scientific groups. Students in the competitive professions group scored higher on the aggressive subscale than students in the helping and scientific groups. Finally, students in the scientific professions group scored higher on the detached subscale than students in the helping and competitive groups.

In addition to establishing the validity of the CAD, the results of this research have implications for using the CAD in academic and career advising. Another rather interesting attempt to validate the CAD while applying Horney's theory to marketing and consumer behavior is presented below in "Applications in Personality Psychology."

APPLICATION

APPLICATIONS IN PERSONALITY PSYCHOLOGY

Personality and Preferences for Personal Grooming Products: Applying Horney's Theory to Buyer Behavior

A rather unique application of Horney's theory of personality is in the area of marketing and consumer behavior. Joel Cohen (1967), professor of marketing at the University of Florida, used Horney's three interpersonal styles to help explain the purchasing behavior of consumers. In this research, 157 males were asked to complete the CAD and a questionnaire assessing their product and brand usage. The men were classified into high- or low-scoring groups on the basis of their scores for each of the three CAD subscales. After classifying the men, Cohen compared the purchasing preferences of the high- and low-scoring groups within each of the three subscales.

Compliant Group Preferred Fresh Breath and No Body Odor

The men who scored high on the compliant subscale of the CAD indicated a greater usage of personal grooming products, such as mouthwash and brand name bath soap (e.g., "Dial"), than those who scored low on the compliant subscale.

Cohen suggests that highly compliant people exhibit consumer preferences that will reassure them that they are capable of being liked by others. Since bad breath and offensive body odors are two very clear barriers to social relationships, it is understandable that compliant people, who seek reassurance by moving toward others, would be more likely to purchase products designed to combat these two personal hygiene problems. They might also be more willing than less compliant people to pay extra for brand name products that are advertised as being highly effective.

Aggressive Group Preferred Smelling Good and Feeling Manly

The men who scored high on the aggressive subscale of the CAD expressed a greater preference for brand name deodorant products with an advertised "masculine image" (e.g., "Old Spice"). They used cologne and aftershave more often, and more of them reported using a manual razor (vs. an electric shaver) for shaving than did the men who scored low on the aggressive subscale.

Cohen suggests that men who scored high on the aggressive subscale exhibit consumer preferences designed to establish a distinct image that attracts attention and projects a sense of masculinity. Because cologne and aftershave are designed to help a person be noticed by others, it makes sense that aggressive men seeking to attract attention would be more likely to purchase these products than would men concerned with blending into the crowd (e.g., compliant group) or the men not overly concerned with interpersonal relationships (e.g., detached group). Also, because projecting a macho image characterized by strength would aid aggressive men in their attempts to move against others, it seems natural that these men would be willing to engage in behavior designed to reinforce this type of self-image, such as shaving with a manual razor and paying more for brand name deodorants advertised as being manly.

Detached Group Had No Real Preferences for Personal Hygiene Products

Cohen's results indicated that men who scored high on the detached subscale demonstrated no clear preferences for personal hygiene products that are designed to achieve certain interpersonal motives or whose advertisements stress interpersonal appeals (e.g., not offending others with bad breath, or feeling manly). This makes sense since men in the detached group, with their desire to move away from others, would be the least likely of the three groups studied to be concerned with the success of their interpersonal relationships.

Finally, comparisons within the three groups indicated no differences in preferences for those personal hygiene products not designed to meet interpersonal needs, such as toothpaste (e.g., advertisements stressing dental health benefits) and hair dressings (e.g., advertisements stressing the benefits of healthy hair), healthcare products (e.g., headache remedies), and products to meet everyday needs (e.g., gasoline brands). Thus, Cohen observed specific consumer preferences only for those personal hygiene products that seem to meet each group's specific interpersonal needs. Such results suggest the importance of considering the specific psychological needs of the consumer when conducting consumer research (Engel, Blackwell, & Miniard, 1993) and of developing effective advertisements (Pride & Ferrell, 1993).

Although the research by Cohen and others (Kassarjian, 1971; Kernan, 1971; Wells & Beard, 1973) supports the validity and utility of the CAD, it is not without its critics. It has been suggested that (1) the CAD is more a measure of just two dimensions (compliant and aggressive) than of three (Munson & Spively, 1982; Noerager, 1979); and (2) the CAD subscales do not consistently correlate with other related measures of personality traits (Munson & Spivey, 1982).

In addition to the work with the CAD, applications of Horney's theoretical principles have been incorporated into other areas, including behavioral correlates of coronary disease (Hamon, 1987), attitudes toward the physically disabled (Jabin, 1987), and the psychobiography of President Lyndon B. Johnson (1989).

Horney's Feminine Psychology: A Reinterpretation of the Female Personality

Horney (1939, 1967) is also known for her contribution to feminine psychology. She reinterpreted Freud's conceptualization of the female personality, with particular reference to the phallic stage and the concept of penis envy. In reinterpreting the dynamics of the phallic stage, Horney (1939) proposed that it is the child's feelings of basic anxiety, hostility, and anger directed at the opposite-sex parent that make the child view this parent as not only a source of competition for the affection of the same-sex parent, but a direct threat to the child's sense of safety and security. Thus, in response to the phallic stage dilemma, Horney proposed a resolution based more on interpersonal dynamics (e.g., differences in social power) than on the more sexual dynamics proposed by Freud (e.g., reduction of tension in the erogenous zone).

In a similar manner, Horney (1967) approached the concept of penis envy by proposing a more cultural interpretation. She pointed out that because of the greater social freedom and opportunities available to men during the time Freud was formulating his viewpoint, it was only natural for women to be envious of and desire the same quality of life as men. Thus, what Freud mistakenly believed to be women's envy of the male penis was nothing more than women wanting to express those very natural needs for success and security characteristic of both sexes. Horney also pointed out that Freud's views of women were biased in that they were, for the most part, based on his interactions with the neurotic women he had as patients.

In taking her discussion and reinterpretation of penis envy one step further, Horney (1967) proposed the notion of **womb envy**: the feeling of admiration and respect men supposedly feel for the female's ability to give birth. She also proposed that since men could not give birth but still had the natural desire to be creative and productive, they expressed their womb envy indirectly through their achievements and successes in other areas. On a more negative side, womb envy could also lead men to express their jealousy by belittling the achievements of women. Men might also engage in various discriminatory practices that make it difficult for women to achieve success and obtain additional status (e.g., systematically overlooking women for promotions).

Westkott (1986a, 1986b, 1989) has also noted that the normative expectations for women to be more nurturing, empathic, and responsible for the maintenance and preservation of interpersonal relationships than men can also serve as cultural constraints on personal growth and fulfillment for women, by reinforcing a particular "idealized" notion of femininity. An example of this situation would be the working mother who is perceived as neglecting the emotional well-being of her children by placing them in a day-care center while she pursues her career aspirations. Such evaluative statements are less likely to be made about men and their career aspirations.

It is no accident that Horney should be one of Freud's critics at a time when his views were enjoying considerable fame. After all, as a career woman and mother, Horney demonstrated that it was possible to be successful in what was at that time clearly a male-dominated profession. It was through her desire to see men and women as psychological equals in their attempts to meet basic security needs, as well as to point out the significance of cultural factors in this process, that Horney probably made her most important contribution to personality psychology.

Evaluation of Horney's Social Psychological Viewpoint: Strengths and Limitations

Characteristic Strengths

Here are some strengths of Horney's viewpoint:

▲ *Reinterpretation of the female personality.* Horney's reinterpretation of the feminine personality is based on a set of needs designed to achieve security in a manner similar to those of males. Such thinking significantly contributed to equalizing the psychology of the sexes.

▲ *Emphasis on the contribution of culture.* Horney's continuous emphasis on the importance of cultural factors in determining the nature of personality was a reminder that in addition to psychological processes operating within the individual, social forces operating outside of the individual must be considered in order to achieve complete understanding of the person.

Characteristic Limitations

The main limitation of Horney's social psychological viewpoint is its lack of empirical evidence. In comparison to the other theorists discussed, Horney's work has generated very little empirical research among personality psychologists. Although her theoretical ideas were presented in a relatively straightforward manner, they have not stimulated much interest in others to investigate their validity. This may in part be due to the rejection of Horney's ideas by the more traditional and influential Freudian tradition operating at the time. But thinking about such ideas as feminine psychology and the importance of social and cultural factors in personality has become more salient. Such changes in thinking have resulted in an increase in an awareness of and research attempting to validate basic concepts of Horney's viewpoint (Cohen, 1967; Munson & Spivey, 1982) and to extend her ideas to areas within (Roemer, 1986, 1987) and outside of (Bergman, Akin, Felig, 1990; Paris, 1989) personality psychology. Perhaps this renewed interest in Horney's unique viewpoint will result in her contribution to personality psychology being fully realized.

Erikson's Psychosocial Viewpoint: The Development of the Ego throughout the Life Span

Erik Erikson's fundamental reaction to Freud was to extend the stages of personality development throughout the life span, to define the stages as more social in nature, and to expand significantly the role of the ego as a component of personality. For a glimpse into the life of Erik Erikson, read "A Closer Look" below.

A Closer Look:

Biographical Background: The Life of Erik Erikson

Erik H. Erikson was born on June 15, 1902, near Frankfurt, Germany. His birth was the result of an extramarital affair by his mother. His parents, both Danish, separated shortly before his birth. Wishing to be near her close friends, Erik's mother moved to Karlsruhe, Germany. When Erik was 3 years old, his mother married a local pediatrician, Theodore Homburger, who successfully treated Erik for a childhood disease. Dr. Homburger adopted Erik and gave him his last name. But in what Erik would later call an act of "loving deceit," his parents concealed his adoption for

Erik Erikson gave meaning to the term "identity crisis" and extended the notion of a stage theory of personality development to include young adulthood, middle age, and late adulthood.

several years. Erik used *Homburger* as his surname until shortly before he emigrated to the United States in 1933. He then adopted the surname of *Erikson,* which means "son of Erik."

Although his stepfather was Jewish, Erik was not easily accepted by his Jewish peers because of his tall, blond, Aryan appearance. At the same time, he was rejected by his German peers because they knew he was Jewish. Having to confront being adopted and then being rejected by his peers may have affected Erikson's later concerns with what he was to call the identity crisis.

Unlike many of the personality theorists discussed so far, Erikson was not a particularly good student. He did show some promise in history and art. After graduating from high school and rejecting his stepfather's suggestions to go to medical school, Erik traveled around central Europe for a year. He then returned to Karlsruhe to attend art school. But he quickly became restless again and, until the age of about 25, spent time wandering through Italy and Germany.

In 1927, an old classmate invited Erikson to join him as a Montessori instructor at a private school run by Anna Freud for children whose parents were receiving psychoanalysis from her father. After Erik had worked at the school for a short time, Anna asked him to consider beginning analysis with her and becoming a child analyst himself. During his training with Anna, which lasted from 1927 to 1933, Erik became a very close friend of the Freud family.

Over the next few years, Erikson distinguished himself as a key figure in psychoanalysis through some of his early publications demonstrating how children could become more aware of themselves through artistic expression. Thus, with just a high school education and a diploma as a Montessori teacher, Erikson combined his early talents in art and history to make a unique contribution to psychoanalysis by trying to understand emotional development during childhood.

On April 1, 1930, Erikson married Joan Serson. In 1933, Erikson moved his wife and two sons to Boston, where he became a practicing children's analyst and accepted a position at the Harvard Medical School. At the same time, he began working on a PhD in the psychology program at Harvard. But realizing that he was not suited for formal education, Erikson withdrew a short time later—after failing his first course. In 1936, he accepted a position at the Yale Institute of Human Relations. In 1938, he spent some time studying child-rearing practices among the Sioux Indians in South Dakota.

In 1939, Erikson moved to San Francisco and continued his practice as a children's analyst. In 1942, he became a professor of psychology at the University of California at Berkeley; but he was released in 1950, along with other faculty members, for refusing to sign a loyalty oath. From 1951 to 1960, Erikson lived in Stockbridge, Massachusetts, where he served as a senior staff member at the Austin Riggs Center, a private hospital for disturbed adolescents, and simultaneously held several other part-time faculty appointments at neighboring institutions.

In 1960, he returned to an academic appointment as a lecturer and professor of human development at Harvard. Although he never actually received a college or university degree, Erikson was considered a very strong intellectual by his colleagues and a very popular teacher by his students. His book, *Gandhi's Truth* (Erikson, 1969), won him a Pulitzer Prize and the National Book Award in philosophy and religion. Although he retired in 1970, Erikson continued to be a productive researcher and writer. His last book concerns personality growth during the later years of life (Erikson, Erikson, & Kivnick, 1986). Erikson died on May 12, 1994, in Harwich, Massachusetts.

For more information about Erikson's life, read his article titled "Autobiographic Notes on the Identity Crisis" (Erikson, 1970) and his obituary (Hopkins, 1995).

Basic Assumptions: Adding New Dimensions to Freudian Thought

Although he was trained in very traditional Freudian psychoanalysis, Erikson formulated certain basic assumptions of personality that were quite different from Freud. Still, Erikson's reaction to Freud extends several aspects of the Freudian viewpoint.

The Nature and Function of the Ego
A major departure from traditional Freudian analysis was Erikson's conception of the ego. Erikson's view of the ego was more in line with that of ego psychology. **Ego psychology** views the ego as being more than just growing out of the id and serving as a mediator for the id and superego (Hartmann, 1958, 1964). Erikson made the ego a central feature in his theory of personality. He believed that it operates as an autonomous structure, giving a sense of meaning and coherence to personal experiences and creating consistency in behavior. The ego serves as the core of the healthy personality and is responsible for creative thinking, artistic expression, logical reasoning, and joyful expression of emotions. Thus, for Erikson, the ego did much more than simply resolve conflict.

The Psychosocial Nature of Ego Development
Erikson proposed that the ego operates in a manner characterized by psychosocial development. **Psychosocial development** refers to Erikson's belief that the ego develops as it successfully resolves crises that are distinctively social in nature. These crises involve establishing a sense of trust in others, developing a sense of identity in society, and helping the next generation prepare for the future.

A Life-Span Perspective of Ego Development
Erikson assumed that ego development through psychosocial crises is a process that continues well into the later years of life. Erikson proposed that preparing for death was the final stage of personality development. This is in sharp contrast to the Freudian view that most of personality development occurs during the first several years of life.

Extending, Not Departing from, Freudian Thought
Although his basic assumptions do differ considerably

from Freud's, Erikson's views are not a departure from Freudian thought but an extension of it. Erikson extends Freudian thought by focusing on the adaptive and creative characteristics of the ego and expanding the notion of the stages of personality development to include the entire life span.

Basic Concepts of Erikson's Psychosocial Viewpoint: The Stages of Ego Development

A significant contribution made by Erikson to the study of personality was his investigation into the development of personality throughout the life span. In this next section, we will consider his views on the nature of ego development.

Characteristic Features of Psychosocial Stages: The Epigenetic Principle, the Psychosocial Crises, and Basic Virtues

Erikson is probably best known for his work on the developmental stages of the ego throughout the life span (Erikson, 1950, 1963). The following paragraphs examine these characteristics of Erikson's developmental stages:

▲   They operate on an epigenetic principle.
▲   They involve the resolution of psychosocial crises.
▲   They result in the acquisition of basic virtues.

The Epigenetic Nature of Ego Development   Erikson's stages of development are said to operate on an epigenetic principle. This **epigenetic principle** assumes that the stages of development occur in a specific sequence and build upon each previous stage. In this manner, the development at one stage is related to development at other stages (Whitbourne, Zuschlag, Elliot, & Waterman, 1992). The sequence is based on certain expectations of the individual by society at certain periods in life. As an example of this sequencing of events, a person must establish a personal identity before being able to establish a meaningful, intimate relationship with another person.

Psychosocial Crises during Ego Development   Like Freud, Erikson assumed that a crisis occurs at each stage of development. For Erikson these crises are of a psychosocial nature, because they involve psychological needs of the individual (i.e., *psycho-*) conflicting with the expectations made by society (i.e., *-social*) (Erikson, 1963; Whitbourne et al., 1992). Successful resolution of each **psychosocial crisis** requires striking a balance between the needs of the individual and the expectations of society. For example, very early in life, people must learn not only to trust others enough to be able to fall in love as an adult but also to mistrust others enough to avoid becoming highly gullible.

The Acquisition of Basic Virtues   With the successful resolution of each of the psychosocial crises comes the acquisition of basic virtues. **Basic virtues** are characteristic strengths that the ego can use to help in resolving subsequent crises. For example, as a child develops a healthy sense of trust, the basic virtue of hope for the future is acquired and incorporated into the child's ego. The greater the amount of these basic virtues the ego is able to acquire during its course of development, the more strength it will have for coping with some of the more difficult crises occurring later in life, such as facing one's death.

The Eight Stages of Psychosocial Development: The Life-Time Development of the Ego

Because Erikson's psychosocial stages of ego development represent his most significant contribution to the study of personality, an appreciation of Erikson's viewpoint can be best achieved by examining these eight stages (see Table 5.2). The following subsections describe the processes and consequences associated with both successful and unsuccessful resolution of each psychosocial stage.

Stage One.   Trust vs. Mistrust: Acquiring Hope   The first psychosocial crisis occurs during the first year of life, as did the oral stage of Freud's psychosexual crises. The crisis is one of **trust vs. mistrust**. During the first year of life, the infant is uncertain about the world in which he or she lives. To resolve these feelings of uncertainty, the infant looks to the primary caretaker for stability, consistency, familiarity, and continuity in the nature of these experiences.

By consistently meeting the child's basic needs over time, parents and other primary caretakers can provide this sense of stability and establish in their

Table 5.2
Erikson's Eight Stages of Psychosocial Development

Stage	Psychosocial Crisis	Basic Virtue	Age
1	Trust vs. mistrust	Hope	Infancy (0 to 1 1/2)
2	Autonomy vs. shame and doubt	Will	Early childhood (1 1/2 to 3)
3	Initiative vs. Guilt	Purpose	Play age (3 to 5)
4	Industry vs. inferiority	Competency	School age (5 to 12)
5	Ego identity vs. role confusion	Fidelity	Adolescence (12 to 18)
6	Intimacy vs. isolation	Love	Young adult (18 to 25)
7	Generativity vs. stagnation	Care	Adulthood (25 to 65)
8	Ego integrity vs. despair	Wisdom	Maturity (65+)

Note: The ages listed are not to be taken as discrete points of development, but are estimates of when each psychosocial crisis is most likely to occur the first time.

children a sense of certainty that their basic needs will be met. In addition, the more a child can generalize these feelings to others (e.g., older siblings, grandparents, and friends), the greater the sense of trust he or she will feel. On the other hand, an infant who experiences inconsistency in the meeting of its basic needs will develop a sense of mistrust.

If the child is able to resolve this crisis in the direction of trust, then comes the belief that the external world is protective and supportive. With this belief, the ego acquires the basic virtue of hope. By developing a sense of trust, the infant can have hope that as new needs and crises arise, there is a real possibility that other people will be there as a source of support. Failing to acquire this sense of hope will result in the development of a sense of fear. This fear involves having to live in an uncertain and unpredictable environment. For example, an individual who has failed to establish a sense of trust as a child may have difficulty establishing friendships as an adult for fear of being rejected.

Stage Two.   Autonomy vs. Shame and Doubt: Acquiring Will   The second psychosocial crisis appears some time around the end of the first year of life and continues through the third year, thus corresponding to the anal stage of Freud's psychosexual crisis. This crisis involves **autonomy vs. shame and doubt**. During these early childhood years, the child is discovering that he or she has many skills and abilities, such as

putting on clothes and shoes, playing with a variety of toys, and manipulating a variety of household objects—from lights to water faucets. All of these activities illustrate the child's growing independence and sense of autonomy.

It is critical for parents and others to let children begin to explore the limits of their abilities in an environment that is supportive, encouraging, and tolerant of failure. Rather than putting on the child's shirt, a supportive parent has the patience to allow the child to continue to try until he or she gets it on or asks for some assistance. As children get the opportunity to demonstrate the extent of their abilities, they begin to develop a sense of mastery over their environment and acquire feelings of being autonomous. On the other hand, if the parents do not allow the child to demonstrate his or her abilities or make expectations well above a child's abilities (i.e., create situations of failure), the child may experience a sense of shame and doubt over failing. This may result in the child becoming very dependent on and/or demanding of others.

If the child is able to resolve this second crisis in the direction of autonomy, the ego acquires the basic virtue of will. By developing a sense of will, the child does not have to fear being controlled and manipulated by surrounding events; he or she has a sense of being able to change them. Failing to acquire this sense of willpower will result in the child's developing a sense of self-doubt. For example, an adult who has failed to establish a sense of autonomy may lack the self-confidence necessary to enroll in college or pursue a particular career.

Stage Three.   Initiative vs. Guilt: Acquiring Purpose The third psychosocial crisis occurs during the fourth and fifth years of life, corresponding to the phallic stage of Freud's psychosexual crisis. The basic crisis at this time involves **initiative vs. guilt**. During this period of life, the principle activities involve the child's going to school and, for the first time, regularly interacting with a large number of people (e.g., classmates).

Erikson believed that central to this period of time is the activity of children playing together. Playing allows children to explore their interpersonal abilities through such behaviors as initiating activities (deciding what to play) and making plans related to the activity selected (deciding on the rules). By taking initiative and making plans, children learn that they can make decisions, propose a course of action, and carry out the plan. With this, they are learning the basic skills of problem solving in the context of working with other people and developing a sense of curiosity. Such basic skills are the cornerstones of coping successfully in society. How others react to these self-initiated actions is also extremely important. For example, if parents respond with excessive verbal or physical punishment when the child tries to take some initiative, the child may begin to feel guilty about taking such actions. As a result, the child may develop feelings of excessive self-consciousness.

Resolving this crisis in the direction of initiative makes it possible for the child to develop a sense of goal-directed behavior. By feeling comfortable with setting and pursuing goals, the ego acquires the basic virtue of purpose. With purpose, people of all ages begin to develop a sense of meaning in their life. An individual who fails to acquire this sense of purpose may develop a sense of unworthiness. For example, a college student without any sense of purpose will probably just wander from one major to another without doing very well or being very happy going to school.

Stage Four.   Industry vs. Inferiority: Acquiring Competency   Erikson's fourth psychosocial crisis, involving **industry vs. inferiority** occurs in children from the ages 6 through 11. This stage corresponds to the latency period in Freud's psychosexual stages. But, while Freud viewed these years as a time of reduced psychic activity, Erikson viewed them as a time of significant development. During these years, the child is in school learning to acquire and develop the basic technical skills needed to be a productive individual in society. In our society these skills include learning to read, write, perform mathematical operations, and engage in deductive reasoning. In another society they may involve learning to set a bear trap or skin a wild animal.

As they begin to master these skills, children develop a sense of industry and start to use these skills in more unique and personal ways, such as writing love notes to each other or reading books of personal interest. While acquiring these skills together with their peers, some children may realize their level of skills may be lower than that of others, or they may discover that they do not have the skills deemed valuable in their social context (e.g., being humorous or very athletic). Such realizations can lead the child to experience a sense of inferiority, and may cause the child to lose interest in his or her school activities. This in turn can limit employment and career opportunities in adulthood.

Resolving this crisis in the direction of industry creates in the individual the belief that he or she has the basic skills to work and compete as a productive member of society. With this belief, the ego develops a sense of competency. This sense of competency helps the person in taking future risks. For example, an individual with a sense of competency has expectations for success during the process of selecting or changing a career. Failing to establish this sense of competency will result in the ego's developing a sense of incompetency. With such a belief, the individual may not be willing to try new experiences (e.g., make a career change) for fear of failing.

Stage Five.   Ego Identity vs. Role Confusion: Acquiring Fidelity   **Ego identity vs. role confusion**, the fifth psychosocial crisis, lasts from around 12 years of age to about 18 or 20. It is during this stage that the individual begins to make the transition from childhood to adulthood. Part of this transition involves an initial attempt to establish a sense of ego identity within the society. Ego identity involves establishing a sense of belonging to a society by determining the extent to which an individual feels he or she "fits into" it. In our society, such fitting in typically involves making some career decisions (e.g., wanting to be a clinical psychologist) and career planning (e.g., majoring in psychology).

Failing to establish a sense of identity within society can lead to what Erikson refers to as role confusion. Role confusion involves the individual's not being sure of his or her place in society. The feelings of uncertainty that such a state creates are referred to as an **identity crisis**. In response to this role confusion and identity crisis, young adults may begin to experiment with different life-styles. Such experimentation might involve a person switching college majors or working at different jobs in an attempt to get some ideas about what he or she enjoys doing.

Forcing an individual to accept an identity inconsistent with his or her own self-perceptions can result in a lot of unhappiness. Consider Sophie, a student who really does not want to be going to college but is there because of family pressures. She is not likely to be very happy, nor will she do very well in college. Pressuring someone into an identity can result in a rebellion in the form of establishing a negative identity. A **negative identity** is one that is in opposition to what others expect. For example, because of being pressured into going to college, Sophie may simply drop out and take a job as an unskilled laborer to demonstrate her independence and free will. To avoid such rebellion, Erikson recommended that parents and significant others simply offer guidance and be supportive of the decisions their children make about what they want to do, instead of trying to make the decisions for them.

Resolving this crisis in the direction of ego identity allows the individual to develop a sense of being accepted by society for the person he or she is, rather than based solely on what others want. With this sense of acceptance, the ego acquires the virtue of fidelity. **Fidelity** involves being able to commit one's self to others on the basis of accepting the individual even when there may be some ideological differences. For example, even when Peter decides not to go into the family sporting goods business as all had hoped, the family still encourages him in his decision to enroll in a culinary arts college to prepare for a career as a chef. Having the support of significant others makes committing to personal decisions and goals in life and establishing a personal identity easier.

Stage Six.   Intimacy vs. Isolation: Acquiring Love **Intimacy vs. isolation** is the sixth psychosocial crisis. This crisis spans the ages of about 20 to 40, or the period of young adulthood. After establishing a sense of social identity, the individual is now ready to begin the task of establishing a meaningful emotional relationship with another person. People need a solid sense of their own personal identity before they are able to make the necessary commitment and sacrifices expected in an intimate emotional relationship (Bellew-Smith & Korn, 1986). An individual who has not established a firm personal identity will have trouble fusing his or her identity with another person and will feel isolated and lonely.

If the individual is able to resolve this crisis in the direction of intimacy, then comes the capacity to fuse his or her identity with that of another person without having to worry about losing it in the process. With this belief, the ego acquires the basic virtue of love. Beyond the traditional romantic sense, the virtue of love involves being able to commit one's self to someone else, even though this may mean compromising some of one's own needs. Expressions of the virtue of love also include showing respect, providing caring, and helping to take responsibility for significant others.

The major advantage of developing the virtue of love is that by fusing their egos in an intimate relationship, two people are able to have twice as much ego strength between them. Failing to acquire this sense of love will result in a lack of emotional commitment. People who fear commitment will avoid getting too close emotionally to others, or may have a series of meaningless love affairs as a way of obtaining a sense of acceptance without commitment.

Stage Seven.   Generativity vs. Stagnation: Acquiring Care   The seventh psychosocial crisis, spanning the ages of about 40 to 45, corresponds to the period of middle adulthood. The principal crisis here involves **generativity vs. stagnation**. During this period of middle adulthood, the individual must realize that it is not only his or her own ego development that is important but also the ego development of the next generation of young people.

With this belief comes the individual's desire to make things better for the next generation by sharing the wisdom and strengths acquired during the years of ego development. Examples of this sense of commitment include caring for one's own children and doing volunteer work in the community. The secondary gain to be achieved by such commitment to the next generation is that the person's ego will continue to develop through them: the lessons parents teach their children are then passed on to their children. This sense of commitment to the future is what Erikson called generativity.

Not establishing a sense of commitment to the future can result in feelings of stagnation. Stagnation produces adults who live to satisfy only their own needs. An example of this might be the adult who simply packs up and leaves family members as part of what has become known as a midlife crisis.

If this crisis is resolved in the direction of generativity, the individual develops the belief that the ego development of others matters. With this belief, the ego acquires the virtue of care. Care produces a sense of involvement and activity that results in the individual's putting back into society some of what he or she has taken out. An example of care might be a retired executive sharing her knowledge with local high school students as an advisor for an after-school junior entrepreneur program. Failing to establish the virtue of care results in feelings of apathy and self-centeredness. For details about a recent attempt to study the concept of generativity, read "A Closer Look" on page 145.

Stage Eight.   Ego Integrity vs. Despair: Acquiring Wisdom   The last psychosocial crisis appears from about 65 years until death, occurring during what might be called late adulthood. This crisis is one of ego integrity vs. despair. During this part of life, the major task is for the individual to take a look at how his or her ego has developed and reflect on the choices that have been made. **Ego integrity** occurs when the individual can look back on the events of the past seven stages with a sense of pleasure about what has taken place and the people one has helped to develop. With ego integrity, the individual can look back over the years and have a sense of having lived a complete life. Despair occurs when the elderly individual looks back on his or her life with a sense of incompleteness about what has not been done or will

never be done and realizes that his or her time on earth is running out. Such despair leads to feelings of bitterness and anger.

Resolving this crisis in the direction of ego integrity results in the ego acquiring the virtue of wisdom. Wisdom makes it possible for people to look back on life with a sense of closure and completeness. The wisdom that we have gained throughout life also makes it possible for us to accept death without fear. An older person showing courage in the face of death can help the younger generation to fear death less and appreciate living more. Without this sense of wisdom, the mature individual experiences a sense of incompleteness and despair over what might have been or the opportunities missed.

In conclusion, Erikson has made it clear that personality development is a lifelong process. He also helped to point out the significance of personality development during the twilight years of life—a time that was previously associated with very little psychic activity and emotional growth. To explore some ways that personality development is associated with successful and unsuccessful adjustment to aging, read "A Closer Look" on page 146.

Applications of Erikson's Psychosocial Viewpoint: Using What Is Known

Although Erikson had some theoretical differences with Freud, he regarded himself as a traditional psychoanalyst. He employed many standard techniques of psychoanalysis (e.g., free association), but with some modifications.

Psychotherapy: Playing through the Conflict
One of Erikson's unique therapeutic techniques was play therapy. In **play therapy**, children take ordinary toy objects (e.g., dolls and blocks) and arrange them any way they want during a period of free play as a means of expressing their conscious and unconscious concerns. Erikson regarded free play as a special form of free association, during which children could express with toys what they could not or dared not say (Erikson, 1963). As a means of expressing Oedipal feelings, a child might create a scene in which the mother doll is on one side of a block wall while the father doll and baby doll are on the other

A CLOSER LOOK

The Validation of the Loyola Generativity Scale: Measuring Generativity by Actions and Words

In their efforts to study Erikson's notion of generativity, Dan McAdams and Ed de St. Aubin, both of Northwestern University, have developed the Loyola Generativity Scale (McAdams & de St. Aubin, 1992). The Loyola Generativity Scale (LGS) is a 20-item, objective self-report personality inventory. The items of the LGS are answered on a four-point fixed-format response scale, ranging from 0 (the statement never applies to you) to 3 (the statement applies to you very often). Here is a sample of items from the LGS:

1. I think I would like the work of a teacher.
2. I have a responsibility to improve the neighborhood in which I live.
3. I think I will be remembered for a long time after I die.
4. Other people say that I am a very productive person.
5. I have made many commitments to many different kinds of people, groups, and activities in my life.

The items contained in the LGS "cover many of the most salient ideas in the theoretical literature on generativity" (McAdams & de St. Aubin, 1992, p. 1007), including

▲ Passing knowledge and skills to others, especially the next generation (see item 1)
▲ Making significant contributions to improve the quality of one's community and neighborhood (see item 2)
▲ Engaging in activities that will have a lasting impact or create a legacy (see item 3)
▲ Being creative and productive (see item 4)
▲ Caring and taking responsibility for other people (see item 5)

Validating the LGS by What People Do

As part of their attempts to validate the LGS, McAdams and de St. Aubin had study participants complete a behavioral checklist containing 49 activities related to generativity (e.g., taught somebody a skill, performed a community service) and 16 activities not related to generativity (e.g., read a nonfiction book, began a diet to lose weight). People ranging in age from 25 to 74 years were asked to indicate the extent to which they had engaged in a given act during the previous 2 months. In support of the validity of the LGS, it was found that LGS scores were positively correlated with the number of generative behaviors and uncorrelated to the number of behaviors irrelevant to generativity.

Validating the LGS by What People Say

These participants were also asked to describe in writing five important autobiographical episodes involving a recent peak experience, a recent nadir (low point) experience, an experience related to commitment, an experience involving a goal, and an imagined future experience. The autobiographic episodes were analyzed on the basis of five generativity themes:

▲ Creativity (e.g., wrote a poem, built a patio)
▲ Maintaining (e.g., kept up a family tradition, followed up on a project)
▲ Offering (e.g., giving one's time or money to others)
▲ Next generation (e.g., purposeful and positive interactions with those of a younger generation)
▲ Symbolic immortality (e.g., doing something that will outlive one's existence)

In support of the validity of the LGS, it was found that the total number of generativity themes expressed across the five autobiographic episodes was positively correlated with the total LGS score and the number of generative behaviors performed within a 2-month period.

The results of this research support the validity of the LGS as a systematic measure of generativity by establishing its relationship with what people do and say with respect to their generative behavior. In addition, subsequent research with the LGS indicated that expressions of generativity were positively associated with life satisfaction (McAdams, de St. Aubin, & Logan, 1993), which is consistent with Erikson's views.

The research by McAdams and de St. Aubin indicates that a sense of generativity and generative forms of behavior appear in life much earlier than previously indicated by Erikson. This kind of research helps to clarify the nature and operation of Erikson's psychosocial stages in general and the stage of generativity in particular.

side. Play therapy enables children to express emotional conflict from a safe distance.

Psychohistory: The Ego Strength of Greatness

Another unique application of Erikson's viewpoint has been his work on the psychohistory of famous people (Erikson, 1974). **Psychohistory** is the study of an individual's life using the methodology of psycho-analysis and history. In his psychohistories, Erikson investigated how the ego strength of famous people contributed to their greatness. He tried to understand how these people took the conflicts from their own lives and resolved them in later life—in ways that in many cases altered the course of history.

Erikson wanted to understand how the ego strength of a great individual can inspire the collec-

A CLOSER LOOK

Successful and Unsuccessful Adjustment to Growing Old: Acquiring a Sense of Acceptance vs. Hostility

In a classic study of personality adjustment in late adulthood, a group of 87 people from ages 55 to 84 was studied extensively (Reichard, Livson, & Peterson, 1962). In this study, three groups of well-adjusted and two groups of maladjusted people were identified by the researchers.

Successful Adjustment to Old Age: Finding a Style of Aging That Fits

The three groups of well-adjusted people shared a sense of acceptance in their lives.

▲ The "mature" group: Having few regrets. The mature group was described as basically self-sufficient, self-accepting, and genuinely satisfied in their personal relationships. They also had well-developed interests. They accepted growing old and had few regrets for what had already happened in their lives. This group was rated as the most well-adjusted to growing old.

▲ The "rocking chair" group: A desire to slow down. This group of people based their level of satisfaction on the more passive aspects of old age (e.g., retirement; more leisure time). They seemed content with the notion of allowing others to meet their material needs and provide emotional support. This group was rated as the second most well-adjusted to growing old.

▲ The "armored" group: Keeping busy. The happiness of this group was associated with their keeping busy. To cope with their fears of growing old, they remained very active by clinging to old habits and interests. This group was rated as the third most well-adjusted group.

People in all three of these well-adjusted groups tended to be happy, sociable, confident, and productive, and to have high self-esteem.

Unsuccessful Adjustment to Old Age: Feeling Hostility

While those who successfully adjusted to growing old shared a sense of acceptance in their lives, those people in the two groups that demonstrated maladjustment shared a great deal of hostility.

▲ The "angry" group: Blaming others for what could have been. The hostility expressed by the angry group had as its basis the blaming of others for preventing them from achieving their life goals. People in this group could not accept that they were growing old, and they were resentful toward the young. A fear of death was also a characteristic feature of this group.

▲ The "self-haters": Regrets for the past. The hostility expressed by people in this group was directed toward themselves. They experienced depression, pessimism, and regret about their past. They viewed death as a release from all their present unhappiness.

The researchers concluded that successful adjustment to growing old was characterized by accepting the way one has lived life in the past and selecting a lifestyle based on one's current state of mind. On the other hand, unsuccessful adjustment to growing old was characterized by having second thoughts about the way one had lived life. Both of these conclusions are consistent with what Erikson said are critical components of the psychosocial crisis of ego integrity vs. despair.

tive ego development of an entire country. In his award-winning book on Gandhi, Erikson (1969) tried to explain how Gandhi's use of a personal hunger strike and other forms of nonviolent protest resulted in transforming the weak and negative identity of many Indians into a collective positive identity that enabled them to break away from British rule. In this case, by showing that he was not afraid to die for something he believed in, Gandhi inspired the ego development in millions of individuals.

Such an act is at the very heart of two of Erikson's psychosocial crises: generativity (i.e., Gandhi's concern for the future) and ego integrity (i.e., Gandhi's acceptance of death inspired others to live). Thus, Erikson was not concerned with tracing the pathological roots of famous people as a means of explaining maladaptive behavior. Instead, he was more concerned with looking to the future (e.g., Gandhi's impact on the future of India) than the past (e.g., what in Gandhi's childhood caused his behavior).

Personality Assessment from Erikson's Viewpoint:
The Measurement of Psychosocial Development
Several assessment techniques have been designed to measure personality development based on Erikson's viewpoint (Constantinople, 1969; McAdams & de St. Aubin, 1992; Walaskay, Whitbourne, & Nehrke, 1983–1984; Whitbourne et al., 1992). One of the most comprehensive is an objective self-report questionnaire developed by Rhona Ochse and Cornelis Plug (1986) from the University of South Africa. The scale consists of 76 statements related specifically to

Erikson's first seven psychosocial stages and 17 validity items designed to assess social-desirability response tendencies. The individual is asked to indicate on a four-point scale the degree to which the statement applies to him or her. A score for each of the seven stages is then calculated. For a sample of items similar to those found in this questionnaire, see "You Can Do It" below.

Results obtained with the psychosocial questionnaire provide supporting evidence for Erikson's viewpoint (Ochse & Plug, 1986). For example, scores on a

YOU CAN DO IT

Assessing Identity vs. Role Confusion: Finding a Place in Society

Instructions
Respond to each of the 10 items below according to how frequently each statement applies to you:
0 = never applies; 1 = applies occasionally;
2 = applies fairly often; 3 = applies very often.

1. Others recognize my worth.
2. The opinion others have of me does not seem to change.
3. I feel sure about how others feel about me.
4. What I am doing in life, I feel, is worthwhile.
5. Wondering about the type of person I am is something I do not do.
6. The type of person I am seems to be agreed upon by most people.
7. Approving of me is something people seem to do.
8. Fitting well into the community in which I live is a feeling I have.
9. My way of life feels like it suits me.
10. Knowing what I should do with my life is something about which I feel certain.

Scoring
Add together the numerical values of your responses. The higher your score, the greater the degree to which you seem to have resolved this psychosocial crisis in the direction of identity.

Note. Adapted from *Cross-Cultural Investigations of the Validity of Erikson's Theory of Personality Development: Journal of Personality and Social Psychology,* by R. Ochse and C. Plug, 1986, *50,* 1240–1252.

Erikson's study of Gandhi's personality illustrated how Gandhi used his own ego strength to inspire the collective ego strength of a nation of Indians. According to Erikson, it was the collective identity of the Indian people that made it possible for India to break away from British rule.

measure of well-being were significantly correlated with scores on the intimacy scale for young adults and the generativity scale for middle-aged adults. This pattern of results suggests that well-being is strongest within groups of people when it is achieved during the critical stage for one's age as outlined by Erikson.

In a similar manner, scores on the identity scale were related more closely to the intimacy scores for young adults and generativity scores for middle-aged adults than the identity and intimacy scores for adolescents. This pattern of results supports Erikson's contention that establishing an identity is critical for successfully resolving subsequent psychosocial crises. Additional research suggests that scores on subscales for earlier stages of psychosocial development are positively correlated with scores on subscales for later stages of development (Whitbourne et al., 1992). This pattern of results supports the epigenetic principle of Erikson's viewpoint that successful resolution of early psychosocial crises is related to successful resolution of later crises.

Evaluation of Erikson's Psychosocial Viewpoint: Characteristic Strengths and Limitations

Characteristic Strengths
The psychosocial viewpoint has the following strengths:

▲ *A comprehensive viewpoint.* A major strength of Erikson's viewpoint is that it combines psychological, social, and historical factors. His viewpoint has general appeal; Erikson has influenced the thinking of not only personality psychologists but also historians, anthropologists, educators, sociologists, and gerontologists. The everyday use of the term *identity crisis* is evidence of just how much Erikson's thinking has ingrained itself in contemporary thinking.
▲ *Extending the periods of personality development.* By extending the notion of personality development across the life span, Erikson portrays a more realistic view of how people develop their personality. This approach has also done much to change the way the later years of life are viewed. Middle and late adulthood are no longer seen as simply the passing of time; because of

Erikson, they are now considered very active and significant times of personal growth.

Characteristic Limitations
Here are some limitations of the psychosocial viewpoint:

▲ *A rehash of Freud.* Erikson has been criticized as attempting to water down Freudian theory. His views on expanding the role of the ego and extending the psychosocial stages are all seen as simply taking ideas already proposed by Freud and giving them labels that the general population would find easier to accept (e.g., *social crises* rather than *sexual conflicts*). Such a criticism makes sense only from the perspective of the traditional Freudian viewpoint.
▲ *Using society as a measure of identity.* Erikson's critics say his viewpoint encourages the development of conformity rather than individuality. More specifically, Erikson has been criticized for maintaining that while the individual needs to establish an identity, that identity must be developed within the context of what is acceptable to society. Anything outside of this range is considered a negative identity. But as an individual who studied such nonconformists as Gandhi, Erikson can hardly be accused of emphasizing the status quo.

For more information about Erikson's rather unique and creative approach to the study of personality, read Erikson's *Childhood and Society* (1963), *Identity, Youth, and Crisis* (1968), and *Gandhi's Truth* (1969).

The Viewpoints of Sullivan and Fromm: Social Psychological Influences on Personality

Two other neo-Freudians who emphasized the role of social factors as critical determinants of personality were Harry Stack Sullivan and Erich Fromm. For a glimpse into these two personality theorists, read "A Closer Look" on page 149.

A Closer Look:

Biographical Background: The Lives of Harry Stack Sullivan and Erich Fromm

Sullivan was born on a farm in New York State in 1882. He was not a particularly good student but managed to receive an MD in 1917 from the Chicago College of Medicine, which was considered a "diploma mill." From the early 1920s until the 1930s, Sullivan held several hospital appointments and specialized in the treatment of schizophrenia. He disagreed with the dominant psychoanalytic view that schizophrenia could not be helped by psychotherapy and was able to show the benefit of such treatment in a number of patients.

During the 1930s and 1940s, Sullivan developed and refined his viewpoint of personality while pursuing a very busy professional life. In 1933, he helped in the founding of the William Alanson White Psychiatric Foundation, named after a neuropsychiatrist who had a great influence on Sullivan. In 1937, Sullivan founded the journal *Psychiatry*, which made it possible to express his own views. He also served his country by acting as a consultant to the Selective Service Board (the draft board) and to the United Nations Educational, Scientific, and Cultural Organization (UNESCO).

The last years of Sullivan's life were characterized by poor health; an adopted son and some devoted students provided his care. In 1949, upon returning from an executive meeting of the World Federation of Mental Health, Sullivan suddenly died. For more details about the life of Sullivan, read *Harry Stack Sullivan: His Life and Work* (Chapman, 1976).

Erich Fromm was born in Frankfort, Germany, in 1900. His childhood was not a happy one. He described his family environment as tense. His father was moody and his mother suffered from frequent episodes of intense depression. As an adolescent, Fromm was troubled by the suicide of a 25-year-old female friend of the family and the changes in the personalities of relatives, friends, and teachers as they began to express the hatred being promoted by the German government through propaganda during World War I. In college, he sought to find answers to the problems of personality adjustment experienced by his family members and friends. He received a PhD in political sociology in 1922 from the University of Heidelberg and obtained additional psychoanalytic training from the Berlin Psychoanalytic Institute.

Fromm immigrated to the United States in 1933 and taught at the Chicago Psychoanalytic Institute. After teaching at other universities, including Yale and Columbia, and establishing a private clinical practice in New York, he moved to Mexico City in 1949. There he joined the faculty of the National University of Mexico, where he established the department of psychiatric training at the medical school. He also became the director of the Mexico Psychoanalytic Institute. In the 1960s and 1970s, Fromm became very active in the peace movement and helped to establish SANE, the Organization for a Sane Nuclear Policy. In 1976, he moved to Switzerland, where he lived until his death in 1980.

Throughout his career, Fromm combined his interests in political sociology, philosophy, and psychoanalytic thinking to try to understand why people would be willing to give up their freedom to accept and support totalitarian leaders (e.g., the German people's support of Hitler). He wrote a number of books outlining his views. As a result of his ability to convey his ideas to the general public, some of his books have become bestsellers. More on the life of Erich Fromm can be found in *Dialogue with Erich Fromm* (Evans, 1966).

Harry Stack Sullivan's viewpoint of personality emphasized the role significant others play in the development of one's personality.

Erich Fromm proposed a viewpoint of personality that emphasized the interpersonal choices individuals make to cope with feelings of loneliness, isolation, and anxiety.

Sullivan's Interpersonal Theory: Recognizing the Power of Other People

Sullivan (1953) defined personality as "the relatively enduring pattern of recurrent interpersonal situations which characterize a person's life" (p. 11). Sullivan's viewpoint of personality is considered an **interpersonal theory** because he placed a considerable emphasis on the interactions among people as critical determinants of personality (Sullivan, 1953, 1964). These interactions could be with people from the past (e.g., a deceased parent) or present environment (e.g., a lover or boss) and/or people who are real or fictitious (e.g., that special person one fantasizes about meeting someday). For example, in times of stress, a person might mentally reconstruct a conversation with a favorite grade school teacher that now serves as a source of strength. The point is that interactions with others can powerfully influence a person's thoughts, feelings, and behaviors.

Basic Concepts: Seeking Stability in Interactions

Two fundamental concepts of Sullivan's theory included dynamism and personification. A **dynamism** is a basic tendency of behavior, such as a habit, in response to particular social interactions. An example might be the tendency of an individual who gets nervous and remains silent when in one-to-one interactions. If this behavior pattern occurs in a wide variety of situations (e.g., at work, school, or parties), such an individual might be described as having a personality (basic tendency) characterized by shyness.

The most extensive dynamism is that of the self. The **self** generates thoughts and integrates behavior patterns designed to maintain security and reduce anxiety. A very insecure individual might construct a sense of self that is extremely rigid so as to avoid new situations and the anxiety and tension they create. On the other hand, a very reassured self may seek out diversity for opportunities to demonstrate a sense of mastery and achievement.

Personification is the manner in which a person perceives himself or herself as a result of repeated interactions with significant others. More specifically, a person's sense of self begins to reflect the appraisals and evaluations offered by significant others. Interactions that are favorable create the person-

ification of the "good me," while negative interactions help to foster the personification of the "bad me."

For example, a child who is criticized repeatedly by parents and teachers is most likely to develop a "bad me" personification and develop a low level of achievement. On the other hand, the many favorable comments a student receives from professors and other students will create a personification of "good me" and increase the likelihood of the student's thinking she has a really good chance of getting a job after college. Interactions with a particular individual that are generally favorable can lead to the personification of this individual as a "good friend."

The personification of the "not me" represents experiences and interactions from which people wish to dissociate (e.g., repression). For example, a student may succumb to cheating on an exam and later try to repress it into his unconscious to avoid feelings of severe guilt.

Modes of Thinking: Three Methods Influencing the Quality of Interpersonal Communications

Sullivan observed that thinking in different ways could influence the nature and quality of interpersonal relations.

The **prototaxic mode** of thinking is characterized by a very primitive form of thinking that seems rather personal and makes communication with others difficult. This mode of thinking is characteristic of very young children and severely disturbed mental patients. But it is also exhibited when people are arguing and seem to be unwilling or unable to see the opposing point of view because of being stuck in their own way of thinking. In such situations, rigid adherence to one's own point of view makes communication with others very difficult.

The **parataxic mode** of thinking is characterized by a very low level of causal reasoning that often makes communication difficult. An example of parataxic thinking would be a woman who expresses anger and hostility toward a coworker for receiving a promotion that she wanted. The faulty causal reasoning in this situation is that the angry woman assumes it is the coworker's fault she did not receive the promotion. In reality, it was the personnel manager who made the decision and toward whom the anger should be addressed.

The **syntaxic mode** of thinking is characterized by a shared level of communication and effective interaction. An example of the syntaxic mode of thinking would be two writers thinking along the same lines when working on a screenplay. The syntaxic mode is considered to be the highest mode of thinking and creates the greatest degree of interpersonal communication.

Interpersonal Stages of Personality Development: Acquiring the Skills to Be a Friend and Lover

Sullivan also proposed that personality development occurs by passing through a series of stages. During the infancy stage (the first year of life), the individual's primary mode of thinking is prototaxic and involves personifications of the environment based on bodily reactions (e.g., "good parent" meets the hunger needs). The end of the infancy period is characterized by the onset of speech.

During the childhood stage (2 to 6 years of age), children are taught basic communication skills (e.g., to say "please" and "thank you") and interpersonal skills (e.g., to share). Parataxic thinking also starts to emerge at this point (e.g., when the child learns that dropping the drinking cup makes a funny sound). Personifications also begin to develop as the child labels those children with whom he or she plays as "friends" or a stranger as "bad."

During the juvenile stage (6 to 8 years of age), children begin to enter school and start to interact with many more people outside the home. Personification of the self (e.g., good me/bad me) is determined to a large degree by feedback from others (e.g., being teased or being selected first when choosing teams for kickball). During this stage, interpersonal interactions become more complex and social skills are refined (e.g., learning to settle an argument among playmates concerning the rules of a game). Thus, the three stages during childhood are characterized by the emergence of skills that are necessary for interacting with others in social settings

During the adolescent years, the development of personal relationships begins to occur. In the preadolescence stage (9 to 12 years of age), the development of more personal relationships often occurs with same-sex children. The personification of such children is usually that of "best friends." Such same-sex friendships provide a relatively secure environment to begin to explore very personal feelings, such as initial discussions of one's sexuality (Carducci, 1986).

During the early adolescence stage (12 to 18 years of age), changes in the bodies of boys and girls with the onset of puberty trigger increased interest in members of the opposite sex and the development of interpersonal behaviors designed to explore this interest (e.g., going steady). Personification of certain special people as "boyfriend" or "girlfriend" helps to direct the appropriate behaviors for fostering more intimate relationships later in life (e.g., considering the needs and desires of a spouse). During the late adolescence stage (18 to 22 years of age), long-term intimate relationships with specific people begin to appear. Personifications of such people might include "lover," "housemate," or "fiance/fiancee."

If these stages are completed successfully, the individual is prepared to form more intimate and complex interpersonal relationships in adulthood (Rychlak, 1981). During the adulthood stage (22+ years of age), relatively permanent relationships begin to be established emotionally and sexually (e.g., get married, start a family) and financially (e.g., start a career, purchase a home). Personifications at this stage might include "loving spouse," "family friends," "precious children," "prestigious office," and "our lovely home."

Thus, like Freud and Erikson, Sullivan also formulated a stage theory of personality development. But even before Erikson, Sullivan proposed that these stages were interpersonal in nature instead of psychosexual.

Fromm's Sociological Theory: Recognizing the Desire for and Fear of Freedom

From a sociological perspective, Fromm proposed that the fundamental dilemma of human nature is the struggle between wanting to be free and the desire to belong (Fromm, 1941).

The Basic Needs: Freedom to Be vs. the Desire to Belong

Freedom of choice brings with it the personal responsibility for the consequences of those choices. Freedom can also increase the sense of separation people begin to feel from each other and can threaten their sense of belonging. Threats to this sense of belonging create feelings of isolation and loneliness and the belief that one is alone or insignificant (Fromm, 1941).

Such feelings of alienation produce anxiety. As an example of this dilemma consider Jacob, who moves away from home to a much larger city in order to accept a promotion within the company. In this case, although the new promotion involves more money and the greater freedom of choice associated with having money, Jacob has much more responsibility than before and less of the hometown social support of his family and long-time friends. Such a situation can create feelings of anxiety and loneliness.

Character Types: Strategies for Coping with Anxiety and Isolation

In an attempt to deal with the anxiety produced by feelings of isolation, Fromm (1947) proposed that people develop certain dominant strategies (i.e., personality styles) that he classified as character types.

The **receptive character type** requires constant support from others, such as family members, friends, and/or the government, but does not reciprocate that support. Such an individual is rather passive and dependent on others and is very willing to give up freedom (e.g., stay in abusive relationships) for the sake of security (e.g., the abuser pays the bills).

The **exploitative character type** also takes from others but does so in a more exploitative and manipulative manner. Such an individual will lie and cheat (e.g., falsely profess love) or seek out people who are vulnerable (e.g., those with very low self-esteem) to fulfill the need for belonging.

The **hoarding character type** deals with insecurity by keeping all they produce and possess to themselves. These people tend to be selfish, aloof, and suspicious of others. They might establish a sense of security by collecting large numbers of possessions (e.g., a big house, many clothes) and forming emotional bonds with them (e.g., establishing an identity by the type of car they drive) instead of with other people.

The **marketing character type** perceives interpersonal relationships based on their exchange value (e.g., marrying for money) and modifies their personality accordingly (e.g., being overly friendly to those who can be of some help). These individuals are characterized by a personality that is shallow, empty, and anxious.

The **productive character type** deals with feelings of anxiety and loneliness by engaging in productive work (e.g., creative self-expression) and fostering loving and compassionate relationships (e.g., being a supportive friend, parent, spouse, employer, coworker, and/or teacher). The personality of this type of individual is characterized by caring, creativity, and being responsible. Of all the various character types, only the productive type is considered to be a healthy strategy for dealing with the issue of freedom vs. alienation.

Like the other neo-Freudians, Fromm's viewpoint of personality emphasizes the critical role social relationships play in determining the development and operation of personality.

Evaluation of the Viewpoints of Sullivan and Fromm: Characteristic Strengths and Limitations

A characteristic strength of both Sullivan and Fromm is the elaborated sense of importance they gave to interpersonal relationships as a critical factor in the development and operation of personality. In addition, both theorists provided considerable insights into the nature and dynamics of the strategies people would develop for fostering these important interpersonal relationships.

The characteristic limitation of the viewpoints of both Sullivan and Fromm is that neither theorist did much to provide empirical support for his respective viewpoint.

As a final comment on the Freud/neo-Freudian relationship, one of the major contributions of Freud's work was the impact it had on the thinking of others. Freud's impact was not limited to his contemporaries, such as Jung and Adler; rather it extended to a new generation—the neo-Freudians. More specifically, Freud's influence appears in Horney's elaboration of feminine psychology, Erikson's extension of the stages of personality development, Sullivan's emphasis on interpersonal relationships, and Fromm's attention to broader societal concerns.

Chapter Summary:
Reexamining the Highlights

▲ KAREN HORNEY'S SOCIAL PSYCHOLOGICAL VIEWPOINT

—*Basic Assumptions*. The basic assumptions of Horney's viewpoint include the individual's personality being motivated by a tendency to seek a sense of security, the importance of early parent-child interactions in determining personality adjustment in adulthood, and the significance of culture in shaping personality.

—*Basic Concepts*. The basic concepts of personality proposed by Horney include feelings of basic hostility and basic anxiety and coping with these feelings through the use of neurotic tendencies, including moving toward people, moving against people, and moving away from people in the form of healthy or maladjusted strategies.

—*The Nature of Personality Adjustment*. The degree of personality adjustment is reflected in the amount of overlap between the real self and the ideal self.

—*The Application of Horney's Social Psychological Viewpoint*. Self analysis is the therapeutic process by which the individual gains insights into the perceptions of the real and ideal self and the strategies used to seek a sense of security. Horney's perspective on the female personality emphasizes the importance of social roles as critical determinants of personality development.

—*Evaluation of Horney's Social Psychological Viewpoint*. The characteristic strengths of Horney's viewpoint include her reinterpretation of the female personality and recognition of the importance of social factors. Characteristic limitations of her viewpoint include a lack of empirical research being generated to test it. Recent applications of Horney's viewpoint have served to offset this criticism.

▲ ERIKSON'S PSYCHOSOCIAL VIEWPOINT

—*Basic Assumptions*. The basic assumptions of Erikson's viewpoint include increasing the role played by the ego, developing the ego in a psychosocial context, and expanding the nature of personality development throughout the life span, all of which serve to extend basic principles of Freudian thought.

—*Basic Concepts of Erikson's Psychosocial Viewpoint*. The eight psychosocial stages are characterized by their epigenetic nature of development, the resolution of crises involving the needs of the person and the expectations of society, and the acquisition of basic virtues when these crises are successfully resolved.

—*Applications of Erikson's Psychosocial Viewpoint*. Play therapy is designed to help children express their emotional concerns through symbolic free-play activities. Psychohistories involve analyzing in a retrospective manner the lives of historical figures through the use of techniques of psychoanalysis and history. Recent research has attempted to develop assessment techniques designed to measure and validate Erikson's psychosocial stages of development.

—*Evaluation of Erikson's Psychosocial Viewpoint*. The characteristic strengths of Erikson's viewpoint are that his thinking combines the importance of psychological, social, and historical factors and the extension of the psychosocial stages of development to the later years. Characteristic limitations include the perception of his viewpoint as just a reinterpretation of basic Freudian thought and an overemphasis on personality development reflecting conformity to the expectations of society.

▲ THE VIEWPOINTS OF SULLIVAN AND FROMM

—*Sullivan's Interpersonal Theory*. The basic concepts of Sullivan's interpersonal viewpoint include the presence of behavior tendencies characterized by dynamisms and the perceptual tendencies of the self and others through personifications.

The three modes of thinking that serve to influence interpersonal relationships are the prototaxic mode, parataxic mode, and syntaxic mode.

Sullivan proposed six stages of personality development through which people pass as they acquire the skills necessary for establishing and maintaining interpersonal relationships.

—*Fromm's Sociological Theory*. Fromm characterized basic human needs as the desire to be free and independent and the fear of responsibility and loneliness such freedom brings.

The different strategies people develop to cope with these basic needs include the receptive, exploitative, hoarding, marketing, and productive character types.

—*Evaluating the Viewpoints of Sullivan and Fromm.* The characteristic strength of the viewpoints of Sullivan and Fromm include their emphasis on interpersonal relationships. A characteristic limitation is that neither of these two viewpoints has generated much empirical support.

Glossary

autonomy vs. shame and doubt   The second psychosocial crisis, involving the extent to which the child acquires an initial sense of independence.

basic anxiety   Feelings of insecurity in response to a threatening social environment.

basic hostility   Feelings experienced by children in reaction to parents when they do not create a secure environment for them.

basic virtues   The personal attributes a person gains after the successful resolution of each psychosocial crisis.

codependency   A tendency to become involved in dysfunctional interpersonal relationships in which personal sacrifices by one person give emotional support to the other person.

dynamism   A characteristic manner of behavior for responding to certain interpersonal situations.

ego identity vs. role confusion   The fifth psychosocial crisis involves the extent to which an adolescent develops an initial sense of belonging to the community.

ego integrity   The sense of satisfaction and little regret over the way life has been lived by the elderly, which reduces a fear of death in one's self and increases the zest for living in others.

ego integrity vs. despair   The eighth psychosocial crisis, involving the extent to which the elderly can look back on life with satisfaction and a lack of regrets.

ego psychology   A viewpoint of personality that emphasizes the importance and independent functioning of the ego.

epigenetic principle   The sequential and progressive development of personality through a specific set of stages.

exploitative character type   Persons who base their interactions on taking advantage of others in a manipulative manner.

fidelity   The basic virtue of being able to commit to the ideals and values of others to establish a sense of belonging.

generativity vs. stagnation   The seventh psychosocial crisis, involving the extent to which knowledge gained through life is shared with younger people as a means of commitment to future generations.

hoarding character type   Persons who maintain a sense of security from others through selfishness.

identity crisis   An individual lacking a sense of place or belonging in the community or society.

idealized self   An assessment of the ideal type of person one would like to be.

industry vs. inferiority   The fourth psychosocial crisis, involving the extent to which the child acquires a sense of mastery over basic technical skills such as reading, math, and reasoning.

initiative vs. guilt   The third psychosocial crisis, involving the extent to which the child acquires the basic skills of planning and problem solving.

interpersonal theory   Sullivan's viewpoint of personality, emphasizing the role played by interpersonal relationships and the strategies for coping with them.

intimacy vs. isolation   The sixth psychosocial crisis, involving the degree to which the identity of one person is combined with that of another within an intimate relationship.

marketing character type   Persons who base their interactions on what can be exchanged in the relationship.

morbid dependency   The seeking of security through excessive dependency on others within exploitative relationships.

moving against people   A behavioral tendency for dealing with feelings of security by responding with aggression and hostility for the purpose of obtaining an emotional advantage over others.

moving away from people   A behavioral tendency for dealing with feelings of insecurity by withdrawing emotionally and physically from others.

moving toward people   A behavioral tendency for dealing with feelings of insecurity by agreeing with people for the purpose of obtaining their affection.

negative identity   Establishing an identity that is the direct opposite of what others expect, as a form of expressing independence.

neo-Freudians   A group of personality theorists emphasizing the importance of interpersonal processes as determinants of personality.

neurotic trends   A set of irrational needs and desires developed in an attempt to establish a sense of security.

parataxic mode   A form of thinking characterized by a misrepresentation of causality.

personification   The perception of certain people or situations in a specific manner based on repeated interactions with them.

play therapy   A form of psychotherapy in which children express their thoughts and emotions through free-play activities.

productive character type   Persons who base their interactions on concern for and care of others.

prototaxic mode   A form of thinking that emphasizes a person's own perspective while ignoring others.

psychohistory   An investigation into the lives of historical figures through the use of methods of psychoanalysis and history.

psychosocial crisis   A developmental task that involves balancing the needs of the individual and the expectations of society.

psychosocial development   A process of personality development that places increased emphasis on interpersonal and social factors.

real self   An assessment of the type of person one perceives himself or herself as being.

receptive character type   Persons who base their interactions on demanding support from others.

self   In Sullivan's theory, a specific dynamism for processing information and generating responses in a manner characteristic of the individual.

self-analysis   Horney's form of psychotherapy, designed to increase the accuracy of self-perceptions and the effectiveness of interpersonal strategies for gaining a sense of security.

syntaxic mode   A form of thinking characterized by reciprocal communication.

trust vs. mistrust   The first psychosocial crisis, involving the extent to which the infant learns to develop a sense of trust and hope that security will be provided by significant others.

tyranny of the should   A set of excessive expectations a person has about the type of person he or she should be.

womb envy   The sense of envy males feel for the ability of women to give birth.

CHAPTER 6

The Phenomenological Viewpoint of Carl R. Rogers: Putting the Person at the Center of Personality

CHAPTER OVERVIEW: A PREVIEW OF COMING ATTRACTIONS

" *The organism reacts to the field as it is experienced and perceived. This perceptual field is, for the individual, 'reality'" (Rogers, 1951, p. 484). This quote illustrates Carl R. Rogers' phenomenological viewpoint of personality. The* **phenomenological perspective** *stresses that a person's feelings and behavior are determined by how the individual perceives and interprets events. The significance of this assumption is that it makes the person the "undisputed expert" on his or her feelings and behavior. Placing the person's perceptions at the center of the study of personality was in sharp contrast to the dominant Freudian viewpoint at the time, which discounted much of the individual's conscious perception and interpretation of events.*

This chapter begins by examining the basic assumptions and concepts of Rogers' viewpoint, followed by a discussion of the motivational properties of the self-actualization tendency. Next is a discussion of personality development from the Rogerian viewpoint, followed by an examination of Rogers' views on the nature of personality adjustment. Some applications of Rogers' viewpoint are then presented. Chapter 6 concludes with an evaluation of the characteristic strengths and limitations of the Rogerian viewpoint.

For a glimpse into the life of Carl Rogers, who proposed a rather revolutionary perspective to the study of personality, read "A Closer Look" on page 158.

A Closer Look:

Biographical Background: The Life of Carl R. Rogers

Carl Ransom Rogers was born on January 8, 1902, in the Chicago suburb of Oak Park, Illinois. He was the fourth of six children in what he described as a close-knit family. His childhood environment was financially secure and characterized by an almost fundamentalist atmosphere stressing hard work and conservative values. Rogers' parents discouraged the children from developing friendships outside of the family, because "outsiders" engaged in activities that they did not approve, including playing cards, smoking, and going to movies. Such solitude resulted in Rogers becoming an avid reader and a socially independent individual.

When Rogers was 12 years old, his parents moved the family to a farm. Because of his father's emphasis on running the farm scientifically, Rogers became very interested in science and agriculture, reading about many agricultural experiments and studying insects on his own. With his tendency toward solitude and a love of reading, Rogers had only two dates in high school, but he was almost a straight-A student. His chief interests as a student were in English and science.

Following in the family tradition of his parents, two brothers, and a sister, Rogers enrolled at the University of Wisconsin in 1919 to study agriculture. While at college, Rogers became active in church work, then switched his academic emphasis and began to prepare for the ministry. In 1922, Rogers was selected as one of ten students to attend the World Student Christian Federation Conference in Peking, China. Having the opportunity to experience a wide variety of cultural backgrounds while at college and during the conference, Rogers found himself slipping away from the fundamentalist beliefs of his parents and becoming more liberal in his philosophy. In 1924, Rogers received his BA degree in history.

Shortly after graduation, Rogers married Helen Elliott, a childhood sweetheart. The two of them drove in a secondhand Model-T coupe to New York, where Rogers was to begin studying for the ministry at Union Theological Seminary in 1924. Becoming doubtful that his seminary training was preparing him to help people, Rogers transferred to Columbia University Teachers College to study clinical and educational

psychology. He earned his MA in 1928 and a PhD in 1931. Rogers' doctoral dissertation was concerned with measuring personality adjustment in children.

Rogers' first professional appointment was at the Rochester Guidance Center in the Child Study Department of the Society for the Prevention of Cruelty to Children. He started as a student intern and eventually became the center's director. The center's highly Freudian approach, stressing unconscious forces, was in sharp contrast to the very scientific and statistical training Rogers received at Columbia. It was during this time that Rogers began to question the effectiveness of psychodynamic approaches to emotional problems. His interactions with the rather diverse staff at the center led Rogers to begin trying to assess and document the critical factors in the therapeutic environment. The outcome of this effort was Rogers' first book, *The Clinical Treatment of the Problem Child* (1939).

In 1940, Rogers left the clinical setting for an academic appointment at Ohio State University, where he began to develop and test his view of personality. Rogers left Ohio State University and accepted a position as professor of psychology and director of the counseling center at the University of Chicago in 1945. While at the counseling center, Rogers, with the aid of many fine research-oriented clinical psychology graduate students, expanded the systematic investigation and verification of his viewpoint. The outcome of this work was a textbook titled *Client-Centered Therapy: Its Current Practice, Implications, and Theory* (1951), which is considered Rogers' most important textbook. In this book, Rogers took a very scientific approach to studying the processes, dynamics, and effectiveness of his approach to psychotherapy.

In 1957, Rogers left the University of Chicago to return to the University of Wisconsin, where he was

Carl Rogers' lasting contribution to the study of personality psychology was his effort to verify and integrate his viewpoint of personality with social concerns of the individual and society.

both professor of psychology and professor of psychiatry. However, becoming disenchanted with the departmental politics of the university environment, Rogers resigned his professorships and accepted a position with the Western Behavioral Sciences Institute in La Jolla, California, in 1963. In 1968, Rogers and several others from the institute left to form the Center for the Studies of the Person, located in La Jolla. At the center, he continued to devote his life to investigating how to make psychotherapy more effective and understanding human nature more completely.

After devoting more than fifty years of his life to the study of the person, Rogers died on February 4, 1987. In recognition of his contribution to psychology, Rogers has received numerous awards. These awards include being elected president of the American Psychological Association (APA) and awarded the APA's Distinguished Scientific Contribution Award and Distinguished Professional Contribution Award.

More about the life of Carl Rogers can be found in an autobiography (Rogers, 1967) appearing in Boring and Lindzey's *A History of Psychology in Autobiography* and in a book chapter by Nathaniel J. Raskin and Carl R. Rogers (1995) titled "Person-Centered Therapy."

Basic Assumptions: The Person = Personality

The assumptions of his theory illustrate clearly the emphasis Rogers placed on the person as being the center of attention in the study of personality (Raskin & Rogers, 1989, 1995; Rogers, 1951, 1959). A discussion of these basic assumptions follows.

The Reality of Subjective Experience

Subjective experience refers to the unique way each person views the world and his or her experiences in it. As a result of each person having a unique way of perceiving these experiences, the responses to these subjective experiences will also be unique: One person might respond to the loss of a job with anxiety and depression due to perceiving this as a great loss of security. Another person may respond with a sense of optimism at the challenges a new job might

bring. Thus, from the phenomenological perspective, it becomes more important to know how the person views the event than it is to know the nature of the event itself. Or in Rogers' own words, "The best vantage point for understanding behavior is from the internal frame of reference of the individual himself" (1951, p. 494).

Emphasis on the Here and Now

Related to Rogers' emphasis on the subjective experience was his emphasis on the here and now of each person's experiences. Rogers stressed the importance of events as they are perceived and experienced by the person now, not as they were perceived in the past. He did not ignore the past; he simply felt that more could be gained by investigating the individual's perception and reactions to events in the present. For example, although the parents of a college student put pressure on her to succeed when she was in grade school, her anxiety over a test next week has more to do with her views of the current state of affairs of her life at college, such as perceiving a lack of time to squeeze in going to work, participating in a volunteer program with friends, and studying for the test.

The Actualizing Tendency

"The organism has one basic tendency and striving—to actualize, maintain, and enhance the experiencing organism" (Rogers, 1951, p. 487). The motivation underlying the desire for self-improvement is the actualizing tendency (Raskin & Rogers, 1989). The **actualizing tendency** motivates the development of each aspect (e.g., social, spiritual, and intellectual) and capability (e.g., physical and mental) of the person in a direction of increasing autonomy through self-awareness. For example, by learning a new job skill (i.e., an occupational aspect of the person) and gaining more confidence in making her own decisions (i.e., a mental capability), a woman who is being physically abused by her husband can start taking more control over her life. Such changes will make it possible for her to live her life with a greater possibility for exploring and expanding her potential for personal growth than in the past.

The Organismic Valuing Process

To help guide the actualizing tendency, Rogers assumed the operation of a mechanism called the organismic valuing process. The purpose of the **organismic valuing process** is to evaluate subjective experiences as to their short-term and long-term potential for helping the individual toward self-enhancement (Raskin & Rogers, 1989; Rogers, 1959). Experiences judged as consistent with the objective of self-enhancement are evaluated positively, while those judged as inconsistent with this objective are evaluated negatively. For example, a person's decision to stop drinking at a party, even when there is peer pressure to continue drinking, is based on an assessment of the organismic valuing process that the short-term gain of peer acceptance is outweighed by the long-term risks to the self associated with getting drunk (e.g., being arrested for drunk driving). Rogers was a firm believer that given the choice between what is good and bad for the individual, the emotionally healthy and highly self-aware individual would *always freely choose* those alternatives evaluated as promoting the actualizing tendency.

Basic Concepts: Defining Your Sense of Self

Like his basic assumptions, the concepts upon which Rogers developed his viewpoint of personality also emphasized the perceptions of the individual as being central to any attempt to understand personality (Raskin & Rogers, 1995).

The Phenomenal Field

Linked to subjective experience is what Rogers referred to as the phenomenal field (Rogers, 1951, 1959). The **phenomenal field** represents all of the possible sensory experiences that a person is aware of at any given moment. They can be occurring both inside (e.g., test anxiety) and outside (e.g., the announcement of a test) the individual. An impor-

tant feature of the phenomenal field is that it is constantly changing. These changes can significantly affect the thoughts, feelings, and behavior of the individual. For example, the depression experienced by a firefighter can be lessened during group therapy when feedback from others helps her come to the realization that, even with the best of efforts, not everyone can be saved every time. By changing the phenomenal field in the direction of bravery instead of failure, the therapist is able to remove the depression and raise the person's self-esteem.

Subception

Rogers also assumed that the perceptual processes of the phenomenal field could operate at a level outside of conscious awareness, in the form of subception. Rogers (1951) defined **subception** as "a discriminating evaluative physiological organismic response to experience, which may precede the conscious perception of such experience" (p. 507). This means that the individual may respond to something before it is actually consciously perceived. For example, sensing anxiety, a college student represses information about an assignment due early next week and agrees to participate in social events. Thus, to avoid the conscious-level feelings of anxiety, the student becomes preoccupied with other activities. The point is that decisions and actions are influenced by emotional and mental factors about which the person may not be completely aware.

The Self-Concept

"A portion of the total perceptual field gradually becomes differentiated as the self" (Rogers, 1951, p. 497). For Rogers, the unique sense of self is something that does not just happen; it is part of a continuous process forged through the experiences with the phenomenal field. Thus, a sense of self is achieved through the individual's encounters with and interpretations of life's events. The establishment of a sense of self involves the dynamic interaction of two somewhat different components of the self-concept: the organism and the self.

Closely related to the organismic valuing process is that aspect of the self-concept referred to as the organism. The **organism** is that part of the self-concept concerned with helping the individual to evaluate and categorize various experiences. The information gained from these experiences is used in helping the individual to define a sense of self. Suppose that in one semester, an individual takes courses in history, geology, and psychology but finds that only the psychology course is really enjoyable. In the next semester, the individual takes courses in math, psychology, and political science, and again enjoys only the psychology. After a few more favorable encounters with psychology, being a "psych major" becomes part of the individual's self-image. Thus, when experiences are incorporated into the individual's self-image by the organism, they become part of what Rogers called the "self."

The **self** is the sense of personal identity represented within the phenomenal field. The pronouns *I, me,* and *my* are all used to distinguish between each person's sense of self and all other objects in the phenomenal field. The unique perception of the individual's sense of self is a result of the ongoing organismic evaluative process and the interpretation of the information it provides. For example, through a variety of experiences and affective reactions to them, an individual's self could be represented by such labels as philosophy major, animal-rights activist, movie buff, lover of art, reader of mystery novels, hospital volunteer, and environmentalist. These various aspects of the self all help to produce personal opinions (e.g., views on fines for environmental polluters) and patterns of behavior (e.g., visiting certain types of museums while on vacation) that make each person unique.

Congruence and Incongruence

The different components of the self-concept are also related to the extent to which the individual is motivated to maintain a degree of consistency between the evaluative nature of the experiences by the organism and their incorporation into the individual's sense of self. When there is a close match between how a person feels about something and how these feelings are related to the sense of self, Rogers (1959) described this as a state of **congruence** within the individual. For example, having feelings of outrage over discrimination practices in the workplace is congruent with an individual's self-perception of not being a sexist or racist.

On the other hand, Rogers believed that a state of **incongruence** exists when there is some degree of discrepancy between a person's feelings about something and the sense of self. For example, a happily married individual might find feelings of sexual arousal for a coworker as being incongruent with the self-perception of being a faithful spouse and moral individual. Incongruence leads to feelings of anxiety that the individual is motivated to reduce in order to bring the sense of self together (Rogers, 1959). The self-concept seeks to reduce this incongruence through the process of self-actualization.

Self-Actualization: The Motivational Component of Personality

The actualizing tendency reflects Rogers' belief that people are motivated in the direction of self-understanding and self-enhancement (Raskin & Rogers, 1995). **Self-actualization** refers to the motivational process by which this actualizing tendency is expressed. The principal objective of self-actualization is to help the individual meet this fundamental need of self-enhancement by maintaining continuous progress toward personal growth and improvement.

The process of self-actualization is facilitated by openness to emotional experiences and characterized by being ongoing in nature, expressed in a unique way by each person, and holistic in its response. These four features of the self-actualization process are discussed next.

▲ *The necessity of experiential freedom and openness.* Rogers believed that the process of self-actualization is most likely to occur when the individual is willing to be completely free and open to his or her emotions and other experiences in the phenomenal field. For example, without having to distort and deny the reasons for selecting a particular major (e.g., to please family members), a college student is in a much better position to select a course of study that will allow personal interests and talents to flourish. Thus, experiential freedom reflects an honest and unbiased approach to the events in one's life.

▲ *The ongoing process of self-actualization.* Self-actualization is an ongoing process because the individual is innately motivated to move continuously in the direction of self-enhancement and personal growth. In this regard, as the individual experiences self-enhancement and personal growth, there is the tendency to want to become better. For example, no matter how good they are, outstanding teachers always search for ways to improve their teaching effectiveness.

▲ *The unique expression of self-actualization.* The uniqueness feature of the self-actualization process reflects Rogers' belief that each of us seeks self-enhancement in our unique way. For example, when trying to get better grades in school, one student might enroll in a memory improvement course, another might seek out the professor after class for some special study tips, and a third student might endeavor to spend more time studying by working fewer hours at an off-campus job.

▲ *The holistic nature of self-actualization.* The holistic nature of self-actualization refers to people's tendency to use all of their capabilities in a coordinated effort when moving toward self-enhancement. For example, in order to succeed in college, a student must coordinate cognitive abilities (e.g., studying for exams) with psychological abilities (e.g., the motivation to find time to study), and physical abilities (e.g., eating right and getting enough rest to stay healthy). If any aspect of this coordinated effort breaks down (e.g., losing the motivation to study), the student's progress toward personal growth is affected.

The self-actualization process is a fundamental part of each person's expression of uniqueness and desire for personal growth. It is facilitated through successful personality development. Rogers' views on personality development are presented in the next section.

Personality Development: Developing Experiential Freedom

In a very general sense, the principal theme in Rogers' views on personality development concerns the reciprocal interaction between those needs reflecting the individual's desire for the regard of others and those needs reflecting a desire for personal regard (Mruk, 1995; Rogers, 1961). Central to this process are the concepts of need for positive regard, conditional and unconditional positive regard, need for self-regard, and conditions of worth.

The Regard of Others: External Considerations in the Development of the Self

For Rogers, an important part of personality development is the relationship we have with others and the nature of the feelings they have for us.

Need for Positive Regard

The **need for positive regard** is the basic desire each person has for receiving the warmth, acceptance, sympathy, liking, and respect of others (Rogers, 1959). To put it simply, as an individual begins to develop and accept a sense of self, he or she wants others to accept it as well. For example, children engage in behaviors (e.g., clear their plates) that will elicit a smile or praise from their parents. As adults, we might express this need by buying some new clothes with the hope that our friends will say how much they like them too. The experience of positive regard can take one of two forms: unconditional or conditional positive regard.

▲ **Unconditional positive regard** is when a person receives the positive regard of others without any limitations attached to it. Unconditional positive regard is the acceptance of people for who they are, not for what others would like them to be. For example in successful relationships, good friends realize that they will not agree on all issues. With children, unconditional positive regard occurs when they realize that even though they may be afraid of the dark or dislike eating broccoli, their parents still love them. In both instances, unconditional positive regard involves giving acceptance with no strings attached. When such a situation exists, people are free to experience openly and freely the true nature of their feelings.

▲ **Conditional positive regard** involves placing limitations on the regard people give to others. For example, when a parent says, "I won't love you if you keep making that noise," the child can interpret this to mean that conditions of acceptance are being imposed. In a more complex example, when someone says, "If you really love me, you'd have sex with me," this person is really putting a price tag on the affection and acceptance to be granted. Such examples come close to what might be called emotional blackmail. As people become more and more responsive to conditional positive regard, they run the risk of having their sense of self defined by others and being the type of person others want them to be, not the type they really want to be. Such a situation is a serious barrier to the process of self-actualization.

The Regard of Self: Internal Considerations in the Development of the Self

So that personality development is not based totally on our relationships with others, Rogers also stipulated the need for positive regard.

The Need for Positive Self-Regard

The **need for positive self-regard** is the desire we have as individuals to be accepting of our own experiences based on an internal valuing process. In this sense, everyone begins to judge for themselves what they like and dislike and what they will—and will not—incorporate into the sense of self. Based on the need for positive self-regard, each person develops self-acceptance and a unique identity. This process is most likely to occur when the individual experiences

unconditional positive regard from others. An example would be supporting a spouse's decision to quit work for two years to pursue a lifelong dream of a career in acting.

Conditions of Worth

People can facilitate the process of self-actualization in others; they can also hinder it. More specifically, **conditions of worth** develop when significant others (e.g., parents, a lover, or a spouse) give a person labels that become incorporated into that person's self-concept. This occurs because the person begins to equate conditional positive regard and positive self-regard. That is, a person experiences a sense of self-acceptance only when meeting the expectations others have set as a condition of acceptance. An example of this process would be a young man who feels a sense of manhood only when he goes along with peer pressure to engage in various petty crimes. Because conditions of worth can undermine the true organismic valuing process, Rogers (1959) felt that conditions of worth can threaten the efforts toward self-actualization.

From Rogers' perspective, personality development is a continuous process by which the person strives to promote self-actualization by acquiring a degree of experiential freedom (i.e., openness to experience) for the organismic valuing process. In the next section, you will learn about some benefits of successful personality development by considering the nature of personality adjustment.

The Nature of Personality Adjustment: Some Characteristics and Consequences of Experiential Freedom

For Rogers, the degree of successful personality adjustment was directly related to the amount of experiential freedom available during the process of personality development. Rogers defined quite clearly the characteristic features and consequences associated with successful and unsuccessful personality development.

Personality Adjustment and the Fully Functioning Person: Living the Good Life

Being free and open to experience maximizes the possibility that the individual will maintain congruence within the self-concept. Rogers (1959, 1961, 1964) referred to the **fully functioning person** as an individual constantly experiencing a high degree of congruence. The fully functioning person, according to Rogers, has a high degree of mental health and personality adjustment. Rogers (1959, 1961, 1964) identified the following characteristic features of the fully functioning person:

▲ *Congruence of self and experience.* Fully functioning people can incorporate the true nature of their experiences into their sense of self. For example, the loving parent recognizes that sometimes anger will be expressed toward and punishment given to misbehaving children.

▲ *Open to experiences.* Because these people are self-accepting, they are not threatened by their experiences and are able to experience them openly. For example, the happily married individual can accept the sexual arousal he or she feels when looking at a picture of a favorite movie star.

▲ *Existential living.* Being open to experience makes it possible for such people to encounter each new experience as unique while minimizing the need for preconceived categories. For example, when making out a class schedule, a student selects an unknown class because it sounds interesting.

▲ *Organismic trust.* Because of their tendency to have a high degree of self-acceptance and openness to experience, fully functioning people trust their feelings and judgments. For example, an individual who does not want to take drugs refuses to give in to peer pressure to engage in such behavior while attending a party.

A consequence of being a fully functioning person is living what Rogers (1961) called "the good life." From this point of view, the good life involves more than having a big house and a fancy car. For Rogers, some of the benefits that go along with living the good life include

▲ *Increased freedom.* This increase in freedom involves being able to make decisions based on a personal sense of self and the organismic valuing process, thereby demonstrating a sense of independence. An example might be the college student taking courses based on personal interest, rather than because of parental pressure to go into a certain academic field.

▲ *Creativity.* The sense of increased freedom and organismic trust makes it possible for the fully functioning person to perceive and adjust to events in novel ways. A good example of this type of creativity would be the police chief who promotes family and community education programs in combating drug use, instead of just arresting drug users.

▲ *Basic trustworthiness.* Because such people react on the basis of true organismic processing, others can trust them to respond to situations in a manner that is both realistic and constructive. For example, although they are basically peace-loving individuals, loving parents can be trusted and counted on to respond with physical aggression, if needed, when danger threatens those they love.

▲ *A richer life.* Such freedom, confidence, and openness make it possible for the individual to live a life that includes having a wider range of experiences, and those experiences will be richer. For example, because of the decision to participate in a variety of student organizations, a graduating senior was able to meet and interact with a greater number of students and faculty members. The result of this decision is a much richer college experience than would have been possible if all this student did was to go to class and socialize at the student union.

Thus, the good life is characterized by a greater degree of independence, creativity, trust by others, and richness of experience. But as Rogers (1961) warns,

> This process of the good life is not, I am convinced, a life for the faint-hearted. It involves the stretching and growing of becoming more and more of one's potentialities. It involves the courage to be. It means launching oneself fully into the stream of life. Yet the

deeply exciting thing about human beings is that when the individual is inwardly free, he chooses as the good life this process of becoming. (p. 196)

Thus, living the good life and developing a high degree of personality adjustment are the consequences of being a fully functioning person. For those who are unwilling or unable to do so, the consequences are a life characterized by a certain degree of personality maladjustment.

Personality Maladjustment: Living the Incongruent Life

Developing a sense of self based too much on the conditional positive regard of others results in a sense of self that has attached to it conditions of worth. A person who relies too much on external influences for determining the nature of his or her experiences minimizes experiential freedom and maximizes the possibility of incongruence within the self-concept. This state of incongruence is at the core of psychological maladjustment (Rogers, 1959). It is likely to occur when conditional positive regard and conditions of worth are pitted against the need for positive self-regard. When the self-actualization process is hindered, the individual begins to experience anxiety and tries to cope with it by engaging in defensive behavior. This defensive behavior reflects personality maladjustment and is expressed in some of the following forms:

▲ *Distortions in awareness.* Distortions in awareness involve the person modifying the perception of threatening experiences in order to make them less imposing. For example, by stating "I don't stand a chance of getting the job," an individual can avoid the threat of rejection by not even showing up for the interview.
▲ *Denying awareness.* Denial is characterized by not acknowledging the existence of those experiences that are a threat to the self-concept. An example of denial is the individual who deals with an unhappy marriage by spending a lot of time working to avoid thinking about the problems at home.

▲ *Intensionality.* Behaving in an intensional fashion reflects responding to threatening situations in a very rigid and overgeneralized manner. An example would be the individual who stays at a very boring job because of the risks associated with making a job or career change.

Thus, while such defensive behaviors help the individual to gain a certain degree of perceived congruence by distorting the situation, the actual level of incongruence produces feelings of anxiety and unpleasantness. When this level of anxiety gets to be too great, the individual may become disorganized. In a state of disorganization, feelings of anxiety resulting from incongruence come into conscious awareness (Rogers, 1959). When disorganization becomes too severe, the individual is motivated to seek psychotherapy in an attempt to regain congruence and positive self-regard. Rogers' views on psychotherapy are discussed in the next section.

The basic concepts of Rogers' viewpoint of personality adjustment are summarized in Figure 6.1. Also illustrated in Figure 6.1 is the relationship between Rogers' views on personality development and his views on personality adjustment.

Applications of Rogers' Viewpoint: Using What Is Known

Like any other comprehensive and influential theory of personality, Rogers' viewpoint has found its way into many different applications. You will learn about three areas of application in this section: psychotherapy, education, and personality assessment.

Person-Centered Therapy: Reestablishing Congruence

Rogers is best known for the application of his viewpoint to the type of psychotherapy he developed, called client-centered therapy (Rogers, 1951), which he later retitled **person-centered therapy** (Rogers, 1977). As with everything else related to Rogers' viewpoint, the individual is the essential element in the therapeutic process. There is also a considerable

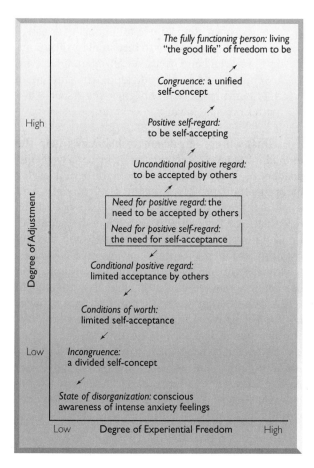

Figure 6.1
From Rogers' viewpoint, experiential freedom is positively related to personality adjustment.

amount of emphasis on the working relationship between the client and therapist (Raskin & Rogers, 1989, 1995). Finally, a basic premise is the belief that people are motivated to seek therapy by their desire to continue the process of self-actualization.

The Reintegration of the Self-Concept as the Basic Object of Person-Centered Therapy
Since personality maladjustment is characterized by the conscious awareness of intense anxiety, which signals a state of incongruence, the goal of therapy should be to minimize this state of affairs. In person-centered therapy, the major objective is to reintegrate the self-concept by helping the individual to freely experience events in the phenomenal field. Once the individual can make judgments based on a true organismic valuing process, the barriers to the self-

actualization process are removed. To achieve this objective, Rogers specified those conditions necessary to analyze the therapeutic process.

The Necessary Conditions of the Therapeutic Environment
As a means of helping the individual to begin establishing a state of congruence, Rogers (1957, 1959; Raskin & Rogers, 1989, 1995) felt that the therapeutic environment must include the following six conditions:

▲ *Client and therapist establish contact.* Having **contact** implies a purposeful relationship between the client and the therapist. For the client, contact involves being able to share intimate experiences with the therapist. For the therapist, contact requires attempting to understand these experiences from the client's point of view. Their shared contact stresses trying to communicate in a manner that will bring about experiential freedom for the client.

▲ *The client is in a state of incongruence.* The client has to be experiencing a certain amount of emotional pain (i.e., incongruence) prior to therapy. It is the state of vulnerability and anxiety that motivates the individual to want to become more congruent and seek therapy. For example, as long as an unhappy spouse continues to distort the situation at home by simply hoping things will get better, it is unlikely that he or she will seek counseling.

▲ *The therapist is congruent in this relationship.* To accurately understand what the client says, and to react in a true and unbiased manner, the therapist should be operating with a unified self-concept when interacting with the client. That is, the therapist's own conditions of worth should not interfere with the therapeutic process. For example, although the therapist may be going through a very emotional divorce at the time, personal feelings should not bias his or her therapeutic responses to what a client may be saying about a spouse. The therapist is free, however, to express personal feelings that might help strengthen the relationship with the client (e.g., the therapist reveals having similar feelings of anxiety as a result of the divorce) (Rogers & Sanford, 1985). In such situations, the therapist is responding to the client with genuine feelings and "avoiding the temptation to hide behind a mask of professionalism" (Rogers & Sanford, 1985, p. 1379).

▲ *The therapist expresses unconditional positive regard for the client.* The therapist should promote unconditional positive regard by not passing judgment on what the client says or by conveying conditions of worth. This point is crucial because unconditional positive regard is an important preliminary step in developing experiential freedom and critical for forward movement in the therapeutic process (Rogers, 1986). If the client senses that the therapist is conveying conditions of worth, even through nonverbal behavior (e.g., looking away when infidelity is discussed), the client might begin to modify statements about his or her true feelings. This situation only hinders the therapeutic process. Even if the therapist does not approve of the client's behavior, it is important that unconditional positive regard be expressed. As an example, the therapist might disapprove of the emotional abuse of a spouse by the client. But the therapist still can express acceptance of the client as a person for seeking therapy to change this destructive behavior.

▲ *The therapist demonstrates empathic understanding.* The therapist should express empathic understanding by trying to experience what is said from the client's perspective. The therapist must realize that what is important is how the client perceives the events. For example, although the therapist can see that the client has many personal strengths, it is the client's perceived sense of helplessness that is creating much of the anxiety about the unhappy marriage.

▲ *The client is able to perceive the therapist's sense of unconditional positive regard and emphatic understanding.* It is not enough for the therapist to attempt to be accepting and understanding. The client must be able to see that this is the case. For example, sitting face-to-face with the client, the therapist might rephrase what the client has just said so that the client can see that what is being disclosed and discussed is being understood in a manner that is not judgmental.

While Rogers (1959) admits that other elements are usually present, he maintains that "These seem to be the necessary conditions of therapy . . ." (p. 213). Rogers believed that these six basic conditions are at the core of any form of successful therapy, not just person-centered therapy. In addition to identifying these necessary conditions, Rogers developed a number of techniques for creating a therapeutic atmosphere of empathy and unconditional positive regard for the client.

Techniques for Making Contact in Person-Centered Therapy

As part of his research, Rogers investigated the factors involved in how people communicated in face-to-face interactions (Rogers, 1952). This information was used to formulate a set of verbal response techniques that the therapist could use to communicate a sense of acceptance and understanding to the client:

▲ *Probing response.* A probing response would be used to obtain additional information from the client in a manner that does not give the impression of prying. An appropriate probing response might be, "Would you like to talk more about your feelings concerning the pressures you are experiencing at school?" In this case, the client can respond if he or she feels comfortable.

▲ *Interpretative response.* The interpretative response is designed to offer the client a tentative explanation for the nature of the problem being experienced. A therapist might say to a client, "Do you think it is possible that the pressure you feel is related more to pleasing your family than to the amount of work assigned by your professors?"

▲ *Reassuring response.* The reassuring response is designed to convey a sense of the therapist's acceptance and encouragement of the client. The therapist might say, "It is only natural for you to feel such pressure when you go to those family gatherings. Perhaps if you tried to explain to your parents all that you have to do in addition to your school work, they would be more understanding." In this case, the therapist acknowledges the client's feelings without passing judgment while also encouraging a new behavior that might help to alleviate the problem.

▲   *Reflective response.* Reflective responses are designed to communicate that the therapist is attempting to understand the client's point of view. This is achieved by the therapist trying to convey the nature of the emotion being expressed by the client. For example, a client might say, "I'm really upset about seeing my parents next weekend." A reflective response by the therapist might be "Given what you have said up to now, I can imagine how you might be upset. What about the situation seems to upset you the most?" The therapist can also use reflective responses to encourage the client to explore or elaborate the nature of the feelings being expressed, as well as to let the client know he or she is being listened to and understood.

These four verbal responses form the most fundamental techniques of person-centered therapy. Although they may look and sound easy, it takes a considerable amount of training and practice to be able to use them effectively. For example, an interpretative response offered too early might provoke a defensive reaction on the part of the client.

Measuring the Outcome of Treatment: Assessing the Effects and Effectiveness of Person-Centered Therapy

Given his long association with some of the nation's most prestigious research universities, Carl Rogers was well aware of the valuable information that could be gained from rigorous research. It is through research that Rogers has made many significant contributions to the field of psychotherapy.

Rogers was the first major figure to systematically assess the effects and effectiveness of psychotherapy. In his research on psychotherapy, Rogers was concerned with assessing changes that occurred in the individual as a result of a successful therapeutic experience and identifying the factors associated with successful psychotherapy. Rogers employed a number of methods to assess the effectiveness of person-centered therapy. For example, he and his colleagues would record the verbal dialogue of treatment sessions and perform content analysis on the type (e.g., belittling vs. self-affirming) and nature (e.g., blaming the self vs. blaming others) of statements clients made as therapy progressed. To assess changes in the clients, Rogers and his colleagues used various rating scales for measuring self-perceptions (e.g., ratings of the real and ideal self) and the nature of feelings expressed (e.g., degree of anxiety vs. happiness) at various points in the treatment process.

Assessing the Effects of Person-Centered Therapy
Rogers (1958, 1959, 1961; Meador & Rogers, 1973) noted several changes in the person, both during and after a successful therapeutic experience.

In the course of psychotherapy, one of the first changes clients begin to show is a greater tendency to express their feelings in words (e.g., an angry tone of voice) and behavior (e.g., pounding on the arm of the chair). Clients also begin to make more references to the self (e.g., my feelings of anger) than to others (e.g., my spouse's disappointment) as therapy progresses. Clients would show a greater awareness of the incongruence within the self-concept and begin to express freely feelings that were directly related to it (e.g., anger with one's self for being so conforming). Clients also displayed a reduction in the distortion and denial of experiences related to feelings of incongruence (e.g., less likely to express anger for their own disappointments at a spouse or the children).

One of the most important breakthroughs that occurs during therapy is when the client becomes able to experience, without threat of removal, the therapist's unconditional positive regard. For example, sensing unconditional positive regard from the therapist, a client trying to make a career change might reveal deep feelings of disappointment related to the lack of support given by family members. Such changes within the person are at the basis of an increased level of congruence that Rogers believed would last after the successful therapeutic experience. A survey of the research on these and other changes within the individual following successful therapy can be found in Rogers & Dymond's (1954) classic textbook *Psychotherapy and Personality Change.*

The Effectiveness of Person-Centered Therapy

To maximize the possibility of achieving these positive outcomes, Rogers and others have concerned themselves with identifying the factors contributing to treatment effectiveness. In a rather extensive review of the research investigating certain therapist interpersonal skills (Truax & Mitchell, 1971), it was noted that therapists or counselors who are accurately empathic (e.g., sensitive), nonpossessively warm in attitude (e.g., not dominating), and genuine (e.g., open-minded and lack defensiveness) contribute to treatment effectiveness regardless of the type of treatment context (e.g., individual or group therapy), therapist's theoretical orientation (e.g., person-centered or psychoanalytical) and type of client (e.g., college underachievers, juvenile delinquents, or hospitalized schizophrenics). To consider two somewhat different sources of evidence in support of the relationship between treatment effectiveness from the Rogerian viewpoint, see "A Closer Look" on page 170.

Although the effectiveness of person-centered therapy is well documented, this therapeutic approach is not without its critics (Mitchell, Bozarth, & Krauft, 1977). However, the extensive systematic research Rogers conducted and helped to inspire—investigating the effects of and factors responsible for effective person-centered therapy—can be used to support the validity of the Rogerian viewpoint of personality and psychotherapy.

Encounter Groups: Living Laboratories for Intrapersonal and Interpersonal Exploration

Encounter groups have their origin in what were called T-groups in the late 1940s. Originally, **T-groups** were designed to help train managers and executives to improve their human relations skills. In these early T-groups, groups of people were taught to observe the nature of their interactions and then given the opportunity to receive feedback from other members of the group and trained group leaders. Thus, the *T* in T-groups stands for training. However, Rogers expanded the nature of the original T-group into what has become known as encounter groups.

What Are Encounter Groups?

Encounter groups have as their principal objective an emphasis on "personal growth and the development and improvement of interpersonal communication and relationships through an experiential process" (Rogers, 1970, pp. 4–5). Encounter groups are designed to increase the group members' sense of awareness in themselves and their relationships with others. In a rather eloquent expression of this objective, Elliot Aronson, a famous social psychologist, comments on his group experience by noting that in addition to learning about himself, "I also learn how others see me, how my behavior affects them, and how much I am affected by others" (Aronson, 1972, p. 239).

As an example of increased self-awareness, a rather lonely middle-aged man might discover, based on feedback from group members, that his rather defeatist outlook toward the world makes them feel bad too and makes them want to avoid him. Thus, encounter groups are designed to help people enhance their self-awareness and interpersonal effectiveness. The nature of this enhancement comes from the experiences provided by the encounter group process.

What Effects Do Encounter Groups Have?

Based on personal testimonials from many people who have participated in encounter groups, Rogers (1970) provides a number of examples illustrating the positive changes that have resulted from an encounter group experience. More systematic evaluations of the effects of encounter groups indicate that positive outcomes are typically reported by their participants (Bednar & Kaul, 1978; Gibb, 1971; Lieberman, Yalom, & Miles, 1973). Some of the positive changes reported include increases in self-liking, openness, self-ideal, congruence, creativity, self-direction, interpersonal orientation, self-awareness, and coping skills (Bednar & Kaul, 1978; Kendall & Norton-Ford, 1982).

But one limitation of the changes just noted is the degree to which they can be transferred from the encounter group to the "real world" (Rogers, 1970). The direct and often confrontational feedback provided in an encounter group might provoke physical attacks when performed in day-to-day interactions.

A Closer Look:

The Impact of Therapist Warmth and Empathic Understanding: Learning to Touch Snakes and Love Yourself

The Impact of Therapist Warmth

The importance of the "therapist warmth" variable was demonstrated in a rather interesting study done by Morris and Suckerman (1974). They looked at the effect of "therapist warmth" on the treatment of snake phobias using a form of behavior therapy known as graduated practice. **Graduated practice** involves helping clients to overcome their fear of a specific object (e.g., dog) or situation (e.g., public speaking) by gradually bringing them into closer proximity to it.

In their study, Morris and Suckerman initially assessed how close 23 snake-phobic female college students would be willing to get to a live, harmless 3-foot king snake (e.g., be in the same room, touch the glass cage, or touch the snake) as a pretest measure of snake avoidance. Over the next couple of weeks, approximately two-thirds of the 23 women were then given six 20-minute sessions involving a standard treatment for snake phobia based on graduated practice. One group of these women received the treatment session by a therapist who behaved in a rather warm and compassionate manner. Another group received the *same* treatment by the *same* therapist who, for these women only, behaved in a cold and rather matter-of-fact manner. After completing all of the six sessions with either the "warm" or "cold" therapist, the extent to which the women were willing to approach the snake was assessed once again as a posttest measure. A third group of the women did not receive any type of treatment. The posttest measure of willingness to approach the snake for these women was obtained concurrently with that for the women in the warm and cold therapist conditions. For all of the women in the study, a second posttest measure was taken approximately $2^{1}/_{2}$ months after the first measure.

The study results indicated that the women treated by the warm therapist exhibited a greater tendency to approach the snake during the posttest measures than those treated by the cold therapist or those receiving no treatment at all. In addition, no difference was found between the approach behavior of the women treated by the cold therapist and those receiving no treatment at all. Such results demonstrate the significance of therapist warmth in affecting positive behavioral changes with treatment procedures other than the person-centered therapy approach.

The Impact of Empathic Understanding

One of the many sources of evidence Rogers used to evaluate the effectiveness of person-centered therapy was to look at the changes it brought about in clients. The following passage indicates that one important impact of empathic understanding is the greater level of self-acceptance and personal responsibility it can create in clients.

> ROGERS A vivid example of this comes from a young man who has been the recipient of much sensitive understanding and who is now in the later stages of his therapy:
>
> CLIENT I could even conceive of it as a possibility that I could have a kind of tender concern for me. Still, how could I be tender, be concerned for *myself*, when they're one and the same thing? But yet I can feel it so clearly—you know, like taking care of a child. You want to give it this and give it that. I can kind of clearly see the purposes for somebody else, but I can never see them for myself, that I could do this for me, you know. Is it possible that I can really want to take care of myself, and make that a major purpose of my life? That means I'd have to deal with the whole world as if I were guardian of the most cherished and most wanted possession, that this *I* was between this precious *me* that I wanted to take care of and the whole world. It's almost as if I *loved* myself; you know, that's strange—but it's true.
>
> ROGERS It is, I believe, the therapist's caring understanding—exhibited in this excerpt—which has permitted this client to experience a high regard, even a love, for himself. (Rogers, 1980, p. 153)

Although these two sources of evidence are quite different, they have in common their support of the treatment effectiveness of a person-centered approach to therapy.

For example, under the supervision of a trained group leader, one member of the group might begin to question in a very persistent manner another member's reasons for having extramarital affairs. Additional information on encounter groups can be found in *Carl Rogers on Encounter Groups* (Rogers, 1970), especially Chapter 2, and *Joy: Expanding Human Awareness* (Schultz, 1967).

It is safe to say that not since Freud has any single person influenced the field of psychotherapy as much as Carl Rogers. His development of person-centered therapy and his emphasis on investigating the therapeutic process and its outcomes are unparalleled contributions to psychotherapy.

The Rogerian Viewpoint in the Classroom: Developing the Freedom to Learn

In addition to concerning himself with the learning that takes place within the context of psychotherapy and encounter groups, Rogers was also concerned with the learning process as it occurred in the classroom (Raskin & Rogers, 1995). For him, the aim of education was "the facilitation of learning" (Rogers, 1969, p. 105). As with the other types of learning with which he concerned himself, Rogers (1969) felt that

> the facilitation of significant learning rests upon certain attitudinal qualities which exist in the personal *relationship* between the facilitator and the learner. We came upon such findings first in the field of psychotherapy, but increasingly there is evidence which shows that these findings apply in the classroom as well. (p. 106)

Qualities That Facilitate Learning: The Student-Centered Method
The **student-centered method** of learning reflects Rogers' view of a system for maximizing the quality of education using those same principles he found to be so effective for learning during the successful therapy experience. As in person-centered therapy, the student-centered method focuses on those factors in the teacher-student relationship that facilitate learn-

ing (Rogers, 1983). Discussed next are the attitudinal qualities that characterize the facilitation of learning from the Rogerian viewpoint.

Realness in the Facilitator   Realness involves entering into a relationship with the learner without presenting a facade. This means teachers can be real people in their relationships with students, expressing enthusiasms, boredom, anger, and interest. Because such teachers are able to accept their own feelings, they are more accepting of the feelings of the students.

In sharp contrast to this are those teachers who play the role of "teacher" in class—they do all the talking and the students do all the listening. Students are likely to enjoy a class more when the instructor seems to be really enjoying what he or she is talking about than when the teacher simply appears to be going through the motions. In short, teachers who seem to be the best facilitators of learning are those who can be real people in their relationships with students. But as can be seen in Figure 6.2, sometimes students have a hard time accepting their teachers as real people.

Exhibiting a Prizing Attitude   A prizing attitude exists when teachers treat students with respect and

Carl Rogers proposed that success in education, like success in psychotherapy, required facilitators (i.e., teachers) to be "real people," prize their students, and display empathic understanding.

Figure 6.2
From the student-centered approach, the inability to see teachers as real people is a barrier to the facilitation of learning. Reprinted with special permission of King Features Syndicate.

accept them for the individuals they are, not what the teachers would like them to be. This type of acceptance promotes seeing students as unique individuals with distinctive likes and dislikes, feelings, and aspirations. It means giving students the freedom to express their opinions. The prizing teacher realizes that when students disagree, it should not be taken as a personal attack on the teacher's authority. Sensing defensive reactions to their disagreement will lead to students learning only to memorize and repeat what the teacher wants. Thus, a characteristic feature of the prizing attitude is an acceptance of students as real people too.

Developing Empathic Understanding   Empathic understanding within the context of the classroom denotes being able to see the process of learning as it appears from the perspective of the student. Much of the dissatisfaction students express while in school relates to their having to memorize material they feel has little relevance to their everyday lives. Realizing this, effective teachers try to include in their teaching some material related to the everyday living experiences of the students (e.g., examples from popular movies, contemporary music, or important social issues). Such actions represent making an attempt to know something about what goes on in the lives of students.

Becoming a Learning Facilitator   Acquiring the attributes of a successful teacher do not just happen by accident. Rogers believes it comes from being willing to take some risks and includes the ability to

trust others, particularly students. A lack of trust is illustrated by a teaching philosophy that involves cramming into students only what teachers want them to know because students cannot be trusted to think for themselves. An example of a more trusting philosophy involves exposing students to a number of different perspectives and allowing them to choose their own direction for classroom discussion. The major risk to be taken here by the teacher involves acting on the assumption that students can be trusted to make such decisions. Rogers noted that only by taking such risks will the teachers be able to discover for themselves the extent to which certain teaching methods will be effective for a particular group of students.

Does the student-centered approach work? Rogers (1969) and others (Bradford, 1976; Schmuck, 1963, 1966) provide some supporting evidence that it does. Aspy (1965; cited in Rogers, 1969, p. 119) found that third-graders who were taught reading by teachers who were high in their degree of realness, prizing attitude, and empathic understanding showed greater improvement in their reading scores than students who were taught by teachers possessing a low degree of these qualities. Does this approach work for you? To find out, try for yourself the exercise described in "You Can Do It" on page 173.

In summary, at the core of the student-centered method of teaching and learning is Rogers' belief in giving the student the freedom to learn. Additional information about the student-centered

YOU CAN DO IT

Grading the Teacher: A Student's Assessment of the Student-Centered Method of Learning

Now that you know what seem to be the characteristic features of successful teachers, take the time to list in the spaces below five professors you have had in your college career. Rate each professor on a scale from 1 (very low) to 10 (very high) on his or her degree of realness, prizing attitude, and empathic understanding. Finally, using the same rating scale, indicate the degree of enjoyment and amount of learning in that course.

Professor's Name	10-Point Ratings				
	Realness	Prizing	Empathy	Enjoyment	Learning
1. _____	____	____	____	____	____
2. _____	____	____	____	____	____
3. _____	____	____	____	____	____
4. _____	____	____	____	____	____
5. _____	____	____	____	____	____

Is there any relationship between these three teacher qualities and your ratings of enjoyment and learning? If so, is it consistent with what was said about the effects of the student-centered method? Without giving the names of the professors, discuss your results with those of some of your classmates. In addition, if you have time, repeat this exercise with a friend or two, after you have explained to them the nature of realness, prizing attitude, and empathic understanding.

method of learning can be found in *Freedom to Learn* (Rogers, 1969), *Freedom to Learn for the 80's* (Rogers, 1983), or *Human Forces in Teaching and Learning* (Bradford, 1976).

Personality Assessment from the Rogerian Viewpoint: Measuring the Personal World

The focus of personality assessment from the Rogerian viewpoint is an attempt to measure the individual's personal world. Measuring this personal world involves trying to understand how the individual views his or her sense of self. The Q-Sort technique is a method most often associated with personality assessment from the Rogerian viewpoint.

The Q-Sort Technique

The **Q-Sort technique** (Stephenson, 1953) is designed to systematically assess the way people perceive themselves through the use of a set of self-descriptive statements (Ozer, 1993). When performing a Q-Sort, the individual is given a rather large number (i.e., 100) of self-descriptive statements printed on separate cards and asked to sort them into a limited number of piles (i.e., nine) ranging from "least like me" (i.e., "1") to "most like me" (i.e., "9").

Although there are a number of different instructional sets for sorting the statements, one of the most common is the self-ideal sort. With the **self-ideal sort**, the individual is asked first to perform a self-sort. In a **self-sort**, the individual sorts the statements according to how he or she perceives him- or herself now. After it has been noted into which pile each statement is placed, the individual is then asked to perform an ideal sort. In an **ideal sort**, the individual sorts the statements into the piles based on the ideal person he or she would like to be. Again, it is noted into which pile each statement is placed. Because each statement is assigned a number based on the pile into which it was placed after each sort, it is possible to calculate the correlation coefficient between the ratings of the statements for the different sorts. The higher this correlation, the greater the degree of similarity between how the individual sees him- or herself and how he or she would like to be.

A high degree of similarity in self-perceptions was seen by Rogers as a measure of personality adjustment. Thus, from the Rogerian viewpoint, the significance of the Q-Sort technique is that it makes it possible to quantify objectively the subjective perception of the self-concept. As a means of obtaining some firsthand experience with a Q-Sort type of activity, try for yourself the exercise outlined in "You Can Do It" on page 174.

The Q-Sort technique has been used extensively to measure the effectiveness of psychotherapy by assessing changes in the degree of congruence that

YOU CAN DO IT

Using a Q-Sort Exercise: What "Sort" of Person Are You?

Instructions
Using the nine-point scale listed below, perform the following self-sort.

Self-Sort
For each of the 20 items listed below, rate the extent to which you feel each statement is characteristic of how you perceive yourself now.

After you have completed the self-sort, cover your responses with a piece of paper and complete the following ideal sort using the same nine-point scale.

Ideal Sort
For each of the 20 items below, rate the extent to which you feel each statement is characteristic of how you perceive your ideal self.

RATING SCALE

not at all characteristic		moderately characteristic				extremely characteristic	
1	2	3	4	5	6	7	8	9

	Self-Sort Rating	Ideal Sort Rating
1. Relate well with opposite-sex others	____	____
2. Demonstrate a sense of humor	____	____
3. Accept others' faults	____	____
4. Tendency to procrastinate	____	____
5. Sensitive to the feelings of others	____	____
6. Handle criticism well	____	____
7. Exhibit sudden mood fluctuations	____	____
8. Optimistic about most things	____	____
9. Talkative in social situations	____	____
10. See myself as physically attractive	____	____
11. Express opinions openly	____	____
12. Relate well with same-sex others	____	____
13. Like to engage in daydreaming	____	____
14. Basically anxious	____	____
15. Attract the confidence of others	____	____
16. Tendency toward self-indulgence	____	____
17. Prefer to be alone than with others	____	____
18. Feel self-confident	____	____
19. Trust the motives of others	____	____
20. Possess a sense of direction in life	____	____

Interpretation
Note that it is not the size of the numbers that is important (e.g., having all 8s or 9s), but the degree of similarity between the numbers in the self and ideal columns. The greater the similarity between the two sets of numbers, the closer you are to the type of person you would like to be. If you are like most other college students, your responses for the two sorts are probably close on some statements but far apart on others. It should be noted that this is not a true Q-Sort technique, since only a rather limited number of self-descriptive statements are used and the items are rated rather than sorted.

have occurred within individuals as a result of receiving therapy. The logic has been that if the therapy is effective, a higher correlation between the self- and ideal-sorts should be observed after therapy than before it.

One of the most frequently cited studies using the Q-Sort technique for this purpose is a study by Butler and Haigh (1954). In their study, they reported a self-ideal average correlation of $r = -.01$ for a group of clients before therapy. When the self-ideal sorts were examined after therapy, the average correlations were $r = .34$ for the post-counseling sort and $r = .31$ for a follow-up sort obtained a period of time after therapy. As a basis of comparison, self-ideal sorts were also obtained for a control group of individuals not requiring therapy at approximately the same time. The correlations between the self-ideal sorts were $r = .58$ for the pre-therapy sort and $r = .59$ for the follow-up sort. A more extensive example of the application of the Q-Sort technique to assess the effectiveness of psychotherapy is presented in "Applications in Personality Psychology" on page 175.

Although the Q-Sort technique is used to study the effectiveness of psychotherapy (Cohen, Montague, Nathanson, & Swerdlik, 1989; Rogers, 1959; Rogers & Dymond, 1954), it is not limited to this single application. Research involving theory testing used the Q-Sort technique to investigate the basic structure of personality and the stability of personal-

APPLICATION

APPLICATIONS IN PERSONALITY PSYCHOLOGY

The Q-Sort Technique in Psychotherapy: "Sorting" Out the Outcome of the Therapeutic Experience

In a rather elaborate application of the Q-Sort technique to assess the effectiveness of psychotherapy, a study was done that included four different therapy groups and two separate control groups (Butler, 1968). Three of the therapy groups received traditional person-centered therapy. The fourth therapy group received treatment based on Adlerian therapy. The two control groups included a "normal" group and a "client" group. The normal control group consisted of a group of people who did not appear to need therapy. The client control group consisted of people who had sought psychotherapy but were placed on a 10-week waiting list. This client control group was tested at the onset of the 10-week period and then again 10 weeks later. The inclusion of the client control group is important because it provides a more valid test of the effectiveness of therapy by directly comparing those individuals who needed therapy and received it (i.e., the four therapy groups) with those who did not (i.e., the client control group).

The results of this study are summarized in Figure 6.3. The nature of the correlations for the pre- and posttest sorts for those receiving therapy increased in a positive direction. This pattern of results indicates a greater degree of congruence within the individual after therapy than before it. The correlations for those clients requiring but not receiving therapy remained relatively low and unchanged. In addition to validating the Q-Sort technique, these results make it clear that it was the therapy, not just the passage of time, that produced the positive changes within the clients. Without the client control group, this conclusion would not have been possible.

The Q-Sort technique has also been used to help distinguish career from noncareer naval officers, assess the importance of various aspects of nurses' work, obtain students' evaluations of teachers, study the views about children and family life held by the mothers of schizophrenic patients, and examine the services provided by a counseling agency over a four-year period (Wittenborn, 1961). Other more general areas of application of Q-Sort techniques are educational psychology (Stephenson, 1980), leadership values (Cassel, 1958), and vocational and occupational counseling (Tyler, 1961; Williams, 1978). In short, a major strength of the Q-Sort technique is its versatility. For more information about the various applications of the Q-Sort technique, Brown lists some 277 references from which to choose among the over 580 references in his "Bibliography on Q Technique and Its Methodology" (Brown, 1968).

Although it has been used extensively in a number of areas, a major criticism of the Q-Sort technique is the extent to which people can provide

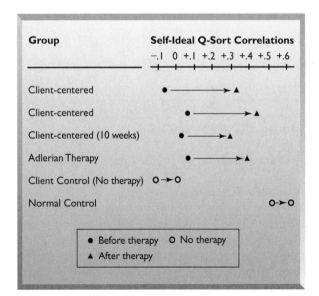

Figure 6.3

A comparison of the mean correlations for self-ideal Q-Sorts before and after therapy for the treatment and control groups

*The higher and more positive the correlation, the greater the degree of congruence within the self-concept.

Note: Based on *Psychotherapy: Theory, Research, and Practice,* J.M. Butler, 1968, Vol. 5, 13-17.

ity over time (Bem & Funder, 1978; Block, 1971; Funder & Block, 1989; Funder, Block, & Block, 1983; Funder, Parke, Tomlinson-Keasey, & Widaman, 1993; McCrae, Costa, & Busch, 1986; Ozer & Gjerde, 1989).

reliable and valid self-report information that is not biased by the desire to make themselves look good (Cohen, Montague, Nathanson, Swerdlik, 1989; Jackson & Messick, 1958; Lanyon & Goodstein, 1971). However, others have found self-report information to be extremely useful in the study of personality, treatment effectiveness, and other related areas (Bem & Allen, 1974; Bem & Funder, 1978; Mischel, 1972, 1981; Merluzzi, Glass, & Genest, 1981).

Additional Applications of Rogers' Viewpoint
Although only three major applications of the Rogerian viewpoint were discussed in this section, Rogers made very serious attempts to extend the application of his views to a wide variety of other areas. Some of these areas of concern include social issues (Rogers, 1977), marriage and family life (Rogers, 1972), play therapy for children (Axline, 1947; Ellinwood & Raskin, 1993), medical education (Rogers, 1980), the reduction of interracial and intercultural tension (McGaw, Rice, & Rogers, 1973), and world peace (Rogers, 1982, 1987).

Evaluation of the Rogerian Viewpoint: Strengths and Limitations

Characteristic Strengths

Here are some strengths of the Rogerian viewpoint.

Emphasis on Research
Probably the most significant strength of Rogers' viewpoint is the emphasis he placed on systematic research as a means of verifying all aspects of his theory and applications. Rogers wanted to understand and investigate systematically the underlying processes and dynamics that contributed to a successful therapeutic experience. In his research, Rogers employed a number of innovative techniques (e.g., content analysis of recorded therapy sessions, Q-Sort methodology). His use of the therapy session as a "research laboratory" did much to take some of the mystery out of psychotherapy for the general public. It is probably safe to say that Rogers' emphasis

on research, and the impact of that emphasis on the field of psychotherapy, is only second to the influence of Freud.

An Emphasis on the Person
Rogers promoted the view of people as having free will and responsibility over their actions. He also emphasized the conscious and subjective experiences of the individual as critical factors in determining behavior. While such views seem rather straightforward today, they were extremely different from the Freudian and behavioristic (see Chapter 10) viewpoints of the 1940s and 1950s that were so dominant at the time Rogers was formulating his theory of personality and psychotherapy.

The Impact of the Rogerian Viewpoint
The impact of the Rogerian viewpoint is significant inside as well as outside the field of personality psychology. In personality psychology, the Rogerian viewpoint offered a totally different way of viewing the individual and expressed this view most clearly in person-centered therapy. Not since psychoanalysis has a specific form of therapy so significantly influenced the way psychotherapy is conducted. The overall impact of the Rogerian viewpoint was facilitated by Rogers' dedication to systematic research and the respect this brought him—and his ideas—in the academic and psychotherapeutic communities.

In addition to having its substantial impact on psychotherapy, the Rogerian viewpoint can be found outside of personality psychology in such areas as education, child-rearing practices, management training, and employee relations. In short, the Rogerian viewpoint has made quite a name for itself through its extensive application in a wide variety of areas.

Characteristic Limitations

The Rogerian viewpoint has the following limitations.

Emphasis on the Subjective Experience and Self-Report
A major limitation of the Rogerian viewpoint is its emphasis on the subjective experiences and self-

reports of individuals. The basis of this limitation is the extent to which we can rely on what people say about themselves. For example, how much should the therapist rely on the subjective experiences and self-perceptions of clients to identify the source of their problems? How much should a therapist rely on clients to tell the truth as opposed to what they think the therapist wants to hear? In defense of Rogers' position, it should be known that he was aware of such possibilities. Rogers felt, however, that if a warm and nonjudgmental therapeutic environment were created, a skillful therapist would be able to help clients see the true nature of their problems and elicit honest responses. But the validity of what others say about themselves is still in question.

Theoretical Simplicity

The Rogerian viewpoint is said to be theoretically rather simplistic and naive. It has been labeled simplistic because of its reliance on a relatively few number of theoretical constructs. Much of what Rogers says about the nature and dynamics of personality can be summarized with two concepts: congruence and self-actualization.

The theoretical simplicity of Rogers' viewpoint is also reflected in its rather limited explanation of the nature of personality development. Although Rogers has specified which factors are important (e.g., unconditional positive regard and positive self-regard), he has not discussed or examined in much detail the specifics of the processes and dynamics involved in the development of personality. Instead, he assumes that the same processes and dynamics that foster the development of an adjusted personality in adults during therapy will operate in a similar manner for children. The naiveté of Rogers' viewpoint is also said to be reflected in his emphasis on the conscious mind and the validity he attributed to self-report information while almost completely ignoring the unconscious mind. Thus, Rogers' view of human nature has been characterized as being somewhat superficial.

Criticisms of Person-Centered Therapy

Person-centered therapy has come under attack as being a technique more than a therapy. Critics say that anyone who can learn how to make reassuring and reflective responses is in a position to perform person-centered therapy. As more fuel for this argu-

ment, training in the person-centered therapy approach is very popular in educational programs for social workers, counselors, and seminarians. These programs tend to be relatively brief (e.g., two-year programs), are conducted outside of psychology programs (e.g., schools of sociology, education, and religious studies), and require only a minimal amount of education in psychology. Sometimes the training is viewed as nothing more than hand-holding that treats all clients alike regardless of their disorder.

In his defense, Rogers spent more than 20 years in association with the Center for the Studies of the Person in La Jolla, California, a training and research institute for person-centered therapy. He was deeply committed to training qualified therapists and examining the dynamics of psychotherapy. He would certainly not accept the argument that simply being able to reflect what was said back to the client would constitute "doing therapy."

A final criticism of person-centered therapy is that its effectiveness seems to be limited to helping people suffering from mild to moderate emotional problems of adjustment related to everyday living (e.g., loneliness, family or business stress, and problems of self-esteem). However, like any other form of treatment, person-centered therapy was never meant to be a therapeutic cure-all.

Rogers' Phenomenological Viewpoint of Personality: Some Closing Remarks

Rogers' ideas were unique in that he, like Freud, proposed a viewpoint of personality that sharply contrasted with the dominant thinking at the time. Rogers' attention and devotion to systematic research made contributions to the study of personality that will remain for many years. More information about the Rogerian viewpoint can be found in *A Way of Being* (Rogers, 1980), a very readable account of Rogers' general theory, his thoughts on many important social issues, and recent developments in his philosophy. Of particular interest are his thoughts concerning "the person of tomorrow" (pp. 348–356).

Chapter Summary: Reexamining the Highlights

▲ *Basic Assumptions.* The basic assumptions of Rogers' viewpoint include an emphasis on the subjective experience of the individual, focusing on the importance of the here and now as the critical cause of behavior, having the actualizing tendency as the primary source of motivation, and considering the organismic valuing process as the basis of evaluating the value of subjective experience.

▲ *Basic Concepts.* The basic concepts of the viewpoint of personality proposed by Rogers include the phenomenal field, the process of subception, the self-concept as consisting of the organism and the self, and the states of congruence and incongruence.

▲ *Self-Actualization.* The motivational process by which the actualizing tendency is expressed requires freedom and openness of experience. It also is ongoing in nature, manifests itself uniquely in each person, and is holistic in its reaction.

▲ *Personality Development.* The process of personality development involves satisfying the need for positive regard from others and positive self-regard. Positive regard from others can be expressed in the form of unconditional or conditional positive regard. The need for positive self-regard can be altered by conditions of worth.

▲ *The Nature of Personality Adjustment.* The fully functioning person reflects a high degree of personality adjustment and is characterized by a congruence of self and experience, openness to experience, and organismic trust. The maladjusted personality is characterized by distortions in awareness, denial of awareness, and intensionality.

▲ *Applications of Rogers' Viewpoint.* The most extensive application of Rogers' viewpoint includes person-centered therapy and the identification and development of the conditions necessary for an effective therapeutic experience. The Rogerian viewpoint has also been applied to education through the development of the student-centered method of learning and the identification of those characteristics that facilitate learning. The application of the Rogerian viewpoint to personality assessment is best reflected by the Q-Sort technique and its use to assess the outcome of psychotherapy.

▲ *Evaluation of the Rogerian Viewpoint.* Characteristic strengths of the Rogerian viewpoint include its emphasis on research, the promotion of humanism, and the extensive impact of Rogers' ideas both inside and outside the field of personality psychology. Characteristic imitations include its emphasis on the subjective experience and self-report information, theoretical simplicity, and criticism of person-centered therapy as a therapeutic technique.

Glossary

actualizing tendency   An internal inclination for continuous personal growth and development.

conditional positive regard   Being accepted by others only to the extent that the individual meets certain conditions.

conditions of worth   Self-acceptance based on the conditions of acceptance by others.

congruence   A state of consistency between internal feelings and an individual's external perception of the self.

contact   A heightened and meaningful relationship between the client and therapist.

encounter groups   A form of group therapy designed to increase a person's self-awareness by receiving feedback from others in the group.

fully functioning person   An individual characterized by a high degree of mental health and personality adjustment.

graduated practice   A form of therapy used to help people overcome extreme fears.

ideal sort   A Q-Sort technique in which the individual makes ratings of the self along various dimensions as he or she would like to perceive the self as being.

incongruence   A state of inconsistency between internal feelings and an individual's perception of the self.

need for positive regard   The desire to be accepted by others.

need for positive self-regard   The desire to accept one's self.

organism   The evaluative dimension of the self-concept.

organismic valuing process   A personal standard by which actions are evaluated by their ability to promote self-enhancement.

person-centered therapy   A form of psychotherapy developed by Rogers to help treat an incongruent self-concept.

phenomenal field   An individual's total sensory aware-ness at any given moment.

phenomenological perspective   Stresses that the subjec-tive interpretation of events is the critical determinant of thoughts, feelings, and behavior.

Q-Sort technique   An assessment technique designed to measure various forms of congruence of the self-concept.

self   The individual's sense of reference in the external environment.

self-actualization   The source of motivation for self-enhancement.

self-ideal sort   A type of Q-Sort assessment technique measuring the degree of overlap in the perceptions of the real self and ideal self.

self-sort   A Q-Sort technique in which the individual makes ratings of the self along various dimensions as he or she perceives the self as being now.

student-centered method   A method to facilitate learn-ing, stressing experiential freedom and empathic under-standing.

subception   The process of formulating an affective reac-tion to an event before the event reaches total conscious awareness.

T-groups   A semiformal organized group discussion for the purpose of improving interpersonal communication skills.

unconditional positive regard   Being accepted by others without any limitations.

CHAPTER 7

The Humanistic Viewpoints of Maslow and Kelly: A Motivational and Perceptual Perspective

CHAPTER OVERVIEW: A PREVIEW OF COMING ATTRACTIONS

*T*he **humanistic viewpoint** *is characterized by a belief about people as being basically good, active, and creative individuals who live in the present and base their actions on the subjective perception of experience. The humanistic viewpoint stresses the positive and healthy aspects of personality and the uniqueness of the individual (Hall & Lindzey, 1978; Monte, 1991). People are seen as active agents in the perception and modification of their own reality (Buss, 1978) and motivated to move in the direction of personal growth and self-fulfillment (Maslow, 1962).*

There are many similarities between the humanistic viewpoint and the phenomenological viewpoint of Rogers discussed in the previous chapter (Monte, 1991). You will observe some very concrete similarities between the two viewpoints, including an emphasis on the uniqueness of the individual, the importance of subjective experience, and the notion of self-actualization. Because of these and other similarities, Rogers' ideas are often labeled as humanistic (Hall & Lindzey, 1978; Monte, 1991).

The viewpoints of the two personality theorists to be discussed in this chapter, Abraham H. Maslow and George A. Kelly, reflect humanistic beliefs. The viewpoints of Maslow and Kelly are considered by examining the basic assumptions, concepts, and various applications of their ideas.

Maslow's Motivational Viewpoint: Meeting the Needs of the Person

Like Carl Rogers, Abraham Maslow formulated his viewpoint of personality in reaction to the rather pessimistic views of the unconsciously controlled individual proposed by the Freudian perspective and that of the environmentally controlled individual formulated by the behavioral perspective (Maslow, 1970b). Maslow felt that the individual is motivated by the desire for self-enhancement and self-actualization in a manner that goes well beyond satisfying base unconscious needs and simply reacting to external stimuli. He emphasized the creative, spontaneous, and optimistic side of human nature over its dark, more pessimistic side. For a glimpse into the life of a man who formulated a viewpoint of personality based on the strengths of people, see "A Closer Look" below.

A Closer Look:

Biographical Background:
The Life of Abraham H. Maslow

Abraham H. Maslow developed a viewpoint of personality that attempted to explain the motivation behind what makes great people great and good people want to be the best that they can possibly be.

Abraham H. Maslow, the first of seven children, was born on April 1, 1908, in a Jewish district of Brooklyn, New York. His parents, who were Russian immigrants, owned a barrel manufacturing company. As the business improved, the Maslows moved their family out of the slums and into a lower-middle-class neighborhood. In the new neighborhood, Maslow was the only Jewish boy and the target of much anti-Semitism. As a result, he spent much of his time alone reading books in the library. His relationship with his parents was also somewhat difficult. He talked about being afraid of his father, and he talked about his mother as probably being schizophrenic. Despite Maslow's strained relationships with his parents, he developed a very close relationship with his mother's brother. He attributes his mental stability to the care and attention he received from his uncle.

After high school, Maslow was persuaded by his father to attend college to study law. Because he was not particularly interested in being a lawyer, Maslow's grades were not very good. He was also troubled by career uncertainty and his love for a woman of whom his parents disapproved. Maslow dealt with these troubled times by leaving New York and enrolling at the University of Wisconsin. Shortly after moving to Wisconsin, Maslow (who was then 20) returned to New York to marry his childhood sweetheart, 19-year-old Bertha Goodman. The newlyweds then returned to Wisconsin. As an indication of the emotional difficulty of his early life, Maslow stated that he really did not start living until he married Bertha and moved to Wisconsin.

Maslow stayed at Wisconsin to earn his BA (1930), MA (1931), and PhD (1934). The educational training he received at Wisconsin emphasized the very rigorous and objective scientific approach to the study of psychology that was so popular at that time. His doctoral dissertation, which dealt with the sexual behavior of monkeys, was under the direction of the famous experimental psychologist Harry Harlow. Upon completing his PhD degree, Maslow returned to New York and accepted a position at Columbia University as a research assistant to Edwin L. Thorndike, another famous psychologist. He also started teaching at Brooklyn College, where he stayed until 1951. During this time, Maslow began to extend his early research on the establishment of dominance in monkey colonies to the study of dominance in humans.

Because many of Europe's leading psychologists, psychiatrists, and other intellectuals were settling in New York to escape the Nazis, Maslow was able to meet, interact with, and learn from such personality theorists as Karen Horney and Alfred Adler. Such a stimulating environment would be enough to affect most people's thinking, but Maslow reported that it was the birth of his first child that significantly affected his views. He proclaimed that all of his academic knowledge and training and scientific research with rats and monkeys did little to prepare him for the wonder and mysteries of an infant child. As a result, Maslow shifted his attention away from the study of animals and began to study what he felt were the motivating forces behind personality out of a sincere desire to discover how to improve it.

In 1951, Maslow left Brooklyn College to accept a position at Brandeis University. He remained there until 1969. During that time, Maslow continued to develop and refine his theory on the nature of human motivation, which attracted a considerable amount of recognition.

In 1967, Maslow was elected to the prestigious office of president of the American Psychological Association. He left Brandeis University to become a resident fellow of the Laughlin Charitable Foundation in California, where he began a large-scale study applying his theory of human motivation and the philosophy of humanistic psychology to such topics as politics, economics, religion, and ethics.

Having had a history of heart trouble, Maslow died of a heart attack on June 8, 1970. More information about the personal side of Maslow's life and sources of his ideas can be found in a semi-autobiographical account titled *The Farther Reaches of Human Nature* (Maslow, 1971).

Basic Assumptions: Looking at the Positive Personality

Maslow felt the study of personality had a tradition of looking at the individual in somewhat negative terms. Such a view of personality portrayed people as being governed by either unconscious or environmentally determined forces. In response to this, Maslow proposed a viewpoint of the individual that has become known as the third force in psychology, with the psychodynamic and learning (see Chapter 10) viewpoints being the other two. The emphasis of this **third force** has been to enhance the dignity of people by studying the internal processes contributing to their self-enhancement.

A Positive View of the Individual
Like Rogers, Maslow viewed the individual as constantly striving for a sense of self-enhancement at a level of conscious awareness. He viewed people as basically good but somewhat weak in that they can easily fall victim to diversions that distract them from self-enhancement. For example, while going to school is an activity that reflects a desire for self-enhancement, any student would have little trouble listing those occasions when he or she might have gotten distracted by going out with friends instead of studying for a test or working on a term paper in the library. Fortunately, in the end, most students do get back on track and do the required work, even if it means staying up all night. Thus, while he recognized that people have faults, Maslow felt that people are basically good and motivated toward self-enhancement.

An Emphasis on Investigating the Healthy Personality
Maslow felt the emphasis on studying clients within the context of psychotherapy resulted in a restricted view of people that revealed little about the characteristics of the healthy personality. As a result, Maslow reasoned that to better understand emotionally healthy people, the emphasis should be on studying in detail those people who best exemplify the emotionally healthy personality. Much of Maslow's own research focused on an in-depth analysis of what he defined as "the best of the best individuals" in various disciplines, including Albert Einstein, Abraham Lincoln, and Ludwig van Beethoven.

The Motivational Nature of Personality and the Dynamic Satisfaction of Needs
Maslow viewed people as rarely being in a state of complete satisfaction. Instead, he believed that we are constantly being motivated to meet a variety of biological and psychological needs. The meeting of these biological and psychological needs was assumed to operate in a dynamic process rather than in isolation. For example, while doing well in college will make it possible to obtain a comfortable salary to help meet basic biological needs for food and shelter, it also meets the psychological needs of self-respect and gaining the respect of others.

Basic Concepts: The Nature and Structure of Human Needs

The basic concepts of Maslow's viewpoint include his conceptualization of the nature and structure of human needs and their motivational impact on the individual. These needs have as their principal objective the motivation of the individual to reach a state of self-actualization. For Maslow, the **state of self-actualization** involves people's attempts to reach their full potential by using their talents and abilities to the fullest extent while trying to achieve personal growth, satisfaction, and fulfillment. Maslow organized human needs in a manner designed to promote the achievement of this state of self-actualization. He grouped them into two basic types and arranged them into a hierarchy of five basic needs.

The Types of Needs: Deficiency and Being Needs

Maslow (1970b) made the distinction between deficiency needs and being needs:

▲ **Deficiency needs** are the lower, more basic needs necessary for the survival of the individual, including hunger, thirst, and safety. The deficiency needs motivate the individual to engage in behavior designed to bring about their satisfaction.

▲ **Being needs** are considered the higher needs necessary for the achievement of a state of self-actualization, including those needs reflecting a desire for wisdom and a sense of aesthetics.

The being needs motivate the individual to engage in behavior designed to bring about their fulfillment (e.g., going to college or an art museum). Deficiency needs are characterized by a lack of something the individual is motivated to supply. Being needs are characterized by an ongoing motivational process of self-enhancement, not a deficiency in a need requiring only satisfaction. The lower needs are considered to be more potent and to have a greater influence on behavior than the higher needs. As a result of these features, the lower needs are also generally satisfied before the higher needs. When your stomach is making loud, grumbling noises, it is difficult to fully appreciate a Van Gogh painting. In this case, a quick trip to the snack bar will satisfy the hunger, making it possible to once again focus more attention on the higher aesthetic needs and pleasures. As this example illustrates, both types of needs are important in helping to motivate people in their attempts to achieve the state of self-actualization.

The Hierarchy of Needs: The Road to Self-Actualization

Maslow (1970b) categorized human needs into five basic groups and organized them in a hierarchical fashion. The logic of the **hierarchy of needs** is that the needs at the lower end of the hierarchy exert more power to be satisfied than the needs at the next level. Progressing up the hierarchy of needs results in the individual coming closer to achieving the state of self-actualization. Figure 7.1 illustrates Maslow's hierarchical arrangement of needs.

Physiological Needs: The Most Basic Needs At the bottom of the hierarchy are the physiological needs. **Physiological needs** are those directly related to the survival of the individual. They include the need for food, water, sleep, and elimination. Such needs are extremely potent and when unfulfilled can dominate

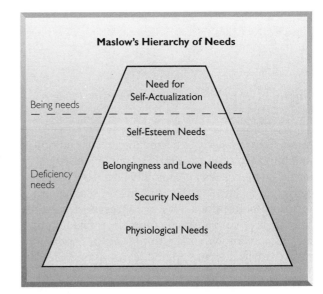

Figure 7.1
Maslow's hierarchy of needs is organized with the lowest, most potent needs at the bottom and the highest, least potent needs at the top.

the life of the individual. For example, ideals like democracy and justice mean little to people who are on the brink of starvation. When physiological needs are routinely met, people can devote more of their energies to meeting the next level of needs—safety needs.

Safety Needs: The Desire for Stability **Safety needs** are those directly related to creating an environment for living that is free from the threat of danger. They include the need for order, predictability, and structure. For most people, safety needs are met by the dwellings in which they live and by the security and predictability they provide. No matter how hectic your day might have been, settling into an evening routine adds a sense of stability and security to your life. On the other hand, the trauma of being burglarized probably stems from the fact that the one place most people feel has a sense of security has been violated.

Thus, by developing certain daily routines in our life, and order in our living environment, we are able to regularly meet these safety and security needs. The consistent satisfaction of safety needs allows us to begin considering the next cluster of needs—belongingness and love needs.

Belongingness and Love Needs: The Desire to Be with Others **Belongingness and love needs** are directly concerned with the basic desire to feel accepted by and have meaningful interpersonal relationships with others. They include the need to feel a part of some reference group (e.g., family, neighborhood, a gang, religious group, or professional organization) and the ability to both receive and give love (e.g., establish meaningful friendships). Belonging to various social organizations (e.g., the Psychology Club), community service groups (e.g., Parent-Teacher Association or Jaycees), and leisure organizations (e.g., bowling league), as well as being a member of a family, gives us a sense of acceptance and belongingness and helps to meet this category of needs.

With the changing nature of the social structure in our society (e.g., high divorce rate, the constant transferring of families for business reasons, and urbanization), the meeting of these needs has become more and more difficult, creating increases in feelings of loneliness and alienation. Maslow felt that failing to meet belongingness and love needs was at the core of most, if not all, forms of maladjust-

ment. Once people are able to achieve a satisfactory sense of acceptance, they can devote some of their attention to meeting the fourth level of needs in the hierarchy—the esteem needs.

Esteem Needs: The Desire to Be Recognized by Others **Esteem needs** are concerned with the desire to have the respect of others and possess a sense of self-respect. Included in having the respect of others are achieving status and recognition within those significant groups and being perceived as a worthy and able member.

For example, when trying to meet this aspect of the esteem needs, it would not be enough to simply be a member of a community service group. You would demonstrate a caring for and an interest in the group by running for a position on the board of directors. Pursuing a seat on the board requires a sense of self-confidence and self-esteem. Being elected to the board reflects the confidence and esteem other members have for your abilities. Included in possessing a sense of self-respect is having a level of self-esteem that reflects a feeling of confidence in your personal abilities.

Thus, gaining the respect of others and achieving and developing a sense of self-respect seem to be reciprocal processes. People who are able to consistently satisfy the esteem needs can direct their motivation at the highest level of the hierarchy of needs—self-actualization.

Self-Actualization: Developing the Individual's Full Potential **Self-actualization** involves the individual's desire to develop his or her abilities to their fullest potential. Such development involves obtaining a deeper sense of one's own desires and abilities and maximizing their expression in an attempt to bring them together. As an example, for a young woman interested in acting, self-actualization would require participating in acting to the fullest extent of her ability. If she has only limited acting ability, this might involve acting in the local theater productions, as well as possibly attempting to direct some of the productions. If she has greater ability, self-actualization may involve moving to a large city and pursuing a full-time career in acting by devoting literally all of her time to this ambition.

For others, the expression of the self-actualization desire might involve designing clothes, working on cars, bodybuilding, or gardening. The point is that whatever the person feels is a vital part of his or her human nature should be pursued with the idea of doing it as well as can possibly be done. Such a sentiment was stated in an extremely eloquent manner by Maslow (1954) when he said:

> A musician must make music, an artist must paint, a poet must write if he is ultimately to be at peace with himself. What a man *can* be he *must* be. This need we may call self-actualization. (p. 91; Note: In this statement, Maslow was referring to both men and women.)

However, while the self-actualization need is at the highest level of the hierarchy, it is also the least powerful. It is for this reason that Maslow felt that very few people are able to completely satisfy this need. For such a need to be achieved, the individual must be extremely motivated from within himself or herself. For example, although many may have the ability to be an Olympic figure skater or the heavyweight boxing champion of the world, very few have the internal desire required to devote the many years it takes to achieve such a goal.

A Final Comment on the Hierarchy of Needs: Some Points of Clarification Many people have some misunderstandings about the hierarchy of needs that should be addressed. First, although the needs are arranged hierarchically, this does not mean that the person must completely satisfy one group before moving on to the next level. Instead, the lower needs should be satisfied only to the extent that the individual has some relief from them and can devote more attention to the higher needs. The more relief a person has from lower needs, the more attention that person can give to the higher needs. For example, the less time a man has to spend concentrating on job security (i.e., threats to physiological and safety needs), the more time he has for personal sources of pleasure, such as improving his stamp collection (i.e., esteem needs) and being an active member of the local stamp-collecting club (i.e., belonging needs).

Second, because it is possible to experience more than one need at a time, it is also possible to satisfy more than one need at a time. For example, becoming the chairperson of a neighborhood block watch crime-prevention program involves the individual maximizing a sense of security (i.e., safety needs) but also obtaining status and recognition (i.e., esteem needs) within the neighborhood (i.e., belongingness and love needs).

Finally, even though the lowest needs are most powerful, they can be superseded by the higher needs. For example, an individual skips lunch (i.e., physiological need) to attend a club meeting or drive a friend to the airport (i.e., belongingness and love needs, respectively). More extreme examples of this are individuals who go on hunger strikes, often until death, as a means of expressing their deep commitment to a particular cause; and the starving artist who would rather spend money on paints than on food. The concluding point to be made here is that the hierarchy of needs is not as cut-and-dried as many people might assume.

Maslow's Study of Self-Actualizing People: In Search of Excellence

Although Maslow was extremely interested in the nature and organization of human needs, he was particularly interested in the self-actualization need. It is for this reason that he attempted to identify the characteristics of exceptional people. In the true tradition of studying the "best of the best," Maslow launched a rather ambitious study of self-actualizing people. In this study, he selected a relatively small number of subjects who he felt were operating at their maximum abilities. Some were rather contemporary figures (e.g., Franklin D. Roosevelt and Sigmund Freud); others were historical figures (e.g., Ludwig van Beethoven and Thomas Jefferson). In studying these people, Maslow took a rather clinical approach, collecting information from a variety of sources. He conducted personal interviews with the subjects who were living at the time or with people who knew them well, and he analyzed historical and personal documents. In analyzing this information, Maslow looked for characteristics shared by these people in their approach to work, interpersonal relationships, and life in general.

Some Self-Actualizing People:
A "Who's Who" of the Best of the Best
Some of the people Maslow considered as coming closest to what he meant by self-actualization included

▲ *Albert Einstein (1879–1955).* German physicist, formulator of the theory of relativity, and winner of the 1921 Nobel prize for physics
▲ *Eleanor Roosevelt (1894–1962).* U.S. diplomat, author, lecturer, and wife of President Franklin Delano Roosevelt
▲ *Jane Addams (1860–1935).* U.S. social worker, writer, and winner of the 1931 Nobel peace prize
▲ *William James (1842–1910).* U.S. psychologist and philosopher, and the father of psychology in the United States

▲ *Albert Schweitzer (1875–1965).* Alsatian doctor and missionary in Africa
▲ *Aldous Huxley (1894–1963).* English novelist, essayist, and critic
▲ *Baruch Spinoza (1632–1677).* Dutch philosopher
▲ *Abraham Lincoln (1809–1865).* 16th president of the United States
▲ *Thomas Jefferson (1743–1826).* U.S. architect, statesman, diplomat, and 3rd president of the United States

Such a list reads like a "who's who" of the best of the best. However, more impressive than the names of these people are the characteristics they shared.

Some of the individuals Maslow considered to be self-actualizers are presented in this collection of photographs (left to right from the upper left): Albert Einstein, Eleanor Roosevelt, Jane Addams, William James, Albert Schweitzer, Aldous Huxley, Abraham Lincoln, and Thomas Jefferson.

Characteristics of Self-Actualizing People: Some Common Threads of Excellence

While self-actualizing people can be found in all areas of life, Maslow (1970b) found that they seem to share certain characteristics:

▲ *More accurate perception of reality*. Because they are secure in their needs, self-actualizing people can judge events in an unbiased, less defensive manner. For example, being secure in their sense of self, they can make decisions based on the issues at hand, not based on some self-serving bias.

▲ *Greater acceptance of self and others*. Their realistic perception of the world makes it possible for self-actualizing people to see both the good and bad side of themselves and others. As a result, they tend to be more understanding and accepting. They also tend to view people more democratically, responding to the behavior rather than the personal characteristics of the individual. For example, they treat people fairly and equally, regardless of race, class, religion, or level of education.

▲ *Nonhostile sense of humor*. Their nonhostile sense of humor is characterized by a dislike for jokes that might be degrading to others. Self-actualizing people would not find jokes that feature the stereotypes of ethnic minorities funny. Instead, they prefer to laugh at themselves or at more philosophical or satirical forms of humor.

▲ *True to themselves*. Self-actualizing people tend to have a spontaneous, natural, and fresh approach to experiencing the world. They tend to say what they feel and feel what they are experiencing in a natural manner indicative of their inner self. Such naturalness also produces a high degree of spontaneity and freshness in their behavior. For example, a self-actualizing person might still be deeply moved by a scene from a favorite movie, even after seeing it many times, and express this feeling by crying openly in the theater.

▲ *Peak experiences*. Their openness and naturalness of experiencing the world allow self-actualizing people to have a greater number of peak experiences. **Peak experiences** involve a heightened sense of wonder, awe, or ecstasy over an

YOU CAN DO IT

A Personal Look at Peak Experiences: Experiencing a Natural High

In his own attempt to understand the nature of peak experiences, Maslow (1962) used written descriptions of such experiences provided by college students. Polyson (1985) has developed a written exercise designed to help students gain a better understanding of the construct of peak experiences by looking for them in their own lives.

To examine possible peak experiences in your own life, write on a separate sheet of paper what you might consider a peak experience. To help you identify such an experience,

> think of the most wonderful experience of your life: the happiest moments, ecstatic moments, moments of rapture, perhaps from being in love, or from listening to music or suddenly "being hit" by a book or painting, or from some creative moment (Maslow, 1962, p. 67)

To give you some point of reference, based on the written descriptions provided by his students, Polyson (1985) reports:

> Most of the peak experiences had occurred during athletic, artistic, religious, or nature experiences, or during intimate moments with a friend or family member. There were a number of peak experiences in which the students achieved an important personal goal or collective goal. There were also peak experiences in which the students overcame some adversity or danger or helped someone in need. (p. 212)

Thus, peak experiences are associated with very special moments in our lives when we are able to achieve an intense and unique feeling that can only be described as a "natural high." For a closer look at some more extensive research of peak experiences, consider the information in "A Closer Look" on page 189.

experience. For example, the tremendous sense of emotional elation you might feel when falling in love is a form of peak experience. While

Maslow believed that we are all capable of having peak experiences, self-actualizing people tend to have more of them and experience them to a greater degree than other people. To understand what is meant by a peak experience, try for yourself the exercise outlined in "You Can Do It" on page 188.

A Closer Look:

Research on Peak Experiences: Objective Attempts to Investigate Subjective Experiences

It would seem that the rather subjective nature of peak experiences would make their investigation difficult. But a number of researchers are attempting to study peak experiences using many of the standard research techniques (e.g., clinical interview and factor analysis) discussed throughout this book. The following are some examples of this research.

Frequencies of Peak Experiences

Research on the frequency of peak experiences indicates that they are not all that rare (Alexander, Rainforth, & Gelderloos, 1991; Wulff, 1991). For example, mild forms of peak experiences were reported by 35% of a national sample of 1,460 Americans (Greeley, 1975), 36.4% of a British national sample of 1,865 persons (Greeley, 1975), and 30% of a group of 139 upper-divisional and graduate students (McClain & Andrews, 1969). But when a more stringent (e.g., less spiritual) definition of peak experiences emphasizing transcendental experience (James, 1958) is used, and follow-up interviews with the respondents are conducted, only 2% of the individuals were classified as having peak experiences (Thomas & Cooper, 1977). Thus, the frequency at which peak experiences occur tends to depend on how they are defined.

Correlates of Peak Experiences

Wulff (1991) notes there is a somewhat small but expanding body of research on correlates of peak experiences. When people who did and did not have peak experiences were given a number of personality tests, the results indicated that "peakers" tend to be more intelligent, assertive, expedient, tender-minded, imaginative, forthright, experimenting, self-sufficient, placid, and relaxed; and they tend to be less dogmatic and authoritarian than "nonpeakers" (McClain & Andrews, 1969). Those who report deeper and more lasting peak experiences tend to engage in meditative practices and tend to be less materialistic, less status-conscious, and more socially concerned (Wuthnow, 1978). Peak experiences are positively correlated with psychological well-being and negatively correlated with poor mental health (Greeley, 1975; Margoshes & Litt, 1966). Although peak experiences (described in different ways) and various indices of psychological health are positively related, the causal link between them is still undetermined (Alexander, Rainforth, & Gelderloos, 1991).

Identifying the Distinguishing Characteristics of Peak Experiences

To identify the distinguishing features of peak experiences, 123 male and female upper-level college students completed the *Experience Questionnaire* (Privette, 1984), which is designed to assess the unique and shared qualities of peak experiences and other intense, self-directed emotional experiences (Privette, 1983). Peak experiences were found to be characterized by three distinguishing factors: fulfillment, significance, and spirituality (Privette & Bundrick, 1991).

- ▲ Fulfillment involves respondents describing peak experiences as intrinsically rewarding, providing an enduring positive feeling, and related positively to their own performance.
- ▲ Significance involves the respondents describing peak experiences as being turning points in their lives and featuring increases in personal understanding, expressions, and values.
- ▲ Spirituality involves respondents describing peak experiences as creating a sense of unity of self and the environment and a loss of time and space.

This represents only a brief listing of the research on peak experiences. A more extensive discussion of peak experiences can be found in the *Handbook of Self-Actualization* (Jones & Crandall, 1991) and *Psychology of Religion: Classic and Contemporary Views* (Wulff, 1991).

▲ *Other-centered rather than self-centered.* Self-actualizing people tend to demonstrate a concern for problems and issues that go beyond themselves and have the potential to affect many people. A self-actualizing student might be actively involved in organizations dealing with the issues of the homeless or teenage pregnancy. In the Adlerian sense, these people have a high degree of social interest.

▲ *Autonomous in behavior and values.* Because they are motivated by the desire to fulfill their personal sense of self, self-actualizing people are less influenced by what others say or do. They also have a strong personal sense of ethics, which they use in deciding for themselves what is right and wrong. As a result, they tend to be nonconformists in their behavior and attitudes.

▲ *Selective in their interpersonal relationships.* The autonomous nature of self-actualizing people creates in them a desire for privacy and detachment. Because they are inner directed, they do not feel the need to constantly be around other people. As a result, they tend to have few friends. But the friendships they do develop tend to be very deep and rich. Self-actualizing people tend to seek out the friendship of other self-actualizers.

▲ *Being creative.* The creativity of self-actualizing people is not limited to such traditional forms as writing books or producing art; it is evident in the way they live their lives. For example, they might demonstrate the tendency to come up with creative solutions for the political bickering going on in the office. Or they might come up with rather novel ideas for party games or costumes that do not cost much money. In short, they tend to have a unique perspective on things in all aspects of life.

Included in this set of rather positive characteristics of self-actualizing people are some negative characteristics. Because they tend to be such emotionally strong people, they are capable of exhibiting detachment from those who they feel have done them wrong in a manner that might be described as cold, heartless, and ruthless. As you will recall, Freud severed his long-time friendships with Jung and Adler with almost surgical precision and coldness. Like so many other people, some self-actualizers have been described as boring, silly, wasteful, and capable of temper outbursts. Thus, even while operating at their maximum potential, such self-actualizing people are not perfect.

Some Final Comments on the Study of Self-Actualizing People

Self-actualizing people seem to share certain characteristics that set them apart from most other people. But it should be made clear that having these characteristics has little to do with intelligence and more to do with how the person chooses to live his or her life. Self-actualizing people tend to experience life to the fullest of their ability, and they search for excellence within themselves and in their experiences with other people and events in their lives.

Applications of Maslow's Viewpoint: Using What Is Known

As with most other profound theories, Maslow's views have been applied to a wide variety of areas, including psychotherapy (1970b), religion (1970a), education (1971), and stereotypes (1968, 1970b). But a major application of Maslow's viewpoint has been to the world of work. In fact, an article by Maslow (1943) titled "A Theory of Human Motivation" was rated second among some 1,964 articles in a survey by Matteson (1974) of significant contributions to the literature on management. In this section, you will learn about the application of Maslow's viewpoint to the world of work and personality assessment.

Maslow in the World of Work: "Working" Your Way Up the Hierarchy of Needs

Maslow felt that our needs should be met in all aspects of our lives. For many people, probably one of the most significant aspects of life, outside of family, is the world of work. In his own concern with human needs in the world of work, Maslow advocated what he called eupsychian management (Maslow, 1965).

Applying Eupsychian Management: An Employee-Centered Approach **Eupsychian management** stresses that managers should concern themselves with becoming more aware of the needs of employees and creating a work environment designed to facilitate the satisfaction of these needs in their quest for self-actualization.

For example, while employees may have a high degree of job security and earn a substantial hourly wage (e.g., physiological and safety needs are met), if they feel exploited by the company (e.g., belongingness needs not met) or are bored or not sufficiently challenged by their job (e.g., esteem needs not met), both the worker and the company will suffer. Worker suffering might include increases in alcohol or drug abuse and various types of physical illnesses, such as ulcers and high blood pressure. The company suffers in that the quality of products produced by such employees is rather low, which translates into loss of sales.

Maslow suggested that one way to assess the extent to which employee needs were being met was to examine the nature of their complaints. When employees complain about the office being too crowded or noisy, Maslow proposed that this should be a clue to management that safety needs are not being met. If they complain about office furnishings as being too drab or dehumanizing, this may be a sign that while their safety needs are met, their belongingness needs are not being satisfied. As employee complaints become more advanced in the nature of the need concerned, management can see that the employees are getting that much closer to being self-actualized. Thus, the point of eupsychian management is to listen to what employees are saying and act on this information in a manner that will help employees to move up the hierarchy of needs within the world of work.

Research Evaluating Eupsychian Management   The eupsychian approach to management makes a lot of intuitive sense, which may explain the impact it has had on the management literature. But testing the value of a theory involves more than just intuitive appeal; it involves systematic research. In this regard, the empirical evidence is not as strong as the intuitive appeal.

In a study examining the relationship of Maslow's need hierarchy in the work context of some 892 Canadian accountants, scientists, and engineers, it was reported that the security needs form a distinctively different category from the remaining needs, while the self-actualization need was rated similar to lower needs (Mitchell & Moudgill, 1976). Thus, instead of finding five categories of needs, only two were noted: security needs and the other needs, including self-actualization.

While Maslow also proposed a two-category need classification (see Figure 7.1), he had the self-actualization need in the being needs category all by itself, and the security needs were grouped with the others in the deficiency needs category. This classification of needs is just the opposite of what was observed in Mitchell and Moudgill's (1976) study. Other studies have also failed to identify the five categories of needs proposed by Maslow (Alderfer, 1972; Friedlander, 1963; Lawler & Suttle, 1972).

In a rather extensive review of Maslow's hierarchy of needs in the workplace, Wahba and Bridwell (1976, p. 233) state, "This literature review shows that Maslow's Need Hierarchy Theory has received little clear or consistent support from the available research. Some of Maslow's propositions are totally rejected, while others receive mixed and questionable support at best."

Wahba and Bridwell (1976) also note that part of the difficulty in assessing the validity of Maslow's hierarchy of needs is that he was not very specific about certain vital points. Because Maslow did not specify a timetable for meeting these needs (Muchinsky, 1983), researchers are hard-pressed to know if they are allowing enough time to accurately assess the actual changes in the individual's progress within the hierarchy. In addition, because the satisfaction of needs depends on so many psychological, social, and situational factors, specifying the "right combination of events" is probably impossible. In this sense. "Maslow's Need Hierarchy Theory is almost a nontestable theory" (Wahba & Bridwell, 1976, p. 234).

Nontestable though it may be, Maslow's concept of the hierarchy of needs has profoundly influenced our thinking. In a survey of the bibliographical citations of the hierarchy of needs, Roberts (1972) noted over 200 listings after 1965 by over 140 authors in such diverse areas as organizational behavior and systems, teacher education, employee needs and expectations, leadership and management, political behavior, job performance, and psychological needs and satisfaction. It is very hard to dismiss something that has had the impact of Maslow's hierarchy of needs; but it should be judged on its empirical evidence, not just its intuitive appeal.

Personality Assessment from Maslow's Viewpoint: The Assessment of Self-Actualization

The significance Maslow and others interested in his viewpoint gave to the concept of self-actualization is also reflected in its application to personality assessment. While the concept of self-actualization is supposedly very subjective and unique to each person, attempts have been made to develop objective measures for assessing an individual's degree of self-actualization (Jones & Crandall, 1986; Shostrom, 1975, 1977).

The Personal Orientation Inventory: A Measure of Self-Actualization An objective measure most often associated with assessing self-actualization is the Personal Orientation Inventory. The **Personal Orientation Inventory (POI)** was developed by Everett L. Shostrom (1963, 1964, & 1975) as an objective means of measuring some of the behaviors and values related to Maslow's concept of self-actualization. The POI contains 150 items, arranged in pairs of opposing statements. From each pair of statements, the individual is asked to select the one statement that best describes him or her. The scoring of the POI involves assessing two major scales and 10 subscales. The major scales are Inner Directiveness (ID) (i.e., autonomy) and Time Ratio (TR) (i.e., oriented in the present and effectively utilizes time). The 10 subscales consist of characteristics indicating self-actualization, including self-acceptance, spontaneity, synergy (i.e., flexibility in thinking), and capacity for intimate contact (Shostrom, 1963, 1964, 1975). To assess your own level of self-actualization, complete the exercise in "You Can Do It" below.

YOU CAN DO IT

The Assessment of Self-Actualization: Measuring Maximum Potential

Listed below is a sample of items similar to those in the Personal Orientation Inventory. For each pair of items, select the alternative that seems to be most characteristic of how you feel.

1. (a) I do what others expect me to do.
   (b) I choose freely what I want to do.
2. (a) Jokes that make fun of others are not something I enjoy hearing.
   (b) Jokes that make fun of others are something I do enjoy hearing.
3. (a) It is my belief that people basically care about others.
   (b) It is my belief that people basically care about themselves only.
4. (a) Justifying my actions is something I must do in the pursuit of my own interests.
   (b) Justifying my actions is something I do not feel I must do in the pursuit of my own interests.
5. (a) The rules and standards of society guide the way I live my life.
   (b) The rules and standards of society are not always needed to guide the way I live my life.
6. (a) I need reasons to justify my feelings.
   (b) I do not need reasons to justify my feelings.
7. (a) Warm feelings are the only ones I feel free to express to my friends.
   (b) Both warm and hostile feelings are feelings I feel free to express to my friends.
8. (a) Being myself is the best way to continue to grow.
   (b) The only way to continue to grow is by setting my sights on a high-level goal that is socially approved.
9. (a) The anger people feel should always be controlled.
   (b) The anger people feel should be expressed honestly.
10. (a) Criticism can provide a welcomed opportunity for growth.
    (b) Criticism does not provide a welcomed opportunity for growth.

Interpretation

Give yourself one point each time your response agrees with the following scoring key: Item 1 = b, 2 = a, 3 = a, 4 = b, 5 = b, 6 = b, 7 = b, 8 = a, 9 = b, 10 = a. The higher your score, the more consistent your responses are with those characteristic of self-actualization.

Note. From *Personal Orientation Inventory* (POI): *A Test of Self-Actualization.* by E. Shostrom, 1963. San Diego, CA: Educational and Industrial Testing Service.

Research Assessing the Validity of the POI The validity of the POI has been investigated by assessing how closely it correlates to other personality inventories that measure traits and values related to the characteristics of self-actualizing people. For example, the ID scale was correlated positively with inventories measuring self-esteem, faith in people, purpose in life, and empathy; but it was correlated negatively with rigidity, social anxiety, hopelessness, and narcissism (Leak, 1984). POI scales have also been correlated positively with tests of creativity (Braun & Asta, 1968) and academic achievement (LeMay & Damm, 1968; Stewart, 1968). Supporting the notion of personal growth occurring within successful therapeutic experiences, greater increases in POI scores were found for people who participated in encounter groups than for those who did not (Guinan & Foulds, 1970).

Limitations of the POI include the apparent interrelatedness of the various scales (Silverstein & Fisher, 1968, 1972; Hattie, 1981) and findings inconsistent with Maslow's thinking (Maddi, 1989). Although there appear to be certain shortcomings, "the POI has shown impressive group differences following growth experiences and also impressive correlations with related trait measures" (Leak, 1984, p. 38).

In fact, the amount of research on the POI is extensive. Over 700 studies on the POI were listed prior to 1979; in 1982, over 390 references were identified in a separate computer search of the POI literature (Hattie, Hancock, & Brereton, 1984). More extensive reviews of research investigating the psychometric properties of the POI can be found in several other sources (Hyman, 1979; Knapp, 1976; Tosi & Lindamood, 1975).

Evaluation of Maslow's Motivational Viewpoint: Characteristic Strengths and Limitations

Characteristic Strengths
Here are some strengths of Maslow's motivational viewpoint:

▲ *An emphasis on the best of the best.* While many of the personality theorists discussed in this book developed viewpoints of personality based on their clinical work involving people with maladjusted personalities, Maslow took just the opposite approach. His approach was to learn about the healthy personality by studying the healthiest personalities he could find. Maslow's emphasis on studying the best of the best represents a welcome alternative in an attempt to better understand the operation of the healthy personality.

▲ *A realistic view of human nature.* Maslow maintained a relatively realistic view of human nature. He saw people as basically good and motivated in the direction of self-enhancement. But he also realized that such a process of self-enhancement did not just happen automatically; it required some desire and effort on the part of the individual. Maslow realistically pointed out that as the level of self-enhancement becomes higher, more personal effort and desire on the individual's part are required. His basic point was that people will improve to the extent that they want to improve.

▲ *The impact of Maslow's idea.* Because Maslow's hierarchy of needs makes so much intuitive sense, it is discussed in a wide variety of disciplines, from religion to work. It is also very easy for people to apply the needs hierarchy to their own lives as a means of explaining and understanding their own behavior. Thus, because it is something that can be easily used, the hierarchy of needs concept has been applied in various disciplines.

Characteristic Limitations
Maslow's motivational viewpoint has the following limitations:

▲ *An almost nontestable theory.* Central to Maslow's viewpoint is his hierarchy of needs. But much of what he said about this theoretical concept is rather ambiguous, with the exception of the ordering of the need categories. Maslow was unclear about all of the needs that were included in each category. He also left unspecified the exact nature by which these various needs could be satisfied. In short, many important questions about the hierarchy of needs remain unanswered—and the farther up the hierarchy you go, the more ambiguity you tend to find. Such ambiguity creates an almost non-testable theory.

▲ *The subjective nature of self-actualization and self-actualizers.* Although Maslow defined the characteristics of the self-actualizing individual in a rather detailed and specific way, he selected these features primarily based on his own subjective judgment, using very little objective statistical analyses. The extent to which other researchers would come to the same conclusions as Maslow about what characteristics constitute the best of the best remains unanswered. In all fairness, however, the research on the POI does represent an attempt to objectively assess the concept of self-actualization.

▲ *Limited empirical research.* Because of the problems noted in the preceding two limitations, Maslow's viewpoint has generated very little empirical research. And as noted earlier, the research that has been done seems to offer only minimal support for many of Maslow's principal concepts.

More information about Maslow's views on personality can be found in *Toward a Psychology of Being* (Maslow, 1968) and *Motivation and Personality* (Maslow, 1970b).

Kelly's Personal Construct Perspective: The Construing of Events and Alternatives

Like Abraham Maslow, George Kelly felt that the individual was motivated by the desire to achieve a sense of mastery over his or her environment. For Kelly, this mastery took the form of trying to create a greater sense of predictability and understanding of the people and events in the individual's world. Such increases in understanding and predictability involved the individual categorizing and organizing his or her perceptions and interpretations of events in meaningful ways.

Kelly stressed the humanistic tradition in his holistic approach to the study of personality (Cloninger, 1993; Kelly, 1955a, 1955b, 1969). Consistent with the humanistic tradition, Kelly was optimistic in his assumptions about human nature and viewed people as basically good by nature and rational in their thinking (Kelly, 1969; Schultz, 1990). Kelly also stressed the importance of subjective perception of experience as a determinant of an individual's actions (Cloninger, 1993; Monte, 1991; Pervin, 1993), which is consistent with both the humanistic and phenomenological viewpoints. For a glimpse at some of the personal highlights in the life of a unique thinker, read "A Closer Look" below.

A Closer Look:

Biographical Background: The Life of George A. Kelly

George A. Kelly was born on April 28, 1905, in the wide-open plains of Peth, Kansas. He was the only child of parents who were deeply committed to their fundamentalist religious beliefs, which included being opposed to such "wastes of time" as dancing and card playing. In 1909, Kelly's father converted a lumber wagon into a covered wagon and moved his family to Colorado. But shortly afterward, they moved back to their farm in Kansas because they were unable to find water on the land they were given as new settlers. Kelly's return to Kansas began for him an educational background and professional career that were as electric as they were impressive.

Kelly's education began in a one-room schoolhouse, and he was also taught at home by his parents. At the age of 13, he was sent to Wichita, where he eventually attended four different high schools before graduating. Upon graduating from high school, Kelly attended Friends University, a Quaker school in Wichita, where he was active in debate and music. After three years at Friends University, he transferred to Park College, where in 1926 he received his BA degree in physics and mathematics.

After working for a short time in aeronautical engineering, Kelly found his interests turning toward education and social problems. He enrolled at the

George Kelly's view-point of personality reflected his eclectic educational back-ground, experience, and interests.

University of Kansas, where he pursued a master's degree with a major in educational sociology and a minor in labor relations. His master's degree thesis, which he received in 1928, was a study on how workers in Kansas City spent their leisure time.

Over the following year, Kelly had several different academic experiences: holding a part-time position at a labor college, teaching speech classes for the American Bankers Association, and conducting Americanization classes for future citizens. While teaching at a junior college in Sheldon, Iowa, where he was also coaching dramatics, Kelly met his future wife, Gladys Thompson, who taught English and also coached drama.

In 1929, Kelly was awarded an exchange scholarship. This scholarship allowed him to study at the University of Edinburgh with the eminent statistician and educator Sir Godfrey Thomson. While working with Sir Thomson, Kelly earned a bachelor's degree in education in 1930. His thesis involved predicting teaching success. It was during this time that Kelly developed an interest in psychology. Upon his return to the United States in 1930, he enrolled at Iowa State University to start working on a PhD in psychology. As a graduate student in psychology, Kelly was interested in physiological psychology, doing his dissertation on the common factors in speech and reading disabilities. Two days after receiving his PhD in 1931, Kelly married Gladys Thompson.

With the stock market crash and the subsequent depression in America, the early 1930s were not the best of times for a newly wed, young PhD recipient to be looking for an academic position. But Kelly did obtain an academic position in 1931 at Fort Hays

Kansas State College. Kelly soon realized, however, that his training in physiological psychology had not prepared him very well for the problems being experienced by the students he encountered at Fort Hays during the depression. As a result, Kelly decided to move away from physiological psychology and devote his attention to more humanitarian efforts by shifting his interest to clinical psychology. During the next 13 years at Fort Hays, Kelly made a number of significant contributions to the field of clinical psychology. One contribution was the development of a program of traveling psychological clinics that served the state's schools. Through this unique program, Kelly and his students experimented with various approaches for treating the problems they encountered. Another significant contribution was the progress Kelly began to make in his own theory of construct alternativism.

Working as an aviation psychologist during World War II, Kelly headed a training program for local civilian pilots and did much to improve the quality and effectiveness of clinical psychology in the armed services. In 1945, he accepted a faculty position at the University of Maryland, but left in 1946 to accept a position as professor of psychology and director of the clinical psychology program at Ohio State University (the director's position was previously held by Carl Rogers). Kelly, along with his colleague Julian Rotter (see Chapter 11), took the relatively small clinical psychology program at Ohio State and developed it into one of the finest programs in the country. Kelly spent 19 years at Ohio State University.

In response to an invitation by Maslow, Kelly left Ohio State in 1965 to accept a position at Brandeis University, where he was appointed the Riklis Chair of Behavioral Science. The position allowed him to devote all his time to the development and application of his theory of personality.

In addition to his dedication to teaching and research, Kelly also was very involved in the development of clinical psychology as a profession. He was extremely instrumental in the development of the American Board of Examiners in Professional Psychology, and served as its president from 1951 through 1953. The American Board of Examiners in Professional Psychology is an organization devoted to the professional development of psychologists. Kelly's service to his profession also included being a member of the Training Committee of the National Institute for Mental Health and the National Institutes of Health from 1958 to 1967. Kelly died on March 6, 1967, at the age of 62.

The educational and professional diversity of Kelly's training and experiences is nothing short of remarkable. It was this diversity that helped Kelly to develop his unique viewpoint of personality. More information on the life of George Kelly can be found in Brendan A. Maher's *Clinical Psychology and Personality: The Selected Papers of George Kelly* (1969) .

Basic Concepts of Kelly's Personal Construct Perspective: The Foundation for Formulating Alternatives

At the core of Kelly's perspective is the idea that an individual's personality reflects the choices that person makes based on the perception of surrounding events. The basic concepts of Kelly's theory lay the foundation for explaining how these choices are determined.

Constructive Alternatives

Constructive alternativism is a cornerstone of Kelly's viewpoint of personality. The basic logic of **constructive alternativism** is that any one particular event can have several different interpretations. From this perspective, there is no absolute truth or objective reality, but simply different ways of viewing the same event or situation. For example, when trying to explain why a student got a "C" on a test, the professor might say it was due to a failure to answer the questions appropriately; the student might say the test was unfair and too picky. The point to be made here is that the same event can be construed from various alternatives, depending on who is doing the perceiving.

Personal Constructs as the Core of Construct Alternativism

The basic elements involved in this process of construct alternativism are what Kelly referred to as personal constructs. A **personal construct** is a category of thought by which the individual interprets and labels experiences in his or her personal world. Some examples of constructs might include "friendly-

unfriendly," "helpful-harmful," "masculine-feminine," "exciting-boring," and "sensitive-callous."

It is possible for people to be using a different personal construct system even though they may be using the same dimensions. For example, to one student a "tough" professor might be one who does not allow any work to be turned in late. To another student, a "tough" professor may be one who requires a lot of reading and library work before giving a good grade in his or her course. Thus, while the words (e.g., *tough, smart, lazy,* etc.) may be the same, the meaning of the construct for the individual is personal. It is the personal nature of these constructs that Kelly believed helped to account for the differences in people's personalities. In addition, as more experience is gained, personal constructs can be refined. For example, as the student gets to know the professor better, the tough professor may be perceived as impartial and concerned with helping students perform beyond their own expectations.

The Fundamental Postulate

While the nature of personal constructs involves a system that people can use to classify and categorize perceptions of the events occurring around them, the purpose of personal constructs is to help develop a course of action related to these events. Kelly summarized the purpose of personal constructs in what he referred to as his fundamental postulate.

The **fundamental postulate** states that "A person's processes are psychologically channelized by the ways in which he anticipates events" (Kelly, 1955a, p. 46). A key element in this statement is the word *anticipates*. The nature of the course of action an individual decides to take depends upon the nature of the construct used and how the construct influences (i.e., "channelizes") what the person thinks is going to happen.

For example, based on previous experiences with going to parties, Margaret might use the constructs "good-bad" and "exciting-boring" to anticipate whether an invitation to a party this weekend will result in yet another unpleasant experience. If she enters the party with a bad attitude and the expectation of having an unpleasant time, this will probably result in her not smiling at many people, standing in a corner, and being critical of the refreshments and music. With such a negative attitude, Margaret is probably going to have a bad time. In this sense, her perceptions (e.g., the food is bland) and behavior (e.g., standing in the corner) are determined not by the reality of the situation (e.g., it may be a really good party for everybody else), but by the constructs that Margaret uses to create expectations of the situation (e.g., she is not going to have fun).

The Corollaries of Constructs

In addition to the fundamental postulate, Kelly also outlined a number of corollaries that clarify the nature and operation of constructs:

▲ The **range corollary** stipulates that a construct has a limited range in which it might be useful. For example, an individual might use a "dangerous-safe" construct to decide whether a situation is perceived as a threat and requires withdrawal or is harmless and permits continued forward movement. The range corollary highlights the adaptive and flexible nature of successful constructs.

▲ The **experience corollary** states that a person's construct system changes as he or she successfully perceives events over time. For example, each time the person is in a hostile situation and successfully anticipates when to take a stand or when to give ground, he or she gains experience that helps to refine when and where certain constructs and responses are useful.

▲ The **modulation corollary** is used to help explain the idea that changes in an individual's system of constructs can occur only to the extent that the constructs are flexible enough to accommodate new information. For example, to be successful, a personnel manager must be able to construe an effective district sales manager as someone other than a white male applicant. The modulation corollary points out that successful constructs are adjusted to fit the experience that has been acquired.

▲ The **sociability corollary** states that the extent to which two people will be able to interact successfully with each other is determined by the extent to which they are using similar construct systems (i.e., the same perception of reality) to perceive the same event. For example, based on the sociability corollary, it is easy to see how parents might argue with their teenagers over the merits of sleeping outdoors in front of the concert hall box office all night in order to get tickets to a rock concert. In this case, the arguments are due to their different usage of the "danger-safety" construct. Thus, the sociability corollary is at the core of our interactions with others.

The basic concepts Kelly outlined in his viewpoint of personality were designed to help explain how personal constructs are used to determine the perceptions of reality and the alternatives for dealing with it.

The Nature of Personality Adjustment: Successful and Unsuccessful Utilization of Personal Constructs

For Kelly, successful adjustment to the real world requires more than just the ability to generate and classify alternatives based on a system of personal constructs. The extent to which people are able to put these alternatives and explanations into actions reflect differences in successful and unsuccessful personality adjustment.

Successful Personality Adjustment: Cycles of Success

From Kelly's viewpoint, successful personality adjustment involves the extent to which we are able to generate, implement, and modify our system of personal constructs based on experiences. Two processes that he believed characterized successful personality adjustment were the C-P-C cycle and the creative cycle.

The C-P-C Cycle   The **C-P-C cycle** is the process by which people cope with situations and experiences in a propositional manner. The propositional nature of this process involves a sort of "if-then" approach, with the constructs being the "if" aspect and the course of action, and its outcome, being the "then" aspect. The process by which the C-P-C cycle is carried out involves passing through what Kelly (1955a) labeled the circumspection, preemption, and control phases.

▲ The **circumspection phase** involves using propositional constructs to generate several possible alternatives to a situation as it is being perceived by the individual. **Propositional constructs** are *if-then* statements made based on the interpretation of the situation. For example, when asking for a raise, an individual might reason: *If* I perceive my boss as being in a good mood, *then* I'll take a direct approach when asking for a raise. However, *if* I perceive my boss as being in a bad mood, *then* I'll take a more indirect approach.

▲ The **preemption phase** involves selecting one course of action over all the alternatives that have been generated. For example, the individual may conclude that the boss seems to be in a somewhat bad mood this morning and decide on the indirect approach.

▲ The **control phase** involves a specific course of action being developed based on the decision in the preemption phase. In the example, the course of action in the indirect approach might involve the individual thinking up an amusing story to help engage the boss in some small talk before asking for the raise.

At the end of the C-P-C cycle, Kelly stated that the individual would evaluate the outcome of the course of action and modify the constructs accordingly. For example, if the course of action resulted in success (i.e., the raise was obtained), this would be used as evidence to strengthen the validity of the individual's ability to use a set of personal constructs to perceive and respond to the situation in the future (i.e., read the boss's mood). But if it was not successful, the individual would then either try another of the available alternatives (i.e., return to the preemption phase) or start generating new ones (i.e., return to the circumspection phase). In this regard, the C-P-C cycle represents a description not only of how people select their actions but also of how they strengthen and modify the nature of their system of personal constructs. From Kelly's point of view, being able to recognize when you are right and when you are wrong and make the proper modifications in your constructs are at the cornerstone of the well-adjusted personality.

The C-P-C cycle was not the only process by which constructs were generated. Another means by which Kelly believed people generate possible alter-

natives for coping with the events in their life is the creativity cycle. To examine how you can cultivate your own level of creativity by using the creativity cycle, read "A Closer Look" below.

A Closer Look:

The Creativity Cycle: Cultivating Creative Constructs

The **creativity cycle** involves using constructs in a much less rigid and critical manner as a means of discovering novel or unique alternatives for coping with the events in our life (Kelly, 1955a). By applying less rigorous standards to the way they perceive or think about an event, people can "loosen up" constructs to include alternatives that they might not have thought about before. Along these lines, much of what is considered artistic or creative thinking involves being able to see an object or situation using constructs in a way that most people might overlook..

In contrast to the if-then logic of constructs found within the C-P-C cycle is the what-if logic characteristic of the creative cycle (Rychlak, 1981). The what-if logic is a more preliminary form of construing alternatives. Its main objective is not necessarily to find a specific course of action, but simply to explore some new possibilities without really having to worry about their actual validity.

For example, when deciding what to wear for a job interview, a man might pick a blue suit from the closet. When trying to decide what to wear with it, he puts a bright red silk handkerchief in the pocket, instead of the same old conservative navy blue one. In the privacy of his home, the man is able to dabble with different variations on the blue suit because the consequences for doing so are not costly at all. On the other hand, wearing the red silk handkerchief with this outfit to the interview may be a little too loud and risky for business purposes. Even if the man decides not to wear the red handkerchief with the blue suit to the job interview, he might discover that it looks striking enough to wear to a party this weekend. As a result, the "conservative-striking" construct for perceiving the blue suit as only something to wear to work has been modified and expanded to include it being a party outfit as well.

Thus, although it does not always have to occur, dabbling with constructs in the looser, what-if framework during the creative cycle can lead to unique solutions (e.g., combining a bright red handkerchief with a drab blue business suit to a party). Kelly felt that using the creative cycle in this manner was a characteristic of the well-adjusted personality.

Unsuccessful Personality Adjustment: Catastrophic Construing

In its most basic form, unsuccessful personality adjustment is what we might consider to be characteristic of someone experiencing a psychological disorder. In this regard, Kelly (1955b) defined a psychological disorder as "any personal construction which is used repeatedly in spite of consistent invalidation" (p. 835). Stated more specifically, unsuccessful personality adjustment is when an individual continues to think and behave in a particular manner even though such thoughts and actions are ineffective.

The construct system of the individual with a psychological disorder, as well as the process by which this system is based, reveals certain characteristics. Features of such a system include the individual's ignorance of interpretations, a restrictive range of convenience, impermeability, and incompleteness.

▲ *Ignoring interpretations.* People experiencing psychological disorders typically feel that their problems are a result of certain "facts" in their life rather than their perceptions of these problems. For example, Ingrid may feel extremely lonely and attribute this lack of popularity to the "fact" that all of her co-workers are jealous of her superior skill, instead of her actual tendency to dominate every conversation with her opinions.

▲ *Restrictions in the range of convenience.* As a characteristic of unsuccessful personality adjustment, anxiety is due to the individual feeling that life events are operating outside the range of convenience of his or her system of personal constructs. In this regard, the individual feels anxious because the available constructs in his or her system are not sufficient to help predict and cope with these life events. For example, an individual may become anxious in social situa-

tions because he does not feel he has anything interesting or amusing to say to others.

▲ *Impermeable constructs.* The personal construct system of people suffering from psychological disorders is also characterized by impermeable constructs. A construct that is impermeable is one that does not change as new evidence becomes available. For example, even after others at the party laugh at a story he told, Jorge still sees himself as not having anything amusing to say and remains reluctant to share other stories or attend other parties. Such impermeability tends to put limits on the development of the individual's personal construct system.

▲ *Incomplete constructs.* An incomplete construct is one that lacks sufficient information or details to help the individual categorize, predict, and/or cope with life's events. For example, a man may experience a considerable amount of hostility because his construct of "supervisor-worker" does not include the possibility of a supervisor being a female, particularly one from a racial minority. The hostility felt may be due to the confusion and uncertainty created by his construct system not being organized in enough depth to help him cope with the reality that he is working for a woman.

Thus, the primary difference between successful and unsuccessful personality adjustment has to do with how the construing is done, not why (i.e., to help predict and cope with events). Successful personality adjustment tends to be characterized by the modification of the personal construct system based on the consequences of actions and new experiences. Unsuccessful personality adjustment is characterized by people who have a construct system that is inflexible and who fail to learn from experience.

Applications of Kelly's Personal Construct Perspective: Using What Is Known

Like all other aspects of his viewpoint, the applications of Kelly's viewpoint center upon the notion of personal constructs. In the clinical applications of his viewpoint, Kelly developed an approach to psychotherapy designed to modify maladaptive personal constructs. Kelly also applied his ideas to the development of an assessment technique designed to measure personal constructs. Business applications of Kelly's ideas have focused on identifying and measuring personal constructs.

Psychotherapy: A Reconstruing Process

While most people are able to correct any limitations in their personal constructs themselves, other people with problems of personality adjustment may need some assistance. Kelly developed an approach to psychotherapy designed to help people correct the shortcomings in their system of personal constructs.

Because Kelly believed that faulty construct systems were at the core of psychological maladjustment, the basic goal he established for psychotherapy was to help the client reconstruct a system of personal constructs that would foster better prediction of and adjustment to life's events. Kelly viewed the therapy session as a laboratory where clients could experiment with new constructs and variations of old ones as a means of reconstructing their system of personal constructs. In short, Kelly (1955b) viewed "psychotherapy as a reconstructing process" (p. 937).

1. The first step in the process of psychotherapy involves the client presenting the complaint by stating what he or she perceives as being the problem. For example, a client might say that he has trouble establishing a meaningful relationship because the women with whom he gets involved keep breaking up with him.
2. After the client has stated the complaint, the second step involves what Kelly referred to as "elaborating the complaint" (Kelly, 1955b, p. 937). **Elaborating the complaint** involves the therapist working with the client to determine more specifically the underlying construct system that seems to be operating. Such an examination might reveal the extent to which the incomplete and impermeable nature of the constructs might be contributing to the problem (e.g., his "dominant male-submissive female" construct may be pushing these women away).
3. The third step in the process would then involve the therapist employing various therapeutic

techniques designed to help the client modify the nature of his or her personal construct system.

Techniques of Psychotherapy: Procedures for the Reconstruction of Constructs

A distinguishing feature of Kelly's approach to psychotherapy is the use of some very novel techniques, many of which reflected Kelly's early experiences as a teacher of drama.

Enactment as a Role-Playing Technique **Enactment** is a therapeutic technique that involves the client acting out with the therapist, or with other clients in group therapy, roles specifically designed to illustrate or test a particular perspective. For example, the client might be asked to act out a recent date he had, with the therapist playing the role of his date, to demonstrate how his domineering tendencies can make people upset with him. Enactment might also involve role reversal in which the client acts out the role of another person as a means of being exposed to a different perspective (e.g., seeing what it is like to be on a date with someone who is so domineering). The major purpose of enactment is to make salient the construct system and allow the client to experiment with and experience different constructs in a therapeutic environment that is safe and comfortable.

Fixed-Role Therapy Kelly believed that role playing would be even more valuable when it was performed within the real world. This belief was reflected in the development of fixed-role therapy. **Fixed-role therapy** involves the client acting out in the real world a specific role as a means of learning to construe himself or herself differently. The logic of fixed-role therapy is that the view people have of themselves is not only based on how they perceive themselves but also what they do. Thus, by getting people to behave differently, it is possible to get them to alter the nature of their system of personal constructs.

The first step in the process of fixed-role therapy is generating a self-characterization sketch. A **self-characterization sketch** is a description the client writes about himself or herself in the third person by noting various characteristics, behavioral tendencies, and relationships with others. For example, the client may start his self-characterization sketch by writing, "Sid is a 29-year-old single male who would like very much to establish a long-term, meaningful relationship. However, he seems to express just the opposite kinds of feelings to others." The self-characterization sketch is designed to get the client to view the nature of his or her construct system from a different and more objective perspective.

Based on the self-characterization sketch, the therapist then assists the client in writing a fixed-role script. The **fixed-role script** is a description of a fictional person reflecting a construct system that is more therapeutically beneficial to the client than the present one. The fixed-role script is written by the therapist. The client is instructed on how to construe events differently while practicing the script. To facilitate the acceptance of the script, the client might also be given a new name to use. For example, while practicing his fixed-role script, Sid might be told that his name will be Arthur, and he is to think of himself as someone who is really trying to establish a meaningful relationship. In the fixed-role script, "Arthur" spends more time listening to what others have to say, instead of focusing on only his opinions. The fixed-role script is designed to help the client become exposed to a more adaptive construct system.

After the client has had a chance to practice this script and can accept what is being expected, the script is then presented as a fixed role. The **fixed role** involves the client acting out in the real world the constructs described in the fixed-role script. In this case, Sid will be instructed to behave as "Arthur" would when meeting new people at a business reception later this week, and to observe the extent to which people respond when the other-centered emphasis of the personal construct system is being exhibited. In this context, clients can then experiment with a new construct system in the real world to see how others would react to them if their behavior was different. Observing their own reactions, as well as the reactions of others, also gives clients an alternative way of viewing themselves in a rather safe and nonthreatening manner because, after all, they are "only playing a role."

Fixed-role therapy displays a tremendous degree of originality and creativity in Kelly's approach to psychotherapy. For some firsthand experience with many of the dynamics of fixed-role therapy, consider the information presented in "Applications in Personality Psychology" below.

APPLICATION

APPLICATIONS IN PERSONALITY PSYCHOLOGY

All the World's a Stage: An Exercise in Fixed-Role Therapy

To gain some firsthand experience with fixed-role therapy, think of some aspect of your personality that you would like to change. Suppose you would like to be more outgoing or assertive. Take a moment to think about what it would be like to be more outgoing or assertive. What would you say or do differently? Next, start to write down some of the things you would say and do if you were more outgoing or assertive, also noting under what circumstances and with whom such behaviors might occur.

Now that you have some actions written down, practice them in front of a mirror, or see if you can get a good friend to role play with you. After you have some practice with speaking and behaving in a more outgoing or assertive way, take this role and play it in the real world—someplace where you might not know too many people so that you will not feel self-conscious.

You might try practicing this newly adopted construct system by going to a mall located away from your home where you know there will be a lot of people but few, if any, who will know you. When the day is over, try to think about how you felt while playing this different role. Note the extent to which people responded to you differently. Did you happen to notice anything different about yourself, or were you too busy concentrating on your role?

Regardless of what aspect of your personality you elected to explore in this exercise, if you have taken it seriously, you should have learned something about how you can expand the nature of your construct system, which can make it possible to see yourself in a manner that you might previously have overlooked.

Dream Analysis and Controlled Elaboration as Supplemental Therapeutic Techniques   In addition to the fixed-role therapy, Kelly used several other techniques, such as dream analysis and controlled elaboration. Instead of analyzing dreams for their symbolic content, Kelly preferred to think of them as very loose constructs that could be explored in therapy to help the client modify his or her construct system. For example, a dream of flying might be used in helping a client who is frustrated in her current job to loosen her construct of "job security-insecurity" by exploring some possible career alternatives that might involve moving (e.g., flying) to another city.

In **controlled elaboration**, the therapist would verbally "walk through" the C-P-C cycle with clients in order to help them experiment with certain aspects of their system of personal constructs. When working with a client who is experiencing a high degree of loneliness, the therapist might suggest to the client several alternatives that are available besides just hoping that he will meet someone (e.g., joining a book discussion club for singles or starting small talk with someone who is also alone at a party). Through controlled elaboration, the therapist might tell the client to think about what is the worst and/or best thing that could happen if he pursued such an alternative. And if this did happen, what could the client do about it? Both dream analysis and controlled elaboration are used to help clients loosen up their system of personal constructs.

Personality Assessment: The Role
Construct Repertory Test

The concern for determining the nature of constructs was also embedded in Kelly's approach to personality assessment. The **Role Construct Repertory Test** (*Rep Test* for short) is an assessment device designed to measure the nature of constructs that people use to construe the important people in their lives (Kelly, 1955a).

In the Rep Test, the individual is given a list describing 22 people relevant to that person's life (e.g., self, mother, sister, medical doctor, and influential teacher). The individual is then asked to choose three of these people and indicate how two of them are similar to each other but different from the third. For example, the self and doctor might be construed as being analytical but the mother as being intuitive. From this comparison, what is learned is that the

construct of "analytical-intuitive" is used in how the individual construes himself or herself, other people, and events in the world.

In making more comparisons, it is possible to begin to examine the complexity of the individual's construct system by considering the number, variety, and breadth of the constructs reported in the test. For example, if the individual also uses the "intuitive-analytical" construct in 10 of the 22 comparisons made, the conclusion would be that the person's construct system is rather simple and rigid. As a supplemental therapeutic technique, the therapist might use the results of the Rep Test with controlled elaboration to help the client learn to construe people and events in additional dimensions.

To gain some experience with the procedures of the Rep Test, try for yourself the exercise "You Can Do It" on page 203.

Business Applications: Constructs in the Workplace
Kelly's ideas have also found several different business applications (Stewart & Stewart, 1982).

Applications to Marketing Research   In the area of marketing research, variations of the repertory grid technique are used to help assess the subjective dimensions consumers use when evaluating products and making purchasing decisions (Stewart & Stewart, 1982). By determining what specific constructs consumers of a particular product see as salient, marketing researchers can work with advertisers to develop advertising campaigns. Information about perceived negative features of products identified through consumer testing with the repertory grid technique can be utilized by those working in product development to redesign or modify present or future products.

Applications to Management Training   In the selection and training of management personnel, it is important for businesses to convey the many beliefs, values, and corporate expectations of the senior administrators to newly hired junior managers if they are to be effective within the organization. As noted by Jankowicz (1987), "If the information is part of the corporate culture and if it is essential to be aware of it, if only to test it out and plan one's actions appropriately, then the manager had better discover it quickly" (p. 484). To facilitate the transmission of

YOU CAN DO IT

Considering Your Constructs: An Illustration of the Construct Repertory Technique

You can gain some insight into the nature of your construct system by completing the following comparisons, which are modeled after those found in Kelly's Rep Test. For each of the 10 people listed, compare those three in each row (indicated with the circles) by considering how two of them are similar but different from the third. In the column labeled "Construct," write the term that represents how these two people are similar. In the column labeled "Contrast," write the term that represents how the two similar people are different from the third. Finally, put a checkmark in the column of any other numbers in that row that indicate other people who might also be described by the term in the construct column (e.g., in the first row, you might add a check under column 2 for "mother" as being similar to "close friend").

	1	2	3	4	5	6	7	8	9	10	Construct	Contrast
1. self	o		o	o							___	___
2. mother	o	o			o						___	___
3. father			o		o	o					___	___
4. close friend	o		o	o							___	___
5. worst enemy	o	o				o					___	___
6. most successful person you know	o			o	o						___	___
7. most influential teacher					o	o	o				___	___
8. person for whom you feel sorry		o				o	o				___	___
9. your physician		o	o			o					___	___
10. person who makes you feel uncomfortable					o	o	o				___	___

After completing all of the comparisons listed, you can then begin to examine the nature of your construct system. To do this, start by examining the number of different constructs used. You might also consider the extent to which you made comparisons based on such factors as physical appearance (e.g., pretty vs. ugly), status (e.g., doctor and teacher are different from friend), or personal needs (e.g., comforting vs. unpleasant). Such an examination can be used to indicate the range of a particular construct. Examining the number of checks you placed in each row can be used to indicate the flexibility of the construct.

If you like, compare your results with other members of the class, or repeat this exercise with your friends, spouse, and/or children. If you like, use the results as a starting point from which to employ the C-P-C and creative cycles as a means of modifying or expanding the nature of the constructs noted in this exercise.

corporate philosophy, microcomputer programs designed to elicit and analyze construct systems have been developed that allow senior managers to expose new managerial employees to such vital information (Eden & Sims, 1981).

Applications to Product Quality Control   Quality control inspectors are employed to make judgments about the quality of merchandise before it is shipped to retailers. Repertory grid techniques have been used to help experienced inspectors articulate the constructs they use in their evaluative judgments of merchandise quality. Once these constructs have been stated in a more objective manner, they can then be shared when training new inspectors. In a toy factory that manufactured teddy bears, Stewart and Stewart (1982) noted the constructs quality inspectors used when judging the soft toy to be defective or acceptable. Through careful interviews with the inspectors, in which their constructs were discussed, it was discovered that a teddy bear was judged not to be defective if: (a) there was symmetry in the facial features such that the distance between the eyes and nose equals the distance between the nose and the mouth, and (b) the piece of black material used for the pupil of the eye is glued in the center of the white of the eye. Prior to this systematic assessment, the process by which the inspectors made their judgments of quality was intuitively defined as an unspecific set of "feelings of rightness" based on experience. With a more specific set of standards, the training of future inspectors is made much easier and the consistency of the judgments enhanced.

Other business applications based on Kelly's repertory grid techniques are found in such areas as the assessment of loan applicants made by loan agents (Jankowicz & Hisrich, 1987), job analysis and performance appraisal (Jankowicz, 1985), the development of employee training programs (Easterby-Smith, 1980), and occupational and career counseling (Jankowicz & Cooper, 1982), to name just a few.

Additional information on the clinical and business applications of Kelly's viewpoint can be found in "Whatever Became of George Kelly? Applications and Implications" (Jankowicz, 1987). More information about Kelly's viewpoint can be found in *Personal Construct Psychology: Psychotherapy and Personality* (Landfield & Leitner, 1980).

Evaluation of Kelly's Personal Construct Theory: Characteristic Strengths and Limitations

Characteristic Strengths

Here are some strengths of Kelly's personal construct viewpoint:

▲ *Viewing individuals as analytical.* Kelly's emphasis on the individual engaging in the analytical process of formulating constructs to help explain and predict events makes salient the role of cognitive factors (e.g., beliefs, expectations, if-then reasoning) when trying to understand personality. Thus, Kelly viewed people as being analytical when attempting to understand and cope with events in their world.

▲ *Novel and adventurous applications.* Kelly's approach to measuring constructs using the Rep Test represents a unique approach to personality assessment, on a level of originality comparable with that of the Rorschach Test. Kelly's approach to psychotherapy also represents an extremely novel and creative approach that, although not as popular, is no less unique than Roger's person-centered approach. In addition, while Kelly's approach to treatment has not received widespread clinical acceptance, "it had a profound influence on the development of subsequent interventions" (Hollon & Beck, 1994, p. 429). Kelly's ideas have been applied to help resolve problems in several different areas of business.

Characteristic Limitations

Kelly's personal construct viewpoint has the following limitations:

▲ *Kelly's overemphasis on rationality.* Kelly's approach has been criticized because of the unrealistic expectations he had about the rationality of human beings. More specifically, his view that we seek to behave in a logical manner designed to predict and control our world is somewhat inconsistent with a lot of the irrational behavior that is observed in the way people actually think and behave (Plous, 1993; Ross & Nisbett, 1991). The point here is that people are probably a little more emotional and less rational than Kelly might have assumed.

▲ *The problem of assessing the existence of constructs and determining their predictive validity.* The somewhat abstract nature of constructs makes them difficult to measure, because the reliability and validity of the Rep Test have not been sufficiently documented. In addition, because constructs are unique to each person, it is difficult to design programs of research to test the utility of constructs in predicting behavior and for establishing general laws of behavior. In short, Kelly's viewpoint seems to be better suited to explain behavior on an individual level than to predict it on a general level.

More information on Kelly's views of personality can be found in Brendan Maher's *Clinical Psychology and Personality: The Select Papers of George Kelly* (1969) and in A. D. Jankowicz's "Whatever Became of George Kelly? Applications and Implications" (1987).

Chapter Summary: Reexamining the Highlights

▲ Maslow's Motivational Viewpoint
—*Basic Assumptions.* The basic assumptions of Maslow's viewpoint include a rather positive and humanistic view of the individual, an emphasis on investigating the healthy personality, and perceiving the operation of personality to meet a combination of biological and psychological needs.
—*Basic Concepts.* The state of self-actualization involves the individual maximizing the satisfaction of personal needs. These needs are classified into deficiency needs and being needs and arranged into a hierarchy from most to least potent. The hierarchy arrangement includes physiological, safety, belongingness and love, esteem, and self-actualization needs.
—*The Study of Self-Actualizers.* As identified by Maslow, characteristics of self-actualizers include a more accurate perception of reality, a greater acceptance of self and others, being true to themselves, having peak experiences, being other-centered and autonomous, having a limited number of very close personal friends, and being creative in everyday matters.
—*Applications of Maslow's Viewpoint.* Maslow's ideas have been extended to worker motivation with the philosophy of eupsychian management. However, research of the effectiveness of eupsychian management has produced mixed evidence. Applications of Maslow's ideas to personality assessment have focused on the development and validation of measures of self-actualization, such as the Personal Orientation Inventory.

—*Evaluation of Maslow's Viewpoint.* Characteristic strengths of Maslow's viewpoint include his emphasis on studying the exceptionally healthy personality, his realistic view of human nature, and the diverse extension of his ideas. Characteristic limitations of Maslow's viewpoints include the untestable nature of many of his principal concepts, the subjective description of self-actualizers based only on his standards, and the limited amount of empirical research his ideas have generated.

▲ Kelly's Personal Construct Perspective
—*Basic Constructs.* The basic concepts of Kelly's viewpoint include the underlying logic of construct alternativism, the utilization of personal constructs, the fundamental postulate, and the supplemental corollaries of personal constructs.
—*The Nature of Personality Adjustment.* Successful personality adjustment is characterized by the effective use and modification of personal constructs through the C-P-C cycle and creativity cycle. Unsuccessful personality adjustment is characterized by continued usage of invalid or ineffective constructs.
—*Applications of Kelly's Viewpoint.* Fixed-role therapy represents the principal application of Kelly's viewpoint to psychotherapy, while the Role Construct Repertory Test represents the principal application to personality assessment. Kelly's ideas have been utilized in a number of business applications.
—*Evaluation of Kelly's Viewpoint.* Characteristic strengths of Kelly's viewpoint include his perception of people as being analytical and the innovative nature of his applications. The characteristic limitations include his unrealistic expectations about the analytical nature of people, the abstract and individualistic nature of constructs, and the difficulty this creates for researchers trying to validate his ideas.

Glossary

being needs   A category of needs related to personal growth.
belongingness and love needs   A basic desire to establish and maintain meaningful interpersonal relationships.

circumspection phase   The generation of possible alternatives during the first step in the C-P-C cycle.

constructive alternativism   The logic that any particular event can be perceived in many different ways.

control phase   The implementation of a specific course of action during the third step of the C-P-C cycle.

controlled elaboration   The process of a therapist and client verbally going through the C-P-C cycle when formulating new constructs in the therapeutic setting.

C-P-C cycle   A systematic process for formulating, selecting, and implementing constructs to cope with various situations.

creativity cycle   A system for formulating constructs in a more tentative manner for experimenting with possible ideas and solutions.

deficiency needs   A category of needs related to basic survival.

elaborating the complaint   The process of the client outlining a problem of personal concern and the underlying constructs.

enactment   The role playing of certain situations for the purpose of testing various constructs.

esteem needs   A basic desire to establish and maintain self-respect and the respect of others.

eupsychian management   An approach to worker motivation based on meeting both the deficiency and being needs of people.

experience corollary   A statement of the extent to which a construct is modified based on experience.

fundamental postulate   A rule of thinking stating the tendency for events to be perceived in a manner consistent with expectations.

fixed role   The acting out of the actions in the fixed-role script by the client in real-life situations.

fixed-role script   A specific set of actions written for a client for the purpose of testing new styles of interacting with others.

fixed-role therapy   A form of psychotherapy emphasizing playing various roles for the purpose of increasing self-awareness.

hierarchy of needs   A systematic arrangement of needs based on their potency and influence on the individual's behavior.

humanistic viewpoint   A perspective of human nature emphasizing personal growth and the development of one's full potential.

modulation corollary   A statement of the extent to which an individual's system of constructs is flexible.

peak experiences   Moments of intense emotional reactions and self-awareness.

personal construct   A personalized manner by which an individual gives meaning to and gains a sense of understanding experiences.

Personal Orientation Inventory (POI)   An objective self-report method of personality assessment designed to measure self-actualization tendencies.

physiological needs   A set of needs required for basic survival.

preemption phase   The selection of a specific alternative during the second step of the C-P-C cycle.

propositional constructs   Constructs formulated in an "if-then" manner for generating possible solutions to a problem.

range corollary   A statement of the extent to which a construct can be utilized.

Role Construct Repertory Test   An objective method of personality assessment designed to measure an individual's construct system.

safety needs   A basic desire for security and stability.

self-actualization   The tendency to develop one's potential to its fullest when meeting personal needs.

self-characterization sketch   A summary statement written by the client outlining his or her basic characteristics and interactions with others.

sociability corollary   A statement of the extent to which two people share the same construct system.

state of self-actualization   The utilization of a person's abilities to their full potential. **hird force**   A perspective of people emphasizing the study of those processes facilitating self-enhancement.

CHAPTER 8

The Trait Viewpoint: Psychological Dispositions of Personality

CHAPTER OVERVIEW: A PREVIEW OF COMING ATTRACTIONS

*I*n this chapter, you will examine the trait viewpoint of personality, including the trait theories of Gordon W. Allport, Raymond B. Cattell, and Hans J. Eysenck. After considering the perspectives of these three theorists, you will learn about some central issues associated with the operational influence and structural organization of traits.

Personality Traits: The Foundation of Personality

Although there are various trait viewpoints, they all tend to be guided by certain basic beliefs about personality traits. These basic beliefs include the principal assumption that traits define the nature of personality, and the principal logic that traits determine the operation of personality.

Traits are dimensions of personality that influence in a particular way the thoughts, feelings, and behaviors of the individual. The principal assumption of the trait viewpoint is that people differ in the degree to which they possess certain traits (Funder, 1995). From the trait viewpoint, the characteristics of an individual's personality are assumed to reflect the nature and degree of traits possessed. Thus, traits define the nature of an individual's personality. As an illustration of how this aspect of the trait viewpoint is expressed in everyday life, consider the exercise in "You Can Do It" on this page.

The principal logic of the trait viewpoint is that behavior is influenced in a manner consistent with the traits possessed by the individual (Funder, 1991; Kenrick & Funder, 1988). For example, if an individual is very pushy about borrowing your class notes, parks in a handicapped zone, and smokes a cigarette in a nonsmoking section of the student activities center, we would probably assume that this person is very inconsiderate. From the trait viewpoint, the explanation of this tendency to behave in such an inconsiderate manner is that the individual's personality contains the trait of self-centeredness to a high degree. Thus, an individual's personality is defined by the nature of the traits it consists of (e.g., self-centered and dishonest); these traits then determine the individual's behavior (e.g., behaving selfishly and inconsiderately).

YOU CAN DO IT

How Do I Describe Thee? Let Me Count the Ways: An Everyday Example of Behaving Like a Trait Psychologist

Think of a friend you know well. After you have selected someone special, describe that person by writing in the space below those words or phrases that seem to be essential characteristics of your friend.

_____

_____

_____

_____

In a similar exercise with some of his students, Gordon W. Allport, a very famous trait psychologist to be discussed in this chapter, found that the number of central traits used to describe the essential characteristics of an individual was generally between 5 and 10, with an average of around 7. Does your description support this hypothesis? As a further test of Allport's hypothesis, you might also ask a few of your friends to complete this exercise. Using traits to describe the behavior of others in everyday life is similar to how trait psychologists approach the study of personality.

Allport's Personalistic Viewpoint: In Search of the Uniqueness of Individuals

Allport's theory of personality is **personalistic** in nature. **Personalism** is the psychology of the person (Allport, 1960). As a personalistic theorist, Allport's emphasis was on trying to understand and explain the complexity and uniqueness of the total individual. His principal concern was to develop a theory of personality that would help to explain what makes each of us unique. Thus, as a personalist, Allport was trying to understand "real people" rather than the so-called average person who is supposed to represent what "most people" are like. For a more personal look at an individual who tried to promote personalism, consider the material in "A Closer Look" on page 209.

A Closer Look:

Biographical Background:
The Life of Gordon W. Allport

Gordon W. Allport is considered to be the founder of personality psychology in the United States.

Gordon W. Allport was born in Montezuma, Indiana, on November 11, 1897. He was the youngest, by some five years, of four boys. Allport's father was a country doctor who turned to the study of medicine rather late in life (e.g., after a career in business and having three sons). Allport believed that he and his mother were his father's first patients.

Allport grew up and received his early education in Cleveland. Although describing himself as a "good routine student, but definitely uninspired and uncurious about anything beyond the usual adolescent concerns" (Allport, 1967, p. 5), Allport did graduate second in his high school class of 100. Not sure what to do about further schooling after graduation, Allport followed the advice of his oldest brother, a Harvard graduate, and applied to Harvard. Although he applied late in the summer and just squeezed through the entrance exams, Allport was admitted to Harvard. In his first set of examinations at Harvard, Allport received an array of D's and C's. However, by stiffening his efforts, he finished the first year with A's.

After receiving his AB in 1919, majoring in economics and philosophy, Allport accepted a teaching position at Roberts College in Istanbul, Turkey, where he taught English and sociology. The year of teaching at Roberts College was a very enjoyable one for Allport and convinced him "that teaching was not such a bad career for me" (Allport, 1967, p. 7). Allport's newfound enjoyment of teaching resulted in his accepting a fellowship for graduate study at Harvard.

On his way back from Turkey, Allport stopped in Vienna to visit one of his brothers who was working there. While in Vienna, Allport wrote a letter to Freud announcing that he was in Vienna and requesting a visit with the great psychoanalyst. Allport received a handwritten invitation from Freud to visit him at his office at a certain time.

Upon entering Freud's office, Allport found the great man sitting in silence, waiting for the young Allport to state the purpose of his visit. Feeling uncomfortable with the silence, Allport began relating to Freud an incident he had observed on the streetcar en route to Freud's office. The specific incident involved a little boy who seemed to possess an intense fear of dirt and an extreme desire to avoid a "dirty man" sitting next to him.

When Allport finished the story, Freud asked, "And was that little boy you?" Allport realized that Freud's misunderstanding of his motivation for telling the story, which was to break the uncomfortable silence, was probably a result of the psychoanalyst's extensive contact with his clinical patients and their neurotic defenses. For Allport, this experience was significant; it taught him that psychoanalysis placed too much emphasis on the unconscious motivation of the individual and that more might be gained by studying the individual's surface motives.

Upon returning to Harvard, Allport continued his studies and completed the requirements for his PhD two years later in 1922. His doctoral dissertation, titled "An Experimental Study of the Traits of Personality," is believed to be the first American dissertation concerned with personality traits. In addition, a course he taught at Harvard in 1924 and 1925, titled "Personality: Its Psychological and Social Aspects," is believed to be the first course to be offered at an American college that dealt with the subject of personality.

In 1937, Allport published a textbook, which he said had been "'cooking' in my head since my graduate days" (Allport, 1967, p. 15), titled *Personality: A Psychological Interpretation*. According to Allport, he wrote this book because he wanted to "give a psychological definition of the field of personality as I saw it" (Allport, 1967, p. 15). For almost 25 years, this classic textbook was more or less standard reading in the field of personality psychology. Some 24 years later, Allport (1961) revised the textbook to reflect new movements in the field of personality, as well as to update his ideas, and titled it *Pattern and Growth in Personality*.

Allport spent virtually all of his academic life, from 1924 to his death on October 9, 1967, on the faculty at Harvard. During his illustrious career, he made numerous significant contributions linking his research interests in personality and social psychology to issues and concerns having real social relevance. Such contributions included his work in the area of rumor analysis during World War II (Allport & Postman, 1947), the problems of group conflict and prejudice (Allport, 1954), and personal values (Allport, Vernon, & Lindzey, 1960). For his efforts, Allport received virtually every professional honor given by psychologists. Some of these honors included being elected president of the American Psychological Association and receiving the gold medal of the American Psychological Foundation and the American Psychological Association's award for distinguished scientific contributions. More information on the life of America's founder of personality psychology can be found in an autobiography (Allport, 1967) appearing in Boring and Lindzey's *A History of Psychology in Autobiography*.

Basic Assumptions: Allport's Definition of Personality

According to Allport (1961), "Personality is the dynamic organization within the individual of those psychophysical systems that determine his characteristic behavior and thought" (p. 28). To clarify his definition, Allport went on to discuss what he considered to be its key concepts:

▲ *Personality is a dynamic organization in a state of continuous growth.* The concept of "dynamic organization" stresses that while an individual's personality consists of an orderly system (i.e., an organization) of components, the system is in a constant state of change and personal growth (i.e., a dynamic state). Within such a state, each experience that is encountered serves to modify and/or strengthen, even in the slightest way, various aspects of the individual's personality. For example, honesty in law-abiding students is strengthened when they read about dishonest students being disciplined for cheating.

▲ *Personality is psychophysical in nature by combining the mind and body.* "Psychophysical" is a concept used by Allport to stress that personality consists of an integration of the capacities of the mind (i.e., psycho-), such as feelings, ideas, and beliefs, and the body (i.e., -physical), such as hormones and the nervous system. For example, the thrill-seeking personality exhibited by certain people has been linked to various biological characteristics (Zuckerman, Bushsbaum, & Murphy, 1980).

▲ *Personality is a determinant of behavior.* Allport uses the term *determine* to emphasize that personality serves an activating and directive function in the individual's adaptive and expressive thoughts and behavior. Stated more simply, according to Allport (1961), "personality *is* something and *does* something" (p. 29).

▲ *Personality is an expression of each person's uniqueness.* The phrase "characteristic behavior and thought" refers to whatever people may do or think as they reflect on, adjust to, and/or strive to master their environment in a manner that is "unique" (i.e., characteristic of) to each person. For example, the way different people react and adjust to being turned down for a job reflects the characteristic nature of their personality.

In summary, Allport's definition of personality clarified the nature, operation, and purpose of the concept of personality as an expression of uniqueness.

Basic Concepts: Helping to Express Our Uniqueness

The basic concepts of Allport's theory reflect the emphasis he placed on traits to help define and express each person's unique personality. Allport's viewpoint focused on the classification and operation of traits.

Traits Are the Basic Unit of Personality
For Allport, the trait is the basic unit of study for personality (Allport, 1958). He defined a trait as "a neuropsychic structure having the capacity to render many stimuli functionally equivalent, and to initiate and guide equivalent (meaningfully consistent) forms of adaptive and expressive behavior" (Allport, 1961, p. 347). Thus, Allport assumed that traits are real within the individual, and that they consistently guide the individual's thoughts and behavior across a variety of situations. For example, the extent to which Jack, a newspaper reporter, possesses the trait of aggressiveness will determine his behavior when charging the net in a game of tennis, honking the horn when cut off by another driver on the expressway, and being forceful when trying to get to the front of a crowd of other reporters to get a statement from a political candidate. Thus, the trait of aggressiveness influences Jack's behavior in a rather consistent manner across many different situations.

Common Traits and Personal Dispositions as Expressions of Uniqueness among People
Allport made a distinction between common traits and personal dispositions (or individual traits). The importance of this distinction has to do with attempts to understand the personality of an individual. **Common traits** refer to those traits possessed in varying degrees by all people. In the study of personality, comparing the common traits of different people (e.g., the shyness of two friends) or groups (e.g., freshmen are more anxious than seniors) is part of what Allport referred to as the **nomothetic approach** to investigating the nature of personality and establishing general laws of behavior. Thus, common traits give us information involving comparisons between people rather than information about the personality of specific persons.

   Personal dispositions are traits *unique* to the individual and create a personalized style of behavior. In this context, the term *unique* means that an individual's system of personal dispositions is specific to that person alone. The phrase *equalizing a variety of stimuli* means that the individual's unique system of personal dispositions interprets or perceives a wide variety of information in a similar

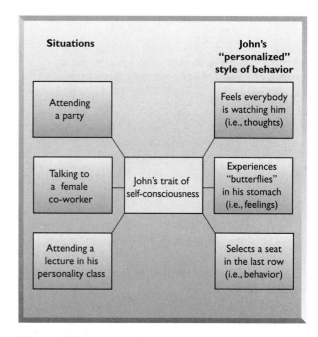

Figure 8.1
An example of John's trait of self-consciousness "equalizing" a variety of situations, resulting in a rather consistent pattern in his thoughts, feelings, and behavior

(i.e., equalized) manner, resulting in a consistent pattern of behavior. Figure 8.1 illustrates how the personal disposition of self-consciousness results in the individual (John) interpreting all of these situations in a similar manner (e.g., threatening), which produces a pattern of consistency across his thoughts, feelings, and behaviors. Thus, Allport used the concept of personal dispositions to explain the uniqueness of each person and the consistency of the individual's behavior. To study personal dispositions and unique experiences, Allport recommended the **idiographic approach** to investigating the nature of personality.

   Just as common traits and personal dispositions differ in their nature, so did the methods by which Allport felt they should be studied. To examine some of Allport's research on common traits and personal dispositions based on the nomothetic and idiographic approaches, read "A Closer Look" on page 212.

A Closer Look:

Allport's Nomothetic and Idiographic Research: Two Methods Are Better than One

Allport was a master at letting the problem at hand define the method of study. He demonstrated great ingenuity in his research. A major methodological distinction he made in his research was between the nomothetic and the idiographic approach.

Allport used the nomothetic approach primarily when comparing the personalities of different people. The typical nomothetic study might involve having groups of people complete a survey, questionnaire, or personality test and then comparing the scores of people in the different groups. An example of Allport's research in the nomothetic tradition is his classic work on values. In this research, Allport and his colleagues (Allport et al., 1960) developed a personality test that assessed six basic values:

▲ Theoretical (e.g., discovering truth)
▲ Economic (e.g., being pragmatic)
▲ Aesthetic (e.g., seeking and appreciating beauty)
▲ Social (e.g., value helping others)
▲ Political (e.g., interested in power)
▲ Religious (e.g., desiring spiritual fulfillment

Allport assumed that each person would combine these six values in a particular fashion to form a "philosophy of life." This philosophy of life would give meaning to the things people do and decisions they make. More will be said about Allport's work on values later in this chapter.

While the nomothetic approach was considered appropriate for studying and comparing groups, Allport did not consider it an appropriate method for studying the unique individual. As an alternative, Allport recommended the idiographic approach. The idiographic approach represents an in-depth analysis of a particular person. Some methods included in this approach are the examination of expressive behaviors (e.g., body-movement and facial and vocal expressions), the case study method (discussed in Chapter 1), individualized questionnaires, and the content analysis of personal documents (e.g., letters and

The testing of groups of individuals to obtain an average is characteristic of the nomothetic approach.

diaries). An example of Allport's research using the idiographic approach is the structural and content analysis of some 300 letters written by Jenny, a middle-aged woman, to a young, married couple over a period of 12 years (Allport, 1965). Following are two of Jenny's letters.

Sunday, March 4/34

Isabel, my dear:

  It is quite evident that you have never been an indigent, aged female, or your splendid St. Patrick's Day box which arrived Saturday (March 3rd) would have been more wisely chosen, altho' certainly not with more kindly thought. Possibly you have never lived in one room. This house is largely made up of old women from 75 to 90 something; as a result it is kept unusually warm—very uncomfortably warm for me. I nearly faint in the dining room.

  Whatever made you send me *a quart* of thick tomato juice? What did you suppose I could do with it? I always supposed tomato juice was an appetiser, to be taken before dinner, and frequently get it as such when I go to town. It is not appetisers we need here, it is something to eat. Yesterday I went to a restaurant on Broadway, and met 6 of our women, indigent females, all having something to eat. Our meals are a joke, or would be if we felt funny enough to see them that way. When the weather is severe and I cannot go out I lie awake until 3 or 4 am knowing I need food.

But could I get up to drink lukewarm thick tomato juice, or eat very salty crackers? If it were only plain crackers, sweet, wheat, graham, social tea, arrow root, but salt? And by the way, I have never seen them served anywhere—in what way are they used? They would probably be ok with a glass of beer if one had no pretzels or with cold meat. Had the sardines been in individual tins which contain 4 or 5—I often buy them that way—but in such a large tin! I could not eat a whole tin at one sitting, and what could I do with what was left? My room is so hot. I have never eaten preserved meat of any kind—I couldn't. And the cheese is too soft for me.

I hope and pray you will be sensible and understand. Drop a line and say you're not vexed.

Lady M

N.Y.C. March 13/34
My dearest Girl:

Ah! I can breathe again—what a relief. You have written, and you are not blazing mad. The Gods are not so bad after all.

You see, the letter was hardly out of my hand when I felt sorry for sending it—you might feel hurt, and be angry and the box wasn't worth that.

Lady M.
(Allport, 1965, pp. 116–117)

Note: From *Letters from Jenny*, by G.W. Aldport, 1965, New York: Harcourt, Brace, and World.

To analyze Jenny's personality, Allport asked 36 people to read the letters and indicate what traits they believed Jenny possessed. The total number of traits listed by all of the judges was close to 200. However, Allport was able to group them into eight categories: suspiciousness, self-centered, autonomous, dramatic, artistic, aggressive, cynical-morbid, and sentimental. The traits of suspiciousness, self-centered, and autonomous were identified as the most prominent traits of Jenny's personality.

The analysis of personal documents, such as letters and diaries, for the purpose of studying the personality of an individual in great detail is characteristic of the idiographic approach.

Using Cardinal, Central, and Secondary Traits to Account for the Uniqueness of the Individual

While personal dispositions were used to account for the unique variation of one individual from another, Allport (1961) used cardinal, central, and secondary traits to explain the unique variation *within* the individual.

Cardinal traits represent the most significant and dominant features of the individual's personality. They seem to express themselves in virtually all aspects of the person's behavior. For example, if someone is called a "social climber," it means that everything the individual does reflects his or her desire to "get ahead" (e.g., selection of friends and a spouse and organizations joined). Allport (1961, p. 365) referred to such a personal disposition as a "ruling passion" of life. Examples of cardinal traits are the pervasive sense of power so dominant in Hitler's personality and the pervasive sense of justice so dominant in the personality of Martin Luther King.

Not all people organize the nature of their personality around dominant cardinal traits. Instead, the personality of most people is defined by a set of central traits. **Central traits** are less pervasive and dominant than cardinal traits, but still highly characteristic of the individual's personality. Central traits might be exemplified in a letter of recommendation or in a description of an individual's most salient features. When describing a potential blind date to a friend, you might say that the individual is somewhat shy and slightly self-conscious when meeting people for the first time but really friendly and witty after getting to know them. For Allport, central traits described the "outstanding characteristics of the individual" (Allport, 1937, p. 338). In one study, Allport (1961, p. 366-367) reported that the traits used to describe the essential features of an individual generally numbered between 5 and 10, with the average being 7.2 traits. As an example of this point, compare these results with the number of traits you used to describe the essential characteristics of a good friend in "You Can Do It" on page 208.

Secondary traits are personal dispositions having a much more limited influence on the individual's behavior. Secondary traits tend to express themselves in the context of specific situations and circumstances. For example, the normally outspoken government official may become tongue-tied when being questioned in front of a congressional ethics committee.

The Proprium as the Core of Personality

If traits are considered the basic units of personality, then the proprium might be considered the core of personality for Allport (Maddi, 1989). For Allport (1955), the **proprium** includes all aspects of the individual's personality that are considered "personally" his or her own. In a general sense, the proprium helps the person define a sense of self. It includes the vital and essential physical, psychological, and social aspects of life that are considered to be "part of you." For example, some people consider their car, house, and/or job as being vital to their sense of who they are. Other people have *their* room decorated with all of their personal belongings as an important reflection of their sense of individuality. Seeing someone at a party wearing the same outfit as yours might trigger a reaction such as "What is that person doing with *my* outfit on?" Thus, a key function of the proprium is that it helps to establish a unifying feeling of what is really a part of you.

In summary, the basic concepts proposed by Allport within his personalistic viewpoint were designed to help explain how each person is able to express his or her personality in a unique way.

The Dynamics of Personality: Developmental and Motivational Processes of the Proprium

In this section, we will consider Allport's views on the operational dynamics of personality. Central to Allport's views on the dynamics of personality are the development of the proprium and the process of functional autonomy.

Personality Development: The Emergence of the Proprium

Something as complicated and detailed as a sense of who you are does not develop overnight. In an attempt to account for such a complicated developmental process, Allport (1961) outlined a lifelong pattern of development associated with the emergence of the seven aspects of the proprium. The unified development of each of the seven aspects of the proprium results in the formation of a mature and healthy personality. More specifically, the emergence of the proprium involves a process of development ranging from the discovery of "I am" to "What shall I be?" With the development of each aspect of the proprium, people discover a little more about their unique self. Such a process is dynamic and continuous. Table 8.1 summarizes each aspect of proprium development.

Thus, proprium development is characterized as being a continuous and evolutionary process. Throughout life, the individual will continue to add to the development of his or her own sense of personal self-awareness and uniqueness.

Functional Autonomy: The Motivational Force behind Personality

The energy and motivational source behind the development and operation of the proprium is what Allport referred to as functional autonomy. Allport (1961) defines **functional autonomy** as "any acquired system of motivation in which the tensions involved are not the same as the antecedent tensions from which the acquired system developed" (p. 229). Stated more briefly, this concept simply means that in a mature adult, the motivation behind current actions is independent (autonomous) of early childhood motivation.

Table 8.1
The Developmental Aspects of the Proprium

Aspect of Proprium Development	Specific Knowledge of the Self Acquired
INFANCY (Years 1 to 3)	
Bodily Self (year 1)	I am separate from the environment. (e.g., I won't bite my own toe.)
Self-Identity (year 2)	I am separate from other individuals. (e.g., I am John.)
Self-Esteem (year 3)	I can manipulate and master my environment. (e.g., I can turn on the TV.)
CHILDHOOD (Years 4 to 12)	
Self-Extension (years 4 to 6)	I can exist beyond my physical self. (e.g., This is my bike.)
Self-Image (years 4 to 6)	I see myself as being like this. (e.g., I am good at naming my colors and afraid of the dark.)
Self as a Rational Coper (years 6 to 12)	I can solve my problems by using my "brain." (i.e., I can think logically.) (e.g., I'll get my kite untangled by shaking the branches of the bush.)
ADOLESCENCE (Years 12 and above)	
Propriate striving (years 12 through adolescence)	What will I be in the future? (e.g., I will take accounting in high school to help get my college degree in business.)

As an example, think about why adults attend college (i.e., "go to school"). As children, people go to school because they "have to." But as mature adults, some people are still going to school, although for completely different and independent reasons (e.g., self- and/or career enhancement). Functional autonomy is Allport's way of saying that to understand the actions of the emotionally healthy and mature individual, we must look at present motives and future expectations and not just into the individual's "ancient past," as Freud proposed.

As a way of further clarifying this motivational concept, Allport (1961) described two levels of functional autonomy: perseverative functional autonomy and propriate functional autonomy.

▲ **Perseverative functional autonomy** is a rather primitive motivational system that accounts for the expression of many repetitive behavior patterns and a desire for routine and familiarity. An example would be an office manager who refuses to use new, more efficient computerized equipment to run the office because of the comfort and security associated with running the office the "old way."

▲ **Propriate functional autonomy** represents a higher level of motivation that helps people to develop beyond their original level those aspects of their lives most significantly related to their sense of self-awareness (e.g., interests, abilities, values, and desires). For example, as a child Freida may originally be externally motivated to practice the piano because her parents tell her to. But as an adolescent, her practicing may be motivated by the sense of internal satisfaction and accomplishment she experiences when playing a musical piece well. Thus, the energy source for practicing the piano now comes from the sense of self-pride Freida develops as learning to be a better pianist becomes a vital part of her total sense of self.

The proprium and functional autonomy operate dynamically in the developmental process of the emotionally healthy and mature individual. An overall level of an individual's maturity might be measured by the extent to which the person's motives are functionally autonomous. Table 8.2 is a more specific list summarizing the six major features Allport considered to be characteristic of a mature personality.

Applications of Allport's Viewpoint: Using What Is Known

In addition to trying to understand the uniqueness of the individual through the study of traits, Allport was interested in other psychological features that contribute to the unique expression of each person.

Table 8.2
Six Characteristics of the Mature Personality

Characteristic*	Example
Extension of the sense of self. The mature individual is involved in activities outside of himself or herself.	By participating in community activities (e.g., volunteering to serve meals to the homeless), mature people are able to give of themselves to others.
Warm relating of the self to others. The mature individual is able to show compassion for the rights, needs, and values of others.	Mature people do not make jokes about another person at the expense of that individual's self-esteem.
Emotional security (self-acceptance). The mature individual is able to tolerate the frustrations of life without overreacting.	After going through a divorce, the mature individual does not jump immediately into another relationship just to make sure he or she is still able to be accepted by others.
Realistic perception, skills, and assignments. Mature people live in the "real world" and react to the problems of life rationally, not in a defensive or self-centered way.	After getting a low grade on a test, instead of just blaming the professor, the mature individual might reflect on how his or her study habits might have contributed to the poor test performance in order to avoid such mistakes in the future.
Self-Objectification: Insight and humor. Mature people have a realistic self-image of what they can do and are not threatened by their weaknesses. They are also able to laugh at their weaknesses.	Realizing that he is not a very good tennis player, a mature individual is able to make a joke about his slipping and being hit by the ball on his "behind" as he tries to charge the net.
Unifying philosophy of life. Mature people have a clear sense of how they wish to live their lives.	A unifying philosophy of life for a mature individual might involve treating others as you would expect them to treat you, or operating on the assumption that all men and women are created equal and should be treated accordingly.

*Note the similarity between the characteristics of Allport's view of the mature personality and Maslow's self-actualizing people discussed in Chapter 7 (pages 188–189).

Note. Data from *Pattern and Growth in Personality,* by G. W. Allport, 1961. Boston, MA: Holt, Rinehart and Winston, Inc.

In his work on the study of human values, Allport applied his viewpoint to meeting this objective.

Personality Assessment: Measurement of Values as Dominant Interests in Personality

The six categories of values Allport used in his work were originally adapted from the work of the German philosopher Eduard Spranger (1928). Following are brief descriptions of the six categories of values:

▲ *Theoretical.* A desire to discover truth and systematize one's knowledge. An example of this type of value might be seen in the thinking of scientists and philosophers.

▲ *Economic.* A basic concern for what is useful and practical. Such a bottom-line philosophy might be seen in the thinking of people in the business world.

▲ *Aesthetic.* An appreciation of the artistic beauty, harmony, and form for its own sake. This type of value might be dominant in the thinking of artists.

▲ *Social.* A basic concern for the well-being of other people. This type of thinking might be a dominant force in the lives of many teachers, social workers, and others in a variety of helping professions.

▲ *Political.* A basic interest in power related to any field, not just to politics. Such a value might be a guiding force in the thinking of a domineering spouse or an unscrupulous career-minded individual.

▲ *Religious.* A desire to unite the self with a higher sense of reality. Such spiritual awareness might be exemplified by people who regularly attend religious retreats and, to some degree, by those who take drugs to achieve a sense of expanded self-awareness.

The Study of Values Scale   To assess these six basic value categories, Allport and his colleagues developed a personality inventory they called the **Study of Values Scale** (Allport et al., 1960). This inventory consists of 45 forced-choice items, in which a response indicating each value is paired an equal number of times with each of the remaining five values. Here is a sample of items similar to those found in the Study of Values Scale (the values being compared are in parentheses):

> Should great artists, such as Mozart or Leonardo da Vinci, be allowed to be selfish and ignore the feelings of others? a. yes; b. no (artistic vs. social)
>
> Which of the two disciplines would you consider more important to further our understanding of mankind? a. mathematics; b. theology (theoretical vs. religious)
>
> Assuming your ability and the salary were the same for each of these occupations, would you prefer to be a—a. mathematician; b. sales manager; c. clergyman; d. politician (theoretical vs. economics vs. religious vs. political)

The relative strength of each value for the individual is obtained by adding the number of times that person selects a particular value throughout the test. The more times the person selects a particular value (i.e., the higher the score), the more dominant the value is in his or her personality.

Research on the Study of Values Scale   Evidence supporting the validity of the values scale is demonstrated by comparing the scores of groups of people whose characteristics are known and upon which it would be expected to find differences on certain values. For example, the religious dimension was the dominant value score for members of the clergy, while business students tended to score highest on the economic dimension (Allport et al., 1960).

Scores on the different value scales were also correlated with the speed with which people could perceive certain value-related words (Postman, Bruner, & McGinnies, 1948). For example, people scoring high on the economic scale might be able to perceive the word *dividend* sooner than those scoring high on the aesthetic scale.

For information about other studies supporting the validity, as well as reliability, of the values scale, read the reference manual that accompanies the *Study of Values Scale* (Allport et al., 1960).

The Application of Values Assessment: Marital and Vocational Counseling

The utility of Allport's Study of Values Scale can be illustrated by considering its applications to two of life's most important issues: marriage and career counseling.

The Study of Values Scale and Marital Counseling   In discussing the various applications of the Study of Values Scale, Allport et al. (1960) noted that the assessment of values has been found to be helpful to marriage counselors, especially among the clergy, in preparing and counseling prospective marriage partners. In one of the first studies investigating marital compatibility, an early version of the Study of Values Scale was used to assess personality similarity in married couples (Schooley, 1936). "Veteran" couples, those who had been married from 5 to 20 years, showed more similarity in economic and religious values than "newlywed" couples, who had been married 4 years or less. But the veteran couples showed greater dissimilarity in theoretical and aesthetic values than the newlywed couples. Thus, it seems that the key to longevity in marriage is for spouses to have a high degree of similarity on values about money (i.e., economic) and unity (i.e., religion) and a low degree of similarity on values related to a concern for such abstract and ideal notions as the seeking of truth (i.e., theoretical) and beauty (i.e., aesthetic).

Such findings seem to be as true today as they were back then. Similarity in religious and economic backgrounds and realistic expectations about marriage still seem to be some of the most important factors associated with long and successful marriages (Kieren, Henton, & Marotz, 1975; Rosen & Hall, 1984; Steinmetz, Clavan, & Stein, 1990). Similarly, a study of marital adjustment among nurses, based on the assessment of values, indicated that religious, economic, and theoretical values, in that order, were the values most related to successful marital adjustment (Nimkoff & Grigg, 1958). In this same study, a greater emphasis on monetary issues (i.e., high economic value score) was the factor most highly related to a lack of marital adjustment.

The Study of Values and Vocational Counseling   In the area of vocational counseling, the assessment of values has been used to help differentiate between various occupational groups. In one study, students pursuing graduate training in clinical psychology were found to express values reflecting a love for people (i.e., high social value) to a greater degree than students pursuing graduate training in other areas of psychology (Kelly & Fiske, 1950). Combining their general competitive nature with their occupational expectations of working in some type of community setting (e.g., physical education teachers or leaders of community recreation centers), males majoring in health and physical education at a college with a religious emphasis displayed peak scores in the political (e.g., competitiveness), social (e.g., working with people), and religious value categories (Seashore, 1947). In the same study, students majoring in the applied social sciences displayed peak scores in the social and religious value categories.

The utility of the Study of Values Scale in occupational and vocational counseling is enhanced by research suggesting the possibility that different vocational groups have distinctive value profiles (Allport et al., 1960). Overall, these studies seem to indicate that the assessment of values plays an important part in the process of vocational counseling.

Evaluation of Allport's Personalistic Viewpoint: Strengths and Limitations

We will conclude our discussion of Allport's viewpoint of personality by considering its characteristic strengths and limitations.

Characteristic Strengths
Allport's personalistic viewpoint has the following strengths:

▲   *Versatility in the research methodologies employed.* As noted earlier, Allport was inclined to let the nature of the problem dictate the methodology used to study it. As a result, few psychologists have demonstrated as much versatility in their research as Allport. In a career of research spanning almost fifty years, Allport used investigation methods including surveys, questionnaires, case studies, content analysis, experimental methodology, and the analysis of personal documents (e.g., letters and diaries).

▲   *An emphasis on the "person" in personality.* Although Allport is classified as a trait theorist because of his extensive conceptual usage of traits in developing his viewpoint, he was also

one of the first personality theorists to emphasize studying the uniqueness of the individual. Thus, consistent with Rogers, Maslow, and Kelly, Allport's personal philosophy reflected the belief that each person in his or her own right, functioning at a conscious level of awareness, is the most legitimate object of study in personality psychology.

Characteristic Limitations
Here are some limitations of Allport's personalistic viewpoint:

▲   *The invisibility of traits.* While traits played a central role in Allport's viewpoint, the concept of traits has certain limitations. Allport clearly assumed that traits existed, but his critics like to point out that no hard evidence exists to identify and locate a personality trait anywhere in the brain or rest of the body. His critics accuse Allport of building a theory around the invisible structure of the trait, which makes formulating and testing such a theory almost an empirical impossibility. In all fairness, the same criticism can be applied to other personality theorists (e.g., Freud's use of the ego and Rogers' use of the ideal self) and other areas of psychology (e.g., long-term memory is a concept used in the study of learning and memory).

▲   *Focusing on the discontinuity of development by failing to link the present with the past.* One major limitation noted in Allport's viewpoint has to do with his notion of functional autonomy and the emphasis it placed on the discontinuity of personality. Allport's critics stressed that he tended to downplay, if not ignore, the relationship between personality development in childhood and that of personality development in adulthood.

▲   *Too much emphasis on the individual created an "unscientific" approach to studying personality.* Allport has also been criticized for the emphasis he placed on studying the individual (i.e., idiographic approach) over trying to establish more general laws of behavior by studying groups of people (i.e., nomothetic approach). Studying groups of people to establish general laws of behavior is believed to be more consistent with what is considered the "scientific" approach to the study of personality. To be fair, Allport did spend a considerable amount of time studying groups of people in many different aspects of his research.

As the founder of the systematic study of personality in this country, Allport's contributions are monumental and continue to influence contemporary thinking in personality psychology (Funder, 1991). For more information about Allport's views on personality, read "Allport's Psychology of the Individual," in Hall and Lindzey's (1978) *Theories of Personality*; or Allport's (1961) classic textbook *Pattern and Growth in Personality*.

Cattell's Structural Trait Viewpoint: The Search for Source Traits

"Science demands measurement! Measurement began in personality at the end of the Freudian, Jungian, and Adlerian phase of clinically derived theories" (Cattell, 1990, p. 101). To further appreciate this quote by Raymond B. Cattell, you should know that he strongly rejected "armchair speculation" as a means of defining the nature of personality. As an alternative to such speculation, Cattell favors what is best described as a "data-based" approach to defining the nature and operation of personality. Cattell prefers to base his study of personality on empirical observations, which are then used to generate specific hypotheses to be confirmed or rejected based on additional research. For a glimpse into the personal life of Raymond Cattell, read "A Closer Look" below.

A Closer Look:

Biographical Background: The Life of Raymond B. Cattell

Raymond B. Cattell was born on March 20, 1905, and raised in the Devonshire area of England. As a young boy, he read widely and was keenly interested in

Raymond B. Cattell's emphasis on a systematic and empirical approach to personality research did much to raise the scientific status of personality psychology. Cattell is also noted for applying his ideas to a variety of areas both inside and outside of personality psychology.

chemistry—he once made gunpowder in his "chemistry shed." At the tender age of 16, he entered London University, graduating with honors in physics and chemistry. Yet he decided not to pursue a career in chemistry and physics:

> A variety of circumstances conspired in my last year of work in the physical sciences to crystallize that sense of a serious concern with social problems which had been awaiting germination in the five years since the war. (Cattell, 1974, p. 64)

As a young lad, Cattell had seen soldiers, still in their blood-soaked bandages, coming back from the front lines. This experience was one of the turning points that would increase his concern with changing social conditions:

> Gradually I concluded that to go beyond human irrationalities one had to study the workings of the mind itself . . . I realized that psychology was to be my life interest. (p. 64)

His friends tried to persuade Cattell against a career in psychology (they and others saw psychology as a field for cranks). But he would not be persuaded, even though prospects for gainful employment for psychologists were dismal at best.

As a graduate student at London University, Cattell studied with the eminent psychologist and statistician Charles Spearman, well known for his study of the structure of human intelligence and development of the early techniques of factor analysis—a technique that would play a crucial role in Cattell's career.

In 1929, after graduating from London University with his PhD, Cattell found that his friends had been correct—there were no positions for those with a new PhD in psychology. A succession of "fringe" jobs followed, but so did extreme poverty. But in 1937, E. L. Thorndike, a famous American psychologist, invited Cattell to come to America as a research associate for one year. While he described leaving England as being as painful as a tooth extraction, Cattell consoled himself with the thought that it was only for one year and accepted the offer. However, the year at Columbia with Thorndike was followed by two years at Clark University and then a position at Harvard.

For Cattell, life really began at age 40. In 1945, he was invited to the University of Illinois. He was also married to Karen Schuettler, a mathematician who would assist him in his research in many ways, including being a subject. It was at the University of Illinois that most of Cattell's approach to personality blossomed. An example of his dedication is the truly impressive volume of research and other publications Cattell has produced: over 30 books and approximately 400 publications thus far.

After spending almost thirty years at the University of Illinois, Cattell retired from there and is currently a member of the faculty of the University of Hawaii. More information on the life of Raymond Cattell can be found in his autobiography appearing in Lindzey's *A History of Psychology in Autobiography* (Cattell, 1974).

Basic Assumptions: Cattell's Definition of Personality

The basic assumptions of Cattell's viewpoint focus on using empirical measures to predict people's behavior. For Cattell, that which predicts behavior also defines personality.

Predicting the Person as the Principal Assumption of Personality

Cattell defined personality as "that which permits a prediction of what a person will do in a given situation" (1950, p. 2). Cattell's major objective is to be able to predict the behavior of an individual using information about that person's personality. Cattell's approach is based firmly on using empirical data,

combined through a statistical formula, to predict the behavior of an individual.

Constructing a Definition of Personality Based on Three Types of Empirical Data

In defining and studying the nature of personality, Cattell used three primary sources of empirical data: L-data, Q-data, and T-data.

▲ **L-data** consist primarily of records of life events, located in such places as public records (e.g., a college transcript) or archives (i.e., a diary) and the ratings made by others (e.g., the contents of a personnel file).

▲ **Q-data** include self-ratings on questionnaires or personality tests (e.g., the six separate scores on Allport's values scale).

▲ **T-data** involve observations of an individual in a limited situation designed to assess some aspect of personality. Examples of T-data include measuring the time required to complete a complex set of hand-eye coordination tests, or recording the amount of stuttering during a job interview.

While these types of data are discussed individually, the ability to predict a person's behavior is increased by combining them. For example, in selecting candidates for jet pilot training school, Air Force trainers ask potential recruits to provide college transcripts (i.e., L-data), complete a variety of intelligence and personality tests (i.e., Q-data), and perform on a flight simulator (i.e., T-data) as a means of predicting how well they would perform under actual combat conditions. No matter how the three types of data are combined, Cattell believes that they are the data upon which you begin to construct your definition of personality and predict the behavior of the individual.

The Basic Concept of Traits: Cattell's Structural Units of Personality

Like Allport, Cattell reflects the significance he places on traits by the way he defines them. According to Cattell, "A trait may be defined as that which defines what a person will do when faced with a defined situation" (Cattell, 1979, p. 14). Thus, Cattell uses the individual's behavior to define traits. To account for the diverse nature of the personalities observed among people, Cattell identifies different categories of traits and the effects each has on behavior.

Surface and Source Traits:
Creating Differences in Personality
The uniqueness of each person's personality is due to what Cattell conceptualized as surface and source traits.

▲ **Surface traits** are related elements of behavior that, when empirically measured and intercor-related, tend to cluster together. They are also the most visible evidence of a trait. For example, studying long hours, making sure all of the references in a term paper are correct, and showing up early to work might be considered visible evidence of the following surface traits: perseverance, conscientiousness, and punctuality, respectively. But surface traits are in turn controlled by underlying source traits.

▲ **Source traits** are responsible for the diversity seen in the personalities of those around us. In the preceding example, differences in perseverance, conscientiousness, and punctuality across individual students is explained by differences in the degree to which they possess the underlying source trait of ambitiousness.

Because of the major influence source traits have on behavior, Cattell maintains that the understanding of personality and the prediction of behavior are increased by studying how their surface traits are collectively related to certain underlying source traits instead of simply studying each behavioral element in isolation. For example, a greater understanding of people's personalities is gained by studying differences in the source trait of ambitiousness than by studying separately the surface traits of perseverance, conscientiousness, and punctuality.

Categorizing Traits: Conceptualizing the
Similarities and Dissimilarities of Personality
In addition to the surface-source trait distinction, the depth of Cattell's conceptualization of traits is reflected in the detailed manner in which he categorizes traits.

Common and Unique Traits   Cattell made the distinction between common and unique traits to account for the general nature of certain aspects of personality and the idiosyncratic nature of certain people's personalities.

▲ Like Allport, Cattell considered **common traits** to be certain traits assumed to be possessed by everyone to some degree. Examples of common traits are intelligence and anxiety.

▲ **Unique traits** are traits that are specific to one person and can take the form of peculiar interests (e.g., a friend who can watch reruns of "The Monkees" for hours) and/or beliefs (e.g., an individual who believes kids under 18 years old should be banned from shopping malls). Unique traits are similar to what Allport defined as personal dispositions.

Ability, Temperament, and Dynamic Traits   The individual nature of personality is also reflected in what Cattell referred to as ability, temperament, and dynamic traits.

▲ **Ability traits** (e.g., being insightful) involve a person's skill in dealing with complex problem-solving situations.

▲ **Temperament traits** reflect the general manner or style of an individual's behavior (e.g., relaxed or intense).

▲ **Dynamic traits** relate to what is often referred to as motivation (e.g., a desire to learn or being an underachiever).

Constitutional and Environmental-Mold Factors
Another way of categorizing traits involves considering the degree to which a trait is the result of biological or environmental factors.

▲ **Constitutional factors** are traits that are primarily dependent on biological factors. For example, an individual's degree of nervousness might be related to the arousal level of the person's nervous system, which is a biologically determined characteristic.

▲ **Environmental-mold factors** are traits that are influenced primarily by environmental factors. For example, a person's degree of morality is highly influenced by such environmental factors as peer groups or family background.

Of course, few traits are either-or. Most traits are due to the joint effects of biological and environmental factors.

Consistent with this point, Cattell has determined what he calls the nature-nurture ratio for many traits. The **nature-nurture ratio** represents the degree to which a trait is due to biological or environmental factors. For example, while intelligence is generally believed to be a biologically determined factor, it is possible to raise an individual's intelligence to some extent by placing the person in an environment that offers plenty of intellectual stimulation.

With all of the different ways to categorize traits, students commonly ask, "How did Cattell identify the presence of these diverse traits?" To examine the technique he used to identify traits, read "A Closer Look" below.

A Closer Look:

Factor Analysis: Cattell's Tool of the Trade

A very important part of Cattell's work in personality is the statistical technique of factor analysis. In basic terms, **factor analysis** is a data-grouping and data-reduction technique based on the logic of the correlation coefficient (see Chapter 1). Factor analysis can be used to determine how a large number of surface traits can be clustered into a smaller number of groups related to specific source traits.

The Process of Factor Analysis: A Step-by-Step Approach

The manner in which the researcher believes various surface traits will cluster is based on a specific theoretical framework and/or previous knowledge of the operation of these surface traits. Factor analysis is used to determine the extent to which the researcher's ideas about the clustering of the surface traits are confirmed. Although there are many ways to perform a factor analysis, they require the aid of a computer and usually involve the following basic steps:

1. *Data collection.* The first step in factor analysis is to collect data (e.g., L-, Q-, and T-data). For example, suppose information on some 500 stu-

dents is obtained in the seven different situations listed in the "Measures" column of Table 8.3.

2. *Establishing an intercorrelation matrix.* An **intercorrelation matrix** summarizes the correlation coefficients between each measure of behavior with every other measure of behavior being investigated. Table 8.3 is an intercorrelation matrix illustrating the correlations among the seven measures of interest in our discussion. For example, in this table, item B, "nervous mannerisms of the hands," correlates .63 (i.e., strongly related) with item A, "butterflies in the stomach," while "number of captions" (item E) correlates .00 (i.e., unrelated) with "heart rate" (item D).

Table 8.3

The Intercorrelation Matrix for Seven Measures: An Example

Measure	A	B	C	D	E	F	G
A. "Butterflies in stomach' while talking to an attractive member of the opposite sex	—						
B. Nervous mannerisms of the hands during a job interview	.63	—					
C. Amount of rocking back and forth while giving a talk in class	.50	.55	—				
D. Rapid heart rate during exam	.72	.63	.61	—			
E. Number of captions written for a cartoon	.08	.03	.04	.00	—		
F. Number of uses suggested for common objects	.02	.15	.11	.68	.81	—	
G. Number of suggestions for activities the "gang" could engage in this weekend on a group date	.10	.00	.03	.72	.78	.68	—

3. *The identification of factors.* The third step in factor analysis is the identification of factors. A **factor** is defined as a cluster of related behavior measures. A **factor loading** is a numerical index of the extent to which each specific behavioral measure is related to each factor. Factor loadings are calculated with the aid of a computer and the statistical technique of factor analysis. The results of the factor analysis are summarized in a factor matrix. A **factor matrix** is the listing of the factor loadings for each separate factor. Like a correlation coefficient, the higher the factor loading, the more a particular measure is related to the factor. Table 8.4 is an example of a factor matrix.

The factor matrix in Table 8.4 illustrates what might be likely to happen if the data in Table 8.3 had been subjected to a factor analysis. The most striking feature of Table 8.4 is the extent to which the seven separate measures are grouped together into two separate clusters, or factors. This illustrates the data-reduction and data-grouping characteristics of factor analysis. More specifically, instead of the seven separate measures to consider in an attempt to understand the nature of the personality of the 500 students, a researcher now has only two factors.

4. *Naming factors.* The final step in a factor analysis involves naming the factors that have been iden-

tified in the factor matrix. In Table 8.4, Factor I has high factor loadings for "butterflies," "nervous mannerisms," "rocking," and "heart rate." Perhaps "anxiety" might be an appropriate label that would capture the essence of the underlying relationship among these four behavioral measures. Since Factor II has loadings on "captions," "uses for common objects," and "activities suggested," perhaps "creativity" is a label that might capture the essence of the underlying relationship among these three behaviors. While the identification of factor structures is a rather empirical process, the naming of factors is rather subjective.

The Yield of Factor Analysis Is "Real" Source Traits

For Cattell, the major purpose of factor analysis is to identify source traits. The source traits are then used to define the nature of personality and predict people's behavior. In support of this search, Cattell (1979) notes that certain source traits (i.e., factors) have been identified consistently regardless of the type of data used (e.g., questionnaire, personal records), have been found in many different cultures, and have been used to predict real-life behavior (e.g., academic achievement).

In summary, performing a factor analysis is a highly complicated mathematical process that requires a certain amount of training and experience. However, having an understanding of the "basic logic" of factor analysis that is presented here is enough to be able to comprehend the approach taken by Cattell in his attempt to identify source traits within his study of personality.

Table 8.4
A Factor Matrix with Factor Loadings on Two Factors: An Example

Measure	Factor Loadings	
	Factor I	**Factor II**
A. "Butterflies"	.53	.03
B. Nervous mannerisms	.66	.10
C. Rocking	.61	.02
D. Heart rate	.72	.07
E. Captions	.00	.68
F. Uses for common objects	.09	.77
G. Activities suggested	.00	.73

The Behavioral Specification Equation: A Formula for Predicting What People Will Do

As stated in his basic definition of personality, Cattell stressed that personality research can aid in the understanding of the individual because it can be used to *predict* behavior. To facilitate the prediction of behavior, Cattell combines information (i.e., L-, Q-, and T-data) related to underlying source traits into the behavioral specification equation. The **behavioral specification equation** is a formula that combines information about traits, along with the degree of importance assigned to each type of information, in a mathematical manner for the purpose of predicting a particular behavior. The equation takes the following form:

$$B = w_1T_1 + w_2T_2 + w_3T_3 + w_4T_4 + \ldots + w_iT_i$$

The "B" in this equation stands for the behavior to be predicted. The "T's" stand for the various source traits that are deemed relevant to the behavior being predicted. The information represented by the different traits would be scores obtained from the various types of records (i.e., grades), tests (i.e., responses to a self-esteem inventory), and behavioral indices (i.e., ratings of hostility in a group discussion) available to the personality researcher trying to predict the behavior. Finally, the "w" is the weight factor that indicates the degree to which a given trait is involved in controlling the expression of a particular behavior. The larger the weight factor for a particular trait, the more influence that trait is believed to have on the expression of the behavior under investigation.

As an example of how the behavioral specification equation is used to predict behavior, suppose a personality researcher wanted to predict which students would be most likely to speak up to answer questions in class. To predict this behavior, the researcher might generate the following equation, based on three source traits identified by Cattell:

B (answering = (.4) Intelligence score
questions)   (i.e., high mental capacity)

+ (.2) Surgency-Desurgency score
        (i.e., talkativeness)

+ (.6) Parmia-Threctia score
        (i.e., boldness)

After inserting the values for each source trait and completing the mathematical operations in the equation, it would be predicted that those students having the highest values for the equation would be the most likely to answer questions in class. Additional information about other relevant source traits and their corresponding weight factors can be added to the equation in an attempt to increase the accuracy of the prediction.

In this section, you have learned the basic concepts of Cattell's viewpoint, his conceptualization and identification of source traits, and the utilization of source traits to predict behavior. Figure 8.2 summarizes the major points of this discussion and shows their interrelatedness.

Applications of Cattell's Viewpoint: Using What Is Known

The significant role of traits is illustrated further by the extent to which they are involved in the application of Cattell's viewpoint. Two areas in which this point is clearly illustrated include personality assessment and marriage counseling.

Personality Assessment: Measurement of Source Traits

Cattell's passion for identifying and classifying source traits also manifests itself in the application of his viewpoint to personality assessment. The most well-known of the many personality tests Cattell has

Figure 8.2
The basic concepts of Cattell's viewpoint are designed to achieve what he felt was the basic goal of personality—to predict what an individual will do in a specific situation.

developed is the **Sixteen Personality Factor Questionnaire**, or the **16PF** for short.

The Sixteen Personality Factor Questionnaire   The 16PF (Cattell, Eber, & Tatsuoka, 1970) is a multidimensional personality inventory containing 187 questions designed to assess 16 different source traits. The questions are arranged in several types of forced-choice formats, illustrated by the three items presented here. These three items are similar to others measuring the "parmia-threctia" factor (similar to shyness) of the 16PF, which Cattell et al. identified by the letter *H*.

> On social occasions I would rather:
>   a. come forward,
>   b. stay quietly in the background.
>
> If I should suddenly become the focus of attention in a social situation, I would become slightly embarrassed.
>   a. yes,
>   b. no.
>
> Having "stage-fright" in different social situations is something I have experienced:
>   a. quite often,
>   b. occasionally,
>   c. hardly ever.

The 16 source traits measured by the 16PF are presented in Table 8.5. The 16 traits are assigned letters in order of their contribution to the total personality structure. In other words, the traits near the top of the list have a greater influence on behavior than traits near the bottom. In addition, to indicate the types of behaviors controlled by each specific source trait, Table 8.5 includes a set of key words defining the principal characteristics of high- and low-scoring people.

Validity Research on the 16PF   Much of the validation research on the 16PF involves the formulation of various behavioral specification equations to distinguish between and/or predict the behavior of certain groups of people. For example, Knowles (1966) used a previously established specification equation for identifying creativity in scientists to predict the subsequent academic achievement of incoming freshman students. This study suggests that a particular specification equation can be used to predict the behavior of different groups of people.

In another study, Drevdahl and Cattell (1958) identified those traits on the 16PF that were found consistently among several samples of successful American and British artists. The personality of these successful artists included scoring high on the following 16PF source traits (the letters of the source traits found in Table 8.5 are in parentheses): being dominant (E), radical (Q1), emotionally sensitive (I), strongly influenced by inner motivations (A), and self-sufficient (Q2). Low scores on the following 16PF source traits indicated that the personality characteristics of these artists also included being disregardful of rules (G), natural and spontaneous in their behavior (N), and somewhat detached (A). The most striking feature of this study is the extent to which the same trait structure (e.g., being individualistic and free-thinking) was identified across several different groups of artists. This finding suggests that a common set of 16PF source traits can describe the basic personality of these successful artists. Many other interesting examples of studies documenting the validity of the 16PF, as well as additional information on its reliability, are in the *Handbook for the Sixteen Personality Factor Questionnaire (16PF)* (Cattell et al., 1970).

Application of the 16PF to the Study of Marriage: Identifying Marital Stability and Compatibility
Do opposites attract? In a dating relationship, do people actively seek someone different from themselves to balance their own personality? Or is it better to be two similar peas in a pod? In an attempt to answer such difficult questions, Cattell and others have applied their knowledge of traits and their assessment to the study of marriage.

The Study of Marriage Stability Using the 16PF   In 1967, Cattell and Nesselroade studied married couples they identified as either "stable" or "unstable." Stable couples were defined as those who took no steps toward dissolving the marriage. Unstable couples were defined as those who were separated or were undergoing marriage counseling. Cattell and Nesselroade hypothesized "that a positive correlation

Table 8.5
The Traits of the 16PF: A Listing and Description of the Basic Source Traits

Letter	Cattell's Label for the Factor	Description of High Score	Description of Low Score
A	Affectia-Sizia	Warmhearted Outgoing Easygoing	Reserved Detached Critical
B	Intelligence	Bright High mental capacity Fast-learning	Dull Low mental capacity Poor judgment
C	Ego strength	Emotionally stable Mature Faces reality	Affected by feelings Easily upset Changeable
E	Dominance-Submissiveness	Assertive Aggressive Competitive	Obedient Easily led Dependent
F	Surgency-Desurgency	Enthusiastic Happy-go-lucky Talkative	Serious Full of cares Concerned
G	Superego strength	Conscientious Persistent Responsible	Disregards rules Expedient Undependable
H	Parmia-Threctia	Adventurous Bold Impulsive	Shy Restrained Withdrawn
I	Premsia-Harria	Sensitive Overprotected Expects affection and attention	Unsentimental Self-reliant Keeps to the point
L	Protension-Alaxia	Jealous Dogmatic Suspicious	Trusting Understanding Ready to forget difficulties
M	Autia-Praxernia	Imaginative Absent-minded Interested in art, theory, basic beliefs	Practical Conventional Concerned with immediate interests
N	Shrewdness-Naiveté	Worldly Socially aware Exact, calculating mind	Unpretentious Spontaneous Lacks self-insight
O	Guilt proneness-Untroubled adequacy	Apprehensive Insecure Troubled	Self-assured Self-confident Cheerful
Q1	Radicalism-Conservatism	Experimenting Analytic Free-thinking	Not likely to change Respects traditional values Tolerant of old methods
Q2	Self-sufficiency-Group dependency	Self-sufficient Resourceful Prefers own decisions	Group dependent Is a "joiner" Sound follower
Q3	Self-sentiment	Controlled Exacting will power Compulsive	Uncontrolled Follows own urges Careless of social rules
Q4	Ergic tension	Tense Frustrated Driven	Relaxed Tranquil Composed

Note. Data from *The Scientific Analysis of Personality*, by R. Cattell, 1965. Chicago, IL: Aldine and *A Guide to the Clinical Use of the 16PF*, by S. Karson and J. W. O'Dell, 1976. Champaign, IL: Institute for Personality and Ability Testing.

Will this marriage be a success? The Marriage Counseling Report is used in marriage counseling and marriage enhancement therapy to help marriages succeed.

between husband and wife would be found over most of the personality factors for the normal group, but that negative, zero, or significantly lower positive correlations would be found for the unstable than for the normal couples" (p. 352). If their hypothesis was upheld, it would provide little support for the old saying that "opposites attract." As it turns out, their hypothesis was supported. Stable couples tended to have more highly correlated (i.e., similar) personality traits than unstable couples.

Assessing Marital Compatibility Using the 16PF   The Cattell and Nesselroade study is a good example of how research can be very useful in helping us to understand something as important as marriage. In a similar manner, David Madsen and Mary Russell (1982; Russell & Madsen, 1988) have developed the Marriage Counseling Report (MCR). The **Marriage Counseling Report** is a computer-generated interpretation comparing pairs of personality profiles based on the 16PF. With the aid of a trained counselor, the MCR is designed to examine individual and joint strengths and weaknesses found in the personalities of people in marriage counseling and marriage enhancement group therapy settings. The MCR can also be used to compare the personality patterns of people seeking marital counseling with the personality patterns of people experiencing successful marital

adjustment. Based on these comparisons, the MCR provides information about the couple's personality patterns and their relationship which can be explored in greater detail during subsequent counseling sessions.

A sample MCR comparing the paired profiles of a couple is presented in Table 8.6. In the table, the *F*'s represent the scores obtained by the woman on the 16PF while the *M*'s indicate the scores obtained by the man. The dotted lines between the *F*'s and *M*'s indicate the magnitude of the difference in their scores. The *B*'s indicate that both the man and the woman scored identically on the trait.

The results of the paired profiles based on the 16PF is just one element of the overall MCR. Another part of the MCR is titled "Marriage Counseling Data." The interpretation of the counseling data is based upon research identifying personality traits related to adjustment and possible interpersonal difficulties. Following are some summaries of interpretations based on information from the counseling data section of the MCR for the couple whose personality profile is illustrated in Table 8.6.

> He manifests the tendency to react in a negative manner to criticism or critical probing. Rather than express any feeling of hostility through the process of direct confrontation, his tendency might be to do so in more covert, intellectualized ways. To counteract these reactive tendencies, it is suggested that time be spent attempting to develop a more supportive environment.
>
> She seems to be an individual who is unable to handle her feelings in a proper manner. It is likely that under stress she might be apt to develop physical symptoms, such as ulcers or headaches, that would interfere further with her ability to cope with her feelings and interpersonal relationships.

(Based on Madsen & Russell, 1982)

Based on what is known about these two people, how would you rate the likelihood of their creating a successful marital relationship? The value of the MCR is that it gives couples the opportunity before marrying or dissolving a marriage to become aware of personality factors in their relationships and the possible adjustments they may need to make in accommodating them. For more information on other applications

Table 8.6
Assessing Marital Compatibility: A Sample MCR Profile

Trait		1	2	3	4	5	6	7	8	9	10	
A	Cool, reserved			F---	--------	--M						Warm, easygoing
B	Concrete thinking					M---	--------	--------	--F			Abstract thinking
C	Easily upset				M---	------------F						Calm, stable
E	Not assertive		M---	--------	--------	--------	--------	--F				Dominant
F	Sober, serious			M---	----------F							Enthusiastic
G	Expedient				M---	--------	--------F					Conscientious
H	Shy, timid				M---	--------	--F					Venturesome
I	Tough-minded			F---	--------	--------	--------	--------	--------	--M		Sensitive
L	Trusting					M---	----------F					Suspicious
M	Practical			B								Imaginative
N	Forthright		F---	--------	--------	--------	--------	--------	--M			Shrewd
O	Self-assured					B						Self-doubting
Q1	Conservative				F---	--------	--------M					Experimenting
Q2	Group-oriented			M---	--------	--------	--------	-- F				Self-sufficient
Q3	Undisciplined				M---	--------	--------	-- F				Self-disciplined
Q4	Relaxed				F---	--------	--M					Tense-driven

Interpretation: The degree of personality similarity between these two people may be considered extremely low.

Note. From *Marriage Counseling Report*, by D. H. Madsen and M. T. Russell, 1982. Champaign, IL: Institute for Personality and Ability Testing.

of the 16PF, read the relatively short book (160 pages) by Samual Karson and Jerry W. O'Dell (1976), titled *A Guide to the Clinical Use of the 16PF.*

Evaluation of Cattell's Structural Trait Viewpoint: Strengths and Limitations

We will conclude our discussion of Cattell's viewpoint of personality by considering its characteristic strengths and limitations.

Characteristic Strengths
Here are some strengths of Cattell's structural trait viewpoint:

▲ *A quantitative approach.* One of Cattell's major strengths is the objectivity he uses to study the nature of personality. Cattell believes that the best way to determine the structural nature of personality and predict behavior is to use quantitative methods, such as factor analysis, instead of armchair theorizing.

▲ *Cattell as a scientist.* The statistical technique of factor analysis and other techniques used by Cattell allow him to study personality in a rather rigorous manner. Inconsistent with some of the less stringent approaches taken by other personality theorists, Cattell's commitment to rigorous research has done much to earn him the label of "scientist" in every sense of the word.

Characteristic Limitations
Here are some limitations of Cattell's viewpoint:

▲ *The limitations of being too technical.* The statistical techniques that Cattell used to develop his structural trait viewpoint can be very complicated and extremely technical. The language used to explain Cattell's viewpoint is also highly technical and not very appealing to the casual reader. For these reasons, Cattell's approach has not attracted the attention of many people, including personality psychologists. Given the emphasis personality psychologists place on the "scientific approach," it seems almost contradictory that Cattell should be criticized on the grounds of being "too technical."

▲ *An emphasis on identifying the universal personality while losing sight of the individual.* In his effort to establish a scientific approach to predicting behavior (e.g., the identification of 16 source traits), Cattell's research relies primarily on the study of large groups of people. Such an approach tends to reduce the study of personality to a consideration of the "average person." Cattell has been criticized for his attempt to define a universal set of source traits that seems to lose sight of the individual.

More information about Cattell's theory of personality can be found in *The Scientific Analysis of Personality* (Cattell, 1965), which is designed as a basic introduction to his theory and is written to be read by the general public (i.e., it is not too technical) or *Advances in Cattellian Personality Theory* (Cattell, 1990).

Eysenck's Hierarchical Trait Viewpoint: A Type Theory of Traits

In addition to Allport and Cattell, a third individual has contributed significantly to the trait viewpoint of personality. Hans Eysenck's contributions have been in identifying fundamental dimensions of personality and their potential biological bases. For a glimpse into the life of Eysenck, read "A Closer Look" below.

A Closer Look:

Biographical Background: The Life of Hans J. Eysenck

Hans Jurgen Eysenck was born in Germany on March 4, 1916. His mother was an actress in films and his father an actor on the stage. Eysenck did not see much of his parents as a child; he was raised primarily by his grandmother. In reaction to the rise of Nazism and his refusal to join the military at 18, Eysenck left Germany in 1934 and went to study in both France and England. In 1940, he received his PhD from the University of London while studying under the eminent psychologist Sir Cyril Burt. During World War II he served as a research psychologist at the Mill Hill Emergency Hospital, which was a psychiatric institution specializing in the treatment of patients suffering from combat stress. At the end of the war, Eysenck was named the director of the Maudsley Hospital's new Institute of Psychiatry.

Eysenck has demonstrated a most remarkable level of productivity—he has published over 30 books and some 600 articles. Even more impressive is the diversity of topics about which Eysenck has written. Some of these topics include introversion-extraversion, biological bases of personality, learning theory, intelligence, genetics, smoking, criminal behavior, and sexuality. Some of his published works are co-authored with

Hans J. Eysenck is a personality researcher with a wide range of interests who has been at the center of many important issues in psychology.

his second wife, Sybil B. G. Eysenck, and his son, Michael W. Eysenck. Eysenck has also been at the center of many controversies in psychology. These controversies include assessing the effectiveness of psychotherapy and the inheritability of intelligence. More on the life of Eysenck can be found in his autobiography (Eysenck, 1980).

Basic Assumptions: Starting with a Fundamental Idea

Like Cattell, Eysenck relied on factor analysis extensively to help identify the existence of the underlying dimensions of personality. But unlike Cattell, Eysenck did not rely solely on factor analysis to define the outcome of the personality structure. Instead, Eysenck started out with certain ideas about what he thought the dimensions of personality should look like and then used factor analysis to help identify the dimensions. Eysenck relied on the works of others, including Jung and the ancient Greek physicians Hippocrates and Galen, to help guide his thinking (Eysenck, 1967). Eysenck began with the fundamental idea that personality could be conceptualized by two major dimensions of personality. He then used factor analysis to test this idea. Figure 8.3 illustrates the nature of the two major dimensions of personality and the classification of various traits proposed by Eysenck.

Basic Concepts: The Structure and Dynamics of Personality

Like Allport and Cattell, Eysenck demonstrates the significance he attributes to traits in the study of personality by the depth in which he describes their structural organization and dynamics.

The Hierarchical Nature of Traits: From Specific Actions to General Types

Figure 8.4 illustrates Eysenck's view on the basic structural nature of personality (Eysenck, 1947, 1953, 1967, 1982, 1990; Eysenck & Eysenck, 1985).

▲   *Specific response level.* At the bottom of the hierarchical structure are specific responses. **Specific responses** are particular actions

observed in a particular situation. An example of specific response is when an individual smiles and extends a handshake upon meeting someone new.

▲   *Habitual response level.* A **habitual response** is the repetition of the specific response across a number of situations. For example, if the individual smiles and extends a handshake each time he or she meets someone new, this pattern might then be defined as a habitual response to meeting someone new.

▲   *Trait level.* **Traits** are a collection of habitual responses. A person might be considered to have the trait of sociability if he or she also has the habitual response of going to parties, having many friends, and participating in group-type leisure activities (e.g., golf, cards).

▲   *Type level.* At the top of the hierarchy are personality types. A **type** is the interrelationship of many traits to create a general pattern of behavior that exerts a major influence on the individual's response style. Types are also the

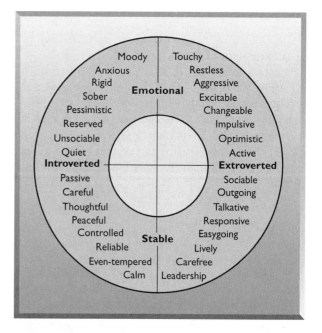

Figure 8.3
Eysenck's two major dimensions of personality and the classification of various personality traits
Note. From The Causes and Cures of Neurosis: An Introduction to Modern Behavior Therapy Based on Learning Theory and the Principle of Conditioning, by H. J. Eysenck and S. Rachman, 1965. London: Hodder & Stroughton.

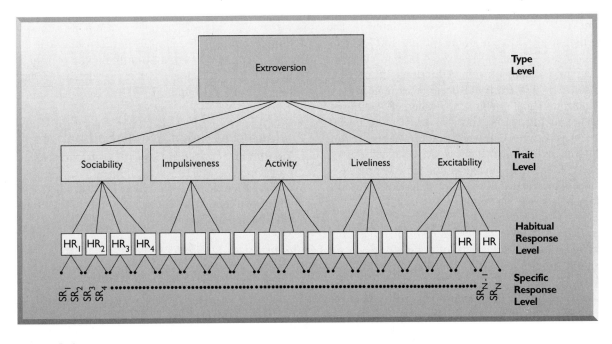

Figure 8.4
Eysenck's organization structure of personality traits

Note. From *The Biological Basis of Personality*, by H. J. Eysenck, 1967. Springfield, IL: Charles C. Thomas.

general dimensions around which Eysenck believed personality is organized. For example, if the individual is an extraverted type, he or she would probably select a career (e.g., sales or management) and elect to live in a location (e.g., in or near a big city) that makes possible the expression of the traits of sociability, impulsiveness, activity, liveliness, and excitability.

Thus, for Eysenck, personality is arranged in a hierarchical structure manner based on the degree of influence each trait level has on behavior.

Personality Dynamics: The Three Basic Types of Personality

Eysenck describes the dynamics of personality as involving the relationship of three basic types of traits. The three basic types of personality proposed by Eysenck are **extraversion-introversion** (E), **neuroticism** (N), and **psychoticism** (P) (Eysenck, 1990; Eysenck & Eysenck, 1985). These dimensions are assessed using the *Eysenck Personality Questionnaire* (Eysenck & Eysenck, 1975).

Extraversion   The extraversion dimension (E) is composed of extraversion at one end of the continuum and introversion at the other (Eysenck, 1975). Extraversion is characterized by people who like to be around other people, enjoy excitement, and are easy-going, optimistic, and adventurous. Introversion is characterized by people who like order and are introspective, emotionally controlled, calculating, and socially distant outside of having a few close friends. In addition to the overt differences between extraversion and introversion types, these people differ in several other ways. Extraverts were found to be more popular (Brown & Hendrick, 1971), report more sexual behavior (Eysenck, 1976), acquire more sexual knowledge (Barnes, Malamuth, & Cheek, 1984) and sexual experience at a younger age (Schenk & Pfrang, 1986), take more risks and have more accidents while driving (Shaw & Sichel, 1971), and consume more alcohol (Edwards, Chandler, & Hensman, 1972) than introverts.

On a more covert level within the individual, extraverts seem to be less sensitive to stimulation (Wilson, 1978), endure pain better (Eysenck &

Eysenck, 1985), show more arousal later in the evening—from 9:00 p.m. to midnight—but less earlier in the day—from 7:00 a.m. to 4:00 p.m. (Wilson, 1990), and display faster reductions in cortical arousal (i.e., less electrical brain wave activity) to stimulation (Haier, Robinson, Braden, & Williams, 1984) than introverts. Many of these more covert differences between extraverts and introverts are due to differences in biological processes (Eysenck, 1967, 1970, 1990). These biological and genetic processes are discussed in the next chapter dealing with the biological bases of personality.

Neuroticism   The neuroticism dimension (N) is composed of emotional stability at one end of the continuum and emotional instability at the other (Eysenck & Eysenck, 1985). Emotionally stable people are characterized as carefree, even-tempered, and calm. Emotionally unstable people are characterized as touchy, restless, moody, and anxious. Emotionally unstable people display greater reactions to stress (Maushammer, Ehmer, & Eckel, 1981) and seem to require a longer period of readjustment following a stressful experience than emotionally stable people (Harvey & Hirschmann, 1980).

As shown in Figure 8.3, Eysenck combined the dimensions of extraversion and neuroticism to formulate a description of personality. Someone scoring more in the direction of extraversion and emotional stability might exhibit the personality traits of being responsive and easygoing; someone scoring more in the direction of the introversion and emotional instability dimensions might exhibit the personality traits of being sober and pessimistic. Thus, with Eysenck's system it is possible to describe various personality patterns and not just the extreme cases of general personality types.

Psychoticism   The psychoticism dimension (P) is composed of psychoticism at one end of the continuum and superego control (i.e., a sense of morality) at the other (Eysenck, 1990; Eysenck & Eysenck, 1976). Psychoticism is characterized by people who are impulsive, cold, not empathic, unconcerned about the rights and welfare of others, and antisocial. Psychoticism is associated with more severe forms of personality pathology (e.g., schizophrenia) and is less important in the study of the healthy per-

sonality. For example, people scoring high on the P dimension displayed a pattern of sensory sensitivity and arousal to visual stimuli similar to that of schizophrenics (Claridge, 1983; Claridge & Birchall, 1978; Claridge & Chappa, 1973).

Evaluation of Eysenck's Viewpoint: Characteristic Strengths and Limitations

We will conclude our discussion of Eysenck's viewpoint of personality by considering its characteristic strengths and limitations.

Characteristic Strengths
Here are some strengths of Eysenck's viewpoint:

▲ *Eysenck's emphasis on empiricism eclecticism.* Like Cattell, one of Eysenck's principal strengths is his emphasis on developing the scientific perspective of personality psychology based on empirical data. Eysenck relies heavily on factor analysis and other rather complicated statistical techniques to support his ideas.

▲ *Eclectic thinking.* Another of Eysenck's significant strengths is his eclectic thinking style and ability to integrate a variety of areas of knowledge within his viewpoint. His perspective on personality has combined the study of genetics, biological and physiological processes, learning theory, and societal and cultural factors.

Characteristic Limitations
Here are some limitations of Eysenck's viewpoint:

▲ *Eysenck's emphasis on just three dimensions of personality.* A major criticism of Eysenck's approach centers on his assumption that personality can be reduced to just three principal types or factors. As discussed in the next section, a central issue in the study of traits is identifying the number of dimensions or factors necessary to describe personality. The research on this issue suggests that three factors are probably too few to describe the underlying structure of personality.

▲ *Concerns about the nature of Eysenck's dimensions of personality.* In a related matter, there are also questions concerning the validity of the extraversion-introversion dimension as a single dimension. It has been suggested that the extraversion-introversion dimension might be more accurately described as two separate dimensions of personality, such as sociability and impulsiveness.

Additional aspects of Eysenck's viewpoint of personality are discussed in the next chapter concerning the biological bases of personality. For more information about Eysenck's viewpoint, read his books *Psychology Is About People* (1972) and *The Inequality of Man* (1973).

Special Issues in the Study of Traits: The Consistency and Organization of Traits

Although only the trait theories of Allport, Cattell, and Eysenck are discussed in this chapter, you should know that many people are working in the trait tradition today. Even though many of them do not offer their own definitions of traits, most "would probably agree that trait terms refer to stylistic consistencies in interpersonal behavior" (Hogan, DeSoto, & Solano, 1977, p. 256) and that traits are personality psychology's "unique and therefore defining characteristic" (Buss, 1989, p. 1378). The work of some of these people involves addressing issues related to the specific nature and operation of traits (Buss & Cantor, 1989).

Two issues of central concern for contemporary personality psychologists working in the trait tradition involve the consistency of traits in influencing behavior and the structural organization of traits.

The Issue of Cross-Situational Consistency: The Ability of Traits to Predict Behavior

As noted at the beginning of this chapter, trait theorists assume that traits exist and that people differ in the degree to which they possess certain traits. With the idea that traits exist comes the expectation that they should operate in a rather stable manner to influence an individual's behavior over time and across various situations. The stability of most concern is often referred to as cross-situational consistency.

The Search for Cross-Situational Consistency: Traits as a Stabilizing Influence in Life

The basic assumption of cross-situational consistency is the stabilizing influence of traits on behavior over time and place. The basic assumption of **cross-situational consistency** is that the behavior of an individual should be expected to be relatively consistent across a wide variety of situations (e.g., at work, school, and home) due to the stabilizing impact of traits. For example, an extraverted individual was extremely social last week at a party, is talkative today while attending a business conference, and is expected to be very friendly two months from now when on vacation. While no one is really expected to be perfectly consistent, people are expected to maintain their relative ranking across situations by exhibiting behaviors consistent with their level of endowment (e.g., high, medium, or low) of the trait. For example, attending a funeral will make even the most extraverted individual somewhat less sociable. But the individual high on the trait of extraversion will probably be more sociable (e.g., talk to more people) at the funeral home than an individual low on the extraversion dimension.

Documenting a Lack of Cross-Situational Consistency: Classic and Contemporary Evidence

In this section, we will consider the evidence suggesting a lack of cross-situational consistency in behavior.

Some Classic Evidence Documenting a Lack of Cross-Situational Consistency

A classic example of research addressing the issue of cross-situational consistency is that of Hartshorne and May (1928). They investigated the cross-situational consistency of moral behavior (e.g., lying, cheating, cooperativeness) in more than a thousand children across a variety of situations (e.g., home, school, party games, and athletic competitions). The results of this extensive research indicated that the average correlation between the moral behavior in any two situations was only about $r = +.30$. Such results suggest very little cross-situational consistency.

Dudycha (1936) observed a similar pattern of results when studying punctuality of college students (e.g., arriving on time to class, social events, meals, and appointments) by examining more than 15,000 observations for over 300 college students. The average cross-situational correlation was calculated to be only $r = +.19$, which indicates a rather low degree of cross-situational consistency.

Some Contemporary Evidence Documenting a Lack of Cross-Situational Consistency

More contemporary evidence examining the issues of cross-situational consistency of behavior has been summarized by Mischel (1968) in his now-classic book titled *Personality and Assessment*. In this book, Mischel reviewed and summarized much of the past and present research on the ability of personality tests (i.e., trait measures) to predict behavior across a variety of situations. He noted that there was little evidence to suggest that trait measures do a very good job of predicting behavior in different situations. More specifically, he noted that correlations between various personality tests (e.g., shyness) and observed behaviors (e.g., avoiding others at a party) rarely exceeded the magnitude of $r = .30$.

So consistent was this finding that Mischel (1968, p. 78) coined the phrase "personality coefficient" to describe it. **Personality coefficient** describes the correlation of around $r = .20$ to $.30$ that is typically found whenever attempts have been made to correlate a measure of a trait (e.g., aggressiveness) or other personality dimensions (e.g., an immediate sense of anger) assessed by personality tests with some observable behavior (e.g., number of hostile statements made in a group discussion). The inability of traits to predict behavior across situations has brought into question their overall value and importance (Kenrick & Funder, 1988).

In Support of Cross-Situational Consistency: Predicting Some of the People Some of the Time

In contrast to the early findings and conclusions about the inability of traits to predict behavior, con-

temporary research has documented a greater degree of cross-situational consistency than is represented by the personality coefficient. This research tends to make more realistic assumptions about the nature and operation of traits. It also uses more sophisticated research methodologies than simply calculating the correlation between the trait measure and behavior in various situations.

One of the more realistic assumptions made by contemporary researchers is that not everybody is equally consistent for each personality trait. As a test of this assumption, Bem and Allen (1974) had people indicate the extent to which they demonstrated consistency in behavior for the traits of friendliness and conscientiousness. Bem and Allen then selected groups of highly predictable and unpredictable people and obtained ratings of the individual's behavior across a number of situations related to being friendly and conscientious (e.g., sociability and promptness). The results indicated that the correlations between the trait of friendliness and the overall behavioral friendliness rating were $r = +.57$ for the predictable group and $r = +.27$ for the unpredictable group. For the trait of conscientiousness, the overall correlations were $r = +.45$ for the predictable group and $r = +.09$ for the unpredictable group.

This consistency between personality traits and behavior gets even larger when people are given the opportunity to select those specific traits for which they feel they are most consistent (Kenrick & Stringfield, 1980). Thus, as more realistic assumptions about traits are made (e.g., not all people are equally predictable) and more sophisticated procedures are employed (e.g., identifying predictable people and letting people select their predictable traits), there is considerable evidence to document cross-situational consistency in personality traits (Buss, 1989; Kenrick & Funder, 1988; Zuckerman et al., 1988).

Clarifying the Consistency Issue: Situational, Cognitive, and Aggregation Alternatives

With the impact of personality traits on behavior established, three general categories of approaches have been proposed to further clarify how traits might be used to help account for the cross-situational consistencies in behavior. These include what might be labeled as the situational, cognitive, and aggregation alternatives.

The Situational Alternative: It's Not Only Who You Are, but Where You Are That Counts

The situational alternative to the cross-situational consistency issue stresses that behavior occurs in a particular situation. The assumption here is that situational factors (e.g., posted rules) serve to modify behavior and create inconsistency across situations.

Situationism and External Constraints on Behavior
Situationism proposes that certain characteristics of the situation dictate what are acceptable or possible forms of behavior in a given situation (Bowers, 1973; Moos, 1973; Price & Bouffard, 1974). For example, although an individual may be extremely talkative at school and parties, the formality of visiting a funeral home produces a much more somber display of behavior. In addition, posting a sign in a hallway at school that says "Quiet Please" might also produce uncharacteristic silence in this individual. Thus, the inconsistencies in the individual's degree of talkativeness are a result of the implicit (e.g., social customs) and explicit (e.g., instructions) constraints of the situation on behavior.

The Concept of Interactionism   An extension of the situational alternative is the concept of interaction-ism. **Interactionism** states that it is not the person (i.e., personality traits) or the situation (i.e., characteristics of the environment) independently but the interaction (i.e., combination) of these two factors that best explains and predicts the behavior of individuals (Bowers, 1973; Ekehammer, 1974; Endler, 1973, 1982; Higgins, 1990; Magnusson & Endler, 1977; Ozer, 1986; Pervin, 1984). The logic behind interactionism is that the combination of personal and situational components have a much greater effect than when they are considered separately.

As an example of interactionism, consider how shy and not-shy people might rate their enjoyment of small (i.e., 20 people) or large (i.e., 75 people) social gatherings. If only the shyness of the individual (i.e., personality factor) is considered, the results might look like those in the left chart of Figure 8.5. If only the size of the party (i.e., situational factor) is considered, the results might look like those in the middle chart of Figure 8.5. But if both the personality and situational factors are considered, the results might look like those in the right chart of Figure 8.5. Shy people may prefer large parties because it might be easier for them to blend into the crowd and feel less self-conscious. On the other hand, less-shy people might prefer smaller parties where there is less competition for them to be the center of attention. Thus, by considering both situational and personality factors, researchers can achieve a more complete understanding of behavior than by considering these factors separately.

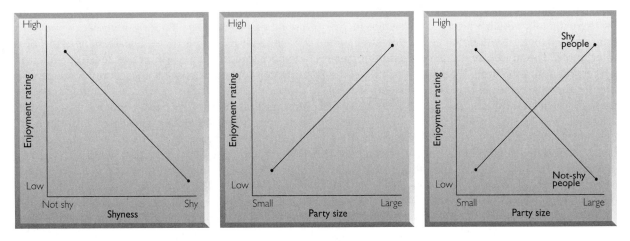

Figure 8.5
An example of interactionism: Enjoyment ratings of different-size parties by shy and not-shy people

While interactionism stresses the benefits of combining both personality and situational factors, sometimes the effects of situational characteristics or the personality of the individual considered separately do a better job of predicting behavior and explaining cross-situational consistency (Diener & Larsen, 1984; Diener, Larsen, & Emmons, 1984; Sarason, Smith, & Diener, 1975). Sometimes the person-situation interactions are more complex than simply adding together the personalities of the people and the characteristics of the situation. Personality psychologists must more systematically consider when and why characteristics of the situations, the personality of the individual, and/or the interaction of these two variables are most important (Buss, 1989; Diener & Larsen, 1984; Higgins, 1990; Magnusson & Endler, 1977; Mischel, 1973, 1984, 1985; Moskowitz, 1982). Thus, because situational and personality factors considered alone tend to be equally moderately correlated with specific behaviors (Funder & Ozer, 1983; Mischel, 1968), the situational alternative proposes that cross-situational consistency can be better explained by considering both of these factors and their combination.

The Cognitive Alternative: Perceptions and Interpretations of Situations

The cognitive alternative to the cross-situational consistency issue stresses the role of cognitive factors in the perception and interpretation of situational cues that determine what behaviors will be performed. The basic assumption here is that the degree of cross-situational consistency will be determined by the extent to which there is consistency in the manner in which situational cues are perceived and interpreted. The more likely different situations are perceived and interpreted as being similar, the greater the degree of behavioral consistency across these different situations.

Cognitive Factors as a Determinant of Behavior Consistency   **Cognitive factors** refer to various mental processes that influence the thoughts people have about being in a particular situation and how they might respond to these thoughts (Mischel, 1973, 1984, 1990). Examples of cognitive processes include the selective perception to certain cues in a situation (e.g., what other people are doing) and the

specific interpretation of these cues (e.g., these people seem to be having fun). The selective perception and specific interpretation of these cues serve to clarify the situation and determine the individual's behavior.

The behavior of others in a situation is a very powerful cue that can determine an individual's behavior (Lamm & Myers, 1978; Zimbardo, 1970). Even a very introverted person might start to yell and scream at a football game after being caught up in the excitement and emotion of the other fans. Thus, the inconsistency in behavior of this introverted person is due to the perception and interpretation of certain cues (e.g., screaming is perceived and interpreted as appropriate and desirable).

Powerful vs. Weak Situations as Determinants of Cognitive Clarity   To pinpoint more accurately the role of cognitive factors, Mischel (1973, 1984) describes the power of situations to determine specific behaviors. The power of a situation is characterized by its cognitive clarity. Cognitive clarity is the extent to which everyone will perceive a particular situation in a similar manner and emit a similar response. A very powerful situation has a considerable amount of clarity and serves to minimize the contribution of personality traits (i.e., individualistic expression). On the other hand, a very weak situation is characterized by a high degree of ambiguity and makes possible a greater role for personality traits to influence the response.

The power of a situation can be determined by such factors as its context (e.g., formal vs. informal; public vs. private), the amount of choice available to the individual (e.g., little vs. considerable), duration in the situation (e.g., brief vs. extensive), and the range of responses possible (e.g., narrow vs. broad) (Buss, 1989). A very powerful situation might be one in which a military recruit is ordered by the drill instructor to hit other recruits as part of a hand-to-hand combat exercise. In this very formal, public, low-choice, and brief situation with a narrowly defined range of possible responses, even a very nonviolent individual will behave aggressively. A much weaker situation might be when the recruit is at home and is trying to decide what to do while on a two-week pass. Given this set of circumstances, the true nonviolent nature of the recruit's personality might result in the individual leaving a bar when a fight starts to break out. Thus, according to the cognitive alternative, inconsistency in behavior can be attributed to differences in the perception and interpretation of situational characteristics.

The Aggregation Alternative: "Adding Up" the Consistency in Behavior

For Seymour Epstein (1979, 1980, 1983; Epstein & O'Brien, 1985), the problem with trying to identify consistency in behavior has to do with the way personality psychologists have been looking for it. Personality psychologists have searched for consistency by examining single units of behavior as they relate to a particular personality trait. For example, suppose a researcher was investigating the degree of extraversion exhibited by a female college student in three different situations. If the researcher were to look at each of these situations separately, it might be noted that the student talks a lot to others at work, but not while on the bus, and only slightly to her classmates before class. Such evidence taken separately suggests a rather low degree of consistency between the trait of extraversion and her tendency to talk to others. But a more accurate picture of her consistency along the trait of extraversion might be obtained by combining all of the behaviors to form a more global index of social interaction.

Aggregation Research and Playing the Law of Averages

The logic of **aggregation research** is to document the stability of behavior by combining (i.e., aggregating) various measures of the behavior and determining

Seymour Epstein's research on the aggregation alternative has done much to help clarify the issue regarding the ability of traits to influence behavior across a variety of situations.

an average level of its occurrence over time. A similar logic is applied when calculating a student's grade for a specific course. The grade for the course is determined not by a single test score but by a series of test scores obtained throughout the semester. The logic of aggregation is not a new idea by any means. As far back as 1910, the eminent psychologist Charles Spearman said, "Let each individual be measured several times with regard to any characteristics to be compared" (pp. 273-274).

Considerable evidence supports the ability of aggregation research to identify consistency in behavior (Cheek, 1982, Eaton, 1983; Epstein & O'Brien, 1985; Moskowitz & Schwarz, 1982; Rushton, Brainerd, & Pressley, 1983). This has also been found to be true for situations in which such consistency was thought to be lacking (Epstein & O'Brien, 1985). For example, the logic of aggregation research was applied to the data from the classic work of Hartshorne and May (1928) by combining several specific measures of honesty to form a more global index of honesty. With this procedure, the average correlation coefficient for predicting honesty across situations increased to $r = .73$, which represents a rather large increase from the average of only $r = .23$ when each measure of honesty was considered individually (Epstein, 1979). The intuitive nature of the aggregation alternative is also supported by evidence suggesting that people are aware of and employ the principles of aggregation when judging the cross-situational consistency of others in everyday life (Epstein & Teraspulsky, 1986).

The Act Frequency Approach to Confirming Consistency

Similar to aggregation research is the act frequency approach proposed by David Buss and Kenneth Craik (Buss, 1984, 1985; Buss & Craik, 1983, 1984, 1985). The **act frequency approach** says that the nature and consistency of an individual's personality should be determined by calculating the frequency with which acts from a particular class of action occur. The more frequent the act, the more indicative that behavior is of the individual's personality and the greater the degree of behavioral consistency. For example, the degree of aggressiveness in an individual's personality would be determined by assessing the frequency and extent to which behaviors defined as aggressive are exhibited in different situations.

The aggregation alternative suggests that it is possible to find consistency in behavior across a variety of situations by adding up behaviors. But critics of both aggregation research (Mischel, 1984, 1985; Mischel & Peake, 1982) and the act frequency approach (Block, 1989; Mischel & Peake, 1982; Moser, 1989) do exist.

In summary, there is cross-situational consistency in the influence of personality traits on behavior. As a result, the original issue of whether traits affect cross-situational consistency seems to have transformed into issues related to developing more realistic assumptions about traits and research methodologies for assessing their influence.

The Classification of Traits: The Big Five Factors

Traits have been used to describe, predict, and understand behavior. But what seems to be missing is a structure by which all of the many different personality traits studied by personality psychologists can be organized. The issue centers on the extent to which an organizing structure can be found and the nature of this structure.

Classic Contributions to Classifying Traits Made the Classification Process 900 Times Simpler

In one of the first attempts to identify and classify the number of personality traits, Allport and Odbert (1936) counted the number of words in the 1925 edition of *Webster's New International Dictionary*, which contained some 550,000 terms, that could be used to distinguish the behavior of one human being from another. Their research yielded some 18,000 terms! Upon further inspection, however, they determined that only about 4500 of the terms met the criteria of personality traits (e.g., being causal and internal and having stable tendencies).

A few years later, Cattell used these 4500 trait terms and added another 100 terms to reflect certain temporary states that could also be used to explain behavior (e.g., frightened). Using the technique of factor analysis, Cattell (1943) was able to organize these terms into 35 trait variable categories of words that seemed to be similar. In subsequent research, Cattell (1945) took the 35 trait variables and used

factor analysis to even further reduce the organization of traits into 12 factor categories. Additional reanalysis and extensions of Cattell's work further simplified the structural organization of personality traits into five basic categories (Fiske, 1949; Tupes & Christal, 1961).

In a return to the work of Allport and Odbert (1936), Norman (1967) used the 1961 *Webster's Third New international Dictionary* to identify some 18,125 personality terms, and he was eventually able to reduce the list to 2800 stable trait terms. These terms were then organized into five basic categories. Thus, through continued replications and refinements in techniques and procedures, the organizational nature of traits went from 4500 individual terms to 5 basic factors. This represents a reduction of 90,000 percent, or 900 times, in the classification structure of traits.

Contemporary Contributions to Classifying Traits and the Validation of the Big Five Factors

Although others had documented five factors in their attempt to identify the organizational nature of trait structures, it was Goldberg (1981) who coined the term the "Big Five." **The Big Five** is a descriptive model used in analyzing and classifying terms used by people to describe themselves and others (Digman, 1990; John, 1990). Table 8.7 lists the Big Five factors and some characteristics associated with each one.

There is a considerable amount of evidence to document the presence of the Big Five factor model (Costa & Widiger, 1994; Digman, 1990; Goldberg, 1990, 1993; John, 1990; McCrae, 1989; Wiggins, 1996). For example, support for the Big Five model has been found for personality trait terms in both Dutch (Brokken, 1978; De Raad, Mulder, Kloosterman, & Hofstee, 1988) and German (Angleitner & Ostendorf, 1989; Angleitner, Ostendorf, & John, 1990). Based on translations of American terminology, the Big Five model has also been documented with samples of Japanese, Chinese, and Philippine people (Bond, Nakazato, & Shiraishi, 1975; Katigbak, Church, & Akamaine, 1996; McCrae, Zonderman, Costa, Bond, & Paunonen, 1995).

The presence of the Big Five structure has been identified using various factor analysis techniques (Goldberg, 1990). In addition to its use with the classification of trait terms, the Big Five structure has

Table 8.7
The Big Five: Factor Labels and Characteristic Traits

Factor Label	Characteristic Traits
1. E-Factor: Extraversion, energy, enthusiasm	Adventurous, assertive, dominant, quiet,* reserved,* retiring,* shy, sociable
2. A-Factor: Agreeableness, altruism, affection	Cooperative, cruel,* generous, quarrelsome,* sympathetic, unfriendly*
3. C-Factor: Conscientiousness, control, constraint	Careless,* deliberate, efficient, frivolous,* irresponsible,* precise
4. N-Factor: Neuroticism, negative affectivity, nervousness	Anxious,* calm, contented, self-pitying,* stable, temperamental*
5. O-Factor: Openness, originality, open-mindedness	Artistic, commonplace,* insightful, intelligent, narrow interests,* shallow*

*These traits are negatively related to the factor.

Note. Table adapted from The "Big Five" Factor Taxonomy: Dimensions of Personality in the Natural Language and Questionnaires, by O. P. John, 1990. In L. A. Pervin (Ed.), Handbook of Personality: Theory and Research. New York: Guilford Press.

also been found in different forms of data, including the frequency of acts (Botwin & Buss, 1989), self- vs. other ratings (Goldberg, 1990), and various questionnaires (Costa & McCrae, 1988; McCrae & Costa, 1987; Peabody, 1987; Peabody & Goldberg, 1989).

The NEO Personality Inventory (NEO-PI) (Costa & McCrae, 1985) is a widely used personality test designed to measure the five major dimensions of personality. The NEO-PI has been used to validate the existence of the five-factor model in other personality inventories (Costa & McCrae, 1995) and their stability over extended periods of the life span (Costa & McCrae, 1994; McCrae, 1989). The NEO-PI has also been used to investigate the Big Five model within attachment styles and romantic relationships (Shaver & Brennan, 1992), career decision making (Holland, 1996), and the tendency for academic success and juvenile delinquency in African American and Caucasian adolescent boys (Robins, John, Caspi, Moffitt, & Stouthamer-Loeber, 1996). Finally, the five-factor model has also been incorporated into other aspects of personality, such as mood, needs,

psychological types, heredity, and interpersonal behavior (John, 1990; Wiggins, 1996). Taken together, this research does seem to "provide a good answer to the question of personality structure" (Digman, 1990, p. 436).

Some Reservations Concerning the Big Five Model
While there are many supporters of the five-factor model, it does have its critics (Livneh & Livneh, 1989; Waller & Ben-Porath, 1987). One criticism is that although the Big Five factors are observed consistently, there seems to be no guiding explanation as to why they exist and how they came to be (Briggs, 1989). More specifically, the Big Five model describes the structure of personality. It does not, however, explain the operation of personality regarding such principles as learning, environmental influences, genetics, and motivation.

Another reservation is that the Big Five model does not really predict differences between people (e.g., achievement in college). In addition, the rather broad nature of the Big Five factors can make it difficult to distinguish among more subtle but important aspects of personality (e.g., shyness vs. introversion).

Yet another criticism is that a Big Seven model (Almagor, Tellegen, Waller, 1995; Tellegen, 1993; Tellegen & Waller, 1987; Tellegen & Waller, in press; Waller & Zavala, 1993), which includes two additional evaluative dimensions, one positive and the other negative, provides a more complete description of personality variability and clinical emotional

Paul Costa and Robert McCrae developed the NEO-PI.

states than the Big Five model (Waller & Zavala, 1993). The Big Seven model also provides a more consistent representation of the way in which people commonly characterize personality than does the Big Five model (Tellegen, 1993). But recent evidence seems to suggest that the dimensions of the Big Five model and Big Seven model are actually quite similar and represent two different ways of organizing the structure of personality (Church, 1994).

A final criticism of the Big Five model, as well as the Big Seven model, is that such broad categorizations of people can increase the likelihood of losing sight of a major objective of personality psychology, which is understanding the uniqueness of the individual (Lamiell, 1987).

Reconciling the Differences in the Support for and Reservations about the Big Five Model

Probably the best way to reconcile the support for and reservations about the Big Five model is to remember that personality can be studied at many different levels. The five-factor model provides the overall structural organization of personality at the top. The study of specific dimensions of personality (e.g., shyness and achievement) starts from the bottom, laying the foundation upon which the five-factor model will rest and into which these specific dimensions of personality can be organized. Thus, not all trait personality psychologists have to study personality at the same level. But at some point, those working from the bottom up and those working from the top down will meet in the middle. This meeting in the middle will create a more complete understanding of personality from the trait perspective.

Applications of the Big Five Model: Using What Is Known

A principal feature of the Big Five model is the flexibility in its applications. In this section, you will consider the application of the Big Five model to the study of drug abusers and sex offenders.

The Big Five Personality Profile of Drug Abusers: Assessment and Treatment Implications

The Big Five model has been used to help identify the personality profiles of drug abusers and to develop drug treatment programs based on these profiles (Brooner, Schmidt, & Herbst, 1994). In one study, the scores on the five dimensions of the NEO-PI were compared for a group of 203 drug abusers and a normative sample of non-drug abusers (Costa & McCrae, 1989).

The personality profiles of drug abusers tend to be characterized by higher scores on the neuroticism dimension, particularly with regard to hostility, depression, and feelings of vulnerability, and lower scores on the agreeableness and conscientiousness dimensions than the profiles obtained from the normative sample of non-drug abusers. In addition, although the profile score for the drug abusers on the extraversion dimension was similar to those of the non-drug abusing sample, the drug abusers tended to demonstrate greater excitement-seeking tendencies, as measured within the extraversion dimension. Consistent with the results of other studies (Alterman & Cacciola, 1991), the profiles of these drug abusers suggest that they are prone to high levels of emotional distress, interpersonal antagonism, excitement seeking, and low levels of conscientiousness.

The tendency of the drug abusers to have profiles characterized by a high degree of neuroticism and low degree of agreeableness and conscientiousness is critical because of the influence such features have on treatment planning and effectiveness. It has been noted that people who are disagreeable and unconscientious pose major problems for therapists (Miller, 1991). These people tend to be antagonistic and skeptical of the therapist, making it difficult for the client and therapist to establish an affiliation during treatment. In addition, while a high degree of emotional distress (i.e., neuroticism) can serve as a source of motivation to enter and remain in treatment, the lack of extraversion may be detrimental to the treatment process because effective treatment involves active involvement in the therapeutic process.

With this information in mind, it is important to establish reasonable therapeutic goals that may differ from other client populations. For example, because of the skepticism and antagonism of these drug abusers, more time might have to be allocated to the treatment program for trying to establish an emotional bond between the client and therapist. In addition, the high level of neuroticism suggests that these people are bringing with them to the treatment setting a higher degree of emotional distress, which in turn will probably require longer treatment.

The Big Five Personality Profile of Sex Offenders: A Forensic Evaluation

In an attempt to understand the personality makeup of sex offenders, the NEO-PI has been utilized as part of the forensic evaluation of incarcerated sex offenders. In one study, 99 male sex offenders (e.g., child molesters and exhibitionists) were given the NEO-PI as part of a forensic evaluation (Lehne, 1994).

In comparison to the NEO-PI scores from a normative sample of non-sex offenders, the results indicated that, overall, the sex offender scores were higher on the neuroticism dimension, which also included scoring higher on the anxiety, hostility, depression, self-consciousness, impulsiveness, and vulnerability facets of the neuroticism dimension. But the sex offender scores were similar to the normative sample of non-sex offenders on the extraversion, openness to experience, agreeableness, and conscientiousness dimensions of the NEO-PI. The only exception was that the sex offenders scored higher on the excitement-seeking facet of the extraversion dimension.

This pattern of results suggests that, with the exception of the neuroticism dimension and the excitement-seeking facet of the extraversion dimension, the personality profiles of the sex offenders and non-sex offenders were very similar. Such results have some serious forensic implications. One implication has to do with the identification of sex offenders. More specifically, with the exception of expressing more of an excitement-seeking tendency, the sex offenders appear normal! This is an extremely important point because it helps to explain how these sex offenders are able to intermingle within society and with their potential victims so successfully without being detected. For example, a child molester, with no previous history of arrest, who is very agreeable and extraverted would have little trouble seeking employment in a day care center.

A second implication has to do with the treatment and rehabilitation of sex offenders. More specifically, while sex offenders display a high degree of psychopathology, as indicated by their high scores on the neuroticism dimension and all of its separate facets when compared to the non-sex offenders, it is the perverted sense of pleasure they seem to derive from their activities that makes them so difficult to treat and rehabilitate. An example of the manifestation of this deep-seated psychopathology is the intense arousal and pleasure (i.e., thrill-seeking excitement) of seeing the victim's reactions after an exhibitionist has exposed himself or the arousal and excitement associated with stalking a child for molestation that is most critical to such sex offenders (Comer, 1995). The fact that such behavior patterns exist in the face of some very serious negative social and legal consequences is a statement about their powerful nature and resistance to treatment.

In summary, it is the seemingly normal, social nature of these sex offenders that makes it very difficult to identify them prior to committing their crimes but the deep-seated nature of their psychopathology that makes them so difficult to treat.

This concludes the discussion of applications of the Big Five model. While only two applications were presented in this section, you should be aware that there are many more, such as the study of eating disorders (Ellis, 1994), assessment of employee service performance (Stewart & Carson, 1995), and the diagnosis of various personality disorders (Clark & Livesley, 1994; Harpur, Hart, & Hare, 1994; Widiger & Trull, 1992), to name just a few. This also concludes the discussion of the Big Five model of personality. If you would like more information on the Big Five model, read the relatively short but highly informative book titled *The Five-Factor Model of Personality* (Wiggins, 1996), or a somewhat longer and very thorough book titled *Personality Disorders and the Five Factor Model of Personality* (Costa & Widiger, 1994).

Chapter Summary: Reexamining the Highlights

▲ *Personality Traits.* Traits are underlying psychological structures that predispose people to act in a particular manner.

▲ *Allport's Personalistic Viewpoint*
  —*Basic Assumptions.* Allport viewed personality as being a dynamic organization within the person, psychophysical in nature, determining behavior, and contributing to the uniqueness of each person.

—*Basic Concepts.* Traits are considered the basic unit of personality. They can be classified into common traits or personal dispositions. Cardinal, central, and secondary traits are used to account for the uniqueness expressed by each person. The proprium gives the individual a unifying sense of self.

—*Dynamics of Personality.* Personality development is characterized by the emergence and integration of the separate aspects of the proprium. The source of motivation for personality is that of functional autonomy, which can be divided into preservative and propriate functional autonomy.

—*Applications of Allport's Viewpoint.* The classification and assessment of human values and their utilization in varied counseling settings represents a significant application of Allport's viewpoint of personality.

—*Evaluation of Allport's Viewpoint.* Characteristic strengths of Allport's viewpoint include his utilization of various research methodologies and emphasis on studying the individual. Characteristic limitations of Allport's viewpoint include a failure to provide physical documentation concerning the existence of traits, the discontinuity of personality development, and an overemphasis on studying the individual at the expense of developing general laws of behavior.

▲ *Cattell's Structural Trait Viewpoint*

—*Basic Assumptions.* Cattell assumed that the principal function of personality was to help in predicting behavior. Cattell used L-data, Q-data, and T-data as sources of empirical information to help in predicting behavior.

—*Basic Concepts.* Traits are considered the basic units of personality and are reflected in the behavior of the individual. Traits are classified into surface and source traits, common and unique traits, and ability, temperament, and dynamic traits. Constitutional factors and environmental-mold factors are used to explain the contribution of inherited and environmental influences on personality traits. Factor analysis is the statistical technique used by Cattell to identify and classify traits. The behavioral specification equation is a formula developed by Cattell for predicting behavior based on the relative contribution of various traits.

—*Applications of Cattell's Viewpoint.* Cattell developed the Sixteen Personality Factor Questionnaire (16PF) to assess major source traits. The Marriage Counseling Report (MCR) is an application of the 16PF designed to assess marital compatibility.

—*Evaluation of Cattell's Viewpoint.* Characteristic strengths of Cattell's viewpoint include his quantitative and rigorous approach to the study of personality. Characteristic limitations of his approach are that it is too technical, and it overemphasizes understanding the global personality while losing sight of the individual.

▲ *Eysenck's Hierarchical Trait Viewpoint*

—*Basic Assumptions.* Eysenck assumed that two major dimensions serve as the underlying structure of personality.

—*Basic Concepts.* Eysenck organized the hierarchical structure of personality to include specific responses, habitual responses, traits, and types.

—*Personality Dynamics.* The dynamics of personality involve the interrelationship of the personality types of extraversion-introversion, neuroticism, and psychoticism.

—*Evaluation of Eysenck's Viewpoint.* Characteristic strengths of Eysenck's viewpoint include his empirical emphasis and the diversity of knowledge he tried to integrate within his viewpoint. Characteristic limitations of Eysenck's viewpoint include the rather limited number of factors he used to conceptualize personality and validity of these factors.

▲ *The Issue of Cross-Situational Consistency*

—*The Search for Cross-Situational Consistency.* Cross-situational consistency assumes that personality traits provide a stabilizing influence on behavior over time and situations.

—*Documenting a Lack of Cross-Situational Consistency.* The personality coefficient summarized the tendency of personality measures to correlate around $r = .30$ with observable behavior.

—*In Support of Cross-Situational Consistency.* Increases in cross-situational consistency can be achieved by identifying consistent people and specific dimensions upon which they are highly consistent.

—*The Situational Alternative.* A greater understanding of cross-situational consistency can be achieved by considering the situation in which the behavior occurs. Situationism considers the constraints placed on behavior by the characteristics of the situation. Interactionism proposes that behavioral consistency is best understood by considering both the personality of the individual and the situation in which the behavior occurs.

—*The Cognitive Alternative.* Cognitive factors affect the way that we perceive and interpret situations. Powerful situations provide clear cues for behavior; weak situations allow for personality factors to determine individual responses.

—*The Aggregation Alternative.* Aggregation research documents cross-situational consistency by averaging the occurrence of behavior over time. The act frequency approach determines cross-situational consistency by calculating the number of times a particular class of behavior occurs.

▲ *The Classification of Traits*

—*Classic Contributions to the Classification of Traits.* The number of trait-like terms used to describe behavior was reduced from some 4500 terms to five basic factors.

—*Contemporary Contributions to the Classification of Traits.* The Big Five factor model is used to describe the structural nature of the classification of traits. Evidence supporting this model has been found in different languages, using different factor analytic techniques and forms of data, various questionnaires, and other aspects of personality.

—*Some Reservations Concerning the Big Five Model.* A criticism of the Big Five factor model is that although it describes a basic trait structure, it does not explain why it exists. In addition, the Big Five factor model does not predict specific behaviors, make distinctions among more subtle dimensions of personality, nor promote an understanding of the individual.

—*A Point of Reconciliation.* The Big Five factor model is the general classification system by which the study of individual traits can be organized. Organizing a general classification system of traits and studying individual traits are both necessary for a complete understanding of personality from the trait viewpoint.

—*Applications of the Big Five Model.* Applications of the Big Five factor model include the study of the personality profiles of drug abusers and sex offend-ers, as well as how such information can be used in the development of treatment programs for such people.

Glossary

ability traits   Manifestations of the specific skills of an individual.

act frequency approach   A procedure for estimating the consistency of behavior across situations by counting its occurrence over time.

aggregation research   A procedure for estimating the consistency of behavior across situations by averaging its occurrence over time.

behavioral specification equation   A procedure for combining trait information to predict behavior in specific situations.

cardinal traits   Traits having a dominant influence on the expression of an individual's personality.

central traits   Traits representing salient characteristic features of an individual's personality.

cognitive factors   Mental processes that determine the behavioral reactions to situations.

constitutional factors   Biologically determined traits.

common traits   Traits possessed by all people in varying degrees.

common traits   Traits possessed by all people to some degree.

cross-situational consistency   The assumption that traits stabilize behavior across a variety of situations.

dynamic traits   An individual's motivational source of behavior.

environmental-mold factors   Environmentally determined traits.

extraversion-introversion   A basic personality type identified by Eysenck and characterized by varying degrees of sociability.

factor   The intercorrelation of a group of behavioral measures reflecting an underlying source trait.

factor analysis   A statistical procedure for identifying trait structures.

factor loading   The extent to which a specific behavioral measure is related to a certain factor.

factor matrix   The identification of different factors.

functional autonomy   The motivational source in adulthood that is separated from the motivational sources in childhood.

habitual response   Specific behaviors performed across a number of different situations.

idiographic approach   The study of the personal dispositions of an individual.

intercorrelation matrix   A summary of individual correlation coefficients used in factor analysis.

interactionism   The assumption that behavior is determined by a combination of personality and situational factors.

L-data   Forms of information about an individual that are a matter of public record.

Marriage Counseling Report (MCR)   An inventory, based on the 16PF, designed to assess marital compatibility.

nature-nurture ratio   An estimation of the extent to which a trait is determined by biological and environmental factors.

neuroticism   A basic personality type identified by Eysenck and characterized by varying degrees of emotional stability.

nomothetic approach   The study of common traits by comparing the personality of different people.

personal dispositions   Traits that are unique to the individual.

personalism   An approach to psychology emphasizing the study of the person.

personalistic   An emphasis on the understanding of the individual.

personality coefficient   The tendency for personality test scores and behavioral measures to be only moderately correlated.

perseverative functional autonomy   The motivational source for basic routine and repetitive behavior.

propriate functional autonomy   The motivational source for the development of a sense of self-awareness.

proprium   A psychological structure creating a sense of self in the individual's personality.

psychoticism   A basic personality type identified by Eysenck and characterized by varying degrees of personality pathology.

Q-data   Information about an individual obtained from questionnaires and personality inventories.

secondary traits   Personal dispositions that influence an individual's behavior in very specific situations.

situationism   The tendency for behavior to be determined by the characteristics of the situation.

Sixteen Personality Factor Questionnaire (16PF)   A personality inventory used to assess major source traits.

source traits   Underlying psychological dispositions that influence behavior across a wide variety of situations.

specific responses   Behaviors observed in particular situations.

Study of Values Scale   A measure of the six basic human values identified by Allport.

surface traits   Interrelated forms of behavior serving as observable evidence for the presence of certain underlying traits.

T-data   Information about an individual obtained while observing the person in specific situations.

temperament traits   Manifestations of an individual's general behavioral style.

The Big Five   A model for describing the organizational structure of personality traits into five major dimensions.

trait   A psychological construct assumed to predispose people to respond in a particular manner.

traits   For Eysenck, a set of related behaviors performed across a variety of situations.

types   For Eysenck, the grouping together of related traits.

unique traits   Traits specific to the particular individual.

CHAPTER 9

The Biological Viewpoint: Biological Perspectives on Personality

CHAPTER OVERVIEW: A PREVIEW OF COMING ATTRACTIONS

*T*he biological viewpoint of personality assumes that certain biological factors influence the development and operation of personality. The biological factors to be discussed in this chapter include genetic, physiological, neurological, and evolutionary determinants of personality. You will learn about their theoretical formulations and examine illustrations of their applications. Before discussing these biological influences, this chapter opens with an overview of some basic issues related to the biological viewpoint of personality.

The Role of Biological Processes in the Study of Personality: Some Basic Issues

As psychologist David Buss (1990) states, "Many misunderstandings surround the biological study of personality" (p. 2). This section is designed to help clarify some of these misunderstandings.

The Nature-Nurture Controversy: A Basic Issue

A basic issue surrounding the biological perspective of personality is the nature-nurture controversy (Plomin, DeFries, & McClearn, 1990). In its most elementary form, the **nature-nurture controversy** concerns the extent to which personality and other complex behaviors are determined by biological or environmental factors. On the nature side of the argument is the assumption that inherited biological factors are the principal determinants of personality. On the nurture side of the argument is the assumption that environmental (e.g., parenting styles, socioeconomic status, educational opportunities, and sibling and peer relationships) and cognitive factors (e.g., perceptions, beliefs, and reasoning) are major determinants of personality. While there is evidence suggesting that both nature and nurture contribute to the formulation of personality (Bourchard & McGue, 1990; Eysenck, 1990b), more emphasis has traditionally been given to the nurture side of the argument by personality psychologists (Kenrick, Montello, & MacFarlane, 1985).

Genetically Determined Does Not Equal Genetically Fixed

For various reasons, personality psychologists tend to lean away from the biological study of personality (i.e., nature side). One reason has to do with the misperception that the biological perspective is at odds with the environmental side of the study of personality (Buss, 1990). One major source of this misunderstanding is the value placed in our society on all people being equal. The idea of endorsing the nature position has been viewed as acknowledging that some people are born more gifted (e.g., more intelligent or extraverted) and, as a result, will have a greater advantage than others. The major error in this type of reasoning is assuming that "genetically determined" means "genetically fixed" (Pervin, 1984).

As a point of clarification, **genetically determined** means that certain biological factors with which the individual is born combine with other factors in the environment to influence how the individual adjusts and responds to the events in his or her world. An individual born with very poor eyesight might not be able to be a fighter pilot or police officer. But with the right educational opportunities and encouragement by family members, he or she can become independent and live a full life as a financial planner at a bank. Another individual born with very poor eyesight might receive lots of pity and coddling from family members and end up becoming an extremely dependent and self-centered person. As this example illustrates, biologically determined factors affect the *possible range of opportunities* available to the individual. They do not fix the individual on a "predetermined" course of action.

In deciding which position to take on the nature-nurture issue, you will see that the most realistic position, based on the evidence to be presented in this chapter, is that they both contribute significantly to the development and operation of personality (Buss, 1990; Eysenck, 1990a, 1990b; Gangestad, 1989; Loehlin, Horn, & Willerman, 1990; Plomin, Chipuer, & Loehlin, 1990; Plomin, DeFries, & McClearn, 1990).

The Logic of the Biological Viewpoint

The goal of the biological viewpoint to the study of personality is to investigate how such biological factors as genetics, evolution, biochemistry, and bodily processes contribute to the operation and development of personality (Buss, 1990). But you should understand that the contributions made by such biological factors *are not* designed to replace those offered by environmental, psychological, or cognitive factors. Instead, the study of both types of factors should be viewed as complementing and supplementing each other in order to achieve a greater understanding of personality.

Consider how biological factors might contribute to the socially withdrawn behavior typically associated with the personality of introverts. Because introverts seem to show greater nervous system sensitivity and reactivity to relatively low levels of noise than extraverts (Eysenck, 1990a; Stelmack, 1990), they may elect to deal with the noise at a party by not talking to others or by leaving the party early. Thus, a more complete understanding of the social withdrawal characteristic of introverts involves considering how biological (reactivity of the nervous system), environmental (noise level at the party), psychological (emotional discomfort), and cognitive (deciding to leave) factors operate together.

The Biosocial Interaction

Like the situational interactionism viewpoint discussed in Chapter 8 (see page 235), the biological viewpoint also assumes that biological factors combine with the social environment in what might be defined as a biosocial interaction (Kenrick, Montello, & MacFarlane, 1985; Loehlin, 1977). The basic assumption of a **biosocial interaction** is that the biological and social factors operate reciprocally. This implies that both factors are of some importance in determining the personalty of an individual. It also implies that each factor may make a different contribution at different points in an individual's life (Plomin & Nesselroade, 1990).

For example, a child born with a very sensitive nervous system might elect to spend more time alone than playing with others while growing up. As a result of this social isolation, the person has less opportunity to acquire the social skills necessary to interact successfully with others. To cope with the lack of social skills and feelings of loneliness experienced as an adult, the person might elect to join a "singles club" that advertises itself as being for "quiet and gentle people." Thus, although this introverted person may be relatively shy and reserved most of the time, the quiet and gentle nature of this club allows the person to display a more socially expressive personality style. This example illustrates how biological factors (e.g., sensitivity of the nervous system) and environmental factors (e.g., a club for quiet and gentle people) operate reciprocally in a biosocial interaction to meet both the biological (e.g., desire for low stimulation) and emotional (e.g., desire to socialize) needs that make up the individual's personality.

A Summary of the Basic Issues of the Biological Viewpoint

The principal point to be made in this section is that in addition to being social organisms (i.e., nurture), people are also biological organisms (i.e., nature). These two aspects of the individual do not operate independently; they operate interactively and reciprocally. Thus, the major objective of the biological viewpoint is to bring the studies of personality and biology together to enhance the understanding of personality, not to turn personality psychology into a biological analysis of the individual.

Constitutional Viewpoint: The Early Roots of a Biological Basis of Personality

Constitutional psychology has as its objective the identification of underlying biological processes within the individual that are important in explaining human behavior. The notion of trying to relate an individual's personality to various biological processes has a long and colorful history, dating as far back as the ancient Greeks. This section places current approaches to understanding personality from the biological viewpoint in a historical context by discussing some early attempts to identify the biological bases of personality.

Ancient Beginnings of the Biological Viewpoint of Personality: It's All Greek to Me

Some of the earliest attempts to identify the underlying biological bases of personality were made by the ancient Greeks. The great Greek physician Hippocrates (460?–377 B.C.), the "father of medicine," and—five centuries later—the Roman physician Galen (A.D. 130–200) were among the first to postulate a biological basis of personality.

According to Hippocrates and Galen, different temperaments (personality types) were associated with the four basic body fluids, called **humors**. The four basic humors were blood, black bile, yellow bile, and phlegm. These four biological elements supposedly corresponded to the four basic cosmic elements of nature (i.e., air, earth, fire, and water). A person with too much blood had a **sanguine** personality, characterized by being hopeful and excitable. A person with too much black bile had a **melancholic** personality, characterized by sadness and depression. A person with too much yellow bile had a **choleric** personality, characterized by anger and irritability. A person with too much phlegm had a **phlegmatic** personality, characterized by calmness and apathy. The well-adjusted personality had a balance of all of the four basic humors.

While only of historical interest today, the influence of the humoral theory is reflected in the contemporary biological viewpoint by current investigations into the role of hormones in personality. However, for information about a recent study of relationship between a basic body fluid and personality, read "A Closer Look" on this page.

The famous Greek philosopher Aristotle (384–322 B.C.) proposed to understand personality through physiognomy. **Physiognomy** is the practice of inferring personality traits from physical features, particularly as they relate to the features of animals (Allport, 1937). A person with a slender face and long nose might, like a fox, have a personality characterized by cleverness and deviousness (i.e., sly as a fox). Figure 9.1 illustrates the assumed relationship between physiognomic features and the four basic temperaments.

Some 2000 years later, Italian criminologist Cesare Lombroso (1836–1909) theorized a relationship between facial features and criminal behavior. Because Lombroso believed that criminals represented a lower level of evolutionary development, he assumed they would possess characteristic features of this level of development, including squared jaws and protruding foreheads.

Although not considered seriously today, the physiognomic theme can be seen in the contemporary evolutionary perspective of personality. For

A Closer Look:

The Personality and Blood Type of Nations: A Contemporary Constitutional Cross-Cultural Comparison

The ancient humoral theory of personality linked differences in personality with variations in certain types of bodily fluids. More recently, a link between personality and blood type has been established. The personality of introversion is found more frequently among persons having the AB blood type, while the characteristic of emotionality is found more frequently among persons having the B blood type (Angst & Maurer-Groeli, 1974).

In an extension of these findings, Eysenck (1982a) classified countries based on the personality scores of thousands of people (Hofstede, 1976, 1980; Lynn, 1981) and assessed the percentage of persons having different blood types. His results indicate that countries classified as introverted by scoring low on extraversion (e.g., Egypt, France, Japan, and Yugoslavia) had a higher percentage of persons with AB blood type than countries scoring high on extraversion (e.g., Australia, Canada, Greece, United Kingdom, United States, and Italy). Countries classified as emotional by scoring high on neuroticism (e.g., Egypt, West Germany, Japan, and Poland) had a higher percentage of persons with type B blood than countries scoring low on neuroticism (e.g., Australia, Italy, United States, and Sweden).

Because blood type is genetically determined, these results suggest that personality differences between nations and cultures may in part be due to biological and genetic factors. Thus, in addition to suggesting certain regional geographic and weather conditions (Pennebaker, Rime, & Blankenship, 1996) and cultural variations in norms and values (Triandis, 1996) as important determinants of cross-cultural differences in personality, researchers must now include the possibility of biological factors.

example, a relationship between facial structure and an inhibited temperament (i.e., shyness) has been identified, with inhibited children having a somewhat longer and more narrow face than uninhibited children (Kagan & Arcus, 1996).

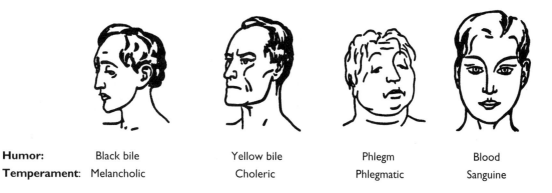

| **Humor:** | Black bile | Yellow bile | Phlegm | Blood |
| **Temperament:** | Melancholic | Choleric | Phlegmatic | Sanguine |

Figure 9.1

Some illustrations of physiognomy and its relationship to the theory of humors

Note. From *Personality: A Psychological Interpretation*, by G. W. Allport, 1937, p. 68. New York: Henry Holt and Co.

Early Biological Viewpoints from the 19th Century

In the late 18th century, the German anatomist Franz Joseph Gail (1758–1828) and his student Johann Gaspar Spurzheim (1776–1832) developed phrenology. **Phrenology** proposed a relationship between the bumps and contours on a person's head and the nature of that person's personality and mental abilities. According to phrenology, bumps on the head correspond to overly developed parts of the brain, and the personality and mental abilities associated with these parts of the brain would be dominant features of the individual's personality. A phrenologic mapping of the brain and listing of the corresponding affective and intellectual abilities are illustrated in Figure 9.2. Although no scientific evidence was ever presented in support of phrenology, the relationship between brain functioning and personality is considered in the contemporary physiological perspective of the biological viewpoint of personality.

Biological Viewpoints of the Early 20th Century

Modern constitutional approaches to the study of personality include the work of the eminent German psychiatrist Ernst Kretschmer (1888–1964). Kretschmer attempted to establish a relationship between an individual's physique and personality type (Kretschmer,

1925). In the United States, the name most often associated with constitutional psychology is that of William Sheldon. Sheldon, like Kretschmer, also tried to establish a relationship between physique and personality type.

Through extensive research involving the ratings of over 4000 people, Sheldon (1942, 1954) determined that the classification of physiques (i.e., body types) could be done using only three dimensions: endomorphy, mesomorphy, and ectomorphy. The rating along the **endomorphy** dimension involved the extent to which the individual's body structure was characterized by being soft and round (see the left panel in Figure 9.3). The rating along the **mesomorphy** dimension involved the extent to which the individual's body structure was characterized as being hard and muscular (see the middle panel in Figure 9.3). The rating along the **ectomorphy** dimension was used to indicate the extent to which the individual's body structure was characterized as being linear and fragile (see the right panel in Figure 9.3). Sheldon believed that an individual's physique was based not only on the outward shape of the body but also on the person's underlying bone structure. As a result, Sheldon assumed that while the shape of a person's body might change over time (e.g., due to illness, dieting, or exercise), the bone structure remains the same, which adds consistency to the body structure (i.e., somatotype).

Sheldon (1942, 1954) classified individual physiques by a somatotype rating. A **somatotype**

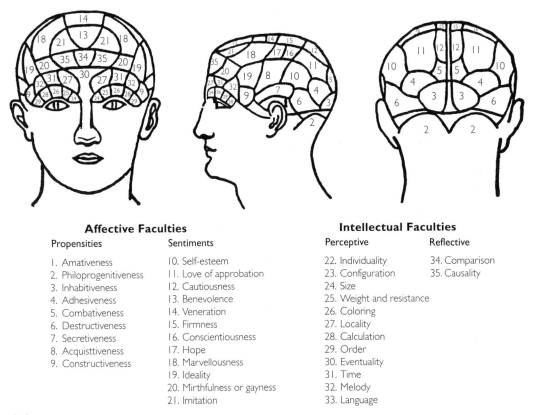

Affective Faculties

Propensities | Sentiments

1. Amativeness
2. Philoprogenitiveness
3. Inhabitiveness
4. Adhesiveness
5. Combativeness
6. Destructiveness
7. Secretiveness
8. Acquisttiveness
9. Constructiveness

10. Self-esteem
11. Love of approbation
12. Cautiousness
13. Benevolence
14. Veneration
15. Firmness
16. Conscientiousness
17. Hope
18. Marvellousness
19. Ideality
20. Mirthfulness or gayness
21. Imitation

Intellectual Faculties

Perceptive | Reflective

22. Individuality
23. Configuration
24. Size
25. Weight and resistance
26. Coloring
27. Locality
28. Calculation
29. Order
30. Eventuality
31. Time
32. Melody
33. Language

34. Comparison
35. Causality

Figure 9.2
An illustration of the mapping of emotional and mental abilities as defined by phrenology

Note. From "Powers and Organs of the Mind," According to J. G. Spurzheim. *Phrenology, or the Doctrine of Mental Phenomena*, 1834, Boston: Marsh, Capen, and Lyons.

rating is a method of assessing an individual's physique using a three-digit number corresponding to the endomorphy, mesomorphy, and ectomorphy dimensions. The first digit indicates the extent to which the individual's body is characteristic (i.e., 1 = *not characteristic* to 7 = *very characteristic*) of the endomorphy dimension. The second digit indicates the extent to which the individual's body is characteristic of the mesomorphy dimension. The third digit indicates the extent to which the individual's body is characteristic of the ectomorphy dimension. In Figure 9.3, corresponding three-digit somatotype ratings are given under the drawings of the individuals. Although there are 343 possible somatotype rating combinations with the three-digit system, Sheldon reported initially that he was able to identify only about 80 distinctively different somatotypes. But he

increased his estimation to 267 with further refinements of his rating technique (Sheldon, Lewis, & Tenney, 1969). As a point of interest, you might take a moment to calculate your own somatotype rating.

To establish a link between body type and personality, Sheldon developed a personality test identifying three major dimensions of **temperament:** viscerotonia, somatotonia, and cerebrotonia.

▲ **Viscerotonia** consists of a cluster of traits relating to a love of food, comfort, people, and affection (e.g., the character of Bluto, played by John Belushi in the movie "Animal House").

▲ **Somatotonia** consists of a cluster of traits related to a high desire for physical adventure, risk-taking activities, and muscular activity (e.g., the character played by Harrison Ford in

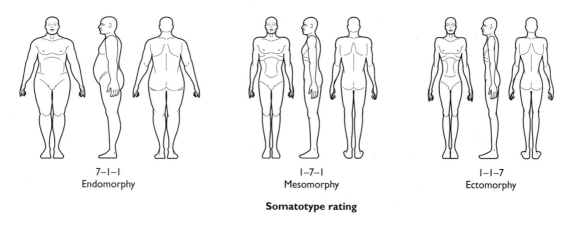

7–1–1
Endomorphy

1–7–1
Mesomorphy

1–1–7
Ectomorphy

Somatotype rating

Figure 9.3
Illustrations of Sheldon's dimensions of physique and somatotype ratings

Note. Adapted from *Atlas of Men: A Guide for Somatotyping the Adult Male at all Ages*, by W. H. Sheldon, 1954. New York: Harper.

the "Indiana Jones" movies, or Ripley as played by Sigourney Weaver in the "Alien" movies).

▲ **Cerebrotonia** consists of a cluster of traits related to emotional restraint, self-consciousness, and a preference for solitude and privacy (e.g., the character of Clark Kent, the public identity of Superman, played by Christopher Reeve).

Sheldon assumed that as with somatotype ratings, the three dimensions of temperament affect each person to a certain degree.

To establish the link between body type and personality, Sheldon (1942) calculated the correlations between somatotype ratings and temperament scores. The results indicate that the rating of the endomorphic body type correlates most strongly with the viscerotonia temperament rating ($r = +.79$). The rating of the mesomorphic body type correlates most strongly with the somatotonia temperament rating ($r = +.82$). The rating of the ectomorphic body type correlates most strongly with the cerebrotonia temperament ($r = +.83$). The consistency and magnitude of these results support Sheldon's theory.

Additional research assessing the relationship between somatotype and temperament ratings involving the school performance of children (Sanford, Adkins, Miller, & Cobb, 1943), behavior of delinquent and nondelinquent boys (Glueck & Glueck, 1950, 1956), and performance of wartime pilots (Damon, 1955) also supports Sheldon's position. However, a major shortcoming of Sheldon's work is its assumption that body type *causes* temperament. The correlational nature of the research does not support such a conclusion. For example, the athletic activity of the somatotonic type may be reinforced by the cheers and praise of others, which are environmental factors.

The various constitutional theories probably seem strange by today's standards. But the work of these researchers within the constitutional perspective help set the stage for the more contemporary biological viewpoint of personality.

The Behavioral Genetics Viewpoint: The Basic Biological Unit of Personality

The study of **behavioral genetics** attempts to determine the extent to which behavioral differences among people are due to genetic as well as environmental differences (Plomin, DeFries, & McClearn, 1990). In a similar manner, the biological viewpoint of personality incorporates behavioral genetics to examine the extent to which various aspects of the individual's personality, such as extraversion

(Eysenck, 1990b), are determined by genetic and environmental influences (Plomin, Chipuer, Loehlin, 1990). The study of behavioral genetics in personality also examines the role of genetics in determining the structure of personality (Rowe, 1989) and personality consistency and variation across the life span (Plomin & Nesselroade, 1990; Rowe, 1989).

Behavioral genetics has as its historical roots the more traditional study of genetics by such noted figures as naturalist Charles Darwin (1809–1882) and the Augustinian monk Gregor Mendel (1822–1884). Both Darwin and Mendel attempted to ascertain the inherited nature of such physical characteristics of organisms as eye color and blood type.

Methodological Considerations in Behavioral Genetics: Tracking the Genetic Influence in Personality

A valuable research tool in studying the genetic bases of physical characteristics is selective breeding. In the **selective breeding experiment**, organisms (e.g., rats or flies) with certain characteristics (e.g., fur texture or eye color) are selected specifically and bred to determine exactly how these characteristics are passed from one generation to the next. Because selective breeding of people to determine the transmission of personality traits is unethical, researchers using the behavioral genetics approach to studying personality must rely on other methods. Some of these methods include family studies, twin studies, adoption studies, and model fitting.

Family Studies
Family studies investigate the inheritability of personality by examining the family history to determine the extent to which certain personality characteristics are found to occur more often within the various family members (e.g., mother, grandfather, third cousins) than in the general population. Proponents of family studies hold that the closer the relationship between the people (parent-child vs. stranger-child), the greater the shared genetic makeup and the more similar the personalities. For example, although the incidence of schizophrenia is only about 1% in the general population, it is almost

13% for children of schizophrenic parents and about 3% for the grandchildren of schizophrenics (Gottesman & Shields, 1982).

A shortcoming of the family studies, however, is that because family members share not only similar genes but also a similar social environment, it is difficult to separate how much of the family similarity is due to a common gene pool (i.e., the nature argument) or to a common home environment (i.e., the nurture argument). As a result of such confounding of information sources, family studies are considered to provide the weakest type of evidence concerning the inheritability of personality characteristics.

Twin Studies
Twins can be classified as identical or fraternal twins. **Identical twins**, also called **monozygotic twins**, develop from the same fertilized egg and share the same (i.e., identical) genetic structure. **Fraternal twins**, also called **dizygotic twins**, develop from two separate fertilized eggs and are no more similar in their genetic structure than any two brothers or sisters.

Researchers in behavioral genetics using **twin studies** compare the personality similarity of identical twins with the similarity of fraternal twins. The principal logic of twin studies is that because identical and fraternal twins share the same environment, any increase in similarity in personality between the identical twins can be attributed to genetic factors. The degree of similarity between any set of twins on any personality dimension is referred to as the **concordance rate**. In a review of several twin studies, researchers found that identical twins showed a higher degree of personality similarity (concordance) than fraternal twins (Eysenck, 1990b).

A limitation of twin studies is that the greater personality similarity found with identical twins can also be attributed to the possibility that because they look alike, identical twins are treated more similarly by their parents, siblings, other relatives, and teachers than are fraternal twins. Such a state of affairs can be interpreted as supporting evidence for an environmental contribution to personality. But in support of the behavioral genetics position, some evidence suggests that although identical twins are treated with greater similarity than fraternal twins, this special treatment is not a significant factor in the greater degree of personality and behavioral similarity of identical twins over fraternal twins (Loehlin & Nichols, 1976).

Adoption Studies

To avoid the complications presented when considering the similarity of environments between identical and fraternal twins, researchers in behavioral genetics attempt to gather information about twins who grow up in different environments as a result of being adopted into separate families. **Adoption studies** compare the similarities in a child's personality with those of his or her biological parents and adopted parents. It is reasoned that although the adopted child shares the same social environment with the adopted parents, he or she shares the same gene structure only with the biological parents. Thus, if the child's personality is similar to those of the adopted parents, this can be considered as evidence supporting a strong environmental influence. On the other hand, if the child's personality is more like those of the biological parents, this suggests a strong genetic influence.

Another possibility is to combine the logic of twin studies and adoption studies by comparing identical twins who were separated at birth and raised in different families. Finally, there is the possibility that adults with their own children might also elect to adopt additional children. In such cases, it is also possible to compare the degree of similarity between the biological children and the adopted children with the parents to determine the effects of people with different genetic structures (e.g., adopted children vs. biological children) being raised in a similar environment. The more similar the adopted children are found to be to the biological children of the parents, the stronger the evidence for the environmental position.

Biases in selective placement are limitations associated with adoption studies (Plomin, DeFries, McClearn, 1990). Biases in **selective placement** can include the procedures used by adoption agencies in selecting families who are allowed to adopt children and biases in the assignment of children to these families. Another source of bias comes from the possibility that only certain types of families are selected to adopt children. The bias here is that the information obtained from adoption studies may be based on the effects of being adopted into more favorable and affluent environments. Yet another bias is that adoption agencies tend to place the children with parents who are similar in such dimensions as race, physical features, and intelligence. Thus, any contribution of the environment is maximized by creating a certain amount of similarity to the adopted parents from the very beginning. Fortunately, research on such biases seems to suggest that while they do have an impact when trying to assess intelligence, their effect is minimal when it comes to assessing personality variables (Loehlin, Willerman, & Horn, 1982).

Model Fitting

Model fitting is a mathematical procedure for testing the proposed relationship among a variety of variables. In behavior genetics, model fitting involves assembling a model reflecting the relative contribution of various genetic and environmental factors and comparing it with observed correlational relationships.

Figure 9.4 presents three models outlining the influence of shared environmental (E) factors (e.g., home of adopted parents) and genetic (G) factors (e.g., biological parents) on the personality (P) of two adopted people. In Figure 9.4a, it is assumed that environmental factors are the only determinants of personality. In Figure 9.4b, it is assumed that genetic factors are the only determinants of personality. Figure 9.4c indicates that both environmental and genetic factors are important. The models are tested by calculating the separate correlational relationships (indicated by the arrows) and then comparing them statistically to determine which model comes closest to explaining the observed relationships. An excellent example of model testing is the work of Michael Stallings and his colleagues, who compared 1287 twin pairs and tested 14 different models to determine the relative contribution of genetic and environmental factors to an assortment of personality dimensions (Stallings et al., 1996).

The major advantage of model fitting is that it enables researchers to combine variables from many different types of information, such as family, twin, and adoption studies (Plomin, Chipuer, & Loehlin, 1990; Plomin, DeFries, & McClearn, 1990). A limitation of model fitting is that because it is primarily correlational, it cannot be used to determine definite causal influences of genetic or environmental

(a)

(b)

(c)

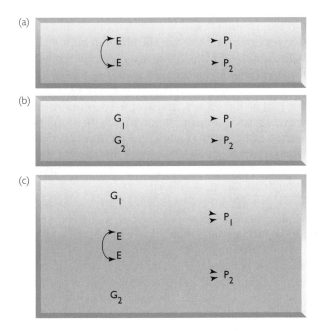

Figure 9.4
Three models outlining the influence of shared environmental factors (E) and genetic factors (G) on the personalities of two adopted people (P$_1$ and P$_2$)

factors. Model fitting can be used only in determining how well the model being proposed explains the observed relationships when compared to other models. In this regard, the model being tested is only as good as the theorist proposing it.

The Interaction Temperament Model: A Dynamic Behavioral Genetics Perspective

While considerations of the inheritability and genetic foundations of personality have a place in contemporary personality psychology (Diamond, 1957; Thomas, Chess, Birch, Hertzig, & Korn, 1963), a significant development involving this viewpoint has been the work of Arnold H. Buss, of the University of Texas at Austin, and Robert Plomin, of Pennsylvania State University, in the framework of what they call the interaction temperament model (Buss & Plomin, 1975, 1984).

The basic feature of the **interaction temperament model** is the reciprocal and dynamic nature of genetic and environmental contributions to personality. The implication is that it is not just genetic factors *or* environmental factors that determine the nature of personality, but the dynamic interaction of these two factors working with and on each other. This dynamic interaction suggests that not only do our inherited personality tendencies modify the environment, but the environment can also modify our inherited personality tendencies.

For example, a rather sociable person can change the environment of a dull party into an enjoyable one by making others feel comfortable. In the same way, a highly sociable person can become extremely quiet and withdrawn if shunned by everyone at the party. These two very simple examples show how in the first case the personality of the individual modifies the situation, while in the second case the environment modifies the personality of the individual. Thus, one of the unique features of the interaction temperament model is its attempt to specify and assess when, how, and to what degree genetic and environmental factors influence each other.

Basic Assumptions: The Bottom Line of the Interaction Temperament Model
In this section, a discussion of the basic assumptions of the Interaction Temperament Model will be presented, along with some supporting examples.

The Inheritability of Some Personality Traits as a Fundamental Assumption   Buss and Plomin (1984) state,

Arnold Buss and Robert Plomin (pictured here) have made important contributions to understanding the role genetics plays in determining the nature of personality.

"A fundamental assumption in our theory is that some personality traits are inherited" (p. 4). They warn that such a statement should not be interpreted as meaning that all personality traits are inherited, nor that inherited personality traits cannot be modified. But they do suggest that a highly developed inherited trait might be very difficult to modify. For example, it might be more difficult to create a sense of extraversion in an adult who demonstrated tendencies toward being shy and withdrawn as an infant, child, and teenager than if such efforts to change the individual were made at a very early age. Thus, although some aspects of personality are inherited, they can be modified.

A Limited Number of Inherited Dispositions   Another assumption made by Buss and Plomin (1975) is "that children start life with a small number of inherited personality dimensions" (p. 2). An example of this might be that because of the genetic nature of an infant's nervous system, the child may be slow to react to stimulation and may have to be told several times to settle down when banging a toy drum loud enough to create an enjoyable level of stimulation. Such a child might be considered to have inherited a basic personality dimension defined as "active." Buss and Plomin have identified emotionality, activity, and sociability as being the three basic inherited dimensions of personality within the interaction temperament model of personality. But you should be aware that the nature and number of dimensions of temperament is still a topic of much debate (Cloninger, Svrakic, & Pzybeck, 1993; Stallings et al., 1995).

Inherited Dimensions Form the Basis of Individuality   Buss and Plomin also assume that these few inherited personality dimensions form the basis of many of the individual differences in personality across people. The idea here is that because each of us inherits a specific combination of the basic personality dimensions to varying degrees, this unique combination determines each person's distinctive pattern of behavior. For example, an individual who inherits a personality characterized by a high degree of activity and sociability will demonstrate a style of behavior (e.g., goes to parties and plays volleyball) that is different from an individual who inherits a personality characterized by

a high degree of activity but a low degree of sociability (e.g., goes to many movies and collects stamps). Thus, Buss and Plomin believe that the uniqueness of each person is determined by a specific combination of inherited personality dimensions.

Inherited Dimensions of Personality Are Modifiable and Determine the Range of Behavior   Buss and Plomin assume that because inherited dimensions of personality are modifiable, they serve to determine the range of an individual's behavior. They do not serve to create a specific, preprogrammed pattern of action. For example, although two people may both inherit a high degree of activity and low degree of sociability, the range of their behaviors may vary. The first person might choose to engage in many activities that are done alone but are of a very physical nature, such as hiking or jogging. The second person might decide to engage in many activities that are also done alone but are much more sedentary in nature, such as writing poetry and painting landscapes. The choice of activities that each elects to pursue, although having an inherited basis, is molded by the environment. For example, the hiker might have had parents who took her camping as a child, while the poet might have had parents who read poetry to her as a child. Thus, the environment can modify inherited personality dimensions to some degree.

Personality Can Modify the Environment   A unique assumption of the interaction temperament model states that temperaments can also affect the environment (Buss & Plomin, 1975). There are three ways through which the environment can be shaped by personality:

▲ The personality of one individual can set the tone for the second individual's behavior. An example of this would be a highly emotional individual triggering argumentative reactions in others.
▲ One person can use a more direct process of initiating certain types of behaviors in others. For example, a highly active and social individual can create a highly active and social environment by seeking out people who are also very active and social.

▲   One person can modify the environment through the use of rewards. For example, a highly social and active individual can offer praise and support each time other people behave in a very sociable manner, which then creates a social environment consistent with the individual's highly sociable personality.

Thus, the individual's personality can shape the environment by setting the tone of people's interaction ahead of time, initiating behaviors designed to seek out a certain type of environment, and rewarding the behaviors of others for behaving in a manner consistent with the nature of the individual's personality.

The Basic Nature of Temperament: What's It Like?
Buss and Plomin are also very explicit in describing the basic nature of temperament. They assume that temperament is inherited, present in early childhood, and stable throughout development.

Temperament Is Inherited   Buss and Plomin (1975) based their concept of temperament on Allport's (1961) definition:

> Temperament refers to the characteristic phenomena of an individual's nature, including his susceptibility to emotional stimulation, his customary strength and speed of response, the quality of his prevailing mood, and all the peculiarities of fluctuation and intensity of mood, these being phenomena regarded as dependent on constitutional make-up, and therefore largely hereditary in origin. (p. 34).

Buss and Plomin (1984) also agree with Allport that inheritance is a significant criterion upon which to define temperament, and that evidence obtained from twin studies and other behavioral genetics methods can be used to document the validity of such a claim (Plomin, Chipuer, & Loehlin, 1990).

Temperament Is Present in Early Childhood   Buss and Plomin (1984) extend the inheritance criterion by providing a more objective basis for their view on temperament. For them, "inherited personality traits are present in early childhood" (p. 84) and define temperament. By focusing on manifestations of behavior found in early childhood, Buss and Plomin are setting an empirical criterion for the assumed presence of a genetic basis of temperament. The underlying logic is that if such individual differences in style of behavior are there from the very beginning (e.g., active vs. passive babies), given their limited exposure to environmental influences, these differences must reflect an inherited component. Thus, Buss and Plomin stress the empirical verification of these differences in personality early in life as a second criterion upon which they define temperament.

Temperament Is Stable throughout Development   A third criterion for Buss and Plomin's definition of temperament is that it demonstrates some stability throughout the various stages of development in the individual's life. For example, the temperament of sociability first identified in a very responsive baby should also be found in the individual when interacting with friends during secondary school, being elected to various social committees in a college dorm, and making a career decision to become a personnel manager as a way to "work with people." Buss and Plomin do not rule out the possibility that certain types of genetic influences might manifest themselves differently at different points in an individual's life (Plomin & Nesselrode, 1990). However, they do tend to be more interested in those genetic aspects of temperament that show some stability across the life span. For example, while being an "early or late bloomer" during adolescence might determine when certain romantic interests in others first appear, the individual's level of emotionality remains stable through development. Thus, the final criterion used by Buss and Plomin to define the genetic nature of temperament is that it should show some stability throughout development.

In summary, Buss and Plomin conceptualize temperament as those aspects of the individual's personality that are inherited, observed early in childhood, and manifest their presence throughout development across the life span when validated by behavioral genetics methodology. For details about a recent investigation into the presence and operation of a dimension of temperament, read "A Closer Look" on page 257.

A Closer Look:

Biological Indicators of Shyness in Children: Some Support for Inhibition as a Dimension of Temperament

Are people born shy? Is it possible to predict which infants will grow into shy children? In an attempt to answer such questions, the research by Harvard psychologist Jerome Kagan and his colleagues (Kagan, 1994; Kagan, Reznick, & Snidman, 1988) provides some rather interesting evidence for a biological basis to shyness in a manner consistent with the Buss and Plomin notion of temperament (i.e., the behavioral tendency is observed very early in childhood and stable over time). The dimension of temperament they have investigated is inhibition in infancy and childhood.

The Selection of Inhibited and Uninhibited Children as Early Indicators of Shyness

Kagan and his colleagues observed over 400 young children from approximately 21 to 31 months of age. Their observations included rating the children on such behaviors as prolonged clinging to or remaining near the mother during the sessions, level of verbal and play activity, and tendency to approach or retreat from unfamiliar events (e.g., an unfamiliar child and woman). On the basis of these observations, two groups of children who exhibited rather extreme behavior patterns were selected and classified as either consistently inhibited (*n* = 54) or consistently uninhibited (*n* = 53) children, with a similar proportion of boys and girls in each group (Kagan, Reznick, & Snidman, 1988). The children were then observed along these and other related measures again when they were approximately 3.5 to 4, 5.5, and 7.5 years of age.

Subsequent Observations of Inhibited and Uninhibited Children and the Prediction of Shyness 5 Years Later

At 7.5 years of age, the children were observed in two laboratory situations. One situation involved the extent to which the child would engage in spontaneous verbal interaction with a female experimenter who was administering a battery of tests to the child. The second situation involved the child playing with seven to ten unfamiliar children in structured, competitive games for 50 minutes and a total of 30 minutes of free-play intervals between the structured games. In the play situation, researchers observed the extent to which the child would spontaneously speak and play or stand near the other children.

Overall, the results indicated that those children who displayed extreme forms of inhibited and uninhibited behaviors at around age 2 exhibited similar behavior patterns some five years later. For example, the children classified originally as inhibited children tended to talk less to the experimenter at 4, 5.5, and 7.5 years of age than those children classified originally as uninhibited. In addition, the inhibited children tended to show more isolated play than the uninhibited children. Figure 9.5 indicates that when the two laboratory measures of behavior were combined,

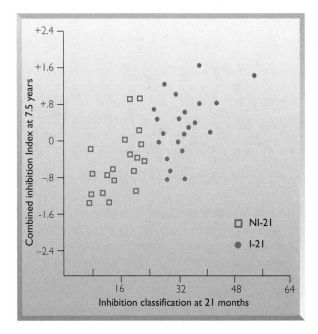

Figure 9.5
The relationship between being classified as inhibited (I-21) and not inhibited (NI-21) at 21 months and the combined index rating of inhibition at 7.5 years of age

Note. From *Biological Bases of Childhood Shyness*, by J. Kagan, J. S. Reznick, and N. Snidman, 1988, *Science*, Vol. 240, p. 169.

those children who were classified as inhibited tended to display a greater degree of inhibition some five years later than those classified as uninhibited.

Biological Correlates of Inhibition and Childhood Shyness

A number of physiological processes also consistently distinguished the inhibited and uninhibited children. For example, at every age, the inhibited children displayed a higher heart rate than the uninhibited children. In addition, when being tested, the inhibited children displayed a greater increase in heart rate (about 10 beats per minute) than the uninhibited children. The inhibited children displayed more pupil dilation when being tested and between testing sessions than uninhibited children. The inhibited children displayed greater levels of muscle tension in the larynx and vocal cords than uninhibited children.

When these and other physiological measures were combined, there was a significant relationship between the composite physiological index and level of inhibition at every age. It is important to note that increased heart rate, pupil dilation, and muscle tension in the larynx and vocal cords are all indices of stress. Differences in the level of symptoms of stress can also be traced back to very early in the children's lives. The mothers of the inhibited children reported that the infants experienced excessive irritability, colic, and sleeplessness during the first year of their lives.

The Question of Being Born Shy, and a Return to the Nature-Nurture Issue

The results of the research by Kagan and his associates seem to suggest that a tendency toward shyness may be based on the inhibited temperament that is observed very early in life and displays some consistency over time. The physiological correlates indicate that inhibited children may display a somewhat greater level of bodily stress than uninhibited children.

While it might be easy to attribute these behaviors and physiological differences to biological sources, Kagan and his associates also acknowledge the contribution of environmental factors that might act upon the original dispositional temperament present at birth. One such environmental factor is birth order. More specifically, in this research, two-thirds of the inhibited children were later born while two-thirds of the uninhibited children were firstborn. Having older siblings who tease, yell, and seize toys unexpectedly might increase the level of emotional arousal in a child with a biological constitution leaning toward excitability (e.g., high heart rate) and create a constant level of stress that might develop into a style of coping characterized by behavioral inhibition.

Thus, consistent with the views of Buss and Plomin, even temperaments that supposedly have a biological basis and appear very early in life can be influenced by environmental factors. This seems to suggest that people are not actually born shy, and that shyness is a product of the interaction of both biological and environmental factors. For more information on the interactive impact of biological and environmental influences on shyness, read Jerome Kagan's (1994) book titled *Galen's Prophecy: Temperament in Human Nature*. This book is written in a thorough but clear manner.

The Dimensions of Temperament: Emotionality, Activity, and Sociability

Buss and Plomin have identified three dimensions of personality they feel meet the criteria to be defined as temperament: emotionality, activity, and sociability.

Emotionality: The Degree of Intensity **Emotionality** is the general intensity of an individual's responses. Characteristics of the intensity of the individual's reactions include being easily aroused and demonstrating excessive affective reactions. Examples of people high in emotionality might include a child who throws temper tantrums, a teenager who frightens easily, or an adult subject to extreme mood swings. Someone exhibiting a combination of these characteristics of emotionality might be a famous but moody singer. Fearing disapproval from the audience, the star explodes in a fit of anger just before going on stage, but becomes depressed shortly after coming off the stage. Table 9.1 gives some examples of items used to assess emotionality in children and adults.

Activity: The Level of Behavior **Activity** refers to the general energy level of the individual. Characteristics of an active individual might include being very busy, constantly in a hurry, speaking rapidly, and displaying

Temperament can help to account for variations in the emotional and behavioral expression seen in young children. Intense emotional reactions, such as crying, are characteristic expressions of the emotionality dimension of temperament. Extensive involvement with various activities, particularly physical activities during play, is characteristic of the activity dimension of temperament. A desire to participate in activities involving other people is characteristic of the sociability dimension of temperament.

vigorous actions. A person high on the temperament of activity might be the teenager who joins the French club, the spirit squad, and the debate team, and also takes ballet lessons. As an adult, such an individual might be a member of the Junior League, a player on a softball team, a Sunday school teacher, and a volunteer firefighter. Table 9.1 also gives examples of items used to measure activity in children and adults.

Sociability: The Tendency to Affiliate **Sociability** refers to the tendency to prefer and desire the presence of others instead of being alone. Characteristics of sociability include considering social rewards (e.g., friendship and sympathy) obtained from interacting with others more valuable than most nonsocial rewards (e.g., money) and being responsive to others. The sociable child might want to have other children sleep overnight more, and make more effort to con-

sider what the other children want to do, than might a nonsociable child. As an adult, a sociable individual might prefer going out with groups of people, but listens to what others have to suggest about where to go for the evening. Thus, more than simply wanting to be around others, sociable people also tend to be more responsive to them as well. Table 9.1 gives examples of items used to assess sociability in children and adults.

Validation Research on Temperament Buss and Plomin have used various behavioral genetics methods in an attempt to find support for the contention that emotionality, sociability, and activity contain some proportion of inheritability. Using the twin methodology, Buss and Plomin (1975) reported that correlations for male and female identical twins were consistently higher than male and female fraternal

Table 9.1
Assessing Emotionality, Sociability, and Activity Dimensions:
Measuring Temperament in Children and Adults

For children, assessing temperament typically involves observing their behavior while at home, school, on the playground, or in a laboratory setting. Following are some types of observations made for each dimension.

Dimension	Observation
Emotionality	*Frequency:* Observe the number of times the child cries, shrinks back, throws temper tantrums, and exhibits other affective behaviors (e.g., how often does the child smile and laugh?).
	Threshold: Observe the verbal or physical stimulus level required to elicit a response from the child (e.g., how loud does a noise have to be before the child cries?).
Activity	*Frequency per unit time (rate):* Observe how quickly the child runs, crawls, or talks (e.g., how quickly does the child speak when asking for a favorite toy?).
	Choice: Observe the extent to which the child selects high-energy games or toys (e.g., does the child prefer to play with wooden blocks or on the jungle gym?).
Sociability	*Frequency:* Observe the number of attempts made by the child to initiate contact (e.g., how often does the child sit next to others?).
	Restriction: Observe the extent to which, when isolated, the child exhibits emotional or behavioral responses designed to contact others (e.g., how long will the child cry when its primary caretaker is out of the room?)

For adults, in addition to employing a modified version of the observational technique used with children, temperament can be assessed by having them complete the EAS Temperament Scale, a 20-item, forced-choice personality inventory (Buss & Plomin, 1984). On a five-point scale, the individual is asked to indicate the extent to which each item is or is not very characteristic or typical of him- or herself. Following are items similar to those in the EAS for each dimension.

Dimension	Choice
Emotionality	I am troubled by and fretful of everyday events.
	I am easily upset emotionally.
Activity	I lead a fast-paced life.
	I often feel like I have an overabundance of energy.
Sociability	Nothing is more stimulating to me than people.
	I would rather work with people than work alone.

Note. From *Temperament: Early Developing Personality Traits*, by A. H. Buss and R. Plomin (1984), pp. 93–94 and Table 7.3. Hillsdale, NJ: Lawrence Erlbaum Associates Publishers.

twins on the measures of emotionality (rs = .68 and .60 vs. .00 and .05, respectively), sociability (rs = .65 and .58 vs. .20 and .06, respectively), and activity (rs = .73 and .50 vs. .18 and .00, respectively).

Similarly, more recent data indicate that identical twins living together or apart displayed higher correlations on the three dimensions of temperament than fraternal twins living together or apart (Plomin, Pedersen, McClearn, Nesselroade, & Bergeman, 1988). Using parental ratings of twins,

Plomin and Rowe (1977) reported that the correlations for identical twins were consistently higher than those for fraternal twins on measures of emotionality (rs = .60 vs. .27), activity (rs = .73 vs. .05), and sociability (rs = .56 vs. .05). In a study of temperament of identical twins in late adulthood reared apart, the correlations reported for the twins were .30 for emotionality, .27 for activity, and .20 for sociability (Plomin, DeFries & Fulker, 1988). Model-fitting methodology using twin studies has also documented heritability estimates of about 40% for emotionality, 25% for activity, and 25% for sociability (Plomin, DeFries & Fulker, 1988).

Thus, behavioral genetics data from investigations during infancy, childhood, adolescence, and adulthood provide considerable support for the genetic basis of the three major dimensions of temperament specified by the Buss and Plomin (1984) interaction temperament model (Plomin, 1986; Plomin, DeFries, & McClearn, 1990). However, emotionality, activity, and sociability are not the only dimensions of personality considered to have a genetic basis. To examine the genetic influence on other personality traits, read "A Closer Look" below.

A Closer Look:

Additional Evidence for a Genetic Basis of Personality: The Examination of Many Personality Traits Using a Diversity of Techniques

In addition to emotionality, activity, and sociability, behavioral genetics research has also found support for a genetic component of many other personality traits as suggested by the interaction temperament model (Plomin, 1986; Plomin, DeFries, & McClearn, 1990; Plomin, Chipuer, & Loehlin, 1990).

In a study involving 181 families whose adopted children had been with them for 10 years, Loehlin, Willerman, and Horn (1987) found that the personalities of adopted children do not resemble their adoptive families, even though they have lived with them since birth. But there was a modest degree of personality similarity to their biological mother, whom they never had the opportunity to know.

A similar pattern of results has been reported in a study of 115 adopted and 120 biological families by investigating the personality dimensions of introversion-extraversion and neuroticism (Scarr, Webber, Weinberg, & Wittig, 1981) and between unwed mothers and their adopted-away offspring in 300 adopted families for the personality dimension of extraversion (Loehlin, Willerman, & Horn, 1982).

In a study involving 850 pairs of twins, Loehlin and Nichols (1976) compared male and female identical and fraternal twins on a variety of personality and ability dimensions. Their conclusion was that the correlation for identical twins was about .20 higher than fraternal twins, whether the measure was for dimensions of ability, personality, or the self-concept.

Finally, Tellegen et al. (1988) compared separate samples of identical twins reared apart, fraternal twins reared apart, and identical and fraternal twins reared together along a number of different personality dimensions. Following is a summary of the correlations for identical twins reared apart for the various personality dimensions:

- ▲ Absorption (imagination) = .74
- ▲ Achievement (hard working, seeks mastery) = .38
- ▲ Aggression = .67
- ▲ Alienation = .59
- ▲ Control (cautious, sensible) = .56
- ▲ Harm avoidance (takes low risks) = .45
- ▲ Sense of well-being = .49
- ▲ Social closeness (intimate) = .15
- ▲ Social potency (a leader desiring to be the center of attention) = .57
- ▲ Stress reaction (neuroticism) = .70
- ▲ Traditionalism (tendency to follow rules and authority) = .59

These correlations, with an average of .54, are higher than those for identical twins reared together. Analyses of this data based on model-fitting techniques indicate 50% of the variability can be accounted for by inheritability. Thus, the results of these many different studies using a variety of techniques do seem to provide supporting evidence for a genetic basis of personality.

A Summary Statement Concerning the Extent of the Genetic Contribution to Personality   This discussion presents only a fraction of the research supporting the contribution of genetics to personality (Plomin, 1986). But a general conclusion seems to be that about 25% of the variability observed in personality can be explained by genetics (Loehlin et al., 1987; Scarr et al., 1981). With this in mind, you should realize that the remaining 75% is probably best explained by considering the family and social environments and how they might interact with genetic and other biological processes to be discussed in this chapter.

This concludes the discussion of the dynamic behavioral genetics perspective based on Buss and Plomin's interaction temperament model. More information about behavior genetics can be found in *Behavioral Genetics: A Primer* (Plomin, DeFries, & McClearn, 1990). For more information about the interaction temperament model, a recommended reading is Arnold H. Buss and Robert Plomin's (1984) *Temperament: Early Developing Personality Traits*.

The Psychophysiological Viewpoint: The Biological Processes of Personality

The psychophysiological perspective attempts to investigate the extent to which underlying physiological processes can be used to help explain differences in personality. Some of the psychophysiological processes investigated include the orienting reflex, averaged evoked response, neurotransmitters, and hormonal production (Davidson, 1991; Eysenck, 1990a; Stelmack, 1990; Zuckerman, 1990).

▲   The **orienting reflex** is defined as the physiological and behavioral reaction to stimuli presented at a moderate level of intensity (Zuckerman, 1983). The orienting reflex includes muscle tension, heart rate, and skin conductance (i.e., "sweating"). An example of an orienting response might be an increase in muscle tension, perspiration, and heart rate when you see a large truck coming straight at you.

▲   The **averaged evoked response** (AER) is a change in the electrical activity of the brain in response to external stimulation (e.g., a loud noise or bright lights). In recording AERs, the stimulus is presented several times and the average response is calculated. For example, during certain stages of sleep and relaxation, the level of electrical activity in your brain is low. But when you are watching a tense murder mystery, the level of electrical activity in your brain is probably quite high.

▲   **Neurotransmitters** are chemicals in the body used to help pass information between neurons and eventually to the brain and muscles. Neurotransmitters help coordinate a person's responses to external stimuli. For example, when you get excited by the sight of your car on a roller coaster getting ready to go over the highest hill, the neurotransmitter acetylcholine is released and helps the neurons to signal your brain and muscles to get ready to hold on tight.

▲   **Hormonal production** refers to the release of various hormones into the body in response to external stimuli. For example, when you are under the stress of having to turn in a term paper the next day, the hormone adrenaline is released into the body and gives you the added bit of strength it takes to pull an all-nighter to complete the paper.

While this list certainly does not exhaust all of the possible psychophysiological responses used to investigate differences in personality (Davidson, 1991; Eysenck, 1967, 1982b, 1983, 1990a; Eysenck & Eysenck, 1985; Zuckerman, 1983, 1990), these responses have been used fairly regularly in studying the psychophysiological bases of major dimensions of personality. Two rather comprehensive approaches to the study of the psychophysiological basis of personality are provided by Marvin Zuckerman's research on the personality dimension of sensation seeking and research on Eysenck's theory of personality.

The Sensation-Seeking Personality: Seeking the Psychophysiological Bases of Thrill Seekers

Why do some individuals enjoy skydiving or driving fast cars while others are more content to go to a museum to get their thrills? In this section, we will attempt to answer these questions by considering the sensation-seeking personality.

Defining the Sensation-Seeking Personality: The Specification of Thrill Seekers

For over twenty years, Marvin Zuckerman of the University of Delaware has been investigating the personality dimension of sensation seeking. As a trait of personality, **sensation seeking** is "a trait defined by the need for varied, novel, and complex sensations and experiences and the willingness to take physical and social risks for the sake of such experience" (Zuckerman, 1979, p. 10). From this perspective, sensation seeking is not merely the searching for stimulation but the achievement of unique and powerful sensory experiences *within* the individual as critical sources of arousal. For example, although watching television can provide a rather high degree of visual and auditory stimulation, you are not very likely to achieve any unique and powerful emotional sensation, since most of what is shown on television is very similar (e.g., all detective shows are about the same). On the other hand, driving a car at 80 miles per hour with your eyes closed produces very little external stimulation but a tremendous degree of internal stimulation due to the risk and danger involved. This example points out that the decision to seek a very powerful level of internal sensation is a critical component of sensation seeking. Thus, sensation seeking can be considered the active search for experiences designed to produce unique and powerful sensations *within* the individual.

The Sensation Seeking Scale: Assessing the Sensation-Seeking Personality

In investigating this dimension of personality, Zuckerman has developed the **Sensation Seeking Scale** for the purpose of assessing the degree to which people have the trait of sensation seeking (Zuckerman, 1971; Zuckerman, Eysenck, Eysenck, 1978). In its latest version, the Sensation Seeking Scale (SSS) consists of 40 items arranged in a two-option, forced-choice format. The 40 items are divided so that 10 of each are classified as falling into one of the four subscales: Thrill and Adventure Seeking, Experience Seeking, Disinhibition, and Boredom Susceptibility (Zuckerman, 1983; Zuckerman, Buchsbaum, & Murphy, 1980).

▲ The Thrill and Adventure Seeking subscale measures the extent to which the individual

Marvin Zuckerman's study of the sensation-seeking personality has made a significant contribution to our understanding of the biological processes underlining personality.

expresses a desire to engage in activities of a physical nature involving speed, danger, novelty, and defiance of gravity (e.g., riding a motorcycle, parachuting, bungie jumping, or hang gliding).

▲ The Experience Seeking subscale measures the extent to which the individual expresses a desire to engage in activities designed to produce novel experiences through travel, music, art, meeting unusual people, or nonconforming life styles with other similar people (e.g., going to a nudist colony, taking mind-altering drugs, or listening to avant-garde music).

▲ The Disinhibition subscale measures the extent to which the individual seeks release through uninhibited social activities with or without the aid of alcohol (e.g., going to parties, sexual promiscuity, or high-stakes gambling).

▲ The Boredom Susceptibility subscale measures the extent to which the individual expresses displeasure for routine activities, repetitive experiences, and predictable people (e.g., an aversion to attending another company social function or seeing the same movie twice).

In addition to a score on the four separate subscales, a general measure of sensation seeking is obtained from the SSS by combining scores from the four subscales. To get a feel for your own level of sensation seeking, consider the material presented in "You Can Do It" on page 264.

YOU CAN DO IT

Are You a Thrill Seeker? Assessing Your Sensation-Seeking Tendency

To what extent are you a thrill seeker who shares a personality similar to the likes of such thrill seekers as Rambo or Indiana Jones? As a means of getting a slight glimpse of that possibility, answer the 6 items listed here.

1. A. My preference would be for a job requiring a lot of traveling.
   B. My preference would be for a job that required me to work in one location.
2. A. I would prefer to be indoors on a cold day.
   B. I am energized by being outdoors on a brisk, cold day.
3. A. Being a mountain climber is a frequent wish of mine.
   B. People who risk their necks climbing mountains are individuals I just can't understand.
4. A. I find body odors unpleasant.
   B. I find some of the earthy body smells pleasant.
5. A. Seeing the same old faces is something that bores me.
   B. I find comfort in the familiarity of everyday friends.
6. A. My preference would be to live in an ideal society where safety, security, and happiness are experienced by everybody.
   B. My preference would be to live in the unsettled days of our history.

Scoring:
Each time your response agrees with the following answers, give yourself one point: 1–A, 2–B, 3–A, 4–B, 5–A, and 6–B. The higher your score, the more your responses reflect a tendency for sensation seeking. But since only a very limited number of items were presented, these results are not meant to be an actual measure of sensation seeking.

*From Sensation Seeking: Beyond the Optimal Level of Arousal, by M. Zucker (1979), pp. 388–389. Hillsdale, NJ: Lawrence Erlbaum Associates Publishers. "Dimensions of Sensation Seeking," by M. Zuckerman, 1971, Journal of Consulting 2nd Clinical Psychology, 36, 45–52.

Behavioral and Psychophysiological Correlates of Sensation Seeking: The Behavior and Body of Thrill Seekers

In this section, we will consider the behavior differences of high and low sensation seekers and the underlying physiological processes that account for these differences.

Behavioral Correlates of Sensation Seeking There is considerable evidence that high sensation seekers tend to engage in behavior characterized as involving greater risk and stimulation than low sensation seekers. For example, high sensation seekers tend to engage in physically dangerous activities—such as parachuting, motorcycle riding, scuba diving, and fire fighting—to a greater degree than low sensation seekers (Zuckerman, Buchsbaum, & Murphy, 1980). It has been documented that high sensation seekers report participation in a greater variety of sexual activities with a greater number of partners than low sensation seeking individuals (Zuckerman, 1979). High sensation seeking scores are also associated with greater drug usage, gambling, and financial risk-taking behavior (Zuckerman, 1979; Wong & Carducci, 1991). High sensation seekers also tend to be attracted to professions involving relatively high risks, such as crisis intervention worker, rape counselor, air traffic controller, police officer, psychologist, and assorted other helping professions (Zuckerman, 1979).

Low sensation seekers tended to express vocational interest involving somewhat less risky occupations, such as pediatric nurse, accountant, pharmacist, banker, and mortician. As you can see from even this relatively short list of the behavioral correlates of sensation seeking, high sensation seekers might be described as "living in the fast lane."

Psychophysiological Correlates of Sensation Seeking In addition to the distinct behavioral differences between high and low sensation seekers, there is considerable evidence that high and low sensation seekers differ in their psychophysiological responses. When examining the orienting reflex to novel auditory and visual stimuli, it has been found that high sensation seekers respond with a greater degree of skin conductance (i.e., perspiration) than low sensation seekers (Neary & Zuckerman, 1976; Zuckerman,

1989). But no difference was found in habituation to the stimuli. This suggests that while high sensation seekers get really excited at first to a novel stimulus, they tend to get bored in a manner similar to low sensation seekers. In such situations, high sensation seekers might need to seek additional novel stimulation to a greater degree than low sensation seekers. For example, while high sensation seekers might be more likely to fall "head-over-heels" for someone right away, as these feelings begin to level off, the high sensation seeker would probably be more likely to seek a new partner sooner than low sensation seekers.

The searching for an optimal level of arousal refers primarily to cortical arousal (i.e., the amount of electrical activity in the brain) and is measured by the average evoked response (AER). Examination of the degree of cortical arousal seems to suggest that people respond with what might be defined as a style of **augmentation** (viz., increasing their level of arousal) or reduction (viz., reducing their level of arousal) to novel stimulation. While the general level of sensation seeking has been found to be significantly correlated to cortical arousal (Zuckerman, Simons, & Como, 1988), the relationship seems to be strongest for people scoring high on the Disinhibition subscale of the SSS who tend to respond to novel stimulation with a pattern of augmentation (Zuckerman, 1979, 1990). As you will recall, the Disinhibition subscale measures the extent to which people seek release through uninhibited social activities, such as dancing, going to concerts, or simply listening to loud music. From this research on AER, it is clear that such uninhibited behavior might have as its basis a desire for high levels of stimulation.

A neurotransmitter found to be consistently related to sensation seeking is that of monoamine oxidase (MAO) (Zuckerman et al., 1980). The basic function of **monoamine oxidase** is to prevent other neurotransmitters responsible for getting actions started from being released into the body. Thus, high levels of MAO would be associated with an individual who might be described as being inactive. Consistent with this reasoning, high sensation seeking scores have been found to be negatively correlated with the level of MAO in the body of the individual (Schooler, Zahn, Murphy, & Buchsbaum, 1978; Zuckerman, Ballinger, & Post, 1984). Thus, it is possible that this low level of MAO in high sensation seekers makes it possible to maintain a higher level of behavioral activity than that of people whose level of behavioral activity is reduced by the disinhibitive effects of MAO.

Investigations of the relationship between sensation seeking and hormonal production indicate that the Disinhibition subscale of the SSS is positively correlated with levels of the sex hormones of androgen, estrogen, and testosterone (Daitzman & Zuckerman, 1980; Daitzman, Zuckerman, Sammelwitz, & Ganjam, 1978). The hormones androgen and testosterone have been found to be related to the sex drive and behavior of both males and females. Estrogen is a hormone involved in regulating the menstrual cycle. While cultural factors also play a significant role, it is interesting to speculate about the role increased levels of these hormones might play in determining the intense level of emotional arousal associated with engaging in sexual behavior and high-risk activities. It is possible that increased levels of these hormones serve to heighten the emotional experience associated with engaging in such behaviors, which would increase the likelihood that the individual will repeat them.

This concludes the discussion of the psychophysiological perspective as illustrated within the context of the personality dimension of sensation seeking. For more information about the trait of sensation seeking, a recommended reading is *Sensation Seeking: Beyond the Optimal Level of Arousal*, by Marvin Zuckerman (1979).

Neurological Basis of Extraversion and Introversion: The Ascending Reticular Activating System and the Arousal Hypothesis

In addition to his work in classifying traits, as discussed in Chapter 8, Hans Eysenck has also examined the biological bases of personality (Eysenck, 1967; Eysenck, 1990a). At the center of Eysenck's biological perspective of personality is the neurological structure known as the ascending reticular activating system.

As seen in Figure 9.6, the **ascending reticular activating system** (ARAS) is a collection of nerve fibers located at the base of the spinal cord and the lower portion of the brain. The basic function of the ARAS is to help regulate the level of arousal in the brain in order for the individual to function most effectively. For example, as indicated by the ascending arrows in Figure 9.6, the level of arousal in the brain is increased when an individual is excited by the music and conversation at a party or concentrating intensely while studying for an important test. But, as indicated by the descending arrows, the brain may inform the ARAS to reduce the level of arousal under certain conditions. Such conditions might include when an individual is trying to fall asleep or when being too excited interferes with the person's ability to answer questions on a test. Thus, depending on the feedback it receives from the brain, the ARAS can either increase or decrease the level of arousal.

Linking Extraversion/Introversion with the ARAS through the Arousal Hypothesis

To establish a biological link with personality, Eysenck (1967) proposed that introverts have a lower threshold of arousal (or higher levels of activity) in the ARAS than extraverts. Based on this relationship, a general formulation of the **arousal hypothesis** proposes that introverts should react with greater responsiveness along those physiological processes regulated by the ARAS than extraverts. Because they are already somewhat more aroused (i.e., higher level of ARAS activity), introverts should react sooner and to a greater degree than extraverts to various forms of external stimulation.

Support for the Arousal Hypothesis: The Contrasting Arousal Styles of Extraverts and Introverts

There is a considerable amount of evidence to support the proposed relationship between extraversion/introversion and the ARAS formulated by the arousal hypothesis (Eysenck, 1990a; Stelmack, 1990). For example, when using an electroencephalogram (EEG) to measure cortical arousal, introverts exhibit more brain wave activity than extraverts in response to stimulation (Gale, 1983).

As Figure 9.7a indicates, while introverts display a greater degree of skin conductance response (SCR) to auditory stimulation of moderately intensity than extraverts, just the opposite is true at the

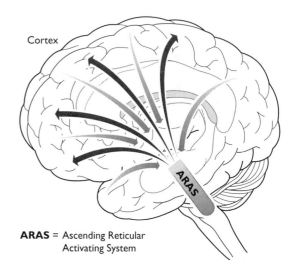

ARAS = Ascending Reticular
Activating System

Figure 9.6
The location of the ARAS and the ascending and descending pathways of cortical arousal

Note. Adapted from *Biological Basis of Personality* by H. J. Eysenck, 1967, p. 231. Springfield, IL: C. C. Thomas.

high level of stimulus intensity (Wigglesworth & Smith, 1976). A similar pattern of results occurs when the level of arousal is created (Figure 9.7b) by having groups of introverts and extraverts consume various drugs that serve as nervous system stimulants, such as caffeine (Smith, 1983) and nicotine (O'Connor, 1980, 1982). On the other hand, because of their heightened level of arousal, introverts require a larger dose of a depressant drug (e.g., alcohol) to produce sedation effects than extraverts do (Shagass & Kerenyi, 1958). The lower level of cortical arousal found in extraverts is consistent with other research indicating that MAO levels are negatively related to extraversion (Zuckerman, Ballinger, & Post, 1984). Because a heightened level of arousal can interfere with task performance, particularly if the task is a difficult one, introverts have been observed to perform less effectively on a task of learning than extraverts (McLaughlin & Eysenck, 1967). Finally, in addition to responding with greater intensity, introverts also tend to respond faster to external stimulation than extraverts (Stelmack, 1985; Stelmack & Geen, in press; Stelmack & Wilson, 1982). Such actions may represent an effort to reduce the aversive nature of excessive arousal.

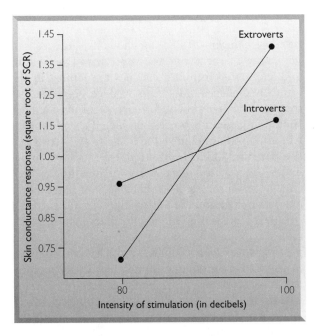

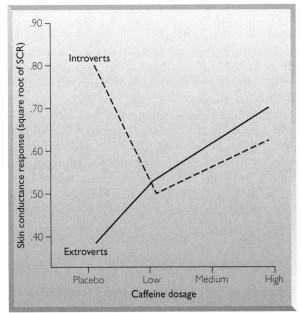

(a) Introverts respond more intensely to a moderate level of external stimulation, while extraverts respond more intensely to a high level of stimulation.

(b) The response intensity of introverts decreases as caffeine dosage increases; the opposite pattern of response occurs for extraverts.

Figure 9.7
The skin conductive response of extraverts and introverts in reaction to external auditory stimulation and caffeine

Note. Adapted from *Biological Bases of Extraversion: Some Evidence*, by R. M. Stelmack, 1990, *Journal of Personality*, Vol. 58, pp. 296 and 301.

Thus, in support of the arousal hypothesis, extraverts and introverts appear to have rather contrasting styles of arousal.

A Concrete Illustration of the Arousal Hypothesis
The preceding results provide a number of convergent pieces of information in support of the arousal hypothesis and the ARAS as a biological basis of the extraversion/introversion dimension. But, as a more concrete example, consider how these results might be applied to the behavior of introverts and extraverts at a party. In general, introverts may find parties more stressful than extraverts. This may be a result of the level of arousal of introverts increasing more quickly and to a greater degree than the arousal level of extraverts in response to the excessive amount of stimulation provided by such external events at the

party as music, conversation, and cigarette smoke. Such excessive arousal may also reduce the effectiveness of introverts to engage in such social skills as trying to make conversation or thinking of witty things to say. To reduce such stimulus overload, introverts may leave the party early (respond quicker) or avoid parties altogether (social avoidance).

On the other hand, extraverts may enjoy parties more because they have a greater tolerance for various sources of external stimulation (see Figure 9.5a), require less alcohol to experience reduced inhibitions (lower sedative threshold), and are predisposed to being more active because of a generally lower MAO level than introverts. While this explanation is only speculative, the general differences in the arousability and other corresponding biological processes can be used to help explain some of the variation in the behavior patterns exhibited by extraverts and introverts. More information about the biological bases of Eysenck's perspective on personality can be found in his book *The Biological Basis of Personality* (Eysenck, 1967), and a book chapter titled "Biological Dimensions of Personality" (Eysenck, 1990a).

The work by Zuckerman and Eysenck represents only two examples of the psychophysiological perspective to personality. These viewpoints were selected because of their rather comprehensive nature and extensive research support. Information on other psychophysiological perspectives can be found in the *Handbook of Individual Differences: Biological Perspectives* (Gale & Eysenck, in press).

The Biosocial Viewpoint: The Evolutionary Approach to Personality

The biosocial perspective has as its foundation the classic theory of evolution proposed by Charles Darwin (1859/1958) and works of the contemporary biologist Edward O. Wilson (1975). A central feature of the biosocial perspective is Darwin's notion of sexual selection (Darwin 1859/1958).

The following is the underlying assumption of **sexual selection**: "Traits that increase the probability of successful reproduction will tend to increase in frequency" (Kenrick, Sadalla, Groth, & Trost, 1990, p. 97).

Basic Assumptions of Biosocial Viewpoint: Sexual Selection and Differential Parental Investment

A process related to sexual selection is that of differential parental investment (Buss, 1994; Fisher, 1992; Trivers, 1985). **Differential parental investment** is generally defined as "the contributions a parent makes to one offspring's reproductive success at a cost to its own ability to invest in other offspring" (Kenrick et al., 1990, p. 100). According to the process of differential parental investment, females have a greater investment for each offspring because of having to carry the fetus and nurse the infant; and, compared to males, females are limited in the number of offspring they can produce. As a result of their greater investment for each offspring, females should engage in a process of sexual selection that will attempt to maximize the benefits and reproductive potential for each offspring. On the other hand, males, having less of a parental investment, will engage in a process of sexual selection designed to maximize the number of offspring.

Based on this fundamental difference between males and females in the process of differential parental investment, females would be more inclined to select as potential mates the males with personality characteristics most likely related to success within the species, while males would be more inclined to select as mates the females with successful reproductive ability.

In the animal kingdom, male traits associated with success of offspring within the species have traditionally been related to providing indirect economical resources. Traits linked to the ability to provide food and protection (e.g., size, muscles, and aggressiveness) are male traits related to economic success for animals. For females in the animal kingdom, traits associated with reproductive success within the species have traditionally been related to more direct physical resources. Traits linked to reproductive success in female animals include the presence of certain biological cues (e.g., scent from the genital area) and ability to nurse.

For humans, the potential for providing indirect economical resources by males as mates tends to be associated with their earning potential, while the potential for providing direct physical resources for females as mates tends to be associated with their physical attractiveness (Buss & Barnes, 1986). Thus, for humans, if earning potential is equated with providing economical resources in males, and physical attractiveness (e.g., youth and good health) is equated with reproductive ability in females, there is some possibility that the differential parental investment process found to operate in the animal kingdom can also be found within the mate selection of humans as well.

Impact of the Biosocial Viewpoint on the Person: Traits, Mates, and to Procreate

In investigating the differential parental investment hypothesis, Kenrick et al. (1990) had men and women undergraduates rate their minimum criteria on 24 partner characteristics at four levels of relationship involvement: dating, sexual relations, steady dating, and marriage. At every level of involvement, females were more selective with respect to traits related to what Kenrick et al. 1990) referred to as "earning capacity," such as powerful, wealthy, high social status, dominant, ambitious, popular, wants children, good heredity, good housekeeper, religious, and emotionally stable (p. 108). On the other hand, at every level of involvement, males tended to be more selective about physical attractiveness.

Additional research has documented that women report physical attractiveness to be less important in their selection of mate preferences than males do (Feingold, 1990, 1991, 1992). Women also report that they value socioeconomic status and ambitiousness more than men do (Buss, 1989; Feingold, 1992; Kenrick et al., 1990). If "earning capacity" can be equated with providing indirect economic resources by males and physical attractiveness equated with direct physical resources associated with youthfulness and reproductive success, such results are consistent with the differential parental investment hypothesis and other research related to the evolutionary approach (Buss, 1989; Buss & Barnes, 1986; Kenrick & Dengelegi, 1988; Hastie & Park, 1986; Sadalla, Kenrick, & Vershure, 1987).

The biosocial perspective assumes that certain personality characteristics are a result of the contribution they make to the successful reproduction of the species. Does this mean that the development and operation of the human personality is governed by the same principles of evolution that supposedly guide the physical and instinctive characteristics found in the animal kingdom? The answer to this question is no. What it does suggest is that personality characteristics and social behavior are in part a result of "naturally selected genetic mechanisms" (Kenrick, 1989, p. 316), and there are some unique opportunities for personality and social psychologists to "enrich the existing evolutionary literature" (Kenrick, 1989,

p. 317; Kenrick & Trost, 1987). For example, some evidence indicates that environmental factors (e.g., divorce, father-absence, infant day care) during childhood influence attachment patterns in such areas as sexual maturation, mating, and parenting in a manner consistent with the evolutionary approach to personality (Draper & Belsky, 1990). Thus, the biosocial perspective is just another element to consider when examining the interaction of biological and environmental factors in the development and operation of personality (Kenrick, Montello, & MacFarlane, 1985). For additional information about evolutionary processes in personality, read "A Biosocial Perspective on Mates and Traits: Reuniting Personality and Social Psychology," by Douglas T. Kenrick (1989).

Applications of the Biological Viewpoint: Using What Is Known

Information from the biological viewpoint has been applied to several different areas: the assessment of prenatal development, somatic treatments for emotional disorders, and occupational choice.

Assessment of Prenatal Development: Promoting Positive Prenatal Growth

Advances in the biological perspective have been used in assessing prenatal development in order to detect disease and genetic defects in the fetus. Such early detection increases the likelihood of promoting healthy prenatal and postnatal development. Two forms of prenatal assessment include genetic counseling and prenatal diagnosis.

Genetic Counseling
Genetic counseling is a service designed to help couples determine the likelihood of genetic or other related biological defects in their offspring (Papalia & Olds, 1992). Genetic counselors obtain information about the couple's genetic family history, including information about diseases, birth defects, mental

disorders, and causes of death of parents, siblings, grandparents, and other family relatives. Sophisticated laboratory techniques use the client's blood, skin tissue, urine, and sometimes fingerprints, to obtain additional information about the possibility of certain diseases and genetic defects. Based on all of this information, the genetic counselor calculates the mathematical odds of a couple transmitting a genetic defect to their offspring. If the risks of disease or genetic defect in the offspring are too high, a couple may decide to adopt children or consider artificial insemination.

Prenatal Diagnosis

In addition to obtaining a genetic family history, various medical techniques can be used to test the fetus while it is still in the womb to determine the presence of diseases and genetic defects. **Amniocentesis** is a medical technique, usually conducted at the 14th or 15th week of pregnancy, in which a sample of amniotic fluid is obtained from the amniotic sac containing the fetus and analyzed. In a **chorionic villus sampling** (CVS), a small sample of tissue is taken from the amniotic sac for analysis.

In addition to identifying the sex of the fetus, such medical techniques can be used to assess such genetics-related diseases and defects as Tay-Sachs disease (a fatal degenerative disease of the nervous system mostly afflicting Jews of Eastern European ancestry), sickle-cell anemia (a blood disorder found mostly among African Americans), Down syndrome (a cause of mental retardation), and muscular dystrophy (a disease that produces progressive muscular deterioration), to name just a few.

Fortunately, 98% of the women who have amniocentesis find no abnormality in the fetus (Plomin, DeFries, & McClearn, 1990). For some of the other cases, prenatal surgery or the injection of nutrients, vitamins, or hormones into the amniotic fluid can be used to treat these genetics-related diseases. However, some of these diseases have no known cure. In such cases, the possibility of abortion might be considered. Such decisions raise a number of critical ethical concerns involving moral and religious issues and the rights of the fetus to be born healthy, the rights of the parents, and the rights of society (Omenn, 1978).

Somatic Treatments of Emotional Disorders: Treating Troubled Minds from a Biological Perspective

Biological approaches have also been applied to the treatment of emotional disorders. But some of the most dramatic and controversial treatments of emotional disorders involve somatic treatments. **Somatic treatments** are those involving bodily (i.e., somatic) processes in the treatment of emotional disorders. Two somatic treatments are electroconvulsive therapy and chemotherapy.

Electroconvulsive Therapy

One of the most controversial somatic treatments is **electroconvulsive therapy** (ECT), also known as "shock" therapy. Although initially thought to be a cure for schizophrenia, as well as being used to treat various other emotional disorders, ECT has been found to be most successful in treating certain forms of severe depression and suicidal behavior (Comer, 1992; Rathus & Nevid, 1991). An ECT session involves administering a very mild electric current of 70 to 130 volts to the forehead or temple region of the head for a half second or less. This procedure produces a seizure similar to that of a grand-mal epileptic seizure. The patient also receives a muscle relaxant to control the excessive movements of the body during the seizure. Within the hour, the client is awake and the session is over. A client will receive about 6 ECT sessions over a two-week period, with a maximum of about 12 sessions within a year (Comer, 1992).

While ECT has been found to be successful in treating certain forms of depression and suicidal behavior, a source of controversy is that the process by which it works is still unknown. One explanation is that the induced seizures increase the release of certain hormones and neurotransmitters in the brain, altering the thoughts and behavior of certain depressed and suicidal people. Another source of controversy involves the side effects of ECT. Some undesired effects of prolonged use of ECT include memory loss, personality alteration, and permanent organic changes (Taylor & Carroll, 1987). Because of these undesired effects and the advancements made in the use of various drugs designed to treat major depression and suicidal behavior, the use of ECT has been declining since the 1950s (Comer, 1992). Today ECT is used primarily as a last resort after all other treatments have failed to produce the desired outcome.

Chemotherapy

Chemotherapy involves the use of drugs as a treatment for certain emotional disorders. **Minor tranquilizers** are a category of drugs used to treat feelings of anxiety and tension. Probably the most popular of the minor tranquilizers is Valium (generic name, diazepam). **Major tranquilizers** (also called "antipsychotic" drugs) are a category of drugs used in treating schizophrenic patients by reducing the agitation, delusions, and hallucinations associated with various forms of this disorder. **Antidepressants** are a category of drugs used in treating more serious forms of depression by altering the nature of certain neurotransmitters in the brain associated with the physical (e.g., sleep disturbances) and vegetative (e.g., lack of energy) features of the disorder.

While chemotherapy has enabled many people suffering from various emotional disturbances to experience fewer symptoms of their disorders, its use has some shortcomings (Rathus & Nevid, 1991). A major problem is the possibility of the individual becoming physically and/or psychologically addicted to the drug used to treat the disorder. Another major problem is that the symptoms of the disorder return once the drug is discontinued. In addition, the use of drugs does not help the client acquire more effective forms of coping behavior. It is for this reason that chemotherapy is often more effective when combined with other forms of psychotherapy that stress examining and altering maladaptive behavior patterns.

Work and the Biological Viewpoint: Some Biological Contributions to Occupational Choice and Satisfaction

Next to sleeping, there is probably no single activity that people spend more time participating in than working. There is evidence that certain biological dispositions play a role in influencing job attitudes and satisfaction (Arvey, Bouchard, Segal, & Abraham, 1989; Staw & Ross, 1985). For example, behavioral genetics research with monozygotic twins reared

apart (average age at separation and reunion being .45 and 31.71 years, respectively) indicates "a significant genetic component to intrinsic job satisfaction as well as to general job satisfaction" (Arvey et al., 1989, p. 190). This research also indicates that the jobs held by the twins were similar in their complexity level, motor skill requirements, and physical demands. Such a pattern of results suggests "a genetic component in terms of the jobs that are sought and held by individuals" (Arvey et al., 1989, p. 190).

One biological factor to be linked with occupational choice has been that of testosterone. **Testosterone** is the principal male sex hormone, but it is present in both sexes. In studies with both humans and animals, testosterone has been associated with a variety of characteristics such as dominance, aggression, persistence, and sensation seeking, to name just a few (Dabbs, de La Rue, & Williams, 1990).

In relating testosterone to occupational choice, it has been observed that women working in somewhat more traditionally masculine occupations (e.g., lawyers, managers, technical workers) were higher in testosterone than women working in somewhat more traditionally feminine occupations (e.g., clerical workers, nurses, teachers, housewives) (Purifoy & Koopmans, 1979; Schindler, 1979). For males, actors and professional football players were higher in testosterone than physicians, professors, and firemen, who were higher than salesmen and ministers (Dabbs, de La Rue, & Williams, 1990).

In more specific occupational comparisons, missionaries, who work to build new congregations, were higher in testosterone than pastors, who work with already-existing congregations. Stand-up comedians, who succeed or fail alone, had higher testosterone than stage actors, who work with groups of other actors (Dabbs, de La Rue, & Williams, 1990). It is suggested that high-testosterone occupations are associated with the personality characteristics of competition and dominance (Mazur, 1985; Mazur, Booth, & Dabbs, 1992).

It is not clear how biological factors and occupational choice and satisfaction operate. For example, it is not clear whether the testosterone causes people to enter certain professions, or whether once people enter a particular occupation, their level of testosterone increases. It is also possible that people seek out occupations that are compatible with their genetic makeup (e.g., testosterone level). But their choice of occupations may be a function of the kind of environment they inhabit.

For example, a female with high testosterone growing up in a family environment where nontraditional sex roles are supportive but money is lacking may have fewer occupational choices than a similar individual whose family can afford to help her with college tuition. In these cases, the female in the former environment might seek employment in some technical field, while the female from the latter environment might elect to attend law school. Additional research needs to be done to explore the processes by which biological factors influence occupational choice and the dynamics by which it can contribute to job satisfaction (e.g., employee training, work assignments).

Chapter Summary: Reexamining the Highlights

▲ *Biological Processes in the Study of Personality*
Some basic issues associated with the study of personality from the biological viewpoint include the nature-nurture controversy; the limitations of genetics in determining behavior; the role of the biological processes in conjunction with psychological, cognitive, and environmental processes; and the concept of biosocial interaction.

▲ *The Constitutional Viewpoint*
An initial biological approach to the study of personality is the constitutional prospective. Early constitutional approaches included humoral theories, physiognomy, and phrenology. Sheldon's approach attempted to link dimensions of physique (endomorphy, mesomorphy, and ectomorphy) with dimensions of temperament (viscerotonia, somatotonia, and cerebrotonia).

▲ *The Behavioral Genetics Viewpoint*
—*Methodological Considerations.* The study of genetic influences on behavior and personality characteristics involve family studies, twin studies, adoption studies, and model fitting.
—*The Interaction Temperament Model.* The dynamic interaction of genetic and environmental factors as determinants of personality are at the core of the interaction temperament model. Basic assump-

tions include the inheritability of a limited number of personality traits, the basis of individuality being attributed in part to some inherited traits, and the ability to modify both environmental and inherited dimensions of personality. The basic nature of temperament includes being inherited, appearing early in childhood, and displaying stability throughout life. The dimensions of temperament are emotionality, activity, and sociability.

▲ *The Psychophysiological Viewpoint*
—*Methodological Considerations.* The psychophysiological perspective involves explaining differences in personality by investigating underlying physiological processes, such as the orienting reflex, average evoked response, neurotransmitters, and hormonal production.
—*The Study of Sensation Seeking.* As an example of the psychophysiological approach, the study of sensation seeking attempts to explain the tendency to take risks to achieve novel stimulation. The tendency for sensation seeking is measured using the Sensation Seeking Scale and has been found to be correlated with risk-taking behaviors. Psychophysiological correlates of sensation seeking include augmentation in cortical arousal, a low level of monoamine oxidase, and an excess of certain hormones.
—*The Neurological Basis of Extraversion and Introversion.* Eysenck has examined the operation of the ascending reticular activating system as a psychophysiological basis of extraversion and introversion. Extraverts and introverts differ on several measures of arousal in a manner consistent with the arousal hypothesis.

▲ *The Biosocial Viewpoint*
The biosocial perspective investigates the selection and development of traits for the purpose of reproductive success. Based on the differential parental investment of males and females, certain traits in potential mates are sought.

▲ *Applications of the Biological Viewpoint*
—*Assessment of Prenatal Development.* Genetic counseling, amniocentesis, and chorionic villus sampling are assessment techniques used to detect the presence of diseases and genetic defects in the fetus.
—*Somatic Treatments of Emotional Disorders.* Electroconvulsive therapy is used in treating certain forms

of severe depression and suicidal behavior by inducing seizures in the brain. Chemotherapy involves the use of various groups of drugs, including minor tranquilizers, major tranquilizers, and antidepressants, in the treatment of emotional disorders.

—*Work and the Biological Viewpoint.* Possible genetic factors and certain hormones, especially testosterone, have been linked with the selection of and satisfaction with occupational choice.

Glossary

activity   A dimension of temperament characterized by energized activities.

adoption studies   A comparison of people with their biological and adopted parents to examine genetic transmission of various characteristics.

amniocentesis   A procedure for sampling and screening amniotic fluid for genetic defects and diseases in the fetus.

antidepressants   Drugs used in the treatment of depression.

arousal hypothesis   A proposed relationship between extraversion/introversion and the general level of arousal in the brain.

ascending reticular activating system   A neurological structure that regulates the level of arousal in the brain.

augmentation   The tendency to increase or intensify stimulation.

averaged evoked response   Changes in the electrical activity of the brain.

behavioral genetics   The assessment of behavioral differences due to genetic and environmental factors.

biosocial interaction   The combined operation of biological and environmental factors to influence personality.

cerebrotonia   A dimension of temperament characterized by emotional restraint.

chemotherapy   The treatment of emotional disorders with medication.

choleric   A tendency to be angry and irritable.

chorionic villus sampling   A procedure for sampling and screening fetal tissue for genetic defects and disease in the fetus.

concordance rate   The extent to which sets of twins share certain characteristics.

constitutional psychology   A viewpoint of psychology emphasizing bodily processes and characteristics to explain behavior.

differential parental investment   Gender differences in the degree and nature of parenting.

dizygotic twins   Individuals who are fraternal twins.

ectomorphy   A dimension of physique characterized by frailness.

electroconvulsive therapy   A procedure for passing an electrical current into the brain to treat certain emotional disorders.

emotionality   A dimension of temperament characterized by intensity of expression.

endomorphy   A dimension of physique characterized by softness and roundness.

family studies   The systematic investigation of family histories to assess the occurrence of certain individual characteristics.

fraternal twins   Two people conceived from different fertilized eggs and not sharing the same genetic makeup.

genetically determined   Personality, behavioral, or physical characteristics appearing as a result of certain genes.

genetic counseling   Advice given to people concerning their likelihood of having offspring with genetic defects and diseases.

hormonal production   The release of hormones for the purpose of triggering bodily responses.

humors   Fluids of the body, as defined by the ancient Greeks.

identical twins   Two people conceived from a single fertilized egg and sharing the same genetic makeup.

interaction temperament model   A proposed dynamic relationship between genetic and environmental factors in determining personality characteristics.

major tranquilizers   Drugs usually used to treat schizophrenia.

melancholic   A tendency to be gloomy and sad.

mesomorphy   A dimension of physique characterized by high muscle tone.

minor tranquilizers   Drugs used to treat anxiety and tension.

model fitting   The comparison of various mathematical models to assess the proposed contribution of genetic and environment factors to various characteristics.

monoamine oxidase   A neurotransmitter that inhibits actions.

monozygotic twins   Individuals who are identical twins.

nature-nurture controversy   The debate over the role of heredity vs. environmental factors as determinants of personality.

neurotransmitters   Chemicals used to send neurological information within the body.

orienting reflex   A general response to a new stimulus.

phlegmatic   A tendency to be quiet and reserved.

phrenology   An early attempt to understand personality and mental abilities by relating them to the shape of a person's head.

physiognomy   An early attempt to understand personality by relating it to physical features of the person.

sanguine   A tendency to be cheerful.

selective breeding experiment   The systematic breeding of organisms to study the genetic transmission of certain characteristics.

selective placement   Certain biases in the placement of children during the adoption process.

sensation seeking   A tendency for excessive, novel stimulation.

Sensation Seeking Scale   A personality inventory to measure the sensation-seeking tendency.

sexual selection   The selection of mates for the purpose of maximizing successful reproduction.

sociability   A dimension of temperament characterized by the preference to be with others.

somatic treatments   The treatment of emotional disorders using medical techniques.

somatotonia   A dimension of temperament characterized by physical and risk-taking activities.

somatotype   A system for rating an individual's physique along the endomorphy, mesomorphy, and ectomorphy dimensions.

temperament   An inherited dimension of personality.

testosterone   A masculine hormone that can be found in both sexes.

twin studies   The investigation of twins to study the genetic contribution to various individual characteristics.

viscerotonia   A dimension of temperament characterized by sociability.

CHAPTER 10

The Behavioral Viewpoint: Perspectives of Personality Based on Principles of Learning

CHAPTER OVERVIEW: A PREVIEW OF COMING ATTRACTIONS

*T*he *viewpoints of personality presented in the preceding chapters have focused on psychological (e.g., dynamics of the unconscious mind and traits) or biological (e.g., hormonal levels and neurotransmitters) dimensions existing inside the individual. In direct contrast, the focal point of study for the behavioral viewpoint of personality stresses factors existing in the external environment.*

In this chapter, you will first consider the basic assumptions of the behavioral viewpoint of personality. The assumptions are followed by detailed discussions of the two major perspectives within the behavioral viewpoint; classical conditioning and operant conditioning. The sections on classical and operant conditioning include descriptions of the basic principles, processes, and applications associated with each perspective. At the end of this chapter, you will find a discussion of the characteristic strengths and limitations of the behavioral viewpoint.

Basic Assumptions: The Behavioral Nature of Personality

Although the behavioral viewpoint encompasses a variety of perspectives (Loevinger, 1987; Wilson, 1989; Wilson, 1995), they all share certain basic assumptions about the fundamental nature of personality (Kenrick, Montello, & MacFarlane, 1985; Liebert & Spiegler, 1990; Pervin, 1989):

▲ The behavioral nature of personality
▲ An emphasis on principles of learning
▲ The importance of the learning history
▲ An emphasis on environmental factors

Personality Equals Behavior: You Are What You Do

One assumption of the behavioral viewpoint is that an individual's personality is defined by the person's overt behavior. Instead of relying on internal psychological (e.g., traits), motivational (e.g., self-actualization), or biological (e.g., inherited temperament) explanations, personality psychologists working within the behavioral viewpoint describe an individual's personality by noting what the person is doing or has done in the past. For example, rather than defining someone as having the trait of aggressiveness as measured by items on a personality test (e.g., when angry I strike out; yes or no), behavioral psychologists would consider an individual as having an aggressive personality based on the extent to which he or she behaves aggressively in various situations (e.g., honking the car horn, yelling at a coworker, and watching violent movies). Thus, from the behavioral viewpoint, "personality equals behavior."

Personality Is Learned: Learning to Be You

A principal assumption of the behavioral viewpoint is that personality is learned. More specifically, the complex behavior patterns making up an individual's personality are nothing more than a series of separate, learned responses based on such fundamental principles of learning as the concepts of reinforce-

ment and punishment. For example, the simple responses of glancing away, folding your arms, and lowering your head are easily learned and very simple acts that do not mean much when considered separately. But they become much more meaningful when combined in a complex response pattern, such as each time someone tries to talk to you at a party or every time you are called on in class. A person who consistently exhibits this particular response pattern might be labeled by others as having a shy personality. Thus, the point to be made here is that an individual's personality consists of pieces of learned behavior combined into complex response patterns.

Personality Is Acquired Over Time: You and Your Learning History

The complex behavior patterns making up an individual's personality are not learned overnight; they are acquired over time as a result of being performed again and again. To expand on the preceding example, the behavior pattern labeled as shyness that was observed at the party or in class probably developed over many years. The person may have shied away from relatives at family reunions as a child, schoolmates on the playground in elementary school, and classmates at dances in high school. This individual has learned that shying away from people in social situations reduces feelings of anxiety.

Based on the learning principles of reinforcement and repetition, behaviors producing a positive outcome tend to be repeated. Thus, from the behavioral viewpoint, to gain insight into an individual's personality, you must look at the **learning history** of the individual.

The Environment Is Emphasized: External Influences on Personality

Rather than relying on internal psychological and/or biological processes to explain the nature and dynamics of personality, the behavioral viewpoint tends to emphasize the influential nature of the external environment. The emphasis is on how the individual learns to respond in specific ways to particular cues in the external environment. For example, the sight of an attractive stranger approaching you at a party might make you exhibit the pattern of shy behavior. But the sight of this same attractive person verbally attacking a good friend of yours might trigger your very outspoken response in defense of the friend. The point here is that from the behavioral viewpoint, personality (i.e., behavior) can be better understood by looking at the surrounding environment than by searching for various dynamics within the individual.

Internal Personality Dynamics and the Behavioral Viewpoint: A Point of Clarification

A common misinterpretation of the preceding statement is to assume that personality psychologists working within the behavioral viewpoint deny the existence of internal dynamics of personality (DeBell & Harless, 1992; Lamal, 1995). What this statement really means is that proponents of the behavioral viewpoint do not consider internal structures and processes as important as environmental factors when trying to understand and explain an individual's personality. For example, while internal psychological (e.g., fear and anxiety) and biological (e.g., an increase in heart rate) processes might trigger an individual to take action (e.g., running away), it is the external factors (e.g., being alone and the threat of physical assault from another) that are the principal determinants of the nature of these internal processes and behavioral outcomes.

The following chart summarizes the relationships between environmental factors and behavioral responses and the role of internal processes in the expression of personality from the behavioral viewpoint:

$$\begin{array}{ccc} \text{environmental} & \rightarrow \text{internal} & \rightarrow \text{behavioral} = \text{personality} \\ \text{factors} & \text{processes} & \text{response} \\ \text{[observed]} & \text{[inferred]} & \text{[observed]} \end{array}$$

Thus, unlike the other personality viewpoints, a central theme of the behavioral viewpoint is the emphasis it places on the external environment as a principal determinant of observable behavior when trying to explain and understand personality. Two major perspectives within the behavioral viewpoint are classical conditioning and operant conditioning.

The Classical Conditioning Perspective: The Learning of Associations

In this section, we will discuss the basic principles and processes of classical conditioning and the contribution they have made to the study of personality psychology.

Basic Principles: The Basics for Building a Personality

At the core of understanding the classical conditioning perspective to the study of personality is an understanding of its basic principles. Our examination of the classical conditioning perspective will begin with a discussion of these basic principles.

The Generality of Classical Conditioning
A vivid memory most students have of their introductory psychology course is the picture of one of Pavlov's dogs being conditioned to salivate to the sound of a bell. While it may not be readily apparent, there are many things about people in general (e.g., who they might find attractive or what products they buy) and their personality in particular (e.g., their attitudes and fears) that can be understood based on the salivation of Pavlov's dogs (Brehm, 1992; Clore & Byrne, 1974; Cohen, 1981; Davison & Neale, 1994; Engel, Blackwell, & Miniard, 1993; Hawkins, Best, & Coney, 1989; Lohr & Staats, 1973; Ost & Hugdahl, 1981). But regardless of whether the focus is the salivation of dogs or the acquisition of attitudes, the basic elements and principles of classical conditioning as a process of learning are the same. These elements and processes are described next.

The Basic Elements of Classical Conditioning
Through his monumental work on classical conditioning, the Russian physiologist Ivan Pavlov (1927)

identified four basic elements that are required for the process of classical conditioning to work: unconditioned response, unconditioned stimulus, conditioned stimulus, and conditioned response (Domjan, 1993).

▲   An **unconditioned response** (UCR) is a natural response that the individual or organism is able to perform prior to the conditioning process. In Pavlov's original experiments, the dog's salivation response was the UCR. For humans, it might be something like the ability to express various emotions (e.g., fear, happiness, and anger), certain reflexive avoidance behaviors (e.g., eye blink), or turning to run away.

▲   An **unconditioned stimulus** (UCS) includes any stimuli that are capable of eliciting the UCR with no previous training. In Pavlov's experiments, the meat powder was capable of making the dog salivate from the very first time it was placed on its tongue. For humans, a UCS might be something like the smile from another person or a slap on the face.

▲   The **conditioned stimulus** (CS) is any object that prior to the conditioning process would not generate the UCR. In the original experiments, Pavlov sounded a bell, but got no salivation response from the dog. In humans, a CS might be the scent of a new perfume or a telephone number.

▲   The **conditioned response** (CR) is the response by the organism that occurs when the CS is presented alone. In Pavlov's experiments, the conditioned dog salivated upon seeing the bell. For humans, a CR might be the sense of joy we experience when dialing a friend's phone number.

The Process of Classical Conditioning

In the process of classical conditioning, the first step is to demonstrate the existing relationship between the UCS and the UCR and the lack of relationship between the CS and the UCR. This is done by repeatedly presenting the UCS and observing the presence of the UCR, as well as by separately presenting the CS and noting the absence of the UCR. In Figure 10.1, phase 1 illustrates the basic relationship existing between the UCS, CS, and UCR before the conditioning process.

The next step in the process of classical conditioning is the acquisition phase. The **acquisition phase** involves repeatedly presenting the UCS immediately after the CS and observing the presence of the UCR. It is during the acquisition phase of the conditioning process that the organism learns to make the association between the CS and the UCR. Pavlov originally presented the bell first, then the meat powder, to the dog; and then observed the dog's salivation. For humans, it might involve a feeling of joy (UCR) we feel when hearing a very friendly voice (UCS) after calling a particular telephone number (CS). Thus, the next step in the process of classical conditioning involves establishing an association between the CS and the UCR. The existence of this relationship is demonstrated by observing that the presence of the UCR after the presentation of the CS is followed by the UCS. Phase 2 in Figure 10.1 illustrates the basic relationship between the UCS, CS, and UCR during the acquisition phase of the classical conditioning process.

The third step in the process of classical conditioning involves testing for the existence of conditioning by observing the presence of the conditioned response (CR). The CR is the final element required in the process of classical conditioning. In the example, the CR is the sense of joy now experienced while dialing a friend's telephone number. In this case, the original source of these feelings (i.e., the friendly voice) does not need to be present for the feelings to occur, just a stimulus now associated with the original feelings (i.e., dialing the telephone number). Thus, the last step in the conditioning process involves testing the extent to which the CS, when presented alone, is capable of eliciting the CR. Phase 3 in Figure 10.1 illustrates the basic relationship that exists between the CS and the CR after the conditioning process.

Contingency Theory: An Explanation of Classical Conditioning

Although outlining the basic elements involved in classical conditioning provides a description of how a previously neutral CS now comes to elicit the CR through its association with the UCS, it does not nec-

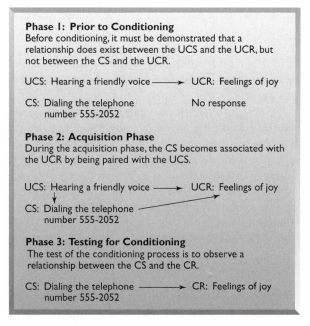

Phase 1: Prior to Conditioning
Before conditioning, it must be demonstrated that a relationship does exist between the UCS and the UCR, but not between the CS and the UCR.

UCS: Hearing a friendly voice ———→ UCR: Feelings of joy

CS: Dialing the telephone   No response
     number 555-2052

Phase 2: Acquisition Phase
During the acquisition phase, the CS becomes associated with the UCR by being paired with the UCS.

UCS: Hearing a friendly voice ———→ UCR: Feelings of joy

CS: Dialing the telephone ————————↗
     number 555-2052

Phase 3: Testing for Conditioning
The test of the conditioning process is to observe a relationship between the CS and the CR.

CS: Dialing the telephone ———————→ CR: Feelings of joy
     number 555-2052

Figure 10.1
An example of the basic principles of classical conditioning, illustrating the process by which dialing a telephone number becomes a conditioned stimulus

essarily explain why this association takes place (Barker, 1994; Rescorla, 1967, 1968, 1988). In explaining the process of classical conditioning, **contingency theory** (Rescorla, 1988), proposes that what is critical is not simply the pairing of the CS and the UCS, but the information value that the CS (i.e., the bell) provides about the subsequent appearance of the UCS (i.e., meat powder).

For example, although there were several other possible CSs in the laboratory when Pavlov was conditioning his dogs (e.g., color of the walls or temperature of the room), the dogs focused on the bell because it was a salient feature of the environment. In classical conditioning, **saliency** refers to the relative likelihood that a particular CS will be associated with a particular UCS. In Pavlov's original work, the bell represented a very salient feature of the environment because its audible presence gave the dog valuable information that the meat powder was soon to follow. Thus, although many other potential stimulus cues appearing in the environment at the same time

as the bell (e.g., color of the walls), it was the bell that provided the most valuable information to the dog. In a similar manner, although many other cues appear along with the dialing of the telephone number (e.g., the color of the carpet or a picture hanging on the wall near the phone), the telephone number becomes the most salient feature because it is what the individual most readily associates with hearing the friendly voice. Thus, contingency theory helps to explain more thoroughly how (e.g., the appearance of salient cues) and why (e.g., the information value of the CS) the process of classical conditioning occurs.

As summarized in Figure 10.1, the basic elements in the process of classical conditioning are designed to help establish new associations between objects based on old associations. But these are not the only principles associated with classical conditioning; additional principles are discussed next.

Some Additional Principles of Classical Conditioning: Expanding the Nature of Personality

The four basic principles discussed in the preceding section can be combined with other principles to gain a more complete understanding of personality from the classical conditioning perspective. Some of these additional principles, discussed in the following subsections, include stimulus generalization, stimulus discrimination, higher-order conditioning, and vicarious conditioning.

The Principle of Stimulus Generalization
After an individual has been conditioned to respond to a particular CS, other stimuli *similar* to that CS also tend to trigger a response. For example, an individual might also experience joy when seeing the friend's name, in addition to the original response of joy when dialing the friend's telephone number. Thus, **stimulus generalization** is the extent to which the individual responds to other stimuli based on how similar they are to the original CS used in the conditioning process.

It is important to note that the degree of generalization can become quite extensive. For example, the feelings of anxiety (CR) triggered in a shy person by a particular individual (e.g., a very overbearing person) at a party (CS) might also be triggered by other people with similar characteristics at the party, co-workers on the job, and/or classmates at school. This extensive pattern of stimulus generalization results in a high degree of social anxiety and shyness appearing in many different situations. As this example illustrates, the principle of stimulus generalization can help to explain personality consistency.

The Principle of Stimulus Discrimination

Related to stimulus generalization is the principle of stimulus discrimination. **Stimulus discrimination** refers to the extent to which the individual makes specific decisions to limit responses only to certain stimuli related to the original CS. For example, at the party, the shy person might distinguish between those people who are perceived as an interpersonal threat (e.g., ask very direct questions) and those who are not (e.g., speak in quiet tones). Based on this classification, the feelings of social anxiety are triggered only whenever someone at the party, work, or school asks this shy person very direct questions.

The Principle of Higher-Order Conditioning

Higher-order conditioning is a process in classical conditioning in which a new CS is paired with the old CS so that it too will eventually elicit the CR (Domjan, 1993). In higher-order conditioning, however, the original UCS is not presented at all. For example, if you have a tendency to call a friend at around seven o'clock, the sound of a wall clock striking seven (new CS) might now come to elicit feelings of joy (CR) similar to those originally triggered by actually dialing the number (old CS) and hearing the voice (UCS). At the party, if the shy person happens to remember that the person (CS) who elicited the feelings of anxiety and nervousness (CR) by asking the very direct questions was wearing a red jacket, he or she might now become nervous each time someone at the party comes near wearing a red jacket (the new CS), even before the person says anything.

The Principle of Vicarious (secondhand) Conditioning

Vicarious conditioning occurs when a person learns CRs by observing the nature of other people's responses to a particular stimulus. For example, without having any direct experience, the shy person might develop feelings of nervousness toward a particular person at the party by observing that other people seem to exhibit nervousness when speaking to this person.

These four additional principles of classical conditioning make it possible to understand how people begin to acquire certain aspects of their personality, as well as how these aspects are extended to new and different situations. In the next section, you will examine how these basic principles of classical conditioning can shape certain specific aspects of an individual's personality.

The Classical Conditioning of Specific Aspects of Personality: Acquiring Attitudes, Fears, and Preferences

Specific aspects of personality can be explained by the process of classical conditioning. In this section, you will learn about the following specific aspects: attitudes, phobias, and attraction.

The Acquisition of Attitudes and the Conditioning of Prejudice

At a very basic level, there is evidence that the feelings people have about certain objects are acquired based on the principles of classical conditioning (Petty & Cacioppo, 1981; Zimbardo & Leippe, 1991). For example, when people are shown words supposedly representing names of groups of people they have not heard of before, their expressed liking or disliking for these groups is found to be related to the extent to which the group names are paired with positive (e.g., happy) or negative (e.g., dumb) words (Lohr & Staats, 1973).

Evidence also suggests that the positive and negative feelings people acquire about the names of people or groups are expressed in behavior patterns consistent with these feelings. For example, Berkowitz and Knurek (1969) first conditioned people to feel negatively about specific male names (e.g., George) by associating the names with words having negative connotations (e.g., ugly or selfish). Later, when these people were placed in a group discussion with a person having one of the negatively conditioned names, the researchers observed that the people behaved in a more hostile manner toward this person than they did toward people whose names were not among those previously conditioned.

In a much more serious context, if young children hear the words *blacks*, *Jews*, or *Japs* associated with negative connotations (e.g., lazy, stingy, or shrewd) from the adults around them, the children may come to feel and behave negatively toward these groups of people as well.

Thus, based on this and other research (Rajecki, 1989; Zimbardo & Leippe, 1991), it is possible to help explain how people acquire certain attitudes and prejudices based on the process of classical conditioning (Baron & Byrne, 1994; Deaux, Dane, & Wrightsman, 1993).

The Acquisition of Phobias and the Conditioning of Fears

A **phobia** is an intense fear of an object (e.g., a dog) or situation (e.g., enclosed spaces) that is out of proportion to the actual level of danger it presents. Most people have what might be considered mild forms of phobias (e.g., speaking in front of groups). There is evidence to suggest that such phobias might have been acquired based on the process of classical conditioning (Comer, 1992, 1995; Davison & Neale, 1994; Mehr, 1983). This basic process involves some object or situation that was probably neutral to begin with, but was somehow associated with an extremely high emotional reaction by the individual. From that time on, each time the person experiences this stimulus object or situation, he or she responds with a highly charged emotional reaction.

The same is true for situations such as the fear that many people have about public speaking. For example, at some point Beth, a college student, probably began to feel extremely anxious (UCR) after hearing others discuss how unpleasant it was to give a speech in class (UCS). As a result of hearing about the anxieties of these other students, each time Beth now thinks about personally having to give a speech (CS), she begins to feel anxious (CR). Based on higher-order conditioning, Beth also feels anxious at the sight of the speech courses in the class listings during registration, which makes her avoid classes in which speeches are required. On a more personal level, if you examine any intense fear you have, you

will most likely find that it was probably acquired based on the principles of classical conditioning.

The Acquisition of Attraction and the Conditioning of Preferences for People and Products

In addition to developing prejudicial attitudes toward others based on classical conditioning, it is also possible to develop an attraction for others (Baron & Byrne, 1994; Byrne, 1971; Brehm, 1992; Clore & Byrne, 1974; Lott & Lott, 1974). For example, if you are having a great time at a party, you are likely to associate these good feelings (CR) with other people (CSs) attending the party (Freeman, 1977). As a result, if you recognize someone from the party the next week at school and feel favorably toward that person, you are likely to sit with him or her in the student union. The same is true for the products we purchase. The logic is that the good feelings you experience when watching a particular commercial (e.g., Ray Charles selling Pepsi) become conditioned to a particular product (Engel, Blackwell, & Miniard, 1993; Hawkins, Best, & Coney, 1989; Peter & Olson, 1990). When you go to the store and see the product, the good feelings return, which increases the likelihood that you will select that product over other products (e.g., 7-Up or Dr Pepper).

Thus, the attraction people feel for others and certain products may be due in part to the process of classical conditioning. For this reason, when trying to attract the affection of someone special, it is best to be associated with as many positive feelings as possible in this person's presence. In attempting to accomplish this, people do such things as wearing nice clothes, using perfume or cologne, saying amusing things, and going to romantic places with the other person. But the positive feelings acquired based on classical conditioning can also get out of hand and develop into what are called "fetishes" (Comer, 1995). For more insight into this possibility, read "A Closer Look" on page 282.

Applications of the Classical Conditioning Perspective: Using What Is Known

In the preceding section, you examined the process of classical conditioning as it relates to explaining how people might acquire certain aspects of their

A Closer Look:

Developing Fetishes: Attraction That Is Not Appropriate

A **fetish** involves powerful sexual feelings and urges in reaction to a particular object. In some cases, the object of the fetish is required to be present in order to attain sexual arousal and gratification. In very mild and common forms, a fetish might involve an exaggerated preference for a certain type of individual (e.g., models and movie stars) or a particular part of a partner's body (e.g., hairy chest or big breasts).

In more extreme cases, a fetish might involve inanimate objects such as female underclothing, rubber boots, or leather garments. Consider this brief excerpt from a case study of a man with a boot fetish (Epstein, 1965):

> I always seem to have been fascinated by rubber boots. I cannot say exactly when the fascination first started, but I must have been very young. Their spell is almost hypnotic and should I see someone walking along with rubber boots, I become very excited and follow the person for great distances. I quickly get an erection under such circumstances and I might easily ejaculate. I am most excited by boots that are black and shiny and hip length.

> Whenever I see a picture of boots in a magazine, I become excited. (pp. 515–516)

How is it possible to explain such behavior? Although it is not the only possible explanation, the one based on classical conditioning suggests that at some point during this man's sexual history, he might have come to associate the fetish object with sexual arousal. For example, as a young boy, he might have masturbated to pictures in magazines of nude women wearing long boots.

In support of this conditioning explanation, Rachman (1966) repeatedly presented males with sexually arousing slides of nude women, interspersed with showing slides of women's boots. As a result of these associations, viewing the slides of the boots alone was enough to cause these young men to respond with an erection! A similar process tends to occur when a person becomes sexually aroused after hearing a song that has certain sensual memories associated with it because of some special experiences that person might have had with a lover when they first heard the song.

Also note that the inappropriate nature of fetishes tends to occur when it is the only way that the individual can achieve sexual gratification. Many people have also come into contact with the law because of resorting to theft to obtain the object of their fetish.

---

personality. But in some instances, certain aspects about an individual's personality may need to be changed. For example, a shy adult may find it extremely difficult to meet others socially because of a phobia of speaking to people in small social groups. Another person might have difficulty meeting people because he finds himself able to become emotionally interested in others only when he dresses in women's clothing and makeup before going out for the evening. In both cases, these people might elect to seek behavior therapy to help alter certain problematic aspects of their personality.

The Basic Logic and Goal of Behavior Therapy

Generally speaking, **behavior therapy** involves applying basic principles of learning to help a person alter those behaviors that seem to be causing them trouble (e.g., anxiety about speaking to people) (Masters, Burish, Hollon, & Rimm, 1987; Rathus & Nevid, 1992). The basic logic of behavior therapy assumes that because people acquire these problematic behaviors based on general principles of learning, they can use the same principles to unlearn the behaviors and replace them with more appropriate ones (Comer, 1995; Kazdin, 1994; Wilson, 1995). Along these lines, the basic goal of behavior therapy involves working to directly alter the problematic behaviors, instead of searching for deep-seated causes of the problems as is done in psychoanalysis or humanistic psychotherapy. Rather than looking for complex psychological explanations relying on the dynamics of the unconscious mind or incongruence within the self-concepts to explain an individual's anxiety about speaking to others, a behavior therapist would attempt to directly alter those behaviors causing the anxiety, such as associating people with receiving negative evaluations and rejection. The following subsections describe two therapeutic applications of classical conditioning: systematic desensitization and aversive counter-conditioning.

Systematic Desensitization: Replacing Bad CRs with Good CRs

Systematic desensitization is a gradual process by which an individual uses classical conditioning principles in learning to replace unpleasant or maladaptive responses to certain stimuli with more pleasant or adaptive responses (Emmelkamp, 1994; Wilson, 1995; Wolpe, 1958, 1973, 1981, 1987, 1990). As a therapeutic technique, systematic desensitization has been used primarily to help people unlearn phobias or other forms of extreme anxiety reactions (Davison & Neale, 1994; Kazdin, 1994).

Central to the process of systematic desensitization is the notion of reciprocal inhibition (Wolpe, 1973). **Reciprocal inhibition** means that one emotional response can prevent the occurrence of another emotional response due to its incompatible nature. For example, it is hard to feel anxious when you are feeling relaxed, just as it is impossible to study while you are talking on the phone. Thus, the basic logic of systematic desensitization is to replace one response with another that is incompatible with it. This is typically done in three steps: establishing an anxiety hierarchy, learning the new, more adaptive response, and becoming desensitized (Martin & Pear, 1992).

Establishing an Anxiety Hierarchy   The first step in the technique of systematic desensitization is to establish an anxiety hierarchy. An **anxiety hierarchy** is a listing of conditions related to a specific anxiety-provoking object or situation, arranged in order from the least threatening to the most threatening (Wolpe & Lang, 1964). The following anxiety hierarchy might be created by a shy adult who fears speaking to others in small, intimate social gatherings:

1. Standing outside the door just before entering a party.
2. Entering the room where the party is taking place.
3. Seeing a group of people talking about ten feet away from me.
4. Walking over to the group and being about five feet away from them.
5. Walking closer and being right next to the group.
6. Having everybody in the group stop talking and look at me as I stand next to the group.
7. Trying to say something in response to what someone in the group said.
8. Being asked a specific question by someone in the group and having everyone looking at me.
9. Thinking that what I will say in response to this question will be evaluated as being dumb.
10. Having everybody looking at me as I get ready to respond to the direct question.

The items in this hierarchy are arranged according to how much anxiety the person feels when experiencing each specific situation. Depending on how specific the person wants to be, an anxiety hierarchy can include from as few as 10 items to as many as 30 or more.

Learning a New Adaptive Response   The second step in systematic desensitization involves learning a new response that is incompatible with and more adaptive than feeling anxious. This is done through relaxation training. **Progressive relaxation training** involves teaching the individual how to achieve a state of relaxation by systematically tightening and loosening various muscles in the body, and then noting the pleasant sensations that result.

In progressive relaxation therapy, the client is instructed to select a quiet and comfortable environment. The client then receives instructions similar to these:

> Close your eyes and try to make yourself as comfortable as you can. With your eyes closed, make a tight fist so that you can feel your muscles tense up. Notice how tight and tense your muscles feel in your hands, arms, and even in your neck. With your eyes still closed, relax your hand and loosen your muscles. Concentrate on how good and comfortable you feel as the muscles in your hand, arm, and neck are now relaxed. Once again, clench your fist; notice how tense and uncomfortable you feel. Relax and loosen your muscles, and note how comfortable you feel.

Concentrate on how tension-free you are feeling now that the muscles in your hand, arm, and neck are relaxed. (Based on Wolpe and Lazarus, 1966)

The procedure of tightening and relaxing the muscles is repeated for various aspects of the body, such as the facial muscles, leg muscles, and back muscles. The initial training sessions might involve 20 to 30 minutes of instructing the client on how to tense, relax, and concentrate on various muscles. After the training, the client will eventually be able to relax the muscles quickly without first having to tense them. The major advantage of the relaxation response is that it can be done almost any time and place. For example, training in relaxation can be offered to employees in the workplace (Quick, Murphy, & Hurrell, 1992) or even to entire communities (Ingham & Bennett, 1990; Rutter, Quine & Chesham, 1993). The process of muscle relaxation can be done quietly and quickly whenever the individual begins to feel tense.

Becoming Desensitized   The final step in the process is desensitization. It involves pairing the items in the anxiety hierarchy with the new response of relaxation. This is done by first having the client visualize the least-threatening item in the anxiety hierarchy. As the client reports feeling anxious while visualizing this scene, the therapist instructs him or her to begin the progressive relaxation response. The client continues to visualize the situation while trying to relax until the feeling of anxiety fades. With the first item in the hierarchy now associated with feeling relaxed instead of anxious, the client goes on to visualize the next item in the hierarchy. The desensitization process continues in this way until the client has learned to associate all of the situations in the hierarchy with feelings of relaxation.

The desensitization process may require several training sessions, as well as practice at home. In more advanced stages of therapy, the client might be instructed to engage in the relaxation response while actually in the threatening situation. For example, a shy adult might be instructed to go to a social gathering and stand at the edge of the room while engaging in the relaxation response until no longer feeling anxious. Then the person might take a few steps toward a group of people, stopping to relax if feelings of anxiety recur.

There is considerable evidence that systematic desensitization is effective as a treatment of certain anxiety disorders, particularly phobias (Comer, 1992; Davison & Neale, 1994; Kazdin & Wilcoxon, 1976; McNally, 1986; Wilson, 1989). Gordon L. Paul (1966) compared the effectiveness of three different types of therapy for treating the fear that college students have about speaking in public. The treatments compared were insight therapy (e.g., trying to understand why they had the fear), an attention-placebo treatment (e.g., taking a fake tranquilizer), and systematic desensitization (e.g., defining an anxiety hierarchy combined with relaxation training). A fourth group received no treatment. The results indicated that regardless of whether the assessment involved measuring the students' behavior while actually speaking in front of an audience, their self-reported ratings of anxiety, or their physiological responses, those students in the systematic desensitization treatment group indicated a greater decrease in their nervousness and anxiety than students receiving the other two types of treatments or no treatment at all. Even more impressive is that the reduction in anxiety and nervousness for the desensitization group over the other groups was still observable in a follow-up study 2 years later (Paul, 1969).

The effectiveness of behavior therapy is increased even more when the individual's cognitions (e.g., irrational beliefs and attitudes) about the feared situation are also considered (Mattick & Peters, 1988). Because many students suffer from speech anxiety, the following "Applications in Personality Psychology" feature on page 285 presents some ideas for coping with speech anxiety using the classical conditioning perspective.

Counterconditioning:
When Learning to Feel Bad Is Good
As noted in the preceding discussion, the process of systematic desensitization involves learning to replace unpleasant responses to certain stimuli with pleasant ones. Other situations might call for just the opposite reaction. **Counterconditioning** (also known as **aversion therapy**) is the process of using classical conditioning to replace a pleasant but maladaptive or inappropriate response to a certain stimuli with an unpleasant but adaptive or appropriate response (Comer, 1995; Martin & Pear, 1992).

APPLICATION

APPLICATIONS IN PERSONALITY PSYCHOLOGY

Coping with Speech Anxiety: Learning to Relax While Speaking in Public

According to Michael Motley, professor of rhetoric and speech communications at the University of California, approximately 85% of the general public have feelings of anxiety when speaking in public (Motley, 1988). Besides the obvious effect of making you look, feel, and sound nervous when you are actually giving the speech, speech anxiety can affect your speech performance in other ways. The anxiety associated with giving a speech probably prevents you from going to the library to gather information on the topic of your speech, practicing the speech, and concentrating on what you are supposed to be saying while giving the speech. Thus, it is not just the anxiety of actually giving the speech that affects speech performance, but probably a whole variety of actions associated with it as well. Just as it helps people to overcome other forms of anxiety, the process of systematic desensitization can also be applied to help individuals overcome their speech anxiety.

The first step is to construct an anxiety hierarchy associated with various events related to speaking in public. Here is an example of a public speaking anxiety hierarchy:

A Public Speaking Anxiety Hierarchy

1. Hearing the instructor remind you that the next set of class speeches is scheduled for one week from today.
2. Spending time in the library obtaining additional references for your speech.
3. Rehearsing your speech in your room in front of the mirror the night before the class.
4. Thinking about the speech while you are eating breakfast.
5. Thinking about the speech as you are going to school.
6. Thinking about the speech in the class before your speech class.
7. Standing outside the classroom where you will give the speech.
8. Sitting at your desk waiting as the instructor reviews the procedures for giving the speeches.
9. Hearing your name being called as the next speaker.
10. Standing at the podium with everyone watching you and wondering what they are thinking.
11. Starting your speech and feeling like your voice is cracking and your hands are shaking.
12. Losing your place momentarily while giving your speech.
13. Coming to the end of your speech, asking for questions from the other students, and fearing that you will not be able to give satisfactory answers.

This is only one of several possible public speaking anxiety hierarchies. You might want to add other items more specific to your own experiences with public speaking anxiety.

The next step is to practice the progressive relaxation exercise described on page 283. After establishing your relaxation response, the next step is to start the process of desensitization by associating each item in the anxiety hierarchy with the relaxation response.

As a therapeutic technique, counterconditioning has been used to help people in many ways, including

▲ Alleviating or stopping addictive behaviors to substances such as alcohol, cigarettes, and drugs (Blanchard, 1994; Emmelkamp, 1994; Cannon, Baker, & Wehl, 1981)

▲ Treating sexual deviance, including fetishism and making obscene phone calls (Boudewyns, Tanna, & Fleischman, 1975; Emmelkamp, 1994; McConaghy, 1971)

▲ Controlling self-mutilation such as head banging in autistic children (Emmelkamp, 1994; Lovaas & Simmons, 1969)

In the case of addictive behaviors, the individual has learned to associate the pleasant state of being "high" (CR) with the drug (CS). In the case of a fetish, the individual associates the pleasant feeling of being sexually aroused (CR) to an object or thought (CS) that is considered inappropriate (e.g., fantasies of children as sexual partners). In the case of self-mutilation, the autistic child might get a sense of novel stimulation (CR) from hitting its head (CS). As these cases demonstrate, while the CR is pleasant, it is considered maladaptive or inappropriate.

The Logic of Counterconditioning   The basic logic behind counterconditioning is to help prevent the maladaptive or inappropriate behavior patterns from occurring by associating them with unpleasant feelings. In a treatment program using counterconditioning, the client either performs—or is instructed by the therapist to perform—the unacceptable behavior or thought. Immediately after the client performs the unacceptable action, the therapist creates the aversive experience. The aversive experience can be created by any number of methods, including applying electric shock, injecting or ingesting nausea-producing drugs, or introducing unpleasant odors into the environment.

After repeated pairings of the unacceptable behavior with the aversive experience, the original, pleasant response (CR+) is replaced with a negative response (CR−). Thus, the unacceptable action now produces or triggers an unpleasant response.

For example, a client who is being treated for the fetish of becoming sexually aroused by the sight of children might have the therapist show him a series of color slides of children playing. Immediately after showing each slide, the therapist applies an electric shock to the client's arm. After numerous such pairings, the client will associate the thought of children as sexual partners with the unpleasantness of the electric shock. Another example might be treating an individual who has an addiction to alcohol. In this case, the individual might be asked to ingest a drug that when combined with alcohol makes the individual feel extremely nauseous. After repeated pairings of this nature, the individual will associate the drinking of alcohol with getting sick. Still another example might involve an individual who suffers from a problem of overeating. In this case, the individual might be instructed to eat certain foods (e.g., chocolate cake or other pastries) in a room in which a foul smell has been created. As a result, eating such foods will become associated with the unpleasant smell. In all of these cases, the counterconditioning process involves helping people learn to feel bad when feeling bad is good.

The Effectiveness and Limitations of Aversive Counterconditioning: Some Questions of Ethics and Logistics Do counterconditioning techniques work? Although some evidence suggests that it does (Claeson & Malm, 1973), a more general conclusion is that the latest evidence seems to suggest that aversive conditioning as a treatment technique alone is not very effective (Cannon, Baker, & Wehl, 1981; Kendall & Norton-Ford, 1982).

In addition to its limitations as a treatment technique, aversive conditioning has other limitations associated with its therapeutic use. One limitation concerns the ethical nature of such treatment (Kazdin, 1994). The notion of inflicting pain and discomfort on people, even when they seek it voluntarily, is an idea that many people find ethically unacceptable. Such concerns seem to be justified by evidence suggesting that the effectiveness of aversive techniques is not conclusive. For example, counterconditioning was not found to be more effective than placebo treatment control groups in a wide range of aversive treatments (cf. Diament & Wilson, 1975). Thus, if its effectiveness is questionable, then so is the idea of inflicting pain when performing the treatment.

Another limitation associated with aversive counterconditioning is that it loses its effectiveness as the client goes from the therapy sessions to the "real world." For example, the client may get anxious knowing the therapist will be administering the shock during the treatment session. But once the client leaves the office and the therapist is no longer present, the threat of receiving the noxious experience is gone. Not having the association between unacceptable behavior and the noxious stimulus weakens the effectiveness of the counterconditioning treatment program. One solution to this logistical problem has been to design counterconditioning techniques that clients can take with them outside of the treatment setting and into their everyday world. For details about such a counterconditioning technique, read "A Closer Look" on page 287.

A Closer Look:

Covert Sensitization:
Aversive Therapy "To Go"

Covert sensitization is an aversive counterconditioning procedure that involves creating mental images of an aversive stimuli (UCS) and pairing it with mental images of stimuli (CS) that are considered inappropriate (Cautela, 1966; Cautela & Kearney, 1993; Kazdin, 1994; Martin & Pear, 1992; Rathus & Nevid, 1991). Through such a process, the inappropriate stimuli will eventually come to trigger unpleasant feelings (CR) within the individual. Because these mental images are self-induced and can be generated at any time, this process requires very little input from the therapist.

While there is little direct involvement with the behavior therapist, essential to the process is the client being able to generate very vivid images while relaxing (Cautela, 1966). For example, to help people suffering from certain sexual deviations, therapists might ask these clients to imaging themselves vomiting while engaging in the sexually arousing but deviant behaviors (Callahan & Leitenberg, 1973) or to imagine the humiliating consequences of such deviant behavior (Hayes, Brownell, & Barlow, 1978).

The following scenario is based on the use of covert sensitization as part of a treatment program for an adult male who was in a psychiatric facility due to his multiple sexual deviations (exhibitionism and sadistic fantasies involving bondage and forced sex) and criminal sexual behavior (being arrested for exhibitionism and attempted rape). As part of his treatment, the man was asked to imagine the aversive consequences of his exhibitionism:

I see this woman walking up the sidewalk near my car. I call her over to the car in a tone of voice that sounds like I'm in trouble. She can't see that I'm masturbating in the car. When she gets near the window, she notices my erect penis and the look on her face changes from concern to shock and embarrassment. I quickly drive away. But as I look into the rear view mirror, I see her look back and start thinking to myself, "Damn it, she knows my license plate." I begin to get really nervous that she might report me. When I get home, I still have this worried look on my face. My wife asks, "What's the matter with you?" I tell her I just had a really bad day. Just as we are sitting down to dinner, we hear a knock at the door. I open it and three police officers charge into the house and announce that I am under arrest for indecent exposure. My wife starts screaming at me, "How could you! How could you! I am leaving you!"
(Based on Hayes, Brownell, & Barlow, 1978)

Although less extreme, the information in the "You Can Do It" feature on page 288 allows you to try for yourself the process of covert sensitization.

This concludes the discussion of the applications of classical conditioning principles. For more information about the application of classical conditioning principles to different aspects of behavior, read *Behavior Modification: Behavioral Approaches to Human Problems* (Redd, Porterfield, & Anderson, 1979), *Behavior Modification: What It Is and How to Do It* (Martin & Pear, 1992), and *Behavior Therapy: Techniques and Empirical Findings* (Masters, Burish, Hollon, & Rimm, 1987). These textbooks contain a variety of interesting examples and case studies. This section also concludes the discussion of the classical conditioning perspective. In the next section, you will examine the operant conditioning perspective.

The Operant Conditioning Perspective: The Learning of Consequences

In the process of classical conditioning, what is learned is an association between the appearance of some stimulus and the response it triggers. If the stimulus is not presented, either mentally or physically, the response does not occur. For example, the warm feelings you might have dialing the telephone number of that friend with the friendly voice will occur whether someone says the number out loud or you notice a piece of paper with the number on it sitting on the desk. Thus, the response occurs only *after* the stimulus is presented.

In sharp contrast to this process of learning associations is the process of learning involved in

YOU CAN DO IT

Increasing Your Study Time: Using Your Imagination to Get Yourself to Study

For some direct experience with the process of covert sensitization, consider applying the following technique to increase the amount of time you spend studying. Try to imagine the following scene the next time you are distracted while studying:

Imagine that you are sitting at your desk trying to study. However, while studying at your desk, you begin to feel bored. You decide that talking to a friend will give you a needed distraction to make you feel better. As you turn your head away from your books and notes on the desk where you are studying and look toward the phone, you begin to feel a little uneasy in your stomach.

Although you are now feeling a little sick, you begin to reach for the phone. As you stop studying and start to touch the phone, you begin to feel even more nausea in the pit of your stomach. Your stomach now begins to get real tight, as if you are having severe cramps. No longer studying, you begin to dial your friend's number. But as you are dialing the number, you can feel vomit starting to move up your throat. With the phone in your hand, you feel the thick volume of vomit fill your mouth. In the next instant, you begin to vomit all over the phone and the hand dialing your friend's number.

The stench coming from the vomit reminds you of what it smells like as you open up a plastic trash bag that has been sitting in the hot summer sun for three days filled with pieces of raw chicken that you threw out because they were starting to spoil. The stench and sight of the greenish-brown, thick vomit all over the phone, your hand, and the front of your clothes are more than you can take. You decide to put the phone back on the receiver and not call your friend after all.

As you put the phone down and turn your head back to your books and notes, you immediately begin to feel better. You decide now that you will go to the bathroom to get a towel to clean off yourself, the phone, and the desk so that you can immediately return to studying. As you have these thoughts of getting back to studying, you begin to feel more relaxed and refreshed. With everything clean, you are now studying again. As you are studying, notice how good you feel. Notice how this feeling differs from the stench associated with calling your friend on the phone during your study session. You now feel so much better after being back studying. You now look forward to a very pleasant study session.

Notice that in the scenario, careful attention was paid to being as specific as possible regarding the stimulus that is being conditioned. In this case, what is being counterconditioned is the good feeling you have when you *stop studying to call your friend*. The intention is not to make you feel sick each time you begin to call your friend on the phone, but only when you call your friend on the phone when you should be studying. Such considerations are extremely important when formulating images for the purpose of covert sensitization. If you learn how to do it correctly, you will find that the process of covert sensitization can be very helpful. And because it is all done "in your head," aversive counterconditioning is available whenever or wherever you may need it. In this sense, you can think of covert sensitization as "aversive therapy to go."

operant conditioning. In **operant conditioning**, the emphasis is on learning the *consequences* of certain behaviors (Barker, 1994; Domjan, 1993; Kazdin, 1994; Malott, Whaley, & Malott, 1993). More specifically, the behavior that is performed determines whether the individual gets something pleasant or unpleasant as a consequence. While thinking about the telephone number of the person with the friendly voice triggers feelings of warmth and joy, if you dial the wrong number, you will not actually get to hear that voice and will probably have feelings of disappointment. Thus, for operant conditioning, the critical elements are the specific behaviors (e.g., learning to dial more carefully) and the consequences they produce (e.g., hearing the friendly voice).

The Basic Principles: The Determinants of Consequences

In this section, we will discuss the nature and operation of the basic principles of the operant conditioning perspective and the contribution they have made to the study of personality.

The Law of Effect

While Pavlov was teaching dogs to salivate to bells in Russia, a famous American psychologist by the name of Edward Thorndike was trying to get cats to let themselves out of a problem box. The cats had to press a lever that would allow them to get to some food placed outside of the box. What Thorndike found was that the cat would wander around the box until it accidentally stepped on the lever, which opened the door and made the food available. When he put the cat back into the box, Thorndike found that the cat was much more likely to press the lever this time than when placed in the box the first time. After several tries, the cat stepped on the lever immediately after being placed in the box.

A major outcome of this work was what Thorndike (1911) referred to as the "law of effect." As a fundamental concept of operant conditioning, the **law of effect** states that behaviors leading to favorable or pleasant consequences will be strengthened and have a greater likelihood of being performed again (Barker, 1994; Catania, 1992; Domjan, 1993). For example, if an individual finds that smiling at others produces a greater likelihood of them saying "hello" than a frown, the person is much more likely to smile at people than not smile at them. On the other hand, if a person finds that being assertive results in receiving better service at a restaurant, the individual is much more likely to behave in an assertive manner in the future. In using the law of effect to explain personality, the first example indicates that the individual might develop a very friendly personality, while in the second example, the person might develop a rather assertive personality as a result of the consequence of their respective actions.

A reinforcer is anything that serves to increase the likelihood of a behavior occurring again. Making money, eating delicious food, and owning a fancy car all serve to increase the likelihood that individuals will engage in some form of behavior (e.g., go to work) that makes obtaining these items possible. What are some reinforcers for you?

The Concept of Reinforcement and the Strengthening of Behavioral Tendencies

At the very core of the process of operant conditioning is the concept of reinforcement. From the operant conditioning perspective, **reinforcement** is the tendency for a behavior to be strengthened by increasing the likelihood of it being performed.

Central to the concept of reinforcement is what is called a reinforcer. A **reinforcer** is any object that when presented *after* a behavior occurs, increases the likelihood of that behavior occurring again. In the language of operant conditioning, a reinforcer is not the same thing as a reward. While the term *reward* typically has a pleasant connotation, this does not mean it will necessarily increase the likelihood of a behavior occurring. For example, offering to take a little boy to a baseball game if he eats his spinach may not necessarily be effective in increasing the likelihood of eating the vegetable if the child does not like baseball. On the other hand, some adults will work very hard for 50 weeks a year so that they can spend a few days sitting in a cold, muddy swamp at 5:00 a.m. to hunt ducks. While subjecting yourself to that kind of discomfort is not everyone's idea of a reward for working hard all year, for some people it is enough to get them up each day and off to work, thus fitting the definition of a reinforcer. For a better understanding of the concept of reinforcement, think of this very simple rule: *Reinforcers are defined by what they do, not by what they are.* And what reinforcers do is strengthen behavior by increasing the likelihood of it occurring again. Based on this rule, sitting in a muddy swamp is a reinforcer for some people, while sitting in the bleachers on a sunny day may not be a reinforcer for others.

Positive and Negative Reinforcement

In the context of reinforcement, a distinction can be made between positive and negative reinforcers. A **positive reinforcer** increases the likelihood of a behavior occurring again if the reinforcer is presented after the behavior has occurred. For example, receiving a good grade after you studied hard for a test in your personality psychology course would be a positive reinforcer if it increased the likelihood of your engaging in this type of industrious behavior again for the next test.

A **negative reinforcer** increases the likelihood of a behavior occurring again when performing the behavior results in the removal or termination of an aversive stimulus. For example, you might wiggle the antenna on the top of your television again and again because doing so removes the distortion on the screen. In this case, removing the distortion is the negative reinforcer that is a consequence of adjusting the antenna. Another example would be that engaging in the assertive behavior of complaining to the headwaiter is strengthened because doing so results in not having to wait for some service at a restaurant. In this example, not having to wait any longer is the consequence of engaging in the assertive behavior. If such assertive behavior occurs the next time the person has to wait an unreasonable length of time, the assertive behavior would be considered to be strengthened based on negative reinforcement. Thus, reinforcement, whether it is positive (i.e., presenting the reinforcer) or negative (i.e., terminating an aversive stimulus), is defined by what it does—it increases the likelihood of a behavior being performed.

Primary and Secondary Reinforcers

Another way of understanding the concept of reinforcement is to distinguish between primary and secondary reinforcers. **Primary reinforcers** have reinforcement value because of the way an organism is constructed. For example, because of our biological makeup, things like food, water, warmth, and the avoidance of pain can serve as powerful determinants of behavior. **Secondary reinforcers** acquire their reinforcement value through their association with primary reinforcers. For example, money has a high degree of reinforcement value because it can be used to purchase food, shelter, and comfort. Parents might use a weekly allowance and employers could use a monthly bonus as secondary reinforcers for developing a type of personality that includes responsible and conscientious behaviors (e.g., a son cleaning up his room; an employee surpassing her sales quota).

The Concept of Punishment and the Weakening of Behavioral Tendencies

The concept of **punishment** involves reducing the likelihood of a behavior occurring by producing a consequence the individual would rather avoid. For example, an employer is using punishment if he docks employees $10.00 each time they are late for work. The objective here would be to reduce the likelihood of employees showing up late.

A very common misconception is to confuse punishment with negative reinforcement. But from the operant conditioning perspective, they are completely different; punishment is designed to *decrease* the likelihood of a behavior occurring, while negative reinforcement is designed to *increase* the likelihood. In the preceding example, if the boss stops yelling at the employees each time they show up on time for work, this would illustrate the use of negative reinforcement because showing up on time terminates the yelling.

This concludes the discussion of the basic principles of operant conditioning. What seems to be critical to explaining each principle is the consequence it has on behavior. But to examine an application of operant conditioning based on a lack of a relationship between behaviors and their consequences, read the following "Applications in Personality Psychology" feature below.

APPLICATION

APPLICATIONS IN PERSONALITY PSYCHOLOGY

Helplessness, Hopelessness, and Depression: Illustrating the Consequences of Uncontrollability

It is generally agreed that operant conditioning has as its basis the establishment of a relationship between a specific behavior and the consequences that particular behavior produces. But University of Pennsylvania psychologist Martin Seligman and his colleagues have made a rather significant application of operant conditioning to the study of depression based on the absence of a relationship between behaviors and their consequences. According to Seligman (1975), people become depressed when they experience learned helplessness. **Learned helplessness** is a condition characterized by apathy and passivity when people

feel that the negative consequences experienced are independent of their actions. An example of this state of affairs would be the sadness a student feels about believing that there is no relationship between the amount of time spent studying for (i.e., the behavior pattern) and the grade received (i.e., the consequence) in a particular class.

Inducing Helplessness: Creating a Sense of Uncontrollability

In early demonstrations of learned helplessness, Seligman and his colleagues (Overmier & Seligman, 1967; Seligman & Maier, 1967) placed dogs in cages where they received an electric shock through the grid at the bottom of the cage. Some dogs were unrestrained, so they could escape the shock by jumping over a barrier; other dogs were restrained by a harness that made escape impossible. When placed in a different situation, where both groups of dogs could escape the shock by jumping over a barrier, only those dogs who had previously been able to control their fate by jumping over the barrier did so. The other group of dogs sat passively and accepted their fate without trying to escape. The dogs who experienced the initial lack of control displayed behavioral tendencies characteristic of depressed individuals, such as lethargy, lack of motivation, and difficulties in learning new behaviors (Maier & Seligman, 1976).

Similar results have also been observed when humans are placed in experimental situations where they have no control over unpleasant events, such as working on problems or puzzles that could not be solved (Maier & Seligman, 1976). More specifically, people were placed in laboratory conditions where they worked on a series of problems. Some of the problems had solutions; others did not. In subsequent situations where these people were working on problems that *could be solved*, the people who had experienced situations where they did not seem to have control demonstrated a loss in perseverance, problem-solving ability, and sense of humor, as well as an increase in aggression, in comparison to the people who had previously worked on problems that could be solved. Behavioral tendencies such as lowered perseverance, a decrease in problem-solving ability, and reduced sense of humor are all characteristic symptoms of depression (Davison & Neale, 1994; Seligman, 1975).

Hopelessness as an Explanation of Helplessness: The Linking of Helplessness and Depression

While the concept of helplessness can be used to describe the apathetic behavior displayed by those who have experienced uncontrolled negative consequences, it does not necessarily explain why it occurs. Seligman and others (Abramson, Metalsky, & Alloy, 1989; Abramson, Seligman, & Teasdale, 1978; Metalsky, Joiner, Hardin, & Abramson, 1993) proposed that a critical factor in the expression of helplessness is the individual's interpretation of the original uncontrollable events.

People are most likely to exhibit helplessness when they develop a personal sense of hopelessness. **Hopelessness** is a condition that develops when the individual attempts to provide a causal explanation for the negative consequences by assuming an excessive sense of personal responsibility for and perceiving an inability to change them. More specifically, the basis of developing a sense of hopelessness is when the individual assumes that the inability to alter the outcome of the uncontrollable, negative consequences are *internal* (e.g., it's my fault that I don't know what to do), *stable* (e.g., I'm going to be this inept forever), and *global* (e.g., no matter in what situation I am, the same thing will happen—nothing will turn out right) (Metalsky Halberstadt, Abramson, 1987; Peterson, Schulman, Castellon, & Seligman, 1991; Peterson & Seligman, 1984). Thus, it is the sense of hopelessness that contributes to the individual giving up and exhibiting a behavior pattern of helplessness so symptomatic of depression.

Basic Processes of Operant Conditioning: The Acquisition and Maintenance of Consequences

It should be clear that reinforcement and punishment are important determinants of behavior. But just as important is how the reinforcement and punishment are administered within the process of operant conditioning. Four basic processes of operant conditioning involved in administering reinforcement and punishment are schedules of reinforcement, the partial reinforcement effect, shaping, and stimulus control.

Schedules of Reinforcement: Guidelines for Giving

A **schedule of reinforcement** is a plan for deciding when reinforcements will be given during the process of operant conditioning. In addition to helping to plan when the reinforcement will be given, a specific schedule of reinforcement also determines the rate at which the behavior is performed (Barker, 1995; Catania, 1992; Kazdin, 1994; Malott, Whaley, & Malott, 1993). The four major schedules of reinforcement discussed in this section are fixed ratio, variable ratio, fixed interval, and variable interval (Skinner & Ferster, 1957).

Fixed-Ratio Schedule   In a **fixed-ratio schedule**, the individual is given the reinforcement after a fixed number of responses. As seen in Figure 10.2, such a schedule typically produces a rather high rate of responding because the individual knows that after the specific number of responses, let's say 10, the reinforcement is given. As a result, the individual

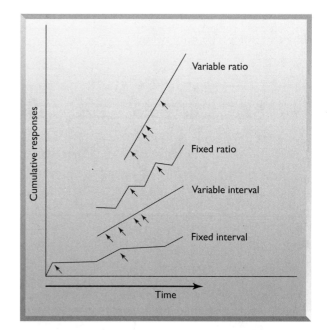

Figure 10.2
An illustration of the distinct response patterns produced by the different schedules of reinforcement. The presentation of the reinforcer is indicated by each arrow ➤.

Doing piece work, in which the individual is paid for each item or a fixed number of items produced, is an example of a fixed-ration schedule. The individual shown above is paid a fixed price for each computer he tests.

Playing a slot machine is a good example of a variable-ratio schedule of reinforcement. While playing, these people must continue to pay to pull the level but do not know how many times they must perform this action before they are reinforced with a payoff. The pattern of the payoff varies.

quickly performs the 10 responses, gets the reinforcement, and starts performing again. A good example of a fixed-ratio schedule is when factory workers are paid $2.00 for every six boxes of tools they can pack. As a result of such a schedule, the most money goes to those who have learned to be ambitious.

Variable-Ratio Schedule   In a **variable-ratio schedule**, the number of responses to be performed before giving the reinforcement is varied. This type of schedule also tends to produce a rather high rate of responding (see Figure 10.2). The reason seems to be that because receiving the reinforcement is less predictable, the more responses the individual produces, the greater the possibility of receiving the reinforcer. As a result, the variable-ratio schedule does tend to produce a rather steady rate of responding. A good example of a variable-ratio schedule is playing a slot machine. Because people never really know when the slot machine will pay off, they continuously drop money into the machine at a rather steady pace for hours (or until they run out of money). This steady rate of behavior occurs because people are "sure" that on the next play, or maybe the next, they will win the jackpot. With such a schedule, what people are doing is playing the odds.

A good example of behavior being regulated by a fixed-interval schedule is the study behavior of most college students. Because college examinations tend to come at specific times in the semester (e.g, about once every 5 weeks), students tend to concentrate their study efforts just before the test.

Fixed-Interval Schedule   A **fixed-interval schedule** involves the reinforcement being presented after a specific amount of time has passed. For example, being paid once a week or once a month is an example of a fixed-interval schedule. As seen in Figure

10.2, such a schedule tends to produce only a moderate rate of responding. What typically happens is that the individual maintains a relatively low rate of responding, with short bursts of activity occurring just before and just after being given the reinforcement. For example, employees who are paid once a week on Friday tend to work the hardest on Friday and Monday. Another example would be the student who tends to study hard just before the test, as well as a few days after it, and does very little studying in between. Since tests are typically scheduled at specific times during the course (e.g., one test every three to four weeks), such a situation, and the pattern of study behavior it produces, is characteristic of the fixed-ratio schedule.

Variable-Interval Schedule A **variable-interval schedule** involves varying the amount of time required before the reinforcement is given. Variable-interval schedules tend to produce a moderate but rather steady rate of responding (see Figure 10.2). The reason is that as long as the individual is uncertain of how much time must pass before the reinforcement will occur, he or she will continue to respond. An example of this would be the patience seen in people who like to fish. In most cases, they do not know if they will have to wait 10 minutes or 2 hours before their next catch (e.g., reinforcement). As a result, it is not uncommon to observe anglers sitting patiently for hours.

Extinction and the Partial Reinforcement Effect:
The Benefit of Being Inconsistent
In the process of operant conditioning, **extinction** refers to a situation in which a learned response is no longer reinforced when it is emitted. With extinction, what typically happens is that this behavior then tends to occur with less frequency. For example, when a child is crying for some candy, the parent can begin to ignore the child's screams as a means of eliminating this behavior. But one of the most interesting aspects of operant conditioning is what is referred to as the partial reinforcement effect.

The **partial reinforcement effect** refers to the tendency for behaviors that have been reinforced intermittently to persist longer in the face of extinction than behaviors that have been reinforced regularly (Barker, 1995; Catania, 1992; Martin & Pear, 1992).

Because the person shown fishing does not know how long the line must be kept in the water before a fish takes it, the time between casting the line and catching the fish, which serves as the reinforcer, will vary.

On the surface, this statement seems counterintuitive in that *less* reward produces *more* resistance to extinction. But this effect tends to occur because when a reinforcer is given regularly, the person comes to expect it at a particular time (e.g., fixed interval) or after a fixed pattern of behavior (e.g., fixed ratio). If the regularly appearing reinforcement is no longer given, the person quickly concludes that it is not coming.

When the reinforcement appears irregularly, the person is never really sure if the reinforcer is no longer coming, if it will appear on the next response (e.g., variable ratio), or if he or she will have to wait just a little longer for it (e.g., variable interval). In a situation like this, since the person is so uncertain, it will take him or her a much longer time to conclude that the reinforcer is no longer being presented.

A familiar example is the child crying for candy. In most situations like this, what typically happens when the parent tries to ignore the child (i.e., the process of extinction) is that the child screams even louder. The child does this because in the past, sometimes screaming louder has worked (i.e., partial reinforcement). So the child reasons that if he screams louder, the parent will give up and buy the candy. If the parent tries to resist, the child screams louder and louder, until the child either realizes that the parent means business this time or the parent, out of a fit of embarrassment, gives in and buys the candy. In the former case, the next time the child cries for candy and the parent says "no", the child will stop crying right away. In the latter case, the next time the child cries for candy, it will scream even louder and longer.

The next time you are waiting in line at the supermarket and you see a child asking a parent for candy, you might try to assess the child's learning history for this behavior based on the level and duration of the screams. As this example illustrates, one of the outcomes of being inconsistent with reinforcement is that it produces behavior that is rather resistant to extinction.

Shaping: Molding Behavior One Step at a Time

To help people learn complex behavior patterns, operant conditioning uses the process of shaping. **Shaping** is a process by which a target behavior is broken down into smaller steps so the individual is reinforced for performing behaviors that are closer and closer approximations of the desired behavior (Barker, 1995; Kazdin, 1994; Malott, Whaley, & Malott, 1993). The logic here is that what is important in the process of learning a new behavior is to be reinforced constantly for the efforts made, even if the first attempts are not perfect. The secret to the successful use of shaping is to gradually increase the expectations for giving the reinforcement as the person masters the individual steps.

The process of shaping has been quite valuable when used in the therapeutic setting to help people learn new, more adaptive forms of behavior. When trying to help a woman overcome her shyness about speaking to new people, a therapist might first verbally reinforce (e.g., praise) the client for going out of her house to lectures, plays, and other social events. Next, the therapist would reinforce her only for going up to strangers at these social events and saying "hello." The next step might involve reinforcing her whenever she makes a comment to the stranger, such as "What did you think of the speaker?" She would then be reinforced only when she carries on a conversation for at least two minutes, followed by reinforcement only for conversations longer than five minutes. The point is that if the therapist had waited to reinforce the woman for engaging in a five-minute conversation in the early stages of the therapy process, she might never have received reinforcement

and would have become discouraged and terminated the therapy.

Thus, a major advantage of shaping as an operant conditioning process is that it enables people to experience success very early in the process of learning a new behavior. You might keep this bit of information in mind the next time you are getting a little frustrated trying to learn something new. It could be that all you need to do is to break the target behavior down so that you are learning it "one step at a time."

Stimulus Control: Learning the Limits of Consequences

A point that has been continually emphasized in this section is that the reinforcement or punishment must follow the behavior. **Stimulus control** refers to the tendency for the individual to perform a certain behavior because of the cues that are present in the surrounding environment. Such cues are the stimuli that dictate what behavior is most likely to produce the reinforcement. Two important aspects of stimulus control are generalization and discrimination.

Generalization   **Generalization** refers to the tendency to extend a particular behavior pattern from the situation in which it was originally learned to other similar situations. For example, initially, you might have learned that using assertive behavior results in receiving better service when you dine at a local Greek restaurant. At a local Italian restaurant, you also find that speaking assertively to the headwaiter results in receiving a very good table and fast service. Finally, after receiving unsatisfactory service at an auto dealership, you decide to get assertive with the service manager. Although the situations are different, you have gradually learned that certain cues (e.g., being mistreated) call for a specific behavior pattern (e.g., being assertive) that will have a similar consequence (e.g., getting satisfaction). Thus, the degree of generalization is determined by the extent to which the cues from one situation are perceived as calling for a similar pattern of behavior in other situations. What is learned here is that the utility of specific behaviors can be extended to other situations.

Discrimination   **Discrimination** refers to the tendency to respond differently to different situations based on the available cues. For example, while being assertive has gotten you satisfaction at the auto dealership, you might discover that it only works with the evening service manager. With the daytime manager, you might have discovered that being assertive also involves speaking in very loud tones and threatening to write a letter to the dealership's owner. From such experience, you have learned to alter your behavioral response (e.g., assertive vs. angry and threatening) depending on what cues are present (e.g., daytime vs. evening service manager) in a particular situation in order to achieve the desired consequence (e.g., getting satisfaction). In another situation, you might find that behaving in an angry and threatening manner results in getting punched in the nose. In such a situation, you would be wise to use the process of discrimination to learn when to just keep quiet.

This concludes the discussion of some basic processes of operant conditioning. In the next section, you will learn how these principles are used to help explain certain aspects of personality.

The Shaping of Specific Aspects of Personality: Becoming Superstitious, Altruistic, Compulsive, and Even More Prejudiced

This section describes how the basic principles and processes of operant conditioning can shape specific aspects of personality, including superstitious, altruistic, compulsive, and prejudicial behavior.

Becoming Superstitious

In some cases, the principles and processes of operant conditioning can be used to explain superstitious behavior (Skinner, 1948). The logic is that if a person happens to receive a reinforcer after engaging in some behavior, the person will tend to do that behavior again, even if the behavior had nothing to do with getting the reinforcer. As an example, some basketball fans may cross their fingers when a player from their team is shooting a crucial basket. If the ball goes into the basket, the fans will probably cross their fingers the next time a crucial shot is taken. In a similar manner, a student gets a good grade as a consequence of wearing his "lucky socks," or a passenger sits in the same seat on a plane to make sure she will

arrive at her destination safely. What seems to be critical to developing superstitious behavior is that a specific action (e.g., crossing fingers or wearing lucky socks) *seems* to be related to the favorable consequence and is thus repeated.

Becoming Altruistic

From the operant conditioning perspective, altruistic tendencies are based on the extent to which individuals have previously been reinforced or punished for helping others (Buss, 1995; Schroeder, Penner, Dovidio, & Piliavin, 1995). For example, people who were rewarded with verbal praise when giving directions to a stranger (e.g., "Thanks. I really appreciate your help.") were much more likely to help subsequent strangers than were people who received punishment in the form of negative comments (e.g., "I can't understand you. I'll ask someone else.") (Moss & Page, 1972). Thus, whether a person chooses to lend a helping hand probably depends on the extent to which that hand has been shaken or bitten when offered in the past.

Becoming Compulsive

An **obsessive-compulsive disorder** is when an individual feels compelled to think about or carry out a particular act to reduce feelings of anxiety. In minor forms of this disorder, many people feel compelled to check all of the doors twice before being able to go to sleep; others feel compelled to check the answers on their test four times before handing it in to the professor. In more extreme forms, compulsive behaviors may involve having to wash one's hands a hundred times a day, or having to put on clothes in exactly the same order each day before being able to go to work. From the operant conditioning perspective, compulsive behaviors occur because performing them produces negative reinforcement (Carr, 1971; Comer, 1992, 1995; Davison & Neale, 1994; Hodgson & Rachman, 1972). For example, each time a woman washes her hands, she eliminates her feelings of anxiety. Because the reduction of anxiety tends to occur immediately after the compulsive behavior is performed, it tends to acquire a high probability of occurring the next time the woman feels anxiety.

Maintaining Attitudes and Strengthening Prejudice

While principles of classical conditioning could be used in explaining the development of certain attitudes, the evidence also suggests that operant conditioning can maintain and strengthen these attitudes (Baron & Byrne, 1994; Petty & Cacioppo, 1981; Zimbardo, Ebbesen, & Maslach, 1977; Zimbardo & Leippe, 1991). For example, an office manager's negative attitudes toward Italians could be strengthened by co-workers smiling or laughing each time she makes a derogatory statement about members of this group. Such favorable consequences for expressing these negative attitudes will certainly strengthen and increase the likelihood of their occurring again, as well as increasing the possibility of these attitudes being generalized to related forms of behavioral discrimination (e.g., refusing to hire Italians).

In this section, you explored a few of the many ways the principles and processes of operant conditioning can be used to shape personality. In the next section, you will learn about some applications of the principles and processes of operant conditioning.

Applications of the Operant Conditioning Perspective: Using What Is Known

The term **behavior modification** is typically used to describe the application of operant conditioning principles to practical problems, because the main objective is to modify the problematic behavior (Kazdin, 1994; Martin & Pear, 1992; Rathus & Nevid, 1991; Ullmann & Krasner, 1965, 1969; Krasner & Ullmann, 1965). In the following section, you will consider some applications of operant conditioning principles to several practical problems: self-control, token economies, biofeedback, and the use of punishment.

Self-Control: Adding That Personal Touch to Behavior Modification
A very personalized form of behavior modification is the technique of self-control. **Self-control** involves a program of behavior modification in which people use operant conditioning to alter their own behavior (Martin & Pear, 1992). Regardless of the behavior being modified, the technique of self-control can be divided into three phases: self-monitoring, self-evaluation, and self-reinforcement/punishment.

Self-Monitoring Phase   During the self-monitoring phase, the individual is required to observe his or her behavior to determine the nature of its stimulus con-

trol. Self-Monitoring requires the individual to keep a record of what stimuli seem to trigger a specific or problematic behavior, and what reinforcers seem to maintain it. This record might include the time of day, the location, and any other thoughts or feelings the individual may have had when the behavior occurred. For example, when applying the self-control technique to the problem of overeating, a man might note when, where, and why snacking on fatty foods seems to occur. Attempting to keep accurate records during the self-monitoring phase is extremely important, for two reasons: (a) it gives the individual a better picture of the nature and severity of the problematic behavior, and (b) research indicates that just keeping track of the problematic behavior can help in reducing its occurrence (Johnson & White, 1971; Kazdin, 1994).

Self-Evaluation Phase   The self-evaluation phase involves the individual determining a realistic goal for the existence of the target behavior. In some cases, this may involve decreasing (e.g., the amount of time the person spends thinking depressing thoughts) or increasing (e.g., the amount of time the person will spend studying) the target behavior. In the preceding example, the man might have discovered, based on self-monitoring records, that he tends to eat a lot of snacks during the evening (i.e., when) while in front of the TV (i.e., where), particularly right after returning from the kitchen with a snack during the commercials (i.e., why). In this case, the target behavior might be to have only two after-dinner snacks during the evening. It is important that the target behavior be realistic, so that the individual stands a reasonable chance of experiencing success in the beginning of the program. Seeking the assistance of a therapist who uses behavior modification might be helpful in determining a realistic goal.

Self-Reinforcement/Punishment Phase   In the self-reinforcement/punishment phase, the individual then decides the reinforcement or punishment to be received if the behavior is performed. In selecting the reinforcement or punishment, it is important to select something that can be administered easily and immediately. For example, it does little good to promise yourself ten dollars for a desired behavior if you do not have the ten dollars. In the preceding example, the man might decide that if he does not eat during a commercial, he will allow himself to watch television until the next commercial. If he eats during the commercial, he must turn off the television for 10 minutes.

Do such self-control techniques work? Although it is not conclusive (Kazdin, 1994), some evidence indicates that self-control techniques have been effective in the following problematic behaviors:

▲ Treating depression (Fuchs & Rehm, 1977)
▲ Alleviating uncontrollable eye-twitching (Ollendick, 1981)
▲ Reducing cigarette smoking (Belles & Bradlyn, 1987)

▲ Achieving weight gain (Gulanick, Woodburn, & Rimm, 1975)
▲ Achieving weight loss (O'Leary & Wilson, 1975)

In fact, in a survey of different behavior treatment programs for weight loss, the inclusion of a self-control component was considered important, regardless of the program (O'Leary & Wilson, 1975).

If you are considering applying the technique of self-control to some aspect of your own behavior, the material in "You Can Do It" on this page may help you succeed in your program of behavior modification.

YOU CAN DO IT

Strategies for Successful Self-Control: Giving Yourself an Added Advantage

In their book *Adjustment and Growth: The Challenges of Life*, Spencer Rathus and Jeffrey Nevid (1992) offer some excellent suggestions for maximizing the success of a self-control program. These suggestions include the following strategies:

▲ Strategies for controlling the environment
—*Restrict the stimulus field.* Gradually begin to eliminate the undesirable behavior from your environment. For example, eat only at the table, not in front of the television, or study only when you are at your desk, not in bed.
—*Stay away from stimuli that trigger the undesired behavior.* Avoid placing yourself in situations where you will be tempted to engage in undesirable behavior. For example, don't go window shopping if you don't have the money to spend, or don't drive by your favorite "pig-out" place.
▲ Strategies for making performing undesirable behaviors more difficult
—*Engage in competing responses.* Perform behaviors that are incompatible with undesired behaviors. For example, drink fruit juice instead of a milk shake, or put a piece of celery in your mouth instead of a cigarette.

—*Breaking the chain.* Make it harder to engage in undesirable behaviors. For example, place two chairs in front of the refrigerator, or put your credit cards in the back of the highest cabinet at home.
▲ Strategies for controlling the consequences of undesirable behaviors
—*Make responses cost.* Pay a penalty each time you engage in the undesirable behavior. For example, each time you smoke a cigarette, crumble up three more. Mail $2.00 to your least-favorite charity each time you snack at school.
—*Reinforce desired behavior.* Make something you like doing contingent on something you do not like doing. For example, watch television only after you have studied for one hour, or have a snack only after you have had three glasses of water or tomato juice.
—*Use covert reinforcement.* Give yourself mental rewards after engaging in a desired behavior. For example, after you resist eating during a commercial, imagine how good you are going to look this summer with a better body. Or imagine how much greater you will feel after not giving in to the urge for a cigarette.

As you can see, these strategies are all relatively easy, inexpensive, and self-controlled. The more of them you can build into your own self-control program, the greater the likelihood that you will achieve your desired behavioral objectives.

The Token Economy: Living in an Operant World

While the self-control technique involves applying operant conditioning principles to one person at a time, the token economy involves applying these principles to several people at the same time. In a **token economy**, people are given tokens (e.g., poker chips or play money) having different values whenever they engage in desirable behaviors (Comer, 1995; Kazdin, 1994; Martin & Pear, 1992; Masters, Burish, Hollon, & Rimm, 1987). These tokens can then be redeemed for various objects (e.g., candy) or privileges (e.g., playing pool). In token economies, the tokens are secondary reinforcers given for performing appropriate behaviors.

In a classic example of the use of a token economy, Ayllon and Azrin (1965) set aside an entire ward of a mental hospital, where patients were given plastic tokens for performing such behaviors as making their beds, combing their hair, mopping floors, washing dishes, serving meals, and following instructions. Tokens were taken away when a patient acted bizarre or did not participate in ward activities. After having the opportunity to earn up to 70 tokens a week for various work assignments, the patients could then spend them for such things as leaving the ward for a 20-minute walk (two tokens), their choice of a television program (three tokens), selected reading materials (two to five tokens), and a trip to town with an escort (100 tokens), to name just a few.

Does such a technique work? In Ayllon and Azrin's experiment, the result of introducing a token economy was that these previously uninvolved and apathetic patients, who had been hospitalized an average of 16 years, responded immediately to the program by demonstrating a dramatic increase in the amount of on-ward performance (Ayllon & Azrin, 1965). This dramatic increase can be seen in Figure 10.3 (at 0–20 days). When the token economy was removed (20–40 days), the amount of ward participation dropped considerably. Finally, as a test of its effectiveness, when the token economy was reintroduced (40–60 days), the amount of on-ward participation, as shown in Figure 10.3, again increased dramatically.

Similar successes with token economies have been documented with prisoners (Kazdin, 1994), drug addicts (Budney, Higgins, Delaney, Kent, & Bickel, 1991), hyperactive children (Wulbert & Dries, 1977), juvenile delinquents (Wolf, Phillips, Fixsen, Braukmann, Kirigin, Willner, & Schumaker, 1976), and retarded children in community-type environments (Birnbrauer, Wolf, Kidder, Tague, 1965), as well as with children in regular classrooms (O'Leary & Drabman, 1971). But critical to the success of a token economy is the ability of the operators to consistently control the dispersement of the tokens. For example, if only some staff members reinforce the patients for combing their hair while others do not, the patients will learn to comb their hair only some of the time.

The Problem of Generalizing from the Token Economy to the Real World   While token economies have been quite successful, one problem seems to be the extent to which the behavior learned within the token economy generalizes to the real world (Comer, 1995; Martin & Pear, 1992). For example, hospitalized patients are less likely to comb their hair outside of

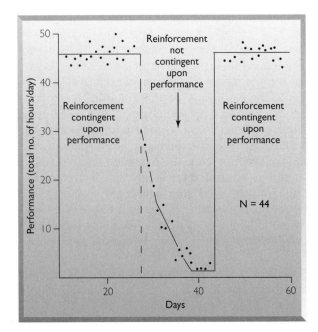

Figure 10.3

The effects of a token economy on institutionalized patients when receiving the tokens were contingent (0–20 days), not contingent (20–40 days), and reintroduced as being contingent (40–60 days) on appropriate on-ward behavior.

Note. The Measurement and Reinforcements of Behavior of Psychotics From *Journal of Experimental Analysis of Behavior, Vol. 8,* by T. Ayllon and H. H. Azrin, 1965, pp. 357–383.

the hospital where tokens are not given (Levine & Fasnacht, 1974). One method for dealing with the generalization problem is to provide naturally occurring reinforcements (e.g., a smile or self-praise) along with the tokens (Kazdin, 1994; O'Leary & Drabman, 1971). For example, by encouraging schoolchildren to engage in a process of self-evaluation and praise (e.g., what a good learner I am) along with giving them tokens for desirable behavior, the desirable behavior was maintained even on those days when the tokens were not presented (Drabman, Spitalnik, & O'Leary, 1973). Thus, to increase the likelihood of successfully moving the desired behavior from the token economy to the real world, generalization must be incorporated into the planning of any token economy (Baer, Wolf, & Risley, 1968).

Legal and Ethical Concerns about Using Token Economies   Legal and ethical concerns have also been raised regarding the use of token economies (Emmelkamp, 1994; Wilson, 1995). A number of court decisions have made it clear that patients have certain legal rights, such as free access to food, storage space, and furniture, as well as a certain degree of freedom of movement, that cannot be violated by clinicians regardless of the potential for positive treatment outcome (Emmelkamp, 1994). The use of token economics has also come under attack for ethical reasons, because clinicians have been accused of simply teaching patients to mimic normal behavior at the expense of the patients' freedom of private thought (e.g., reducing delusional thinking) and behavior (e.g., getting them to dress a certain way). Thus, although no longer as popular as they once were (Glynn, 1990), token economies, in conjunction with other forms of therapy (e.g., chemotherapy, individual psychotherapy, or group therapy), are still used in many mental health, educational, correctional, and business settings.

Biofeedback: Getting in Touch with Your Inner Self through Technology
Biofeedback is a technique by which electronic equipment is used to give an individual information about a certain physiological function (e.g., heart rate or muscle tension) within the body so the individual can eventually gain a greater degree of control over that function. Electrodes are placed on the surface of the skin to measure such bodily processes as muscle tension, skin conductance (e.g., "sweating"), body temperature, heart rate, and brain-wave activity (Kazdin, 1994; Stern, Ray, & Davis, 1980). The information received from the electrodes is then passed through an amplifier and displayed in the form of visual or auditory feedback to the individual.

As it relates to operant conditioning, the feedback presented to the individual is used as a form of reinforcement to indicate the extent to which the individual is engaging in behavior designed to control the particular bodily function. For example, if a red light flashes each time a person is able to think about something that reduces the muscle tension being measured, seeing the red light would serve as positive reinforcement for thinking the comforting thoughts and increase the likelihood of them occurring again. On the other hand, if a tone was lowered each time that person was able to think comforting thoughts, the lowering of the tone would serve as negative reinforcement for thinking the comforting thought and increase the likelihood of those thoughts occurring again. Thus, the logic of biofeedback is that it is possible to get in touch with bodily functions more effectively using electrical technology.

In addition to treating people with some of the direct consequences of stress (Barker, 1994; Hovanitz & Wander, 1990; Shahidi & Salmon, 1992), biofeedback technology has many interesting therapeutic applications. For example, people with a history of headaches were given biofeedback in the form of a lower tone when they engaged in behavior designed to reduce muscle tension. Compared with a group of people not given the feedback, the people given the feedback reported significantly fewer headaches (Kondo & Canter, 1977).

In one form or another, here are some other ways that biofeedback has been used:

▲ To help people suffering from epilepsy in learning to control brain waves to reduce the frequency of seizures (Kuhlman & Kaplan, 1979)
▲ To increase control of muscle loss due to a stroke (Fernando & Basmajian, 1978) or paralyzing disease (Basmajian, 1977)
▲ To reduce asthmatic episodes (Harver, 1994)
▲ To increase control of muscles involved in speech for stutterers (Lanyon, Barrington, & Newman, 1976)

▲ To modify heart rates of people suffering from irregular heartbeats and to reduce hypertension (Blanchard, McCoy, Musso, & Geraridi, 1986)

▲ To reduce the stress associated with insulin-dependent diabetes (McGrady & Gerstenmaier, 1990)

▲ To reduce lower back pain (Wolf, Nacht, & Kelly, 1982)

In addition to affecting health-related behaviors directly, biofeedback is being used to affect such behaviors indirectly by teaching people preventative measures. For example, asthmatics can use biofeedback to help them recognize when their breathing passageways are narrowing, thus allowing them to take their medication beforehand and avoid asthmatic episodes (Harver, 1994).

While biofeedback techniques have been effective, there is also evidence to suggest that for some types of ailments, just as much relief can be obtained by much simpler and less expensive muscle relaxation training (see page 283) as with the rather elaborate and often costly biofeedback equipment (Barker, 1994; Lichstein, 1988; Rimm & Masters, 1979; Schwartz, in press). Another issue is the ability of clients to sustain the treatment on their own after the supervised biofeedback training is completed (Kazdin, 1994). In support of this reasoning, biofeedback is found to gain effectiveness if it is combined with some home practice (Gauthier, Cote, & French, 1994). Thus, the effectiveness of biofeedback seems to be enhanced when it is combined with relaxation training or other forms of therapy (Blanchard, 1992).

Some of the Dynamics and Consequences of Punishment: The Punishment for Using Punishment

While the applications discussed so far tend to emphasize reinforcement, as most people are well aware, punishment is a principle of operant conditioning that is used all too often to modify behavior. Parents spanking their children, police giving speeding tickets, and judges' rulings on capital punishment are just a few of the many applications of punishment. Rather than listing all the applications of punishment, this discussion focuses on some of the dynamics and negative consequences of using punishment to modify behavior. This approach will give you a better understanding and appreciation of the dynamics of punishment as a technique for modifying behavior.

In a rather interesting presentation of operant conditioning principles, Albert Bandura (1969) discusses some of the consequences of using punishment to modify and control behavior. Presented next are some of the negative consequences for using punishment, as noted by Bandura and others (Kazdin, 1994; Masters, Burish, Hollon, & Rimm, 1987).

Failure to Suggest a More Effective Alternative Behavior One of the biggest shortcomings of using punishment is that it does not suggest an alternative form of behavior. Without being able to produce an alternative behavior, there is a very good possibility that the undesirable behavior will occur once again. For example, when a child is punished for interrupting when his parents are talking but is not told when and how it is appropriate to intervene, he will probably interrupt them again.

The Suppression of Undesirable Behavior To state that nothing is learned when using punishment is actually too simplistic. What tends to be learned is for the individual to suppress the undesirable behavior *only* in the presence of the punishing agent. For example, when a child is punished for sneaking cookies out of the cookie jar, what she probably learns is not to sneak cookies when her parents are home. The same is true for getting speeding tickets; we learn to observe the speed limit only when we see a patrol car.

Creating Bad Feelings While punishment may suppress unwanted behavior, it also tends to create negative feelings within the individual being punished. Expressing these negative feelings at the punishing agent would most certainly bring on additional punishment. As a result, these negative feelings are also likely to be suppressed and eventually displaced against a safer target. For example, an angry child may displace his suppressed anger toward other children. An angry parent punished by the boss may exhibit his displaced anger in the form of child or spouse abuse.

The Conditioning and Generalization of Negative Feelings toward the Punishing Agent A possible side effect of the unpleasant feelings punishment generates is that these feelings may become conditioned to the punishing agents as well. For example, after being given a speeding ticket, a person may also begin to develop a dislike for the officer issuing the citation, as well as for other members of law enforcement agencies. In another example, the child punished by the teacher for not doing an assignment correctly may eventually generalize the unpleasant feelings toward other teachers and toward attending school in general.

Promoting Escape and Avoidance   To prevent punishment from occurring, a person may engage in escape and avoidance behavior. For example, to escape parental criticism, a teenager may simply walk out the door in the middle of an argument. To avoid future parental criticism, the teenager may simply avoid coming home. Effective avoidance and escape behaviors are negatively reinforced because they result in the termination of aversive stimuli (e.g., criticism from parents). Since negative reinforcement tends to strengthen a behavioral response, escape and avoidance become more likely to occur in the future.

In addition, such escape and avoidance behaviors make it very difficult to learn a more appropriate and effective alternative response. For example, because the teenager and parents are no longer talking to each other, they are unable to work out what can be done to make the situation better.

Punishment as a Model for Aggression   When parents use punishment in response to the aggressive behavior of their children, they may be unwittingly demonstrating the exact behavior they are trying to eliminate. For example, children observing their parents using aggression to control them may learn to use punishment in controlling the behavior of their peers. Because such aggressive behavior is likely to succeed, it tends to be reinforced. Thus, punishment originally intended to reduce undesirable behavior may actually increase its likelihood.

These are just some of the negative consequences for using punishment as a behavior modification technique. But even knowing these consequences will not keep people from using punishment. As a result, if punishment must be used, a few precautions can be taken to minimize these negative consequences and maximize its effectiveness (Kazdin, 1994). For additional insight into

using punishment more effectively, consider the information in "Applications in Personality Psychology" below.

APPLICATION

APPLICATIONS IN PERSONALITY PSYCHOLOGY

If You Must Use Punishment, at Least Do It Right: Helpful Hints for Using Punishment

In their book titled *Learning to Change: A Self-Management Approach to Adjustment*. Robert Martin and Elizabeth Poland (1980) offer some very helpful hints for maximizing effectiveness when using punishment. The following is a summary of some of their suggestions.

Specify the Undesired Behavior: This Is What's Wrong

It is very important to let the individual know what specific behavior is being punished. For example, if a child is eating cookies and watching television before dinner, the parent must indicate the behavior that is considered undesirable. Is it undesirable to be eating the cookies before dinner, watching television before homework is completed, or both? Punishment is not effective if the individual does not know what behavior is undesirable and to be avoided.

Make It Immediate: Do It Now!

For punishment to be effective, it should be administered immediately after the undesirable behavior occurs. It is not very effective for a parent threatening to punish a child screaming for candy in the supermarket to say, "Wait till I get you home; you're really going to get it then." Chances are good that the child has already experienced some immediate reinforcement for his undesirable behavior in the form of receiving the candy to "shut up," which the parent does to avoid an embarrassing situation. A more effective response might be to remove something the child wants, like cookies, from the basket and return them to the shelf while informing the child that this is the punishment for misbehaving. Such a response is more likely to be effective because the delay between the undesirable behavior of crying and the punishment of losing the cookies is minimal. Thus, for punishment to be effective, it must be done immediately.

Make It Consistent: Do It the Same Way Every Time

Allowing undesirable behavior to go unpunished sometimes is essentially rewarding it on a variable-ratio schedule. As noted previously in the discussion of the partial reinforcement effect, behavior that is rewarded intermittently is very difficult to eliminate. For example, because most people do not expect to be pulled over when driving after drinking, such behavior is fairly common. Each time the person is not pulled over, driving while intoxicated is reinforced. If drunk drivers expected to get pulled over each time they attempted such undesirable behavior, the number of people who drink and drive would probably drop dramatically. Thus, for punishment to be effective, it must be administered consistently.

Use "Time Out" or "Response Cost": Removing the Reinforcements

Two alternatives to punishment are time out and response cost. With **time out**, the individual is removed from the source of reinforcements when undesirable behaviors are performed. Examples of time out are making a child stand in the corner for misbehaving, or suspending a person's drivers license for driving while intoxicated. With **response cost**, the individual is required to surrender some form of reinforcement as a consequence of the undesirable behavior. Examples of response cost would be taking away a child's TV video game privileges, or taking money from speeders by having them pay fines.

Suggest an Alternative Behavior and Reinforce It: Here's How to Avoid the Punishment and Get Reinforcement

Punishment is more effective when it is combined with reinforcement. Immediately after administering the punishment, telling the individual what alternative behaviors they can perform to avoid the punishment, time out, or response cost—as well as what they can do to obtain reinforcement—increases the effectiveness of the punishment. For example, after punishing the child by returning the cookies to the shelf, the parent might tell the child, "If you stop crying, I'll put the cookies back into the basket." Thus, for punishment to be effective, it must be combined with a suggestion for and the reinforcement of an appropriate alternative behavior.

In addition to its many negative consequences, the effective administration of punishment is a little more difficult than most people might expect. Although it does serve a purpose, the role of punishment in behavior modification programs should be to supplement the reinforcement of more appropriate behaviors (Kazdin, 1994; Martin & Pear, 1992).

This concludes the discussion of the applications of operant conditioning principles. Additional information on and illustrations of applications based on the operant conditioning perspective can be found in *Behavior Modification in Applied Settings* (Kazdin, 1994), *Elementary Principles of Behavior* (Malott, Whaley, & Malott, 1993), and *Behavior Modification: What It Is and How to Do It* (Martin & Pear, 1992).

Evaluation of the Behavioral Viewpoint: Characteristic Strengths and Limitations

This section presents the characteristic strengths and limitations of the behavioral viewpoint.

Characteristic Strengths

The major strengths of the behavioral viewpoint include its strong research tradition and the variety of its uses and applications.

▲ *A Strong Research Tradition.* The commitment of the behavioral viewpoint to rigorous research also extends to its many applications, based on both the classical and operant conditioning perspectives. For example, as was illustrated in Figure 10.3, documenting the effectiveness of the token economy involved demonstrating that its presence produced an increase in ward participation while its removal resulted in a decrease in ward participation. Such commitment to empirical documentation is at the core of the behavioral viewpoint.

▲ *A Variety of Uses.* The behavioral viewpoint has gained in popularity and acceptance because it has been shown to be of considerable value in solving a variety of behavioral problems, including treating drug addiction, overcoming shyness, teaching employment skills to the mentally retarded, reducing absenteeism, and counseling people experiencing marital problems. Such diversity in applications shows no signs of diminishing.

Characteristic Limitations

The major limitations of the behavioral viewpoint include its perceived lack of a theoretical nature, situational emphasis, and emphasis on overt behavior.

▲ *The Viewpoint Lacks a Theoretical Perspective.* The behavioral viewpoint has been criticized for lacking a unifying theoretical framework. Critics argue that instead of developing a theory of personality, the behavioral viewpoint is represented by a series of principles of behaviors that merely describe the behavior without actually explaining it. For example, the principle of reinforcement is defined by the ability to increase the likelihood of a behavior occurring. Such an account does not explain *why* reinforcement has the effect it does. From the behavioral viewpoint, the counterargument is that if behavior can be predicted with a high degree of accuracy, little is gained by trying to explain *why* it occurs. As an example, if it can be predicted that giving children $1.00 will get them to clean their rooms, what difference does it make why they are doing it, as long as the job gets done? Thus, from the behavioral viewpoint, what seems to be critical is predicting the behavioral outcome, not necessarily explaining the underlying psychological processes. However, theoretical extensions of the behavioral viewpoint, discussed in Chapter 11, do consider the *why* of these principles.

▲ *The Situational Emphasis Removes the Person from the Study of Personality.* The behavioral viewpoint has also been criticized for placing too much emphasis on the nature of the surrounding environment to explain behavior while portraying the individual as more or less reacting to the environmental cues in the situation. For example, regardless of why the individual displays fetish behavior, the technique for treating it involves an emphasis on getting the person to simply respond negatively whenever the activating cue (e.g., rubber boots) is present in the situation. Thus, the behavioral viewpoint ignores the individual's capacity to be an active agent in the surrounding environment. Again, recent theoretical extensions of the behavioral viewpoint (contingency theory and hopelessness) consider more specifically the significant role played by factors within the person (e.g., expectancies and beliefs).

▲ *The Emphasis on Overt Behavior Fails to Consider the Holistic Nature of Behavior.* Another point of contention with the behavioral viewpoint is that its emphasis on the individual's overt behavioral response to the environment tends to ignore the basic cognitive, psychological, and biological processes operating within the individual. For example, we do not just react to the cues presented in our external environment. Our responses are determined by the thoughts and expectations (e.g., cognitive processes), feelings and motivational state (e.g., psychological processes), and hormonal levels and neurological structures (e.g., biological processes) operating within us. Thus, to ignore the holistic nature of behavior is a serious limitation.

More information about the basic principles, processes, and applications of the behavioral viewpoint can be found by reading Michael D. Spiegler and David Guevremont's (1992) *Contemporary Behavioral Therapy*, Robert A. Martin and Elizabeth Y. Poland's (1980) *Learning to Change: A Self-Management Approach to Adjustment*, or Alan E. Kazdin's (1994) *Behavior Modification in Applied Settings*. These clearly written books include a number of interesting applications of the behavioral viewpoint.

In the next chapter, you will examine the social learning-cognitive viewpoint of personality. Many of the strengths—and efforts to overcome the limitations—of the behavioral viewpoint are expressed in the social learning-cognitive viewpoint.

Chapter Summary: Reexamining the Highlights

▲ *Basic Assumptions*. The basic assumptions of the behavioral viewpoint include defining personality by overt behavior, accounting for personality processes based on principles of learning, accounting for the gradual acquisition of personality through a learning history, and emphasizing environmental influences on personality.

▲ *The Classical Conditioning Perspective*
 —*Basic Elements and Processes*. The classical conditioning perspective emphasizes the learning of associations as major components of personality. The basic elements of the classical conditioning perspective include the unconditioned stimulus, unconditioned response, conditioned stimulus, and conditioned response. The additional classical conditioning principles of stimulus generalization, stimulus discrimination, higher-order conditioning, and vicarious conditioning help to account for more complex personality processes. Some aspects of personality that are explained, based on classical conditioning, include the acquisition of attitudes, phobias, and attraction.
 —*Applications of the Classical Conditioning Perspective*
 —*Systematic Desensitization*. The process of systematic desensitization employs the principle of reciprocal inhibition to replace a maladaptive response. The three steps in this process include establishing an anxiety hierarchy, conducting progressive relaxation training, and administering the desensitization process.
 —*Counterconditioning*. The process of counterconditioning is used to replace pleasant but inappropriate responses with more adaptive responses using aversive conditioning. Limitations of this procedure include its inconclusive effectiveness, ethical concerns, and generalizability beyond the treatment setting.

▲ *The Operant Conditioning Perspective*
 —*Basic Principles*. Operant conditioning emphasizes the consequences of behavior. The law of effect, positive and negative reinforcement, primary and secondary reinforcers, and punishment are basic principles that serve as consequences of behavior.
 —*Basic Processes*. Schedules of reinforcement determine how reinforcement is presented. Four schedules of reinforcement are fixed ratio, variable ratio, fixed interval, and variable interval. The extinction of behavior is affected by the partial reinforcement effect. The performance of behavior is influenced by the processes of shaping, stimulus control, generalization, and discrimination. Some aspects of personality that are explained—based on operant conditioning—include superstitious, altruistic, compulsive, and prejudicial behavior.
 —*Applications of the Operant Conditioning Perspective*
 —*Self-Control*. The behavior modification technique of self-control is designed for personal use in altering an individual's behavior. The phases of this technique include self-monitoring, self-evaluation, and self-reinforcement/punishment.
 —*Token Economy*. The behavior modification of people in a collective setting using secondary reinforcers is the main objective of a token economy. Its effectiveness is determined by the consistency of implementation and degree of generalization.
 —*Biofeedback*. The technique of biofeedback uses electrically measured information as reinforcement to help people gain control over bodily processes. The effectiveness of biofeedback is restricted to having the necessary equipment and to the ability of people to maintain the treatment beyond the supervised training.
 —*Punishment*. As a behavior modification technique, punishment can result in a number of negative consequences, which include failing to suggest an alternative form of behavior, suppressing undesirable behavior, creating bad feelings within the individual and toward the punishing agent, promoting escape and avoidance behavior, and serving as a model for aggression.

▲   *Evaluation of the Behavioral Viewpoint*
  —*Characteristic Strengths.* The strong research tradition and the many uses and applications are some characteristic strengths of the behavioral viewpoint.
  —*Characteristic Limitations.* The perceived lack of a theoretical nature and emphasis on the situation and overt behavior are some characteristic limitations of the behavioral viewpoint.

Glossary

acquisition phase   A period in classical conditioning in which the unconditioned and conditioned stimuli are paired repeatedly.

anxiety hierarchy   A systematic arrangement of anxiety-provoking stimuli in reverse order of the amount of fear they elicit.

behavior modification   The process of using operant conditioning principles for the therapeutic alteration of behavior.

behavior therapy   A classification of treatment for emotional and behavior disorders based on principles of learning.

biofeedback   A technique for providing information about bodily processes for the purpose of their therapeutic control.

conditioned response   A response elicited by the conditioned stimulus as a result of the conditioning process.

conditioned stimulus   A neutral stimulus paired with an unconditioned stimulus.

contingency theory   An explanation of the process of classical conditioning, focusing on the information value of the CS in signaling the appearance of the UCS.

counterconditioning (aversion therapy)   A classical conditioning procedure for replacing pleasant feelings with unpleasant feelings.

covert sensitization   A form of counterconditioning that uses vivid mental images to generate unpleasant feelings.

discrimination   Limiting a response only to certain situations.

extinction   The termination of the presentation of a reinforcer.

fetish   An exaggerated, irrational sexual attachment to an object.

fixed-interval schedule   The presentation of a reinforcer after the passage of a specific amount of time.

fixed-ratio schedule   The presentation of a reinforcer after a specific number of responses.

generalization   An extension of a response to similar situations.

higher-order conditioning   The ability of a new conditioned stimulus to elicit the original conditioned response.

hopelessness   A consequence for assuming an excessive amount of personal responsibility for negative consequences and believing that the uncontrollable nature of the situation is not likely to change.

law of effect   The tendency for behaviors producing favorable consequences to be repeated.

learned helplessness   A behavior pattern characterized by a lack of effort to change a situation; acquired from experience with uncontrollable events.

learning history   An individual's experiences involving principles of learning; used to help explain behavior patterns.

negative reinforcer   The termination of a stimulus consequence that decreases the likelihood of a behavior being repeated.

obsessive-compulsive disorder   The pathological preoccupation with a particular thought or behavior pattern to reduce anxiety.

operant conditioning   A type of learning based on voluntary actions and emphasizing the consequences of behavior.

partial reinforcement effect   Following extinction, the greater persistence of intermittently reinforced behavior than consistently reinforced behavior.

phobia   An exaggerated, irrational fear reaction to an object or situation.

positive reinforcer   The presentation of a stimulus consequence that increases the likelihood of a behavior being repeated.

primary reinforcers   Any reinforcers that have innate value.

progressive relaxation training   A technique of systematically tensing and relaxing muscles for the purpose of relaxation.

punishment   The act of presenting a stimulus consequence that decreases the likelihood of a behavior being repeated.

reciprocal inhibition   The tendency of one response to prevent an incompatible response from occurring.

reinforcement   The consequence of a behavior that increases the likelihood of that behavior being performed again.

reinforcer   Any stimulus serving as a consequence of a behavior that increases the likelihood of repeating that behavior.

response cost   The permanent removal of reinforcers as a consequence of undesirable behavior.

saliency   A descriptive feature of a CS that accounts for its increased likelihood of being associated with a UCS.

schedule of reinforcement   The presentation of reinforcers in a specific pattern.

secondary reinforcers   Any stimulus that maintains value as a reinforcer because of its association with a primary reinforcer.

self-control   The personal application of behavior modification.

shaping   The acquisition of a behavior based on the reinforcement of gradual approximations of that behavior.

stimulus control   The prompting of behavior by surrounding cues.

stimulus discrimination   The extent to which a response is elicited by only a particular stimulus.

stimulus generalization   The extent to which a response to a particular stimulus is elicited by other similar stimuli.

systematic desensitization   A treatment for the progressive elimination of extreme fear reactions to particular stimuli.

time out   The temporary removal of the source of reinforcement as a consequence of undesirable behavior.

token economy   A system involving the exchange of secondary reinforcers for specific objects and privileges.

unconditioned response   An already existing response to a particular stimulus, usually a reflexive behavior.

unconditioned stimulus   A stimulus capable of eliciting a particular response without prior exposure to it.

variable-interval schedule   The presentation of a reinforcer after variations in the passage of time.

variable-ratio schedule   The presentation of a reinforcer after a varying number of responses.

vicarious conditioning   The indirect acquisition of conditioned responses as a result of observing the responses of others.

CHAPTER 11

The Social-Cognitive Viewpoint: Cognitive Processes and Personality

CHAPTER OVERVIEW: A PREVIEW OF COMING ATTRACTIONS

*T*he focus of this chapter is the social-cognitive viewpoint and the emphasis given to the role of cognitive processes in the study of personality. **Cognitive processes** are the mental processes that people use to help give meaning to events and experiences, as well as to help determine how we will respond to these events and experiences (Baker, 1994; Cantor, 1990; Cantor & Zirkel, 1990; Fisk & Taylor, 1991; Kazdin, 1994). For example, people with violence-prone personalities demonstrate a tendency to perceive hostility in the actions of others and view aggression as an appropriate response (cf. Berkowitz, 1993). On the other hand, people with a high need to evaluate attempt to give meaning to events and experiences by demonstrating a chronic tendency to engage in evaluative and analytical responses and activities (e.g., discuss and debate issues) (Jarvis & Petty, 1996).

In this chapter, you will consider some basic assumptions of the social-cognitive viewpoint of personality. You will also study the social-cognitive perspectives of Julian Rotter, Albert Bandura, and Walter Mischel, three influential contemporary social-cognitive personality theorists. This chapter presents basic concepts and processes of personality and personality adjustment as described by each of these theorists, along with some applications based on their respective perspectives.

Basic Assumptions: The Role of Cognitive Processes in Personality

In Chapter 10, you discovered that a characteristic limitation of the learning viewpoint was its failure to consider the holistic nature of behavior. For example, while discussing how a specific object, such as a dog, might trigger avoidance behavior characteristic of a phobic reaction in a small child, the learning viewpoint does not explain the process by which the individual comes to decide on how to cope with the threatening situation. In a similar manner, when people display prejudiced actions against others, the learning viewpoint does not really explain why a certain group is selected and/or how prejudiced people come to attribute certain personality traits (e.g., lazy, sneaky) to these group members.

To help overcome these limitations, the social-cognitive viewpoint emphasizes the role of cognitive processes in the study of personality. In the study of personality, such cognitive processes might include the nature of the encoding strategies people use to organize information about themselves and others, the decision-making strategies we use in self-regulation of our behavior, and the subjective evaluation of the consequences of various actions in response to a given situation. For example, as a law student, Kathy's level of self-confidence is determined by how good she perceives her classroom comments are in comparison to those of the other students (i.e., encoding information about herself and others), whether she believes joining a study group and/or seeking the aid of a tutor will help her do better in class (i.e., subjective evaluation of various actions), and the amount of time she spends studying each night (i.e., self-regulation of behavior). Thus, the major characteristic of the social-cognitive viewpoint is its emphasis on our mental processes and how these processes can be used to influence the nature of our thoughts, feelings, and behavior.

At the core of the cognitive viewpoint are the following four basic assumptions:

▲ The significance of the personal perspective
▲ The presence of a need for cognition
▲ People's desire to seek further understanding and clarification of their personal world
▲ The significance of subjective probabilities

The Significance of the Personal Perspective: The Importance of Perceptions and Beliefs

An important assumption of the social-cognitive viewpoint is the significance attributed to an individual's perceptions and beliefs about events and the impact such cognitive processes have on the individual's behavior. The logic of this assumption is that much of what we do, feel, and think is related to our perceptions and beliefs (Isen, Niedenthal, & Cantor, 1992). For example, a shy person decides not to talk to others at a party because he may assume that what he has to say is not very interesting and that others are more amusing than he is. In this example, the shy person withdraws from others as a result of the beliefs (i.e., his contribution is not interesting) and perceptions (i.e., others are more amusing) he has about himself and others. In another example, when trying to determine whether to stay at a boring but secure job or to quit, a female sales manager might decide that she is not very likely to look for a more exciting job as long as she has her present one. As a result, she decides to quit her job without having another one waiting for her. While many people may not consider this a very systematic approach to career planning, from her personal perspective, this is the most "logical" course of action.

Thus, similar to the views of Carl Rogers (see Chapter 6) and George Kelly (see Chapter 7), the social-cognitive viewpoint assumes to truly understand personality, that you have to consider the nature and structure of the person's perceptions and belief system. This is in sharp contrast to the learning viewpoints, which emphasize external or environmental factors as the primary regulators of personality.

The Presence of a Need for Cognition: The Desire to Think

Rather than simply viewing ourselves as passively responding to our environment, the social-cognitive viewpoint describes people as actively seeking information in a direct attempt to give meaning to our experiences and cope with the demands placed on us, particularly in the presence of causal uncertainty (Weary & Edwards, 1994). Once we obtain this information, we each process it to determine the most meaningful course of action from our personal perspective (Cantor & Harlow, 1994; Cantor & Zirkel, 1990).

But people differ in their **need for cognition**, which refers to the amount of time and effort an individual is willing to put forth when processing information to prepare a course of action in response to external stimuli (Cacioppo & Petty, 1982; Cacioppo, Petty, & Morris 1983). For example, when trying to decide which liquid diet program is likely to be most effective for its cost, an individual with a high need for cognition would read the claims made in the advertising brochures more closely than an individual with a low need for cognition, who may simply skim through the claims and focus on the photographs in the brochures. People with a high need for cognition tend to be willing to engage in considerable cognitive processing while analyzing information, even when there is no extrinsic reward (e.g., money or recognition) for doing so (Petty, Cacioppo, & Kasmer, 1985).

For some firsthand experience with how the need for cognition is assessed, read "You Can Do It" below.

YOU CAN DO IT

The Need for Cognition Scale: "I Think, Therefore I Am Having Fun"

The Need for Cognition Scale (NCS) is a 45-item instrument assessing the expressed desire people have for engaging in and enjoying various cognitive activities (e.g., problem solving, seeking to understand something, having a desire to know). The following is a subset of the Need for Cognition Scale (Cacioppo & Petty, 1982). Try it yourself by using the response format described.

Instructions:
Indicate the extent to which you agree or disagree with each of the 10 statements presented below by using the following scale:
  A. Very strong agreement
  B. Strong agreement
  C. Moderate agreement
  D. Slight agreement
  E. Neither agreement nor disagreement
  F. Slight disagreement
  G. Moderate disagreement
  H. Strong disagreement
  I. Very strong disagreement

____ 1. I really enjoy a task that involves coming up with new solutions to problems.
____ 2. Learning new ways to think doesn't excite me very much.

____ 3. I would prefer a task that is intellectual, difficult and important to one that is somewhat important but does not require much thought.
____ 4. I prefer to let things happen rather than try to understand why they turned out that way.
____ 5. I take pride in the products of my reasoning.
____ 6. The notion of thinking abstractly is not appealing to me.
____ 7. I prefer my life to be filled with puzzles that I must solve.
____ 8. I prefer to think about small, daily projects to long-term ones.
____ 9. I enjoy thinking about an issue even when the results of my thought will have no effect on the outcome of the issue.
____ 10. Thinking is not my idea of fun.

Scoring:
The scoring for items 1, 3, 5, 7, and 9 is A = +4, B = +3, C = +2, D = +1, E = 0, F = −1, G = −2, H = −3, and I = −4. For items 2, 4, 6, 8, and 10, the scoring is reversed (e.g., A = −4, B = −3, etc.). Add the numbers corresponding to your responses together. The higher the score, the higher your expressed need for cognition.

For details about some research assessing the validity of the Need for Cognition Scale, read "A Closer Look" on page 312.

Note. From The Need for Cognition. *Journal of Personality and Social Psychology*, Vol. 42, by J. T. Cacioppo and R. E. Petty, 1982, pp. 116–131. Copyright 1982 by the American Psychological Association.

A Closer Look:

Validation Research on the Need for Cognition Scale: Confirming the Desire to Think

In some of the earliest research into the development of the Need for Cognition Scale (NCS), John T. Cacioppo and Richard E. Petty (1982) conducted a series of four studies to examine how NCS scores were related to certain personality, cognitive, and affective measures.

In the initial validation study, Cacioppo and Petty compared the NCS scores for a group of university faculty members with a group of assembly line workers. As expected, the group of faculty members scored much higher on the NCS than the group of assembly line workers. In a second study involving over 400 college students, NCS scores were positively correlated with solving spatial ability problems (e.g., finding an embedded figure hidden within other figures) and were not related to experiencing test anxiety (Cacioppo & Petty, 1982). In a third study, Cacioppo and Petty examined the relationship between NCS scores and those on a measure of the personality dimension of dogmatism (i.e., the degree to which an individual is open- or closed-minded in their thinking). As you might expect, higher NCS scores were associated with more open-minded thinking (e.g., less dogmatism).

In the final study in this series, college students identified as having either a high or low need for cognition, based on their NCS scores, were asked to perform either the simple or complex version of a number-circle task. In the simple version of the task, students were asked to circle all of the 1's, 5's, and 7's found in three pages of a notebook containing 3500 random numbers on each page. In the complex version of the task, students were asked to circle all of the 3s, any 6 preceded by a 7, and every other 4 found in three pages of a notebook containing 3500 random numbers on each page. Although the students did not enjoy the tedious number-circling task very much, the high-need-for-cognition students enjoyed the complex version more than the simple version; and just the opposite pattern of enjoyment was found for the low-need-for-cognition students. Thus, even with a very boring task that involves a mental challenge, people high in the need for cogni-

tion will manage to find some fun and enjoyment in it simply because they like to think.

In a separate set of two studies, Cacioppo, Petty, and Morris (1983) also demonstrated that people with a high need for cognition not only spend more time thinking but also are better able to evaluate the quality of what they are thinking about than people with a low need for cognition. In addition to spending more time thinking about arguments contained in persuasive messages, people with a high need for cognition evaluated strong arguments more favorably than weak arguments, while people with a low need for cognition evaluated the weak arguments more favorably than the strong arguments.

Taken together, the results of these and other studies (Chaiken, 1987; Lassiter, Briggs, & Bowman, 1991; Lassiter, Briggs, & Shaw, 1991) tend to support the validity of the NCS in its ability to identify people who differ in the amount of time spent thinking, quality of thinking, and degree of enjoyment derived from thinking.

A Desire to Seek Further Understanding and Clarification of One's Personal World: The Pursuit of Precision

Another basic assumption of the social-cognitive viewpoint is that people are motivated to make their understanding of their personal world more accurate and precise. That is to say, we assess the outcome of our actions to determine the present effectiveness and future viability of these actions. For example, suppose a student believes that cramming is a very effective method for getting a good grade on a test. But if the student crammed for a test and got a *D*, she would probably then have to reconsider the validity of this hypothesis when studying for the next test. In this case she may decide that cramming is still a good idea, but that the cramming session must start earlier in the evening. For the next test, she decides to start cramming at 8:00 p.m., instead of at midnight after coming home from a movie, as she did for the previous test. The point to be made here is that although you may not agree with the cramming method, this individual does. And from her viewpoint, she will continue to seek information (e.g., cramming longer) that will help to maintain the accuracy of this belief. Thus, regardless of our beliefs, the cognitive viewpoint assumes that we are motivated to determine the accuracy and utility of these beliefs.

The Nature and Value of Subjective Probabilities: Playing the Odds

In an earlier paragraph, the significance of the personal world as a powerful determinant of behavior was noted. A variety of cognitive processes contribute to the individual's view of his or her personal world. One of these processes is the subjective probability that a particular course of action will produce a desired outcome. The logic here is that based on our experiences, each of us begins to develop "odds" that in a particular situation, each different course of action will result in a specific outcome or set of consequences. After considering the various response alternatives, as well as their respective outcomes, we decide what course of action to take.

For example, while riding on a bus, a shy man observes that the people who are most likely to carry on successful conversations with total strangers seem to know something about current events. As a result, he decides to read the current issue of *Time*, *Newsweek*, and *People Magazine* before going to a singles dance that weekend. Based on what happens at the dance, the man will then establish new odds about the effectiveness of keeping up with current events in helping him to meet new people. This revised subjective probability will then influence his behavior in other social situations, such as starting conversations with people while riding on a bus or while waiting in line at the cinema.

The point is that from the social-cognitive viewpoint, the subjective probabilities we establish for certain courses of actions are influenced by the interaction between what we perceive as being the right course of action and the nature of the change it produces in our world. Thus, rather than viewing the individual as passively reacting to the environment, the social-cognitive viewpoint sees the individual as "playing the odds" by actively calculating the subjective probability of a course of action, based on both internal (e.g., personal experiences) and environmental (e.g., the present outcome) factors.

This concludes the discussion of the basic assumptions of the social-cognitive viewpoint.

When considering these basic assumptions, you probably noted a few similarities with some basic assumptions proposed by Carl Rogers, George Kelly, and Harry Stack Sullivan—most notably, the importance these theorists gave to how we perceive events and to our interpersonal relationships with others. This is because the historical roots of the social-cognitive viewpoint involve these and other theorists, such as Freud and Alfred Adler (Cantor & Zirkel, 1990). In the next section, you will consider the social learning theory of Julian Rotter, one of the pioneers in the social-cognitive viewpoint of personality.

Rotter's Social Learning Theory: An Integration of the Learning and Cognitive Viewpoints

Julian Rotter has spent almost 50 years developing and refining his social learning theory of personality (Rotter, 1993). A cornerstone of his theory is the emphasis he gives to how our experiences (i.e., learning) and our perceptions and beliefs about the present situation (i.e., cognitive processes) are interrelated in determining our individual responses to life's challenges. Rotter also emphasizes the relationship between scientific research and clinical applications in the development of his social learning theory of personality. For a glimpse into the life of this influential personality theorist, read "A Closer Look" on page 314.

For almost fifty years, Julian Rotter has made many significant contributions to personality theory, personality assessment, and psychotherapy.

A Closer Look:

Biographical Background: The Life of Julian B. Rotter

Julian Rotter was born in 1916 in Brooklyn, New York. During his youth, he spent a considerable amount of time in the Avenue J Library in Brooklyn, demonstrating a particular fondness for fiction. During his junior year in high school, while searching the library stacks for something new to read, he came across some books by Freud and Adler (Rotter, 1982; 1993). He became so engrossed with his new-found interest in psychoanalytical thought that by his senior year, he was interpreting the dreams of his high school friends. As a senior in high school, he wrote a thesis titled "Why We Make Mistakes" and dreamed of having a career in psychology.

Rotter pursued psychology during his undergraduate years at Brooklyn College, but he took it only as an elective. Because the climate of the Great Depression offered few career opportunities in psychology, and the college did not have a formal psychology department, he could not major in psychology. Instead, Rotter selected chemistry, a more practical major that promised a greater likelihood of a job after college. Even so, he took more courses in psychology than chemistry. One of Rotter's teachers was Solomon Ash, whose classic research on conformity and group influence would eventually make him an influential social psychologist.

In addition to taking courses from Ash, Rotter had the opportunity to meet Alfred Adler. In his junior year at Brooklyn College, Rotter learned that Adler was teaching at the Long Island College of Medicine, where he was a professor of medical psychology. Rotter attended some of Adler's lectures and several of his clinical demonstrations. While still in college, Rotter got to know Adler personally. He attended monthly meetings of the Society of Individual Psychology at Adler's home, where Adler spoke on individual psychology. In response to Adler's passionate lectures, the young Rotter became even more convinced that his future would be in psychology. Although Adler's influence on Rotter had begun when he read Adler's books during high school, it did not end with these lectures. Some forty years later, Rotter stated that Adler had been "a strong influence on my thinking.

I was and continue to be impressed by his insights into human nature" (Rotter, 1982, p. 1).

Rotter graduated from Brooklyn College in 1937. Inspired by Adler and encouraged by two of his undergraduate professors, Rotter decided to pursue graduate study in psychology at the University of Iowa, in Iowa City, Iowa. He arrived at the University of Iowa with enough money to last a few weeks. However, the chair of the psychology department was able to obtain a research assistantship for Rotter, giving him enough money to survive. At the University of Iowa, he took a seminar in social psychology taught by the noted and very influential social psychologist Kurt Lewin. Lewin was famous for his work on how people use personal and environmental factors to determine their perceptions and reactions to the world around them. The critical importance of personal and situational variables in the interpretation of events and as determinants of action were to become central features of Rotter's own theory of personality.

In 1938, Rotter received his MA and moved to Massachusetts to attend Worcester State Hospital, at that time a major training and research center in clinical psychology. At Worcester, he participated in one of the first-ever internships in clinical psychology; he also met Clara Barnes, his future wife. Hoping to be one of the first clinical psychologists, Rotter left Worchester to attend Indiana University, where in 1941 he received his PhD in clinical psychology; he was married to Clara that same year.

After receiving his PhD, Rotter wanted an academic position. But he soon discovered that the warnings he had been given since his days at Brooklyn College about Jews not being able to obtain academic jobs, regardless of their credentials, were now becoming reality. Rotter accepted a position at Norwich State Hospital as a clinical psychologist. At Norwich, his responsibilities included the training of interns and assistants from the University of Connecticut and Wesleyan University. In 1942, Rotter was drafted into the army. He spent the next three years as a military psychologist, where he served as a consultant, helped with officer candidate selection, and—among his many contributions—developed a method for reducing the incidence of absence without leave (AWOL).

After his military service, Rotter returned briefly to Norwich State Hospital. But he soon discovered that the shortage of clinical psychologists after World

War II created a need for his services sufficient to overcome the anti-Semitism that had once prevented him from obtaining an academic position. Rotter had many universities from which to select. He soon accepted a position at Ohio State University, where George Kelly was the director of the clinical psychology program, and from which Carl Rogers had recently departed. Together, Kelly and Rotter built a clinical psychology program rated among the best in the country. Rotter became the director of the clinical psychology program when Kelly gave up the position in 1951.

During his stay at Ohio State University, Rotter formulated and, along with a group of outstanding graduate students, tested and developed the basic framework of his social learning theory. The culmination of this work was his classic textbook titled *Social Learning and Clinical Psychology* (Rotter, 1954). Although he was very happy and extremely productive at Ohio State, Rotter was quite disturbed by the political climate created in the Midwest by the Communist-baiting Senator Joe McCarthy. As a result, Rotter left Ohio State in 1963 and moved to the University of Connecticut, where he continues to refine his theory, conduct research, supervise the training of clinical psychology graduate students, and see clients in his private practice as a clinical psychologist. A significant characteristic of Rotter's distinguished career has been his emphasis on training clinical psychologists to be both researchers and practicing clinicians. This is a philosophy Rotter has maintained during his 50 years as a clinical psychologist.

Rotter retired in 1987 from his faculty position at the University of Connecticut. But true to his life-long philosophy as a scientist-practitioner, Rotter continues to teach and supervise the research and clinical training of graduate students at the University of Connecticut. In addition, throughout his career, Rotter has been active in many professional associations, serving as president of the Eastern Psychological Association, as well as president of Division 8: Personality and Social Psychology and Division 12: Clinical Psychology of the American Psychological Association (APA). He also served as a member of the Educational and Training Board of the APA, the APA Council, and the United States Public Health Service Training Committee. In recognition of his many signifi-

cant contributions throughout his lifetime of work, Rotter received the prestigious APA Distinguished Scientific Contribution Award in 1988.

More information on Rotter's life can be found in a chapter he wrote titled "Expectancies," which appears in *The History of Clinical Psychology in Autobiography* (Walker, 1993).

Basic Assumptions: Combining Experience with Expectations

Your understanding of Rotter's perspective can be enhanced by knowing the four basic assumptions of his social learning theory. These four assumptions include learning from meaningful experiences, the reciprocal nature of life experience, the motivational nature of personality, and the role of expectancies (Rotter, 1954, 1982, 1990; Rotter, Chance, & Phares, 1972; Rotter & Hochreich, 1975).

Learning from Meaningful Experiences: Live and Learn

One assumption Rotter makes is that personality is developed based on the individual's interaction with the environment. The idea here is that people learn by adjusting their perceptions and expectations based on meaningful experiences with their environment. As a result, if you want to know something about how an individual is going to behave, you need to know something about the person's experiences. For example, a student's decision to study by cramming all night before the exam probably depends considerably on the extent to which such a pattern has been successful in the past. If it was not successful, the student is likely to formulate another strategy, such as studying a little each night. Thus, Rotter believes that we learn from living and adjust our behavior accordingly.

The Reciprocal Nature of Life Experience: A Mixing of the Old and New

A second assumption of Rotter's perspective emphasizes the interactive nature of new and old experiences. Rotter believes that our reactions to new experiences are influenced to a certain degree by our old experiences, and the perceptions we have of our old experiences are influenced by our new experiences. For example, your reaction to the first few weeks of college was probably influenced to a tremendous degree by the experiences you had in high school (e.g., both situations involve using basic learning skills). On the other hand, once you established the feel for what college is all about, you began to see how much different it is from high school (e.g., a greater amount of freedom to select what you want to study and when you want to study it). Thus, for Rotter, the nature of personality development is not just simply a list of our experiences, but the outcome of a process of the reciprocal influence of these old and new experiences.

The Motivational Nature of Personality: In Search of Rewards

Rotter also assumes that behavior is goal directed. More specifically, he believes that we are motivated to maximize reward and minimize punishment. For example, based on the experiences you had in high school, you conclude that taking notes in class will maximize the probability of obtaining good grades. But based on the feedback from your first test, if your technique for taking notes is not very good, you will probably need to go to the student development center to upgrade your skills. In this assumption, Rotter suggests that we modify our behaviors based on our experiences to maximize success of achieving a desired outcome (e.g., getting better grades).

The Role of Expectancies: The Effect of Anticipation on Rewards

While the emphasis Rotter places on rewards and punishments might make him sound like a learning theorist espousing principles of operant conditioning, his position on the role of expectancies clearly separates his perspective from traditional learning perspectives. More specifically, Rotter assumes that the importance an individual gives to a reward is determined not only by its nature (e.g., $5000.00) but also by the expectancies the person has about the possibility of obtaining the reward (e.g., 1 chance in 50 million). Thus, when trying to understand and predict the behavior of an individual with any degree of success, Rotter believes you have to know not only the nature of the reward but the extent to which the person feels he or she can obtain it.

A reward is of little motivational value if the individual perceives the likelihood of getting it to be very low. For example, one of the reasons many school-age children living in ghettos do not spend much time studying is that their expectations for such behavior making a difference in their life are very low. The important point to note from this example is not whether higher education leads to better-paying jobs—we know it does—but how these children anticipate the likelihood of receiving such rewards. Thus, Rotter's emphasis on the importance of an individual's expectancies about reward outcome illustrates quite clearly the cognitive nature of his social learning theory.

In summary, the basic assumptions of Rotter's social learning theory tend to emphasize combining experience with expectancies as important factors in understanding the nature of personality.

Basic Concepts: The Specifics for Predicting Behavior

Social learning theory outlines four basic concepts used to help explain and predict behavior. These four basic concepts include behavior potential, expectancy, reinforcement value, and the psychological situation, as well as their combination into the basic formula for predicting behavior (Rotter, 1954, 1982; Rotter & Hochreich, 1975).

Behavioral Potential: What Are My Options?

Like Kelly, Rotter believes that we have various options when it comes to the way we respond to the events in our life. The term Rotter uses to describe this state of affairs is *behavior potential*. **Behavior potential** refers to the likelihood of a specific behavior occurring in a particular situation as a means of achieving a specific goal. The higher the probability of a behavior occurring in a given situation, the greater its behavior potential is said to be. For example, when studying for a test, you might choose one of these options: studying your notes, studying the chapter summaries and definitions, and/or looking for similarities between the book and the notes. Based on what others have told you about how this professor tests, you decide to study only the notes. In this example, studying the notes has a higher behavioral potential than the other two alternatives. But in another class, based on what you have heard about another professor, studying the similarities between the notes and book has the greatest behavior potential. Thus, the more you know about what options are available to an individual, the greater your chances of understanding and predicting that person's behavior.

Expectancy: What Are the Odds?

For Rotter, what we decide to do is influenced not only by the alternatives available to us but also by what we think will happen if we engage in that behavior (Rotter, 1993). The term Rotter uses to explain the subjective nature of what we think will happen is *expectancy*. **Expectancy** refers to an individual's subjective belief that if he or she behaves in a particular manner in a specific situation, certain reinforcements will occur. For example, when deciding to study only your class notes for a test, you are saying that you "expect" to get a better grade in this class by studying the notes rather than the material in the book. You need to keep in mind that expectancies represent subjective perceptions of the situation. In reality, studying the notes may not be the best approach. However, because you believe this to be the case, studying the notes has a greater behavior potential for you than studying the material in the book.

Understanding expectancy also gives us a better understanding of why people behave in ways that seem maladaptive to us. For example, a very lonely person might make no attempt to seek others out at social gatherings, because she simply assumes (e.g., maintains a high expectancy) that she will be rejected. Expectancies can also be considered by examining the extent to which the individual uses them in various situations:

▲ *Specific expectancies* refers to the subjective beliefs an individual has about the relationship between a particular course of action producing a desired outcome in a specific situation. For example, you would be demonstrating a specific expectancy if you believed that studying only the notes would get you a good grade in your history class, but not in your personality course.

▲ *Generalized expectancies* refers to subjective beliefs an individual might possess that are applied to a variety of situations. For example, you would be demonstrating a generalized

expectancy if you assumed that studying only the class notes would get you good grades in all of your courses this semester.

While specific and generalized expectancies are discussed separately, you should realize that they also influence each other. What starts out as a generalized expectancy may develop into a specific expectancy based on experience. For example, when you start college, you may assume that all you need to do is take good notes in all of your classes and study only the notes for the test. But after your first set of midterms, you discover that this strategy works with some professors but not with others. As a result of these experiences, you begin to tailor your expectations so that the nature of your studying behavior is specific to each particular professor.

On the other hand, specific expectancies can also turn into generalized expectancies based on experience. For example, after studying only the class notes for this particular professor's freshman survey course in history, you now take an advanced course from her and study the same way. If you are successful, your expectancies will be generalized; you may conclude that for any course you take from this instructor, all you need to do is have a good set of class notes.

The value of generalized expectancies is that they make adjusting to new situations easier, if the behavior is appropriate. The value of specific expectancies is that they enable us to adjust our behavior to the situation at hand. As you can imagine, people who are not able to employ generalized and specific expectancies successfully are bound to have problems in coping with life. For example, a man who continues to use the same approach in asking women to dance, even though they constantly turn him down, is going to be very lonely—assuming that he is actually trying to get a dance partner. Thus, for Rotter, expectancy means asking yourself "What are the odds of getting what I want with this course of action?"

Reinforcement Value: What Do You Want?

For Rotter, what people want in life is represented by the term *reinforcement value*. More specifically, **reinforcement value** refers to the expressed preference an individual has for one source of reinforcement over others, given that all of them are equally available. For example, suppose Cheng, a college student, has had friends arrange three blind dates for him. One woman is a history major, one a biology major, and one a Spanish major. His selection of the woman who is the history major would indicate that she has a higher reinforcement value than the other two women. In this case, the reinforcement value might be the possibility of establishing a meaningful relationship.

Reinforcement value is determined by a number of factors. One is the expectancy of the reinforcement to meet your needs and objectives. For example, in this case, since Cheng has a history minor, he probably expects to have more in common with the history major than with the other two women. It is also based on the relative choices available. Suppose another friend says that a woman in his tennis club would also be willing to go out with Cheng on a blind date. Given this additional option, and his passion for tennis, Cheng may select the tennis player instead of the history major. Thus, the value we place on what we want is determined not only by expectations we have for selecting them but also by what other choices are available.

The Psychological Situation: Reinforcement in Context

Rotter realized that what is valued in one situation may not be valued in another. As a result, he proposed the notion of the **psychological situation**, which refers to any aspect of the specific situation to which the individual is responding.

Suppose that during his blind date, Cheng discovers that the tennis player is a top-ranked player in the area. Upon knowing this, he becomes tense and nervous due to his own competitive nature. In this context, Cheng's reaction is determined by the fact that his perception of the situation changed once he began to focus on the woman's great tennis ability rather than on the other interests they have in common.

The subjective nature of how people perceive a situation is why Rotter refers to it as psychological. His point is that we are influenced not only by the objective cues in a situation (e.g., Cheng's date is a good tennis player) but also by the psychological reactions they trigger in each of us (e.g., Cheng feels

inferior due to his date's tennis ability). Thus, our responses are determined not only by our expectations and reinforcement values but also by the subjective perception of the cues that are available to us in a particular situation.

The Basic Formula: Combining the Specifics to Predict Behavior

Now that the four basic concepts of social learning theory have been discussed individually, the next step is to examine how Rotter combines them to help predict the nature of an individual's behavior in a particular situation. The **basic formula** states that the behavior potential (BP) in a specific situation (S1) is a function (f) of the expectancy (E) of the occurrence of a certain reinforcement (RVa) following a particular behavior (x). The basic formula might also be expressed in the following way:

$$BP_{S1} = f\,(E_{RVa} + RV_{x,\,S1})$$

Stated more simply, the basic formula proposes that the likelihood of your performing a particular behavior in a given situation is a function of the expectancy you have of this behavior producing a reinforcement that is desirable to you. For example, suppose that you are bored and want to have some fun. You could go to a party or a newly released movie. According to the basic formula, in this context, your decision would be based on your perception of which activity would be more enjoyable. Thus, Rotter's belief is that we can predict behavior more accurately if we know the specifics of the situation, including the choices available, what the person hopes to obtain, what the person believes is the likelihood of obtaining it, and the subjective perception of cues in the situation.

This concludes the discussion of the basic concepts of Rotter's social learning theory of personality. In the next section, you will examine how Rotter conceptualizes the nature of personality adjustment.

Personality Adjustment: The General Nature of Coping

Rotter's basic formula is designed to predict behavior in specific situations, but determining the nature of personality adjustment involves considering behavioral responses on a more general level. In this regard, Rotter defined certain personality processes that are associated with successful and unsuccessful personality adjustment. These processes of personality adjustment include freedom of movement and need value, minimal goal level, and generalized expectancies in problem solving.

Freedom of Movement and Need Value: Having What It Takes to Get What You Want

Freedom of movement refers to the expectancy an individual has about a set of behaviors being able to achieve a group of related reinforcements. **Need value** is the average value an individual places on this group of related reinforcements. For example, you may assume that taking good notes, keeping up on your reading assignments, asking questions in class, and studying regularly are behaviors having a high probability of helping you to obtain a group of rewards after graduating from college that might include a stimulating job, a fancy car, and stylish clothes.

Successful personality adjustment requires that the individual has the skills necessary (i.e., high freedom of movement) to obtain those things he or she wants so much (i.e., need value). On the other hand, unsuccessful personality adjustment is characterized by not having the required skills (i.e., low freedom of movement) necessary to obtain the rewards an individual desires or disproportional need values that are too high (e.g., you expect every person you meet at the party to like you) or too low (e.g., getting an *A* in an easy class gives you little satisfaction).

As you would imagine, not being able to get what you really want could lead to such maladaptive behavior as defensiveness, the manipulation of others, and/or excessive fantasizing. For example, an individual who will not admit to his lack of study skills is likely to blame others (e.g., the instructors are unfair, or other students cheat) in a defensive manner for his lack of academic success. He might also engage in manipulative behavior by borrowing notes or copying other students' answers to the test. Finally, in a more serious sense, the individual may spend more time fantasizing about living the good life than actually doing what it takes (i.e., studying) to get what is desired. Thus, as it relates to personality

adjustment, freedom of movement and need value involve having what it takes to get what you want.

Minimal Goal Level: What Is the Least You Will Settle For?

When considering what different people believe is reinforcing, Rotter found it valuable to introduce the term **minimal goal level**, which he defines as the lowest level within a category of reinforcements an individual will consider as being reinforcing. For example, when you are considering job offers, you might tell yourself that you will not work for anything less than $23,000 a year. In this example, $23,000 represents your minimal goal level. The same can be said for the student who believes that nothing less than an *A* is an acceptable grade. In this case, the minimal goal level is an *A*.

It is important to note that minimal goal level is a relative term. For example, while one student might be perfectly willing to work for $20,000 a year, given the salary expectations for people with his college degree, another individual with a different college degree would not even acknowledge a job offer paying less than $28,000 per year. Based on the experiences of this author when passing back exams, it is interesting to note the reactions students have due to the variations in their minimal goal levels. For example, some students feel happy, almost relieved, when they receive a *C*; others are visibly upset with themselves because they only received a *B+*. Thus, different people have different minimal goal levels in the same situation.

Successful personality adjustment is associated with having the freedom of movement necessary to achieve the minimal goal level you have set for yourself. For example, expecting only *A*'s makes sense if you have the set of studying skills and motivation (i.e., high freedom of movement) that makes such demands on yourself possible.

On the other hand, personality maladjustment is most likely to occur when an individual does not have the freedom of movement to obtain the minimal goal level set for him- or herself. For example, an individual might become easily depressed if he is constantly turned down for jobs because he lacks the necessary educational requirements and relevant experience. Thus, an individual's level of adjustment is related to the extent to which the person sets realistic expectations for what he or she is able to achieve—and willing to settle for.

Generalized Expectancies and Personality Adjustment: The Appropriate and Inappropriate Generalization of Expectancies

In addition to being used to help predict behavior in a specific situation, generalized expectancies also have implications for understanding personality adjustment from the social learning perspective. People with a high degree of personality adjustment are able to determine when a certain course of action will lead to the expected reward and when it will not. People with a low degree of personality adjustment are not able to make such discriminations and tend to overextend the nature of their generalized expectancies.

For example, suppose that Peter receives rejection letters from the first five companies to whom he has sent job applications. As a result of these five rejections, he becomes depressed and decides to stop sending out job applications because of the overextended generalized expectancy he now has that "nobody is ever" going to hire him. The maladjusted nature of Peter's generalized expectancies is that he has overgeneralized the possibility of rejection from these five companies to *all* companies. Thus, the degree of personality adjustment is also reflected by the appropriateness of the generalization of a person's expectancies.

This concludes the discussion of personality adjustment from the social learning perspective. As a practicing clinical psychologist, Rotter was extremely concerned with helping people to overcome any problems of personality adjustment. In the next section, you will learn how the basic principles of social learning theory are utilized by Rotter in his own unique form of psychotherapy and other assorted applications.

Applications of Social Learning Theory: Using What Is Known

As a scientist and practitioner, Rotter was not only interested with testing his theoretical ideas, but was also very concerned with finding useful applications for them. Rotter and others have found many impor-

tant applications for his ideas. In this section, you will read about applications of Rotter's social learning theory to psychotherapy, personality assessment, and marital satisfaction and adjustment to divorce.

Psychotherapy: Therapy as a Learning Process
Rotter (1970, 1978; Rotter & Hochreich, 1975) viewed psychotherapy as a learning process. In this regard, inappropriate behaviors and attitudes are not only eliminated but are replaced with more constructive and adaptive alternatives that are taught to the client during the course of psychotherapy. As in other learning situations, clients enter therapy with very different attitudes, motives, and experiences. As a result, a characteristic of social learning psychotherapy is the flexibility it requires of the therapist. For example, for some clients, the therapist may have to work one-on-one to help them focus on clarifying their goals; other clients may require working in a group therapy setting in order to acquire certain interpersonal skills. For still others, a combination of treatment techniques, including behavior therapy and family therapy, might be what is required.

Thus, rather than trying to fit the client's problem into a specific therapeutic technique, Rotter believes that the nature of the client's problem should dictate the type of therapeutic technique to be employed. In the true social-cognitive tradition, social learning psychotherapy can be construed as a problem-solving process that involves trying to determine the optimal way for the client to learn those behaviors that will bring the greatest likelihood of obtaining rewards.

The Basic Goal: Increasing Freedom of Movement   The goal of psychotherapy from the perspective of social learning theory is to help increase the client's freedom of movement. Enhancing freedom of movement increases the client's likelihood of achieving the minimal goal level for those reinforcements that contribute to greater life satisfaction (Rotter & Hochreich, 1975). Rotter did not specify a particular set of techniques for achieving this objective; instead, he took a more problem-solving approach. This approach relies on the therapist developing an individualized treatment program designed to help the client obtain the necessary cognitive and behavior changes that would produce more freedom of movement. Depending on the degree of the client's personality maladjustment, the treatment program may involve teaching the client how to explore new alternatives for goal attainment, focus on the consequences of his or her behavior, or develop a more appropriate system for generalizing expectancies, to name just a few. Regardless of its nature, the basic goal of social learning therapy is to increase the client's freedom of movement.

Techniques for Teaching: Some Examples of Social Learning Therapy   Some people may be experiencing emotional problems because they have set minimal goal levels that are too high. In such cases, social learning therapy would involve helping the client to establish a more realistic minimal goal level. For example, a female bank executive might be creating an excessive amount of tension for herself because she feels she must personally do all of the work in her office to achieve complete acceptance by her male peers. In this case, the therapist would work with her on possibly lowering the goals she has set for herself by helping her to understand that it is not a sign of failure or weakness to delegate some of the less important work to her staff. This example demonstrates how freedom of movement can be increased by altering the cognitions held by the client.

Sometimes the minimal goal level set by a client is realistic, but he or she may lack the skills necessary to achieve it. The therapist would then work with the client to identify and acquire the necessary skills. For example, suppose that Paul, a sales representative, has developed feelings of depression because of his inability to close sales after his group presentations. In this case, the therapist might ask the client to participate in group therapy. By working within the group, the therapist might determine that when talking to a group, Paul rarely makes eye contact and tends to talk nonstop, or until someone interrupts him. After identifying these shortcomings, the therapist then works with Paul on how to make eye contact and summarize points that will stimulate questions, both of which can be practiced in the process of group therapy. This example demonstrates how freedom of movement can be increased by learning more adaptive skills.

The maladaptive use of generalized expectancies by clients is another common problem addressed during social learning therapy. For example, after being turned down by several women he has asked out for dates, a client may develop the generalized expectancy that he is an unworthy person. In this case, the therapist may help the client to focus on his positive characteristics during one-on-one therapy sessions and then involve him in group therapy where he can experience a more general level of acceptance by the other group members. The therapist may then recommend that the client join a local volunteer organization as a means of extending his generalized expectancies of being accepted by others. But the therapist would also help the client to determine the limitations of his expectancies by making him realize that he does not have to be liked by everyone and helping him to recognize which type of people seem to like him and which do not. Making such discriminations will help the client to minimize those situations in which he is going to be rejected. Thus, learning how to use generalized expectancies more appropriately can also lead to an increase in freedom of movement.

Since an individual's emotional problems might also be caused by his or her relationship with significant others (e.g., spouse, parents, teachers, or children), social learning therapy might also require involving these people in therapy as well. For example, a female client's low self-esteem may be due to her inability to tell her parents that she wants to make her own decisions about college and a career. In this case, the parents may be asked to attend the therapy sessions so that the dynamics of the total family situation might be examined more closely. It could be that the control the parents are exerting on the adult daughter may be a result of their own loneliness and unhappiness. As a result, the therapist might have all of them work on developing more effective communication patterns to express their needs, rather than trying to control each other with emotional tactics. Thus, helping all of the family members learn to communicate more effectively gives them greater freedom of movement not only as individuals but also as a family unit.

As you can see from these examples, psychotherapy from the perspective of social learning theory involves trying to identify the therapeutic technique that will best help the client achieve a greater degree of freedom of movement. Because of the variety of techniques necessary and the emphasis on helping the client to learn new skills and alternatives, a successful social learning therapist must also be an effective problem solver and teacher. In the next section, you will see how the eclectic nature of social learning theory has also been utilized in its application to personality assessment.

Personality Assessment: The Measurement of Generalized Expectancies

In developing a comprehensive theory of personality, Rotter also applied the basic principles of social learning theory to the area of personality assessment. More specifically, Rotter developed two measures of personality that are designed to assess generalized expectancies: The Interpersonal Trust Scale and the Internal vs. External Control of Reinforcement Scale.

Interpersonal Trust Scale: Identifying Suspicious Minds As conceptualized by Rotter (1967, 1971, 1980), **interpersonal trust** is a generalized expectancy held by an individual that the words and promises of others can be relied on when there is no evidence for believing otherwise. The *Interpersonal Trust Scale* (Rotter, 1967, 1971) is designed to assess the extent an individual possesses a generalized sense of trust in the words and promises of others. The trust scale is a 40-item forced-choice questionnaire containing 25 trust items and 15 filler items. People respond to each item by indicating the extent of their agreement. Here is a sample of trust items from the scale:

> Most people can be counted on to do what they say they will do.

> Most elected officials are really sincere in their campaign promises.

> In dealing with strangers, one is better off to be cautious until they have provided evidence that they are trustworthy.

Consistent with the proposed notion of interpersonal trust, research shows that people with high trust scores are less likely to lie, cheat, steal, and be unhappy. They are more prone to give people a second chance, respect the rights of others, and be sought out as friends than people with low trust scores (Phares, 1988; Rotter, 1980). In one rather interest-

ing study, people scoring low on the trust scale tended to view the Warren Commission Report on the assassination of President Kennedy as part of a cover-up conspiracy (Hamsher, Geller, & Rotter, 1968).

Low-trusting people also demonstrated their sensitivity to negative stimuli related to trustworthiness by more quickly recognizing negative words (e.g., *deceitful, malicious*) than positive (e.g., *sincere, truthful*) and neutral words (e.g., *slender, healthy*) when presented with the words for just a fraction of a second. High-trusting people showed no difference in their ability to respond to the three categories of words (Gurtman & Lion, 1982). Finally, when contacted by researchers to serve as participants in a study, high-trusting people asked fewer questions (e.g., How did you get my name? What is the experiment about?) than low-trusting subjects. Thus, this body of research, as well as other works (Rotter, 1971, 1980; Wrightsman, 1971), seems to provide evidence that supports the Interpersonal Trust Scale in identifying suspicious minds.

The Internal-External Control of Reinforcement Scale: Where Do You Believe Your Reinforcements Come From? The **Internal-External Control of Reinforcement Scale** (I-E Scale) (Rotter, 1966) is designed to measure the extent to which an individual holds the generalized expectancy that reinforcements in life are controlled by internal factors (e.g., what you do) or external factors (e.g., luck, fate, or the power of others). The I-E Scale contains 29 question pairs, six of which are filler questions, presented in a forced-choice format. For each pair of questions, the person is asked to select one that best represents his or her belief about the operation of events in the world. In each item pair, one statement reflects belief in internal control of reinforcement (e.g., what you get out of life depends on how much you put into it) and one reflects belief in external control of reinforcement (e.g., it's not what you do but who you know that determines what you get out of life). People who tend to express a belief reflecting a generalized expectancy of an internal locus of control are referred to as "internals," while those who express an external locus of control are referred to as "externals." To sample the I-E Scale for yourself, answer the questions in "You Can Do It" on page 323.

YOU CAN DO IT

The I-E Scale: Measuring One of the Most Studied Variables in Psychology

Of the different scales for assessing personality that he developed, Rotter is probably most highly associated with the I-E Scale. The following 10 items are a sample of the response pairs found in the I-E Scale* (Rotter, 1966). For each pair of statements, select the one that best represents your opinion.

1. a. Many of the unhappy things in people's lives are partly due to bad luck.
   b. People's misfortunes result from the mistakes they make.
2. a. One of the major reasons why we have wars is because people don't take enough interest in politics.
   b. There will always be wars, no matter how hard people try to prevent them.
3. a. Without the right breaks one cannot be an effective leader.
   b. Capable people who fail to become leaders have not taken advantage of their opportunities.
4. a. In the case of the well-prepared student there is rarely if ever such a thing as an unfair test.
   b. Many times exam questions tend to be so unrelated to course work that studying is really useless.
5. a. Who gets to be the boss often depends on who was lucky enough to be in the right place first.
   b. Getting people to do the right thing depends upon ability; luck has little to do with it.
6. a. Becoming a success is a matter of hard work; luck has little to do with it.
   b. Getting a good job depends mainly on being in the right place at the right time.
7. a. It is hard to know whether or not a person really likes you.
   b. How many friends you have depends on how nice a person you are.
8. a. With enough effort we can wipe out political corruption.
   b. It is difficult for people to have much control over the things politicians do in office.
9. a. Sometimes I can't understand how teachers arrive at the grades they give.
   b. There is a direct connection between how hard I study and the grades I get.
10. a. People are lonely because they don't try to be friendly.
    b. There's not much use in trying to please people; if they like you, they like you.

Scoring

Each time you selected "a" for items 1, 3, 5, 7, and 9, give yourself one point; each time you selected "b" for items 2, 4, 6, 8, and 10, give yourself one point. Add up the number of points. The higher your score, the more your responses reflect belief in an external control of reinforcement. Because only a small sample of items were presented, however, do not consider this an extremely accurate measure of your locus of control.

*Copyright by American Psychological Association, 1966.

Validation Research on the I-E Scale: A Tradition of Support Continues   The topic of internal versus external control of reinforcement is currently one of the most studied variables in psychology and the other social sciences (Rotter, 1990). Since its original publication in 1966, Rotter's original monograph on internal-external control has been cited in other texts more than 4700 times, "a number far in excess of any other article for the same period of time" (Rotter, 1990, p. 492). It is also interesting to note that the current research on locus of control continues at approximately the same pace as it did over 20 years ago (Rotter, 1990). Such longevity implies that the locus of control concept is just as relevant today as it was then.

As you might imagine, trying to summarize all the research validating the I-E Scale and internal-external control of reinforcement construct would be next to impossible in the very limited space available in this section. But, to illustrate the diverse uses of the I-E Scale, here is a sample of some of the validation research:

▲ *Information processing and I-E.* Since internals believe they have a greater degree of influence over what happens to them, it is expected that they would pay more attention to—and retain more—information that would be useful to them later. Consistent with this logic, hospitalized tuberculosis patients identified as internals retained more information about their condition than those identified as externals (Seeman & Evans, 1962). A similar pattern of results was found for prisoners with regard to retaining information related to achieving parole successfully (Seeman, 1963). When making decisions, internals tend to give reasons based more on previously learned information than externals, even though both originally had equal access to the information (Phares, 1968).

▲ *Taking responsibility and I-E.* The belief that they have some control over the events in their lives seems to result in internals taking more action than externals. For example, among sexually active single college females, internals were more likely to be practicing some form of birth control than externals (MacDonald, 1970). It has also been reported that participation in civil rights demonstrations and other forms of political actions tended to be associated with an internal locus of control (Abramowitz, 1973; Gore & Rotter, 1963; Strickland, 1965). Thus, internals not only believe that they can make a difference in their lives but also tend to take action to make such changes possible.

▲ *Academic achievement of I-E.* The tendency of internals to take more action than externals also translated into greater academic success. In research with college students, internals tend to study more, perform better on tests, and get better grades than externals (Nord, Connelly, & Daignault, 1974; Prociuk & Breen, 1975). Thus, from elementary students to graduate students, there seems to be a rather consistent relationship between internality and academic success (Bar-Tal & Bar-Zohar, 1977; Findley & Cooper, 1983; Lefcourt,

1982). Some possible reasons for the greater academic success of internals over externals are that internals appear to be better than externals at planning and working toward long-term goals, such as a grade that may be two months away or an advanced degree that may take five years to obtain (Lefcourt, 1982). Internals are also better than externals at establishing reachable goals for themselves (Gilmor & Reid, 1978, 1979). For example, while an external might decide to take four courses per semester with a 35-hour-per-week work schedule, an internal might more realistically decide to take just two courses.

Some rather interesting evidence validating the I-E Scale also comes from its application to the world of work, as described in "Applications in Personality Psychology" below.

APPLICATION

APPLICATIONS IN PERSONALITY PSYCHOLOGY

The I-E Scale in the World of Work: Making Your Locus of Control Pay Off

Numerous studies have been conducted in industry to determine the role of locus of control and worker behavior. In a study using female factory workers, Giles (1977) found that internals who were dissatisfied with their jobs were more likely to volunteer for a job enrichment program than externals. In a related finding, a survey of over 3000 workers in six countries indicated that an internal locus of control was associated with greater work involvement (Reitz & Jewell, 1979). When it comes to using pay incentives to increase performance, as you might expect, internals respond with greater performance than externals (Spector, 1982). As a result of this tendency, another suggested application of the I-E Scale involves using it in the personnel selection process to help identify internals for jobs with incentive systems (e.g., sales or piecework pay schedules) (Lawler, 1971).

The belief that internals have on making a difference in their world of work, as reflected in greater job involvement and performance, does seem to have some positive consequences in terms of career advancements and promotion. In a 5-year longitudinal study conducted on a national sample of some 4330 people, it was reported that internals made greater job progress than did externals (Valecha, 1972). Finally, although there are some specific exceptions, internals have been found to be generally more satisfied with their jobs (Spector, 1982) and to show a higher degree of business ethics (Baehr, Jones, & Nerad, 1993) than externals.

In an extremely interesting study, Carl Anderson (1977) examined the relationship between the locus of control of business owners and their financial recovery following a flood (caused by Hurricane Agnes) that destroyed almost all of the businesses in a small Pennsylvania community in 1972. Anderson followed the problem-solving strategies and financial recovery of 90 business owners over a period of 3½ years following the flood. Externals were found to use more emotion-directed coping strategies (e.g., withdrawal and/or hostility) and fewer problem-solving coping methods (e.g., task-oriented strategies) and to perceive their circumstances as being more stressful than internals. The most noteworthy finding of this analysis, however, was the more favorable credit rating of the internal business owners in comparison to the externals at the end of the 3½ years. Based on the results of this study, it was concluded that "the task-oriented coping behaviors of internals are apparently associated with a more successful solution of the problems created by the stressful event, since the performance of the internals' organizations is higher" (Anderson, 1977, p. 450).

When it comes to the world of work, believing that you can make a difference seems to pay off. This seems to be the case for both employees and business owners alike.

The few areas of research described here are a very limited sampling of the research validating the I-E Scale. For more comprehensive reviews of the I-E Scale and locus of control construct, consider the following sources: Burger (1991), Lefcourt (1981, 1983, 1984), Phares (1976), and Strickland (1989). As you will learn in the next section, the I-E Scale has also been used in addressing a number of significant personal and social issues.

Applications of Locus of Control to Matrimony and Divorce: Enhancing Marital Satisfaction and Adjustment to Divorce

The locus of control construct and I-E Scale have been used in various important applications, including helping to understand how people cope with and recover from unpleasant human conditions such as war, natural disasters, illness, and disease; treating alcoholism; studying the implications for child-rearing practices; and promoting health-related behaviors, to name just a few (Lefcourt, 1982, 1983, 1984; Snyder & Forsyth, 1991). The application of locus of control to issues related to marriage and divorce is especially noteworthy and is featured in this section.

Locus of Control and the World of Matrimony: Understanding Marital Interaction and Satisfaction   In looking at how couples resolve marital conflict, researchers have discovered that internal husbands behave more assertively than external husbands; however, assertiveness is not related to the locus of control of the wives (Doherty & Ryder, 1979). In observing the ways that couples try to communicate in marital problem solving, it was discovered that external husbands respond with more verbal and physical aggression than internal husbands, while external wives resort to more indirect forms of communication, such as teasing and kidding around, than internal wives (Winkler & Doherty, 1983, cited in Doherty, 1983b). These results seem to suggest that because they believe that their direct (e.g., assertive) forms of communication have no effect, external husbands and wives must resort to less mature forms of communication when trying to resolve marital conflicts.

Additional research indicates that internal husbands and wives are more aware of and sensitive to potential marital problems than external spouses, more willing to discuss them openly, and more likely to use problem-solving strategies that involve trying to understand and alter the conditions that were the source grievance for their spouses (Miller, Lefcourt, Holmes, Ware, and Saleh, 1986). One possible reason for this pattern of response to marital problems is the rather active and direct problem-solving orientation of internals. Because internal spouses perceive themselves as more responsible for the outcome of their marriage and view marital outcomes as being controllable by their actions, they are much more likely than externals to be willing to engage in problem-solving coping strategies (e.g., open discussion of the problem and/or carrying out alternatives) (Miller, Lefcourt, Holmes, Ware & Saleh, 1986). In addition, because externals seem to feel rather uncomfortable with adopting problem-solving methods for dealing with stress, they tend to employ emotional-focused methods for dealing with stress (e.g., suppression) (Parkes, 1984; Strentz & Auerbach, 1988). In the case of marital problems, since external spouses feel that they have less control over their marital outcome, they are probably more likely to employ an emotional-focused method of coping, such as suppression (i.e., ignoring the problem), and assume that the problem will simply work itself out.

Because locus of control is related to how effectively couples settle their marital conflicts, you would also expect it to be related to marital satisfaction. In support of this reasoning, internality has been found to be positively associated with marital satisfaction (Miller, 1981; Miller, Lefcourt, Holmes, Ware & Saleh, 1986) and marital intimacy (Miller, 1981). Research also seems to suggest that marital dissatisfaction is highest in those marriages where the wife is relatively more external than her husband and the husband relatively more internal than his wife (Mlott & Lira, 1977; Doherty, 1981). The explanation for this relationship seems to be that while these external wives may need a high degree of outward, expressive support, they tend to be married to men who are critical, impatient, and not creative, and who they perceive as not being intellectual or outgoing (Doherty, 1981, 1983b). These internal husbands tended to be married to women who are aggressive, selfish, and talkative, and they described their wives as being aggressive and trying. Couples with little difference in their locus of control scores seem to experience the least marital dissatisfaction (Doherty, 1981). In short, couples in the more external wife or more internal husband marriages have nothing good to say about each other, which would certainly contribute to their high degree of marital dissatisfaction.

Locus of Control and Understanding Adjustment to Divorce: When Breaking Up Is Hard (and not so hard) to Do   When marital dissatisfaction is high, the possibility of ending the relationship becomes very likely. If this is the case, what is the relationship between locus of control and divorce? In one study involving over 904 people from a national probability sample, divorced people were found to have higher internal scores on the I-E Scale than those who were married or had never been married (Doherty, 1980). While it might be tempting to conclude that internal people are more likely to get a divorce, the data do not support this conclusion. In a study involving people from a national probability sample whose I-E scores were obtained twice over a nine-year period, the results generally indicated no relationship between those staying married and those who split up (Doherty, 1983a).

An alternative explanation for the relationship between divorce and internality suggests that successful coping with the rigors of a divorce may produce a stronger belief in people's personal control over their lives (Doherty, 1983a). To test this explanation, in 1969 William Doherty obtained the I-E scores from a national probability sample of 5393 women, ages 30–44. He later obtained I-E scores from these women in 1972 and 1977. When examining the relationship between I-E score and marital status, once again Doherty found that locus of control was not related to subsequent likelihood of getting a divorce during the period from 1969 to 1977. But the I-E scores for those who were divorced during the period from 1967 to 1972 were significantly more external than for those who stayed married (see Figure 11.1). Just the opposite pattern was observed for the period from 1972 to 1977: those who stayed married became more external than those who were divorced (see Figure 11.1). If we assume that rapid movement toward externality is an undesirable experience, then the pattern of results suggests that "divorce has a short-term negative effect on the average woman but that this negative effect does not endure because those who divorce become indistinguishable later from those who remain married" (Doherty, 1983a, p. 838).

In a related study, Helen Barnet (1990) examined the level of pre- and post-divorce stress in a sample of 107 divorced men and women, who had been

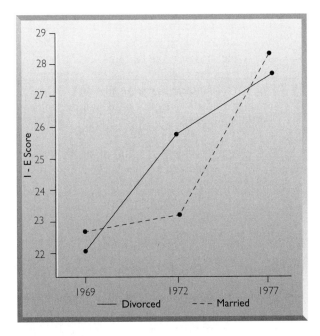

Figure 11.1
Changes in the scores on the locus of control scale for groups of married and divorced women over a 9-year period: The higher the score, the more external the orientation

Note. From Impact of Divorce on Locus of Control Orientation in Adult Woman: A Longitudinal Study, by W. J. V. Doherty, 1983a. *Journal of Personality and Social Psychology,* Vol. 44, pp. 834–840.

married on the average of 10 years (with a range from 1 to 25 years). The survey questions examined how long it took them to decide to get a divorce, the stress due to the divorce, their adjustment to the divorce, and their locus of control score. The results indicated that internals displayed more pre-divorce decision stress but less post-divorce decision stress than externals. In addition, internals displayed less overall stress than externals. It seems that because they feel a greater sense of control, the increased level of pre-divorce decision stress found in internals may be due to their experiencing more agony over the decision to get a divorce than externals. But thinking more about and agonizing more over the decision to get a divorce may have contributed to the internals experiencing less post-divorce decision stress and greater overall adjustment to the divorce than externals.

Thus, when considering the relationship between locus of control and divorce, it seems that divorced people, particularly internals, experience an immediate crisis period. Their long-term reaction, however, might be more accurately described as a recovery period characterized by a greater sense of personal control.

This concludes the discussion on the applications of Rotter's social learning viewpoint. If you would like to know more about other applications of social learning theory, consider reading *Applications of a Social Learning Theory of Personality,* by Julian Rotter, June Chance, and Jerry Phares (1972), or "Locus of Control and Health," a book chapter by Herbert Lefcourt and Karina Davidson-Katz (1991). This discussion of social learning theory concludes with an evaluation of its strengths and limitations.

Evaluation of Rotter's Social Learning Theory: Strengths and Limitations

Our discussion of Rotter's social learning theory will conclude with a summary of its characteristic strengths and limitations.

Characteristic Strengths
Here are some strengths of Rotter's social learning theory:

▲ *Inclusion of cognitive variables: Looking beyond behavior.* Rotter has been a true pioneer in the social-cognitive viewpoint of personality. In addition to acknowledging the significance of cognitive factors in personality, he has developed a theory of personality that specifies explicitly what the factors are (e.g., reinforcement value) and how they are related to each other (e.g., the basic formula) to predict behavior in specific situations. His use of generalized expectancies also represents an extension of the use of cognitive variables to predict behavior in a broader sense. Thus, Rotter's use of cognitive variables involves looking far beyond just behavior to predict behavior.

▲ *Emphasis on research: Verification of constructs.* Because of his affiliation with major research universities, Rotter has always been very concerned with the validation of his theory through basic and applied research. Research on social learning theory has been stimulated by the fact that the basic concepts within the theory can be easily measured. For example, the verification of the effectiveness of social learning therapy can be assessed by noting the extent to which a client lists a greater number of alternative courses of action as the therapy progresses. The ease to which such generalized expectancies as locus of control and interpersonal trust can be measured has also contributed to the tremendous amount of research that has been done to verify the validity of social learning theory. Thus, the clarity with which the basic concepts are stated has contributed to the large amount of research done on social learning theory.

Characteristic Limitations

Here are some limitations of Rotter's social learning theory:

▲ *On being too cognitive: Ignoring the objective situation.* Social learning theory has been criticized for placing too much emphasis on the cognitive side of the individual. For example, critics from the more traditional learning viewpoint have expressed displeasure with the emphasis social learning theory has given to subjective perceptions by the individual. For example, social learning theory tends to rely on such subjective concepts as reinforcement value and specific and generalized expectancies at the expense of attention to objective environmental factors (e.g., schedules of reinforcement). Thus, social learning theory has been criticized as being too subjective by traditional learning theorists.

▲ *More on being too cognitive: A theory with no feeling.* From the more humanistic viewpoint, social learning theory has been criticized as placing too much emphasis on the cognitive side of human nature at the expense of the emotional side. For example, such basic emotions as anxiety are not found anywhere in the language of social learning theory. In its defense, social learning theory uses such terms as *high reinforcement value* and *low freedom of*

movement to describe situations in which an individual would experience what might be considered feelings of anxiety. Thus, while social learning theory has been criticized as lacking a concern for emotions, it actually chooses to consider emotional expressions in more objectively stated terms.

This concludes the discussion of social learning theory. To learn more about social learning theory, consider reading Rotter's (1982) *The Development and Application of Social Learning Theory: Selected Papers.* This text summarizes the major concepts and the overall development of social learning theory over the past 30 years. Rotter's (1954) original formulation of social learning theory in *Social Learning and Clinical Psychology* is also highly recommended to any student interested in obtaining a greater understanding of this major influence on the study of contemporary personality psychology. Along these lines, in the next section, you will consider the perspective of Albert Bandura, another contemporary social-cognitive personality theorist who shares Julian Rotter's emphasis on cognitive factors and systematic validation research.

Bandura's Social-Cognitive Theory: Outlining the Reciprocal Nature of Personality

When describing the basic nature of his social-cognitive theory, Albert Bandura notes that

> people are neither driven by inner forces nor automatically shaped and controlled by external stimuli. Rather, human functioning is explained in terms of a model of triadic reciprocality in which behavior, cognitive and other personal factors, and the environment all operate as interacting determinants of each other. (Bandura, 1986, p. 18)

Bandura believes that to understand an individual, you have to consider the synergism of how what people do affects what they believe and what they believe affects what they do, and how what people both think and do is interrelated with the situation in which they find themselves (e.g., their present physical location or the subculture or society in which they live). Such comprehensiveness characterizes Bandura's approach to his theorizing, research, and applications of his social-cognitive theory. For a glimpse into the life of one of the world's best known and respected psychologists, read "A Closer Look" below.

A Closer Look:

Biographical Background: The Life of Albert Bandura

Albert Bandura was born on December 4, 1925, and grew up in the beautiful but cold and rugged region of northern Alberta, Canada. Like many other children growing up in a small village, Bandura attended the same school from elementary school through high school. But because of a shortage of teachers and resources, Bandura and many of his classmates were almost required to teach themselves. The summer after his graduation, Bandura worked on the Alaskan Highway, which was built during World War II to connect the United States with the Alaskan territory. During that time, the young Bandura came into contact with a variety of coworkers with an assortment of psychopathologies and rather "colorful" pasts, including parole violators, debtors, and ex-husbands trying to avoid paying alimony. His observations of and interactions with these people sparked his interest in clinical psychology.

After graduating from high school, he entered the University of British Columbia. In addition to clinical psychology, Bandura also developed a very strong interest in learning theory. In 1949, after only three years in college, Bandura received a BA degree in psychology. When selecting a graduate school, Bandura followed his interest in learning theory and entered the University of Iowa, which at that time was one of the premier centers for the study of learning, with the leadership of the influential learning theorist Kenneth W. Spence.

Although he was interested in clinical psychology, Bandura, under Spence's influence, became exposed to the rigor of experimental research and had first-hand experience with Spence's theoretical conceptualization of learning, which was a dominant force in psychology at that time. Bandura received his MA

degree in 1951 and his PhD in clinical psychology in 1952 from the University of Iowa.

In addition to being educated by a major figure in psychology, attending the University of Iowa changed Bandura's life in another important way—he met his future wife. Bored with his reading assignments, Bandura decided one day to play some golf with a friend. On the course, Bandura and his friend were playing behind a female twosome. Eventually the male and female twosomes became a foursome. One of the women in the twosome was Virginia Varns, whom Bandura would soon marry.

After leaving the University of Iowa, Bandura accepted a one-year clinical internship at the Wichita Guidance Center. In 1953, at the end of his internship in Wichita, he accepted a position as an instructor at Stanford University in Palo Alto, California, where he has remained for all but one year of his academic career.

At Stanford, Bandura began what was to turn into an extremely distinguished career. His early research and publications involved clinical psychology, including the Rorschach test and the interactive processes underlying psychotherapy and the role of family patterns in the development of aggression in children. Working with Richard Walters, his first graduate student at Stanford, Bandura developed a program of rigorous research investigating the role of the modeling process in the development of aggression in children. Bandura expanded his research in modeling to include the role of observational learning in personality development (e.g., sex-role development), social issues (e.g., television violence), and psychotherapy. His most

Albert Bandura is one of personality psychology's most innovative and influential thinkers. His work has made significant contributions to our understanding of the process of observational learning, the impact of media violence on the behavior of children, and psychotherapy.

recent research focuses on the influence of the self as a determinant and regulator of behavior.

Although he began as only a lecturer, Bandura later served as the chairman of Stanford's exceptional psychology department, where he held the distinguished title of David Starr Jordan Professor of Social Science in Psychology. Based on his scholarly and voluminous research contribution to psychology, Bandura has received numerous awards, including the prestigious Guggenheim Fellowship and the Distinguished Contribution Award from the Division of Clinical Psychology (Division 12) of the American Psychological Association in 1972. In 1974, Bandura was elected to the distinguished position of president of the American Psychological Association, as well as awarded the David Starr Jordan Professor of Social Science in Psychology endowed chair at Stanford University. In 1980, he received the extremely prestigious Award for Distinguished Scientific Contribution from the American Psychological Association, as well as the Distinguished Contribution Award from the Society for Research on Aggression. Bandura also received the James McKeen Cattell Award for outstanding contributions to psychology in 1977, and he was elected to Fellow status of the American Academy of Arts and Sciences in 1980.

Bandura is still at Stanford University, where he continues to conduct a great deal of research, refine his theory, and teach both undergraduate and graduate courses. More information about the life of Albert Bandura can be found in a brief biography appearing in the *American Psychologist* (American Psychological Association, 1981, January), in a book chapter titled "Albert Bandura" (Evans, 1976), or in a book titled *Albert Bandura, the Man and His Ideas—A Dialogue,* by Richard I. Evans (1989).

Basic Assumptions: Linking the Learning and Cognitive Viewpoints

In his social-cognitive theory, Bandura has developed a perspective on personality that combines the contemporary emphasis on cognitive processes with traditional principles of learning (Bandura, 1986). This rather eclectic approach can be illustrated by two basic assumptions: the self system and reciprocal determinism.

The Self System: Subjective Filters of Objective Stimuli

Like the other social-cognitive theorists in this chapter, Bandura does not believe that the individual simply reacts to the objective stimuli in the environment as a robot might. Instead, Bandura suggests that the individual processes information about the stimuli in the environment through a self system (Bandura, 1978, 1986). The **self system** is a set of cognitive functions within the individual that help in the perception and evaluation of the environment and regulation of behavior. For example, when you see a sign that says the speed limit is 65 mph, your speed is determined by several cognitive processes operating within your self system, including the extent to which you perceive others around you as speeding, your evaluation of the likelihood of getting caught speeding today, and how much of a hurry you are in to get to your destination (e.g., level of motivation). Thus, as in traditional learning theory, Bandura recognizes the influence of environmental stimuli in determining behavior (e.g., punishment in the form of a ticket for speeding), but conceptualizes this influence as being filtered through a series of cognitive processes (e.g., the perceived likelihood of being caught speeding). In this manner, Bandura acknowledges the significant contribution made by both learning and cognitive theories.

Reciprocal Determinism: Reacting to the Reaction of Others Reacting to Your Reactions

In addition to the cognitive processes operating on environmental stimuli, Bandura assumes that the environment operates on the self system. **Reciprocal determinism** is the term Bandura uses to describe the back-and-forth influence between the environment and the self system on the regulation of behavior (Bandura, 1978, 1986). For example, if you are generally a speeder and go 65 mph in a 55-mph zone, but then enter a 65-mph zone, you are probably going to increase your speed to around 70 or 75 mph. In this case, the new speed limit sign serves as an external stimulus that influences your driving behavior. In response to the increased number of speeders on this stretch of road, the highway patrol may increase their surveillance of it. In this case, the behavior of the highway patrol is influenced by the behavior of the speeders. With the belief that you are more likely to get caught based on your perception of more patrol officers in the area, you then slow down your speed. Once again, as the number of speeders is reduced, the highway patrol will shift its emphasis to another stretch of road. As this example illustrates, the behavior of both the highway patrol and speeders is influenced reciprocally by their separate but interrelated sets of perceptions and beliefs based on environmental cues.

Thus, while other cognitive theorists have discussed the systematic interrelationship between cognitive and environmental factors on the behavior of the person, Bandura has introduced the idea of combining the separate systems (e.g., the speeders and the highway patrol) to demonstrate more realistically the reciprocal manner in which behavior in the "real world" is determined. To help clarify the notion of reciprocal determinism, Figure 11.2 is a graphic illustration of the speeder-highway patrol example.

With the assumptions of the self system and reciprocal determinism, Bandura has been able to acknowledge the influence of both external stimuli and cognitive process. By incorporating these two assumptions, Bandura has brought together the learning and cognitive viewpoints in a manner that realistically explains the operation of behavior. The

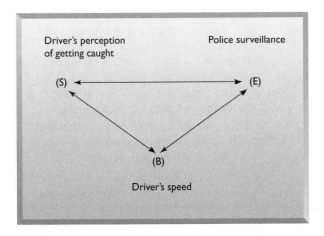

Figure 11.2
According to reciprocal determinism, behavior (B) is a result of the interrelatedness of the individual's self system (S) and the nature of the cues found in the environment (E)

next section describes some major concepts and processes of Bandura's social cognitive theory.

Basic Concepts and Processes: Imitation, Expectations, and Regulation

To give you a better understanding of the fundamentals of Bandura's social-cognitive theory, a discussion of the theory's basic concepts and processes will be presented.

Observational Learning: Learning by Looking
Although his training in learning theory was very traditional, Bandura's position on observational learning clearly places him outside the category of a traditional learning theorist. Bandura has argued that the learning of most of the more significant and complex aspects of behavior is not based solely on principles of operant and classical conditioning, but on observational learning (Bandura, 1977b, 1986).

For Bandura, **observational learning** involves acquiring complex behaviors by watching, hearing about, or reading about the behavior of others. His reasoning is that much of the behavior that plays a significant role in our everyday living is too complex and costly to be learned on the basis of the trial-and-error method involved in the more traditional methods of learning. For example, falling in love is a behavior that cannot be explained by basic principles of learning. Instead, we rely on what we see in the movies, read in books, or hear from our family and friends to help us know when and how to behave when we are in love. In a more global sense, it is difficult to explain how we transmit such complex phenomena as language, social norms, and cultural traditions without acknowledging the contribution that observing others plays in the acquisition of these very important aspects of all of our lives. In a more pragmatic sense, observational learning is also the logic behind many of the self-help videos, books, and seminars that seem to be so popular today.

The Distinction between Learning and Performance: Knowing vs. Doing   One point related to observational learning that separates Bandura from the traditional learning theorists is the distinction he makes between learning and performance. Proponents of the more traditional learning viewpoints believe that a behavior has to be performed before it can be confirmed that it has been learned. In sharp contrast, from the social-cognitive viewpoint, a behavior does not necessarily need to be performed in order to imply that it is learned. In many cases, simply observing someone doing something is enough to learn how to do it.

For example, although most 10-year-old children have not done so, most of them probably know what it would take to start the family car, put it in gear, and back it out of the driveway. The same is probably true for adults regarding what we may have learned from the movies about firing a gun, stopping a bullet wound from bleeding, indirectly trying to bribe a police officer, or participating in unconventional sexual practices. The point is that you do not have to perform a behavior to demonstrate that you have learned it. In fact, it is probably better that we do not attempt many of the behaviors (e.g., bribing a police officer) that we actually know how to perform.

The Role of Vicarious Reinforcement: Direct vs. Vicarious Payoffs   Another point of deviation of the social-cognitive theory from traditional learning viewpoints is the role played by reinforcement (Bandura, 1986). From the traditional learning viewpoint, behavior is strengthened or weakened to the extent that a certain behavior is followed by a reinforcer. Bandura disagrees; he assumes that simply observing someone being rewarded or punished for a particular behavior is enough to increase the likelihood of the observer performing a certain behavior.

For example, most of us do not have to be put in jail to know that shooting someone will lead to punishment. We have learned to expect punishment from reading about and seeing on the news what happens to those who have done so. On the other hand, if we know of people who get away with cheating on their income tax, we are more likely to cheat as well. The point is that increasing or decreasing the likelihood of a behavior being performed can be influenced not only by actually experiencing the consequences but also by developing certain expectancies about the consequences based solely on watching what happens to others. Thus, it is not really necessary to have had a payoff in order to engage in a behavior; just seeing that it might pay off seems to be enough.

The Processes of Observational Learning: The Essentials of Learning by Looking   In addition to suggesting that observational learning does take place, Bandura (1969, 1977b, 1986) also specified four basic processes, divided into four stages, that are involved if such learning is to occur: attentional processes, retention processes, motor reproduction processes, and motivational processes.

▲   *Stage One: Can I have your attention, please? Attentional processes* influence observational learning by determining to what the individual is going to attend. For observational learning to occur, the individual must not only be aware of what the model is doing but also be able to determine what aspects of the behavior are the most relevant. For example, when watching a professional tennis match in an attempt to improve your serve you must concentrate on how high the professionals toss the ball and the arch in their backs, not the color of their tennis outfits. Part of what is involved in discussing attentional processes is considering what factors influence them. Factors such as the age, sex, attractiveness, status, and competence of the model, as well as the motivational state of the observer, all influence the degree of attentional processes. It is for this reason that advertisers hire celebrities to endorse their products; these are the types of people to whom we are most likely to attend.

▲   *Stage Two: Run that by me again, please. Retention processes* influence observational learning by determining the extent to which the individual remembers the model to which he or she was attending. Retention processes are important because in many cases, a person might have only a limited amount of contact with the model and must rely on a memory of what was observed. Bandura asserts that retention processes involve both visual and verbal dimensions. The visual dimension involves being able to generate and maintain a mental image of what was done by the model. The verbal dimension involves being able to describe what was done in words. For example, while you have a mental picture of what the tennis pro looked like while serving, you probably can describe the action by saying something like, "She tossed the ball up slowly about two feet, arched her back about twenty degrees, and bent her elbow slightly as she brought her arm directly over her head when making the serve." The verbal description provides a more concrete set of cues that can be recalled at a later date than the mental image, which tends to fade rather rapidly.

▲ *Stage Three: Try doing that again, please. Motor reproduction processes* involve transforming the information about the model that has been attended to and visually and verbally coded into overt behavior. For example, as a beginning tennis player, you might go to the park with a bucket of tennis balls and begin practicing your serve while telling yourself to "toss the ball slowly about two feet in the air." Transforming the visual and verbal information into actual behavior may not be as simple as it sounds, with the first few serves possibly going right into the net. But with some patience and practice, the motor reproductions soon get smoother and smoother. Without the previously coded information obtained through observation, however, learning to serve would involve a lot of guesswork and trial-and-error behavior.

▲ *Stage Four: What will it take for you to do this? Motivational processes* involve providing the desire to perform those behaviors that have been acquired through the process of observational learning. It is at this point that the distinction between learning and performance comes into play. As noted earlier, the types of factors that influence the performance of learned behaviors include observing the consequences for the model (e.g., did the tennis pro make the serve?), the expectancies of the observer (e.g., will practice improve your serve?), and the motivational level of the observer (e.g., you'll receive a lot of recognition from your peers). While the motivational processes have been discussed as the last stage in observational learning, you should realize that they play a significant role during each of the stages. For example, if you do not really care too much about improving your serve, you may in fact spend more time looking at the color of

the tennis players' outfits than their serving techniques.

You have examined some factors and processes that are involved in observational learning. As you can see, combining the general notion of observational learning—along with its four basic processes—with those basic principles of the more traditional learning viewpoints does a very good job of explaining some of the more complex and significant aspects of social behavior. For some rather significant examples of observational learning, as well as the consequences of the process, read "A Closer Look" on page 334.

A Closer Look:

The Observational Learning of Sex and Violence: What You See Is What You Do— Sometimes

One of the more significant implications of Bandura's emphasis on observational learning is the possibility of learning various forms of antisocial behavior from models that appear on television or in motion pictures. A very serious concern has been the impact of media sex and violence on viewer behavior.

The Watching of Violence in the Media: Modeling Aggressive Behavior
One of the earliest research attempts to investigate the issue of media violence on children's behavior was a series of classic studies known as the "Bobo doll studies," because they used a 5-foot-tall, inflatable plastic clown doll called Bobo. In these studies (Bandura & Walters, 1963), nursery school children were exposed to aggressive or nonaggressive models and then observed for their own level of aggressiveness during free-play periods.

In the aggressive model condition, the children were exposed to an adult who acted very aggressive while playing with the Bobo doll. The aggressive adult model hit the doll with a toy wooden hammer, kicked it, sat on it, and punched it while saying such things as "Kick him" or "Sock him in the nose" (see Figure 11.3). Children in the control model condition were exposed to an adult model who played quietly and passively with other toys in the room. Later, the

Figure 11.3
The top row illustrates the aggressive behavior of the adult model against the Bobo doll. The second and third rows illustrate the children modeling the aggressive behavior.

children were placed in the room containing the Bobo doll and other toys and observed through a one-way mirror for 20 minutes in an attempt to note how similar their behavior would be to that of the model they had seen. As predicted from the social-cognitive theory, those children who had observed the aggressive model behaved more aggressively than those who had observed the quiet, passive model. In fact, the aggressive behavior of the children resembled that of the aggressive model in many cases (see Figure 11.3).

Results similar to those of the "Bobo studies" have also been found in other studies (Berkowitz, 1993; Liebert & Schwartzberg, 1977; Liebert, Sprafkin, & Davidson, 1989; Wood, Wong, & Chachere, 1991). For example, children exposed to excerpts from an actual television show containing a high degree of violence ("The Untouchables") demonstrated a greater willingness to inflict what they believed was pain upon another child than children who were exposed to

excerpts from an arousing but nonviolent track race (Liebert & Baron, 1972).

Similar results have also been obtained with aggressive behaviors in more natural settings (Eron, 1987; Park, Berkowitz, Leyes, West, & Sebastian, 1977). For example, groups of institutionalized delinquent boys were exposed to aggressive commercials every night for a week, while others in the institution were exposed to neutral commercials. The results of this study indicated that the boys exposed to the aggressive commercials engaged in more physical and verbal aggression, even in the presence of institutional staff members, than those exposed to the neutral commercials, (Leyens, Camino, Parke, & Berkowitz, 1975). In a more recent study (Josephson, 1987), young boys exposed to a modified version of a highly violent television show (e.g., a SWAT team killing a group of snipers) displayed more aggressive behavior during a game of floor hockey than boys exposed to an exciting but nonviolent television program (e.g., a motor-cross bike race featuring many exciting stunts). Similar to the results of studies involving televised violence, other research indicates that there is a corresponding increase in aggression in children after playing aggressive video games (Schutte, Malouff, Post-Gorden, & Rodasts, 1988).

The Watching of Sex in the Media: Modeling Sexual Behavior

Some evidence also indicates that certain aspects of sexual behavior may be modeled from the media. For example, in one study (Bryant, 1985), adolescents and adults were interviewed to determine what their reactions were to the first time they viewed X-rated films and magazines. The results indicated that almost 70% of the males and 40% of the females surveyed expressed a desire to imitate the sexual activity portrayed in the X-rated films. Of more importance was the finding that about 30% of the males and 20% of the females actually did imitate the activity portrayed in the film the first time they were exposed to it. But this disinhibition effect seems to be rather short-lived, lasting only about 24 hours.

For example, in one study (Mann, Berkowitz, Sidman, Starr, & West, 1974), 66 married couples were shown erotic or nonerotic films once a week for a month. One group of couples were exposed to the erotic movies for the first two weeks of the month, then the nonerotic films for the second two weeks; another group was exposed to the nonerotic films for the first two weeks. A third group viewed only nonerotic films for the entire month. During the month, all of the couples were asked to monitor their rate of sexual intercourse. The results of this study indicated that during the initial exposure to the erotic films, there was a tendency for the couples to increase the likelihood of sexual intercourse on the movie nights. Thus, there was little carry-over effect of the erotic films to the next day, suggesting that the modeling behavior may have been rather weak. These results are consistent with other research indicating that both males and females reported increases in their frequency of masturbation only within a 24-hour period of watching sexually explicit slides and movies (Schmidt & Sigusch, 1970). Thus, while the initial effect of viewing erotic material may trigger some modeling, in the long run, the novelty seems to wane and people settle into a previously established pattern of sexual behavior.

The Watching of Sex and Violence in the Media: Modeling Violence against Women

Another area of research on modeling that combines the themes of both sex and aggression concerns itself with the role of violence against women in pornography (Baron & Richardson, 1994). A very common theme in the pornographic literature involves a man physically overpowering a woman, forcing her to have sex that she initially finds unpleasant but then comes to enjoy. There is consistent evidence that exposing males to such pornographic literature increases the aggression they exhibit toward women (Donnerstein, 1980; Malamuth & Briere, 1986). More important, males who maintain the belief that the females enjoy the violent sex that is portrayed in pornography are much more likely to admit to the possibility of committing a rape if no one would know and they could get away with it without punishment (Malamuth, 1984). This notion is supported by the finding that when a group of sex offenders was surveyed, 33% of the rapists reported looking at pornographic literature as part of their preparation for committing the crime (Marshall, 1985). Thus, there is some evidence that in a small percentage of males, modeling may play a role in developing and helping to maintain certain attitudes linking sex and violence against women that may contribute to rape.

In a more general sense, another quite significant finding is that after prolonged exposure to pornography involving violence against women, both males and females developed more calloused attitudes and less emotional sensitivity toward the victims of such activities (Linz, Donnerstein, & Penrod, 1984; Zillmann & Bryant, 1984). They felt less sympathy toward the rape victim, perceived violent crimes against women as being less serious, and expressed more agreement with rape myths (e.g., women really want this type of treatment).

As you can see, the role of modeling as a process in acquiring behavior and attitudes has some very important social implications. In a related topic, recent research has begun to focus on the developmental and interpersonal effects of exposure to chronic real-life community violence on young children (Osofsky, 1995).

Thus, observational learning explains the process by which people acquire behavior by imitating what we see others doing. But the performance of this behavior is influenced by various other factors, including beliefs about our ability to execute it and the expected outcome it will produce.

Self-Efficacy: What Do You Think You Can Do?

Observational learning provides a means by which an individual has the opportunity to acquire a particular skill or behavior pattern. But, as noted earlier, simply knowing how to do something is not enough to guarantee that you will perform the behavior. To explain more completely the relationship between what we know and what we do, Bandura utilizes the concept of self-efficacy (Bandura, 1977a, 1977b, 1982, 1986, 1989a, 1991b).

Self-efficacy refers to a person's perceived belief that he or she can execute a specific behavior in an attempt to cope with a particular situation. For example, your decision to go out on the dance floor is a function of the belief that you have of your ability to execute the dance steps and movements successfully enough so that you do not embarrass yourself or your partner. Judgments of self-efficacy determine not only whether you decide on a course of action but also how long you will persist and the extent to which you will prepare for it (Bandura, 1989b; Multon, Brown, & Lent, 1991). For example, if you perceive yourself to be a good dancer, you will probably stay out on the dance floor longer than someone who might not consider himself to be a good dancer.

A concept related to self-efficacy is that of outcome expectation (Bandura, 1986). **Outcome expectations** are the consequences an individual believes will follow the performance of a particular act. For example, a man might believe that if he dances well, he will receive a lot of attention and recognition from his peers. Bandura (1986) summarizes the relationship between self-efficacy and outcome expectations in the following manner: "In social, intellectual, and physical pursuits, those who judge themselves highly efficacious will expect favorable outcomes, self-doubters will expect mediocre performances of themselves and negative outcomes" (p. 392). Thus, if you view yourself as being a good dancer, and believe that dancing well will bring you social recognition, you are much more likely to engage in such behavior than those who do not perceive themselves as being good dancers or believe that dancing will not produce favorable consequences.

The Influence of Self-Efficacy: Affecting Thoughts, Feelings, and Behavior   Self-efficacy influences not only people's behavior but also our thoughts and emotions. For example, if you believe that being a good dancer is very important because of the attention

and popularity it will bring you, and if you also believe you are not a very good dancer and will never be one no matter how hard you try, you are very likely to feel depressed. Such a combination of beliefs and emotions may cause you to not even try to improve your dancing ability. As you might expect, this pattern of self-efficacy is often characteristic of people who experience problems of personality adjustment and psychopathology (Bandura, 1986).

Factors Influencing Self-Efficacy: What You Hear, See, Do, and Feel Makes a Difference   Because of the importance of self-efficacy, it is important to know some of the factors that might influence it (Bandura, 1977a, 1986).

▲   The *verbal persuasion* of others concerning your ability to perform the particular course of action. An example of this might be your friends saying, "Go ahead and go out there. You can dance just as well as all of those other people."

▲   *Vicarious experience*, or simply watching someone else perform the action successfully. Seeing that others who are enjoying themselves dancing are no better at it than you are may be just what is needed to get you out of your chair and onto the dance floor.

▲   Probably the most powerful factor is that of *performance accomplishments*, or simply having performed the behavior successfully in the past. You are more likely to get up and dance if you had a good time and received positive feedback from your friends the last two times you were out on the dance floor.

▲   *Emotional arousal*, or the degree of anxiety you feel in a particular situation that tells you how well you are performing a specific behavior. For example, if you feel very self-conscious and nervous while on the dance floor, you are probably going to assume that it is due to people evaluating you negatively because you are not dancing very well. As a result, you are probably less likely to dance again in the near future.

Although each of these factors are discussed individually, you should realize that in most cases, they operate together to help determine self-efficacy. For example, while your friends may tell you that you dance well enough, and you see that others dance no better than you, your feelings of self-consciousness may be too powerful and keep you sitting in your chair just tapping your feet. Thus, your level of self-efficacy is based on a combination of information obtained from both external (e.g., what we see or others tell us) and internal sources (e.g., our personal thoughts, emotions, and direct experience).

As part of the self-system, Bandura conceptualizes self-efficacy as a subjective mediating process of behavior that is determined by both personal (e.g., beliefs) and external factors (e.g., feedback from others). The concept of self-efficacy also reflects Bandura's emphasis on considering both the person and environment when attempting to explain and understand the dynamics of personality.

Self-Regulation: Doing What You Want to Do

In the more traditional learning perspective, behavior is governed by the consequences of behavior. This view suggests that our behavior is regulated by external rewards and punishments, but it ignores the role played by the individual in regulating his or her own behavior. In a more realistic view of the individual, Bandura also proposes the notion of self-regulation of behavior (Bandura, 1977b, 1978, 1986, 1989b, 1991b). **Self-regulation** involves the process by which the individual establishes and acts upon a set of internally derived standards and expectations. Included in the process of self-regulation are ethical and moral beliefs, standards of excellence, judgments of competency in comparison to the behavior of others, and past performance. For example, whether you decide to stop and try to help an injured person at the scene of an accident depends on the extent to which you feel doing so is the "right" thing to do, you believe that you can make a difference if you do intervene, you assume there are others present who are more qualified to help (e.g., medical personnel) than you, and/or you have been helpful in other situations.

Self-Reward and Self-Punishment: The Consequences of Self-Regulation

At the base of the process of self-regulation are self-reward and self-punishment. When you meet the standards you have set for yourself, you give yourself a pat on the back or feel an increase in your sense of self-worth. As a result, you may try even harder in the future. This often occurs regardless of external consequences. For example, you would assist the accident victim even though the person could not give you any monetary reward, or even though no news reporters were around to put your picture in the paper. As another example, a runner in a marathon may get a sense of reward just for finishing the race. On the other hand, when you fail to meet your own standards, you may blame yourself for not pushing hard enough and feel a personal sense of failure. For example, when you do not get the grade you thought you would, you vow to study even harder for the next test. The point is that it is overly simplistic to assume that only external rewards regulate behavior. Instead, Bandura (1991a, 1991b) proposes that self-regulation is selectively activated based on internal standards of evaluation (e.g., self-efficacy or moral convictions) and environmental conditions (e.g., the presence of other bystanders).

Sources of Origin: From Where Do These Standards for Self-Regulation Come?

Like so many other aspects of our behavior, personal standards of self-regulation are learned through the traditional processes of classical and operant conditioning and observational learning (Bandura, 1977b, 1986). For example, when you fail to meet the expectations of your boss, she may tell you to work harder. As a result, for the next couple of weekends, you regulate your behavior to spend more time working on your assigned report instead of playing tennis. If such behavior does lead to reward, you then come to associate hard work with rewards. You might also observe others being praised by the boss for all the extra time they put in on their reports over the weekend.

Similar processes of learning also occur through our interactions with other significant people in our lives, such as parents, siblings, friends, and teachers. Thus, the standards we acquire from others, to some extent, form the basis of our self-regulatory systems. But understand that it is the individual, and the individual alone, who is responsible for activating the self-regulation system. Thus, regardless of the origin of self-regulating systems, the importance in determining behavior cannot be ignored.

Personality Maladjustment: Maladaptive Modeling, Unrealistic Self-Evaluations, and Inefficacy
According to social cognitive theory, three contributing factors to personality maladjustment are maladaptive modeling, dysfunctional self-evaluations, and perceived inefficacy.

Maladaptive Modeling: Looking but Not Learning Anything   As with other more traditional learning theories, social-cognitive theory assumes that personality maladjustment is a result of faulty learning. But in a departure from more traditional learning theories, Bandura (1968) also believes that maladaptive behavior can be learned by exposure to models displaying maladaptive behavior. For example, consider teenagers who see that their parents simply complain about the difficulties they are facing in life instead of taking some kind of action to improve the situation. Such teenagers will probably model this passive coping strategy when confronted with major problems in their own lives as well.

Dysfunctional Self-Evaluations: Unrealistic Expectations   A category of cognitive processes that can contribute to personality maladjustment is dysfunctional self-evaluations (Bandura, 1977b). **Dysfunctional self-evaluations** involve the failure to establish an effective standard for self-rewards and self-punishments. An example of dysfunctional self-evaluation might include a female executive who sets such high standards for herself that she is never able to experience the satisfaction of doing work that is good enough. Self-evaluation that lacks self-reward but is excessive in self-punishment is probably going to contribute to feelings of depression.

Perceived Inefficacy: Having Self-Doubts   Feelings of anxiety and depression can also be triggered by perceived inefficacy (Bandura, 1977b). **Perceived inefficacy** involves the feeling that you cannot deal effectively with important events (Bandura, 1982). For example, an individual who perceives himself as not having anything interesting to say may feel helpless at parties and other social gatherings and may spend much of his time alone and depressed.

    This concludes the discussion of the basic concepts of Bandura's social-cognitive theory. With a general understanding of the basic elements of Bandura's theory, you can now turn your attention to some of its applications.

Applications of Social-Cognitive Theory: Using What Is Known

In the process of developing a comprehensive theory of personality, Bandura has also directed his attention to the application of social-cognitive theory. While there are many applications of Bandura's social-cognitive theory, and other related cognitive perspectives, the common thread in the applications featured in this section is the emphasis on the modification of behavior and cognitions through modeling and changes in self-efficacy. The three areas used to illustrate the diversity of these applications are therapeutic modeling, cognitive therapy, and self-defense training.

Social-Cognitive Therapeutic Intervention: Promoting Self-Efficacy and Behavioral Change through Modeling
Bandura believes that psychotherapy must go beyond simply talking to clients about their problem. He believes that the therapeutic process should be a learning experience resulting in a change in the client's behavior. In his approach to therapeutic intervention, Bandura (1961, 1986, 1995) promotes combining fundamental principles of learning with his own specific concerns for promoting self-efficacy as a critical element in the changing of behavior. A critical component in Bandura's approach to therapeutic intervention is the use of modeling to help clients acquire new skills and a sense of increased confidence (Bandura, 1977a, 1986).

Modeling Techniques of Therapeutic Intervention: Facilitating the Acquisition of Competencies and Confidence
In its most basic form, the therapeutic use of modeling involves the client observing various models, either live or via videotape, participating in some desired behavior that results in favorable consequences (Nietzel, Bernstein, & Milich, 1994). For example, an individual with low self-esteem might watch a film or observe a live model receiving a

refund after making a request to the salesclerk in a very assertive manner.

In **mastery modeling**, the client is assisted by the therapist or live model in performing the desired behavior (Bandura, 1986, 1988). Although similar to role playing, mastery modeling involves breaking down the desired behavior into subskills and progressively more difficult behaviors. Guiding the client step by step through the problematic behavior increases the client's likelihood of experiencing continuous progress and success. For example, working with an excessively shy client, the therapist might "walk through" the steps of how to approach a stranger at a social gathering in order to initiate and maintain a conversation. In this case, the therapist might first work with the client on making eye contact and smiling when being introduced to someone new at a party. Next, the therapist might show the client how to ask questions in order to keep a conversation going. Finally, the therapist might show the client how to end conversations but leave open the opportunity for future interactions (e.g., asking for a date). Thus, by systematically arranging what needs to be learned and how to learn it most effectively, the therapist is much more likely to help the client experience success and acquire a sense of self-efficacy.

For therapy to be successful, Bandura believes that therapists have to create in clients a sense of confidence that they can succeed. This is facilitated by demonstrating what people need to do through modeling techniques and offering them the opportunity to practice these skills (Evans, 1989). In fact, a very interesting application of modeling technique presents videotaped models of parents using various behavior modification techniques, in order to help parents watching these videos use these same techniques more effectively with their own children. In this case, increasing the competencies and confidence of parents to use these techniques resulted in improved performances by the children at home and at school (Webster-Stratton, 1992). But as you will find in reading "Applications in Personality Psychology" (see next column), one of the most frequent and successful therapeutic applications of social-cognitive theory has been in the treatment of phobias (Bandura, 1986; Kazdin, 1994; Rathus & Nevid, 1991).

APPLICATION

APPLICATIONS IN PERSONALITY PSYCHOLOGY

Curing Phobias: Overcoming What Scares You

A classic example of social-cognitive learning therapy involved the treatment of people suffering from snake phobias who answered a newspaper ad placed by Bandura and his colleagues (Bandura, Blanchard, & Ritter, 1969). These phobic people were divided into four groups. In the live model/participation group, the people watched a model handle the snake and were then guided through the actual handling of the snake by the therapist. In the symbolic modeling group, the people simply watched a film showing adults and children handling a snake. In the systematic desensitization group, the people were taught relaxation training while watching the film. Finally, a control group received no special training or treatment at all. The degree to which all of the people would approach and/or handle the snake was recorded before and after treatments were given. As can be seen in Figure 11.4, the treatment program involving the people observing a live model and then being guided through snake handling proved to be the most effective.

The effectiveness of modeling to reduce a fear of dogs (Bandura, Grusec, & Menlove, 1967), as well as a fear of medical and dental procedures (Melamed & Siegel, 1975; Melamed, Hawes, Heiby, & Glick, 1975), has also been documented. In addition to the treatment of phobias, modeling has been used to treat various other clinical problems, including obsessive-compulsive disorder, antisocial behavior, social withdrawal, and early infantile autism, to name just a few (Rosenthal & Steffek, 1991).

Cognitive-Behavior Therapy:
Learning to Think and Behave Better
The emphasis given to the role of cognitive factors in the therapeutic process led to the development of what are called cognitive therapies (Hollon & Beck, 1994). **Cognitive therapies** have as their basis the development of techniques designed to modify cognitions and the effects they have on behavior. Some of the major

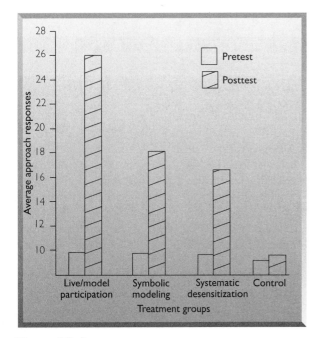

Figure 11.4

The average number of approach responses for clients receiving different treatments for a snake phobia

Note. From Relative Efficacy of Desensitization and Modeling Approaches for Inducing Behavioral, Affective, and Attitudinal Changes, by A. Bandura, E. B. Blanchard, and B. Ritter, 1969. *Journal of Personality and Social Psychology*, Vol. 13, pp. 173–199.

approaches to cognitive therapy include Ellis's rational-emotive therapy (Ellis, 1962, 1980, 1987, 1989, 1995) and Beck's cognitive therapy (Beck, 1976; Beck & Weishaar, 1995; Hollon & Beck, 1994).

A good example of this approach is the cognitive-behavioral therapies developed by Donald Meichenbaum (1977, 1985). The major objective of Meichenbaum's approach to cognitive-behavior therapy is to help clients handle anticipated stressors by teaching them new coping responses (e.g., relaxation training) while making them aware of the way negative self-statements influence their behavior. For example, a woman who has recently experienced the end of a long-standing love affair might now express the negative self-statement that "No one else will ever love me." As a result, she may not try to establish another relationship. After making the client aware of the effects of her negative self-statements, the cog-

nitive-behavioral therapist then begins to replace them with more appropriate and realistic self-statements and teach the client more effective responses to coping with the stress of meeting new people. The therapist might instruct the client to engage in a relaxation exercise if she becomes anxious while attending a social gathering. The therapist might also help the client replace the negative self-statements with others, such as "Not everybody I meet is going to like me right away," of "If I don't meet someone I like here today, I'll try someplace else." Thus, the major goal of Meichenbaum's cognitive-behavior therapy is very consistent with Bandura's emphasis on developing competencies and confidence during the therapeutic process.

Self-Defense Training: Enhancing Empowerment through Self-Efficacy

In a rather unusual application of social-cognitive theory, Elizabeth Ozer and Albert Bandura (1990) have incorporated the principles of mastery modeling and self-efficacy into a self-defense program designed to help women learn to defend themselves successfully against unarmed sexual assailants. In this program, mastery modeling is used to teach women the necessary self-protective skills to escape the hold of and/or disable an assailant. The skills include eye strikes, biting, kicks, foot stomps, and elbow, knee, and palm strikes, as well as how to deliver these defensive behaviors to vital parts of the body such as the eyes, head, throat, knees, and groin. Since many sexual assaults involve throwing the woman to the ground, the women are also taught safe ways to fall and how to strike the assailant while being pinned on the ground.

Graduated Mastery: The Process for Ensuring Success
To ensure mastery of the skills and increase self-efficacy, the skills were taught to the women in a graduated manner through simulated assaults. As illustrated in Figure 11.5, the simulated assaults were carried out by a male assistant wearing a heavily padded headpiece and specifically designed protective body gear. At first, the women watch as the instructor delivers the blows in the simulated assault. Next, each woman is guided through the self-protection maneuvers by the instructor. Finally, each woman participates in a series of simulated assaults

Figure 11.5
Action photographs of some of the types of disabling blows modeled by the instructor (top two rows) and delivered by a student while other members of the self-defense class participate vicariously (bottom row)

Note. From Mechanisms Governing Empowerment Effects: A Self-Efficacy Analysis, by E. M. Ozer and A. Bandura, 1990. *Journal of Personality and Social Psychology,* Vol. 58, pp. 472–486.

depicting various situations, such as a frontal assault, while lying down, being thrown to the ground, and being pinned down. To increase the reality of the assaults, as well as to help increase a sense of confidence and mastery, the simulated assaults are structured so that the assailant gradually increases the amount of the force and constraint of the assault as each woman begins to acquire more skill at delivering the self-protective blows. As shown in Figure 11.5, while each woman in the program participated in the simulated assaults, the rest of the class remained active vicariously by watching the assaults and shouting out the most effective defensive blows for disabling the assailant.

In addition to the physical defense skills, mastery modeling is used to teach the women attitudinal and verbal techniques for halting potential assaultive encounters. For example, through modeling and simulated enactments, the women are taught how to project a sense of confidence, speak assertively when dealing with unwelcome advances, issue stern verbal warnings if the unwelcome advance continues, and yell to frighten off an attacker. Cognitive restructuring is also included as part of this program; more specifically, the women are taught how viewing themselves as defenseless can be a barrier to their self-protection and freedom of movement.

The Outcome of Mastery Modeling: Increased Self-Efficacy in Self-Protection   To assess the effectiveness of the self-defense mastery modeling program, Ozer and Bandura (1990) surveyed the women before their participation in the course, right after completing the course, and again six months later. In comparison to their views before participating in the program, the women completing the program expressed a greater sense of confidence in their ability to protect themselves, viewed themselves as less vulnerable to assault, and demonstrated greater freedom of movement by their willingness to attend more recreational, social, and cultural activities. Thus, the findings indicated that these women certainly benefitted as a result of their participation in this program based on the principles of social-cognitive theory.

This concludes the discussion of applications based on the social-cognitive theory. To end this section on Bandura's theory, you will next consider some of its characteristic strengths and limitations.

Evaluation of Bandura's Social-Cognitive Theory: Characteristic Strengths and Limitations

Presented in this section is a summary of the characteristic strengths and limitations of Bandura's social-cognitive theory.

Characteristic Strengths

Here are some strengths of Bandura's social-cognitive theory:

▲ *Identifying the importance of modeling and self-efficacy: Taking a realistic look at behavior.* A major strength of Bandura's theory is the rather realistic view he takes of behavior. Going beyond traditional learning viewpoints, Bandura's use of such concepts as observational learning, mastery modeling, and self-efficacy makes it possible to more realistically explain how many complex patterns of behavior are acquired and the reasons they may or may not be performed (e.g., an individual's lack of self-confidence).

▲ *An emphasis on research: An appreciation of systematic evaluation.* The emphasis on scientific research is also a characteristic strength of Bandura's theory. Whether it involves testing basic concepts of his theory or applying these concepts to a variety of settings, Bandura continues to emphasize the importance of systematic evaluation of his ideas.

▲ *A concern for social relevance: Putting his ideas to work.* In addition to his theoretical work, Bandura has actively applied his theory to issues of social relevance. His work in the area of aggression modeling has contributed significantly to what we know about the impact of media violence on children's aggressive behavior. The treatment of phobias and other problems of personality adjustment have been enhanced by developments in social-cognitive theory. Most recently, Bandura has begun to examine the role of self-efficacy in the development of educational programs designed to promote self-control over behaviors that carry the risk of contracting AIDS (Bandura, 1990).

Characteristic Limitations

Here are some limitations of Bandura's social-cognitive theory:

▲ *On ignoring the unconscious: Concentrating too much on cognition.* While Bandura has done much to increase our awareness of cognitive variables in the study of personality, he has been criticized for ignoring some of the more complex psychological components of personality. For example, he has been criticized for putting too much emphasis on the conscious aspects of cognitive processes while ignoring unconscious dynamic processes. Like Rotter, Bandura has also been criticized for developing a theory of personality that places little emphasis on the emotional components of personality.

▲ *Overlooking the developmental component of personality: A theory with no growing pains.* Bandura's viewpoint has also been criticized because it does not give much attention to the developmental aspects of personality. For example, Bandura discusses principles of modeling as if they occur the same way for children and adults.

This concludes the presentation of Bandura's social-cognitive theory. More information about Bandura's ideas can be obtained by reading *Social Foundations of Thought and Action: A Social-Cognitive Theory* (Bandura, 1986).

Mischel's Cognitive-Social Person Variables: A Personalistic Cognitive Perspective

The final perspective to be considered in this chapter is one proposed by Walter Mischel. Like Rotter and Bandura, Mischel is another contemporary personality theorist who has been quite influential in promoting a more cognitive view of personality. For a glimpse into the life of Mischel, read "A Closer Look" on this page.

A Closer Look:

Biographical Background: The Life of Walter Mischel

Walter Mischel was born on February 22, 1930, not too far from Freud's office in Vienna. With the Nazi invasion of Austria, Mischel's family left Vienna in 1938 to avoid Nazi persecution and came to the United States. The Mischel family spent two years living in various parts of the United States before settling in Brooklyn in 1940.

Upon completing secondary school, Mischel was to attend college on a scholarship. But before he could start college, his father became ill. Mischel had to delay going to school in order to earn money for his family. During that time, Mischel had several odd jobs (including working as a stock boy, as an elevator operator, and in a garment factory), but he continued to pursue his interest in art and psychology by attending New York University. While he fueled his interest in painting and sculpture by spending time in Greenwich Village, Mischel was rather turned off by his psychology classes, which tended to emphasize the study of learning in animals (e.g., the laboratory rat and pigeon) that was so popular in psychology then. Mischel saw little relevance of this type of psychology to everyday problems. Mischel's early interest in personality psychology was in what he read about Freudian psychoanalysis as an undergraduate student, which, at the time, seemed to have some relevance to his desire to understand people.

Upon graduating from college, Mischel decided to pursue clinical psychology and entered the Masters of

Walter Mischel has been at the center of some of contemporary personality psychology's most heated controversies, as well as a central figure in the cognitive viewpoint of personality.

Arts program at the City College of New York. While working on his master's degree, Mischel held a job as a social worker in the Lower East Side of New York, working with troubled teens and helping the poor and the elderly. It was during this time as a social worker that Mischel came to the conclusion that the writings of Freud and the use of projective tests were of very little help in understanding the real-life problems of people living in the slums. As a result, he began to search for a more practical and empirically based approach to psychology. This research led him to Ohio State University where he became a student of both Julian Rotter and George Kelly.

Mischel received his PhD in clinical psychology in 1956 from Ohio State University. He spent the years from 1956 to 1958 in the Caribbean, studying religious cults that practiced spirit possession and investigating the cross-cultural nature of delay of gratification. In his research, he examined the beliefs, fantasies, and behavior of people while they were in possessed and normal states in an effort to determine why some people prefer immediate rewards but others do not.

After working in the Caribbean, Mischel spent the next two years on the faculty of the University of Colorado before taking a position at Harvard University. At Harvard, Mischel benefitted from his interactions with such eminent personality psychologists as Gordon Allport, David McClelland, and Henry A. Murray, further developing his interest in personality processes and personality assessment. While at Harvard, Mischel met and married Harriet Nerlove, also a psychologist. In 1962, the couple and their three children moved to California, where Mischel accepted a position at Stanford University. At Stanford, Mischel came into close contact with Albert Bandura. After more than 20 years at Stanford, Mischel accepted a faculty position at Columbia and returned to New York City in 1983, where he continues to be very active as a teacher and researcher.

In much of his early work, Mischel attempted to evaluate the effectiveness of personality traits and psychodynamic concepts to predict behavior. He summarized this work in his very influential textbook titled *Personality and Assessment* (1968). Recently, however, Mischel has devoted more attention to integrating personality psychology with cognitive psychology by considering individual differences in the way people process information as a major determinant of their behavior (Mischel, 1973, 1977, 1979, 1984, 1990, 1993).

Over the years, Mischel has been a leading figure in promoting a more critical look at the nature of personality theories and personality assessment. For his efforts, he has won not only the respect of many personality psychologists but also the 1978 Distinguished Scientist Award from the Clinical Psychology Division of the American Psychological Association (APA) and the APA's award for Distinguished Scientific Contribution in 1982. Mischel (1993) is also the author of a highly successful undergraduate personality psychology textbook. More information about the life of Walter Mischel can be found in a brief biography appearing in the *American Psychologist* (American Psychological Association, 1983, January).

Basic Concepts: Cognitive Social Learning Person Variables

At the core of Mischel's viewpoint is what he refers to as cognitive social-learning person variables (Mischel, 1973, 1990, 1993). **Cognitive social learning person variables**, also referred to as cognitive person variables, are certain qualities of the person that influence how the individual processes information about the environment and generates complex patterns of behaviors in reaction to it. For example, your decision to apply for a job will depend on, among other things, how you interpret the job description and how qualified you feel. Mischel lists five such variables: competencies, encoding strategies, expectancies, subjective values, and self-regulatory systems and plans.

Competencies: What You Know and Can Do
Competencies refer to what the individual knows and can do. Cognitive competencies refer to the amount and types of information an individual possesses. For example, a professional basketball coach possesses information that is quite different from that of the average fan. Behavioral competencies refer to differences in abilities to perform certain actions. For example, a professional basketball player is better able to generate certain complex behavior patterns on the court than the average street–ball player. Competencies are determined by several factors,

including age, health, psychological maturity and adjustment, strength, intelligence, and training.

Encoding Strategies: How You Put the Pieces Together

Encoding strategies refer to the different ways people organize, store, and transform the information they receive or possess. For example, a trained detective might see the information at a crime scene differently than a professional photographer. Differences in encoding strategies are determined by such factors as attention, level of motivation, personal values, and training, to name just a few. The point is that the same information can mean different things to different people because of the way each encodes it.

Expectancies: The Outcomes

What people decide to do is most often influenced by what they believe their actions will produce. For Mischel, there are three types of expectancies.

▲ **Behavior-outcome expectancies** refer to the relationship an individual perceives between a particular behavior and the specific outcome it is likely to produce. For example, you believe that if you dress appropriately, you will make a favorable impression on the interviewer.

▲ **Stimulus-outcome expectancies** refer to the tendency for people to use certain pieces of information in their environment to predict future outcomes. For example, the failure of the interviewer to shake your hand at the end of the interview may be viewed as a sign that you probably will not be offered the job.

▲ **Self-efficacy expectancies** refer to an individual's beliefs that he or she can perform the behavior that will produce a desired outcome. For example, the confidence you feel about having a favorable interview will depend on how effectively you believe you will be able to answer the questions you are likely to be asked.

Subjective Values: What Do You Prefer?

Subjective values refer to the preferences we have for certain objects or outcomes over others. For example, the extent to which you select a high-paying, boring job over a low-paying, stimulating job reflects the greater value you give to money over intellectual

challenges. An individual with a greater value for stimulation might make just the opposite decision. Thus, much of the variety we see in human behavior is a reflection of the tremendous differences in subjective values people possess.

Self-Regulatory Systems and Plans: How Can You Get What You Want?

Self-regulatory systems and plans refer to the internal processes that the individual uses to control the nature of his or her behavior.

▲ **Self-regulatory systems** refer to internal standards we use to guide our behavior. For example, because of your strong beliefs against nuclear arms, you turn down the opportunity to interview with an engineering firm that specializes in nuclear defense contracts.

▲ **Self-regulatory plans** include the specific course of action you may decide to take in order to achieve a desired outcome. Such plans are a critical part of how people cope with life's problems (Miller, Shoda, & Hurley, 1996). For example, you might decide that in order to get a job, you need a new suit. As a result, your plan of action might include looking through magazines to see what is in style and then seeking out clothing stores that carry the latest suits. Another person's plan might include seeking the advice of a career counselor.

Like Rotter and Bandura, Mischel's approach to understanding personality is to acknowledge that our behavior is not just governed by situational factors (Miller, Shoda, & Hurley, 1996).

As you can see, the cognitive social learning person variables are what Mischel uses to account for the individual differences in human behavior. Mischel addresses two specific personality processes employing cognitive person variables: delay of gratification and conditions of behavioral consistency.

Basic Processes: Delay of Gratification and Conditions of Behavioral Consistency

Two important personality processes Mischel uses to help explain personality and predict behavior include the ability to delay gratification and the matching of cognitive person variables with situational demands.

Delaying Gratification: The Expression and Consequences of "Willpower"

One important personality process studied by Mischel is delay of gratification and the consequences it has on behavior. (Mischel, 1990; Mischel & Rodriguez, 1993; Mischel, Shoda, Rodriguez, 1992).

Expressing Delay of Gratification: Showing Willpower
Delay of gratification is the tendency to forgo a smaller but immediate reward for a larger reward in the future. In his study of delay of gratification in children and adolescents, Mischel has been concerned with the factors affecting the ability to delay gratification and the strategies people can use to help increase this delay.

A typical example of Mischel's research on delay of gratification involves giving children the choice of receiving a smaller reward (e.g., cracker) immediately for the asking or a larger reward (e.g., several pieces of candy) later. Delay of gratification is made more difficult if the rewards are present and visible to the child (Mischel & Ebbesen, 1970), and if the child is thinking about how crunchy the cracker is or how sweet the candy tastes (Mischel & Baker, 1975).

Increasing Delay of Gratification: It's All in Your Head— Well Most of It Is   Mischel and colleagues found that the ability to delay gratification is increased in children through the use of various behavior (e.g., playing with one's shoe) and cognitive (e.g., thinking of fun things) strategies that take the child's mind off the desired object and help pass the time (Mischel, Ebbesen, & Zeiss, 1972; Mischel, Shoda, & Rodriguez, 1989; Moore, Mischel, & Zeiss, 1976; Rodriguez, Mischel, & Shoda, 1989). For example, having the children think about the reward in front of them as something else (e.g., the pieces of candy as being small stones) increases delay of gratification.

In a more realistic sense, for adults who are tying to delay their gratification and not eat between meals, various behavior strategies might include dusting the furniture or clearing out the closet; cognitive strategies might involve thinking about a party you'd like to have or fantasizing about a loved one. In

commenting on his delay of gratification research, Mischel notes, "Thus what is in the children's head—not what is physically in front of them—determines their ability to delay" (Mischel, 1993, p. 457). To help you resist temptation, keep this important piece of information in mind the next time you find yourself being confronted with the desire to light up your next cigarette while trying to stop smoking, snack between meals while on your diet, or get up to watch television instead of doing your homework.

Consequences of Delaying Gratification: The Interpersonal and Academic Benefits of Willpower   Mischel has noted the importance of delay of gratification as a core component of successful personality adjustment (Mischel, 1990; Mischel, Shoda, & Rodriguez, 1989, 1992; Mischel & Rodriguez, 1993; Rodriguez, Mischel, & Shoda, 1989). A lack of delay of gratification can be implicated in a variety of addictive and antisocial behaviors. For example, in a study of adolescents in a summer residential treatment facility, the inability to delay gratifications was associated with aggressiveness (Rodriguez, Mischel, & Shoda, 1989).

On the other hand, the ability to delay gratification is associated with a number of favorable consequences for adolescents. More specifically, Mischel and his colleagues examined the academic and social competencies of adolescents whose ability to delay gratification was first assessed when they were in preschool. In comparison to those adolescents who demonstrated a lack of delay of gratification when measured in preschool, those who exhibited an ability to delay gratification had higher Scholastic Aptitude Test (SAT) scores and were rated by their parents as being more mature, better able to cope with stress and frustration, more likely to respond to and use reason, and more likely to think and plan ahead (Shoda, Mischel, & Peake, 1990). Thus, developing the ability to delay gratification does seem to have some very favorable consequences.

The Perception and Prediction of Behavioral Consistency: The Matching of Conditions and Competencies

Mischel and his colleagues have also been interested in those cognitive person variables that help explain and predict the behavioral consistency of people across situations (Mischel, 1990). A central theme of this work is the match between the expectations regarding competencies people feel they possess, or others believe they possess, and the demand for these competencies to be performed in certain situations (Shoda, Mischel, & Wright, 1989; Wright & Mischel, 1987, 1988). The degree of behavioral consistency across situations is determined by the extent to which the different situations make similar demands for specific competencies (Shoda, Mischel, & Wright, 1993).

For example, an individual who is skilled at making people laugh will be more likely to demonstrate consistency in this behavior across those situations where this skill is demanded by the situation (e.g., at parties, while on a date, or sitting in the student union with friends) than in those situations where such a skill is less important (e.g., at funerals, in church, or while in class). In a similar manner, if we perceive someone is good at making people laugh, we would expect this person to be funny in casual conversation, at parties, and while on a date.

But a problem can develop when the perceptions of an individual's competencies by others are different than the individual's own expectations. For example, fans of Jackie, a famous comedian, may be very disappointed when they accidentally meet her in an elevator and she does not speak to them, much less say anything funny. In this situation, her fans' perceived inconsistency of Jackie's behavior is due to their expectation that she should be funny in all social situations. But Jackie may feel that riding in an elevator on her day off is sufficiently different from the demands of being on stage or at a party with friends and, therefore, may not feel it is necessary to be funny. As a result of this interaction, the fans may now think of Jackie as being a real snob and not as funny the next time they see her on television.

You can most likely think of some examples from your own life when the perceptions that others (e.g., parents, teachers, or friends) had of your competencies were quite different than your own, as well as the interpersonal difficulties these differences produced. Thus, by considering both cognitive person variables (e.g., competencies and expectancies) and situational demands on these variables, Mischel has demonstrated how you can gain a better understanding of yourself and those around you.

Applications of Mischel's Cognitive-Social Perspective: Using What Is Known

In this section, we will discuss the application of Mischel's social-cognitive perspective to the process of personnel selection and adjustment to college life.

Personnel Selection: The Matching of Employee Competencies with Employment Conditions

As mentioned previously, Mischel and his colleagues (Shoda, Mischel, & Wright, 1993) have noted the importance of matching personal competencies of the individual with situational demands to improve the prediction of cross-situational consistency in behavior. An excellent application of this logic is the process of **personnel selection**.

In the process of personnel selection, information from various psychological tests is used to help predict job performance (Murphy & Davidshofer, 1994). Personnel managers use various psychological tests to assess the specific cognitive, social, and self-regulatory competencies of people for the purpose of matching them with the specific situational demands of the position outlined in the job description.

For example, a personnel manager for a company that sells industrial solvents and cleaners has identified the following situational demands for people working as field sales representatives:

▲ Have the cognitive competencies to retain a considerable amount of knowledge about the different products sold by the company
▲ Be able to calculate estimates in helping customers determine how much of the company's products they might need
▲ Possess the social competencies to make conversation and establish rapport with different types of customers.
▲ Possess sufficient self-regulatory competencies to be able to work without being monitored directly by a supervisor

In selecting the sales representative, the personnel manager might use a general intelligence test to measure memory and mathematical abilities defined as important cognitive competencies. To measure the social competencies of potential sales representatives, the personnel manager might administer a social skills test (Riggio, 1986), which supposedly measures an individual's ability to assess a social situation and modify his or her behavior accordingly. Self-regulatory competencies might be assessed by administering any number of **integrity tests** (*Personnel Selection Inventory:* London House, Inc. 1980), which attempt to measure such behavior as employee theft of money, supplies, or time (i.e., taking unscheduled breaks or days off), work values, customer relations, and drug avoidance.

Thus, by defining what the company feels are the important situational demands to be made on their sales representatives, and then having the personnel manager select people who are most likely to possess the necessary cognitive, social, and self-regulatory competencies, the company is predicting that these competencies will be demonstrated consistently across a variety of situations involving customer/sales representative interactions. Briefly, in the company's eyes, matching competencies of the sales representatives with the situational demands of selling in the field will produce customer satisfaction and big profits for the company.

Coping with Life Tasks: Meeting the Challenges of College Life

Social Intelligence: Knowledge for Day-to-Day Problem Solving   Similar to Mischel's emphasis on cognitive social learning person variables and cognitive processes in the study of personality is the emphasis on social intelligence proposed by Nancy Cantor, of Princeton University, and John Kihlstrom, of the University of Arizona (Cantor & Kihlstrom, 1985, 1987). **Social intelligence** refers to the skills, abilities, and knowledge people bring to various social situations. Social intelligence can include knowledge about what to say and do that has been acquired over time through experience in similar circumstances (e.g., it is appropriate to be witty at parties but quiet and polite at funerals), knowledge about specific events and people (e.g., Uncle Joe does not like salt on his food), and knowledge about strategies for forming impressions of others in order to explain and predict their behavior (e.g., the way she looked away makes me think she is lying and can't be trusted).

The work on life tasks by Nancy Cantor and Julie Norem helps us to understand how college students cope with academic stress. Such research illustrates the importance of applying what we know about personality psychology to helping individuals deal with real-life concerns.

Life Tasks: The Significant Issues in Day-to-Day Living
An important application of social intelligence is its use in helping people to deal with what Cantor and Kihlstrom refer to as life tasks (Cantor & Kihlstrom, 1985, 1987; Cantor, 1990, 1994; Cantor & Harlow, 1994; Cantor & Zirkel, 1990). **Life tasks** are defined as the problems people see themselves as working on in a particular period of life transition. Life tasks come in various forms, but are characterized by the significance each person attributes to them; that is, the amount of time and energy devoted to the tasks, and the extent to which they dominate daily life (Cantor & Malley, 1991; Cantor et al., 1991; Cantor, Zirkel, & Norem, 1993). For example, a life task for an adolescent might involve struggling to be accepted by peers through experimentation in dress and after-school activities. A life task for a middle-aged single parent returning to school might include trying to develop a strategy for dealing with child care and finding enough time to study. For an elderly individual, life tasks might involve trying to deal with the increased amount of free time now available as a result of being retired or coping with the death of a spouse.

Optimism and Defensive Pessimism Strategies: The Bright and the Dark Side of Coping with Academic Anxiety   In her own work on life tasks, Nancy Cantor and her colleagues have focused on various issues facing college students during this significant period of transition, including dealing with independence (Zirkel, 1992; Zirkel & Cantor, 1990), academic performance (Cantor, Norem, Niedenthal, Langston, & Brower, 1987), friendships (Langston & Cantor, 1989) and romantic intimacy (Cantor, Acker, & Cook-Flannagan, 1992).

For example, in a two-year longitudinal study of how college students cope with the life task of academic stress, it was noted that the students utilized two somewhat different coping strategies (Cantor, Norem, Niedenthal, Langston, & Brower, 1987). One group of students used a strategy characterized by optimism. The strategy of optimism is characterized by an "illusory glow" of optimism (Norem, 1989; Norem & Illingworth, 1993). That is, students using the optimistic strategy tended to view academic tasks as difficult and challenging but not something that would overwhelm them. They did not view themselves as overly anxious or out of control before having to perform academically (e.g., take a test, turn in a paper, or give a speech). They were able to avoid a sense of failure by setting realistically high goals for themselves based on past success. Finally, as a means of maintaining a positive sense of self-image, they tended to assume control over their academic successes (e.g., I studied hard) while denying having control over their academic failures (e.g., the professor's questions were too picky). Thus, "optimists" used a number of encoding strategies (e.g., seeing themselves as in control) and stimulus-outcome expectancies (e.g., setting goals based on past success) to cope effectively with the life tasks associated with academic stress.

A second group of students used a strategy described as defensive pessimism (Norem & Cantor, 1986a, 1986b; Norem & Illingworth, 1993). Students using the defensive pessimism strategy had a history of academic success but guarded against threats to their self-esteem by setting unrealistically low expectations for themselves and creating "worst-case scenarios." For example, they tended to feel anxious and reported a lack of control with respect to their performance in academic situations.

What is most interesting about these two different strategies for coping with life tasks in academic settings is that they seem to be successful for both groups. The optimists tend to deal with their academic anxieties by "looking on the bright side." The defensive pessimists tend to use "worst-case scenarios" to motivate themselves to deal with their academic anxiety. The point is that different people use different—but equally effective—strategies to deal with significant life tasks. For more information on life tasks experienced by college students and the coping strategies they employ, read a book chapter by Nancy Cantor and Robert E. Harlow (1994), titled "Social Intelligence and Personality: Flexible Life Task Pursuit."

Evaluation of Mischel's Cognitive-Social Perspective: Strengths and Limitations

Our discussion of Mischel's Cognitive-Social Perspective will conclude with a summary of its characteristic strengths and limitations.

Characteristic Strengths

The basic strength of Mischel's perspective is his attempt to integrate several of the major viewpoints in personality. His emphasis on cognitive person variables as units of individual differences is consistent with that of the trait viewpoint. The significance he gives to behavioral- and stimulus-outcome relationships utilizes concepts from the learning tradition. His use of subjective values and expectancies is consistent with the social learning theories of Rotter and Bandura. Finally, the use of encoding strategies is very characteristic of the cognitive viewpoint. Because of such integration, Mischel can be viewed as a real "builder of bridges" in the study of personality. Another strength of Mischel's perspective is the emphasis he gives to the use of empirical research to validate and develop his ideas.

Characteristic Limitations

A basic limitation of Mischel's perspective is that, with only a few exceptions (e.g., encoding strategies), it is not really that much different from the perspectives of Rotter and Bandura. In addition, while Mischel emphasizes the significance of such cognitive person variables as encoding strategies, he does not specify them in any detail; they simply exist and influence behavior. Be aware, however, that the use of cognitive person variables is a perspective of personality that is still evolving. As Mischel continues to develop and refine his theory, he will become more specific about the details that distinguish it from other cognitive perspectives.

This concludes the presentation of Mischel's cognitive-social theory. For more information about Mischel's ideas, read a book chapter he wrote titled "Personality Dispositions Revisited and Revised: A View after Three Decades" (Mischel, 1990).

Chapter Summary: Reexamining the Highlights

▲ *Basic Assumptions of the Social-Cognitive Viewpoint.* The social-cognitive viewpoint emphasizes the role of cognitive processes in the study of personality. The basic assumptions of the social-cognitive viewpoint include the significance of the personal perspective, the presence of a need for cognition, a desire on people's part to seek further understanding and clarification of their personal world, and the significance of subjective probabilities.

▲ *Rotter's Social Learning Theory*
—*Basic Assumptions.* Four basic assumptions of Rotter's social learning theory include people learning from meaningful experiences, the reciprocal nature of life experience, the goal-directed motivational nature of personality, and the role of experience.
—*Basic Concepts.* Four basic concepts used by social learning theory to explain and predict behavior include behavior potential, expectancies, reinforcement value, and the psychological situation, as well as their combination into the basic formula.
—*Personality Adjustment.* The processes of personality adjustment include freedom of movement and need value, minimal goal level, and generalized expectancies in problem solving.
—*Applications of Social Learning Theory Psychotherapy.* The basic goal of psychotherapy is to increase the client's freedom of movement. Some techniques for achieving this goal include altering cognitions, teaching more adaptive inter-

personal skills, modifying maladaptive generalized expectancies, and participating in group or family therapy.
—*Personality Assessment.* The Interpersonal Trust Scale assesses an individual's degree of trust in others. The Internal-External Control of Reinforcement Scale (I-E Scale) assesses the extent to which an individual believes life's rewards are influenced more by internal or external forces.
—*Applications of Locus of Control to Matrimony and Divorce.* The I-E Scale has been used examine marital interaction and satisfaction, as well as the process of adjusting to divorce.
—*Evaluation of Rotter's Social Learning Theory.* Characteristic strengths of Rotter's social learning theory include its inclusion of cognitive variables and emphasis on research; characteristic limitations include too great an emphasis on cognitive variables at the expense of external forces and affective reactions.

▲ *Bandura's Social-Cognitive Theory*
—*Basic Assumptions.* The influence of the self system and the role of reciprocal determinism are two principal assumptions of Bandura's theory.
—*Basic Concepts.* Basic concepts used by Bandura to explain the nature and operation of personality involve observational learning, including the role of vicarious reinforcement and the effects of media violence, the nature and influence of self-efficacy, and the process of self-regulation.
—*Applications of Social-Cognitive Theory.* Therapeutic interventions based on social-cognitive theory include the use of various modeling techniques and cognitive modification. Self-defense training programs based on principles of mastery modeling and self-efficacy help to empower women against physical assault.
—*Evaluation of Bandura's Social-Cognitive Theory.* Characteristic strengths of Bandura's theory include its rather realistic view of the role of modeling and self-efficacy as determinants of behavior, emphasis on empirical research, and relevance to a variety of social issues. Some of its characteristic limitations include an overemphasis on cognitive processes at the expense of unconscious processes and a lack of emphasis on personality development.

▲ *Mischel's Cognitive-Social Theory*
　　—*Basic Concepts.* Mischel relies on the role of cognitive person variables in the study of personality, which include competencies, encoding strategies, expectancies, subjective values, and self-regulatory systems. and plans.
　　—*Basic Processes.* The process of delay of gratification and conditional determinants of behavioral consistency, as well as those factors affecting them, are important basic concepts of Mischel's theory.
　　—*Applications of Cognitive-Social Theory.* The process of personnel selection illustrates important aspects of Mischel's emphasis on understanding the conditional determinants of behavioral consistency. The study of social intelligence as it applies to coping with life tasks illustrates the utility of cognitive person variables.
　　—*Evaluation of Mischel's Cognitive-Social Theory.* Characteristic strengths of Mischel's theory include his attempt at integrating various theoretical perspectives and emphasis on systematic research. Characteristic limitations include its similarity to other cognitive viewpoints and a rather limited explanation of the operational nature of the cognitive variables he discusses.

Glossary

basic formula　A formula utilizing expectancies and reinforcement values to predict behavior in specific situations.

behavior-outcome expectancies　An individual's beliefs about the relationship between specific actions and outcomes.

behavior potential　The probability of performing a particular behavior.

cognitive processes　Mental activities involving the manipulation and modification of information.

cognitive social learning person variables　A set of internal factors that influence an individual's perceptions of events and behavior.

cognitive therapies　A group of therapeutic approaches designed to modify maladaptive cognitions.

competencies　An individual's beliefs about his or her abilities.

delay of gratification　The refusing of a smaller but immediate reward for a larger but postponed reward.

dysfunctional self-evaluations　Maladaptive strategies for administering self-rewards and punishment.

encoding strategies　Strategies for processing information.

expectancy　The belief that a particular behavior will produce a specific outcome.

freedom of movement　The possession of skills that make it possible to achieve what you desire.

integrity tests　A category of psychological tests designed to assess and predict employee antisocial behavior.

Internal-External Control Reinforcement Scale (I-E Scale)　A personality inventory designed to measure the generalized expectancies about the source of reinforcements.

interpersonal trust　A generalized belief in the word of others.

life tasks　A significant problem, or category of activities, during a specific period of life requiring a considerable amount of time and energy from an individual.

mastery modeling　A technique for acquiring new behaviors by observing others and/or with their assistance.

minimal goal value　The lowest value assigned to a reinforcer.

need for cognition　A desire to engage in thinking, reasoning, and other mental activities.

need value　The average value assigned to a specific collection of reinforcers.

observational learning　Acquiring information and skills by watching the behavior of others.

outcome expectations　The assumed outcome following specific behaviors.

perceived inefficacy　Assumed feelings of self-doubt.

personnel selection　The systematic selection of employees to maximize worker satisfaction and productivity.

psychological situation　All aspects of the environment that produce a response in an individual.

reciprocal determinism　The interrelatedness of personal and environmental factors to influence behavior.

reinforcement value　The expressed preference of one reinforcer over others.

self-efficacy　An individual's perceived level of skill.

self-efficacy expectancies　An individual's belief about having the skills to obtain certain desired outcomes.

self-regulation　The use of internal standards for governing behavior.

self-regulatory plans　Specific strategies for obtaining specific outcomes.

self-regulatory systems   Internally generated rules for governing behavior.

self system   An organizational framework by which external stimuli are personalized.

social intelligence   The personal abilities that help people to cope with social situations.

stimulus-outcome expectancies   An individual's beliefs that certain stimuli are associated with specific outcomes.

subjective values   An individual's preferences for certain outcomes.

Selected Topics in the Study of Personality Psychology

In Part Two, a survey of the major viewpoints of personality psychology was presented. The approach of Part Two was to present a discussion of various topics (e.g., personality development and adjustment), issues (e.g., consistency of behavior), and applications (e.g., business and therapeutic implications) within the context of each viewpoint. Such an approach makes it possible to appreciate the complexity of personality and the diversity in viewpoints used to help understand the complex nature of personality. In Part Three, our focus will shift from the different viewpoints of personality to some selected topics in the study of personality. These topics were selected because they have a rich tradition in the study of personality psychology, they address some very important personal and social issues, and they have been the source of some interesting applications. Thus, while the focus of Part Three has changed, the principal objective remains the same—to demonstrate to you the importance of the study of personality psychology in our everyday living experiences.

CHAPTER 12

The Self-Concept: The Core of Personality

CHAPTER OVERVIEW: A PREVIEW OF COMING ATTRACTIONS

*P*robably no other concept comes closer to encompassing the core of personality psychology than the concept of the self. The significance of the concept of the self is evident in the attention it has been given by such eminent personality theorists as Freud, Jung, and Rogers, as well as other eminent psychologists such as William James and Kurt Koffka, and other great social thinkers who were not even psychologists, including sociologists Charles H. Cooley, George Herbert Mead, and Erving Goffman (Hermans, 1996). In fact, the great personality psychologist Gordon Allport (1961) described the self as "some kind of core in our being" (p. 110). A more objective measure demonstrating that the self continues to hold a "center-stage position in psychology" (Banaji & Prentice, 1994, p. 297) is that since 1987, over 5000 articles on the subject of the self have been published.

In this chapter, you will explore several different aspects of the self. You will start by considering how the self-concept is defined and when it begins to develop. Next, you will learn about the personal/private and social/public dimensions of the self-concept. Finally, you will examine the cultural and historical influences on the self.

The Self-Concept: Its Definition and Origin

Our discussion of the self-concept will begin with two very fundamental issues. The first issue to be addressed will be to define what the self-concept is, as well as what it is not. The second issue addressed will be to consider the origin and emergence of the self-concept.

The Self-Concept Defined: Some Points of Clarification

The term *self-concept* means many different things to many different people. To help you understand how personality psychologists use this term, a description of how the term *self-concept* differs from *self-esteem* and one's *identity* is presented next.

The Self-Concept: What You Believe You Are

The **self-concept** refers to what a person believes about himself or herself (Baumeister, 1991, 1995). Within the self-concept are beliefs the individual has with respect to his or her physical characteristics and personality attributes. Beliefs about physical characteristics might include the extent to which you believe your height and weight are proportional, your hair is too blond or too short, and your face is too round. Beliefs about personality attributes might include the extent to which you perceive yourself as being friendly, assertive, active, emotional, and sensitive to the needs of others. Other information included as part of the self-concept might be related to how smart you think you are, your interests (e.g., I like baseball and disco dancing but not in-line skating), and your political beliefs (e.g., I believe in strong local government), and religious beliefs (e.g., I believe there is a supreme being). In short, your self-concept is what you know and believe about yourself.

Self-Esteem: The Evaluative Component of the Self-Concept

Self-concept should not be confused with self-esteem. **Self-esteem** refers to a person's overall evaluation of himself or herself (Baumeister, 1991; Buss, 1995).

More specifically, given what you know about yourself, how does this make you feel about yourself? Do you feel good about yourself (i.e., high self-esteem) or bad about yourself (i.e., low self-esteem)? Your self-esteem can also be linked to one specific aspect of the self-concept if that aspect of the self-concept is very important to your definition of who you are. For example, if being a successful business operator is significant to your self-concept, the fact that you pay so little attention to your family is of little relevance to how you feel about yourself, just as long as you are successful at your business. The point is that as part of your self-concept, your self-esteem can be based on a specific aspect (e.g., a particular ability) or on a more global view of yourself. You will read more about self-esteem in the next chapter.

Identity: Who Are You?

Self-concept should not be confused with personal identity. **Identity** refers to definitions a person places on his or her sense of self to help distinguish himself or herself from other people (Baumeister, 1991; Buss, 1995). There are many elements that help each of us establish our own personal identity. But probably one of the most salient features of your personal identity is your name. In a very objective sense, such items as a social security number, a telephone number, a personalized license plate, and an e-mail address can all serve to distinguish you from other people and, therefore, contribute to your identity.

From a physical perspective, identity can be defined through physical characteristics, such as gender (i.e., anatomy), hairstyle (e.g., a pink five-inch mohawk), clothing (e.g., wearing really colorful ties), or more permanent bodily modifications (e.g., a tattoo, or pierced nose or ears). From a social perspective, identity can also be defined by family, political affiliation (e.g., Bill is a Democrat), nationality, (e.g., Gino is Italian), geographic location (e.g., Donna is a northeasterner), group membership (e.g., Brutus is a member of the Hell's Angels motorcycle club), religious affiliation (e.g., Harold is a Mormon), sexual orientation (e.g., Susan is a lesbian), and occupation (e.g., Alice is an accountant), to name just a few.

From a personal perspective, internal beliefs and philosophy are also very critical to a person's sense of identity. In fact, because people tend to conform to external social pressures, such internal beliefs might tell us more about a person than would the various public expressions of that person's identity. For example, while an office manager wears an "Equality in the Workplace Now!" tee-shirt for a unity day celebration at the office, at home this same person might complain vehemently about all the special treatment given to certain minority groups.

Identity conflict can also be a source of much emotional discomfort when aspects of an individual's public and private identities do not match. For example, with respect to gender identity, even though a person is physically a male, psychologically he may view himself as a woman trapped in a man's body. Thus, like self-esteem, personal identity is a component of the self-concept that can be expressed in various ways.

As you can see from this brief discussion of the self-concept, a variety of elements contribute to who you are. Now that you have some basic understanding of what the self-concept is, and how it differs from other components of the self, you might be wondering when the self-concept begins, or at what age the self-concept first appears. This and other related questions are considered in the next section.

The Origin and Onset of the Self-Concept: When You Learn You Are You

If you have ever spent time watching a baby playing, questions you probably have asked yourself are, "Is the baby aware of who it is?" or "Does the baby realize that he or she is a distinct and separate entity? If so, when does a baby first make this realization?" To help answer such questions, in the late 1870s, the great biologist Charles Darwin proposed that the origin of the self begins when a child is able to recognize himself or herself in the mirror. Research indicates that the initial signs of a sense of self first seem to appear at about six months of age, emerging gradually and becoming more refined over a period of about a year or so (Damon & Hart, 1982, 1988; Lewis, Sullivan, Stranger, & Weiss, 1989). More specifically, when placed in front of a mirror, children at around six months of age will reach out and try to touch their image as if it were another child.

At this point you are probably asking yourself, "How do we actually know that the child really recognizes itself in the mirror and is not just reaching out to touch someone else who is willing to do exactly as he or she does?" To answer this question, researchers dabbed some red rouge on the noses of children and then placed them in front of a mirror. At around 15 to 18 months of age, the children would touch their own nose, not the image of it in the mirror, when seeing the rouge on it (Gallup & Suarez, 1986). Thus, it seems that by 15 to 18 months of age, children have some sense of what their face should look like and are curious about any variations of it.

This initial recognition the child has of what his or her face looks like is the basis of a blossoming sense of a self-concept. Soon after, children are able to identify themselves and others with respect to gender and age, but not necessarily numerical age (e.g., "I'm a baby but my uncle is old," not "I'm 3 years old and my uncle is 47") (Baumeister, 1991). By school age, children are able to define their sense of self by group membership (e.g., belonging to a certain family group or classroom), psychological traits, and abilities (e.g., "I can kick a ball hard, but I cannot stay inside the lines while coloring").

From about 6 to 12 years of age, children begin to refine their sense of self by comparing their personal characteristics and abilities to those of other children. For example, while a young child's sense of self might hinge more on whether she can ride a bike, an older child's sense of self might hinge more on the extent to which he can ride his bike faster or farther than others (Damon & Hart, 1982). Such comparisons with other children can result in a greater sense of self-consciousness, which increases considerably around 12 to 13 years of age (Baumeister, 1991; Tice, Buder & Baumeister, 1985).

Thus, by around age 8 to 10 years, the child's self-concept is quite stable and becomes a measure by which the sense of self can be compared to others. Given the significance of the self-concept in helping us to define who we are, you might be wondering if humans are the only species to have a self-concept. Do animals have a sense of self? If so, how could you measure it? For some answers to these questions, read "A Closer Look" on page 358.

A Closer Look:

A Comparative Analysis of the Self-Concept: Do Animals Have a Sense of Self?

If you are an animal lover, you will surely admit that your pet dog, cat, or parrot definitely has a distinct personality. But would you also say that it has a self-concept? To answer this rather interesting question, Gallup has extended his work on the onset of the self-concept in children to address this issue for different species of animals.

To study this rather intriguing possibility, Gallup (Gallup, 1977; Gallup & Suarez, 1986) used a variation of the mirror test to investigate the extent to which various animals have a self-concept. In a study using chimpanzees (Gallup, 1977), he had a number of these animals observe themselves in a mirror as a baseline measure. Next, he anesthetized the chimps and dyed one ear and one eyebrow of each chimp a bright red. After recovering from the anesthetic, the chimps were again allowed to observe themselves in the mirror. Upon seeing themselves in the mirror, the animals began to touch themselves on the painted ear and eyebrow. Such behavior seems to indicate that they did recognize themselves and were curious about their altered appearance. Similar results using the mirror/dye test have been observed for orangutans, but not for other lower primates (e.g., rhesus monkeys and macaques) and lower animals (e.g., dogs and rats).

While at least some animals appear to have a sense of self-consciousness (i.e., are aware of changes to their physical self), they lack the second critical component that Gergen (1971) states must be present before a sense of self can be inferred—the ability to be self-reflective. More specifically, animals are not self-reflective in that they demonstrate no knowledge of their traits, thoughts, feelings, or behaviors. Thus, while animals do seem to have distinctive personalities (i.e., differences in temperament) in that some are playful while others are aggressive, they do not have a sense of self. But for people who really love their pets, these results are not really all that important. They love a pet for who it is not for what the pet thinks it is.

Now that you have some sense of what the self-concept is and how it develops, the next step is to give you some information about the different dimensions of the self.

Dimensions of the Self-Concept: The Internal and External Sense of Self

In discussing the dimensions of the self-concept at the turn of the century, William James, the founder of psychology in America, described two different aspects of the self: the spiritual self and the social self (James, 1890). For James, the spiritual self refers to an inner or personal sense of self—the thoughts and feelings that help define your sense of self. The social self refers to an external or public sense of self obtained through the recognition of others. As an indication of its importance, the distinction between the personal and public aspects of the self has gone through many psychological and sociological variations but has managed to survive some 100 years (Hogan & Cheek, 1983; Cheek, 1989). In this section, you will learn about some contemporary views of the public and private dimensions of the self-concept.

In a recent discussion of the self, Davis and Franzoi (1991) make the distinction between public and private self-awareness. **Private self-awareness** refers to an awareness of those aspects of the self that are hidden from the public, such as our thoughts, feelings, desires, dreams, fantasies, and attitudes. **Public self-awareness** refers to an awareness of those aspects of the self that can be viewed by others, such as public statements, overt expressions of emotion, and your appearance. Two contemporary areas of personality research that illustrate the distinction between the private/internal and public/external aspects of the self-concept are the topics of self-consciousness and identity orientation, respectively. It is to these two areas that you will next turn your attention.

Self-Consciousness: Private and Public Perspectives on the Self

Self-consciousness is a personality trait that refers to an individual's tendency to be attentive to his or her sense of self (Davis & Franzoi, 1991). Research on the topic of self-consciousness has been triggered by the work of Michael Scheier, of Carnegie Mellon University; Charles Carver, of the University of Miami; and Arnold Buss, of the University of Texas at Austin. In their work, Scheier, Carver, and Buss (Buss, 1980,

1995; Carver & Scheier, 1981a, 1992) have proposed both private and public aspects of self-consciousness.

Private self-consciousness refers to a tendency of the individual to be in a constant state of internal self-analysis and reflection. For example, people who are very privately self-conscious would regularly try to figure themselves out, examine their motives, and generally focus on the internal aspects of themselves, including their thoughts, fantasies, and emotions. The guiding principle of people who are privately self-conscious might be the old cliche, "Get in touch with yourself."

Public self-consciousness refers to people who are also concerned about seeking self-knowledge, but are more involved in an external self-analysis regarding their public appearance. For example, people who are publicly self-conscious would be very concerned with their social behavior, including how they look, what they say, what they do, and the general impression they make on others. The guiding principle of people who are publicly self-conscious might be "It's better to look good than to feel good." Thus, while privately self-conscious people are more internally focused on their sense of self, publicly self-conscious people are more externally focused on their sense of self.

Measuring Public and Private Self-Consciousness: The Self-Consciousness Scale

Like any other significant personality dimensions, public and private self-consciousness vary from one person to another. Such individual differences in self-consciousness can be assessed using the Self-Consciousness Scale (Fenigstein, Scheier, & Buss, 1975; Scheier & Carver, 1985). The Self-Consciousness Scale (SCS) is designed to assess the extent to which people

▲ Are able to recognize their positive and negative attributes
▲ Display inner sensitivity to their feelings
▲ Are introspective and able to visualize the self
▲ Are aware of the impression they make on others
▲ Are concerned with the evaluations others have of them
▲ Are generally preoccupied with their past, present, and future behavior

The original and most-used version of the SCS consists of 10 items measuring private self-consciousness (i.e., the extent to which an individual habitually engages in internal self-analysis and examination) and seven items measuring public self-consciousness (i.e., the extent to which an individual habitually engages in external self-analysis and examination). People are asked to respond to each item on a five-point, fixed-format scale ranging from 0 (extremely uncharacteristic [not like me]) to 4 (extremely characteristic [very much like me]). Following is a subset of items from the SCS:

Private self-consciousness items:
I'm always trying to figure myself out.
I sometimes have the feeling that I'm off somewhere watching myself.
I'm aware of the way my mind works when I work through a problem.

Public self-consciousness items:
I'm concerned about my style of doing things.
I usually worry about making a good impression.
One of the last things I do before leaving the house is look in the mirror.

Correlates of Self-Consciousness: Characteristics of Private and Public Self-Consciousness

People who score high in private or public self-consciousness reflect specific patterns of thoughts, feelings, and behaviors that are characterized by the

Michael Scheier and Charles Carver, along with Arnold Buss, have made significant contributions to our understanding of the nature, assessment, and dynamics of self-consciousness.

utilization of either an internal or external reference as the point of focus for their sense of self. The following subsections describe some characteristics of privately self-conscious and publicly self-conscious people.

Characteristics of Private Self-Consciousness: Matching an Internal Sense of Awareness with Your Actions and Feelings   Because people who score high in private self-consciousness supposedly know themselves better and are less concerned with the impression they make on others than people who are low in private self-consciousness, you would expect them to engage in a pattern of behaviors that reflects their true internal feelings and beliefs. In support of this reasoning, when college students were given a test to measure their trait of aggressiveness and then given the opportunity to act aggressively toward others (i.e., supposedly by delivering electric shocks to them) as part of a psychology experiment, the students who were also very privately self-conscious demonstrated a closer relationship between their aggressive scores and their aggressive behavior (e.g., highly aggressive people delivered more shocks) (Scheier, Buss, & Buss, 1978).

In a similar manner, when college students were asked to complete a self-report questionnaire on their own degree of altruism and then given an actual opportunity to help another individual, the students who were very privately self-conscious demonstrated a closer relationship between their self-report level of altruism and their actual tendency to help another individual (e.g., highly altruistic people offered more help) then did people who were less privately self-conscious (Smith & Shaffer, 1986). As another measure of their increased sense of self-awareness, high privately self-conscious people were much less likely to change their attitudes and opinions in response to external sources of information than low privately self-conscious people (Scheier, Carver, & Gibbons, 1979; Carver & Scheier, 1981b).

People high in private self-consciousness also demonstrate a greater sense of emotional awareness than people who score low in private self-consciousness. For example, when men were shown slides of nude women and slides of atrocities (e.g., dead bodies piled up) and then asked to give their emotional reaction to these slides, people high in private self-consciousness offer more extreme reactions to the slides than those scoring low (Scheier & Carver, 1977). More specifically, high privately self-conscious people rated the nude slides as more emotionally pleasant and the atrocity slides as more unpleasant than low privately self-conscious individuals.

Other research indicates that high privately self-conscious people exhibit more laughter in response to humorous material (Porterfield et al., 1988), show more aggressive behavior when made angry by others (Scheier, 1976), and display more somatic symptoms in reaction to external stressors (e.g., time pressures) (Frone & McFarlin, 1989) than low privately self-consciousness individuals. Finally, in addition to responding with more extreme emotional reactions, privately self-conscious people are more likely to consume greater amounts of alcohol in response to personal failure (Hull & Young, 1983) and negative life events (Hull, Young, & Jouriles, 1986) than less privately self-conscious people. Apparently, high privately self-conscious people use the alcohol to help reduce the emotional intensity of the unpleasant events brought on as a result of their increased sense of personal self-awareness.

Characteristics of Public Self-Consciousness: Seeking an External Sense of Awareness for Your Beliefs and Actions   While privately self-conscious people are more focused on their internal sense of self, publicly self-conscious people are more focused on an external sense of self. In this regard, you would expect people high in public self-consciousness to be more concerned about and aware of their physical appearance than those who are low in public self-consciousness. Along these lines, you would predict that high publicly self-conscious people would use more makeup to enhance their physical appearance and social interactions than would low publicly self-conscious people. In support of this reasoning, high publicly self-conscious people wore more makeup to an experimental situation in which they were forewarned that their picture would be taken than low publicly self-conscious people (Miller & Cox, 1982).

Consistent with this emphasis on the external sense of self, high publicly self-conscious people are judged to be more physically attractive (Miller & Cox, 1982; Turner, Gilliland, & Klein, 1981), react more quickly when asked to make ratings about their liking and disliking of their physical features (Turner, Gilliland, & Klein, 1981), are better at predicting the impression they will make on others (Tobey & Tunnel, 1981), and are more aware of how much they use expressive gestures, such as moving their hands and arms when talking (Gallaher, 1992) than low publicly self-conscious people.

People who score high in public self-consciousness also demonstrate this tendency toward an external sense of self when interacting with others. More specifically, in their interactions with others, high publicly self-conscious people are more likely to assume personal responsibility for how much others like or dislike them and for the feelings they create in others (Fenigstein, 1979, 1984), more conforming to external norms (Froming & Carver, 1981), more likely to change their attitudes in the direction of their public behavior over private beliefs (Scheier & Carver, 1980), and more concerned about making a good impression than doing what is fair or morally right (Greenberg, 1983; Kernis & Reis, 1984) than are low publicly self-conscious people.

Finally, a rather interesting finding is that high publicly self-conscious people tend to exhibit a tendency toward paranoid ideation (e.g., "I am suspicious of overly friendly people." "Someone has it in for me.") (Fenigstein & Vanable, 1992; Buss & Perry, 1992). Such paranoid ideation is a rather extreme example of the normal tendency of people to focus on the self as a social object, and not equivalent to paranoia in the sense of serious psychopathology (Buss, 1995). Again, what we see in this list of behaviors is the tendency of people high in public self-consciousness to place more emphasis on external factors than internal awareness when interacting with others.

Objective Self-Awareness: A Case of Situationally Induced Self-Consciousness

In addition to individual differences in the trait of self-consciousness, there are also situational conditions that can create an increased sense of public self-consciousness. Some of these situational conditions might include receiving too much attention from others, such as when standing in front of an audience, or when you are receiving too little attention, such as being ignored at a party (Buss, 1995). In both cases, you begin to focus more attention on your sense of self as a social object when you feel as if you are being scrutinized and evaluated by others.

Objective Self-Awareness Defined: Creating a Sense of Increased Self-Reflection

A number of situational conditions have been found to increase an individual's sense of private self-consciousness. For example, filming or taping people with a camera, videotape recorder, or tape recorder can increase their characteristics of private self-consciousness, such as self-analysis and self-reflection.

One of the simplest and most interesting procedures used to increase a person's sense of private self-consciousness is to place them in front of a mirror. According to Shelly Duval and Robert Wicklund (1972), placing people in front of a mirror increases their private self-consciousness by creating a state of objective self-awareness. **Objective self-awareness** is a condition in which people are made more aware of their internal feelings and beliefs. When people are made to feel more objectively self-aware (e.g., see their reflection in a mirror or have their voice tape-recorded), they are also more aware of any discrepancy between their internal feelings and beliefs and their external behavior (Davis & Franzoi, 1991; Duval & Wicklund, 1972).

Coping with Increases in Objective Self-Awareness: Escape and/or Reconciliation

The increased awareness of this discrepancy between internal feelings and beliefs and external behavior creates a state of uneasiness that people try to reduce or eliminate. One way to cope with this discrepancy is to avoid situations that make you feel self-aware. For example, people who were led to believe that they had "failed" to do well on an IQ test spent less time sitting in a waiting room that contained a mirror facing them than did people in the same room without the mirror (Duval, Wicklund, & Fine, described in Duval & Wicklund, 1972). Apparently, it was more comforting for some of these people to leave after a failure than to have to look at themselves in the mirror.

A second way of coping with the discrepancy created by an increased sense of objective self-awareness is to make your external behavior more consistent with your internal standards. For example, people who favored the use of punishment delivered more electric shocks to others when they were supposedly given the opportunity to do so while sitting facing a mirror than did people with similar internal beliefs who were not facing a mirror (Carver, 1975). In a similar manner, people show a greater degree of similarity between their self-reported rating of sociability and their observed sociability when given the opportunity to interact with others when a mirror is present than when the mirror is absent (Pryor, Gibbons, Wicklund, Fazio, & Hood, 1977). When faced with the pressure to conform to the attitudes of others, the people in the presence of a mirror were more likely to "stick to their guns" and stay with their own internal beliefs than were people without the mirror present (Carver, 1977).

As an indication of a greater sense of self-reflection, patients in a Veteran's Administration hospital recalled their medical history more accurately when placed in front of a mirror than did people not exposed to the mirror (Gibbons et al., 1985). In a similar manner, psychiatric patients who responded to questions regarding their feelings of anxiety, hostility, and depression in front of a mirror reported more intense negative feelings than the people who answered the same questions in the absence of the mirror (Gibbons, et al., 1985). Thus, all of these studies seem to indicate that when confronted with an increased sense of objective self-awareness as a result of being exposed to a mirror, people are much more likely to behave in a manner that is consistent with their internal feelings and beliefs than the people who are not exposed to the mirror. This pattern of results is very consistent with the high degree of self-analysis and self-reflection characteristic of privately self-conscious people (Buss, 1995).

From the research just described, it is clear that creating a sense of self-awareness through the use of a mirror can help people to bring their external behavior more in line with their internal feelings and beliefs. Given the consistency of this research, you may want to use this information to your advantage by trying the procedures in "Applications in Personality Psychology" on page 363.

The Control-Theory Model of the Self: Finding Common Ground between the Trait of Self-Consciousness and the State of Objective Self-Awareness

Although discussions of the trait of self-consciousness and the state of self-awareness were presented separately in this chapter, the control-theory model of the self, proposed by Charles Carver and Michael Scheier (1981a), attempts to unify this body of research. The **control-theory model** (CTM) proposes that people regulate their behavior by making a series of comparisons against preexisting standards, until the behavior matches the standards. In the CTM, self-focused attention helps to determine the nature of the preexisting standard to be used. If the self-focus of attention is inward, the individual is likely to use a preexisting internal standard of comparison (e.g., personal beliefs, attitudes, and desires). On the other hand, if the self-focus of attention is outward, the individual is likely to use a preexisting external standard of comparison (e.g., the views expressed by others).

The Self-Focused Attention Feedback Loop: Attention, Comparison, Action, Reexamination, and Termination

According to the CTM, self-focus of attention increases the likelihood of people making a comparison between a current state (e.g., what the person is thinking or doing) and a preexisting standard (e.g., a desire or personal attitude). If there is a discrepancy between the current state and the preexisting standard, the person then takes some action to reduce or eliminate this difference. After taking the specific course of action, the person then reexamines the present state against the standard to determine if the discrepancy still exists. If it still exists, additional action is taken and the comparison made again. If the discrepancy has been eliminated, the person then stops this sequence until another instance of self-focused attention makes salient this new discrepancy between the current state and the preexisting standard.

For example, suppose that a woman is approached by a news reporter on the street and asked about her views on capital punishment. Being confronted in this manner is likely to create a state of self-focused atten-

APPLICATION

APPLICATIONS IN PERSONALITY PSYCHOLOGY

Mirror, Mirror on the Wall: Using Objective Self-Awareness as a Study Aid

If you know that you must study this evening, why not use what you know about objective self-awareness to help yourself possibly study more? Instead of studying the way you normally do, place a small mirror in front of you. The logic here is that having the mirror in front of you will make more salient the internal beliefs you have about your desire to study. Ideally, being in front of the mirror will make it more likely that you will bring your external behavior of studying in line with the internal desire regarding the need to study, and, as a result, you may spend more time studying.

A Note of Caution:

Don't forget what was said earlier about the mirror making you feel uncomfortable if your external behavior is not meeting your increased awareness of your internal standards. In this case, you may feel uncomfortable if you know you have to study, but you see yourself in the mirror not studying (e.g., daydreaming or doodling). Be aware that you may try to deal with this uneasiness by altering your internal standards (e.g., telling yourself that it's not really all that important that you study tonight) or leaving the field (e.g., getting up to call a friend, watching some television, or going to a movie). Instead of avoiding this situation, try telling yourself that this is a new study procedure for you, and that it may just take a little time for you to feel comfortable using it.

Try using the mirror as a study aid for the next couple of weeks, and record the amount of time you spend studying. If this works for you, don't forget to share it with a friend.

action) to the reporter until she feels that her statements reflect her actual views (i.e., the preexisting standard). As illustrated in Figure 12.1, the CTM is based on a feedback loop that involves people attempting to regulate their current behavior to be consistent with some preexisting standard.

CTM and Private Self-Focused Attention: Using an Internal Standard of Comparison

The CTM can be used to explain the behavior of people who are made privately self-aware due to situational circumstances (e.g., being placed before a mirror) or who are high in the trait of private self-consciousness (e.g., based on their SCS score). The CTM predicts that these people are more likely to use an internal standard of comparison to regulate their behavior, because of their increased tendency to engage in a greater degree of self-analysis and self-reflection (Carver & Scheier, 1981a; Davis & Franzoi, 1991; Froming, Walker, & Lopyan, 1982).

For example, a college student who is getting ready for school may be looking at herself in the mirror while listening to a radio talk-show host discuss the issue of using capital punishment as a method of crime prevention. In this situation, she is very likely to reflect on and analyze her personal

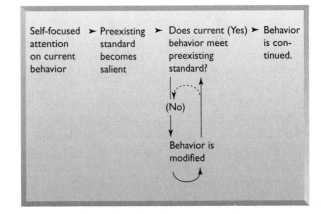

Figure 12.1
According to the control-model theory, self-focused attention creates a feedback loop that results from continuously comparing modifications in behavior to a preexisting standard. When the behavior meets the preexisting standard, the loop is broken.

tion that will prompt the woman to examine her views on capital punishment. If she says she is in favor of capital punishment (i.e., a preexisting standard), she will continue to present her views (i.e., external views in deciding how she will vote on the next state referendum to reinstate the death penalty. In a similar manner, as he listens to this same radio program in his car while driving to school, an individual high in private self-consciousness is also very likely to engage in the process of self-analysis and self-reflection in deciding how he is going to vote on this issue. In these two cases, the state of private self-awareness and the trait of private self-consciousness are both likely to promote the use of an internal standard of comparison when regulating behavior.

CTM and Public Self-Focused Attention: Using an External Standard of Comparison

The CTM also helps to explain the behavior of people who are made publicly self-aware due to situational circumstances (e.g., being in the presence of others who will be judging them) or who are high in the trait of public self-awareness (e.g., based on their SCS score). The CTM predicts that these people are likely to use an external standard of comparison to regulate their behavior, because of their tendency to view the self as a social object that is subject to the scrutiny of others (Buss, 1995; Carver & Scheier, 1981a; Davis & Franzoi, 1991). For example, while one person might use a conversation he had with others about the issue of capital punishment (i.e., a situationally induced state of public self-awareness), another person high in the trait of public self-consciousness might use what she read in the student newspaper (e.g., a tendency of publicly self-conscious people to rely on the views of others) to decide how to vote on this issue in the next election.

In summary, the private and public aspects of the self can be viewed from the perspective of individual differences in self-consciousness or the situationally induced state of objective self-awareness, and both of these aspects of self-focused attention can be linked with the CTM of the self. For more information related to the topics of public and private self-consciousness, read *Self-Consciousness and Social Anxiety* (Buss, 1980), *Attention and Self-Regulation: A Control-Theory Approach to Human Behavior* (Carver & Scheier, 1981a), and/or *Public Self and Private Self* (Baumeister, 1986b). In the next section, you will consider the private and public dimensions of the self as based on identity orientation.

Identity Orientations: Personal and Social Determinants of the Self

Defining Identity Orientations: Internal and External Points of Reference for a Sense of Self

Another approach to the conceptualization of the private and public dimensions of the self is the identity orientation framework proposed by Jonathan Cheek of Wellesley College (Banaji & Prentice, 1994). **Identity orientation** refers to the tendency for people to focus more attention and effort on their internal or external environment in defining their identity (Cheek, 1989; Sampson, 1978).

Identity orientations are labeled as either personal or social. A personal identity orientation would describe a sense of self within an individual that reflects more of an internal emphasis, based on self-knowledge and self-evaluation. For example, such people would focus on their emotions, thoughts, ideas, beliefs, and personal goals to define their sense of self. Thus, personal identity reflects a more private sense of self. On the other hand, a social identity orientation would describe a sense of self within an individual that reflects more of an external emphasis, based on interactions with and the reactions of others. For example, such people would focus on what others say about them, or how others treat them in defining their sense of self. Thus, social identity reflects a more public sense of self (e.g., concerns about your popularity and reputation).

The Aspects of Identity Questionnaire: Measuring Identity Orientations

To help in assessing people's identity orientations, Cheek and a colleague, Stephen Briggs of Rollins College, developed the Aspects of Identity Questionnaire (Cheek & Briggs, 1981, 1982). The Aspects of Identity Questionnaire (AIQ) consists of 18 items, to which people are asked to respond on a 5-point, forced-choice format. Ten of the items assess an individual's tendency toward a personal identity orientation, and eight items assess an individual's tendency toward a social identity orientation. For some firsthand experience with assessing identity orientations, answer the questions in "You Can Do It" on page 365.

For ease of presentation, the personal and social orientations are being discussed separately in this

Jonathan Cheek's work on aspects of identity helps us understand how our sense of identity can influence such important decisions as occupational choices and leisure-time activities.

section. However, Cheek (1989) notes while these two orientations may be considered as independent dimensions, a person's sense of self can reflect both dimensions to varying degrees. For example, since Jane is a very introspective person, her sense of self may be defined based primarily on a personal identity orientation. On the other hand, since Jackie is more of a social butterfly, her sense of self may be defined more by a social identity orientation. Julia, who prides herself on being somewhat independent but also still feels some need for the regard of others, might define her sense of self to a high degree based on the per-

The author's wife expresses the personal aspect of her identity through her work as a dog groomer, where she combines her love of animals with her career. For her, job satisfaction comes from the opportunity to be around animals all day long, not from external sources of reward, such as winning sales awards.

YOU CAN DO IT

Examining Your Identity Orientation: How Do You Define Your Sense of Self?

Instructions
Answer the following eight items* using this scale:
  1 = Not important to my sense of who I am
  2 = Slightly important to my sense of who I am
  3 = Somewhat important to my sense of who I am
  4 = Very important to my sense of who I am
  5 = Extremely important to my sense of who I am

____   1. My emotions, thoughts, and feelings
____   2 The reactions of others to what I say or do
____   3. My moral values and personal standards
____   4. The impression I make on others with my mannerisms
____   5. My private self-evaluations and personal opinions of myself
____   6. How popular I am with other people
____   7. The personal goals and hopes I have for myself in the future
____   8. How attractive other people find me

Scoring
The extent to which your answers reflect a personal identity orientation can be examined by totaling your responses to items 1, 3, 5, and 7. The extent to which answers reflect a social identity orientation can be examined by totaling your responses to items 2, 4, 6, and 8. The higher your score for each set of items, the more your responses reflect that particular orientation.

*A subset of modified AIQ items, adapted from Cheek (1989).

sonal identity orientation but a moderate degree on the social identity orientation. Thus, as Cheek (1989) states, "The degree of balance or conflict between these two identity orientations may have a significant impact on the self-concept processes and social behavior of an individual" (p. 277). With this important point in mind, you will next consider some consequences of identity orientation.

Consequences of Identity Orientation: Personality Correlates of Personal and Social Identity

Each person's identity orientation seems to have an impact on the nature of their personality and other dimensions of the self-concept. For example, in an early validation study of the AIQ, Cheek, Underwood, and Cutler (1985, cited in Cheek, 1989) indicated that while there were no gender differences for social identity, there was a tendency for females to score slightly higher than males on the personal identity orientation.

There also seem to be some developmental differences in identity orientation. In one study, older adults tended to demonstrate a greater tendency for social identity, while younger college students displayed a greater tendency toward personal identity (Leary, Wheeler, & Jenkins, 1986). Such a pattern of results is consistent with Erikson's belief (see Chapter 5) that young adulthood is associated with establishing a personal identity while middle adulthood is more associated with having a social identity established within a community (e.g., generativity).

Personal Correlates of Identity Orientation   Personal and social identity orientations tend to be associated with a somewhat different set of personality characteristics (Hogan & Cheek, 1983; Cheek & Busch, 1982; Cutler, Lennox & Wolfe, 1984). A personal identity orientation tends to be associated with a sense of independence, a lack of concern for social appropriateness, and a need for uniqueness. On the other hand, a social identity orientation tends to be associated with tendencies toward conformity, concerns for social appropriateness, and a desire to help others. With respect to emotional reactions, social identity is associated with a susceptibility to experience shame, which reflects a concern for the public exposure of personal faults or the failure to meet external standards of morality. Personal identity is associated with a susceptibility to experience guilt, which reflects a concern for an individual's own conscience or internal moral standards (Cheek & Hogan 1983).

Identity Orientation and Self-Consciousness   Personal and social identity orientations also seem to be related to other measures of the self-concept, such as public and private self-consciousness. As discussed previously, given that private self-consciousness reflects a more internal emphasis on the self while public self-consciousness reflects a more external emphasis on the self, you would expect personal identity scores to be positively related to private self-consciousness and social identity scores to be positively related to public self-consciousness scores. Such a pattern of results has been found in a number of studies (Cheek & Briggs, 1982; Cutler, Lennox, & Wolfe, 1984; Hogan & Cheek, 1983; Penner & Wymer, 1983).

Occupational and Recreational Preferences and Identity Orientation: Personal and Social Identity Orientations for Work and Play

Next to eating and sleeping, two other very important parts of our lives involve what we do for a living and how we spend our free time. Because work and play are such important aspects of our lives, you would also expect them to be important to our sense of self. As a result, you would also expect identity orientation to play a role in the occupational and recreational choices people make.

Identity Orientation and Occupational Choice   In their analysis of job characteristics, Leary, Wheeler, and Jenkins (1986) proposed that certain occupations offer us greater personal rewards (e.g., self-fulfillment) while others offer greater social rewards (e.g., social status). Based on this distinction, they proposed a relationship between identity orientation and occupational preference. In support of their reasoning, they found that people with a high sense of personal identity expressed a preference for occupations that emphasized personally relevant job outcomes involving self-fulfillment and personal growth. People with a high sense of personal identity expressed a preference for occupations that offered a chance to be creative, a job consistent with personal values, an opportunity to use their abilities to their fullest, the possibility to reach personal goals in life, and the opportunity to have a great deal of input.

On the other hand, people with a high sense of social identity expressed a preference for occupations that emphasized socially relevant job outcomes. These people expressed a preference for occupations that offered social status, high pay, the opportunity to be well known in their field, recognition from others, the possibility of forming friendships with coworkers, and an active social life.

In a similar manner, women who had a stronger sense of personal self-definition were more likely to take more active roles in social and career initiatives, such as starting and leading organizations, than women with a more social sense of self-definition (Jenkins, 1996). The women with the social sense of self-definition tended to choose more traditional female careers, report more career indecision and compromise, and experience more role conflict (e.g., home vs. work role conflicts).

Identity Orientation and Recreational Choice   In their analysis of recreational activities, Leary, Wheeler, and Jenkins (1986) proposed that people would engage in individual and team sports for different reasons. Individual sports, which do not require a teammate (e.g., jogging and swimming), offer the individual complete control over the activity and can be enjoyed for their intrinsic rewards (e.g., the satisfaction of improving your running time). On the other hand, sports requiring teammates (e.g., volleyball, baseball, or soccer) offer the individual a chance to work with others and provide interpersonal rewards (e.g., praise, friendship, and companionship).

Based on this distinction, Leary et al. proposed a relationship between identity orientation and recreational sport preference. In support of their reasoning, they found that people with a high sense of personal identity participated in more individual sports and expressed more personal reasons for doing so (e.g., personal enjoyment, self-satisfaction, and a desire to be physically fit). People with a high sense of social identity participated in more team sports and expressed more interpersonal reasons for doing so (e.g., for the enjoyment of competing with others, to make others notice how physically fit they are, and to increase the possibility for interacting with others).

Thus, as a critical dimension of the self-concept, identity orientation is associated with other relevant personality characteristics and important aspects of the individual's life, such as occupational choice and recreational preferences. For more information on the topic of identity orientations, read a book chapter written by Jonathon Cheek (1989) titled "Identity Orientations and Self Interpretation." This concludes the discussion of private and public dimensions of the self-concept. To help place this discussion in some context, you should be aware that Freud's constructs of the id and superego (see Chapter 3), Adler's concepts of the creative self and social interest (see Chapter 4), Jung's views on unconsciousness/the shadow and consciousness/the persona (see Chapter 4), Maslow's emphasis on belonging needs and esteem needs (see Chapter 7), and Erikson's discussion on identity and generativity (see Chapter 5) all serve as reminders of the significance of people attempting to consider and incorporate personal/private needs of the self and social/public expectations and requirements of the social world when trying to establish a solid self-concept. For more information about the public and private dimensions of the self-concept, read the article titled "The Dynamic Self-Concept: A Social Psychological Perspective" (Markus & Wurf, 1987) and/or "The Self in Social Context" (Banaji & Prentice, 1994).

Cultural and Historical Dimensions of the Self: Views from Around the World and Across Time

In addition to having personal/private (e.g., introspection) and social/public (e.g., your reputation) aspects of the self, Harry Triandis (1989, 1995, 1996) has proposed the concept of the collective self to account for the influence of culture as a determinant of one's identity. The **collective self** refers to an individual's membership in certain social groups. Social groups that contribute to the collective self and social identity include family ties, ethnic identity, religious affiliation, geographic region, and cultural heritage (Baumeister, 1995; Buss, 1995; Pennebaker, Rimé, & Blankenship, 1996).

Cultural Influences on the Self: Collective and Individualistic Cultures

In this section, you will concentrate on cultural influences on the self. The focus of this discussion will be the differential impact of collective and individualistic cultures.

Collective Cultures: Promoting a Strong Public Image

Variations in cultures have different effects on the private, public, and collective aspects of the self

(Triandis, 1989, 1995, 1996). Collective cultures, such as Japanese society, place a considerable emphasis on the public and collective aspects of the self and somewhat less emphasis on the private aspects of the self and individual self-expression. These cultures might be described as "tight" societies because of the high expectations they place on people to conform to societal values, roles, and norms.

Tight societies tend to include people who have a well-developed public and collective self, but give little attention to the private self. For example, even though she may not like studying economics, a young Japanese college student may pursue a career as an economist to fulfill the wishes of elder members of her family. In her culture, it is more important to maintain a proper public image and sense of honor for the family than to express personal desires. The same is true for various religious groups that have very rigid (i.e., "tight") guidelines regarding the behavior of women (e.g., they must remain veiled or modest in their expression).

Individualistic Cultures: Promoting Expressions of Uniqueness

In contrast to collective cultures, individualistic cultures, such as American society, place more emphasis on individual expression and the private self than on the public self (Triandis, 1989, 1995, 1996). These cultures might be described as "complex" societies, because people have considerable societal flexibility to join many different groups and exercise a wide range of choices in the expression of various social roles.

In complex cultures, the collective and public selves are weaker in comparison to the private self, which is given considerable freedom of expression. For example, in American societies, while parents might have certain expectations of their children to go to college, the children are relatively free to choose a major that reflects their personal needs and interests. Although complex cultures allow for greater personal expression, as well as promote a more favorable sense of subjective well-being (Diener, Diener, & Diener, 1995), they also appear to foster more identity problems and confusion (Baumeister, 1995; Katakis, 1984). It seems that greater freedom of choice and expression produces more confusion. For more details about some other cultural consequences for the self, read "A Closer Look" on this page.

A Closer Look:

East vs. West: Cultural Influences on the Sense of Self

Which of these two proverbs do you agree with most?

> The squeaky wheel gets the grease.
> The nail that stands out gets pounded down.

The first saying reflects the views of the American culture, which emphasizes individuality and the expression of unique talents and abilities (Trafimow, Triandis, & Goto, 1991). The second reflects the views of the Japanese culture, which emphasizes the individual as being a part of a collective network of social relationships. These sayings also illustrate some basic differences in the way these two cultures influence the nature and development of the self into what Hazel Rose Markus, of Stanford University, and Shinobu Kitayama, of Japan's Kyoto University, refer to as the independent self and the interdependent self (Markus & Kitayama, 1991; Markus, Kitayama, & Heiman, in press).

The Independent Self: "I've Got to Be Me."
As a reflection of these words from an old tune sung by Sammy Davis, Jr., the American culture emphasizes the independent self. The **independent self** is a sense of the self as a collection of unique feelings, beliefs, and motives possessed by each person and separate from the social context. In the United States, we tend to think of ourselves as being free and independent to act on our own views and desires. According to Kitayama (1992), this comes from the tendency of those in Western cultures to teach their children to be independent of others.

The Interdependent Self: "There Is no *I* in *Team*.
These words from the author's high school football coach seem to reflect the emphasis in the Japanese culture on the interdependent self. The **interdependent self** is a sense of the self as belonging to a group or unit that has an important influence on the individual's behavior. In Japanese culture, people define and develop a meaningful sense of self in the context of social relationships, rather than through independent actions and achievements. Instead of focusing on

The work of Hazel Rose Markus and Shinobu Kitayama make it possible to understand the role culture plays in the development and expression of personality. Such cross-cultural investigations are extremely important as advances in electronic technology and travel make it easier for people from different parts of the world to come together.

unique self-expression, the development of the interdependent self emphasizes considering the consequences of your actions on the feelings and views of others and blending in with them. For example, in the Japanese culture, getting fired from a job would bring shame and embarrassment to one's family; in America, it is more likely to be construed as a sense of personal failure.

Cultural Influences on the Sense of Self: Some Consequences of Independent vs. Interdependent Self

Cultural emphases promoting an independent self or an interdependent self can influence the way people think, feel, and behave (Kashima, Yamaguchi, Kim, Choi, Gelfand, & Yuki, 1995; Triandis, 1996). To illustrate this point, here are some differences observed between an independent and interdependent sense of self:

▲ *Expressions of pride.* Americans take pride in their individual accomplishments, while the Japanese take pride in knowing their efforts helped their group to be successful (Ouchi, 1981).

▲ *Beliefs about personal uniqueness.* In Western cultures, people see themselves as being unique and view others as being more similar to them. In Eastern cultures, people perceive themselves as

being very similar to others and view others as being unique (Kitayama, Markus, Tummala, Kurokawa, & Kato, 1990).

▲ *Beliefs about responsibility.* In Western cultures, people are more likely to hold an individual personally responsible for his or her own behavior (e.g., Dale is really clumsy). People in Eastern cultures are more likely to attribute the cause of an individual's behavior to situational factors (e.g., Pat slipped on the wet floor) (Miller, 1984).

▲ *Explanations for personal success.* In Western cultures, people tend to assume personal responsibility for their success through self-enhancement (e.g., I worked really hard for my raise). People in Eastern cultures tend to perceive their success in a rather self-effacing manner, viewing it as being due to situational factors (e.g., I received my raise because my boss is a generous person) (Takata, 1987).

▲ *Explanations for personal failures.* People in Western cultures are likely to downplay personal responsibility for their failures in a manner that protects their self-image (e.g., I did not get a raise because my boss dislikes me and is cheap). In Eastern cultures, people explain their being outperformed by others as being due to the personal attributes of the other people (e.g., I did not get the raise because I did not work as hard as my coworkers) (Shikanai, 1978).

▲ *Expression of emotions.* People in Western cultures are more likely to experience emotions related directly to a personal sense of self, such as pride (e.g., I did a great job) or frustration (e.g., I was cheated out of a raise) to a greater degree than people in Eastern cultures (Markus & Kitayama, 1991).

▲ *Assertiveness and independence.* Expression of assertiveness and independence are more characteristic of people from individualistic cultures (e.g., Australia and the United States) than collective cultures (e.g., Japan and Korea) (Kashima et al., 1995).

▲ *Sources of self-esteem.* Competitive behavior seems to be linked to high self-esteem for people from a culture that promotes an independent sense of self, while cooperative behavior seems to be linked to high self-esteem for people from a culture that promotes an interdependent sense of self (Kagan & Knight, 1979).

As this summary illustrates, there are some very definite influences of culture on the sense of self. Can you think of other ways in which your culture might have shaped your personality?

The information presented earlier in this section, as well as in the preceding "A Closer Look" feature, illustrates the influence of culture on a person's sense of self. But because of the high degree of mobility people experience today, people have the opportunity to change their cultural context by traveling to different parts of the world, such as an American banker working in Japan or a Pakistani college student studying abroad in Germany. How do people cope with the changes in cultural context? To examine some research that attempts to address this issue, read "A Closer Look" below.

A Closer Look:

Strangers in a Strange Land: Coping with a Clash of Cultural Context at College

Advances in transportation technology available today make it much more likely that people from different cultures will visit other parts of the world, for reasons ranging from the demands of business to the pleasures of vacations. Because new environments can challenge the basic meaning of a person's identity, shifts in cultural context can be stressful (Breakwell, 1986), particularly if they occur for an extended time (e.g., immigration to a new country).

A very common situation that illustrates a shift in cultural context occurs in our own country each year, as American students from diverse cultural and ethnic backgrounds leave home and make the journey to a somewhat different environment—known as college. The journey from home to living away at college is stressful for most students. It can be especially stressful for students whose sense of identity is threatened when they discover they are among an ethnic or racial minority on the campus.

To help understand the psychological and social dynamics of such shifts in cultural context, Kay Deaux (City University of New York Graduate School and University Center) and Kathleen Ethier (Yale University) have been investigating how Hispanic people maintain their sense of ethnic identity when they experience a rather dramatic shift in the context of their culture.

Pre-College Ethnic Identity and Adjustment to College

In their work, Deaux and Ethier (Deaux, 1993a, 1993b, in press; Ethier & Deaux, 1990, 1994) are investigating how Hispanic students attempt to maintain their identity as they go from living at home to going away to college. Ethier and Deaux (1990, 1994) report that the minority status of Hispanic people on predominantly white college campuses poses a serious source of stress to them because of the difficulties it creates for maintaining their sense of ethnic identity and self-esteem. But an important predictor of the nature and degree of how well the Hispanic college students were able to maintain their ethnic identity was the strength of their ethnic identity before going to college (Ethier & Deaux, 1994). Factors in the students' home life that promoted a strong sense of ethnic identity included whether their ethnic language was spoken at home, the ethnic composition of their neighborhood, and the percentage of their friends who were in the same ethnic group. The students who had a strong sense of ethnic identity before going away to college showed the least amount of stress in response to maintaining their ethnic identity while at college. Students with a weak sense of ethnic identity before going away to college experienced drops in their self-esteem and perceived being away at college as threatening.

Remooring as a Strategy for Maintaining Ethnic Identity

A successful strategy for maintaining ethnic identity while away at college is what Ethier and Deaux called *remooring*. With this strategy, the people with a strong sense of ethnic identity before coming to college maintained their ethnic identity by becoming involved with Hispanic activities at college (e.g., club meetings, lectures, or courses) and establishing new friendships with other Hispanic students. These new Hispanic activities and friends at college seem to replace the sources of support for ethnic identity back home.

Such a pattern of action is consistent with those of other ethnic minorities, such as Italian, German, Chinese, and Irish immigrants, as they migrated to the United States from their countries of origin over the decades. For example, most metropolitan cities have

Adjusting to college is never easy. Kay Deaux (pictured above) and Kathleen Ethier are helping explain what strategies ethnic students use to help make a successful transition from their ethnic majority status in their own neighborhoods to their ethnic minority status on campus. Such information will help all of us to cope more effectively with major transitions throughout our lives.

that we move to a different part of the country—or even a different country. To consider how you might apply this research on the remooring strategy, see "Applications in Personality Psychology" below.

APPLICATION

APPLICATIONS IN PERSONALITY PSYCHOLOGY

Personalizing the Strategy of Remooring: Smooth Sailing through College on Your Way to Strengthening Your Sense of Identity

After reading the material in the preceding "A Closer Look" feature, you might wonder if the strategy of remooring can help you to cope with the stress of college life and the threats to your own identity such stress can pose. If you have not already started to remoor, you might consider doing so in response to such stress. A good place to start is by going to the psychology department to see if there is a psychology club, or to the student activities office for a list of clubs and organizations on campus. After finding out what groups or clubs are on your campus, attend a meeting or two to see which of them meet your own needs for developing and maintaining a sense of ethnic, social, and personal identity.

Try to avoid using the excuse that you are too busy or don't have time for this activity. As noted in "A Closer Look," remooring reduces stress and promotes positive self-esteem. Such outcomes will not only increase your likelihood of being a success at college (Gardner & Jewler, 1985, 1992; Jewler, Gardner, & Owens, 1993) but also make remooring worth your while in the long run.

their own "Little Italy" or "Chinatown" where immigrants from these countries gather together to minimize the stress of coming to a new country and to help preserve their ethnic heritage in a new location. The same type of remooring occurs when people join a church upon moving to a new city. Religious affiliation can be a significant component of personal identity. Joining a church is something a person might do to minimize the stress of moving to a new town. A similar pattern of remooring might occur for people with different aspects of their identity that they see as significant. For example, someone with a passion for playing chess or restoring antique cars might also attempt to remoor with people having similar interests when moving to a new part of the country.

Thus, the implication of the research by Deaux and Ethier is that whatever is important to an individual's sense of identity, be it ethnicity, social interests, or sexual preference, finding others who share a similar sense of identity is important for coping with stress and maintaining this sense of identity when moving to a new location (Frable, Wortman, Joseph, Kirscht, & Kessler, 1994). This is an especially important lesson to remember as our society becomes increasingly mobile, and we face a greater likelihood of having to "pick up and go" because a job commitment demands

As you knew all along, people from different countries and cultures do encounter different customs. In this section, you examined how these cultural differences influence the personalities of the people living in them, and considered some of the stress and coping strategies associated with leaving a culture. For more information about cultural influences on personality, read the following:

▲ The Self and Social Behavior in Differing Cultural Contexts" (Triandis, 1989)
▲ "Culture and the Self: Implications for Cognition, Emotion, and Motivation" (Markus & Kitayama, 1991)
▲ "Reconstructing Social Identity" (Deaux, 1993a)
▲ *Identity: Cultural Change and the Struggle for Self* (Baumeister, 1986a)

Roy F. Baumeister has made many significant contributions to the study of the self, including his intriguing analysis of how the concept of the self has changed in response to religious, philosophical, economic, and technical changes throughout history.

A Historical Review of Selfhood: Changes in the Concept of the Self through History

You should be aware that the definitions offered for the various components of the self reflect a contemporary view of the self (Baumeister, 1986a, 1987, 1995). In his research, Roy F. Baumeister of Case Western Reserve University has traced the changes in the concept of the self through history and noted the factors influencing these changes. This section reviews the concept of the self through history.

Late Medieval Period (1000s through 1400s): You Are What You Do

During the late Medieval period, knowledge of the self was not considered very important. There was little concern for introspection and self-reflection about personal behavior. More emphasis was given to people's spiritual soul, to their fate after death, and to the collective salvation of people than to an individual's self-knowledge and understanding while he or she was alive. The sense of self was, for the most part, linked to a person's place in the social hierarchy regarding the services that person provided (e.g., Hans the blacksmith) or the details of his or her family background (e.g., Countess Maria of York). Thus, an individual's sense of self was equated with the social or public self.

Early Modern Period (1500s through early 1800s): Examining the Inner Self of Others

Toward the end of the late Medieval period, the social hierarchy began to weaken as social mobility increased (e.g., commoners gaining access into the aristocracy through marriage). As a result, the emphasis on the sense of self as reflected by birth status or occupation began to play less of a role.

As the emphasis on the public self began to decrease, an emphasis on the private self began to increase. During the 1500s, people began to believe that a hidden aspect of the self resided inside each person and was quite different from the individual's public image. Also during this time, people began to be overly concerned with the notion that people's public behavior did not necessarily reflect their private beliefs and values. It was in this social setting that Shakespeare wrote his great works describing the conflict between the public behavior and private desires and morals of his characters that we still find so enjoyable and relevant today. But the emphasis during this period was on knowing the inner self of others, not one's own.

Puritan Era (early 1800s to late 1800s): The Beginnings of a Concern for Self-Awareness

During the Puritan era, the focus shifted from trying to know others to trying to know one's self. This shift in emphasis was due to the Puritan doctrine of predestination, which proposed that people were destined either to heaven or to hell. As you can imagine, because people wanted to know the direction of their fate, they began to look within themselves for signs that offered a clue to their destination. The Puritans thought one possible clue might have been the degree of success they managed to achieve in their public life. The Puritan emphasis on work as the road to salvation was used to help maximize the direction of a person's fate during this period. It was during this time that such terms as *self-awareness* and *consciousness* began to appear with the meanings they have today (Whyte, 1960).

Romantic Era (late 1800s and early 1900s): Fulfilling the Hidden Self

The Romantic era was characterized by a sense of conflict between the individual and society. During the Romantic era, there was an emphasis on each person having a unique destiny. The individual's task was to discover what that predetermined destiny was and to fulfill it. This concern for self-discovery led to an increased emphasis on self-knowledge and exploration of the hidden self. The idea of the hidden self reflected the notion of what we might consider today as "personality" (i.e., characteristics within the individual), which began to replace social rank and social roles as the central aspect of the self.

In contrast to individual salvation occurring in the afterlife as described in the Puritan era, people in the Romantic era emphasized individual fulfillment while on earth. This took the form of a rich inner life, "focused on work, especially creative arts, and inner passion, especially love" (Baumeister, 1987, p. 167). The focus during the Romantic era on personal fulfillment through living a "rich, full life" based on individual passions and creative efforts sounds very much like the concept of self-actualization proposed by Carl Rogers (see Chapter 6) and Abraham Maslow (see Chapter 7).

Victorian Era (approximately 1830 to 1900): Creating the Right Environment for the Emergence of Freud's Ideas

During the Victorian era, the emphasis on individuality continued to grow. But the excessively high moral standards so prevalent at the time made such self-examination by Victorians difficult. As a result, a tendency developed for the Victorians to become self-deceptive and deny certain aspects of their personality (Houghton, 1957). It was during this time that people began to feel anxious that others would be able to gain access to such aspects of their personality as their private thoughts and wishes by looking at their clothes and/or other assorted behavioral subtleties. In reaction to their fears of unintentionally revealing the private self, people's clothing styles

became rather dull, drab, and inexpensive. In fact, many Victorian women simply refused to be seen in public during daylight for fear of being looked at by others (Sennett, 1974).

As you know from reading Chapter 3, it was during this time that Freud began to discuss his psychosexual stages as a means of describing the intrapsychic conflicts involving people's desires and the constraints placed on them by society. It was also during this time that Freud began to describe the very serious consequences of excessive self-deception (i.e., neuroses) when people failed to successfully resolve their intrapsychic conflicts. Thus, an emphasis on the expression of the individual's desires that conflicted with a rather restrictive society created the right psychological climate for Freud's ideas.

Early 20th Century (1900 to 1940s): The Alienated Self

During the early part of the 20th century, Freud had a tremendous influence on how people began to perceive the self. Freud emphasized the significance of the hidden, unconscious aspects of the self (i.e., the id) while devaluing the conscious aspects of the self. As such, he proposed that due to an assortment of psychological threats and defenses, complete self-knowledge was not possible.

Another general characteristic of the self during the early 1900s was the sense of alienation people began to feel as they perceived self-sufficiency becoming increasingly obsolete. The demise of family-owned farms, small neighborhood businesses (e.g, mom-and-pop groceries), and the economic depression produced by the 1929 stock market crash were some factors that helped to create this sense of alienation. The increasing presence of assembly-line work, which offered little opportunity for individual self-expression or personal identification and satisfaction with the product being made, also contributed to feelings of alienation. People began to experience a loss of their sense of personal identity as they became more dependent on society.

Recent 20th Century (late 1940s through today): The Search for Uniqueness in a Collective Society

Although an ever-increasing bureaucracy continues to foster a sense of self characterized by alienation, people today are still trying to assert their sense of individuality. Most recently, people are searching for their own "special place" in society. The contemporary view of self emphasizes each person's uniqueness. As such, this view also emphasizes self-exploration and self-discovery as a means of finding personal uniqueness within this collective atmosphere. Phrases like "getting in touch with yourself" or "finding out who I really am" reflect this late 20th-century view of the self.

In this period, people have pursued self-exploration and self-discovery through such means as hallucinogenic drugs during the 1960s, encounter groups during the 1970s, and personal growth seminars during the 1980s. The recent resurgence of interest in Native American Indian rituals and Eastern religions as part of the New-Age spiritual movement, as well as the continued proliferation of self-help books and videos, are all signs of a contemporary view of the self that is unlike the views from 50 years ago—and extremely unlike the views that existed some 500 years ago. Thus, as Baumeister (1987) eloquently summarizes the contemporary state of the self, "Recent trends suggest that the individual has accepted the state of being immersed in and dependent on society and is struggling to find meaning and fulfillment within those limitations" (p. 171).

As you can see, the self has changed and evolved over time in a manner that is linked to many different historical factors, including religious, sociological, psychological, and economic influences. For more information on the historical developments of the concept of the self, read the following publications: an article titled "How the Self Became a Problem: A Psychological Review of Historical Research" (Baumeister, 1987), and the book titled *Identity: Cultural Change and the Struggle for the Self* (Baumeister, 1986).

This concludes the survey of the meaning, origins, dimensions, and cultural and historical influences of the self concept. As you can see, the self-concept is extremely complex and influences many important aspects of your thoughts, feelings, and behavior. For more information on the self-concept, read the book chapter by Hazel Markus and Susan Cross (1990) titled "The Interpersonal Self," and one by Roy F. Baumeister (1995) titled "Self and

Identity: An Introduction." In the next chapter, you will continue to explore the self-concept by considering some of its important components.

Chapter Summary: Reexamining the Highlights

▲ *The Self-Concept*
—*The Self-Concept Defined.* Self-concept refers to beliefs an individual has about himself or herself. *Self-esteem* refers to an individual's overall evaluation of himself or herself. *Identity* refers to definitions an individual uses to help distinguish himself or herself from others.
—*The Origin and Onset of the Self-Concept.* Children begin to explore an image of themselves in the mirror at around six months of age, and they demonstrate a solid sense of self at about 15 to 18 months of age. Their sense of self continues to grow as they compare themselves to others at about 6 to 12 years of age, which creates increased self-consciousness.

▲ *Dimensions of the Self-Concept*
—*Private and Public Perspectives on the Self.* Public self-awareness refers to those aspects of the self hidden from the public, while *public self-awareness* refers to those aspects of the self that can be viewed by others. Self-consciousness is the tendency to be aware of your sense of self. *Private self-consciousness* refers to the tendency of an individual to be self-reflective; *public self-consciousness* refers to a tendency to engage in self-analysis regarding a person's public image. The Self-Consciousness Scale is used to measure individual differences in the traits of private and public self-consciousness. The behavior of people who score high in the trait of private self-consciousness reflects internal standards, while the behavior of people high in the trait of public self-consciousness reflects external standards.
—*Objective Self-Awareness.* Objective self-awareness is the sense of heightened self-consciousness created by situational conditions. Private self-awareness is a situationally induced tendency toward internal self-analysis, while public self-awareness is a situationally induced tendency for external self-

analysis. Coping with objective self-awareness involves leaving those situations that create these feelings of objective self-awareness and/or attempting to make overt behavior more consistent with internal standards.

—*The Control-Theory Model (CTM) of the Self.* The CTM links the personality traits of self-consciousness and the state of objective self-awareness. According to the CTM, people regulate their behavior against a preexisting standard. For privately self-conscious people and those in a state of private self-awareness, this preexisting standard is internal. For publicly self-conscious people and those in a state of public self-awareness, the pre-existing standard is external.

—*Identity Orientations. Identity orientation* refers to the extent to which people focus on internal or external environments in defining their identity. A personal identity orientation characterizes people who use self-knowledge and self-analysis to define their identity. A social identity orientation characterizes people who use their interactions with others to define their identity. Personal and social identity orientations are assessed using the Aspects of Identity Questionnaire. Personality, occupational, and recreational correlates of a personal identity orientation reflect a desire for independence and uniqueness, while a social identity orientation reflects a tendency toward conformity and a concern for social appropriateness.

▲ *Cultural and Historical Dimensions of the Self*

—*Cultural Influences on the Self.* Collective cultures emphasize the public aspects of the self and conformity to social norms, roles, and values. Individualistic cultures emphasize individuality and the expression of the private self.

—*A Historical Review of Selfhood.* The history of how people have viewed the self reflects various social, economic, religious, and psychological factors. During the late Medieval period, the self was defined primarily by a person's social position. The early Modern period emphasized knowing the inner self of others, while the Puritan era emphasized an early concern for self-awareness. The Victorian era promoted a view of the self characterized by deception and denial. The early 20th century was characterized by a view of the self reflecting a sense of alienation brought on by the Industrial Age. The recent 20th century is characterized by a view of the self that is seeking a sense of uniqueness in a collective society.

Glossary

collective self   A sense of self determined by group membership.

control-theory model   An explanation for the regulation of behavior based on an internal preexisting standard.

identity   The sense of self that sets you apart from others.

identity orientation   The tendency to use either an external or internal frame of reference in defining your sense of self.

independent self   A sense of self separate from any group membership.

interdependent self   The sense of self determined by an individual's meaningful relationship with others in a group.

objective self-awareness   To be made more aware of internal aspects of the self.

private self-awareness   An awareness of the internal aspects of the self.

private self-consciousness   The increased tendency to engage in internal self-examination.

public self-awareness   An awareness of the external aspects of the self.

public self-consciousness   The increased tendency to engage in external self-examination.

self-concept   Beliefs you have about yourself.

self-consciousness   The tendency for each person to focus on a sense of self.

self-esteem   Your general evaluation of your sense of self.

CHAPTER 13

Special Topics in the Study of the Self: Gender Identity, Self-Esteem, Self-Monitoring, and Self-Schema

CHAPTER OVERVIEW: A PREVIEW OF COMING ATTRACTIONS

*I*n this chapter, you will continue to expand your understanding of the self-concept by considering four special topics in the study of the self. These topics, which represent a diversity of interests displayed by personality psychologists investigating the self-concept, are areas of investigation supported by systematic research and interesting applications.

Beginning with the topic of gender identity, you will examine the processes by which we acquire our sense of gender identity and some consequences of such an identity. Then you will consider the nature and development of self-esteem, with specific attention to the role parenting plays in developing self-esteem in children. Next, you will read a discussion of the personality dimension of self-monitoring, including its characteristics, measurement, and applications. Finally, you will consider the nature and operation of the self-schema.

Gender Identity: The Most Pervasive Aspect of the Self-Concept

Probably the most pervasive aspect of what people consider as our sense of self is that of gender identity. **Gender identity** refers to the individual's private experience of being a male or female (Money & Ehrhardt, 1972). In this section, you will learn what personality psychologists have to say about gender identity and its development, related behaviors, and consequences.

Theories of Gender Identity: Becoming Male and Female

As with anything else that is important and complex, the development of gender identity has been explained in several ways. There are currently two general categories under which the explanations can be classified: psychological and biological explanations.

Psychological Explanations of Gender Identity: The Processes of Identification, Observation, and Categorization

The psychological explanations of gender identity have focused on various psychological processes to account for the acquisition of gender identity. These processes include identifying with same-sex others, receiving and observing rewards for gender-appropriate behavior, the categorization of attitudes and activities along gender lines, and the processing of information according to gender.

Psychoanalytic Theory: The Importance of Identification Psychoanalytic theory proposes that, like all other significant aspects of personality development, gender identity takes place very early in life. More specifically, during the phallic stage (ages 3 to 6 years), boys resolve their Oedipal complexes and girls their Electra complexes by successfully identifying with the same-sex parent (see page 70 for a review). With identification comes the internalization of the attitudes, characteristics, and beliefs of the same-sex parent. Much of which is internalized has to do with what is considered masculine and feminine. For example, in identifying with his father, a little boy imitates his father washing the car by washing his bike. On the other hand, the little girl might imitate her mother going to the office each day by having her "mommy doll" go to work.

While the process of identification is certainly a vital part of the process of acquiring gender identity, more recent research has questioned the underlying dynamics that psychoanalytic theory employs to account for this process. First, many preschool children lack sufficient knowledge about differences in male and female genitalia to make the concerns about castration anxiety for boys and penis envy for girls plausible explanations (Bem, 1989). Second, while Freud proposed that the identification of boys with their fathers was based on fear brought on by castration anxiety, recent research indicates that boys are more likely to identify with fathers who are warm and nurturing, not punitive and threatening (Hetherington & Frankie, 1967; Mussen & Rutherford, 1963). Finally, it is well documented that fathers, as well as mothers, play a significant role in the sex typing of their daughters (Huston, 1983; Lamb, 1981).

Social Learning Theory: Direct Tuition and Observational Learning   Social learning theory explains the process of gender identity by considering the role of direct tuition and observational learning (Bandura, 1969, 1989; Bandura & Walters, 1963; Mischel, 1970). **Direct tuition** involves parents and other individuals directly attempting to influence the child's behavior by using rewards and punishments. For example, it has been observed that for children as young as 20 months, parents respond differently based on the sex of the toddler by encouraging sex-appropriate play and reacting negatively to cross-sex behavior (Fagot, 1977; Fagot & Leinbach, 1989). In such cases, girls were reinforced for dancing, asking for assistance, and playing with dolls while boys were punished for playing with dolls and reinforced for playing with trucks and blocks. Another form of direct tuition is expressed by the toys and furnishings parents buy for toddlers. The rooms of young boys typically contain outer-space toys, sporting equipment, and vehicles, while the rooms of young girls contain dolls, domestic toys, and floral furnishings and ruffles (MacKinnon, Brody, & Stoneman, 1982; Pomerleau et al., 1990). What is most interesting about these findings is that such direct tuition by parents occurs even *before* the children have acquired a basic sense of gender identity and clear preference for male and female activities (Fagot & Hagan, 1991). As children get older and start to socialize with other children at school, the same process of direct tuition can occur when the children are teased by their peers for doing things that involve acting like a "sissy" or gaining acceptance for doing what everybody else is doing, such as young girls wearing make-up to school.

Through the process of observational learning, children gain information about their own gender identity and what behaviors are considered appropriate for it (Bandura, 1989). Children observe that certain behaviors done by certain people lead to rewards, while others lead to punishment. For example, by watching television or reading storybooks, children learn that males are more likely to have important roles, make critical decisions, and be rewarded for taking action, while females are more likely to be rewarded for seeking help and behaving more passively and working at "feminine occupations" (e.g., a nurse or waitress) (Liebert & Sprafkin, 1988; Sternglanz & Serbin, 1974; Weitzman, Eifler, Hokada, & Ross, 1972). As a result, it should come as no surprise to you that children who watch more than 25 hours of television per week express more strongly stereotyped views of men and women than those who watch less television (McGhee & Frueh, 1980). The good news is that as more women are appearing on television in less stereotyped roles, such as detectives or executives, what children will learn about gender roles will change. In support of this reasoning, it has been demonstrated that children who regularly watch nonsexist programs do hold less stereotypical views of men and women (Rosenwasser, Lingenfelter, & Harrington, 1989).

Of particular importance to this process of observational learning is that the child pays more attention to same-sex models than to opposite-sex models (Bussey & Bandura, 1984), suggesting once again the importance of identification. Research has shown, however, that attitudes and other personality characteristics of children do not necessarily mirror those of the same-sex parent (Troll, Neugarten, & Kraines, 1969) and may even be more similar to those of the opposite-sex parent (Tolar, 1968). Still others have reported that the sex of the model is of

little consequence until children are around 6 to 7 years of age (Ruble, Balaban, & Cooper, 1981; Slaby & Frey, 1975). Such variations in opinions and research findings can be viewed as a limitation of the social learning theory of gender identity.

The Cognitive-Development Theory: Categorizing Is Critical The **cognitive-development theory** assumes that gender identity is a result of children being able to categorize what is considered masculine and feminine and then performing those behaviors consistent with their gender (Kohlberg, 1966). More specifically, cognitive-development theory proposes that children pass through a series of stages that involve acquiring the ability to perform increasingly complex cognitive functions. For example, at around 2 or 3 years, young children acquire the ability to use symbols to stand for other objects. As an example, a rock can stand for a car when the child is playing in the sand. At around the age of 5 or 6, children begin to develop not only the ability to define whether they are male or female but also the ability to group other pieces of information into categories that are for "boys" and "girls." For example, they might say that a boy's bike should have a horn but not a white wicker basket. Keep in mind that children as young as 2 years are able to classify themselves as either a boy or a girl. But they do not yet have a clear sense of what is included in this category. For example, a 2-year-old child might assume that if you are a girl and cut your hair short or wear a tie, you are now a boy. Thus, what is critical here is the ability not only to label but also to categorize along gender lines.

According to the cognitive-development theory, after having categorized what is for boys and for girls, and after classifying the self as one or the other, the child then begins to value and express a preference for those attitudes and activities from that category that are consistent with his or her gender identity. The logic is that because I am a boy, I will do boy things; because I am a girl, I will do girl things. These preferences are strengthened even further by the child showing some identification with the same-sex parent and receiving praise and rewards for acting like a "little man" or "little lady." Thus identification is viewed as the end result of the process of gender identity, not as the starting point, as suggested by the psychoanalytic theory. But a criticism of this approach is that the process of gender identity is already under way well before the child begins to demonstrate this ability of categorizing objects and events along the lines of gender consistency. For example, children as young as 3 already show preferences for gender-appropriate activities (Bussey & Bandura, 1992).

Gender Schema Theory: An Information-Processing Approach   Similar to cognitive-development theory, gender schema theory proposes that people use categories based on what they consider to be masculine and feminine to help establish their gender identity and understand their lives and the lives of others (Bem, 1981, 1983, 1987; Martin & Halverson, 1981, 1987). But a critical difference between the two theories is the role of gender schemas.

A **gender schema** is a set of beliefs and expectancies an individual has clustered together with regard to being male and female that influences the type of information to which he or she attends, recalls, and elaborates. According to gender schema theory, the establishment of gender motivates children to begin organizing their experiences and interactions with others into gender schemas (Bem, 1981; Hyde, 1991; Martin & Halverson, 1983). For example, children first develop an **in-group/out-group schema**, which they use to help them classify the extent to which certain objects (e.g., a bat or doll), roles (e.g., teacher or police officer), and behaviors (e.g., fighting or crying) are for "boys" or "girls."

Children also develop an **own-sex schema**, which is a set of thoughts and beliefs people have about their own gender and how such views will be expressed with respect to themselves and in their interaction with others. For example, if a boy learns that playing baseball is for boys (in-group schema) but sewing is for girls (out-group schema), the information-processing nature of gender schema theory assumes that he will be more motivated to seek out and attend to (e.g., watch the way major leaguers hold the bat), recall (e.g., try to imitate a major leaguer when he is playing baseball), and elaborate on (e.g., decorate his room with posters of his favorite players) information related to baseball than sewing.

Support for the information-processing influence of gender schema theory has been reported in research utilizing both children and adults. In one study (Martin & Halverson, 1983), 5- to 6-year-old children were shown 16 pictures in which a child was depicted as engaging in a gender-consistent action (e.g., a boy playing with a truck) or gender-inconsistent action (e.g., a girl chopping wood). When tested a week later, the children were better able to recall, and with greater confidence, those pictures in which gender-consistent actions were depicted than when gender-inconsistent actions were viewed. In addition, the children also demonstrated a tendency to err in the direction of gender consistency (e.g., recall that it was a *boy* chopping wood).

In a study involving adults (Bem, 1981), participants were shown a random list of 61 masculine- or feminine-related words from four categories: proper names (e.g., Henry, Deborah), animals (e.g., gorilla, butterfly), verbs (e.g., hurling, blushing), and clothing (e.g., trousers, bikini). The adults were then given 8 minutes to recall the words in *any* order they could. In support of gender schema theory, the participants with the strongest gender schema, such as highly masculine males and very feminine females, tended to recall the words in clusters based on their gender-relatedness. For example, masculine males tended to recall word clusters having a "masculine theme" (Henry, trousers, hurling, and gorilla) while feminine females tended to recall word clusters having a "feminine theme" (bikini, butterfly, Deborah, and blushing). Non-sex-typed men and women, who supposedly possessed a weaker gender schema, did not display the clustering of gender-related items.

In yet another study, Frable and Bem (1985) had adults listen to 5-minute taped conversations of six separate people. In the "gender condition" of the study, the participants were told that they would be listening to three men and three women. In the "race condition" of the study, they were told they would be listening to three blacks and three whites. While they were listening to the taped conversation of each target person, a picture of that person was projected on the wall. After hearing all six of the conversations, the participants were given a photograph of each person and a written transcript of all of the conversations and then asked to match the conversation with the person. One of the most interesting results of this study was the tendency for those participants who supposedly had a very strong gender schema (i.e., masculine men and feminine women) to make more "opposite-sex errors" than "same-sex errors" when matching the target persons with the appropriate transcript. More specifically, masculine men were more likely to confuse which female target person said what than which male said what, while feminine females were more likely to confuse which male target person said what than which male target person said what. To put it more simply, the traditional masculine males tended to view all the females alike while the traditional females tended to view all the males alike. What is equally interesting is that the same pattern of errors *was not* made for those masculine males and feminine females in the "race condition" of the study. Taken together, these studies tend to demonstrate the information-processing impact of gender schemas on how people attend to (e.g., which female or male said what), recall (e.g., remembering gender-related word clusters), and elaborate on (e.g., reconstructing gender-consistent memories for actions observed) information in a manner consistent with gender schema theory. To examine how gender schemas can play a role in the mistreatment of women, read "A Closer Look" below.

A Closer Look:

The Treatment of Women as Sex Objects: A Gender-Schematic Interpretation

In a rather ingenious study, Doug McKenzie-Mohr, of Wilfrid Laurier University, and Mark Zanna, of the University of Waterloo, examined the role of pornography as a trigger for sexist thinking and behavior in males with a strong gender schema (McKenzie-Mohr & Zanna, 1995). In this study, 30 males classified as gender schematic (expressing very traditional masculine characteristics) and 30 males classified as gender aschematic (expressing a combination of masculine and feminine characteristics) were asked to participate in what were supposedly three independent experiments.

Priming Sexist Thinking Using Pornography
The first of the three experiments involved the men viewing a 15-minute video. The subjects in the "sexually primed" condition were asked to watch a 15-minute pornographic video depicting a heterosexual couple engaging in various sexual acts. In the

"control" condition, the subjects were asked to watch a 15-minute video of a question-and-answer period from the Canadian House of Commons.

Assessing Behavioral Sexism
After viewing the video, each man was escorted into a separate room, where he was interviewed by a female investigator as part of the second study on adjustment to college. In this session, the female interviewer asked each subject a series of questions relating to making the transition from high school to college. During the interview, the female interviewer used a standard set of questions (e.g., was going to college what you expected it to be?) and behaved toward them in a neutral and professional manner.

Assessing Cognitive Sexism
After the subject answered the questions, the interview was ended and he was escorted to a third room, where another male experimenter welcomed him to the third study, which supposedly was a study about memory. In this third study, the subject was given 5 minutes to recall everything he could about the female in the second experiment and the room in which the interview was conducted. After this free-recall task, the individual was placed in front of a computer terminal and asked to respond to a series of seven questions about the female interviewer (e.g., what color was her hair?) and seven questions about the interview room (e.g., what color were the walls in the room?). In addition to assessing the subject's responses to these questions, the computer also measured how fast it took to respond to the questions. It should be noted that in the debriefing session conducted after the third study, none of the men indicated that they believed the three studies were related.

Behavioral Sexism in Gender-Schematic Males
The results of this study support the hypothesis that gender-schematic males exposed to pornographic material would respond to women in a more sexist manner. More specifically, those males with a traditional male gender schema who viewed the pornographic material were rated by the female interviewer as being more sexually motivated and spending more time looking at her body than the other three groups of males she encountered. It is important to note that

the female interviewer *was not* aware of the gender-schematic classification of the subjects nor whether they viewed the pornographic material. This is an important methodological point, because it rules out the possibility of the female's ratings of the males being influenced by her expectations of them. In addition, a measure of how close these men positioned their chairs to the female interviewer indicated that the gender-schematic males who viewed the pornographic material sat closer to the female interviewer than the other three groups of males.

Demonstrating Cognitive Sexism in Gender-Schematic Males

When given the opportunity to recall information about the female experimenter, those schematic males who viewed the pornographic material tended to recall more information about her physical features (e.g., physical appearance and attire) than males in the other three groups. This tendency to recall physical features of the female was particularly strong during the first minute of the five-minute free-recall task for males in the schematic/pornography group.

While those males in the schematic/pornography group were very quick in their recall of information about the physical features of the female interviewer, they recalled much less about what she really had said during the interview and what the interview was about than the other three groups. Finally, it should be noted that the males in the schematic/pornography group tended to take less time to recall the information about the physical features of the female interviewer than the rest of the groups. Thus, these males appeared to be paying more attention to her body and appearance than what she actually said.

Implications for Understanding Sexism

These results are important because they illustrate how males with rather traditional gender schemas perceive and react to women in a rather sexist manner. One important implication of this research is that the processing of gender-schematic information that is sexist in nature, such as focusing on a woman's body or what she is wearing, can prevent the individual from focusing on what the woman is actually saying or doing. For example, if a male personnel director views a female coworker as a sexual object, her on-the-job performance may be overlooked and her continued

employment jeopardized. It also has implications for how sexual intent and the refusal of sexual advances (i.e., rape) may be perceived by men (Shotland & Hunter, 1995).

Another important implication of this research suggests that a potentially harmful effect of pornography is that it can trigger gender-based schematic thoughts and behaviors that are sexist in nature and detrimental to women. Finally, as a point of clarification, recent research in personality assessment is being done to develop a means of measuring individual differences in hostile sexism toward women (Glick & Fiske, 1996). The identification of hostile sexism in certain males will make it easier to develop and direct programs designed to reduce such sexism.

Although the gender-schema approach has produced some rather interesting and supportive research, it is not without its critics. Concerns have been raised regarding how gender schemas are conceptualized (Crane & Markus, 1982; Markus et al., 1982) and measured (Spence, 1984). Other concerns involve disagreement about the underlying cognitive processes that mediate the processing of gender-relevant information (Park & Hahn, 1988) and the inability of others to replicate some of the previous work that is viewed as highly supportive of this approach (Deaux, Kite, & Lewis, 1985).

An Attempt at Integration: Incorporating the Psychological Processes   While each of these four general explanations have been discussed separately, you should realize that psychological processes rarely operate individually. Instead, they tend to operate collectively. The same is probably true for gender identity—that is, identifying with specific models helps the individual to focus his or her attention on certain attitudes and behaviors. These specific attitudes and behaviors are then categorized according to gender, which makes them easier to organize, remember, and reproduce later. Receiving rewards or observing similar others receiving rewards makes the likelihood of expressing these attitudes or performing these behaviors much more likely. Thus, while each explanation emphasizes a slightly different psychological process, it is possible to integrate them.

Biological Explanations of Gender Identity:
Chromosomes, Hormones, and Hermaphroditism
The biological explanations of gender identity have focused on those biological processes within the individual that determine the internal and external physical nature of each person's sex. A distinction is made between internal and external because, as we will see, there are certain people who, internally, have the sexual organs of one sex but the physical appearance of the other (Hyde, 1994). The biological processes to be discussed include chromosomes, hormones, and hermaphroditism.

Sex Chromosomes: The Building Blocks of Gender Identity   **Chromosomes** are genetic structures found within each cell. Each cell in the human body contains a set of 23 pairs of chromosomes. One pair of these chromosomes determines the gender of the individual. A chromosome pair XX designates a female individual and determines the development of the cells of the body in the appropriate physical direction. A chromosome pair XY designates a male individual and determines the development of the cells of the body in the appropriate physical direction. Part of the development determined by these chromosomes is the production of various sex hormones.

Hormones: The Substances of Gender Identity   **Hormones** are chemical substances secreted within the body by a system of glands referred to as the **endocrine system**. The **gonads** are the sexual glands that secrete the hormones that regulate sexual development. For males, the gonads are the **testes**; for females, the gonads are the **ovaries**. For males, the major sex hormones are **androgen** and **testosterone**; for females, the sex hormones are **estrogen** and **progesterone** (Hyde, 1994).

During fetal development, the presence of these hormones influences the development of **primary sexual characteristics** that include the major reproductive organs within the individual. During puberty, the presence of these hormones determines the appearance of **secondary sexual characteristics** that for females involves the development of breasts, broadening of hips, growth of body hair, and other changes in body shape; and for males involves deepening of the voice and the presence of facial and body hair. While these sex hormones have been discussed

separately, you should realize that males and females produce both types of sex hormones. What seems to be critical is the amount that is produced.

Hermaphroditism: A Biosocial Interaction for Deciding Gender   While the discussion of chromosomes and hormones might lead you to believe that the development of gender identity from a biological perspective is pretty straightforward, this is not always the case. A good example of this appears in what is known as hermaphroditism (also referred to as pseudohermaphroditism). **Hermaphroditism** is a biological condition in which the individual possesses the sexual characteristics of both genders. For example, the individual may have a penis but also ovaries and breasts.

The major concern in such cases is whether the individual is to be classified as a male or female. As it turns out, the critical factor is when such a classification is made and how the child is raised. More specifically, in such cases, a decision is made as to whether the child is to be labeled a girl or boy. This decision is typically made after consulting with the parents and a staff of genetic counselors, medical doctors, and mental health professionals.

After the decision is made, depending on the case, there may be some surgery to create the appropriate external organs (e.g., construction of a vagina) and hormonal treatment to simulate appropriate primary and secondary sex characteristics (e.g., the development of breasts at puberty). The individual is then raised based on the assigned gender identity (e.g., put in dresses and called "Mary," and given dolls).

It is recommended that if such gender assignment is to be done, it should occur before the age of 18 months. After that time, the child may have already established a gender identity and may suffer some severe psychological trauma (Ehrhardt, 1985; Money & Ehrhardt, 1982). You should realize, however, that there is some disagreement regarding this conclusion (Diamond, 1982; Imperato-McGinley et al., 1979).

An Attempt at Integration: Incorporating the Biological Explanations with Cultural and Psychological Factors
The integration of the biological explanations involving chromosomes and hormones is relatively straightforward: Chromosomes trigger the release of

certain hormones that, in turn, trigger the development of certain physical features. But the presence of hermaphroditism poses some problems of integration. To account for the process of gender identity based on the assignment of gender involves considering the biological explanations together with cultural and psychological ones. The work with hermaphrodites illustrates just how important cultural (e.g., cultural stereotypes) and psychological (e.g., the process by which these stereotypes are taught to children) factors are when combined with biological factors in the process of the acquisition of one's gender. Once again, you can see that something as significant and complex as gender identity involves many factors and a not-so-simple explanation.

This concludes the discussion of theories of gender identity. For more information on this topic, consult the following sources: a book by Janet Shibley Hyde (1991) titled *Half the Human Experience: The Psychology of Women* (see Chapter 2); a book chapter by Richard D. Ashmore (1990) titled "Sex, Gender, and the Individual"; and John Money and Anke Ehrhardt's (1972) classic book titled *Man and Woman, Boy and Girl*. In the next section, you will consider some consequences of gender identity by examining gender differences in personality and behavior and sex-role stereotypes.

Consequences of Gender Identity: Gender Differences in Personality and Sex-Role Stereotypes

One consequence of differences in gender identity is that the members of each gender might somehow develop certain characteristic personality features or be perceived as possessing these features. The characteristics that develop as a result of gender identity are considered gender differences in personality. The characteristics that members of one gender are assumed to possess are considered sex-role stereotypes (Feingold, 1990; Feingold, A. J., 1992). In this section, you will consider the nature of gender differences in personality and perceived sex-role stereotypes as consequences of gender identity.

Gender Differences in Personality: How Do Males and Females Differ?

As a consequence of gender identity, males and females are subjected to various biological, psychological, evolutionary, and cultural factors that have an impact on their personality development (Buss, 1995; Hyde, 1991; Kashima, Yamaguchi, Kim, Choi, Gelfand, & Yuki, 1995). In this section, you will examine some potential differences in personality that this diversity of factors may produce, as well as some issues related to the magnitude and measurement of these differences (Eagly, 1995; Lippa, 1995). Whenever possible, an explanation is given for why such differences exist. The gender differences in personality to be discussed in this section include aggression, attachment, influenceability, and cognitive functioning.

Aggression: Gender Differences in Hurting   One of the more consistent findings has been that males behave more aggressively than females (Baron & Richardson, 1994; Maccoby & Jacklin, 1974). This difference has been found in animals (Berkowitz, 1993; Archer, 1988; Harlow & Suomi, 1971) and in many different cultures (Shaffer, 1994; Whiting & Pope, 1974). Developmentally, this difference tends to show up at

The pervasive tendency for boys to be more aggressive than girls is, to some extent, a byproduct of learned cultural expectations, which encourage aggressive play by boys with toys linked to aggression. Where do you suppose these two boys learned to play in such a manner?

all age levels. While some of these differences can be explained as a result of hormonal levels, such as testosterone (Glaudue, 1991), it is more likely explained by the processes of learning and social expectations (Baron & Richardson, 1994).

In most cultures, boys are encouraged to engage in more physical activity. It is possible that this increased level of physical activity also carries over into their aggressive behavior. There is also evidence that while girls may not be as physically aggressive as boys, they are just as capable of engaging in passive or indirect aggressive behaviors as boys (Brodzinsky, Messer, & Tew, 1979; Harris, 1992). In this case, indirect aggression might involve ignoring another individual, calling names, or excluding another child from an activity. Thus, this difference in aggression appears to be a consequence of gender identity. You should be aware, however, that the size of this difference is not as large as popular belief might suggest, and that it is determined by several factors, including the type of aggression studied, method of study, age of the subjects studied, and various other cultural considerations (Buss, 1995; Eagly, 1987; Hyde, 1991; Shaffer, 1994).

Attachment: Gender Differences in Wanting Others
The general assumption is that girls and females are more dependent than boys and males. This conclusion is supported by an oft-cited study involving the nature of play of infants 13 months of age. The results of this study indicated that in a free-play situation, infant girls were much more likely to maintain visual (e.g., look at) and physical contact (e.g, play near) with their mothers than infant boys (Goldberg & Lewis, 1969). In contrast to these findings is other research suggesting that at high levels of stress, both boys and girls are just as likely to seek out others. But at low levels of stress, boys are less likely to seek out others (Brooks & Lewis, 1974; Messer & Lewis, 1972). What such results suggest is the possibility that boys learn when it is acceptable to express their fears and when it is not. Thus, at least with children, the conclusion that girls are more dependent than boys is not completely supported (Maccoby & Jacklin, 1974).

In adulthood, other forms of attachment include love, romanticism, and jealousy. Research on gender differences in love has produced inconsistent find-

While both of these individuals seem to be enjoying this romantic dinner, gender differences in attachment indicate that men and women seem to experience love and jealousy differently. Are your experiences with love and jealousy consistent with the results reported in the text?

ings; some studies showed women reporting higher scores on love scales, while others reported no gender differences (Brehm, 1992). When examining scores on scales of romanticism, several studies have indicated that men tend to score higher than women (Sprecher & Metts, 1989). But the inconsistency of the previously noted research becomes more stable when researchers go beyond scores on love and romanticism scales and ask people about their romantic feelings and experiences. Compared to men, women report being in love more frequently and having more intense romantic feelings (Dion & Dion, 1973), as well as more vivid memories of past romantic partners (Harvey, Flanary, & Morgan, 1986). In addition, while females tend to view love as more rewarding than do males, they also tend to report more experience with loving someone without being loved in return (Dion & Dion, 1975).

Threats to one's love or romantic interest can produce feelings of jealousy in both men and women (Buunk, 1982). The assessment of gender differences on jealousy scales indicates that while there are no differences between men and women on global measures of jealousy (White & Mullen, 1989), males tend to experience their jealousy along a cognitive component of jealousy—having thoughts about others being attracted to their partner—and females along an affective component of jealousy—expressing strong feelings about others being attracted to their partner (Carmickle & Carducci, 1993). In addition, expressions of jealousy in females tend to be related more to the expectation that it would be difficult to replace their current relationship, while expressions of jealousy for males are related more to a threat to their self-esteem (White, 1981a, 1981b). In a summary of how men and women cope differently with their feelings of jealousy, it was reported that men were more likely than women to leave relationships, while women were more likely than men to try to preserve the existing relationships (Brehm, 1992).

Thus, with the exception of females being more willing to express their feelings about their love experiences than males, there does not seem to be any clear pattern of gender differences when considering attachment and dependency in adults. Instead, males and females tend to have different reactions to different dimensions of attachment for different reasons.

Influenceability: Gender Differences in Going Along As with dependency, the basic assumption has been that females are more influenceable than males along the lines of being more easily persuaded, more suggestible, and more conforming. This conclusion is based on earlier research comparing the degree of influenceability of men and women in various situations (Crutchfield, 1955; Eagly & Carli, 1981). But a closer look at these studies reveals that there were a number of other factors that could have been used to account for these gender differences in influenceability (Eagly, 1987; Eagly & Carli, 1981). For example, in some of these studies, the tasks used were more familiar to males than to females at that time (e.g., economic or business issues).

As a more valid test of gender differences, subsequent research was conducted (Sistrunk & McDavid, 1971) involving tasks that either favored males (e.g, identifying tools), females (e.g., identifying kitchen utensils), or neither (e.g., identifying celebrities). The results of this research indicated females conformed more than males to the male-familiar tasks, males conformed more than females to the female-familiar tasks, and both were equally conforming in the neutral tasks. These and similar results (Eagly, 1987; Eagly & Carli, 1981) suggest that gender differences in conformity may have more to do with cultural

expectations than underlying abilities between men and women.

Emotional Expressiveness: Gender Differences in the Freedom to Feel It is a common sex-role stereotype that boys don't cry and men do not show their feelings. Research on gender differences in emotional expressiveness indicated that girls and women characterize their emotions as deeper and more intense than do boys and men (Diener, Sandvik, & Larson, 1985). Gender differences in emotional expressiveness solidify rather early. By the time they are 11 or 12 years of age, girls indicate that they are more comfortable than boys about expressing their emotions openly (Fuchs & Thelen, 1988).

Although boys and men seem to demonstrate less emotional expressiveness, this does not mean that they experience less intense emotions than girls or women. In most studies using self-report measures of emotionality, girls are shown to be more fearful, timid, and anxious than boys (Block, 1976). But studies that use direct observation of behavioral responses to threatening stimuli often find no gender differences in fearfulness (Maccoby & Jacklin, 1974). In a more specific sense, recent research suggests that the degree of emotional expressiveness in women may be influenced by the extent to which they possess "certain female gender role traits" (Bromberger & Matthews, 1996, p. 591). Thus, gender differences in emotional expressiveness tend to be less robust than expected and influenced by the individual's particular personality characteristics.

Cognitive Functioning: Gender Differences in Mental Abilities Overall, there appear to be no major differences between males and females on tests measuring general intelligence in the past (Miles, 1935; Terman & Miles, 1936) and in the present (Unger & Crawford, 1992). This is probably because the test developers make every attempt to avoid such biases in performance (Ashmore, 1990; Halpern, 1986; Terman & Merrill, 1937).

But some basic differences in cognitive functions have been reported between males and females. For example, although verbal abilities do not develop until late childhood, girls tend to demonstrate greater verbal abilities than boys (Hyde & Linn, 1988; Maccoby & Jacklin, 1974; Tavris, 1992). In just the opposite manner, males tend to demonstrate

While both the boys and girls in this classroom show an eagerness to respond, research on gender differences in cognitive functioning reports girls demonstrating higher verbal abilities than boys, while boys demonstrate better mathematical and spatial abilities than girls. Such differences have been attributed to different classroom (e.g., responses by teachers) and cultural (e.g., encouraging boys to pursue math and science) expectations. Do you see the men and women in your classes being treated equally?

a greater ability than females in mathematical ability. Although in elementary school, girls tend to do better in math than boys by high school, girls tend to lose their lead. This difference in mathematical ability is reflected in the fact that males are significantly overrepresented in comparison to females in SAT Math Scores above 600 (Benbow & Stanley, 1980; Dorans & Livingston, 1987; Stanley & Benbow, 1982; Tavris, 1992). This difference has been attributed to the tendency for males to take more math and sciences courses as electives during high school than females (Chipman & Thomas, 1985; Unger & Crawford, 1992), since such courses are perceived as masculine and less useful for young girls in their future (Eccles, 1989). Another barrier is that in math and science classrooms, a few males are allowed to dominate class discussion while the females remain silent and/or are ignored by the teacher (Eccles, 1989). However, it is believed that such differences in math ability could be reduced by females perceiving these courses as being consistent with their feminine role and enrolling in such courses (Huston, 1983; West-off, 1979).

Finally, males also seem to show a greater ability than females in the manipulation of spatial relationships (Linn & Petersen, 1985, 1986; Maccoby & Jacklin, 1974). For example, starting in later childhood and continuing into adulthood, males tend to perform better than females on mazes, puzzle boxes, and tests involving fitting pieces together quickly and accurately. It has been suggested that gender differences in spatial ability are due to the tendency to encourage boys more than girls to engage in activities (e.g., video games) that involve greater opportunity to develop spatial abilities (Halpern, 1986) and the gender-typed label associated with the task (e.g., making a dress vs. building a workbench) (Hermann, Crawford, & Holdsworth, 1992).

This concludes the discussion on gender differences in personality. If you would like to read more about gender differences, here are two very informative sources by Alice H. Eagly: a book titled *Sex Differences in Social Behavior: A Social-Interpretation* (Eagly, 1987) and an article titled "The Science and Politics of Comparing Men and Women" (Eagly, 1995). Next, you will consider some of the sex-role stereotypes that appear as a consequence of gender identity.

Sex-Role Stereotypes: How Do the Perceptions of Males and Females Differ?

Sex-role stereotypes are biased beliefs about the behavioral attributes assumed to be associated with being male or female. An example of this type of bias might involve not allowing women to be major league umpires due to the assumed belief that they are not capable of handling the stress and tension of major league competition as well as men. When acted upon, such sex-role stereotypes can result in people being treated unfairly in ways that can range from not being given credit for what they have done to job discrimination and sexual harassment. In this section, you will consider the consequences of sex-role stereotypes for men and women in three different areas: performance evaluation, explanations for successful performance, and the perception of the personality characteristics.

Judgment of Work Quality: Being Just as Good Is Not Good Enough for Females

One of the more pervasive sex-role stereotypes that has been documented is the tendency for work to be judged as being of greater quality if it was done by men than by women, even if the work is *identical*. For example, in one of the first studies to document this tendency, Philip Goldberg (1968) collected articles from various fields (e.g., law, art, business, dietetics, literature) and had people read and then rate the quality of the articles. Half of the subjects read articles that were supposedly written by a male author, while the other half read articles that were supposedly written by a female author. The results were very consistent and extremely clear: regardless of the field and the sex of the individual doing the rating, identical articles written by males were judged as being of higher quality than those written by females.

Such findings triggered a flurry of other studies designed to identify the extent to which such evaluative biases could be found in other areas. Some of the other early studies reporting similar results were found in the judgment of job applicant resumes (Dipboye, Fromkin, & Wiback, 1975), evaluation of job grievances (Rosen & Jerdee, 1975), making of personnel decisions (Rosen & Jerdee, 1974), and ratings of academic intelligence (Lao, Upchurch, Corwin, & Grossnickle, 1975).

But conditions were also identified in which the work of females was considered more favorable than that of males. This seems to occur when the woman's performance is unexpected or out of the ordinary (Abramson, Goldberg, Greenberg, & Abramson, 1977). For example, if the subjects are told that the woman is a successful surgeon, her work is evaluated more favorably than that of a man described in the same way. What seems to occur in this case is that the subjects are rating the work of this particular female as being superior to that of this particular male. That is to say, there must be something about this out-of-the-ordinary woman that makes her work superior, not something about women in general.

A more recent survey of over 100 studies indicates that several important factors must be considered when trying to understand the nature and dynamics of gender differences in performance evaluation (Top, 1991). One factor is the gender typing of the task. Men seem to receive the evaluation advantage for masculine jobs, while women receive the evaluation advantage for feminine jobs. For gender-neutral jobs, men and women receive similar evaluations (Glick, Zion, & Nelson, 1988). Gender biases are also less likely to occur when additional information is provided to the evaluator regarding the individual's abilities (Pazy, 1992). Thus, unless other information is presented, such as information about the nature of a task or an individual's ability, one consequence of sex-role stereotyping is for the work of women to be rated lower than the identical work done by men.

Explanations of Successful Performance: Skillful Men, Lucky Women   Another form of sex-role stereotyping that has been consistently identified is in the way people explain the successful performance of men and women. The successful performance of males on various tasks tends to be attributed to their ability and effort, while the successful performance of females tends to be attributed to luck (Deaux, 1982; Deaux & Emswiller, 1974; Garland & Price, 1977; Unger & Crawford, 1992). This tendency is particularly true when the task is considered masculine in its orientation (e.g., the identification of tools). But even when the task is considered feminine in its orientation (e.g., the identification of household objects), females are rated as being only slightly more skillful than males (Deaux & Emswiller, 1974). A similar gender bias in the attributions of sports performance has also been identified in boys and girls (LeUnes & Nation, 1989). Thus, when it comes to evaluating success, it is assumed that men are successful because of their superior skill and all the hard work they have put in; women are perceived as being just plain lucky.

The consequences of such sex-role stereotyping can have a negative impact for women in the world of work. For example, because of the way their work is evaluated, women may come to expect lower starting salaries than men, and may expect to achieve a lower salary at the height of their careers than men (Jackson, Gardner, & Sullivan, 1992; Major & Konar, 1984). Because of such expectations, competent female employees may actually be undermining their own careers by assuming that such salaries are fair and, thus, settling for lower salaries (Jackson, Gardner, & Sullivan, 1992; Jackson & Grabski, 1988). Consistent with this reasoning is the finding that the higher the starting salaries people requested, the higher their actual salary (Major, Vanderslice, &

MacFarlin, 1985). Fortunately, by focusing more on the actual work of the individual rather than on gender, such biases in the evaluation of job performance can be reduced (Izraeli, Izraeli, & Eden, 1985).

The Perceived Personality Traits of Men and Women: Competent Males, Warm and Expressive Females The reason that men are evaluated more favorably may have something to do with the personality traits believed to be possessed by men and women and the value given to these traits. For example, when asked, college students indicated that the traits most characteristic of men included ambitious, independent, objective, dominant, active, and self-confident (Rosenkrantz, Vogel, Bee, Broverman, & Broverman, 1968). On the other hand, some of the traits considered most characteristic of females included gentle, talkative, interested in own appearance, sensitive to the feelings of others, and able to express feelings of tenderness. Table 13.1 is a more complete list of the traits believed to reflect the personalities of men and women. Thus, while males were perceived as possessing personality traits reflecting competency, females were perceived as possessing personality traits characterized as being warm and expressive. This pattern of results was found to be consistent regardless of socioeconomic class, religion, age, education, and marital status of the subjects (Broverman, Vogel, Broverman, Clarkson, & Rosenkrantz, 1972). A similar pattern of results has also been found in a more recent study (Martin, 1987).

Another example of what might be called a double standard in the perception of the personality traits of males and females was demonstrated in a study of mental health professionals (Broverman, Broverman, Clarkson, Rosenkrantz, & Vogel, 1970). In this study a group made up of social workers, psychiatrists, and clinical psychologists was asked to indicate the characteristics that would describe a mature, healthy, socially competent man; a mature, healthy, socially competent woman; or a mature, healthy, socially competent adult (sex unspecified).

The results of this study were quite consistent and rather surprising. First, while there was considerable agreement among these mental health professionals concerning what they considered to be characteristics of a mentally healthy adult, they dif-

Table 13.1.

Some Favorable Stereotypical Traits for Men and Women: Competency vs. Warmth-Expressiveness Characteristics

Favorable Traits for Men Characterized by Competency	Favorable Traits for Women Characterized by Warmth and Expressiveness
Very aggressive	Very talkative
Very independent	Very tactful
Almost always hides emotions	Very gentle
Very objective	Aware of the feelings of others
Very active	Interested in own appearance
Very competitive	Very neat in habits
Very logical	Very quiet
Very self-confident	Very strong need for security
Very ambitious	Expresses tender feelings

Note. From Sex-Role Stereotypes: A Current Appraisal, by I. K. Broverman, S. R. Vogel, D. M. Broverman, F. E. Clarkson, and P. S. Rosenkrantz, 1972. *Journal of Social Issues,* Vol. 28, pp. 59-78.

fered in their overall perception of the mentally healthy man and woman. More specifically, these mental health professionals tended to view competency-related characteristics (e.g., independent, objective, active) as being more descriptive of the mentally healthy man than the mentally healthy woman. The mentally healthy woman, in contrast to the mentally healthy man, was described as being more submissive, less independent, less adventurous, less competitive, more excitable in minor crises, more emotional, more conceited about her appearance, and more susceptible to having her feelings hurt. Finally, while the ratings by these mental health professionals for the healthy man and healthy adult did not differ, a significant difference was observed for the ratings of the healthy adult and the healthy woman. Thus, these last results suggest that the mental health professionals were equating the description of what is mentally healthy for an adult with that of healthy men, and they were perceiving healthy women as less healthy when using this healthy adult standard. As if this were not enough, these biased perceptions of the mental health of women were found to be expressed by both male and female professionals.

Although the Broverman et al. (1970) study has been criticized on methodological grounds, it still presents some serious implications. Going beyond these sex-role stereotype characteristics of mental health, there is also the possibility that the diagnosis and treatment of mental disorders, especially for women, can be adversely influenced by such sexist biases (Comer, 1995; Kaplan, 1983; Kelly, 1983). For example, the tendency for women to receive the diagnosis of depression more often than men may be based on an extension of the sex-role stereotype concerning what characteristics (e.g., passive, submissive) women are more likely to possess than men (e.g., active, independent). Because of such potential biases, mental health professionals need to be aware that they exist and make a conscious effort to guard against them (Comer, 1995; Williams & Spitzer, 1983). Mental health professionals are not the only people who seem to have their judgments clouded by sex-role stereotypes. For more about this issue, read "A Closer Look" below.

A Closer Look:

The Role of Sex-Role Stereotypes in Sex Discrimination in Hiring: The Matching of Job and Gender Stereotypes

Another serious implication of sex-role stereotypes is in the area of sex discrimination in hiring decisions. A basic problem seems to be that certain jobs are perceived to require a specific set of skills that are believed, based on sex-role stereotypes, to be associated with one gender or the other. For example, the job of nurse is believed to require personality traits involving warmth and nurturance, which are generally assumed to be characteristics of women. On the other hand, the job of executive is typically associated with an individual possessing the personality traits of aggressiveness and competitiveness, which are generally assumed to be characteristic of men. The resulting bias this creates in the hiring process is that one gender is more suited for certain jobs than the other

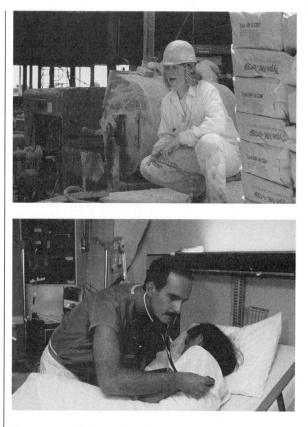

Research indicates that sex discrimination in the workplace exists when it is believed that only individuals of a particular gender possess the physical and personality characteristics that are required for a particular job. The female construction worker and male nurse in these photographs are examples of individuals performing work that is inconsistent with sex-role stereotypes, thus helping to break down certain sex-role stereotypes about what work men and women can do and should be given the opportunity to perform.

because of the traits they are believed to possess. If this is the case, one possible way to reduce such discrimination in the hiring process might be to provide information indicating that the individual applicant does possess those necessary personality traits for performing the job, regardless of his or her gender.

To investigate some ways of reducing sex discrimination in the hiring process, Glick, Zion, and Nelson (1988) sent upper-level managers and business professionals a resume from which they were asked to anonymously evaluate an applicant for three different jobs: sales manager for a heavy machinery company (considered a traditionally masculine job), dental receptionist/secretary (considered a traditionally feminine job), and administrative assistant in a bank (considered a gender-neutral job). The applicant was described as either a male (e.g., "Ken Norris") or female (e.g., "Kate Norris"). The extent to which the applicant possessed certain personality traits was introduced by the gender-related nature of his or her previous experience, as listed in the resume. Masculine work experience included working in a sporting goods store and being captain of the men's or women's varsity basketball team. Feminine work experience included working in retail sales at a jewelry store and being captain of the pep squad. Gender-neutral work experience included working in retail sales at a shoe store and being captain of the men's or women's varsity swim team.

The results indicated that providing the gender-related information on the resume did have an equalizing influence on the evaluation of the applicants. For example, male and female applicants with masculine-related job experience were seen as equally masculine, while applicants with feminine-related job experience were seen as equally feminine. The results also indicated that both the male and female applicants were more likely to be interviewed for the masculine job when they had the masculine-related work experience than when they had feminine-related work experience. On the other hand, they were both more likely to be interviewed for the feminine job when they had feminine-related work experience than when they had masculine-related work experience. But when both males and females were seen as having similar gender-related experience, it was the match between the gender of the individual and the gender-relatedness of the job that seemed to be the most powerful factor in determining the applicant's likelihood of being interviewed.

What conclusions can we draw from this research? On the positive side, providing information about work experience indicating that the individual does possess the type of gender-related personality traits that seem to be appropriate for the gender-related nature of the job can increase the likelihood of being considered for the job. On the negative side,

however, an applicant who is seen as having the right personality (e.g., masculine traits) but the wrong gender (e.g., being a female) for the stereotyped nature of the job (e.g., masculine) may lose out to the individual who is not only perceived as having the right personality traits (e.g., masculine) but also happens to be the right gender (e.g., male). Thus, sex discrimination in hiring seems to be influenced by a matching process that involves both sex-role stereotypes about people and sex-role stereotypes about jobs. Fortunately, as more legal action is taken against those who simply look at gender as the basis of their hiring decisions, less sex discrimination in hiring will take place.

This concludes the discussion of sex-role stereotypes. In the next section, the discussion of sex-roles goes one step further by considering the somewhat controversial notion of androgyny.

Androgyny: The Blending of Masculinity and Femininity

To this point, the discussion of various topics and issues related to sex-roles stereotypes has centered on the distinction between masculinity and femininity. However, a third dimension has been introduced that has contributed to a more complete understanding of sex roles. The concept is that of androgyny (Ashmore, 1990; Shaffer, 1994).

Defining Androgyny: The Blending of Masculinity and Femininity

Broken down, the word **androgyny** means "man" (*andros*) and "woman" (*gyne*). The concept of androgyny is most closely associated with the work of Sandra Lipsitz Bem of Cornell University and Janet Spence of the University of Texas at Austin. In their original conceptualization of androgyny, masculinity and femininity were considered two separate dimensions, and androgyny a combination of the two.

An individual who possesses and exhibits many masculine traits and behaviors but few feminine characteristics was considered a **masculine sex-typed** individual. For example, an aggressive, emotionless office manager, either a man or woman, would be considered masculine sex-typed. An individual who possesses and exhibits many feminine traits and

Sandra Lipsitz Bem and Janet T. Spence have done important work on the assessment, dynamics, and expression of androgyny.

behaviors but few masculine characteristics would be considered a **feminine sex-typed** individual. For example, a compassionate, gentle office manager, either a man or woman, would be considered feminine sex-typed. On the other hand, an **androgynous** individual is one who is described as possessing and exhibiting both masculine and feminine personality traits and behaviors, depending on what is most appropriate for the specific situation (Bem, 1974, 1975). For example, an androgynous office manager would be assertive with an employee who is consistently late for work but also show compassion for the employee who is having difficulties on the job because of some domestic problem. Thus, androgyny is conceptualized as the blending of masculinity and femininity within the individual.

Behavioral and Personality Correlates of Androgyny: A Question of Flexibility and Self-Regard

Because they possess both masculine and feminine characteristics, androgynous people have been found to behave in a more flexible and adaptive manner (Bem, 1974; Prager & Bailey, 1985; Shaffer, Pegalis, & Cornell, 1991). For example, sex-typed masculine, sex-typed feminine, and androgynous people were observed in a situation that involved demonstrating the masculine attribute of independence by resisting social pressure in the ratings of cartoons, or in one that involved the feminine attribution of nurturance

during a 10-minute interaction with a 5-month-old baby (Bem, 1978). The results of this study indicated that the masculine sex-typed and androgynous subjects were more independent in the social pressure situation than feminine-typed people. On the other hand, the feminine sex-typed and androgynous subjects were more nurturing than the masculine sex-typed people when interacting with the baby.

These results are consistent with the notion of greater role adaptability being associated with androgynous people. Androgynous people have also been found to demonstrate their flexibility by performing well in a wide range of tasks and games stereotypically associated with their own sex and the opposite sex. Sex-typed people, on the other hand, tend to perform well and prefer tasks and games stereotypically associated with their own sex (Bem & Lenney, 1976; Bem, Martyna, & Watson, 1976).

In interpersonal situations, some evidence also supports the androgyny advantage. In both childhood and adolescence, androgynous people are perceived by their peers as more likeable and better adjusted than classmates who are traditionally sex

This female police officer exemplifies the concept of androgyny. Her career choice of law enforcement exemplifies masculine sex-role behavior while her nurturing efforts toward the young child exemplifies feminine sex-role behavior. The androgynous individual, like this police officer, successfully combines both masculine and feminine characteristics and expresses them as the need arises.

typed (Boldizar, 1991; Major, Carnevale, & Deaux, 1981). Androgynous men and women are also more comfortable with their sexuality (Garcia, 1982) and more satisfied interpersonally (Rosenzweig & Daley, 1989) than sex-typed people. When meeting for the first time, heterosexual couples that included an androgynous individual expressed a greater liking for each other than did couples that included the more traditional masculine sex-typed male and the feminine sex-typed female, casting doubt on the old saying "opposites attract" (Ickes & Barnes, 1978).

The advantages of androgyny have also been documented in several real-life settings. For example, androgynous college students were also found to receive more honors and awards, date more, and have a lower incidence of childhood illness than low sex-typed masculine and feminine students (Spence, Helmreich, & Stapp, 1975). In a study of Israeli soldiers, masculine and androgynous soldiers received more positive evaluations from fellow officers than did feminine sex-typed soldiers (Dimitrovsky, Singer, Yinon, 1989). This greater role flexibility and behavioral success may be due to the tendency of androgynous people to be less likely to organize information, including information about themselves, in terms of gender and sex-role stereotypes (Bem, 1983). The logic of androgynous people seems to be to classify information and events based on people rather than on gender stereotypes (Bem, 1983, 1985; Fiske & Taylor, 1991).

While the results of the behavioral correlates of androgyny seem to favor clearly the androgynous individual, the results for the personality correlates are less conclusive. For example, research indicates that androgyny is associated with higher levels of psychosocial development (Waterman & Whitbourne, 1982) and self-esteem (O'Connor, Mann, & Bardwick, 1978; Spence and Helmreich, & Stapp, 1975). Androgynous people are perceived by themselves and others as being more well adjusted than masculine and feminine sex-typed people (Bem, 1984; Flaherty & Dusek, 1980; Major, Carnevale, & Deaux, 1981; O'Heron & Orlofsky, 1990; Orlofsky & O'Heron, 1987). Other research, however, suggests that androgynous people do not exhibit higher self-esteem or better adjustment than other people (Lubinski, Tellegen, & Butcher, 1981; Taylor & Hall, 1982; Whitley, 1983). In fact, these studies suggest

that it is possession of "masculine traits" by the sex-typed masculine and androgynous people that contributes most to the expressions of the highest level of self-regard and overall adjustment (Allgood-Merten & Stockard, 1991; Markstrom-Adams, 1989; Taylor & Hall, 1982; Whitley, 1988, 1989). One possible reason for this contradiction in the results is that while the notion of androgyny may be psychologically very appealing, in reality sex-typed masculine characteristics (e.g., aggressiveness, competitiveness, and independence) are associated more with what our society labels as being part of the personality of successful people (e.g., leaders in business and government). Thus, those who possess and exhibit masculine characteristics are much more likely to receive social recognition and, therefore, feel better about themselves.

Another possible explanation for these inconsistencies involves questioning the validity of the scales used to measure androgyny (Spence, 1991; Whitley, 1988). One criticism of these scales is that they are more likely to be a measure of a combination of traits that reflects how people view themselves along the dimension of instrumental-expressiveness of dominance-nurturance/warmth, instead of the specific categories of masculinity and femininity or the combined category of androgyny (Spence, 1983, 1991; Spence & Helmreich, 1978, 1981). Another criticism points out that the concept of androgyny does not exist outside of its relationship with masculinity and femininity, suggesting that there really is not a measure of androgyny but only masculinity and femininity (Pedhazur & Tetenbaum, 1979). Thus, the inconsistency in the results on the behavior and personality correlates of androgyny may reflect the shortcomings in its measurement (Ashmore, 1990; Brown, 1986; Marsh & Myers, 1986).

This concludes the discussion of the concept of androgyny. While androgyny is linked with various controversies, considering it may have helped you to look beyond sex typing as simply involving masculine males and feminine females. If you would like to read more about sex roles and sex-role stereotypes, Carol Tarvis and Carole Wade (1984) have written an excellent book titled *The Longest War: Sex Differences in Perspective*. For more information on the topic of androgyny, an excellent source is a book chapter by Sandra Bem (1985), titled "Androgyny and Gender Schema Theory: A Conceptual and Empirical Integration." This also concludes the discussion of gender identity. If you would like more on the topic of gender and gender identity, an outstanding book is *The Psychology of Gender* (Beall & Sternberg, 1993).

Self-Esteem: Your Evaluation of Your Self

One of the most significant dimensions of the self-concept is that of self-esteem (Baumeister, 1991a, 1995; Buss, 1995; Greenwald, Bellezza, & Banaji, 1988; Harter, 1983; Marsh, 1996; Mruk, 1995; Osborne, 1996). As an objective measure of how important the study of self-esteem is, between 1978 and 1986, there were close to 17,000 publications on just those instruments used to measure self-esteem, self-acceptance, and the self-concept alone (Wylie, 1989). But a more pragmatic example of the importance of self-esteem is the California Task Force to Promote Self-Esteem and Personal and Social Responsibility (1990). The state of California established the committee to develop and implement strategies and programs for increasing the self-esteem of its citizens as a "social vaccine" (1990, p. 4) that would help people and their communities combat such social ills as street crime and violence, abuse within families, alcohol and drug abuse, teen pregnancy, chronic welfare dependency, and educational failure. In short, the task force assumed that enhancement of self-esteem could be used to solve most of the more pressing contemporary social problems.

In support of the task force's efforts, the results of a five-year self-esteem program at Moreland School District in San Jose, California, indicated that

> Moreland had become the highest achieving of 29 districts in Santa Clara County, and the percentage of students going to college had risen markedly, to 89 percent. The dropout rate fell dramatically, while attendance rates soared. Annual vandalism declined from $1000 per school to $178 per school. (Warren, 1996, p. B4)

While the task force's expectations for what self-esteem could do for the entire state of California may be overly ambitious, the evidence suggests that low or impoverished self-esteem is linked to a variety of social ills (Blascovich & Tomaka, 1991). There is also evidence to suggest that threats to the self-esteem of certain people are linked to such acts of violence as murder, assault, rape, domestic violence, child abuse, political terror (e.g., government repression, terrorism, and war), racial prejudice and discrimination, and genocide (Baumeister, Smart, & Boden, 1996).

To emphasize the significance of self-esteem even further, there is evidence to support the valuable contribution self-esteem makes to people's sense of happiness and well-being (Myers, 1992; Roberts, Gotlib, & Kassel, 1996). It was self-esteem, not family life, income, or friends, that was found to be the best predictor of happiness and general life satisfaction. In this section, the nature and determinants of self-esteem are discussed.

The Nature of Self-Esteem: Defining Self-Worth

Self-esteem refers to your personal evaluation of your own sense of self-worth (Baumeister, 1991a; Baumeister, Smart, & Borden, 1996; Blascovich & Tomaka, 1991; Coopersmith, 1967; Hamachek, 1978; Shaffer, 1994). Self-esteem can be expressed in a very general sense (e.g., Joe feels really good about himself these days) or a very specific sense (e.g., Joe is really down on himself for failing his history test). There are two general approaches to conceptualizing self-esteem: (a) the relationship of the real self to the ideal self, and (b) a combination of subjective evaluation and personal significance (Baumeister, 1991a; Buss, 1995).

A Traditional View of Self-Esteem: The Relationship of the Real Self to the Ideal Self
The more traditional approach has its roots in William James's (1890) concept of self-esteem. For James, self-esteem involves two different components of your self-concept as the basis for self-evaluation. These two components are personal success (i.e., what you have actually accomplished) and personal pretensions (i.e., your goals, desires, and aspi-

rations). James viewed self-esteem as a ratio, in which a person's successes were divided by his or her pretensions.

In a somewhat similar manner, Carl Rogers (1951) also based his conceptualization of self-esteem on two separate components of the self, which he referred to as the real self (i.e., what you are actually like) and the ideal self (i.e., the way you would ideally like to be). For Rogers, self-esteem is reflected in the degree of discrepancy between the real self and the ideal self: the less discrepancy between your real and ideal self, the higher your level of self-esteem, or the better you are going to feel about yourself. For example, recall how good you felt about yourself when you reached a goal you had set for yourself. The "warm glow of success" is because there is little discrepancy between what you set out to do and what you actually did. On the other hand, think about how bad you felt when you thought you did really well on a test, only to find that you did rather poorly. This sense of disappointment you have with yourself is a result of a drop in self-esteem created by the rather large difference between what you thought you did and what you actually did.

A Contemporary Viewpoint: A Combination of Subjective Evaluation and Personal Significance

An alternative and more contemporary viewpoint to traditional conceptualizations of self-esteem places somewhat more emphasis on how favorably an individual perceives himself or herself to be with respect to a specific attribute (e.g., helpful) or ability (e.g., solving math problems), while downplaying the significance of how good the individual wants to be (Baumeister, 1991a). This approach also considers how important the specific attribute or ability is to the individual's sense of self.

Attributes and abilities that are important to the individual have a greater impact on the individual's self-esteem than those that are not. Suppose that Patrick has little ability and interest in playing tennis. From the perspectives of James and Rogers, Patrick should have high self-esteem because his actual ability to play tennis is consistent with his ideal level of tennis ability. But if playing tennis is not really important to how Patrick evaluates his sense of self, then the ratio of congruence between the real and ideal self makes no difference to his level of self-

esteem. However, if he now finds himself attracted to someone he met at a party who expresses a strong interest in playing tennis, his tennis ability now has additional importance to his sense of self as it relates to his involvement with this person. The point is that our self-esteem involves more than just the relationship between what we do and want to do; it also includes other subjective personal and interpersonal aspects of the self-concept and their consistency and stability (Campbell et al., 1996).

After considering the different ways personality psychologists define self-esteem, you may now be wondering about the level of your own self-esteem. To gain some insight into this question, you might try completing the exercise in "You Can Do It" on page 396.

Trait vs. State Self-Esteem: Your Fluctuating but Relatively Enduring Sense of Personal Evaluation

While you may have a generally favorable view of yourself most of the time, there are times when your self-esteem takes a drop, such as after hearing you did not get the job you wanted or doing very poorly on an exam. You may even experience a large boost to your self-esteem when your professor or boss gives you a compliment for some work you performed. These examples point out an important distinction between the moment-to-moment sense of self-worth versus a more enduring sense of self-esteem (Heatherton & Polivy, 1991; Kernis, 1993). These transitory states of self-esteem tend to be the result of specific pieces of information you receive from others (e.g., a negative evaluation at work) or your actions (e.g., tripping over a desk and falling flat on your face in front of all of your classmates). On the other hand, your more enduring sense of self-esteem as a personality trait is determined by events that occur very early in life, such as parenting styles (Coopersmith, 1967; Wattenberg & Clifford, 1964; Shaffer, 1994).

In general, the trait of self-esteem is relatively stable over time (Block & Robins, 1993; Braumeister, 1991b). This seems to be true even for that period of life most often associated with a sense of "identity crisis"—adolescence (Harter, 1982; Simmons, 1987). It

YOU CAN DO IT

Examining Your Self-Esteem: A Self-Report Approach

To gain some firsthand experience with how personality psychologists use objective personality tests to measure self-esteem, please answer these 10 questions (Rosenberg, 1965, pp. 17-18), according to the following instructions.

Instructions

For each of the statements below, indicate the extent to which you:

SA=Strongly Agree
A = Agree
D = Disagree
SD = Strongly Disagree

_____ 1. On the whole, I am satisfied with myself.
_____ 2. At times I think I am no good at all.
_____ 3. I feel that I have a number of good qualities.
_____ 4. I am able to do things as well as most people.
_____ 5. I feel that I do not have much to be proud of.
_____ 6. I certainly feel useless at times.
_____ 7. I feel that I am a person of worth, at least on an equal plane with others.
_____ 8. I wish I could have more respect for myself.
_____ 9. All in all, I am inclined to believe that I am a failure.
_____ 10. I take a positive attitude toward myself.

Scoring

For items 1, 3, 4, 7, and 10, the scoring is: Strongly Agree = 4, Agree = 3, Disagree = 2, and Strongly Disagree = 1. For items 2, 5, 6, 8, and 9, the scoring is reversed. To calculate your self-esteem score, add the number of points. The higher your score, the greater your level of self-esteem. However, like most other complicated aspects of personality, your self-esteem is determined not only by internal factors (e.g., self-evaluation), but external factors (e.g., surrounding social groups) as well (Rosenberg, 1979). As a result, consider your score on this brief self-esteem scale as just one piece of information among many that could be used to determine your global level of self-esteem.

seems that for the most part, there is no major downward shift in people's self-esteem as they enter and move through adolescence (Nottelmann, 1987; Petersen, 1988). On the other hand, if there is a change in the direction of an adolescent's self-esteem, it is more likely to be in a positive direction than a negative one (Marsh, 1989). However, for a small minority of young people who experience many life changes all at once (e.g., changing schools, family problems, changing body image, and dating), adolescence can be a period of eroding self-esteem (Simmons, Burgeson, Carlton-Ford, & Blyth, 1987; LaBreche, 1995). Thus, while specific experiences may result in a temporary increase or decrease in self-esteem, it remains a relatively stable personality trait.

Because of the significance of the endurance of self-esteem, the discussion now turns to those determinants of this rather stable dimension of personality.

Determinants of Self-Esteem: The Influence of Parents and Peers

Two critical determinants to self-esteem are parents and peers. For parents, their principal influence on the self-esteem of their children is through child-rearing practices. For peers, their principal influence on the self-esteem of other children is through the process of social comparison.

Child-Rearing Practices:
Getting an Early Start at Home

In a classic study on the early determinants of self-esteem, Stanley Coopersmith (1967) compared the parenting practices of parents of fifth- and sixth-grade boys who had either high or low self-esteem. He found that some rather specific parenting practices were associated with children having high self-esteem and those having low self-esteem. The differences in the parenting practices involved the use of restrictions and discipline, democratic practices, and acceptance (Coopersmith, 1967). Similar findings have also been observed in more recent research investigating the determinants of self-esteem in both boys *and* girls (Lamborn, Mounts, Steinberg, & Dornbusch, 1991).

Consistent Restrictions and Discipline: Drawing the Line and Enforcing It.

One of the most interesting findings of Coopersmith's study was that children having high self-esteem were punished just as often as children having low self-esteem. The difference seems to be in *how* the punishment was done. Parents of the children with low self-esteem tended to be very permissive and inconsistent in setting rules, guidelines, and restrictions for their children. They tended to be rather permissive until they would lose their patience. After losing patience, they would then punish the child by using harsh and humiliating methods (e.g., "How can you be so stupid!") and/or withdrawing love (e.g., "Daddy won't love you any more!"). On the other hand, parents of the children with high self-esteem tended to set specific rules and enforced them in a very firm and consistent manner by punishing the child's behavior, not the child's self-image. For example, if a child failed to clean her room, the parents might say, "Because you didn't clean your room, you will be grounded for a week as you were told." This is in sharp contrast to an attack on the child's self-image by saying something like, "You are such an irresponsible person; you're so sloppy." Thus, one characteristic of a parenting style that fosters high self-esteem in children involves clearly stated restrictions that are consistently enforced.

Democratic Practices: The Use of Reasoning and Rewards

Although the parents of high self-esteem children did provide consistent limits and discipline, they also made an effort to hear the child's reasons and explanations for the behavior, as well as providing the child with an explanation for the discipline. Also, rather than punishing the children to get them to comply with the restrictions, these parents tended to prefer the use of rewards (e.g., praise). On the other hand, the parents of the low self-esteem children spent little time and effort listening to or reasoning with their children. When these parents wanted conformity to the few rules they did have, they simply used force.

Acceptance: Unconditional Love   The parents of children with high self-esteem tended to express a loving acceptance of their child, regardless of what the child had done. Such a sense of unconditional acceptance by the parents seems to carry over into the children's unconditional acceptance of themselves. When disciplined, these children tended to perceive it as an expression of their parents' love and concern for their well-being.

In addition to these differences in parenting practices, parents of the high self-esteem children tended to express more affection toward the children, were more interested in their activities, and had high self-esteem themselves (Coopersmith, 1967).

Social Comparison: Using Others as a
Yardstick for Measuring Your Self-Esteem

In addition to the parental influences that occur inside the home, the process of comparing yourself to your peers and others outside of the home is also a critical determinant of your self-esteem. There is evidence to suggest that at around 6 years of age, children begin to compare themselves to their peers with respect to school performance (e.g., how many questions did you miss?) and physical ability (e.g., I am faster than you in the foot race) (Frey & Ruble, 1985), and that such comparisons are critical in fostering the child's sense of self-esteem (Shaffer, 1994). This pattern of social comparison continues throughout life.

The Theory of Social Comparison: A Framework for Comparing Yourself to Others   According to the **theory of** social comparison (Festinger, 1954), we compare ourselves with others in order to gain insight into our own self-concept. The logic of social comparison is that we use others as a "yardstick" to gauge our own level of competence on those dimensions we consider critical to our sense of self. For example, if being a good tennis player is important to your self-concept, then you are going to want to know just how good a tennis player you are. The fastest way to do that is to compare your ability to the ability of others.

But some evidence suggests that these comparisons can have a positive or negative impact on your sense of self-esteem (Osborne, 1996; Tesser, 1991). In one study that used a job interview setting, students who were interviewed with another applicant who appeared very impressive rated their self-esteem lower on a post-interview survey than those who were interviewed with someone who appeared to be a "real jerk" (Morse & Gergen, 1970). In more recent research, college students with low self-esteem felt better about themselves when they were made aware of other students who were having a more difficult time adjusting to college or had performed worse on a task than they had (Gibbons & Gerrard, 1989; Gibbons & McCoy, 1991). Thus, we use others as a yardstick for measuring our own self-esteem.

Relevance as a Basis of Social Comparison: Looking for What's Important to Your Sense of Self-Esteem   The social comparisons you make are not done haphazardly; they are guided by a few basic considerations (Helgeson & Mickelson, 1995). One critical consideration is how relevant the dimension being compared is to your sense of self. The more important the dimension is to you, the more your self-esteem is affected by the comparisons you make with others (Tesser, 1980, 1991). For example, if being popular is much more important to your sense of self-esteem than the grades you get in school, then observing that others seem to have more friends than you do is going to be a greater blow to your self-esteem than knowing that you are getting mostly B's and A's in your courses.

Similarity as a Basis of Social Comparison: Looking for Others Who Are Like You   Another critical consideration for social comparison is determining whether the individual or group being used as a reference point provides a realistic and fair comparison. For example, if you want to know how good a tennis player you are, you should compare yourself to someone who has been playing tennis for about the same length of time as you and who is about your age, sex, and weight. The same is true for determining the quality of your life (Myers, 1992). It is probably safe to say that you would probably not feel very good about yourself if you seriously compared your lifestyle to those appearing on the show "Lifestyles of the Rich and Famous." While evidence suggests that upward social comparisons can be very beneficial (Collins, 1996), try to avoid comparing apples and oranges when determining your self-esteem.

Cultural Considerations in the Social Comparison Process: Sexism and Self-Esteem   Another factor that can play an important role in determining your self-esteem by comparing yourself to others is sex-role stereotypes. Sex-role stereotypes often result in making unfair comparisons that can produce a negative self-concept. For example, if females are not supposed to be competitive or aggressive, a female who enjoys competing aggressively in her professional career may be perceived in comparisons by her peers as being less than feminine and treated in an unfriendly manner. Such treatment may result in this individual not feeling very good about herself (Yoder, 1985).

A more direct illustration of the relationship between the sexist mistreatment of women and self-esteem is that of sexual harassment. Women who encounter sexual harassment may experience lowered self-esteem, as well as other negative personal and social consequences (Gruber & Bjorn, 1982; Maypole, 1986; Unger & Crawford, 1992). These examples illustrate how something as global as cultural factors expressed in the form of sex-role stereotypes can influence something as specific as an individual's self-esteem. In addition to sex-role stereotypes, racial stereotypes have also been shown to influence self-esteem. To examine how the theory of social comparison has been used to help understand the relationship between racial stereotypes and self-esteem, read "Applications in Personality Psychology" on page 399.

APPLICATION

APPLICATIONS IN PERSONALITY PSYCHOLOGY

Academic Performance, Race, and Self-Esteem: Reacting to a Racial Stereotype

Certain racial stereotypes depict African American students as generally academically inferior (Steele, 1992). While school performance for both white and African American students poses a threat to their self-esteem, such a racial stereotype is a much more serious threat to the self-esteem of African American students, because poor academic performance can confirm this negative stereotype (Steele, 1992). Based on social comparison theory (Festinger, 1954; Wills, 1991), comparisons to others who are performing better than you academically could pose a threat to your self-esteem. In coping with this stereotype, African American students tend to develop a strategy that involves separating their global sense of self-esteem from their academic performance.

In support of this strategy, Osborne (1995) examined the relationship between self-esteem and academic performance outcome in African American and white students as they progressed from the 8th and 10th grade. The results indicated that as African American students progressed in school, there was a weakening of the relationship between self-esteem and academic performance. On the other hand, there was a stable or increased relationship between self-esteem and academic performance for white students as they progressed in school. Such a pattern of results helps to explain why, despite poor academic outcomes, African American students tend to report a level of self-esteem similar to that of white students (Osborne, 1995).

The determinants of self-esteem are rather complex. They involve factors as specific as the consistency of discipline in childhood and as global as cultural stereotypes. They involve how and to whom you compare yourself. Because of this, there is no simple formula for determining an individual's self-esteem. However, psychologists offer some basic suggestions that you can apply with regard to how you think about yourself and behave if you want to enhance your level of self-esteem; read "Applications in Personality Psychology" below.

APPLICATION

APPLICATIONS IN PERSONALITY PSYCHOLOGY

Enhancing Your Self-Esteem: Making a Good Person Even Better

Most students reading this book will have a relatively positive sense of self-esteem. After all, you must have a pretty solid sense of self-esteem to go through all that is required to get into and stay in college these days. But as good as you probably are, with something like self-esteem, there is always room for improvement. Following are just a few recommendations that some psychologists have designed to help enhance your self-esteem (Osborne, 1996; Mruk, 1995; Weiten, Lloyd, & Lashley, 1991).

1. *You control your own self-esteem.* Although a number of forces affect your self-esteem, you

Students who compare themselves with individuals who are performing better than they are academically can create a threat to their own self-esteem.

have to recognize that you are ultimately in control of how you feel about yourself. Following are several recommendations that will make it possible to take control of enhancing your own self-esteem.

2. *Controlling your own standards*. Decide for yourself how you want to be and what you really want to do. Avoid having others tell you that "you ought to get a better job," "you would feel better about yourself if you lost some weight," or "you are not trying hard enough." Part of developing a sense of control over your self-concept is having a sense of what you want for yourself. While you may seek others out as a source of information and for suggestions, learn to trust your own judgment about what is best for you.

3. *Accent the positive*. You have many fine qualities. Learn to accept and take responsibility for them. A characteristic of those with low self-esteem is that they tend to discount their role in positive events that happen to them. For example, when you receive a compliment on your appearance, don't automatically assume that the person was just being nice to you; assume that they meant it and that you really do look nice. On the other hand, when you get a good grade on a test, learn to assume that it was a result of your intellectual ability and the effort you put into studying, not because the test was easy or you were lucky. Keep in mind that you would not have gotten this far in your educational development if you did not have certain positive characteristics, such as perseverance and intellect.

4. *Control your negative self-talk*. **Negative self-talk** refers to the tendency for people with low self-esteem to think and speak of themselves in unflattering terms. For example, they might describe themselves as unattractive, socially inept, and uninteresting. This negative self-talk is often based on the feedback they receive involving others. As an example, you might unfairly compare yourself to others who have much greater experience or ability, causing you to tell yourself that you really are not any good at tennis or giving speeches. You can also minimize negative self-talk by not tolerating people or situations that make you think and feel negatively about yourself. If it is not possible to change these external factors enough to make you feel better, simply stay away from them as much as possible. Life is too short to subject yourself to such unpleasantness.

5. *Set realistic standards for yourself*. By setting realistic standards for yourself, you can create a greater likelihood of experiencing success. But keep in mind that learning to establish a realistic standard might involve a certain degree of failure in the form of a trial-and-error process. It may not be realistic to work 25 hours a week, take care of your children, and manage a full load of courses with the expectation of maintaining a "B+" average. However, you won't know until you try. After going to school under these conditions and getting "C+,s," you might have to adjust your standards. This might involve redefining success as getting "C's" instead of "B's," or working less and taking fewer classes to maintain those "B's." The point is that there are many ways to define success. The key is to define one that is realistic for you.

As you can see, these recommendations are relatively straightforward and do not require a lot of sophisticated training in psychology. All they require is some desire on your part to make a good person like yourself even better.

This concludes the discussion of the nature and determinants of self-esteem. If you would like more information about the nature and development of self-esteem, read Stanley Coopersmith's (1967) *The Antecedents of Self-Esteem*; it is a classic study and a "must read" for anyone interested in the development of self-esteem. Two books, *Self-Esteem: Paradoxes and Innovations in Clinical Theory and Practice* (Bednar, Wells, & Peterson, 1989) and *Self-Esteem: Research, Theory, and Practice* (Mruk, 1995), cover several topics related to the nature, development, and enhancement of self-esteem and are recommended for anyone wanting to know more about the topic of self-esteem.

Self-Monitoring: The Public Appearance and Private Reality of the Self-Concept

As you discovered in the section on self-esteem, the self-concept consists of many different components (e.g., the real self and ideal self). Another interesting relationship that has received considerable attention lately is the relationship between the public appearances and the private realities of the self (Osborne, 1996; Snyder, 1987). The public appearance of the self is the image we present to others through our words and deeds in various social situations. The private reality of the self represents our true feelings and beliefs. For example, while you may be really bored with the conversation at a party (i.e., private beliefs), you continue to nod your head, maintain eye contact, and ask questions to give the public impression of being interested. Just as the construct of self-esteem captures the relationship between the real and ideal aspects of the self-concept, the construct of **self-monitoring** links the relationship between the public appearances and private realities of the self-concept. In this section, you will consider the nature, measurement, and applications of the self-monitoring aspect of the self-concept.

The Nature of Self-Monitoring: Putting Your Best Personality Forward

Much of what we know about the construct of self-monitoring is based on the research of Mark Snyder. According to Snyder (1987), people vary in the extent to which they monitor or regulate the nature of the public appearance they represent to others during their social and interpersonal relationships.

High self-monitors are people who are able to control to a great degree the image they present to others, regardless of how they might actually be feeling or thinking. Research indicates that high self-monitors are less likely to behave in ways that agree with their true attitudes and more likely to publicly express an attitude that they really do not believe (Zanna & Olson, 1982). An example of a high self-monitor might be a politician who agrees with and is very friendly toward whomever he or she happens to be speaking to at the time, regardless of how he or she really feels about these people.

Low self-monitors are people who are less concerned with determining the nature of the situation and generating a public appearance that matches it. Because they are more concerned with expressing their true feelings and behavior, regardless of the social situation, they tend to display more consistent behavior than high self-monitors. In support of this reasoning, research indicates that people identified as low self-monitors tend to express public opinions that are consistent with their private beliefs (McCann & Hancock, 1983; Mellema & Bassili, 1995). An example of low self-monitors might be political protesters who say what they really believe despite the threat of arrest.

The Measurement of Self-Monitoring: The Self-Monitoring Scale

The Self-Monitoring Scale is used to identify people who are considered high and low self-monitors (Snyder, 1974). The **Self-Monitoring Scale** is an objective self-report inventory containing 25 true-false self-descriptive statements that assess the extent to which people feel they are able to use social cues to regulate and control their behavior to look, do, and say what is considered appropriate for any given situation. People who are high self-monitors would tend to endorse items on the Self-Monitoring Scale such as, "In different situations and with different people, I often act like very different persons." On the other hand, people who are low self-monitors would tend to endorse items such as, "I have trouble changing my behavior to suit different people and different situations" (Snyder, 1987, pp. 16–17). To get some firsthand experience with assessing your own level of self-monitoring, try "You Can Do It" on page 402.

To Be or Not to Be . . . a High or Low Self-Monitor: Which Is Better?

The construct of self-monitoring represents a particular style of interacting with others—nothing more. Neither a high self-monitoring nor a low self-monitoring style is better than the other (Osborne,

YOU CAN DO IT

Identifying Interpersonal Actors: Assessment of Self-Monitoring

For each of the following six items, answer "true" or "false" to indicate whether or not the item describes you.

1. I find it hard to imitate the behavior of other people.
2. I guess I put on a show to impress or entertain people.
3. In a group of people, I am rarely the center of attention.
4. I have considered being an entertainer.
5. I am not particularly good at making other people like me.
6. I sometimes appear to others to be experiencing deeper emotions than I actually am.

Scoring

If you answered "false" to items 1, 3, and 5, give yourself one point. If you answered "true" to items 2, 4, and 6, give yourself one point. Now add the total number of points you have received. The higher your score, the more you express opinions characteristic of high self-monitoring.

Interpretation

High self-monitors perceive themselves as being able to convincingly produce whatever self-presentation image seems appropriate for the present situation. They also perceive themselves to be good actors in social situations. On the other hand, low self-monitors see themselves as not being skillful enough actors to present themselves in any other way than "being themselves" (Snyder, 1987). Be aware that most people are not exclusively high or low self-monitors, but typically fall somewhere in the middle when responding to the complete set of items on the Self-Monitoring Scale. Also be aware that there is some disagreement regarding what is being measured by the Self-Monitoring Scale (Briggs & Cheek, 1988; Briggs, Cheek, & Buss, 1980; Osborne, 1996).

1996; Ross, 1992; Snyder, 1987). Rather than a separate construct, self-monitoring must be considered as part of a more general pattern of events occurring during social interactions (Karoly, 1993). In addition to simply being able to monitor a given situation, people must assess what the behavioral alternatives are in that situation, how well they believe they can perform any of these behaviors, and the likelihood of which behavior will produce the greatest reward. An individual may be very good at monitoring what behaviors are appropriate for the situation, but may not be able to perform any of them very well. In certain situations, a high self-monitoring and a low self-monitoring individual might behave in a similar manner just by leaving the scene after realizing that neither has what it takes to operate successfully.

Putting Self-Monitoring in Perspective: A Combination of Personality Characteristics

Rather than trying to decide whether high or low self-monitoring is better than the other, what is more important is how the self-monitoring construct is combined with other personality characteristics in an individual's total personality. For example, a high self-monitoring individual who possesses a low degree of guilt feelings might be someone to avoid. Such an individual would probably be the prototypical "con artist," doing or saying whatever is needed without worrying about the consequences for others. On the other hand, a high self-monitoring individual with a high degree of empathy might be just the person you want to be around if you are distressed. In such a situation, you would want someone to respond by being sensitive to your needs and presenting a comforting demeanor, even if that person was also distressed. A low self-monitoring individual with a high degree of hostility might be prone to expressing these feelings of hostility without regard to the surrounding situation.

While it may not be possible, nor is it necessary, to pass judgment about the nature of high and low self-monitors, this construct is of some value in understanding important aspects of our behavior. In the next section, you will consider some applications of the self-monitoring construct.

Applications of Self-Monitoring: Using What Is Known

One way to determine the value of a construct in personality psychology is to consider how extensively it has been applied to various issues in our everyday living experiences. On this measure, the construct of self-monitoring has demonstrated a rather large degree of utility. In this section, you will learn how self-monitoring has been applied to the areas of advertising, consumer behavior, and career counseling.

Advertising: The "Soft" vs. the "Hard" Sell

Two approaches taken to the advertising of products involve the "hard sell" and the "soft sell" (Fox, 1984). The soft sell is based on images consumers may be able to project as a result of using a particular product. Ads that stress using a particular brand of toothpaste to give you sex appeal or drinking a certain type of beer to make you a "party animal" are soft-sell ads. In contrast, the hard sell is an approach to advertising that involves stressing the quality, merits, and functional value of the product. Ads that stress buying a particular watch because it lasts a long time or the soft-drink taste test challenges that attempt to persuade consumers to base their decision on the taste quality of the drinks are hard-sell ads. Thus, the soft sell stresses a public image for the consumer while the hard sell stresses the inherent features of the product.

As applied to self-monitoring, it has been found that high self-monitors evaluate image-oriented ads more favorably than product-oriented ads, while low self-monitors exhibit just the opposite pattern (DeBono & Packer, 1991; Snyder & DeBono, 1985b). High self-monitors were also willing to pay more for a product if its ads stressed image rather than product quality, but low self-monitors were willing to pay more for quality than image.

The same response pattern was true for ads designed to get consumers *not* to engage in a particular behavior. In this case, the behavior the ads were trying to reduce was smoking. The image-oriented ads stressed "Bad breath, yellow teeth, smelly clothes . . . is smoking worth it?" while the health-quality–oriented ads stressed "Coughing, shortness of breath, sore throat . . . is smoking really worth it?" As you might expect by now, high self-monitors indicated the image-oriented ads to be more favorable

and effective than the health-quality–oriented ads, while low self-monitors indicated just the opposite pattern (Snyder, Nettle, & DeBono, 1985). When asked to select ads that could be used to persuade others to be nonsmokers, once again, high self-monitors selected the image-quality ads while low self-monitors expressed a greater interest in using the health-quality–image ads. The pattern of these results makes it clear that high self-monitors respond to the soft sell while low self-monitors respond to the hard sell. To further explore this phenomenon for yourself, read "You Can Do It" on page 404.

Consumer Behavior: Choosing Form vs. Function

In addition to the types of advertisements (e.g., image vs. quality) we are exposed to, part of the decision to purchase a product involves certain decisions by the consumer. In discussing the role of self-monitoring in consumer decisions, Snyder (1987) distinguishes between form and function. Consumer decisions made on the basis of form emphasize the outward characteristics of the product, not its inherent characteristics. For example, buying a sleek, flashy, imported sports car—even if it does not perform as well as less expensive domestic passenger cars—or drinking a premium beer offering higher status—even if it does not really taste any better than most of the less expensive beers—are decisions based on form. Consumer decisions made on the basis of function emphasize the inherent characteristics of the product. For example, buying the "generic" brand of beer because it is cheaper and tastes about as good as the "premium" brand or buying clothes based on durability rather than "trendiness," are decisions based on function.

Linking self-monitoring to the form vs. function aspects of consumer behavior, Snyder (1987) suggests that high self-monitors are more likely to base their consumer decisions on form, while low self-monitors are more likely to base their decisions on function. In support of this reasoning, it was discovered that low self-monitors are more likely to agree (i.e., 59%) with the statement "I think generic products are just as good as name-brand products" to a greater degree than high self-monitors (i.e., 42%) (Snyder & DeBono, 1984). In another study, the subjects were asked to read one of two car performance test reports that they thought were from *Consumer*

YOU CAN DO IT

Hard Sell, Soft Sell, and Self-Monitoring: The Linking of Personality Psychology and Advertising

To examine the extent to which others you know might respond differently to "image- vs. quality-oriented" ads, have them select from the following four ads the two they believe to be the most effective.

Each time they select one of the image ads, give them 3 points; each time they select one of the quality ads, give them 1 point. Now add up their total points. Next have them answer the self-monitoring questions in "You Can Do It" on page 402. According to what you have read so far, there should be some relationship between their score for this exercise and their self-monitoring score. Is there?

Note. This exercise was adapted from Linking Dispositions and Social Behavior: Self-Monitoring and Advertising Preferences, by M. Jones, 1994. *Teaching of Psychology, Vol. 21*, pp. 160-161.

Reports. In both cases, the car was described as being of average performance. But for some of the subjects, the picture attached to the report was of the very stylish Pontiac Fiero; the other report had a picture of the rather boxy-looking Volkswagen Rabbit. The results of this study indicated that even though there was no difference in the performance reports of the cars, high self-monitors rated the Fiero more favorably and judged it to be of higher quality. On the other hand, low self-monitors rated the Rabbit more favorably and judged it to be of higher quality (Snyder & DeBono, 1985a). In considering the decision-making process that produced such results, it could be that high self-monitors equate looks with quality while low self-monitors may view flashy packaging as a way of covering up product weaknesses (Snyder, 1987).

Career Counseling: Self-Monitoring in the Workplace

One of the most important issues you are probably going to face during your college years is deciding what you want to do once you graduate. Seeking career counseling is one approach to address this issue. One factor that might influence your decision about a job is the job description. For example, is the nature of the job clearly stated in detail (e.g., you will be required to work two weekends a month, entertaining clients in your home) or vaguely stated (e.g., you will be required to work some weekends)? In one study, it was reported that high self-monitors were more likely to accept a job only if they were given a high degree of detail about what they would be expected to do, while low self-monitors gave an equal preference for the job whether it was described in detail or quite vaguely (Snyder & Gangestad, 1982). This difference may reflect the tendency of high self-monitors to want to know as much as possible about the situation beforehand in order to present the most appropriate public appearance.

In addition to wanting to know specific details about a job, high self-monitors also seem to be rather specific in the strategies they use when seeking employment. High self-monitors were found to engage in such activities as setting a precise job goal, taking job interview training, and using reference groups to gain organizational contacts to a greater extent than low self-monitors (Latham,

1985). Once again, the idea seems to be that high self-monitors are more likely to seek specific information that makes it possible to structure the situation so that they can present the most "appropriate" public self.

Finally, when deciding which applicant should receive a job offer, high self-monitors were found to base their personnel decisions to a greater extent on the physical appearance of the applicants than low self-monitors who tended to base their decisions on the personality disposition of the applicants (Snyder, Berscheid, & Matwychuk, 1988). Based on such research, it seems that when making personnel decisions, high self-monitors seem to be more likely "to judge a book by its cover" than low self-monitors. Thus, whether it involves making career decisions for themselves or others, high self-monitors tend to rely more on the public presentation of the self than low self-monitors.

This concludes the discussion of the self-monitoring. If you would like to know more about the construct of self-monitoring, read Mark Snyder's (1987) award-winning book *Public Appearances/Private Realities: The Psychology of Self-Monitoring*.

The Self-Schema: The Organizational Component of the Self-Concept

In this section, you will consider the self-schema. This discussion will focus on the nature of the self-schema and its impact on the self-concept.

The Self-Schema Defined: Determining Your Distinctive Features

A **self-schema** is a set of organized ideas, beliefs, and perceptions you have about the characteristics that comprise your self-concept. For example, you might perceive yourself as being independent, assertive, outgoing while at work but rather shy, passive, and insecure when it comes to social situations. The dimensions that people tend to incorporate into their self-schema generally involve those that are important to them, those upon which they view themselves as being extreme, and those for which they are certain the opposite does not hold true for them (Markus, 1977; Fiske & Taylor, 1984, 1991). For example, you would probably incorporate the dimension of independence when defining your self-schema if being independent is very important to you and you see yourself as being very independent and not dependent. On the other hand, if someone asked you how orderly you are, you might not have as strong a sense of identity to this dimension when defining your sense of self because being orderly has never really been that important to you, you do not think of yourself as particularly orderly, or sometimes you are orderly and sometimes you are not.

The nature of your self-schema development is based on your experiences. While at work, for example, you have repeatedly demonstrated your independence by trying to figure out a problem rather than asking for help from your coworkers, and by assertively expressing your opinions in meetings. Thus, the self-schema serves as an organizational process in determining the distinctive features of your self-concept (Fiske & Taylor, 1991).

Effects of the Self-Schema: Receiving and Recalling Relevant Information Regarding Your Self-Concept

In addition to helping you to determine and organize what you consider to be the distinctive features of your self-concept, the self-schema also influences how you receive and recall information about your self-concept.

The Processing of Our Perceptions: Making Snap Judgments

Incorporating a particular dimension into our self-schema affects the way we perceive ourselves and others (Fuhrman & Funder, 1995; Fiske, 1995). People who incorporate a certain dimension into their self-schema tend to respond more quickly when asked to indicate the extent to which other related dimensions apply to them (Markus & Sentis, 1982). For example, people who view themselves as independent would be quicker to judge themselves as

being self-reliant and unrestricted than people who do not include independence as a characteristic of their self-schema.

In addition to making judgments more quickly about themselves, people who view a particular dimension as a vital part of their self-schema are also more likely to view the behavior of others differently than those who do not possess that dimension in their self-schema (Fong & Markus, 1982). In a meeting, if you view yourself as assertive, you might be more sensitive to the behavior of others that involves expressing an opinion than would someone who does not think of him- or herself as assertive.

Finally, our self-schema also determines the extent to which we think about schema-relevant information (Cacioppo, Petty, & Sidera, 1982; Osborne, 1996). For example, if you consider yourself a "liberal," you are more likely to respond in greater detail to attacks on liberal arguments (vs. conservative issues) on various issues (e.g., education, defense spending, social services). Thus, the underlying logic regarding the effect of self-schema on our perceptions is that if a particular dimension (e.g., independence) is important to the way you view yourself, it may be very helpful to be able to make snap judgments about yourself, others, and related information along that dimension as quickly and efficiently as possible (Bargh, 1982).

But the efficiency by which the self-schema is used to make quick judgments about yourself and others is not always advantageous. People prone to depression may have a self-schema that predisposes them to recall and interpret information about themselves in an automatic, unintended, and negative manner (e.g., just like that relationship two years ago, I can't control what happens in my life) that contributes to their feelings of depression and hopelessness (Bargh & Tota, 1988; Comer, 1995; Dykman, Abramson, Alloy, & Hartlage, 1989).

The Recall of Schema-Relevant Information: Memories of Me

Besides affecting your perceptions of yourself and other people and events, your self-schema also helps you to remember schema-relevant information (Fiske, 1995; Fiske & Taylor, 1991). Having a particular dimension incorporated into your self-schema makes it easier for you to recall information that supports your self-schema (Markus, Crane, Bernstein, & Siladi, 1982; Sweeney & Moreland, 1980). In addition, people tend to recall and seek out information that confirms the view they have of their self-concept (Swann & Read, 1981a, 1981b) in a manner that seems to be biased toward emphasizing its positive aspects (Greenwald, 1980). For example, if friendly and helpful are significant dimensions in your self-schema, it would probably be much easier for you to generate examples of your friendliness and helpfulness from the past, because doing so makes you feel better about yourself than recalling examples in which you did not behave that way. Thus, your self-schema influences the memories you have of yourself, and these memories seem to strengthen the self-schema. As a result, there seems to be a reciprocal relationship between the self-schema and the memories it affects and the memories you have of yourself.

This concludes the discussion of the self-schema. If you would like to know more about the role of the self-schema in determining the self-concept, read Chapter 6 in Susan T. Fiske and Shelley E. Taylor's (1991) book titled *Social Cognition*.

This also concludes the discussion of the four special topics in the study of the self. For more information on these and other topics on the self, read an outstanding book by Randall E. Osborne (1996) titled *Self: An Eclectic Approach*. In the next chapter, you will explore the topic of anxiety as an all-encompassing intrapersonal process of personality.

Chapter Summary: Reexamining the Highlights

▲ *Gender Identity*

—*Theories of Gender Identity.* The psychological explanations of gender identity include psychoanalytic theory and its emphasis on identifying with same-sex others; social learning theory and the role of direct tuition and observational learning; and cognitive-development theory and gender schema theory and the processes of gender labeling, categorization, and information organization. Biological explanations of gender identity include chromosomal and hormonal influences and the interaction of biological and psychological factors in the expression of hermaphroditism.

—*Consequences of Gender Identity.* One consequence of gender identity is the investigation of gender differences in personality along such personality dimensions as aggression, attachment, influenceability, emotional expressiveness, and cognitive functioning. Another consequence of gender identity is the presence of sex-role stereotypes and their effects on the judgment of work quality, explanations of successful performance, and perceived personality traits of men and women.

—*Androgyny.* The personality dimension of androgyny is the expression of both masculine and feminine personality traits and behavior. Behavioral and personality correlates of androgyny include greater sex-role flexibility and interpersonal satisfaction and enhanced self-regard, which has been linked to the possession of masculine traits.

▲ *Self-Esteem*

—*The Nature of Self-Esteem.* The traditional viewpoint of self-esteem is expressed by the relationship between the real self and the ideal self. The contemporary viewpoint of self-esteem emphasizes an individual's evaluation of specific attributes and the personal significance assigned to these attributes.

—*Trait vs. State Self-Esteem.* Trait self-esteem is the overall, enduring evaluation of an individual's self-worth. State self-esteem is the temporary fluctuations of self-esteem in response to external events.

—*Determinants of Self-Esteem.* Parenting practices that affect a child's self-esteem include consistent restrictions and discipline, democratic practices, and acceptance. Social comparison theory suggests that self-esteem is determined by how you compare yourself to others. Such comparisons are based on the personal significance of the attributes being compared, the similarity of the person to whom you are comparing yourself, and sex-role stereotypes.

▲ *Self-Monitoring*

—*The Nature of Self-Monitoring.* The personality dimension of self-monitoring reflects an individual's ability to regulate overt appearances in response to various situations. High self-monitors are more likely to regulate their overt appearance in response to external situations, while low self-monitors are more likely to regulate their overt behavior in response to personal beliefs.

—*The Measurement of Self-Monitoring.* The personality dimension of self-monitoring is assessed with the Self-Monitoring Scale. The evaluation of your degree of self-monitoring must also include the extent to which you are able to generate appropriate responses, as well as to monitor what responses are appropriate.

—*Applications of Self-Monitoring.* High self-monitors are more likely to respond to soft-sell appeals based on the public image the product can create for the individual, while low self-monitors are more likely to respond to hard-sell appeals based on the merits of the product. High self-monitors are more likely to make consumer decisions based on the form or outward appearance of the product, while low self-monitors are more likely to make consumer decisions based on the functional aspects of the product. High self-monitors are more likely to prefer employment positions with a clear job description, seek more job-related information, and emphasize appearances in performance evaluations than low self-monitors.

▲ *Self-Schema*

—*The Self-Schema Defined.* The self-schema is a set of organized personal information and beliefs about the self-concept. The information and beliefs incorporated into the self-schema are those deemed important to the individual's personal sense of self.

—*The Effects of the Self-Schema.* The use of the self-schema increases the speed by which judgments about the self and others are made and the extent to which an individual thinks about schema-relevant information. The self-schema also increases the likelihood of schema-relevant memories, which strengthen the individual's self-schema.

Glossary

androgen   A hormone that regulates sexual development in males.

androgynous   An individual who demonstrates both masculine and feminine traits and behaviors.

androgyny   A Greek word expressing masculinity and femininity together.

chromosomes   Structures within cells that contain genetic information.

cognitive-development theory   The viewpoint of gender identity based on the classification of behaviors into masculine and feminine categories.

direct tuition   The use of rewards or punishment to influence behavior.

endocrine system   The process regulating the release of hormones into the body.

estrogen   A hormone that regulates sexual development in females.

feminine sex-typed   An individual who demonstrates traditional feminine traits and behaviors.

gender identity   The awareness of one's gender.

gender schema   A collection of personal assumptions about the beliefs and behaviors possessed by each gender.

gonads   A gland that secretes hormones, which regulate sexual development.

hermaphroditism   The presence of both masculine and feminine secondary sex characteristics within the same individual.

high self-monitors   People whose behavior tends to reflect situational demands.

hormones   Chemical substances, produced by and secreted into the body, that influence mood and behavior.

in-group/out-group schema   A set of assumptions about which ideas, beliefs, or behaviors go together and which do not.

low self-monitors   People whose behavior tends to reflect personal beliefs.

masculine sex-typed   An individual who demonstrates traditional masculine traits and behaviors.

negative self-talk   To think or speak of yourself in a self-demeaning manner.

ovaries   The gonads of females.

own-sex schema   A set of assumptions about what beliefs and behaviors are appropriate for a person's own gender.

primary sexual characteristics   The presence of specific organs and hormones that make reproduction possible.

progesterone   A hormone that regulates sexual development in females.

secondary sexual characteristics   A collection of body changes that indicate gender-specific sexual maturation.

self-esteem   An individual's overall sense of personal self-worth.

self-monitoring   A personality dimension expressing the tendency for an individual's behavior to reflect personal beliefs vs. situational demands.

Self-Monitoring Scale   A personality test assessing individual differences in self-monitoring.

self-schema   A set of beliefs you have about the nature of your self-concept.

sex-role stereotypes   Assumptions about the behaviors, beliefs, and traits associated with a particular gender.

testes   The gonads of males.

testosterone   A hormone that regulates sexual development in males.

theory of social comparison   A framework by which people compare themselves to others for the purpose of self-assessment.

CHAPTER 14

Anxiety: An All-Encompassing Intrapersonal Process of Personality

CHAPTER OVERVIEW: A PREVIEW OF COMING ATTRACTIONS

Although the concept of anxiety has been mentioned in previous chapters, it was typically treated only as a secondary point of discussion. In this chapter, the concept of anxiety is the primary focus of attention. You will start by considering its core dimensions and the different ways in which they manifest themselves. Then you will learn about the various theoretical viewpoints that have been proposed to explain the nature and dynamics of anxiety. In the next section, you will examine some different types of anxiety, including the distinction between anxiety as a state vs. anxiety as a trait, the nature and dynamics of test anxiety, and the characteristics and causes of anxiety disorders. At the end of this chapter on anxiety, you will consider two areas of application: (a) examining how anxiety has been applied to the world of advertising, and (b) using what is known to help understand and overcome shyness. Thus, in the course of this discussion, you will be exposed to the conceptual, theoretical, and practical sides of anxiety.

Anxiety as an Intrapersonal Personality Process: The Influence of Personality on the Person

In this chapter, anxiety is conceptualized as an intrapersonal personality process. An **intrapersonal personality process** is a specific dimension of personality that is rather encompassing in the effect it has on the individual. The term *intrapersonal* is used because the major effect such a dimension has is primarily within (viz., "intra") the individual (viz., "personal"). Anxiety is considered a personality process because in and of itself, it has specific dynamics that affect the individual differently than other separate dimensions of personality. A personality process is considered encompassing because, as a separate dimension of personality, it influences many different aspects of life. For example, anxiety affects aspects of your life ranging from the thoughts and feelings you have about yourself to the perceptions and reactions you have about the people and products around you. Because the major effect anxiety has as a personality dimension is primarily within the individual, such an effect can be easily conceptualized as "the effect of personality on the person."

The Dimensions of Anxiety: Affecting Your Body, Mind, and Actions

One reason that anxiety has such a profound effect on you whenever it appears is it manifests itself in so many different ways. For example, when you become anxious, you seem to feel it in the form of "butterflies" in your stomach, a sense of "impending doom" in your mind, and a noticeable increase in the clumsiness and awkwardness of your voice while giving a speech to a large group of people. This section devotes some attention to the three specific dimensions of anxiety: the physiological, cognitive, and behavioral dimensions of anxiety.

The Physiological Dimension of Anxiety: The Building of Butterflies in Your Stomach

Whenever you experience an anxiety-provoking situation, your body responds by triggering its **sympathetic nervous system**. The sympathetic nervous system is that aspect of your nervous system that takes over your body to help it prepare to cope with the threat presented in the situation (Groves & Schlesinger, 1982). For example, some of the reactions in your body triggered by the sympathetic nervous system (SNS) involve increasing your heart rate, blood pressure, and respiration, all of which are designed to get more blood and oxygen to the muscles in your body. As your muscles get more oxygen, they become stronger and better able to deal with the threatening situation. The SNS also causes various hormones, such as adrenaline, to be released into the bloodstream, which make you more resistant to and better able to cope with the stress. The SNS dilates (i.e., enlarges) the pupils in your eyes, so that you can better see the source of the threat.

While some reactions are triggered by the SNS, other systems are turned off by it in times of stress and anxiety. For example, the SNS minimizes the functioning of your digestive and sexual systems in response to anxiety-provoking situations, since eating or having sex would probably not be very useful when attempting to cope with the stress. Thus, the physiological dimension of the anxiety involves your body responding in numerous ways to anxiety-provoking situations (Brown, Tomarken, Loosen, Kalin, & Davidson, 1996). In a more subjective sense, it is these dramatic changes in your body that contribute to those feelings of butterflies in your stomach.

The Cognitive Dimension of Anxiety: The Closing of Your Mind

In addition to causing changes in your body, anxiety causes changes in your mind, or more specifically the cognitive processes that occur in your mind (Fischer, 1970; Kiske, Morling, & Stevens, 1996). For example, when you are confronted with an anxiety-provoking situation, your thoughts often become confused and unrelated. You might have experienced such a state of events when you found it difficult to remember what you were going to say next when giving a speech, or when you started to say something from the middle of your speech at the beginning. Your thoughts might also become stereotyped and repetitive when you are anxious. You might not be able to think of a novel answer and simply give the old standby response of "I don't know" when confronted by a traffic officer as to why you were doing 70 mph in a 55-mph speed zone.

In the presence of anxiety, your ability to recall information from your memory also becomes impaired. You have probably experienced the situation in which you couldn't remember an answer to a question when you were rushing to answer it as time was running out during a test, only to have the answer jump out at you while you were driving home from school after the test. Thus, the cognitive dimension of anxiety involves the influence it has on your ability to think effectively in anxiety-provoking situations (Leary & Kowalski, 1995). As you can see, the general effect of the cognitive dimension of anxiety is almost literally the closing of your mind.

The Behavioral Dimension of Anxiety: Fumbling, Fighting, or Fleeing

While the physiological and cognitive dimensions of anxiety are private signals of anxiety to you, the behavioral dimension of anxiety is a public signal to others that you are experiencing anxiety. The behavioral dimension of anxiety is characterized by three response categories: disturbances in the fluency of behavior, attack, and avoidance.

One category of behavioral response to an anxiety-provoking situation is a disturbance in the fluency of behavior. A characteristic of this category is otherwise smooth movements becoming disjointed and awkward when experiencing anxiety. For example, when experiencing anxiety while giving a speech, some signs of such a breakdown in the fluency of behavior might include trembling, shifting your weight from one foot to the other, fidgeting with your hair or clothing, and the cracking or changing of the pitch in your voice, as well as those beads of

perspiration that may form on your forehead. Regardless of their specific nature, one of the behavioral consequences is for you to begin fumbling around.

The other two behavioral categories of anxiety can be conceptualized into a **fight-or-flight reaction** pattern (Cannon, 1929). The basic logic underlying the fight-or-flight reaction is that when confronted with an anxiety-provoking situation, an individual responds by either attacking (i.e., fighting) the situation or avoiding (i.e., fleeing from) it. Suppose that you receive an extremely low grade on a test in your psychology class and begin to feel anxious because you now run the risk of receiving a below-passing grade for the course. You might "attack" this anxiety-provoking situation by launching into a verbal campaign designed to get the professor to feel sorry for you and to change your grade on the test. On the other hand, another student in the class might cope with this threatening situation by avoiding the issue and going to the nearest video store and checking out three movies to help him escape for awhile. The point is that sometimes people respond to an anxiety-provoking situation by fighting it, and at times we elect to take flight from it.

Combining the Dimensions of Anxiety: The Manifest Anxiety Scale (MAS)

One consequence of these three dimensions of anxiety is that they can be combined to create vast differences in the level of anxiety that people experience. One of the most widely used measures of these individual differences in the level of anxiety is the **Manifest Anxiety Scale** (Taylor, 1953). A sample of items from the Manifest Anxiety Scale is presented in "You Can Do It" on page 414.

In support of the validity of the MAS in assessing individual differences in anxiety, people scoring high on the MAS reported experiencing a greater level of anxiety when confronted with a threatening situation than those scoring low on the MAS (Hodges & Spielberger, 1969).

As you can see, the physiological, cognitive, and behavioral dimensions of anxiety involve a wide vari-

YOU CAN DO IT

Selected Items from the MAS: Assessing Physiological, Cognitive, and Behavioral Dimensions of Anxiety

The Manifest Anxiety Scale (MAS) contains 50 true-false items and is designed to measure individual differences in anxiety. Included in the MAS are items indicating the physiological, cognitive, and behavioral dimensions of anxiety. Here are some representative MAS items for you to examine.

Physiological Dimension of Anxiety

T F I have very few headaches. (False)

T F I sweat very easily even on cool days. (True)

Cognitive Dimension of Anxiety

T F I cannot keep my mind on one thing. (True)

T F I find it hard to keep my mind on a task or job. (true)

Behavioral Dimension of Anxiety

T F I am more sensitive than most other people. (True)

T F I am usually calm and not easily upset. (False)

Scoring

Agreement with the choice in parentheses indicates a response characteristic of an anxious person.

ety of systems, processes, and responses that manifest themselves in the body, mind, and actions of the individual. The next section focuses on the theoretical viewpoints of anxiety. But before reading further, you should realize that while the preceding examples focus on the negative effects of anxiety on behavior, believe it or not, anxiety can actually improve the quality of your performance. For example, if you become anxious about the possibility of getting a below-passing grade in a psychology class, you might respond to this threat by attacking your books and studying much harder than you have done in the past. Read "A Closer Look" (page 415) to consider the conditions under which anxiety can help or hinder your performance.

A Closer Look:

The Yerkes-Dodson Law: Using Anxiety to Your Advantage

The **Yerkes-Dodson Law** is a principle of motivation that outlines the relationship between motivation and performance. In its simplest sense, a fundamental point of the Yerkes-Dodson Law is that motivation or arousal may be viewed as existing on a continuum, ranging from very low levels to extremely high levels of excitement. As can be seen in Figure 14.1, at the very low end of the continuum, the individual is viewed as being underaroused or undermotivated (e.g., asleep, drowsy, or bored). At the very high end, the individual is viewed as being extremely aroused and overly motivated (e.g., in a state of frenzy). Within this framework, anxiety is conceptualized as a form of arousal.

Another fundamental principle of the Yerkes-Dodson Law is that arousal affects performance in what is described as an "inverted-U pattern" (see Figure 14.1). At the very low end, your performance is believed to be hindered by a low level of anxiety (arousal) because you become inattentive and careless. Examples of this level might be missing your exit on the expressway because you were tired, or misreading a test question because you just didn't really care that much about it. At the very high end, your level of performance is also believed to be hindered by an extremely high level of anxiety (arousal) because you become disorganized and flustered. An example of this would be when you become so anxious during a test that your mind goes "completely blank" and you end up getting a low grade on the test.

Between these two extremes is a moderate level of arousal, defined as the **optimal level of arousal** because it maximizes the quality of your performance. At this optimal level of arousal, you are aroused or motivated enough that you force yourself to concentrate more intensely on the task at hand, but are not so motivated that you are overwhelmed by your level of arousal. Examples of this level might be the tremendous sense of concentration and determination that goes along with a moderate increase in the level of anxiety you experience while trying to maneuver your car through the scene of a traffic accident, or when you are trying to recall a game-winning question while playing Trivial Pursuit.

Thus, the lesson to be learned here is to try to establish what your optimal level of anxiety is, so that you can use anxiety to your advantage. This might involve trying to calm yourself down or "psyching" yourself up.

Theoretical Viewpoints of Anxiety: Anxiety as a Warning Signal, Acquired Response, and Driving Force

Something as complex as anxiety is not easily explained. As a result, a number of theoretical viewpoints have been proposed to help explain the nature of anxiety. This section focuses on three of them: the psychodynamic, learning, and drive viewpoints of anxiety.

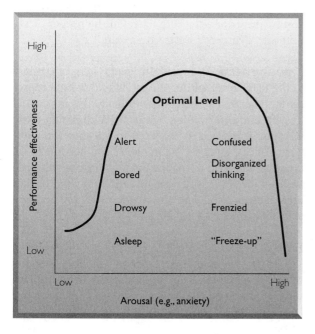

Figure 14.1
The "Inverted-U" relationship of the Yerkes-Dodson Law, describing the relationship between different levels of arousal and performance effectiveness

The Psychodynamic Viewpoint: Anxiety as a Signal of Danger

In one of the earliest formulations of anxiety, Freud (1936), as you will recall from Chapter 3 (page 64), conceptualized anxiety as a warning signal to the ego that some threatening unconscious impulse is on the verge of breaking through and manifesting itself in the individual's conscious awareness. Using this warning signal, the ego can then take evasive action by employing any one of several defense mechanisms. For example, suppose you were taking a test and were not sure of the answer to one question. In such a situation, you might be tempted to take a look at the person's test sitting near you. However, as you think about this possibility, you start to feel a little anxious because of the prospect of getting caught. As a result, instead of cheating, you simply close your eyes and try even harder to concentrate on recalling the answer to the question. In this case, the feeling of anxiety was enough to prevent you from cheating and the possibility of getting caught and suffering an even greater threat to your ego by being labeled a cheater. Thus, from the psychodynamic viewpoint, anxiety is viewed as a warning signal to keep you out of danger.

The Learning Viewpoint: The Acquisition of Anxiety

From the learning viewpoint, anxiety is conceptualized as a learned response to certain stimuli that signals to the organism the imminent onset of an unpleasant event, along with the anticipation of possible suffering (Mowrer, 1950). Although both the psychodynamic and learning viewpoints think of anxiety as a signal of impending danger, the learning viewpoint has extended our understanding of anxiety by more thoroughly explaining the underlying process by which the response of anxiety actually comes to serve as a warning signal of danger.

The fundamental explanation of this process is based on classical conditioning. If you recall, the logic of classical condition is that certain emotionally neutral stimuli can acquire the potential to elicit an emotional response by simply being associated with a stimuli that causes pain or other aversive consequences (see pages 277–287 for a discussion of classical conditioning). For example, suppose you know that whenever employees get fired at work, they typically get a phone call around 4:30 p.m. As a result, you and your coworkers begin to get a feeling of intense anxiety each time the phone rings late in the afternoon. In this case, your anxiety caused by a late-afternoon phone call is an acquired response used to signal the aversive possibility of being fired. Your anxiety in this situation can be considered an acquired response because, as you look back, it was only after starting to work for this company that you began to "fear the phone." You are now probably saying something like, "Come on! Can we really learn to fear a phone and/or other harmless objects based on the process of classical conditioning?" To find out, try for yourself the demonstration in "You Can Do It" below.

YOU CAN DO IT

The Conditioning of Anxiety: Acquiring an Aversion to Air in the Blink of an Eye

For this demonstration, you will need a willing subject (i.e., a good friend), a tube of toothpaste, and a toothbrush. For the sake of your friendship, before doing the demonstration, brush your teeth to make sure you have fresh breath! To start, have your friend sit comfortably in front of you. Sit facing your friend and position your face about 12 inches from his or her face. Next, with your hand to your side and out of the view of your friend, snap your fingers and immediately *afterwards* blow a small puff of air into his or her face. Repeat this about twenty or thirty times. (Now you know the importance of the toothpaste and toothbrush.) The next part of the demonstration involves testing for the conditioning of the anxiety response. To do this, while sitting in the same position, now snap your finger but *do not* blow the puff of air into your friend's face. What you should see now is your friend blinking his or her eyes to the sound of your fingers snapping. In this case, the eye blinking is a conditioned anxiety response to the sound of your fingers snapping, which was used to signal the aversive stimulus of a puff of air into the eyes. As you can see from this very simple demonstration, it is possible to acquire an aversion to air in the blink of an eye.

Thus, from the learning viewpoint, anxiety is an acquired response that serves as a warning signal for the onset of a potentially threatening stimulus and the possibility of suffering by the organism. The process by which such responses are acquired is based on classical conditioning.

The Drive Viewpoint: Anxiety as a Driving Force

Somewhat different from the psychodynamic and learning viewpoints of anxiety is the drive viewpoint (Hull, 1943; Spence, 1956). According to this viewpoint, anxiety is a motivating force that fits into a more general formula for predicting the likelihood of a particular behavior being performed. Here is the basic formula proposed by drive theory:

$$E = D \times H$$

Excitatory Potential: What Are You Likely to Do?   In this formulation, *E* refers to the **excitatory potential** of a response, which represents the likelihood of a particular response being performed by an individual. An example of this would be the likelihood of you turning your steering wheel in the proper direction when your car starts into a spin.

Drive Level: How Motivated Are You to Do It?   *D* refers to the **drive level** within the individual, which represents the extent to which the individual is motivated to perform a particular behavior. Within this basic formula, anxiety is considered to fall into the category of drive level. For example, as you become more anxious when your car begins to go into a spin, the amount of force you use to press on your brakes increases, causing your tires to squeal as you begin to skid, as well as spin.

Habit Strength: How Well Do You Do It?   *H* refers to the **habit strength** of a response, which represents how well a response has been learned by an individual. The habit strength of a response is also further conceptualized into dominant and nondominant responses:

▲   A **dominant response** is one that has been performed routinely and is done very well. An example of this would be the many times you place your foot on the brake pedal of your car whenever you are confronted with a threatening situation while driving.

▲   A **nondominant response** is one that has not been performed very often and is not done very well. An example of this would be the rare situation in which you must turn your car in the direction of a skid to get out of it safely.

Combining E = D x H: Putting It All Together   According to the basic formula, the basic relationship between habit strength and drive level is that any experience that raises the drive level increases the habit strength of a behavior, which in turn increases the excitatory potential. According to this relationship, dominant behaviors become even stronger in habit strength while nondominant behaviors become even weaker. This is the reason that, as your level of anxiety increases, you are much more likely to "stomp" on your brakes when your car starts to go into a spin than turn your steering wheel in the direction of the spin, which is what you are supposed to do. On the other hand, a professional race car driver, because of many years of practicing what to do in a spin, has turning into the spin, rather than braking, as the dominant response in this anxiety-provoking situation. Thus, the role of anxiety in the drive viewpoint is to increase the likelihood of the dominant response occurring.

Integrating the Viewpoints of Anxiety:
Describing Different Aspects of Anxiety
Although this chapter has presented the different theoretical viewpoints of anxiety separately, you should not view them as opposing viewpoints. Instead, they should be integrated according to their ability to help explain different aspects of the total nature of anxiety. For example, the psychodynamic viewpoint describes the basic purpose of anxiety—it serves as a warning signal of impending danger. The learning viewpoint describes the underlying process by which anxiety becomes a warning signal of this impending danger—it is an acquired response based on the process of classical conditioning. Finally, the drive viewpoint provides a basic description of how anxiety affects behavior—it intensifies dominant responses. Thus, when combined, the different viewpoints of anxiety provide a more thorough explana-

tion of the total nature of anxiety than any one viewpoint considered separately.

This concludes the discussion of the theoretical viewpoints of anxiety. Now that you have a basic understanding of the various dimensions and theoretical viewpoints of anxiety, the next section focuses on some different types of anxiety.

Types of Anxiety: An Abundance of Anxieties

As you might expect, something as complex and pervasive as anxiety does not come in one single form or at one level. This section focuses on three types of anxiety. First, you will learn about the very important conceptual distinction between anxiety as a state and anxiety as a trait. Next, you will focus on the nature, dynamics, and measurement of test anxiety, as well as some suggestions for overcoming test anxiety. Finally, you will consider the nature and dynamics of anxiety disorders, a type of anxiety that can be very debilitating to those who experience it.

State vs. Trait Anxiety: Threatening Places and Anxious Faces

There is one distinction that differentiates between two different types of anxiety: anxiety as a state and anxiety as a trait (Spielberger, 1966, 1972).

State Anxiety: Transitory Tension
All of us have experienced a brief period of time when we have felt very uneasy. In this regard, **state anxiety** refers to the temporary emotional change that you experience when confronted with a threatening situation. State anxiety is said to fluctuate and vary in its intensity over time and to be triggered by specific stimuli (Spielberger, 1972). An example of state anxiety would be the state of emotional uneasiness you feel when waiting to get the results back from your first major test in a particular class. On the other hand, as a result of doing well on all of the previous tests, toward the middle of the semester, your state of emotional uneasiness is not as high while you are waiting to get back your third test. As you are

returning to your car after class, however, you notice a rather large dog eating part of a discarded hamburger that was thrown next to your car. Noticing you, the dog growls in an effort to protect its meal, at which point you begin to experience the onset of a rather intense state of emotional uneasiness. As this example illustrates, your level of state anxiety varies from situation to situation, as well as from moment to moment. Thus, a characteristic of state anxiety is its transitory nature.

Trait Anxiety: Always-Anxious Individuals

While state anxiety is considered a response to a situation, trait anxiety is considered a characteristic of the individual. Trait anxiety refers to the fact that some people are simply more anxious than others. More specifically, **trait anxiety** describes individual differences in the tendency to perceive a wide range of situations as threatening and respond to them with anxiety reactions, that is state anxiety (Spielberger, 1972). When used to describe anxious people, this definition attributes two major characteristics to them: the range of anxiety reactions and the intensity of anxiety response.

People with high trait anxiety tend to respond anxiously to a wider range of situations than people with low trait anxiety. For example, people with high trait anxiety might perceive making a decision about changing jobs, applying for new jobs, and going on job interviews as situations that trigger high levels of anxiety, while people with low trait anxiety might only perceive going on interviews as being anxiety-provoking situations. People with high trait anxiety also tend to respond with more intense anxiety reactions to threatening situations than people with low trait anxiety. For example, while waiting for a job interview, people with high trait anxiety will be more anxious than people with low trait anxiety. Thus, the two characteristics of trait anxiety include perceiving more situations as anxiety provoking and responding with a greater degree of anxiety to these situations, or stated more simple, as being "always anxious."

Measuring State and Trait Anxiety: The Assessment of Two Types of Anxiety Together

While state and trait anxiety have been discussed as separate types of anxiety, keep in mind that they can

Actor Don Knotts is famous for his character Sergeant Barney Fife. Barney Fife exhibited all of the characteristic features of trait anxiety; he was easily aroused by a wide variety of situations. Although being overly anxious is nothing to laugh at, it was Barney's tendency to become easily aroused that created most of the comedy that surrounded his character.

operate together. For example, while all of the passengers may experience anxiety when the plane begins to bounce around due to wind turbulence (i.e., state anxiety), some passengers might experience more anxiety than others (i.e., trait anxiety).

To assess these two types of anxiety together, Charles Spielberger and his colleagues have developed the State-Trait Anxiety Inventory (Spielberger, Gorsuch, & Lushene, 1970). The **State-Trait Anxiety Inventory** (STAI, for short) consists of two 20-item scales arranged in a fixed format. The 20 items comprised by the state-anxiety portion of the STAI are designed to assess the *present feelings* of the individual (e.g., I feel calm). In contrast, the 20 items comprised by the trait-anxiety portion of the STAI are designed to assess how the individual *generally feels* (e.g., I lack self-confidence). The ability to conceptualize and accurately assess anxiety into state and trait categories has been the impetus of some rather interesting and significant research (Spielberger, 1972). To examine some of this research, as well as the STAI itself, read "A Closer Look" on page 418.

A Closer Look:

Mixing Athletics with Academics: Research on State and Trait Anxiety Using the STAI

As stated previously, the STAI contains items assessing both how the individual currently feels and how the individual feels in general. Following are sample items from both the state-anxiety and trait-anxiety portions of the STAI, along with their basic instructions.

Assessing State and Trait Anxiety: A Sample of STAI Items

State-Anxiety Items

For each of the following items, circle the number under the statement on the right that best indicates how you feel at this moment.

	Not at All	Somewhat	Moderately So	Very Much So
1. I feel tense	1	2	3	4
2. I feel content	1	2	3	4
3. I feel nervous	1	2	3	4

Trait-Anxiety Items

For each of the following items, circle the number under the statement on the right that best indicates how you generally feel.

	Almost Never	Sometimes	Often	Almost Always
1. I wish I could be as happy as others seem to be.	1	2	3	4
2. I become tense and upset when I think about my concerns.	1	2	3	4
3. I tire quickly.	1	2	3	4

Note. From *Manual for the State-Trait Anxiety Inventory,* by G. D. Spielberger, R. C. Gorsuch, and R. C. Lushene, 1970. Palo Alto, CA: Mind Garden, Inc.

Scoring

Calculate your state-anxiety score and your trait-anxiety scores separately by adding together the value of the numbers you have circled for each set of items. The higher your scores, the greater your level of state and trait anxiety.

Illustrative Research with the STAI: The Similarity of Athletes and Academics

Because separate state- and trait-anxiety scores can be obtained when using the STAI, some rather interesting research in this area involves using both of them together.

Anxiety in Athletics

Coaches speak of "Wednesday All-Americans" as people who perform well at practice during the week but cannot live up to their capabilities on game day because of the debilitating effects of anxiety (Smith & Smoll, 1990). Yet these same coaches also talk about how anxiety can increase performance for some people on game day. A key to this paradoxical effect of anxiety may have something to do with individual differences in anxiety levels across athletes. For example, in one rather novel use of the STAI, Peter Klavora (1975) assessed the trait-anxiety levels of several hundred Canadian high school football and basketball players. Using athletes' trait-anxiety scores, Klavora classified the athletes into high and low trait-anxiety groups. Klavora then measured their state anxiety before a regular practice, a regular season game, and a playoff game. As can be seen in Figure 14.2, overall, the high-anxiety athletes displayed a greater level of anxiety than low-anxiety athletes, and this pattern was seen across all the different situations.

Anxiety in Academia

In another study, college students were asked to complete the STAI several times throughout a course, including just before taking an examination that was worth one-third of their final grade and right after taking this examination (Kendall, Finch, Auerbach, Hooke, & Mikulka, 1976). Once again, based on their trait-anxiety scores, the students were divided into high and low trait-anxiety groups. Figure 14.3 shows that the high trait-anxiety students, like the high trait-anxiety athletes, displayed more anxiety before, during, and after the test than low trait-anxiety students.

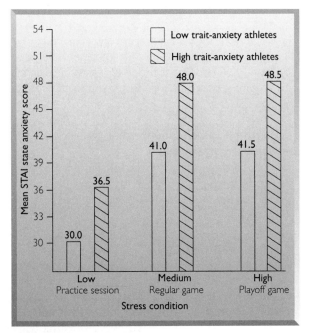

Figure 14.2

Mean STAI state anxiety scores for high and low trait-anxiety athletes as a function of the stress condition

Note. From Application of the Spielberger Trait-State Anxiety Theory and STAI in Pre-Cognitive Anxiety Research, by P. Klavora, 1975. In D. M. Landers, D. V. Harris, and R. W. Christina (Eds.), *Psychology of Sport and Motor Behavior II*, pp. 141–143. University Park, PA: Penn State HPER Series, No. 10.

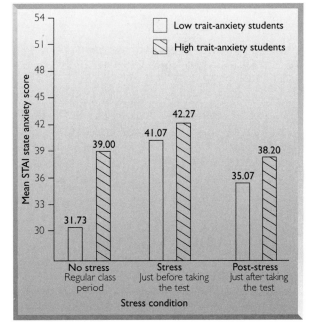

Figure 14.3

Mean STAI scores for high and low trait-anxiety students as a function of the stress condition

Note. From The State-Trait Anxiety Inventory: A Systematic Evaluation, by P. C. Kendall, A. J. Finch, Jr., S. M. Auerbach, J. F. Hooke, and P. J. Mikulka, 1976. *Journal of Consulting and Clinical Psychology, Vol. 44*, pp. 406–412. Washington, D.C.: American Psychological Association.

Although the research just discussed studied two rather different samples of people, the patterns of the results are very similar; they illustrate the two major characteristics of trait anxiety discussed earlier (see pages 418):

Anxious people respond with anxiety to a wider range of situations (e.g., at practice, a regular game, and a playoff game; before, during, and after an examination).

Anxious people respond with an overall greater intensity of anxiety.

Thus, whether you are talking about athletics or academics, the nature and dynamics of state and trait anxiety seem to operate in a rather similar manner.

This concludes the discussion of the state-trait theory of anxiety. As you can now see, this conceptu-

alization makes it possible to view anxiety not only as a transitory emotional response to threatening situations but also as a pervasive behavioral pattern characteristic of people who seem to be anxious all of the time. In the next section, you will consider the type of anxiety that probably has the most relevance to you as a student—test anxiety.

Test Anxiety: Turmoil during Testing

For students, few things are more frustrating than the experience of test anxiety, especially if you have spent time studying diligently. To get a better understanding of test anxiety, in this section you will find some information concerning the assessment and dynamics of test anxiety, as well as some helpful suggestions to help you minimize it.

The Assessment of Test Anxiety: Tabulating Testing Turmoil

When studying test anxiety, researchers have found it helpful to classify people into high and low test-anxiety groups. One of the most extensively used inventories for assessing test anxiety is the Text Anxiety Scale (Sarason, 1972, 1980). The **Test Anxiety Scale** (TAS) includes 37 items, written in a true-false format, designed to assess responses related specifically to testing situations. Thus, unlike the generalized level of anxiety exhibited across a variety of situations measured by the MAS or trait-anxiety dimension of the STAI, the TAS measures state-anxiety responses to the perceived threat and stress related to situations involving taking tests. In this regard, test anxiety is considered a much more specific type of anxiety. To get some idea of how relevant the concept of test anxiety is to you, answer the questions presented in "You Can Do It" below.

A Fundamental Finding: Tests as Ego Threats

A basic finding of research using the TAS is that when the test has some degree of ego involvement (i.e., the results are important to the individual), high test-anxiety subjects perform more poorly on a variety of tasks than low test-anxiety subjects. For example, when told the task they were going to perform was a measure of their intelligence, high test-anxiety

---

YOU CAN DO IT

Measuring Test Anxiety: Assess Your Level Using the Test Anxiety Scale (TAS)

Test Anxiety Scale

For each of the 12 items presented here, circle one letter to indicate whether the statement is true (T) or false (F) for you.

T F 1. While taking an important exam, I find myself thinking of how much brighter the other students are than I am.

T F 2. During tests, I find myself thinking of the consequences of failing.

T F 3. Getting a good grade on one test doesn't seem to increase my confidence on the second.

T F 4. After taking a test, I always feel I could have done better than I actually did.

T F 5. When taking a test, I believe that my emotional feelings do not interfere with my performance.

T F 6. During a course examination, I frequently get so nervous that I forget facts I really know.

T F 7. I seem to defeat myself while working on important tests.

T F 8. I would rather write a paper than take an examination for my grade in a course.

T F 9. On examinations I take the attitude, "If I don't know it now, there's no point worrying about it."

T F 10. Thoughts of doing poorly interfere with my performance on tests.

T F 11. seldom feel the need for "cramming" before an exam.

T F 12. The university should recognize that some students are more nervous than others about tests and that this affects their performance.

Scoring

Each time your response matches the following answer key, give yourself one point.

Answer Key

1 T, 2 T, 3 T, 4 T, 5 F, 6 T, 7 T, 8 T, 9 F, 10 T, 11 F, 12 T

Interpretation

The higher your score, the greater degree of test anxiety you tend to experience during test situations.

Note. From Introduction to test anxiety, by Sarason, I. G. (1980). In I. G. Sarason (Ed.), *Test Anxiety: Theory, Research, and Applications* (pp. 3–14). Hillsdale, NJ: Lawrence Erlbaum Associates, Inc. Copyright 1980 by Lawrence Erlbaum Associates, Inc. Reprinted by permission.

subjects performed worse than low test-anxiety subjects (Sarason & Palola, 1960). In other research, high test-anxiety subjects performed worse than low test-anxiety subjects when told that they were being observed by people behind a one-way mirror (Ganzer, 1968) or when another person was performing the same task in their presence (Pederson, 1970). In these examples, having inferences made about your intelligence, being watched by someone else, or having yourself compared to others all seem to be threats to some people's egos.

On a more personal note, for readers who scored high on the TAS, these findings help to explain why you experience test anxiety while taking a test in class. During a test in class, an inference is being made about your intelligence (i.e., you are being graded), someone is observing you (i.e., the instructor or teaching assistant is watching you take the test), and others are performing the task at the same time (i.e., other students are taking the test in the room and you compare yourself to them). Thus, the experience of test anxiety tends to manifest itself whenever the testing situations present some perceived threat to the individual's ego.

Now that you have some idea of how to identify the people who experience test anxiety, the next step is to consider the underlying dynamics of test anxiety.

The Underlying Dynamics of Test Anxiety: Differences in the Personalities of People with High and Low Test Anxiety

You are already familiar with one of the most fundamental differences between high and low test-anxiety people: high test-anxiety people perceive tests as posing a greater threat to their ego than low test-anxiety people. But some other important differences in the underlying dynamics operating within high and low test-anxiety people also increase our basic understanding of test anxiety and its effects (Sarason & Sarason, 1990). In this section, you will consider some of these additional differences in the underlying dynamics by grouping them into three major categories: behavioral, evaluative, and cognitive differences.

Differences in Behavioral Responses to Test Anxiety: What Are You Doing During the Test?

High and low test-anxiety people differ in their overt and covert behavior during testing situations. At the overt level, high test-anxiety people were found to take longer on problem-solving tasks than low test-anxiety people (Holroyd, Westbrook, Wolf, & Badhorn, 1978; Sarason, 1973). An example of this is the highly anxious student who is the very last one to finish the test because he keeps going over his answers "just to make sure." High test-anxiety people seem to feel they are experiencing more intense emotional reactions during the testing situation than low test-anxiety people. For example, when asked to indicate their level of physiological arousal, high test-anxiety subjects indicated they were experiencing more arousal (e.g., increased heartbeat and skin perspiration) than low test-anxiety subjects (Holroyd & Appel, 1980).

At the covert level, however, when the actual measures of physiological responses are recorded from the subjects during testing situations, the evidence seems to indicate that high and low test-anxiety subjects tend to experience *very similar* levels of physiological arousal (Holroyd & Appel, 1980; Holroyd et al., 1978). Thus, while high test-anxiety people *may believe* they are experiencing a greater degree of anxiety than low test-anxiety people, their levels of anxiety are actually the same. As a result, it is the *perceived* level of physiological arousal experienced by the high test-anxiety people that is distracting them, not the actual level of arousal.

Differences in the Evaluation of Test Performance: How Did You Do on the Test?

Like most of us, people with test anxiety are concerned with their performance on the test. But unlike most of us, people with high test anxiety tend to evaluate their performance differently than people with low test anxiety. This difference is reflected in how they view their potential performance before they actually take the test (Holroyd et al., 1978; Sarason & Stoops, 1978). High test-anxiety people tend to evaluate their performance on a test as being poor regardless of how well they actually performed. For example, even if they seem to know the answers to the test and finish it before many of their classmates, people with high test anxiety would still believe that they did not do very well. On the other hand, people with low test anxiety tend to evaluate their performance by how well they actually did on the test. In this case, people who finish quickly would evaluate their performance as favorable, while people who seem to have difficulty with the test would, justifiably, evaluate their performance as not being very good. Thus, a major difference between people with high and low test anxiety seems to be in how they evaluate their performance.

Don't Remind Me How Well I Did on the Test, Please
What was just said seems to suggest that people with high test anxiety do not respond to performance feedback about how well they are doing while taking a test. You would think that if this were the case, giving them feedback about their performance during the test might enhance their performance on the rest of the test. As logical as this idea might seem, it apparently does not work (Ray, Katahn, & Snyder, 1971). For example, in one test of this possibility, people classified as having high or low test anxiety were asked to perform a task (Mandler & Sarason, 1952). Midway through the testing situation, some people from each group were interrupted and given feedback on their performance, while the remaining people were not interrupted to be given feedback. As honorable as their intentions might have been, these researchers found that providing the feedback during the interruption resulted in a *decrease* (i.e., slower times) in the performance of high test-anxiety subjects but an *increase* (i.e., faster times) in the performance of low test-anxiety subjects on the rest of the test. This pattern of results is summarized in Figure 14.4. Thus, high test-anxiety subjects seemed to perform better when they were not given feedback than when they were given feedback. The reason for this seems to be that anything that reminds high text-anxiety people that they are being tested hinders their performance (Mandler & Sarason, 1952). Reminding high test-anxiety people that they are taking a test focuses their attention on the testing situation itself and the anxiety reactions it is producing, thus decreasing their performance.

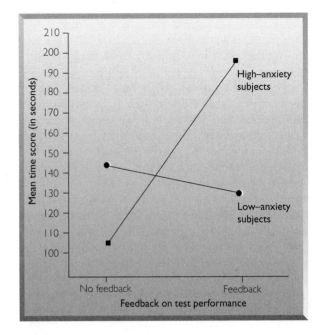

Figure 14.4
Mean time scores for high and low test-anxiety subjects as a function of feedback on test performance

Note. From A Study of Anxiety and Learning, by G. Mandler and S. B. Sarason, 1952. *Journal of Abnormal and Social Psychology, Vol. 47,* pp. 166–173. Washington, D.C.: American Psychological Association.

Differences in Cognitive Processes: What's Going through Your Head during the Exam?
High and low test-anxiety people tend to differ in certain cognitive processes that are critical during the testing situation (Geen, 1980). More specifically, they differ in their attention and utilization of task-relevant information, response to success and failure, and response to physiological arousal.

I Should've Seen That!   One difference in cognitive processes has to do with the attention to and utilization of information required to perform a particular task correctly. High test-anxiety people tend to ignore information on the test that could help them perform better (Geen, 1976). For example, relevant information such as test instructions or critical information provided in a mathematical word problem are much more likely to be ignored or overlooked by high test-anxiety people than low test-anxiety people. We have all had this experience at one time or another; it typically elicits responses such as "Darn it! I should've seen that on the test" when the instructor returns the test.

Fueling Future Failure   High and low test-anxiety people also tend to differ in their responses to previous success and failure. Following failure on one task, high-anxiety people tended to perform more poorly than other high-anxiety people who did not experience failure, while low-anxiety people performed better after failure than other low-anxiety people who did not experience previous failure (Sarason, 1957). Such early failure for those high in anxiety seems to increase the number of self-deprecating thoughts (e.g., I'm so stupid), which results in the lowering of their expectations and overall motivation to succeed in the future (Mandler, 1972; Spiegler, Morris, & Liebert, 1968). Thus, for high-anxiety people, failing seems to fuel future failure.

What Are You Worrying About?   The final difference in cognitive processes involves the way that people high and low in test anxiety respond to the physiological reactions occurring within the body during times of stress. As noted earlier, people with high and low test anxiety tend to experience increased levels of physiological arousal during testing situations. But it has been noted that high test-anxiety people tend to respond to this anxiety by labeling it in a more negative affective manner, and then spending more time worrying about it, than low test-anxiety people (Sarason, 1972). For example, the highly anxious individual might produce a line of reasoning something like this: "My high level of excitement is because I am worrying about my performance on the test." Thus, high test-anxiety people tend to label their physiological arousal during an exam as something to worry about.

Putting It All Together:
Designing Your Own Despair
The picture painted of high test anxiety seems to be one of people who tend to exaggerate the level of their anxiety, evaluate their performance more negatively, and cloud their minds with disruptive thoughts about the test. From this perspective, it should be

very clear that engaging in this pattern of behavior is surely designed to create a sense of despair that would make you feel extremely upset about the prospect of taking a test.

Although you now have a complete understanding of the assessment and dynamics of test anxiety, knowing all about it is not enough for those of you who experience it; you want to know how to reduce it. For some helpful hints on how to reduce your anxiety, read "Applications in Personality Psychology" below.

APPLICATION

APPLICATIONS IN PERSONALITY PSYCHOLOGY

Seven Simple Steps for Overcoming Test Anxiety: Pinpointing the Problems and Practicing the Solutions

Because test anxiety is such a problem for many people, many personality psychologists and other professionals have spent a considerable amount of effort to develop strategies for overcoming it (Sarason, 1980; Sarason & Sarason, 1990). Here are seven simple steps designed to help you overcome your test anxiety (Rathus & Nevid, 1980).

Step 1: Pinpointing Situations That Trigger Test Anxiety
The first thing you must do is to begin to identify those situations that trigger your test anxiety. Here are a few examples of some situations that typically trigger feelings of test anxiety.

1. Waiting for the professor to give you the test.
2. Answering a few questions and then starting to feel unsure about your answers.
3. Changing some of your answers because you feel unsure due to the anxiety.
4. Being completely baffled by one of the questions.

5. Looking around and seeing that everybody else seems to be working as if they know what they are doing.
6. Handing in the test.
7. Hearing some people outside of the classroom talk about their answers to the test as you are walking away after the test.

Although these situations may not be the exact ones that trigger test anxiety in you, they can be used as a starting point to generate situations that are a bit more relevant to you.

Step 2: Pinpointing Self-Defeating Thoughts

The next step involves pinpointing the specific thoughts in the situations identified in step 1 that seem to trigger test anxiety. This is done by using your active imagination. Get comfortable and close your eyes. Now, concentrate on being in each of the situations. Imagine the sights and sounds involved in the situation. After you have conjured up the physical details of the situation, start examining some of the thoughts that might be racing through your mind while in that test-anxiety situation. Try to pinpoint any of these self-defeating thoughts that might be triggering your feelings of anxiety. They are called **self-defeating thoughts** because the anxiety that they generate seems to prevent you from concentrating on answering the test questions. To help you in identifying your own self-defeating thoughts, some of them are presented in the following table, under the heading of "Self-Defeating Thoughts."

Self-Defeating Thoughts vs. Rational Thinking: Some Illustrative Examples

Self-Defeating Thoughts	Rational Thinking
"I should have studied more. I'm not prepared enough to pass the test."	"I've done as much studying as I can. All that is left to do now is take the test."
"There's not going to be enough time for me to finish the test. I'm going to run out of time, I just know it."	"Don't start to rush. Just take one question at a time and answer all those I can first, then go back to those that might require more time."
"I can't answer this question. Now I am going to blow the whole test."	"It's only one question. The grade for the whole test does not rest on this one question."
"Look at all of those people leaving before me. They all must be really smart."	"Just because people are leaving does not mean they are going to get a better grade. I'll just work at my own pace. This is a test, not a race."
"Why do I feel like such a loser after I hand in the test?"	"The test is over. There's no sense worrying about it now. I feel pretty good."

Step 3: Practicing Rational Thinking

As just noted, the problem with self-defeating thoughts is that they get in the way of concentrating on the test. To overcome this problem, you should begin to generate rational thoughts as alternatives to these self-defeating thoughts. Some examples of rational thinking as alternatives to certain self-defeating thoughts are presented in the table column titled "Rational Thinking." The primary purpose of rational thinking is to help you eliminate self-defeating thoughts and minimize the interfering anxiety they create, thus allowing you to focus more of your attention on taking the test.

Step 4: Practicing Rational Test Taking

As with trying to learn any other new form of behavior, in learning to overcome your test anxiety, you must practice doing it. And the best way to do this is to create situations that are as close to the actual testing situation as possible. For example, when studying for a test, do not just study your notes; write out test questions and try to answer them. When answering these questions, set some time limits so that you can get used to organizing your thoughts and working under pressure. While taking the practice test, if you start to experience self-defeating thoughts, practice replacing them with the rational alternatives you generated in the previous step. Again, as with anything else, the more you practice, the easier you will find it is to perform these rational behaviors. And the more you practice them, the more likely they are to become a dominant response in your test-taking repertoire.

Step 5: Practicing the Process of Overlearning

In order for you to feel more comfortable with the material you are studying for a test, as well as the rational test-taking behaviors, it is a good idea to overlearn the material. **Overlearning** involves going over the material you have already mastered again and again. Rehearsing information again and again makes it easier to recall when you need it and less likely to be interfered with by other distractions, such as anxiety.

Step 6: Practicing the Process of Relaxation

If you start to feel tense and nervous during the test, try to calm yourself down by using the relaxation technique to cope with test anxiety discussed on pages 283–284 in Chapter 10.

Step 7: Practicing Self-Reward

Because tests are associated with the unpleasant experience of anxiety, it would be beneficial to associate them with something more pleasant. As you will recall from Chapter 10, it is possible to replace negative associations with pleasant ones by using the process of classical conditioning. This is done by associating taking tests with as many pleasant and positive emotions and experiences as possible. For example, as you replace a self-defeating thought with a rational alternative, concentrate on how good it makes you feel. Pat yourself on the back for being able to use the relaxation technique to calm yourself down during the test. During the test, do not punish yourself by focusing on those questions about which you are unsure. Instead, make yourself feel good by focusing your attention on all of the material that you are able to answer with some degree of ease and confidence. Finally, once the test is over, let it be over. Do not continue to punish yourself with thoughts of what you should have done. Instead, reward yourself by doing something enjoyable. Although this may sound strange, if you get really good at the process of practicing self-reward, you may find that you will actually enjoy taking tests because of the favorable emotions and events that you have come to associate with them.

As you can see from these seven simple steps, the process of overcoming test anxiety is relatively straightforward. All it requires is some practice.

This concludes the discussion of test anxiety. If you would like to learn more about test anxiety, read *Test Anxiety: Theory, Research, and Applications*, edited by Irwin G. Sarason (1980), one of the foremost authorities on test anxiety. It is full of helpful strategies for controlling test anxiety.

The discussion of the various types of anxiety will focus next on anxiety disorder, a type of anxiety reaction that is rather extreme and can disturb a person's entire life.

Anxiety Disorders: Anxiety of Pathological Proportions

To this point in the chapter, you have been examining the types of anxiety that are familiar to everyone, because we have all probably experienced them to some degree. For example, we have all had experience with being in a state of anxiety, known someone who seems to be the "anxious type," or experienced test anxiety at one time or another. Some types of anxiety are well within what you might consider normal levels of anxiety. But this section introduces another type of anxiety, one that is considered abnormal. This type of anxiety is referred to as anxiety disorder (Comer, 1995).

Anxiety Disorder: A Matter of Degree

Like the anxiety that is considered a normal part of life, anxiety that is defined as abnormal is also characterized by nervousness, fear, apprehension, perspiration, muscle tension, rapid heartbeat, and debilitating effects on behavior. But anxiety is considered to be abnormal when its level of intensity begins to interfere with personal goals or interpersonal relationships and causes a great degree of fear and/or pain. At such a level of intensity, the anxiety is considered an anxiety disorder. Thus, an **anxiety disorder** is characterized by a level of anxiety being experienced by the individual that is more intense, frequent, and debilitating than normal anxiety (Napoli, Kilbride, & Tebbs, 1988).

Although extreme in nature, anxiety disorders are relatively common. For example, it has been estimated that about 15% to 17% of the general population has at some time been diagnosed as having an anxiety disorder (Comer, 1995). In fact, as you read about anxiety disorders in this section, you will probably be surprised at how much you already know about them as a result of their appearance in your everyday conversation. The anxiety disorders discussed in this section include panic disorder, generalized anxiety disorder, obsessive-compulsive disorder, and phobic disorder.

Panic Disorder: Having an "Anxiety Attack"   A **panic disorder** is characterized by a sudden, very brief, but extremely intense feeling of fear, doom, uneasiness, and panic that creates a sense of terror within the individual. This sense of panic is so strong that it literally causes the individual to "freeze up" to the point where taking any action is almost impossible. Lasting anywhere from just a few seconds to an hour or more, this "anxiety attack" is unpredictable. That is to say, the individual can begin to experience this high level of anxiety without the presence of any external threat. For example, you have probably heard stories of people freezing up when their car gets stuck on the train tracks. While the emotional state probably resembles that of a panic disorder, it would not be considered an anxiety disorder because the oncoming train does represent something about which you really should be feeling anxious.

Generalized Anxiety Disorder: The Experience of Chronic Anxiety   A **generalized anxiety disorder** is characterized by a chronic feeling of apprehension, worry, uneasiness, and nervousness that lasts for at least one month and often lasts for several months or more. While the level of anxiety is not intense enough to render the individual completely immobile, as is the case with the panic disorder, the constant pressure of the anxiety is enough to affect the emotional and motivational state of the individual to the point that just trying to maintain everyday living activities becomes a chore. As an example of what it is like to experience a generalized anxiety disorder, think about what it would be like to feel the level of test anxiety you experience before a very important exam all day long, day in and day out for months.

Obsessive-Compulsive Disorder: Uncontrollable Thoughts and Behavior   An **obsession** is characterized by a persistent preoccupation with a particular thought, idea, or feeling that the individual seems unable to control. The thought, feeling, or idea typically involves a rather bizarre or irrational theme, such as

drowning one's child while bathing it. Anxiety is created because the individual is unable to stop such thoughts from recurring and/or worries about the possibility of actually executing them. You have probably had some experience with a minor obsession, such as wondering whether you turned off the iron when you left your house to go on vacation. An obsession becomes pathological when the anxiety associated with it begins to interfere with the individual's daily ability to function.

A **compulsion** is characterized by an irresistible urge to perform a particular act or course of action again and again. The behavior triggered by the compulsion is typically extremely rigid and must follow certain rules developed by the individual. The anxiety is created when the individual fails to carry out the act in the previously specified manner. But if the act is performed in the prescribed manner, the anxiety is reduced and the person feels much better. Because it eliminates the anxiety, the compulsive behavior becomes much more likely to be performed again each time the anxiety reappears. For example, a female lawyer may develop a hand-washing compulsion because she believes germs are all over her office. As a result, she must wash her hands constantly to relieve the anxiety associated with the germs. Again, you have probably had some experience with minor compulsions yourself, such as walking around a ladder or getting up out of bed to make sure you turned off the stove. As with more extreme compulsions, you immediately begin to feel much better after walking around the ladder or getting up to check the stove.

Phobic Disorder: Unrealistic Fears   A **phobic disorder** (or **phobia**) is characterized by feelings of fear and anxiety that are out of proportion to the actual danger present in the situation. There are three basic types of phobic disorders: agoraphobia, social phobia, and simple phobia.

▲ **Agoraphobia** is the fear of being alone or being in a public place, with the feeling that if something should go wrong, no one will be able to help you. As a result, people suffering from agoraphobia often may be limited to their home environment and/or require constant companionship, resulting in a very restrictive existence.

▲ **Social phobia** involves an irrational fear and avoidance of social situations where the individual must interact with others, usually fearing the possibility of humiliation or embarrassment. The most common example of this type of phobia is the excessive anxiety people fear over having to speak in public, resulting in the person being willing to do almost anything to avoid such situations.

▲ A **simple phobia** is characterized by excessive anxiety triggered by an irrational fear of a particular object or situation. The anxiety appears when the feared stimulus is present and is eliminated if it can be avoided. The individual suffering from a phobic disorder will spend a considerable amount of energy and effort trying to organize his or her life around avoiding the fear stimulus. For example, an individual suffering from **ailurophobia** (fear of cats) may spend most of his time at home for fear of encountering a cat while outside.

As Table 14.1 demonstrates, it seems that almost anything can be the source of a phobic reaction.

Explaining Anxiety Disorders: Unconscious Conflict and Faulty Learning

How is it that someone could develop **ergasiophobia** (the fear of writing) or go around with the compulsion of having to touch each wall in a room before feeling comfortable in it? As it turns out, explaining the cause of anxiety disorders is not an easy task. Two of the primary explanations of anxiety disorders are based on the psychodynamic and learning viewpoints (Comer, 1995; Mehr, 1983).

Psychodynamic Explanation: Manifestations of Unresolved Conflicts

According to the psychodynamic viewpoint, anxiety disorders are a result of an unresolved unconscious conflict that is now manifesting itself in the form of the anxiety disorder. As an example of a generalized anxiety disorder, an individual who has never expressed his anger at his parents for forcing him to go to college might spend his entire college career feeling anxious over his desire to quit school. An

Table 14.1
Some Examples of Exotic Phobias

Name of Phobia	Object of Phobia
acarophobia	insects
androphobia	men
aphephobia	being touched
arachnephobia	spiders
chrematophobia	money
erotophobia	sex
gynephobia	women
hypnophobia	sleep
keraunophobia	lightning
linonophobia	string
monophobia	being alone
parthenophobia	virgins
phantasmophobia	ghosts
ponophobia	work
spectrophobia	mirrors
trichophobia	hair
triskaidekaphobia	thirteen
zelophobia	jealousy

Note. From *The Language of Mental Health*, by W. E. Fann and C. E. Goshen, 1973. St. Louis: C. V. Mosby.

obsessive thought of harming her child held by a devoted mother may reflect the unconscious resentment she may actually feel about having to take care of the baby rather than pursuing her own personal goals. From the psychodynamic viewpoint, the treatment of anxiety disorders typically involves helping the individual gain insight into and resolve the unconscious conflicts.

Learning Viewpoint: Learning of a Faulty Nature

According to the learning viewpoint, anxiety disorders are a result of faulty learning. For example, on one very hot day, a veteran may experience a panic disorder for what seems to be no apparent reason. This panic reaction may reflect the feelings of intense anxiety he had while in the hot jungles of Vietnam many years ago. Thus, through the process of classical conditioning, the individual may have come to associate very hot days with intense fear of a debilitating nature.

In another example, as a result of reading about and seeing plane crashes on the news, an individual might develop **aviophobia** (the fear of flying) and now comes to associate the sight of a plane with the possibility of crashing. Further, when the person stays off planes, the anxiety is reduced, thereby—based on principles of operant conditioning—reinforcing the avoidance behavior. In a similar manner, because engaging in the compulsive behavior of washing one's hands reduces the feelings of anxiety, the compulsive behavior is reinforced and is much more likely to appear again.

The treatment of anxiety disorders from the learning viewpoint typically involves learning new emotional associations and more effective behavior patterns (Mehr, 1983). This might involve helping the individual to replace the feelings of anxiety with more favorable or appropriate emotions using the process of systematic desensitization. The maladaptive avoidance behavior pattern of a phobic disorder and ritualistic behavior characteristic of a compulsive disorder are replaced utilizing behavior modification programs to help the individual acquire new, more adaptive behavior patterns.

This concludes the discussion of anxiety disorders. In the author's experience, most students find anxiety disorders a fascinating topic and will want to learn more about them. For more information, read *Anxiety Disorders and Phobias* (1985), written by Aaron T. Beck and Gary Emery. This book provides a very thorough presentation of the types, dynamics, and treatment of anxiety disorders.

Some Closing Remarks on the Types of Anxiety: Covering the Full Range of Intensity

In this chapter's discussion of the types of anxiety, you considered three types of anxiety covering a range that varies in the intensity level of the anxiety and the effect it has on behavior. You began with a discussion of the fundamental distinction between state and trait anxiety at a basic level of intensity and its effect on behavior in general. Next you examined the experience of anxiety at a somewhat more intense level in the form of test anxiety and its effect on test-taking behavior. Finally, you read about the experience of anxiety at its most intense level and most debilitating effect on behavior. Such a wide-ranging discussion should remind you how complex and pervasive anxiety is as an emotion in our lives, and as a subject of study for personality psychologists. This presentation on anxiety ends with a discussion of the specific applications of anxiety in the public world of advertising and the personal world of shyness.

"Aviophobia" is the fear of flying due to an exaggerated belief in the possibility of crashing. Such a fear can be acquired by individuals associating flying with reading about or seeing photographs (above) of plane crashes. Do you have any "exaggerated fears"? If so, how do you explain their existence?

The Application of Personality Psychology: Using What Is Known

In this section, we will discuss two applications based on the study of anxiety. First, we will discuss the role of anxiety in advertising through the use of fear appeals. Then, we will consider the role of anxiety in social situations by examining the topic of shyness.

Anxiety in Advertising: Motivating You with Misery

Fear appeals create a sense of uncertainty, unpleasantness, and unpredictability in people. The ad presented in Figure 14.5 is an example of what is called a fear appeal in advertising. **Fear appeals** are ads designed to motivate people to change their attitudes about or buy a particular product by creating anxiety (Cohen, 1981). Whether it is an ad for life insurance, dental hygiene, shoplifting, smoking, drinking and driving, drug abuse, bad breath, or waxy buildup on your kitchen floor, the use of anxiety in fear appeals is based on the tendency for anxiety to be aroused by events that are uncertain, unpleasant, and unpredictable (Cohen, 1981). An example of a fear appeal based on anxiety would be a life insurance commercial on television depicting a woman questioning (i.e., uncertainty) how she is going to be able to take care of her children adequately (i.e., unpleasantness) after the unexpected death of her husband (i.e., unpredictability).

The Role of Anxiety in Advertising: Bringing You Down, and Then Picking You Up

The basic principle upon which anxiety is used in advertising can be summarized in a two-step process. The first step involves the advertisement creating a

Figure 14.5
An ad illustrating the use of fear appeals in advertising

sense of anxiety, either by utilizing the anxiety that is already present in most people (e.g., fear of rejection) or by creating a state of anxiety (e.g., you could die prematurely). The second step involves providing a message (e.g., "our mouthwash reduces plaque") or a course of action (e.g., "act now and receive our bonus coverage") designed to reduce the anxiety. Thus, the basic role of anxiety in advertising is to make you feel uneasy so the product being advertised can make you feel good. In short, the basic process is designed to bring you down, and then pick you up.

Creating Anxiety through Positive and Negative Appeals: To Use, or Not to Use a Product—That Is the Question

The use of fear appeals to create anxiety in advertisements generally takes one of two forms: positive or negative appeals (Aaker & Myers, 1982; Kotler & Armstrong, 1994; Wheatley & Oshikawa, 1970). **Positive appeals** are designed to *reduce* the viewer's anxiety about "buying and using" the product or service. For example, a commercial for homeowner's insurance might emphasize the positive aspects of buying and using the product, such as its low cost in comparison to other investments, the quickness of service provided, and the friendliness of the insurance agents. By highlighting all the positive aspects of this product, the commercial minimizes the viewer's anxiety about buying insurance.

On the other hand, **negative appeals** are designed to *increase* the viewer's anxiety about "not using" the product or service. For example, in a somewhat different approach, another commercial for homeowner's insurance might emphasize the negative aspects of not buying the insurance, such as losing all of your possessions in a fire, or not being able to rebuild your house to the pre-fire standards due to increased costs of building materials. Thus, by highlighting all the negative aspects of the absence of the product, the commercial maximizes the viewer's anxiety about not buying the insurance. Now that the anxiety has been created, the next step involves trying to reduce it.

Reducing the Anxiety in Advertising: Creating Competence and Stressing Support

To help you cope with the anxiety created by the uncertainty, unpleasantness, and unpredictability in these positive and negative fear appeals, advertisers typically use two basic procedures to help viewers achieve relief (Cohen, 1981).

▲ One procedure is to increase the viewers' sense of mastery of or confidence in the anxiety-provoking situation. For example, a deodorant commercial might show how an individual will feel much more confident and in control under the pressure of a big business meeting knowing that he or she will not have to worry about "those embarrassing perspiration stains."

▲ The other procedure involves securing reassurance or support from others. For example, a commercial for toothpaste might have an actor playing the role of a dentist and reassuring the viewers that the product will help to kill the germs that cause bad breath and tooth decay. Commercials against drinking and driving might show a group of friends providing social support for another friend who decides not to drive home after realizing he or she has had too much to drink.

Because anxiety can be such a powerful motivator, fear appeals are quite popular with advertisers. Just how popular are they? To find out, try for yourself the exercise in "You Can Do It" on this page.

Thus, the role of anxiety in advertising is to create a sense of anxiety, by employing either positive or negative appeals, and to present ways to minimize this anxiety. Now that you have some understanding of the role anxiety plays in advertising, the next step is to consider how it works. To do this, the discussion turns to the underlying dynamics of anxiety in advertising.

The Dynamics of Anxiety in Advertising: Combining the Right Ingredients

The successful utilization of anxiety in advertising is like trying to bake bread. What is most critical in both cases is knowing not only what ingredients to use but also just how much of each to use. In this section, you will examine the "ingredients" that go into the successful use of anxiety in advertising. This discussion covers the specific dynamics created by anxiety

YOU CAN DO IT

The Abundance of Anxiety in Advertising: Pinpointing Positive and Negative Appeals

Now that you have a basic understanding of the difference between positive and negative fear appeals, you can begin to see just how pervasive such appeals are by scanning commercials on television and the radio and/or advertisements in newspapers, magazines, or billboards. In looking for such appeals, first determine if they are positive or negative appeals. Then decide if the message is designed to foster anxiety and then to reduce it. After analyzing the fear appeal ads you have identified, you might present them to some of your friends to see if they can, without any prior knowledge of the role of anxiety in advertising, explain what the ad is trying to do and how it goes about it. Chances are they will be able to tell you that the ad is trying to "scare" them into doing something, but they will probably not be aware of the subtleties by which these ads are designed to have their influence: first scaring you, then reassuring you. It's possible that one of the reasons that these ads are so popular is that most people are unaware of just how such ads operate. Before you leave, make sure you explain to your friends what is going on in these ads.

as a stimulus and a drive, the level of anxiety created, and the effect of a concrete recommendation.

Anxiety as a Stimulus and Drive: The Push and Pull of Anxiety in Advertising

As a complex emotional reaction, anxiety can create both positive and negative consequences. To understand fully the dynamics of anxiety in advertising, you have to first consider the role anxiety plays as a stimulus and drive (Aaker & Myers, 1982).

Anxiety as a Stimulus: Triggering Uneasiness   As a stimulus, anxiety can trigger a variety of negative reactions that can reduce the effectiveness of the advertisement to change the attitudes and/or purchasing behavior of the viewers. Such reactions include withdrawing your attention from the message (e.g., you get up and leave the room or change the channel), developing hostility and disliking for the source of the message (e.g., saying to yourself, "That guy in the commercial is such a jerk"), and/or generating defensive thoughts (e.g., thinking to yourself, "Getting cancer from smoking won't happen to me"). All of these negative reactions interfere with the viewer's ability to process the message that is being communicated by the advertiser, and thus reduce the likelihood of its effectiveness to change attitudes and behaviors.

Anxiety as a Drive: Energizing Behavior   On the other hand, anxiety can also act as a drive, motivating and energizing the individual into action. In this capacity, anxiety tends to increase the viewer's dominant response to the message in the commercial. For example, if you are already buying toothpaste, the anxiety created in a commercial for "Smile Bright" toothpaste can increase the likelihood of your buying this particular brand of toothpaste the next time you are shopping. Thus, if the person is responding attentively to the commercial, the anxiety created can actually energize the individual into taking action.

The Level of Anxiety Aroused in Advertising:
Moderation Is the Key
At this point, you are probably wondering how it is that anxiety can be used effectively in advertising if it pushes people away by creating defensiveness as a stimulus but, at the same time, pulls people into action as a drive. The answer to this paradox is that while anxiety as a stimulus tends to have the negative effect of causing viewers to pay less attention to the commercial, anxiety as a drive tends to have the more positive effect of motivating viewers to take action. The key to this rather contradictory state of affairs, however, is the level of anxiety created by the advertisement. If the level of anxiety is too high, it will trigger negative and defensive reactions. If the level of anxiety is too low, it will not stimulate a drive strong enough to cause the individual to take action. What is required is a moderate level of anxiety that is strong enough to create some concern within the individual and energize him or her into action, but not so strong that it triggers uneasiness, defensiveness, and withdrawal.

The Recommendation: Make It Concrete
Once the fear appeal has created a moderate level of anxiety in the individual, the effectiveness of the advertisement is increased when a concrete recommendation for reducing the anxiety is included as part of the message to the viewer (Leventhal, 1970; Rogers & Mewborn, 1976). For example, an advertisement for life insurance might show the individual calling the insurance company to reduce the anxiety that was created concerning not having enough insurance coverage for his family in the event of accidental death. The point is that by recommending to the individual a specific course of action that is designed to reduce the level of anxiety, the advertisement is going to cause the individual to develop more favorable attitudes about the product or service being advertised (Baron & Byrne, 1977).

As you can see, there is a lot more to the use of anxiety in advertising than simply trying to scare the person with a fear appeal. Those using anxiety in advertising must consider the reactions such anxiety is likely to create, the level of anxiety created, and the recommendations designed to reduce this anxiety. Figure 14.6 summarizes the major points discussed in this section.

Anxiety in Social Situations: Understanding and Overcoming Shyness

Understanding Shyness: The
Components and Types of Shyness
Shyness is conceptualized as a syndrome of affective, cognitive, and behavioral components characterized by social anxiety and behavioral inhibition resulting from the feeling that others are evaluating you (Buss, 1995; Carducci & Zimbardo, 1995; Leary & Kowalski, 1995).

▲   The affective component of shyness reflects the anxiety, muscle tension, increased heart rate, upset stomach, and an assortment of other psychophysiological reactions experienced by shy people.
▲   The cognitive component of shyness reflects the excessive sense of self-consciousness (e.g., everybody is staring at me), negative self-appraisal (e.g., what I said was so stupid), irra-

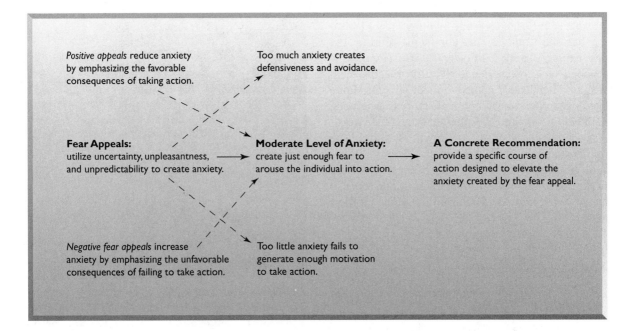

Figure 14.6
The successful application of anxiety in advertising involves three ingredients:
(1) A fear appeal (either positive or negative) designed to create (2) a moderate
level of anxiety, followed by (3) a concrete recommendation for a course of
action to reduce the anxiety.

tional belief system (e.g., nobody at the party will find me interesting) characteristic of the way that shy people think about themselves.

▲ The behavioral component of shyness is expressed by behavioral inhibition (e.g., not speaking to others at a party) and social avoidance (e.g., avoiding eye contact or standing in the corner during a group discussion).

Thus, shyness is not just one or two symptoms but an all-encompassing collection of characteristics that manifests itself in the mind, body, and behavior of shy people.

The Pervasiveness of Shyness: If You're Shy, You're Not Alone Although most shy people feel they are more shy than other people (Carducci & Clark, 1996), shyness is a self-reported characteristic of personality that is expressed by over 40% of those surveyed (Carducci & Clark, 1996; Carducci & Stein, 1988; Zimbardo, 1977). Only about 7% of Americans surveyed indicate

that they have *never* experienced shyness in their entire life (Zimbardo, 1977). Thus, shyness is a pervasive phenomenon; if you are shy, you are not alone.

Types of Shyness: The Shades of Shyness An important development in the understanding of shyness is that shy people are not all the same; there are different types of shyness. **Publicly shy** people express distress as a consequence of more overt manifestations of their shyness, such as through being too quiet, behaving awkwardly, and failing to respond appropriately in social situations (e.g., not acknowledging a compliment) (Pilkonis, 1977). **Privately shy** people express distress as a consequence of more covert manifestations of their shyness, such as through intense psychophysiological arousal (e.g., pounding heart, muscle tension, and anxiety reactions) (Pilkonis, 1977). **Socially anxious shy** people express distress as a consequence of more cognitive manifestations of their shyness, such as being excessively self-conscious (e.g., do my clothes fit right) and overly concerned about being evaluated socially by others (e.g., I wonder what she thinks of my comment) (Carducci & Clark, 1994; Melchior & Cheek, 1990). Thus, while shy people tend to experience all of the affective, cognitive, and behavioral components of shyness, some experience one of the components more than others, which helps to explain the different types of shyness.

Your understanding of shyness should be enhanced now that you know about the multidimensional aspects of how shy people experience and manifest their shyness. In the next section, you will consider what shy people can do to overcome their shyness.

Tips for Overcoming Shyness: Addressing the Multidimensional Nature of Shyness

This section presents a number of suggestions for overcoming shyness. Taken from a variety of sources (Carducci & Zimbardo, 1995; Cheek, 1989; Leary & Kowalski, 1995; Zimbardo, 1977), these suggestions require no complicated treatment procedures. All they require is a desire on the part of the individual to become less shy.

Start with Self-Awareness: Which Shy Type Are You? Because each person experiences his or her shyness in a unique way, the place to start when trying to overcome shyness is to gain some understanding of your own shyness. Begin by looking at what situations seem to make you feel shy, and why. For example, do you become shy when meeting new people, interacting at a social gathering, or speaking to someone to whom you find yourself attracted? Try to understand if your shyness manifests itself cognitively (e.g., excessive self-consciousness or self-deprecating statements), affectively (e.g., overriding feelings of anxiety), or behaviorally (e.g., failure to speak to others at social gatherings).

You might also try to understand how these three different aspects of shyness might interact with each other in your experience of shyness. For example, consider the following situation where the affective and cognitive components of shyness interact to produce avoidant behavior: You are at a party and assume others are evaluating you. As a result, you begin to experience feelings of intense anxiety, which makes it difficult for you to think of anything to say to others. Such lack of involvement in the ongoing conversation makes you perceive yourself as socially

Shyness is characterized by an avoidance of others as a result of excessive feelings of self-consciousness and negative self-evaluation. If you are shy, there are tips for overcoming shyness beginning on this page.

incompetent and not very interesting. As a consequence, you leave the party. Since leaving the party reduces the feelings of anxiety, such avoidance is negatively reinforced (see Chapter 10) and becomes more likely to occur in the future. Thus, you can begin to overcome your shyness by examining the nature of your shyness.

Overcome the Affective Component of Shyness: Eliminate Excessive Emotions   If your shyness manifests itself primarily through affective reactions, such as excessive levels of anxiety, a racing heart, and butterflies in the stomach, then such symptoms need to be brought under control. There are a variety of simple relaxation techniques you can use to reduce your level of psychophysiological arousal. Simple breathing exercises involve inhaling and exhaling deeply and slowly and focusing your attention on the nature of your breathing. Taking the attention away from the physiological symptoms of your shyness and focusing your attention on the nature of your breathing will help you relax. Another relaxation technique involves tightening and loosening your muscles, such as squeezing your hands into a tight fist and then letting go, to reduce some of the tension you are experiencing (see pages 283–284 for additional information on relaxation techniques). The important point is that it is very difficult for you to think or act appropriately if you are overly anxious, as indicated by the Yerkes-Dodson Law (see pages 414–415).

As a word of caution, do not resort to alcohol or other drugs as a means of reducing your level of arousal. The principal reason is that after the short-term effects of the alcohol or drugs have worn off, the level of anxiety is going to return. You'll be right back where you started, but now you'll also have a hangover.

Overcome the Behavioral Deficits of Shyness: Practice What to Say and Do   A common problem with shy people is that they fail to respond appropriately in social situations. If your problem of shyness is manifested as behavioral deficits, there are a variety of strategies you can develop to help you learn to respond more appropriately and effectively. Here are four recommendations:

1. *Start with very, very small talk and simple actions: Getting your feet wet.* Shy people often report that they have trouble talking with people they have just met, particularly those people to whom they might feel attracted. A strategy for helping shy people to overcome this inhibition is to start with relatively nonthreatening situations and very small talk. Nonthreatening situations might include malls, museums, political rallies, or sporting events where you will have the opportunity to interact with a lot of people for a relatively brief period of time. In such interactions, you can start by smiling and saying something simple like "hello" to as many people as you care to make eye contact with and who will smile at you. Asking for simple directions, giving an unexpected compliment, or offering assistance (e.g., offer to hold a door) are three very simple ways to practice talking with people. Thus, the point here is to get used to talking with others.
2. *Develop conversation skills: How to keep talking.* Shy people who have mastered the art of small talk can take the next step by developing their conversational skills. The trick to successful conversation is to *have something to say.* There are a number of very simple strategies that shy people can employ to make sure they have

something to say. You can start by reading the newspaper or magazines and/or listening to information-based radio programs to keep up on the type of current events other people are most likely to be talking about. An important advantage of such information sources is that they also give you the type of in-depth, "behind-the-headlines" analysis that is the basic substance of much social conversation. Shy people can also do their part to help keep the conversation going by asking open-ended questions that require more than a yes or no answer (e.g., What do you think of . . . ?).

3. *Rehearse what you are going to say: Practice makes perfect.* Shy people who want to increase their confidence in the art of making conversation can prepare a "script" ahead of time, based on events that are most likely to be the topic of conversation at the social gathering, and rehearse it in the privacy of their own home in front of the mirror. For example, a shy individual going to a political rally might practice expressing his or her views on the political issues that are most likely to be brought up by others attending the rally.
4. *Perform social graces: Give (kindness) and you shall receive (kindness).* Performing social graces is a safe way to facilitate social interactions. The performance of social graces might include giving a compliment or offering to get someone some refreshments as you are getting some for yourself. Shy people can maximize their likelihood for successful social interactions by looking for others who might appear shy, such as an individual who is standing or sitting alone and would welcome the opportunity to interact with someone.

Planning and rehearsing for social interactions with others might sound a bit trite and artificial. But because shy people manifest their shyness in the form of behavior deficits when interacting with others, what they need is to acquire new social and conversational skills. And the best way to acquire and develop such skills is still to define what the skills are and to practice them beforehand in a comfortable environment.

Overcome the Cognitive Deficits of Shyness: Getting Your Mind Right   For those shy people whose shyness is expressed primarily through negative thoughts about themselves, the key to overcoming their shyness is to change the way they think about themselves. Such change is more difficult than it sounds, because it is not easy to change the thoughts an individual may have had about himself or herself since early childhood. Here are four strategies for reducing the cognitive component of shyness:

1. *Reduce your sense of self-consciousness: The whole world is not looking at you.* Since self-consciousness is a principal cognitive component for many shy people, it is very helpful for such shy people to realize that most people are far more interested in how they look or what they are doing than what anyone else is doing or saying. As an example, realize that if you are dancing on the dance floor, others who are dancing are more interested in how they are doing than how you are doing. And those people who are in their seats around the dance floor are probably wishing they had the courage to be out on the dance floor, and are not just thinking about how well you are dancing. Thus, for shy people, realizing that other people care more about themselves than about you will make interacting in social situations much more tolerable.

2. *Focus on your social successes: Stop whipping yourself.* Shy people tend to be overly self-critical of their performance in social situations. In their view, they are never outgoing enough or witty enough to be satisfied with themselves. To help overcome their shyness, shy people can begin to minimize the anxiety such expectations create by focusing on their strengths, and not only on what they perceive as their weaknesses. For example, rather than being upset with herself for not using the jokes she practiced at home, this shy person should focus on the fact that at the party, she did give a few compliments, carried on a conversation with several new people, and was approached by others while at the party. Thus, focusing on the reactions of others to what she did or said, rather than on the negative statements about herself, will shift her focus of attention to others and make her feel less self-conscious.

3. *Avoid overgeneralizations: It may not be your fault.* A mistake many shy people make is to overgeneralize their social misfortunes in one context to another and often to unrelated, social contexts. Such a tendency magnifies the negativity of the experience and degree to which the shy individual feels personally responsible. For example, after one individual excuses himself while talking to Judy, a shy individual, Judy now assumes that no one else at the party will want to talk to her and decides to leave. Leaving the party early only guarantees that no one else will be able to talk to Judy. Another error in this situation is in Judy's assumption that the other person excused himself because he found her boring. But the other individual could have excused himself because he had someone else to meet. Thus, the point is to avoid overgeneralizing social misfortunes and your responsibility for them.

4. *Avoid perfectionism: Nobody's perfect.* Part of the exaggerated sense of self-criticism experienced by shy people is based on the excessive expectations they set for themselves. Their jokes have to be absolutely funny and their remarks insightful and witty. In short, shy people tend to set standards that are rather impossible to maintain. A simple strategy for overcoming the cognitive component of shyness is for shy people to set more realistic standards for themselves. It's not necessary to be the life of the party in order to categorize your performance as a social success. In some cases, simply talking to four new people at a party might be the mark of a successful performance. Thus, shy people reduce the misery they create for themselves by being less perfectionistic and more realistic.

5. *Learn to take rejection: No one is liked by everyone.* Rejection is one of the risks that accompanies engaging in social interactions. A key to overcoming shyness is not to take rejection personally. There may be a variety of reasons that someone is rejected by someone else, none of which may have anything at all to do with the person being rejected. For example, one person may not like what the shy person is wearing, and another person may be bored with the entire social situation, not just with

her conversation with the shy individual. The point is that sometimes you can control the reactions of others (e.g., by wearing stylish clothes) and at other times you cannot. What's important is that shy people make a realistic attempt to socialize with others. If it doesn't work out and rejection results, simply select someone else and start all over again.

6. Find your comfort zone: Do what fits you. Not all social situations are for everyone. For example, some shy people might be uneasy in a bar or nightclub where physical attractiveness and stylish dress are critical predictors of social success. In other situations, extensive knowledge of politics, art, or murder mysteries might be the key to success. Shy people should seek out those situations that are most consistent with their temperament and interests. It is easier for shy people to overcome or manage their sense of social anxiety and self-consciousness by finding situations in which they feel reasonably comfortable. Volunteering for different organizations is a good strategy for shy people to use in an attempt to find various places where they might feel comfortable. In most cases, being a volunteer requires a low level of skills, offers the possibility of meeting many different types of people, and is easy to terminate if the experience does not turn out to be what was expected. Thus, overcoming shyness can be helped by seeking out an assortment of volunteer experiences as a means of meeting new people, practicing social skills in different situations, and helping to find those social situations that are the most comfortable.

This concludes the discussion on strategies for overcoming shyness. If you would like more information on this topic, read Philip G. Zimbardo's (1977) *Shyness: What it is, What to do about it* or Jonathan M. Cheek's (1989) *Conquering Shyness: The Battle Anyone Can Win*. Both of these books provide sound advice for overcoming shyness. For more information on the general topic of shyness, read *Shyness: Perspective on Research and Treatment* (Jones, Cheek, & Briggs, 1986). This book provides a very scholarly coverage of the topic of shyness and its treatment.

Some Closing Remarks: A Statement of Reiteration

This concludes the discussion of anxiety. As you may now realize, anxiety is truly a distinct dimension of personality, characterized by many different dimensions and dynamics. It seems to exist in levels of intensity on a spectrum ranging from normal to pathological proportions. Because the sphere of its influence seems almost unlimited, as noted earlier, anxiety is considered an "all-encompassing intrapersonal process of personality." In the next chapter, you will consider aggression as a personality process that is more "interpersonal" in its nature and effect.

Chapter Summary: Reexamining the Highlights

▲   *Anxiety as an Intrapersonal Personality Process*
Anxiety consists of a physiological, cognitive, and behavioral dimension. Individual differences in anxiety can be assessed with the Manifest Anxiety Scale (MAS).

▲   *Theoretical Viewpoints of Anxiety*
   —*The Psychodynamic Viewpoint*. The psychodynamic viewpoint conceptualizes anxiety as a warning signal used to indicate the possible expression of certain unacceptable unconscious impulses.
   —*The Learning Viewpoint*. The learning viewpoint conceptualizes anxiety as a conditioned response to certain stimuli. The conditioned anxiety signals the impending aversive stimuli.
   —*The Drive Viewpoint*. The drive viewpoint conceptualizes anxiety as a motivating force that triggers the individual into taking action. The likelihood of a specific response occurring is determined by the strength of the response and level of motivation.
   —*Integrating the Viewpoints of Anxiety*. The different viewpoints of anxiety can be integrated to explain the purpose, acquisition, and influence of anxiety.

▲   *Types of Anxiety*
   —*State vs. Trait Anxiety*. State anxiety is a temporary change in anxiety in response to an external threat. Trait anxiety is an enduring characteristic of the individual's personality. State and trait anxiety can be assessed with the State-Trait Anxiety Inventory (STAI).
   —*Test Anxiety*. Test anxiety is an excessive emotional response to activities associated with taking tests.

Test anxiety can be assessed with the Test Anxiety Scale (TAS). People with high and low test anxiety differ in what they do in response to the test, how they evaluate their test performance, and what they think about during the test.

—*Anxiety Disorders*. Anxiety disorders are characterized by a level of anxiety that is excessive in response to the external threat. Anxiety disorders include obsessive-compulsive disorder and phobic disorder. The psychodynamic viewpoint explanation of anxiety disorders is based on their manifestation as unresolved conflicts, while the learning viewpoint explanation emphasizes the process of conditioning.

▲ *The Application of Personality Psychology*

—*Anxiety in Advertising*. A fear appeal is a form of advertising that utilizes anxiety as a means of motivating the consumer into action. Positive appeals emphasize how the use of the product will reduce the consumer's anxiety, while negative appeals emphasize how failure to use the product will increase the consumer's anxiety.

—*The Dynamics of Anxiety in Advertising*. The successful use of fear appeals involves an ad that creates a moderate level of anxiety, which is followed by a specific recommendation designed to reduce the consumer's anxiety and reinforce acting upon the recommendation.

—*Anxiety in Social Situations*. Shyness consists of an affective, cognitive, and behavioral component. Three types of shyness are public, private, and socially anxious shyness. Overcoming shyness involves different strategies corresponding to the three different dimensions of shyness.

Glossary

agoraphobia   An irrational fear of open spaces.

ailurophobia   An irrational fear of cats.

anxiety disorder   A category of mental disorders characterized by excessive anxiety reactions that interfere with daily living.

aviophobia   An irrational fear of flying.

compulsion   An uncontrollable desire to perform a specific behavior.

dominant response   A well-learned, easily performed response.

drive level   The degree to which an individual is motivated to perform a specific action.

ergasiophobia   An irrational fear of writing.

excitatory potential   The likelihood of a response being emitted.

fear appeals   An approach to advertising that creates anxiety to motivate the consumer into action.

fight-or-flight reaction   The tendency to either engage a threatening stimulus directly or flee from it.

generalized anxiety disorder   A chronic sense of unexplained feelings of anxiety.

habit strength   The extent to which a response has been learned.

intrapersonal personality process   A dimension of personality that influences many aspects of an individual's thoughts, feelings, and behavior.

Manifest Anxiety Scale   A personality test measuring individual differences in anxiety.

negative appeals   Advertisement designed to create anxiety if the advertised product is not utilized.

nondominant response   A novel response that is performed with some difficulty.

obsession   The presence of an intrusive, recurring thought.

optimal level of arousal   The degree of arousal that results in the greatest performance by the individual.

overlearning   The continued rehearsal of a well-established behavior.

panic disorder   The unexpected onset of acute anxiety.

sympathetic nervous system   A portion of the nervous system that is activated in response to stressful events.

phobic disorders   A group of mental disorders characterized by irrational fears that interfere with daily living.

positive appeals   Advertisements designed to reduce anxiety if the advertised product is utilized.

privately shy   The distress of shyness expressed as a consequence of covert reactions.

publically shy   The distress of shyness expressed as a consequence of overt actions.

self-defeating thoughts   Personal beliefs about your abilities that interfere with your performance.

shyness   Perceived distress as a consequence of excessive self-consciousness and a lack of social skills.

simple phobia   An irrational fear of certain objects or situations.

state anxiety   Anxiety in response to an external threat.

State-Trait Anxiety Inventory   A personality inventory for assessing an individual's specific and general feelings of anxiety.

social phobia   An irrational fear of being evaluated.

socially anxious shyness   The distress of shyness expressed as a consequence of ineffective thoughts and beliefs.

Test Anxiety Scale   A personality inventory for assessing individual differences in test anxiety.

trait anxiety   Variations across people in their personal level of anxiety.

Yerkes-Dodson Law   A principle of motivation that explains the "inverted-U" relationship between motivation and performance.

CHAPTER 15

Aggression: A Pervasive Interpersonal Process of Personality

CHAPTER OVERVIEW: A PREVIEW OF COMING ATTRACTIONS

Unfortunately, reports of aggressive behavior are fairly easy to encounter while watching television, listening to the radio, and reading newspapers and magazines. Because of the pervasiveness of aggressive behavior, personality psychologists have spent a considerable amount of effort studying the nature and dynamics of aggression. In this chapter, you will be exposed to the study of aggression from the perspective of personality psychology. You will start by considering the basic components that define aggression. Next, you will consider the various viewpoints that have been proposed to explain the fundamental nature of aggressive tendencies. Following that section, you will examine certain specific situational and personal determinants of aggression. At the end of this chapter, you will consider two very important applications of personality psychology to the study of aggression: the effects of media violence and strategies for controlling and reducing aggressive behavior.

Aggression as an Interpersonal Personality Process: The Effect of Personality on Other People

In this chapter, aggression is conceptualized as an **interpersonal personality process**: a specific dimension of personality that affects how you interact with and treat other people. The term *interpersonal* is used because the major effect of such a dimension is primarily between (viz., *inter*) persons (viz., *personal*). For example, verbal assaults, racial prejudice, child abuse, sexual harassment, and gang violence are just a few examples of how the aggressive tendencies within the personality of one person or group of persons affect the interaction with and treatment of another person or group of persons. Because the major effect aggression has as a personality dimension involves the interaction of people, such an outcome can be easily conceptualized as "the effect of personality on other people."

Aggression Defined: The Heterogeneous Nature of Hurting

How do you define aggression? Would you know an act of aggression if it "smacked you in the face"? To help you answer this question, try performing the exercise "You Can Do It" on this page.

Based on your responses to the situations in "You Can Do It," what seem to be the underlying characteristics of all of the instances of aggression you noted? If you are finding it difficult to come up with a relatively clear-cut answer to this question, you are not alone. Even the experts have some difficulty agreeing on a specific definition of aggression (Berkowitz, 1993). As an example, Roger N. Johnson (1972) notes that "In summary, there are many different kinds of aggressive behaviors, and as a result there can be no single, satisfactory definition" (p. 8).

While this may be true, it is possible to formulate a working definition of aggression that you, your classmates and instructor, and this author can use as a common point of reference from which to discuss the topic of aggression in this chapter. The definition

YOU CAN DO IT

Pinpointing the Pervasiveness of Aggression: What Is and What Isn't Aggression?

For the following ten situations, indicate whether you believe that an aggressive act was performed.

1. The child begins to scream after receiving a flu shot from a doctor.
2. A baseball player throws his bat into the corner of the dugout after striking out.
3. During a boxing match, the challenger gives the champion a bloody nose and a cut about his left eye.
4. An elderly gentleman is accidentally tripped by the Boy Scout trying to help him cross the street.
5. A frustrated office manager daydreams of running over her boss.
6. The prisoner is executed when the prison guard "flips" the switch to the electric chair.
7. A gunner on a tank fires a rocket that kills 15 enemy soldiers.
8. A security officer shoots a drug dealer in the back as he tries to escape.
9. A middle-aged lawyer commits suicide.
10. A "hit man" misses his target.

Now repeat this exercise with a few friends, coworkers, or family members. How much agreement do you find among them? What conclusion can you come to about how people define aggression?

adopted for this discussion is one proposed by Leonard Berkowitz (1993) of the University of Wisconsin-Madison, a leading expert on the psychological study of aggression for almost 40 years. According to Berkowitz (1993), **aggression** is defined "as any form of behavior that is intended to injure someone physically or psychologically" (p. 3). To help you fully understand the depth of this relatively brief but eloquent definition of aggression, as well as the characteristics of aggressive behavior, the following sections examine this definition in some detail.

Aggression as Behavior: The Act of Attacking

Within Berkowitz's definition, aggression is conceptualized as an act, not as an attitude, emotion, or motive. The reason is that attitudes, emotions, and motives do not harm people, but actions do. For example, you might describe a woman you know as being an aggressive salesperson. In this case, you do not really mean that she will do bodily harm to people who enter the store. Instead, you mean that her style of selling is one that is forceful and determined. As a result, this use of the term *aggression* is not consistent with our definition. On the other hand, a professional "hit man" probably does not have any ill feelings about the person he or she has been paid to kill; the motive to do harm probably stems from financial desire, not anger or hostility. But carrying out the contract is clearly an act of aggression, according to our definition.

The Importance of Intention: With Hurting and Harming in Mind

Another important component of our definition of aggression is that the act must involve the intention to harm another individual (Baron, 1977; Baron & Richardson, 1994, Dollard, Doob, Miller, Mowrer, & Sears, 1939; Geen, 1976, 1995). Including the intention component of the definition helps to eliminate those harmful acts that are delivered accidentally. For example, according to this definition, it would not be considered an act of aggression if, as you were rushing out of the mall, you hurriedly pushed open the door and knocked down another person entering the mall from the other direction. In a more extreme example, a drunk driver who inadvertently crosses over to the wrong side of the street and crashes head on into a school bus, killing 27 children, would not have committed an act of aggression, based on our definition.

Although including intention as part of our definition helps clarify the issue by eliminating those harmful acts performed accidentally, it also clouds the issue by forcing us to consider the sticky notion of what is meant by *intention*. Since intention is a pri-

Leonard Berkowitz is one of the world's leading authorities on the nature, dynamics, and expression of interpersonal aggression.

vate matter, some conclusion must be made about a person's intention by examining events before and after the act of aggression (Bandura, 1973; Berkowitz, 1993; Buss, 1971).

Suppose that in the heat of an argument, a man throws a chair at another man, striking the latter in the head and knocking him against a wall, where a large trophy falls off the shelf onto his head, killing him instantly. Because it was the trophy that killed the man, you probably would assume that it was an accident. But the possibility remains that the first man threw the chair with the intention of killing the other man all along. Unless the chair-throwing man told us, we could not be sure if the killing was unintentional—and therefore an accident—or intentional, and therefore an act of aggression. As a result, although considering the notion of intention makes defining acts of aggression somewhat more difficult, if we did not consider it, we would have to include such actions as the harm caused by a dentist drilling into your tooth, the shot given to you by a nurse, or discipline you received from your parents as acts of aggression.

To Injure and Harm as the Basis of Aggression: A Multitude of Ways to Hurt

By considering aggression as "a response that delivers noxious stimuli to another organism" (Buss, 1961, p. 1), the ways by which hurting and harming others could be achieved are almost endless. For example, a very caustic remark, delivered in front of many other people, to someone with whom you are

At the core of all acts of aggression is the intention to harm another individual. As a result, actions such as sexual harassment and gossiping about others can be considered acts of aggression.

arguing can result in harm coming to the person in the form of a high level of anxiety that accompanies severe embarrassment and a loss of face. Making sexually suggestive remarks to a co-worker is not only sexual harassment but also an act of aggression if these remarks are unwanted and cause the person emotional distress. Spreading vicious rumors about the sexual orientation of a club member, which results in the individual's feelings being hurt after being shunned by others, can also be considered an act of aggression. Finally, a teenager pounding his brother's favorite toy to smithereens, just to "get even," is another example of how it is possible to hurt others. Acts of aggression can also include withholding water, food, and rest from prisoners of war as a means of torture. The point is that causing harm and injury can take many different forms.

The Desire to Avoid Harm: "Please Don't Hurt Me"

The final component in the definition of aggression to be considered is that the individual at which the act of aggression is directed should be motivated to avoid receiving it. That is to say, the individual should not want to be hurt or injured. This point is mentioned because it rules out the delivering of painful and noxious stimuli to people who receive it willingly. For example, although it hurts, a heroin junkie willingly accepts the pain that accompanies the heroin being injected into her arm by another junkie. In certain types of sexual practices, **sadomasochists** are people who seem to enjoy having pain inflicted upon them by their sexual partners. Finally, people who attempt suicide are clearly hurting and injuring themselves willfully, and therefore are not considered to be committing acts of aggression. Thus, in order for the delivery of a harmful or injurious stimuli to another person to be considered an aggressive act, there has to be some desire by the other person to avoid being harmed or injured.

Hostile vs. Instrumental Aggression: Hot vs. Cool Aggression

A final point of consideration in the definition of aggression is the distinction between hostile and instrumental aggression (Berkowitz, 1993; Buss, 1971; Feshback, 1970).

▲ **Hostile aggression** is an act of aggression triggered by anger and having as its underlying rationale the specific intention to hurt somebody. An example of hostile aggression would be slapping the face of someone with whom you were arguing.

▲ **Instrumental aggression** involves acts of aggression being performed to achieve some other objective besides hurting somebody. For example, the killing that accompanies war is often done to gain the economic resources of another country, not simply to harm the people of that country out of hatred for them. The murder carried out by a professional "hit man" is done for the money, not out of anger or hatred.

Because hostile aggression typically involves some feelings of anger or hatred, it is described as "hot" aggression. On the other hand, because instrumental aggression typically involves a deliberate and cal-

Parental and governmental concerns for violence on television have resulted in a rating code to indicate the level of violence in a program. Do you believe such a rating code will help to reduce the impact of media violence on the behavior of children? If so, why? If not, why not?

culated course of action, it is described as "cool" aggression.

The discussion of the basic components that go into the working definition of aggression is now complete. As you finish this section, be aware that because of the many considerations that go into describing what we mean by aggression, aggression is not something that can be easily defined. With this in mind, you now have a basic understanding of the comprehensive nature of aggressive behavior. In the next section, you will explore some theoretical explanations proposed to account for the diversity in aggressive behavior.

Theoretical Perspective on Aggression: The Fundamental Reasons for Inflicting Harm

As you have probably come to expect, something as complex as aggressive behavior is not easily explained. To account for the diversity and complexity of aggressive behavior, many different theoretical explanations have been proposed. This section focuses on three viewpoints: the instinct, biological, and social learning perspectives.

Instinct Perspective: An Innate Tendency to Injure

The instinct perspective on human aggression assumes that there is some inborn or innate tendency to aggress. While this innate tendency can take many different forms (Baron & Richardson, 1994; Siann, 1985), this section presents three viewpoints: the psychoanalytical, ethological, and sociobiological viewpoints.

Psychoanalytical Viewpoint: Displacement of the Death Instinct

As with almost everything else, Freud had something to say about why people engage in aggressive behavior. Freud (1959) assumed that aggressive behavior stemmed from the expression of the "death instinct." If you will recall (see page 62), if you do not), the **death instinct** is an innate desire of the individual to return to a tension-free state through self-destruction (i.e., death). Because such a self-destructive tendency is in direct opposition to the "life instinct," the innate tendency toward self-preservation, Freud proposed that the death instinct could be expressed in an indirect manner. This indirect manner involved turning this inward tendency for aggression outward and directing it toward other people. As an extreme example of this position, Freud used his concept of the death instinct to explain the violence associated with World War I and why "it is so easy to make men enthusiastic about war" (Freud, 1963, p. 41). Thus, the psychoanalytical viewpoint proposes that aggression is due to the displacement of our innate tendency toward self-destruction onto others in the form of aggressive behaviors toward them.

Ethological Viewpoint: The Discharge of Destructive Tendencies

Ethology is the study of animal behavior, especially in its natural habitat. The ethological viewpoint is based on observations of aggressive behavior in animals and the contention that human beings are part of the animal kingdom (Geen, 1976). According to the ethological viewpoint, animals have a **fighting instinct** consisting of aggressive energy that builds up within the organism to the point of needing to be discharged (Lorenz, 1966, 1974). The extent to which this fighting instinct needs to be discharged depends on (a) the amount of aggressive energy that has built up, and (b) the presence of an object in the environment that triggers the release of this energy (e.g., one animal sniffing in another's source of food).

In the animal kingdom, there seem to be certain conditions that keep the expression of the fighting instinct from getting out of hand.

▲   Animals have various natural ways of releasing their aggressive energy, so that it does not build up to a dangerous level where it simply explodes. For example, two moose will lock horns and "head wrestle" as a form of aggressive play in which dominance and power can be expressed without either animal getting hurt.

▲   The conditions that trigger the release of aggressive energy seem to be relatively clear. For example, a clear signal is the presence of one animal sniffing around the primary source of food of another animal.

▲   Probably most important is the seemingly built-in natural tendency for animals of the same species to refrain from killing other members of their own species. For example, a submissive dog lies on its back and bares its throat to a more dominant and aggressive dog as a clear signal of nonaggression and retreat, demonstrating a built-in tendency to terminate any aggressive acts. Thus, for the reasons just noted, the fighting instinct in animals is discharged naturally and safely in a well-regulated manner.

The major dilemma facing the fighting instinct within humans is the tendency for us to be the only member of the animal kingdom that regularly engages in violent aggressive attacks against other members of our own species in a magnitude that is nothing short of staggering (e.g., World Wars I and II). There seem to be several reasons for such behavior. One is the tremendous ability we have to harm other human beings (e.g., guns, bombs, torture). Another is that we do not seem to share with other animals the same degree of internal restraint against harming other members of our own species. The nature and number of objects in our environment that can trigger the release of our aggressive energy is almost endless. For example, people have killed others for love, money, country, religion, or "just for kicks." The machinery of war makes it possible for us to harm others from great distances (e.g., long-range artillery, electronic imaging and heat-sensitive missiles) while making it less likely to receive signals of retreat, even if one is given. Finally, unlike animals, we lack the ritualistic forms of aggressive play that would allow us to demonstrate power and strength without doing physical harm to other human beings. For example, there might be a lot less human suffering if we could settle political differences between rival nations by running a series of races instead of going to war. Thus, for the reasons just noted, the fighting instinct in human beings seems to be discharged in a manner that is excessive, characterized by a lack of regard for other members of our own species, triggered by almost anything, and lacking sanctioned forms of aggressive play.

Sociobiology Viewpoint: Aggression as Altruism

Sociobiology can be conceptualized as the study of the biological bases of social behavior (Wilson, 1975, 1978). The basic assumption of the sociobiology viewpoint is that behavior is adapted to maximize the survival of the species. The underlying basis of this tendency toward survival is the genetic predisposition of emotions designed to promote such survival.

What is most interesting about the sociobiology viewpoint is the contention that animals will engage in behaviors that are designed to maximize the likelihood of survival for the species, but at the same time put the animals in situations of great risk or even death. Whenever conditions are present that threaten the potential survival of the species, the preprogrammed emotions trigger the animal into such altruistic actions designed to protect the survival of its species. With respect to aggressive behavior, such preprogrammed altruistic behavior might involve a single animal attacking a much larger animal that is threatening the group's source of food or shelter (e.g., a wolf attacking a large black bear near the wolf's den) or the strongest members of the species having the task of protecting the young (e.g., young, stronger adult wolves sleeping near the opening of the cave). Thus, for animals, altruistic aggression seems to have evolutionary significance—the survival and continuation of the species (Wilson, 1975, 1978).

When applying the sociological viewpoint to humans, the eminent sociobiologist E. O. Wilson (1978) concludes that

> Our brains appear to be programmed to the following extent: we are inclined to partition other people into friends and aliens. . . . We tend to fear the actions of strangers and to solve conflicts by aggression. These learning rules are most likely to have evolved during the past hundreds of thousands of years of human evolution and, thus, to have conferred a biological advantage on those who conformed to them with the greatest fidelity. (p. 119)

Like other animals, we tend to engage in certain forms of aggression that seem to be altruistic: we send only a small percentage of our population off to fight in wars, and these "warriors" are typically our strongest and most powerful members. But overt aggressive behavior is not seen in all people to the same degree; some people, cultures, or parts of the country (Nisbett, 1993; Staub, 1996) are more aggressive than others. To account for such variations, sociobiologists assume that while the predisposition to aggress is present in all of us, it seems to be evoked under a wide variety of circumstances. For example, even if you are a very peaceful person, you would probably not hesitate to take altruistic aggressive action against someone attacking you or a loved one. Thus, the point seems to be that we all have the predisposition to aggress when our own—or our group's—survival is threatened. But this does not explain the seemingly senseless acts of violence that we read about each day in the paper or see in the nightly news.

Regardless of whether it is viewed as a death instinct, fighting instinct, or altruistic aggression, the instinct perspective on aggression assumes that aggressive behavior is a fundamental and innate component of human nature. In the next section,

you will consider the biological perspective of aggression.

The Biological Perspective: Physiological Processes for the Production of Pain

The biological perspective of aggression assumes that there are certain physiological processes within the individual that contribute to aggressive behavior (Baron & Richardson, 1994). One of the first to systematically postulate a biological perspective on aggressive behavior was the 19th-century Italian criminologist Cesare Lombroso. Lombroso (1876) suggested that criminal behavior could be likened to certain physical characteristics, such as the shape of the chin, closeness of the eyes, squareness of the jaw, shape of the skull and forehead, and lobes of the ears. At an elementary level, Lombroso was suggesting that some biological basis seemed to predispose people with certain physical features to display criminal behavior. While no contemporary criminologist would endorse such a simplistic view these days, there is evidence to suggest that certain biological processes are related to aggression. In this section, you will examine three of these biological processes: brain structures, hormonal influences, and genetic transmission.

Brain Structure and Aggression: It's All in Your Head—or Is It?

Certain parts of the brain have been linked to aggressive tendencies. For example, the limbic system (Figure 15.1) is located in the lower portion of the brain. The **limbic system** contains a series of structures that seem to be involved in regulating the fight-or-flight reaction, which is important to the survival of any species. For example, research in which structures of the limbic system in cats have been electrically stimulated have produced attacking behavior in these cats (Egger & Flynn, 1963). Other research indicates that destroying certain parts of the limbic system that seem to regulate aggressive behavior leads some animals to respond aggressively to even the slightest provocation (Carlson, 1988). A similar finding has been reported in a limited number of case studies involving human subjects. For example, electrically stimulating the limbic area of certain medical patients resulted in emotional or behavioral expressions of aggression and violence (Moyer, 1976). On the other hand, creating lesions of specific structures in the limbic system as a means of controlling epilepsy resulted in decreases in violent outbursts (Eichelman, 1983). As you might expect, such research has produced much theoretical debate (Carroll & O'Callaghan, 1981; O'Callaghan & Carroll, 1987), as well as some inconsistent findings (Jasper & Rasmussion, 1958)

Another part of the brain that has been linked to aggressive behavior is the frontal cortex (see Figure 15.1). The frontal cortex is associated with various important functions, including problem solving, reasoning, and planning, as well as emotionality.

People who suffer damage to their frontal cortex are likely to exhibit irritability, short tempers, and impulsive aggressiveness (Heinrichs, 1989; Silver & Yudofsky, 1987). Additional research using an assortment of psychological tests that measure cognitive abilities (e.g., memory, intelligence) indicates that nonviolent prisoners scored higher than violent prisoners, indicating that violent prisoners had impaired frontal cortex functioning (Spellacy, 1978). Taken together, these findings seem to suggest that deficits in the frontal cortex can impair problem-solving and decision-making processes, which may result in some people engaging in antisocial behavior that precludes the possibility of punishment and/or possible harm done to others (Gorenstein, 1990).

It is this presumed link between the limbic system, frontal cortex, and aggression that led to the development of one of the most controversial psychiatric treatments ever practiced—the lobotomy. In a very general sense, a **lobotomy** is a surgical procedure in which the neurological connections between the limbic system and the front portion of the brain (see Figure 15.1) are severed (Comer, 1995). The purpose of the lobotomy as a medical treatment for certain forms of extreme mental disorders was to separate the awareness of the sense of anger and rage from its underlying source. Thus, by severing the connections between the limbic system and the frontal cortex of the brain, the feelings of rage and anger that led to aggressive behavior cannot reach the individual's conscious level of awareness. For more about the use of the lobotomy to control violent behavior, read "A Closer Look" on this page.

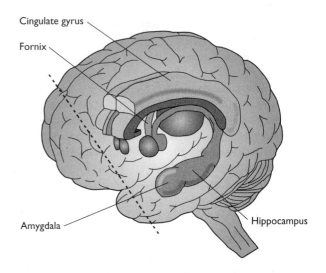

Figure 15.1

The structures of the limbic system are highlighted. This collection of structures is involved in memory, motivation, and emotion. In a lobotomy, the frontal portion of the cortex is surgically separated (see dashed line) from the limbic system.

A Closer Look:

The Case of Clara T: The Successful Subduing of Violent Behavior through Surgery

At the age of 33, Clara T. slipped on a patch of ice and sustained a head injury which soon led to temporal lobe epileptic seizures. Despite anti-seizure medication the frequency and intensity of her seizures increased during the following 29 years. She became more physically assaultive, attacking her mother-in-law, her husband, and many visitors. After being hospitalized, she stabbed a nurse with a scissors during one violent episode. It took six people 45 minutes to subdue this 62 year old woman who weighed only 86 pounds.

Neurological examinations showed that Clara had extensive damage in her temporal lobes, and stereotaxic surgery was performed in which a bank of 40 electrodes was implanted in and around the amygdala. The electrodes were kept in place for several months during which extensive tests were carried out. Abnormal brain waves were discovered in recordings through certain electrodes, and when weak electrical stimulation was applied at these points Clara began having a seizure.

Using radio frequency current, heat was then generated through these electrodes to destroy the cells around the electrode tips. The electrodes were then withdrawn and Clara's behavior was closely observed. She continued having epileptic seizures, but they were much milder and decreased in frequency. For six years following the operation there was a total absence of rage or unprovoked assaults, and once again she was able to resume her normal family and community life. (Johnson, 1972, p. 84)

Although this case demonstrates the successful use of a lobotomy to control violent behavioral tendencies, you should be aware that such success stories were not universal. For example, while lobotomy procedures did reduce violent tendencies and agitation in some people, many unpredictable side effects were also associated with this technique. The side effects included increased hyperactivity, impaired learning ability, reduced creativity, overeating, withdrawal, a loss of emotional expression (e.g., happiness and sorrow), and even death (Coleman, Butcher, & Carson, 1984; Comer, 1995). As an interesting example of one of these unpredictable side effects, Dr. Antonio Egas Moniz, the founder of the lobotomy technique and the winner of the Nobel Prize for Medicine in 1949 for developing this surgical procedure was shot by one of his lobotomized patients.

Although tens of thousands of people in this country and overseas were subjected to lobotomies and other related surgical procedures between the years of 1935 and 1955, these techniques are rarely performed today. In addition to the variety of unpredictable side effects, the major reason for the decline in the number of lobotomies was the development in the 1950s of major tranquilizers and antipsychotic drugs that could be used to control violent people without the irreversible brain damage produced by lobotomies (Comer, 1995; Goumeniouk & Clark, 1992).

Hormonal Influences: "Bad Blood"

As the old saying goes, "Only two things are certain: death and taxes." To this list can be added the tendency for males to engage in more aggressive behavior than females, a difference that has been observed "across species and across cultures" (Baron & Richardson, 1994, p. 252). At the core of this difference may be the hormone testosterone. **Testosterone** is a hormone that is released into the blood system and linked to various masculine characteristics, such as the deepening of the voice and the growth of body hair. There is considerable evidence linking increased levels of testosterone with aggressive behavior. (Julian & McHenry, 1989). For example, infant female monkeys whose mothers were administered testosterone during pregnancy displayed social behavior more characteristic of young male monkeys, such as rough-and-tumble activities, than young females (Goy, 1970). In a similar manner, young girls who were exposed to high levels of testosterone before birth due to a malfunctioning of their adrenal glands tended to engage in more masculine play and initiated more fights than their sisters not exposed to the excessive levels of testosterone (Meyer-Bahlburg & Ehrhardt, 1982).

The relationship between testosterone and aggressive behavior in males has been investigated in various naturalistic settings. For example, in one study normal, healthy, adolescent males were asked to indicate how they might respond to a series of frustrating or threatening events. The results indicated that the degree of self-reported aggressiveness was positively related to their testosterone level (Olweus, 1986). In a massive study involving the records of over 4500 male U.S. military veterans, it was noted that the individual's level of testosterone was positively related to participation in antisocial behaviors (e.g., spouse abuse, assault), with this relationship being particularly strong for those males who were below average in income and intelligence (Dabbs & Morris, 1990). When examining the testosterone level of prisoners, researchers also discovered that inmates who had committed violent crimes had higher levels of testosterone than inmates who committed nonviolent crimes (Dabbs, Frady, Carr, & Besch, 1987). In a very interesting variation of the testosterone-aggression research with female inmates, it was discovered that for those women who were in prison for violent crimes, those who had committed *unprovoked* violent crimes had a higher level of testosterone than females who had committed violent crimes during acts of defense (e.g., a female who kills her husband after years of abuse) or nonviolent crimes (e.g., theft) (Dabbs, Ruback, Frady, Hopper, & Sgoutas, 1988).

Although it is tempting to conclude that the consistency of these results would suggest that testosterone is the direct cause of aggressive behavior, such a conclusion would be overly simplistic. Instead, the relationship between testosterone and aggressive behavior is mediated by an assortment of personality and cognitive factors (Dabbs et al., 1987; Schalling, 1987). For example, since level of testosterone has been found to be correlated with such personality characteristics as sociability, extraversion, nonconformity, and self-assurance, there may be a tendency for such people to use aggressive behavior as a means of gaining status within their peer groups (Schalling, 1987). For example, an adolescent male who uses aggressive behavior to get what he wants from his peers on the playground or schoolyard is probably going to use this same behavior as an adult. In adulthood, however, such behavior is much more likely to result in encounters with law enforcement agencies, which increases the likelihood of the individual being incarcerated.

Genetic Transmission of Aggression: Born to Be Bad?

The study of aggression from a behavior genetics approach emphasizes the possibility that genetic variation can be used to help explain individual differences in aggressive behavior just as it can be used to help explain individual differences in eye color and height (Plomin, DeFries, & McClearn, 1990). In this section, you will examine three of the behavioral genetics approaches to the study of aggression: twin studies, adoption studies, and chromosomal analysis.

Twin Studies on Aggression: Double Trouble?   As noted in Chapter 9, one of the principal ways of studying the genetic basis of any aspect of personality is the use of twin studies (Segal, 1993). In twin studies of aggression, the degree of similarity in aggressive behavior between monozygotic (MZ), or identical twins, is compared with the degree of similarity of dizygotic (DZ), or fraternal, twins. The underlying logic is that if the MZ twins show a greater degree of similarity than the DZ twins, this similarity can be attributed to genetic transmission, because MZ twins have the same genetic structure but DZ twins do not.

Twin studies investigating the genetic contribution to aggressive behavior have been conducted in the controlled environment of the psychology laboratory and with real-life court convictions. In a study conducted as part of the University of London Insti-

tute of Psychiatry Twin Register, 573 twin pairs completed an aggressiveness questionnaire indicating the extent to which they agreed with such items as "Some people think I have a violent temper." In support of the behavior genetics perspective of aggression, the scores on the questionnaire for the MZ twin pairs were much more similar than those for the DZ twin pairs; the relationship was found to be true for both males and females (Rushton, Fulker, Neale, Nias, & Eysenck, 1986).

This relationship was not found when actual aggressive behaviors were examined. In a laboratory using MZ and DZ twins, whose average age was 7½ years, the children first observed an adult model hitting a 5-foot inflatable plastic doll and then were given a chance to aggress against the doll themselves. In this case, MZ twins were found to be no more similar in their aggressive behavior toward the clown doll than the DZ twins (Plomin, Foch, & Rowe, 1981). But, in a review of studies examining the criminal convictions among MZ and DZ twins, a greater degree of similarity was observed in the criminal records (Christiansen, 1974) and criminal convictions of MZ twins than for DZ twins (Mednick, Pollock, Volavka, & Gabrielli, 1982), suggesting a possible genetic link of criminality. Be aware, however, that the methodological weaknesses in the nature of the studies reviewed make it very difficult to separate the genetic contribution from the environmental factors. For example, when only violent crimes were considered, identical twins did not show any greater degree of similarity than fraternal twins (Mednick, Pollock, Volavka, & Gabrielli, 1982).

Adoption Studies: It's All in the Family   Another method of studying the genetic contribution to personality is the use of adoption studies (Segal, 1993). Again, as you recall from Chapter 9, in adoption studies, a comparison is made between the similarity of adopted people and their natural parents and between adopted people and their adopted parents. The underlying logic is that if the adopted people show a greater degree of similarity to their natural parents than to their adopted parents, this similarity can be attributed to genetic transmission, because adopted people and their natural parents share more genetic similarity than adopted people and their adopted parents.

Consistent with the previously mentioned twin studies demonstrating a genetic contribution to criminality, adoption studies have also shown a greater degree of similarity in criminality between adopted people and their natural parents than with their adopted parents (Mednick, Gabrielli, & Hutchings, 1987). But once again, when only violent crimes were considered, adopted people did not show any greater degree of similarity to their natural parents than to their adopted parents.

Chromosomal Abnormalities: Big Bad Boys   A third approach to studying the genetic transmission of aggression has been to examine certain genetic abnormalities. At the point of conception, the mother contributes an X chromosome and the father contributes either another X chromosome, resulting in the conception of a female baby, or a Y chromosome, resulting in the conception of a male baby. But under certain conditions, the father contributes an extra Y chromosome, resulting in the conception of a male baby with an XYY chromosome configuration. Because of their extra Y chromosome, such people have been referred to as "supermales." Characteristics of the **XYY syndrome** include rather excessive height, lower-than-average intelligence, severe acne scars, and occasional outbursts of violence (Baron & Richardson, 1994; Jacobs, Brunton, & Melville, 1965).

What is most interesting about the XYY syndrome is that while its actual birthrate or existence in adult males is relatively low—only about 1 in every 1000 births of normal adult males—it was noted that they were overly represented in prison populations, with estimates ranging from 1 in 35 to 1 in 100 (Court-Brown, 1968; Jacobs, Brunton, & Melville, 1965; Jarvick, Klodin, & Matsuyama, 1973). Such ratios led to the suggestion that this extra Y chromosome was creating "criminal types" with a predisposition toward aggressive behavior.

While the possibility of the XYY syndrome producing a "special criminal class" of people is an intriguing idea, a closer examination of XYY males revealed that most of the crimes of violence were committed by people with the more common XY chromosome combination. In addition, most of the XYY males in prison were there not for crimes of aggression against others, but for other nonviolent crimes such as theft or robbery (Price & Whatmore, 1967). Finally, as you might expect, as with normal XY males, only a very small percentage of the XYY males ever committed or were convicted of crimes.

Probably one of the most important pieces of information linking the XYY syndrome and criminal behavior was that on standard tests of intelligence, XYY males scored lower than XY males (Witkin et al., 1976). The implication seems to be that because they are not as bright as XY males, XYY males are more likely to be caught and convicted of their crimes. For example, because their crimes were poorly conceived, planned, and executed, they were much more likely to be apprehended by the police. There is also the possibility that because they are rather big for their age as children, XYY males may have been much more likely to associate with older people. As a result, XYY males may tend to be exposed to antisocial delinquent role models at a younger age, leading to a greater likelihood of becoming involved in crime (Bandura, 1973). As plausible as this sounds, it has not been totally supported by subsequent research (Witkin et al., 1976). Thus, taken together, the evidence seems to suggest that other cognitive (e.g., lower intelligence) and/or possible social factors (e.g., early association with antisocial role models) that are related to the XYY syndrome, and not the extra Y chromosome abnormality in and of itself, are the significant links in the XYY-aggression relationship.

In concluding this discussion of the genetic transmission of aggressive behavior, a consideration of the inconsistent and inconclusive nature of the results presented in this section seem to suggest that there may be no clear-cut evidence to support genetic transmission of aggressive and violent behavior, or that some people are simply born to be bad.

The Social Learning Viewpoint: The Acquisition of Aggressive Behavior

The basic premise of the social learning viewpoint is that aggression, like other behaviors, is based on principles of learning (Bandura, 1973, 1978). This discussion of the social learning viewpoint focuses on two specific principles of learning that seem to play a critical role in the acquisition of aggressive behavior: reinforcement and social modeling.

*The Role of Reinforcement in the Acquisition of
Aggressive Behavior: Violence, Like Crime,
Seems to Pay*

It should come as no surprise to you that a principal method of acquiring aggressive behaviors involves the reinforcement of aggressive behavior. For example, it was demonstrated that docile rats could be trained to engage in rather aggressive behavior when they were allowed to drink water only after attacking their cage mates (Ulrich, Johnston, Richardson, & Wolff, 1963).

In another study that supposedly involved the effects of punishment on learning a particular task, the "teacher" (who was actually a subject in the experiment) was to give an electrical shock to the "learner" (who was really one of the researchers and never actually received a shock) each time a mistake was made. For half of the "teachers," each time they delivered a shock to the "learner," the supervising researcher provided some verbal reinforcement by saying such things as "Fine" or "Mmm-hmm" while the other half of the "teachers" did not receive any such verbal reinforcement. As can be seen in Figure 15.2, over time, the level of shock intensity given by the verbally reinforced teachers tended to increase to a greater degree than that given by the nonreinforced teachers (Geen & Stonner, 1971).

Finally, in still another example, the aggressive behavior of a group of nursery school children was observed for 10 weeks, along with the consequences of such aggressive behavior (Patterson, Littman, & Bricker, 1967). The consequences of the aggressive behavior were classified into three categories: positive reinforcement (e.g., crying by the other child who received the aggressive act), punishments (e.g., the other child responding with returned acts of aggression), or neutral responses (e.g., ignoring the aggressor). The results of 10 weeks of observations indicated that of those children who showed the highest overall level of aggressive behavior, positive reinforcement was recorded as being the most common consequence following their acts of aggression. From these results, it seems possible to conclude that one reason for people to begin building aggression into their behavioral repertoire is that such behaviors seem to pay.

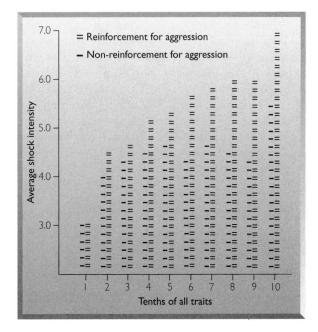

Figure 15.2

The amount of shock delivered tended to increase with the amount of reward given over time for such "aggressive" behavior.

Note. From Effects of Aggressiveness Habit Strength on Behavior in the Presence of Aggression-Related Stimulus, by R. G. Geen and D. Stonner, 1971. *Journal of Personality and Social Psychology,* Vol. 17, pp. 149–153. Washington, D.C.: American Psychological Association.

*The Role of Social Modeling: Look at and Learn
Aggressive Behaviors*

In addition to acquiring aggressive behavior as a result of the direct consequences of reinforcement, people can learn it in a second and somewhat indirect way: social modeling (Bandura, 1973).

Social modeling involves the acquisition of new behaviors by witnessing these behaviors being performed by others. For example, if you are at a fancy dinner party and not sure about what fork to use when eating your salad, you look at what others are doing and model your behavior after theirs. Along these same lines, it is believed that we acquire aggressive behavior in the same way. In a classic example of the role that modeling plays in influencing aggressive behavior, Bandura and his colleagues

(Bandura, Ross, & Ross, 1963) had young children witness a film in which an adult attacked a large inflatable plastic model of a clown by hitting it with a wooden mallet, kicking it, and picking it up and throwing it on the floor while saying things like "Kick him . . . Hit him down . . . Sock him in the nose." After observing the aggressive model in the film, the children were taken into another room and given the opportunity to play with a variety of toys, including the large, plastic doll. In support of the process of social modeling, those children exposed to the film with the aggressive model were much more likely to engage in play that involved "attacking" the clown in a manner similar to what they observed in the film. In a similar manner to what was observed with these nursery school children, college students exposed briefly to an aggressive model assigned more intense shocks as "teachers" to "learners" in a learning situation than students who were not exposed to the aggressive model (Baron & Kepner, 1970). Based on this and other evidence (Baron, 1977; Baron & Richardson, 1994; Berkowitz, 1993; Siann, 1985), it seems clear that witnessing aggressive models does serve as a principal method of acquiring aggressive behavior.

Because social modeling has been found to influence aggressive behavior, personality psychologists and other researchers, as well as concerned parents and government officials, have begun to question the effect of media violence, such as that seen on television and in films, as a source of social modeling in the acquisition of aggressive behavior in children. Because media violence is such a serious issue, it is examined in detail later in this chapter. In that section, you will consider whether watching televised violence increases violent behavior in its viewers, particularly young children.

This concludes the discussion of the theoretical viewpoints on aggression. As you can see, these viewpoints are rather diverse. This should come as no surprise to you, because something as complex and pervasive as aggressive behavior cannot be adequately explained in a simplistic manner. Now that you have a fundamental understanding of the basic theoretical viewpoints of aggressive behavior, you can focus on those factors that seem to trigger aggressive behavior.

Personal Determinants of Aggression: Creating Bad Feelings and Aggressive Tendencies

Aggressive behavior does not just happen; it is typically a response to some determining factor (Berkowitz, 1989, 1990, 1993). In this section, you will consider certain personal determinants of aggression. The personal determinants considered are emotional states residing within the individual that seem to increase the likelihood of expressing aggressive behavior. Three such emotional states identified as facilitators of aggressive behavior include being in a heightened state of arousal, a state of frustration, and a state of intoxication.

Emotional Arousal and Aggression: Exciting Expressions of Hostility

If you will recall from the discussion of the Yerkes-Dodson Law (refer to pages 414–415), one effect of increased arousal is to trigger the individual's dominant response. Along these lines, it seems that with angry people, creating a heightened level of arousal seems to trigger the dominant response of aggression. In such cases, what seems to happen is that the arousal associated with the state of anger facilitates the likelihood of the aggressive behavior. And, for the most part, it does not make any difference whether the feelings of arousal are generated from vigorous exercise, competitive activities, or stimulating drugs (Baron, 1977; Zillmann, 1988).

For example, in comparison with other angry people, it was reported that those who were asked to perform just two minutes of strenuous exercise engaged in a greater level of aggressive behavior against others than angry people who did not exercise (Zillmann, Katcher, & Milavsky, 1972). In this case, it appears that the combined level of arousal associated with the exercise and feelings of anger were enough to trigger the dominant response of aggression. In a similar manner, you are probably much more likely to yell at another driver after being cut off if you are "psyched up" about a test you are going to take that morning and made angry by a story you just heard on the radio while driving to school. This is also why having pep rallies and cheerleaders leading the crowd in cheers are so important to athletic teams. The roar of the crowd increases the arousal in the players and fuels their desire to "beat the heck out of" the opposing team. Thus, it seems the role of arousal is to fuel the flames of anger until they burst into aggression (Baron & Richardson, 1994).

Frustration and Aggression: Hurting Those Who Have Hindered You

In this section, you will consider the role of frustration as a form of emotional arousal that serves to facilitate the expression of aggression.

The Frustration-Aggression Hypothesis: The Basic Relationship

One of the earliest formulations of the role of emotional arousal as a psychological determinant of aggression is the frustration-aggression hypothesis (Dollard, Doob, Miller, Mowrer, & Sears, 1939). The **frustration-aggression hypothesis** suggests that arousing a state of frustration *always* leads to some form of aggressive behavior and that aggression is *always* a consequence of frustration. Assuming that frustration and aggression are always related may be a bit too strong, but it is very easy to find many examples in your own life to support a basic link between frustration and aggression. For example, after hurrying to the mall to buy a jacket on sale that you have been eyeing for weeks, you are informed by the clerk that he sold the last one just 30 minutes ago. In response to your frustration, you pound on the counter, give the clerk a dirty look, and snap, "You shouldn't lie to people and put stuff on sale when you know darn well you don't have enough of them." In this case, your aggressive response to the clerk is a direct result of your being frustrated by the chance to buy the coat on sale.

Aggressive Cues as Releasers of Aggression: Creating a Readiness to Aggress

In a less extreme position, more recent conceptualizations of the frustration-aggression hypothesis (Berkowitz, 1978, 1993) have proposed that frustra-

tion alone is not enough to elicit an aggressive response. Instead, frustration only creates a *readiness* to aggress. Readiness to aggress can be created by a number of factors, including threats to your sense of esteem (Baumeister, Smart, & Borden 1996) and the selective recall of information fueled by anger and retaliation (Taylor, 1992).

In addition, a critical factor that has been found necessary to trigger an aggressive response is an aggressive cue. An **aggressive cue** is any object that has been associated with an aggressive behavior in the past. One obvious example of an aggressive cue is that of a gun (Berkowitz & LaPage, 1967). Other aggressive cues might include a "Rambo" poster, a National Rifle Association sticker, or an advertisement for the type of beer being promoted by a famous television wrestler. The important point to consider is that it is the cue that serves as a release for the aggressive behavior. Another example of an aggressive cue is the association of certain types of people as victims to aggress against in response to your frustration. For example, rather than expressing your hostility at the store buyers for not purchasing enough of the coats the store put on sale, you aggress against the clerk because you have come to associate a lack of merchandise with the store clerks.

A more socially damaging and dangerous aggressive cue is the association of women as victims of aggression in pornographic literature. For more details about this issue, read "A Closer Look" below.

A Closer Look:

Pornography as a Promoter of Violence Against Women: The Danger of "The Resistance-Submission" Scenario

A very common theme in pornographic literature is the depiction of sexual violence against women in what might be called the "resistance-submission" scenario. In a typical resistance-submission scenario, a rapist attacks the woman and attempts forcibly to have sex with her while she actively resists. But while fighting off her attacker, the woman begins to feel a sense of sexual arousal and soon is in a state of extreme passion, pulling her attacker closer while pleading for more. A less extreme version, but probably the most famous example of the "resistance-submission" scenario, is a scene that occurs in *Gone with the Wind*. In this classic scene, Rhett Butler grabs Scarlett O'Hara and, against her will, begins to kiss her passionately. At first she resists, but shortly gives in to her feelings of passion and is returning his kisses just as forcefully. The scene ends with Rhett scooping up Scarlett in his arms and carrying her up the stairs to the bedroom. The next scene shows Scarlett waking up in the morning smiling. As common as such resistance-submission scenarios are in romance novels and movies, it would probably not be very difficult for you to generate a few examples of your own from movies you have seen or books you have read.

Given the commonality of these resistance-submission scenarios, a question of critical importance is the effect they may have on the people viewing such material. Several studies have reported that college men and woman find such forced-sex scenarios arousing, assuming that the female is depicted as enjoying the rape (Malamuth, Heim, & Feshbach, 1980; Stock, 1985). In addition, repeated exposure to forced-sex scenarios increases the likelihood of males endorsing the "rape myth," which is believing that women actually enjoy such treatment (Malamuth &

In a classic scene from *Gone with the Wind*, Scarlet O'Hara at first resists the romantic advances of Rhett Butler. However, as an example of the "resistance-submission," she willfully and passionately succumbs to his advances and is happy and smiling the next morning.

Check, 1981). Such attitudes concerning violence against women are also a very common theme in "hack-'n'-slash" movies, such as "The Texas Chainsaw Massacre." In fact, repeated exposure to this type of "horror-violence" against women seems to make males less sensitive to the pain and suffering brought on these women by these males perceiving them as worthless (e.g., that dumb idiot should have run faster) and making trivial the nature of the injuries (e.g., she really deserved it) (Linz, Donnerstein, & Penrod, 1988).

But in addition to affecting attitudes and perceptions, there is also some research indicating that pornography can contribute to an increase in the level of aggression against women. For example, in one study, male students were exposed to either a neutral film (e.g., a talk show interview containing no sexual or violent content), an erotic film (e.g., a young couple engaging in sexual intercourse), or an erotic-aggressive film (e.g., a gunman forcing a woman to have sexual intercourse with him). After viewing the films, the male students were then asked to participate in a second, but supposedly unrelated, experiment in which they were asked to teach another male or female student a list of words by using electric shock whenever the subject gave wrong answers. The results of this study indicated that exposure to the erotic-aggressive film led to an increase in the level of aggression (e.g., shock) toward only the females (Donnerstein, 1980). In fact, it was reported in another study that it did not make any difference if the female victim in the erotic-aggressive film appeared to be enjoying the treatment (e.g., resistance-submission scenario) or not (e.g., resistance-only scenario) (Donnerstein & Berkowitz, 1981). Finally, in still another related study, the researchers exposed males to an aggressive film (e.g., a violent western), an erotic film (e.g., depicting various forms of sexual intercourse), or no film (Donnerstein & Hallam, 1978) and a second "learning session" that was separated from the first by a 10-minute break. The results of this study indicated that in the first learning session, aggression was greater toward the male learners than female learners in the aggressive film condition, but about the same in the erotic condition. During the second learning session, however, aggression toward the females increased dramatically in the erotic condition only, while all of the levels of aggression remained about the same

(Donnerstein & Hallam, 1978). It seems that during the first session, the male subjects were unsure if it was socially acceptable to aggress against the female learners. But because the experimenter did not seem to show any reaction during the first session, such behavior, along with the experimenter actually having shown the erotic film seemed to be an implicit message to the males that aggression would be tolerated. Thus, although the erotic material was not selected specifically for its aggressive content, as noted by Donnerstein & Hallam (1978), "Given the nature of most erotic films, in which women are depicted in a submissive, passive manner, any subtle aggressive content could act to increase aggression against females because of their association with observed aggression" (p. 1276). Stated more simply, associating women with sexual violence in pornography can serve as an aggressive cue for violence against women when males are sexually aroused.

While these studies were conducted in the controlled confines of the psychology laboratory, their implications are of vital importance. They seem to suggest that by allowing film distributors and theaters to release these films without other citizens voicing an objection to this unrealistic treatment of women in pornography, we may actually be sending the message that it is socially acceptable to treat women in such a manner and, in an indirect way, contributing to an increase in such antisocial behavior as date rape, marital rape, and spouse abuse. In support of this reasoning, recent research indicates that people exposed to sexually violent films expressed less sympathy for victims of domestic violence and perceived their injuries as less severe than people not exposed to such material (Mullin & Linz, 1995).

Thus, while such businesses may have the constitutional right to show such films, there is some research to indicate that making people aware of the false nature of the "resistance-submission" scenario actually reduces the extent to which they believe that such sexual violence is what women desire and find enjoyable (Check & Malamuth, 1984; Malamuth & Check, 1984; Donnerstein & Berkowitz, 1981). Even more disturbing is the research indicating that males who regularly view sexually violent pornography (e.g., rape scenes or women being beaten or tortured) expressed a greater self-reported likelihood of using sexual force or raping a woman (Demare, Briere, & Lips, 1988).

If you would like to read more on this very critical topic in the study of aggression against women, a recommended book—edited by two of the most widely respected researchers in this field, Neil M. Malamuth, of the University of California at Los Angeles, and Edward Donnerstein, of the University of California at Santa Barbara—is *Pornography and Sexual Aggression* (1984).

Alcohol and Aggression: Boozin' and Bruisin'

A considerable amount of evidence exists that associates alcohol with violent behavior. Estimates of crime statistics indicate that alcohol is more likely to be involved in violent crime than nonviolent crime (Murdoch, Phil, & Ross, 1990), and that alcohol is involved in between half and two-thirds of all murders (Steele & Josephs, 1990). In addition, such estimates of violent crime suggest that either the perpetrator, the victim, or both had been drinking (Miller, Downs, & Gondoli, 1989; Muehlenhard & Linton, 1987; Pernanen, 1981). Alcohol consumption has also been linked with family violence (Straus & Gelles, 1990) and sexual aggression and sexual victimization (Koss, Gidycz, & Wisniewski, 1987).

While there is an established link between alcohol and aggressive behavior, this does not mean that alcohol consumption will certainly lead to taking someone's life or beating one's spouse or children. The effects of alcohol on aggression are complex and seem to rely on a combination of situational and cognitive factors.

Situational Expectations: "The Alcohol Made Me Do It!"

It is unfortunate, but one of the consequences of intoxication in our culture is the tendency for people to view such a state as an excuse for inappropriate or unacceptable behavior. This situation is best illustrated with the comment "The alcohol made me do it." For example, when an intoxicated man sexually assaults a woman after having a few drinks with her at a party, or an abusive parent beats her child while in a drunken state, both people might try to minimize personal responsibility for their actions by maintaining that they were not in control of their actions because of their state of intoxication.

The underlying dynamic of the process by which people tend to use alcohol intoxication to minimize personal responsibility for unacceptable actions is the social expectations people have about the effects of alcohol (Berkowitz, 1993). One of the most dramatic examples of such an explanation was a laboratory study in which males were asked to drink a mixture of vodka (which has no taste) and tonic water, or just plain tonic water (Lang, Goeckner, Adesso, & Marlatt, 1975). Half of the participants were given correct information about what they were asked to drink, and the other half were given false information. For example, half were led to believe they were drinking an alcoholic mixture when they were not; the other half were led to believe they were not drinking an alcohol mixture when they actually were. Shortly after drinking the beverage, the subjects interacted with a person who, as part of the study, either insulted or did not insult them. After the interaction, the subjects were given the opportunity to give this person a series of electric shocks, supposedly to test the effects of alcohol on various behaviors. The researchers used the amount of electrical shocks delivered as the measure of aggressiveness in this study.

What is most interesting about the results of this study is that it was the *expectation* that one was drinking alcohol that determined the degree of aggressiveness of the individual, and not if they had actually consumed the alcohol. The basic message here seems to be that people expect that alcohol provides them with a "ready-made excuse" for their aggressive behavior, even when they are unaware of what they are drinking (Bushman & Cooper, 1990; Hull & Bond, 1986). Thus, what seems to be important is not what's in your drink, but what's in your head.

Cognitive Deficiencies: Booze Blindness

The cognitive component of the alcohol-aggression link has to do with the deficient manner in which information is processed by intoxicated people. This pattern of cognitive deficiencies is referred to as alcohol myopia (Steele & Josephs, 1990). **Alcohol myopia** is an intoxication-induced condition in which the individual demonstrates a deficiency in cognitive ability and shortsightedness in the processing of information about his or her actions. Alcohol myopia seems to exist because alcohol: (a) restricts the range of information the individual attends to in a particular situation, and (b) reduces the individual's ability to process

and extract meaning from that information in the situation to which the individual is attending.

For example, when intoxicated, an individual may perceive physically attacking the other person as the only alternative for settling an argument while not fully comprehending the fact that if he hits this person with the bar stool, he could possibly kill him. Thus, in this situation, the individual is "blind" to other ways of settling the argument (e.g., thinking up logical statements to make his point) and to the possibility that although he may succeed in winning the argument in the short run, the long-term consequences of such actions might include some serious prison time and all of the severe consequences that accompany such incarceration. In support of the alcohol myopic explanation of the effects of alcohol on aggression, people who consumed alcohol as part of a laboratory study and then were asked to perform a competitive task as part of the study were much less likely than people who did not receive alcohol to ignore subsequent information about the intentions of their opponent (Leonard, 1989). Anecdotal evidence illustrating such findings include an aggressive individual who continues to fight even when the other person says "I'm sorry," the abusive parent who does not want to hear the child's explanation for its behavior, or the drunk individual who persists in making sexual advances even when such advances are continually rebuffed. In all of these examples, the intoxicated people do not process the subsequent information that could be used to help reduce the feelings of aggression.

The Interaction of Situational and Cognitive Factors: Drinking and Thinking Don't Mix

Alcohol myopia is also enhanced by the tendency of intoxicated people to deal with their cognitive deficiencies by focusing on the most dominant features of the situation (Taylor & Leonard, 1983). Given the very powerful human motive for self-protection, intoxicated people, with their restricted sense of information processing, will most likely focus on this very powerful motive and take aggressive action designed to protect themselves. In support of this reasoning is research suggesting that the effects of alcohol on aggression are more likely to occur when the individual is threatened, provoked, or instigated in some manner (Richardson, 1981; Taylor, Gammon, & Capasso, 1976; Taylor & Sears, 1988).

It must also be noted that providing salient cues that promote nonaggressiveness, such as models who behave in a nonaggressive manner or the presentation of explicit rules against aggressive behavior, can reduce aggressive behavior in both intoxicated and sober people (Baily, Leonard, Cranston, & Taylor, 1983; Jeavons & Taylor, 1985; Leonard, 1989; Taylor & Gammon, 1976). For example, an intoxicated individual is less likely to engage in aggressive behavior following an argument if other people are present and are offering suggestions for and encouraging nonviolent solutions to this tense and threatening situation. On the other hand, if the others present are also intoxicated and encouraging the individual to engage in aggressive actions to settle the argument, then the intoxicated individual is much more likely to see violence as the only course of action.

Thus, as these examples illustrate, the effects of alcohol on aggression involve a combination of situational and cognitive factors. Nowhere is this point better illustrated than in the effects of alcohol on sexual aggression. To illustrate how this information about alcohol and aggression is being used to help us better understand a very important social issue, consider the information in "Applications in Personality Psychology" below.

APPLICATION

APPLICATIONS IN PERSONALITY PSYCHOLOGY

Mixing Alcohol and Sexual Aggression: A Cocktail Made for Disaster

Police reports and other similar types of documents that provide evidence linking alcohol with sexual aggression suggest that the perpetrator and/or victim are often drinking at the time of the rape (Muehlenhard & Linton, 1987; Russell, 1982; Scully & Marolla, 1984). Consistent with criminal reports is experimental evidence suggesting that when compared to sober males, intoxicated males, when given the opportunity, behaved more aggressively against a woman who made negative comments to them in a "get-acquainted session" before the experiment (Richardson, 1981).

Also important in our understanding of the relationship between alcohol and sexual aggression are the sexually related expectancies and myths that link alcohol and sexual aggression. An example of a sexually relevant expectancy related to alcohol is the evidence that suggests that people who believed they had consumed alcohol showed an increased interest in pornographic slides (Lang, Searles, Lauerman, & Adesso, 1980) and watched erotic, violent, and violent-erotic stimuli longer than people who did not believe they had consumed alcohol (George & Marlatt, 1986). In addition to showing more interest in viewing erotic stimuli, people who thought they had consumed alcohol reported and experienced more physiological and self-reported sexual arousal in response to videotapes depicting rape and sadistic aggression than those who did not suspect they had consumed alcohol (Briddell et al., 1978). As noted by Briddell et al. (1978), this pattern of heightened sexual arousal to rape and sadistic erotic stimuli by normal heterosexual males who believed they had consumed alcohol is very similar to patterns of sexual arousal exhibited by convicted rapists. Thus, the expectancy of alcohol consumption led to a greater interest in pornographic and violent/sadistic-erotic stimuli.

Central to the link between the expectancy effect of alcohol and sexual aggression is that "alcohol disinhibits psychological sexual arousal and suppresses physiological responding" (Crowe & George, 1989, p. 384). Thus, the individual may feel he is sexually aroused but may not be able to perform well when expected to do so. Such a situation can lead to a state of frustration, which in turn is likely to lead to acts of aggression against the likely cause of this frustration, namely, but mistakenly, the female. The male is likely to assume that it is the female who is failing to arouse him, and not the depressant effects of the alcohol. In a related finding, it has also been reported that people who consumed alcohol engaged in more aggression against a helpless victim—someone who is less likely to be able to retaliate against them—than those people who did not consume alcohol (Gantner & Taylor, 1992). Thus, in most alcohol-induced, sexually aggressive situations, the victim is usually a woman who is probably smaller, weaker, and less able to defend herself than the intoxicated, sexually frustrated male aggressor.

To account for the relationship between alcohol and sexual aggression, Leif C. Crowe and William H.

George (1989), both of the State University of New York at Buffalo, have suggested that the usual social constraints and inhibitions of a man aggressing against a woman are "sufficiently weakened by such things as rape myths or belief in alcohol's excuse-giving qualities" (p. 383). However, once such social constraints and inhibitions are weakened by the tendency of alcohol to impair reasoning and disrupt normal patterns of information processing, and are combined with sexually related expectancies of alcohol consumption (e.g., "She really wants it," or "The alcohol made me do it."), the stage may be set for an increased likelihood of sexual aggression against women.

To help illustrate how the disturbing effects of alcohol on expectancies, social inhibitions and moral restraints, cognitive processes and decision making, and miscommunication could lead to sexual aggression, consider the following scenario:

> In the prototype of acquaintance rape, a rape during a date, a drunk male may be exposed to a variety of cues. He may have some expectations of sexual activity and of the influence of alcohol on his behavior; the female could presumably be responding to him in a relatively warm and friendly fashion, as would be typical on a date; and if he begins to initiate sexual activity in which she is not interested, her first communication of disinterest may be relatively subtle (e.g., removing his hands from her person, or moving away from him). When he is drunk, he is less likely to respond to subtle inhibitory cues and more likely to respond to more salient cues (some of which may be provided by his imagination). His inability to deal with the complexity of multiple cues in the situation may increase the probability that he will use some form of coercion or force. This situation could be even more instigative if the female also is drunk, because she may be having difficulty reading cues from him; she may be slow to realize his intentions and therefore slow to offer inhibitory signals to discourage him (Richardson & Hammock, 1991, p. 93).

Thus, as this scenario illustrates, the relationship between alcohol and sexual aggression is complex and involves many different emotional, physiological, cognitive, and interpersonal factors. It is only by taking a closer look at this serious social issue that we will be able to reduce its likelihood of occurring.

This concludes the discussion about personal factors that influence aggressive behavior. As you now know, these factors are diverse and complex. Such diversity helps to explain why aggressive behavior is so pervasive in contemporary society. In the next section, you will examine how personality psychologists and others are trying to use what is known to deal with some of the ways aggressive behavior occurs in our society.

The Application of Personality Psychology: Using What Is Known

In this section, you will consider how personality psychologists and others have been using what is known to address the issue of aggression as it occurs in everyday living experiences. Three very important contemporary issues that are considered in this section include assessing and understanding the effect of media violence on aggressive behavior, developing strategies that can be used to prevent and control aggression in our society, and gaining an understanding of cultural-societal violence.

Assessing the Effect of Media Violence: Addressing an Important Social Issue

It was noted earlier in this chapter that social modeling is a process by which people can learn to perform aggressive behaviors by watching others behave in an aggressive manner. One very common source of models behaving aggressively is in the popular media, particularly television. Because of this, personality psychologists and others are busy trying to understand what effect such a steady dose of aggressive behavior has on those who view it.

The Impact of Television Violence: A Modern Medium for Modeling Violence
Although people have always had the opportunity to watch others engage in aggressive behavior, it has only been since the invention of the television that we have had the opportunity to do so on such a grand scale. For example, while the average individual will spend some 11,000 hours in the classroom before graduating from high school, this same person will

spend more than 15,000 hours watching television, with this boiling down to an average of about 7 hours of viewing per day. Within all of this viewing, approximately 80% of all TV dramas and 95% of cartoons contain some form of violence (Oskamp, 1984; U.S. National Commission on the Causes and Prevention of Violence, 1970). More specifically, on the average, prime-time TV programming contains about 8 acts of violence per hour while children's cartoons average about 22 acts per hour (Oskamp, 1984). This means that by the time the average individual graduates from high school, he or she will have witnessed approximately 18,000 murders.

With such a seemingly endless opportunity to witness violence, the question that comes most to our minds is: Does such viewing have an effect on those who watch it? The answer to this question is yes, it does affect the way we behave, feel, and think about violence and aggression (Huesmann & Miller, 1994). More importantly, recent research indicates that the effects of viewing media violence are even more pronounced for people considered to be high on the trait of aggressiveness (Bushman, 1995).

Effect on Behavior: Creating a Tendency Toward Aggressive Behavior

One approach to investigating the effect of televised violence is to correlate the amount of violent television watched with the aggressive behavior of the viewers. Although the relationship is far from being perfect, a consistent body of evidence suggests that the more children watch violence on television, the more aggressive their behavior (Eron & Huesmann, 1984, 1985). For example, in a rather extensive six-year study of the television-viewing patterns of over 1550 London youths, it was noted that the youths who were heavy viewers of violent television engaged in approximately 50% more violent acts within the preceding six months than youths who were light viewers (Belson, 1978). An even more dramatic finding is that youths who viewed a great deal of television violence at age 8 were much more likely to have been convicted of a serious crime at age 30 than subjects who were light to medium viewers during their youth (Eron & Huesmann, 1984).

While such results from correlational studies do seem to suggest that there is a link between watching television violence and aggressive behavior, as you will recall from Chapter 1 (see pages 16–20), the basic limitation of correlational studies is that they do not make possible a *causal* link between the two variables in question: (a) amount of television violence watched and (b) amount of aggressive behavior demonstrated. To investigate more closely the causal link between viewing television violence and aggressive behavior, researchers have also taken a more experimental approach to this problem.

In general, experiments on the effects of televised violence on aggressive behavior conducted in laboratory conditions typically involve one group of subjects viewing a film containing an aggressive theme (e.g., a gangster movie) or a nonaggressive theme (e.g., an exciting car race), followed by the opportunity to "aggress" against another individual. Such laboratory aggression typically involves the chance to deliver a noxious stimuli (e.g., electric shock) to another individual, although no shock is actually delivered (Liebert & Baron, 1982). Overall, the results of these laboratory experimental studies seem to suggest that exposing children and adults to televised violence tends to produce more aggressive behavior than exposing them to nonaggressive programming (Bushman, 1995; Geen, 1976; Baron, 1977; Baron & Richardson, 1994; Siann, 1985). In addition, people with aggressive tendencies are more likely to select violent films when given the opportunity to do so than less aggressive people (Bushman, 1995).

Beyond the confines of the laboratory, experimental studies done in more "real-life settings" have also documented increases in aggressive behavior following exposure to televised violence (Parke, Berkowitz, Leyens, West, & Sebastian, 1977). For example, a study done with delinquent boys enrolled in a private school involved observing their aggressive behavior for one week and then dividing the boys into two groups: televised violence vs. televised nonviolence programming. In the televised violence group, the boys were shown one violent movie (e.g., a gangster or combat movie) each night for the next five days, while the televised nonviolence group were exposed to one nonviolent movie each night for five days. After the week of films, the aggressive behavior of all the boys was observed for another week. The results of this field experiment indicated that, when compared to the week before viewing the films, those

Children are exposed to an alarming amount of violent programming on television. Concerns have been raised about the impact such televised violence has on the thoughts, feelings, and behavior of children. Research is mounting that supports the contention that watching televised violence facilitates the expression of aggressive behavior and feelings of indifference towards violence in children. What are your thoughts on this very important social issue?

boys exposed to the week-long diet of violent programming demonstrated an increase in their aggressive behavior toward their peers, while those exposed to the nonviolent programming did not exhibit any consistent increase in violent behavior (Leyens, Camino, Parke, & Berkowitz, 1975).

In a recent study investigating the long-term effects of viewing violent television on the aggressive behavior of females, researchers traced the viewing habits and aggressive behavior of 211 girls from the late 1970s until they were 21 to 25 years of age. The results of the study indicate that "the more violent shows they viewed back then, the more physically aggressive the girls became, and the more violent they remain even as women in their 20s" ("Violent Television," 1996, p. B6). According to L. Rowell Huesmann, a University of Michigan psychologist and researcher with this study, "girls get desensitized to violence just like boys, and when heroines' aggressive acts are portrayed positively, girls conclude it's a good way to solve problems" (p. B6). Thus, consistent with research done with boys, the results of this study also document the importance of modeling processes and the effect of rein-

forcement for aggressive behavior by these models. And, in a comment on this study, Robert Lichter, of the Center for Media and Public Affairs, says, "Going from Barbie to 'Thelma and Louise' is not necessarily progress. We have equal-opportunity media violence now. This shows parents have to worry about the effects of TV violence on kids regardless of their sex" (p. B6).

In general, the results from correlational and experimental studies (Baron & Richardson, 1994; Berkowitz, 1993; Comstock, Chaffee, Katzman, McCombs, & Roberts, 1978; Huesmann & Miller, 1994; Siann, 1985), as well as government-sponsored reports, such as the 1972 Surgeon General's Report and the United Kingdom's 1977 Home Office Research Study, seem to conclude that observing televised violence tends to facilitate behaving in an aggressive and violent manner.

Effect on Emotional Responses: Creating a Sense of Indifference

Viewing media violence has been found to increase feelings of anger in people high in the trait of aggressiveness (Bushman, 1995). There is also evidence to suggest that heavy doses of viewing televised violence can create a sense of emotional indifference to viewing subsequent acts of violence and aggression (Berkowitz, 1993). For example, people who generally watch a lot of television exhibited less physiological arousal when watching a brutal boxing match than those who tended to watch only a little television (Cline, Croft, & Courrier, 1973). At the affective level, there is evidence to suggest that watching violent television also produces a greater tolerance of aggressive acts and increases in apathy for filmed (e.g., watching a televised brawl) or real-life (e.g., observing two children fighting or victims of domestic violence) violence (Drabman & Thomas, 1974, 1975, 1976; Mullin & Linz, 1995). Thus, whether it is at the physiological or affective level, viewing televised violence tends to create a sense of emotional indifference to violence.

Effect on Beliefs: Creating an Exaggerated Sense of a Violent World

Television also seems to affect the beliefs viewers have about the level of violence that occurs in the real world (Berkowitz, 1993). For example, surveys indicate that adolescents and adults who are heavy viewers of television (four or more hours per day) tend to perceive the real world as being a more violent place and to have a greater fear of being a victim of violence than people who are light viewers (2 to 4 hours per day) (Gerbner, Gross, Morgan, & Signorielli, 1986; Gerbner, Gross, Signorielli, Morgan, & Jackson-Beeck, 1979). To bring such fears even closer to their homes, there is also evidence to suggest that young children who are heavy viewers of television express more fear of "someone bad" entering their house or hurting them when they go outside or to view their neighborhood as being a scarier place than children who are light viewers of television (Peterson & Zill, 1981; Singer, Singer, & Rapaczynski, 1984). Thus, extensive viewing of television tends to create the exaggerated belief that the world, including your home and neighborhood, is a rather violent place.

Looking at the Good Side of TV: In Fairness to the "Boob Tube"

Based on the sampling of research just covered, as well as other sources noted (Baron & Richardson, 1994; Siann, 1985), it seems clear that televised violence does affect the behavior, feelings, and thoughts of those who view it. But in all fairness, programming on television also provides a lot of material that is designed to enlighten and inform, as well as to entertain us. For example, many highly successful prime-time miniseries, such as "Roots" and "The Winds of War," were not only entertaining but extremely informative. Extensive research on the effect of such educational programs as "Sesame Street" and "Mr. Rogers' Neighborhood," indicates that television can serve as a medium for teaching children more constructive attitudes and behaviors (Rubinstein, 1978). Thus, although it has been demonstrated that the introduction of television has reduced the amount of time people spend reading, sleeping, socializing, traveling, and engaging in religious activities (Murry & Kippax, 1979; Robinson, 1972), it would probably be unfair to assume that the effect television has had on viewers' lives is totally negative. But in the author's opinion, it would probably be to everyone's advantage to spend more time living life than watching it on television.

Strategies for the Prevention and Control of Aggression: Alleviating Aggression

In preceding sections of this chapter, you have learned about the pervasiveness of aggression and its complexity. You now realize that explanations and an understanding of human aggression involve an appreciation of the complex interaction of emotional (e.g., perceived sense of threat or frustration), cognitive (e.g., interpretation of situational cues), physiological (e.g., hormonal level), and cultural (e.g., pervasiveness of violence on television) factors. You will end your examination of the topic of aggression on a positive note by considering those strategies that have been proposed as a means of preventing and controlling aggression (Baron & Richardson, 1994; Berkowitz, 1993). In this section, you will focus on the use of punishment, catharsis, cognitive strategies for rethinking aggression, the modeling of nonaggressiveness, and social skills training.

Punishment: The Eye-for-an-Eye Approach

One of the most frequently used approaches to the control and prevention of aggression is that of punishment. Sentiments expressed in the form of such slogans as "three strikes and you're out," "build more prisons," "bring back the death penalty," and "an eye for an eye" all indicate the commonsense belief that punishment is effective in deterring and controlling such crimes of violence as rape, murder, assault, and spouse abuse. At the level of common sense, such an approach works because when people who commit violent crimes are put to death, they cannot commit such crimes again, and people incarcerated for committing such crimes are prevented from repeating these crimes against the general public (they may, however, repeat such crimes against other inmates while in prison). Evidence at the scientific level is much less conclusive, and suggests that for punishment to be effective, certain conditions must be present (Baron and Richardson, 1994; Berkowitz, 1993; Bower & Hilgard, 1981). In the following sections, you will examine these conditions.

Level of Anger: Punishment May Not Cool a Hothead
Punishment is most likely to serve as a deterrent to aggression when the individual's level of anger is low

Punishment in the form of imprisonment is a very common response to acts of aggression. What are your thoughts about the use of prisons in particular, and punishment in general, as a means of controlling aggressive behavior?

to moderate. If the level of anger, frustration, or perceived threat gets too high, punishment may fail to produce the desired restraint in aggressive behavior (Baron, 1973; Rogers, 1980). It seems that experiencing such a strong level of anger arousal interferes with a person's ability to consider the consequences of any impulsive aggressive acts (Berkowitz, 1988, 1989). As an example, it would not be too difficult for any of us to come up with a personal experience in which we hurt someone's feelings by saying something we wish we had not in the "heat of the moment." Fortunately, most of us will never reach that state of severe anger arousal in which we fail to consider the consequences of our actions that might seriously injure or kill someone. And, as a result, punishment—at least for most of us—is an effective deterrent of serious aggressive behavior.

The Purpose of Aggression: Does Aggression Pay?   The ability of punishment to deter aggression is also related to the extent to which something can be gained by behaving aggressively. The greater the magnitude and likelihood of the reward as a consequence of the aggressive behavior, the less likely punishment is to deter such aggressive acts. A disheartening example of this tendency is the amount of violence that is associated with the trafficking of

drugs, even though such behaviors carry with them some very severe legal consequences. The inability of punishment to deter such drug-related violence is due to the tremendous amount of money drug traffickers stand to make. Fortunately, most of us will never be in a position where money and other forms of rewards are more important than the physical and emotional well-being of others and, as a result, punishment will be a successful deterrent to our behaving aggressively.

The Delivery of the Punishment: Make It Swift, Make It Severe, and Make It Certain   For punishment to be an effective deterrent of aggressive behavior, the punishment should follow the aggressive behavior as soon as possible; the longer the delay, the less effective the punishment will be. In addition to being immediate, the punishment should also be severe; the more severe the punishment, the more it will serve as a deterrent. Finally, for punishment to be a deterrent to aggressive behavior, the likelihood of the individual being punished for behaving aggressively should be very high. For example, electric shocks administered immediately to schizophrenic patients after they engaged in surprise physical attacks against staff members was successful in reducing such aggressive attacks (Ludwig, Marx, Hill, & Browning, 1969). In addition, when police officers arrested the perpetrators of domestic violence after being called to the scene, the abusers were less likely to repeat such violence in the future than either abusers who were simply advised by the officers at the scene to settle their differences or abusers who were just told by the officers to get away from the house for several hours and allowed to return (Berk & Newton, 1985; Sherman & Berk, 1984).

The Realistic Effectiveness of Punishment: The Less-than-Perfect Use of Punishment   Unfortunately, while we know that swift, severe, and certain punishment does deter aggressive behavior, it is these same characteristics that are often missing from our criminal justice system. The legal proceedings, which guarantee people due process under the law, may go on for months or even years before a criminal is convicted and punishment is carried out. Or, unfortunately, the severity of the punishment people receive for a crime of violence may not depend solely on the nature of the crime but on their race, gender, financial resources, and the quality of their lawyers. Finally, most people are also aware that many violent crimes go unreported, charges are not pressed, and/or the perpetrators of such crimes are never caught and, as a result, the likelihood of punishment being delivered in all of these cases is uncertain. As a related issue, there is also no evidence that the possibility of severe punishment in the form of capital punishment deters homicide (Peterson & Baily, 1988). Finally, there are those offenders, such as psychopaths, for whom no form of punishment is effective (Newman, 1987).

Although punishment has not necessarily been a perfect solution to controlling and preventing aggressive behavior, it should not necessarily be abandoned. On the contrary, think of how bad things would be if we did not use punishment. Its less-than-perfect degree of effectiveness only means that punishment has not been used in an optimal fashion, and that other means should be employed.

Catharsis: Letting Off Steam
Besides punishment, one of the oldest means of reducing aggression tendencies is through the process of catharsis. The logic of the **catharsis hypothesis** is that those activities that allow you to "let off steam" through the performance of various nonharmful activities will help reduce aggressive tendencies. Activities such as exercising, beating your pillow, yelling at the top of your lungs, and watching football, hockey, or boxing are expressions of catharsis. The logic of catharsis as an aggression-reducing strategy is that the expressing or experiencing of vigorous activity reduces tension or arousal, which in turn, reduces the likelihood of the individual engaging in aggressive acts (Dollard et al., 1939).

As logical as the catharsis hypothesis sounds, its effectiveness has been examined with mixed results. Allowing individuals to watch filmed or televised violence may actually produce *increases* in aggressive behavior (Wood, Wong, & Chachere, 1991). Allowing people to "let off steam" by engaging in such activities as throwing darts at their enemies, breaking objects, or attacking inflatable toys does not necessarily decrease aggressive tendencies against the source of anger (Mallick & McCandless, 1966). Even allowing people to engage in verbal catharsis, such as

yelling at the source of their annoyance, does not seem to reduce aggressive tendencies (Ebbesen, Duncan, Konecni, 1975). Thus, it seems that while catharsis may decrease the likelihood of reducing aggression in the short run by distracting the individual and taking his or her mind off the source of the annoyance, such effects are short lived and may actually increase aggressive acts.

Cognitive Strategies: Rethinking the Aggression
Cognitive approaches to aggression control involve adding alternative sources of information to help lessen the individual's feelings of anger, which in turn reduces aggressive tendencies. One cognitive approach involves simply offering apologies for any annoyance or frustration you may have caused someone and asking for their forgiveness. Apologies are most effective when they are based on factors outside of the individual's control (Weiner, Amirkhan, Folkes, & Verette, 1987), such as "I bumped into your car because the street was too icy."

Another cognitive approach to aggression control involves providing causal accounts. **Causal accounts** are excuses or explanations that can be offered for acts of annoyance or frustration to help reduce an individual's feelings of anger. The more sincere and detailed the causal account is, the more effective it is going to be in reducing feelings of aggression in others (Shapiro, Buttner, & Barry, 1993). If you just bumped into someone and he becomes very angry and threatens to "beat you to a pulp," you might be able to reduce the likelihood of such aggressive acts by informing the individual that you are very sorry that it happened, and that it was unavoidable because you were trying to prevent yourself from slipping and injuring yourself.

As a more preventive measure, Raymond Novaco (1975), of the University of California, Irvine, developed a program of cognitive rehearsal by which people mentally practice how they will respond to situations that have the potential to provoke an aggressive response. For example, the individual might practice thinking such statements as: "I know this is making me mad, but I must do my best to remain calm." "This conversation is starting to escalate, but I must remain patient because sometimes differences take time to resolve." Such statements not only help people to think more clearly but also serve to reduce self-reported feelings of anger and related physiological responses (e.g., blood pressure) (Novaco, 1975).

Modeling Nonaggressiveness: Demonstrating Nonviolence

Earlier in this chapter, material was presented suggesting that watching televised and film violence influenced aggressive behavior. Based on the logic that watching violence serves as a model for such behavior in others, another approach to controlling aggression involves presenting nonaggressive models. Systematic research on the use of nonaggressive models indicates that they are effective as a means of reducing aggressive behavior (Baron, 1972b; Donnerstein & Donnerstein, 1976). Programs designed to teach nonaggressive modeling as a means of reducing conflicts between police and students has met with a certain degree of success (Taylor, 1980, as cited in Baron & Richardson, 1994).

The use of physical discipline by parents as a means of controlling their children's aggressive personality can be viewed as a form of aggressive modeling on the part of the parents. To help minimize such unintended modeling of aggressive behavior, Gerald Patterson and John Reid, of the Social Learning Center of the Oregon Research Institute, have developed a program to teach parents effective patterns of discipline involving techniques of behavior modification that emphasize rewards instead of punishment (Patterson, Reid, Jones, & Conger, 1975). Thus, such programs are beneficial for two reasons: (a) they reduce the child's aggressive behavior, and (b) they employ the modeling of nonaggressive behaviors by the parent.

Social Skills Training: Learning the Art of Diplomacy

It has been noted that people who lack social skills account for a high proportion of violence and criminal behavior in many societies (Ronka & Pulkkinen, 1995; Toch, 1985). People lacking in social skills are typically unable to express their needs or desires effectively to others, thus creating a sense of frustration in themselves and often provoking such feelings of annoyance and frustration in others. Those who lack social skills are also typically unable to pick up the subtle social cues associated with body language or facial expressions that are so much an important part of successful interpersonal relationships. Because they lack the verbal fluency to negotiate social conflict, they must often resort to the use of verbal and physical aggression.

To offset this tendency, programs have been developed to help people master the social skills necessary to reduce their likelihood of becoming involved in aggressive encounters and/or resorting to aggressive behaviors to settle such disputes (Schneider & Byrne, 1987). For example, in one such program (Schneider, 1991), boys and girls (ranging in age from 7 to 14) in a treatment center as a result of exhibiting conduct disorder and aggressive behavior patterns participated in training sessions designed to teach them alternative nonaggressive responses. These training sessions consisted of two to four children and lasted about 40 minutes each for a period of 12 weeks. Within the training sessions, these children participated in various exercises designed to teach them how to respond to teasing in a nonaggressive manner, avoid overreacting in the face of frustrating situations, understand the feelings of others better, and perceive the reactions of others more accurately. Follow-up observations of these children during recess and other periods of free play indicated a clear reduction in their aggressive behavior and an increase in their level of cooperation with each other.

Additional support for the effectiveness of social skills training comes from a program involving 6th graders, who were judged by their peers and teachers to be aggressive and disruptive because they lacked certain social skills (e.g., recognizing the feelings of others, dealing with embarrassment, anger, and teasing by fighting). During 10 one-hour training sessions, the children, in groups of three to seven, were taught social skills by playing games, watching videos in which models illustrated nonaggressive methods for dealing with frustration and conflict, and reading stories in which characters coped successfully or unsuccessfully with various problematic situations. Once again, the results indicated that social skills training resulted in these children not only being rated as more socially skilled by their teachers and peers than they were before the training but also displaying lower levels of aggression than a control group of aggressive children who had not yet received such training (Bienert & Schneider, 1995).

More important, these changes were observed to be still present more than a year later as these children made the transition to various junior high schools.

The findings regarding the success of these social skills training programs are very encouraging, for a couple of reasons. First, they suggest that these "aggressive children" are not bad people who are simply acting out of uncontrolled impulses; instead, they are people who simply lack certain necessary skills. Second, it appears that the children's aggressiveness is not something that represents a permanent characteristic of their personality. Instead, such findings suggest that with the proper training, such aggressiveness can be reduced considerably.

This concludes the presentation regarding how personality psychologists and others have tried to use what is known to help understand, assess, reduce, and control aggression as it appears in the media and in our daily lives. If you would like more information on these topics, read Chapters 7 through 11 in Leonard Berkowitz's (1993) *Aggressions: Its Causes, Consequences, and Control* and Chapters 8 and 9 in Robert A. Baron and Deborah R. Richardson's (1994) *Human Aggression*. In the next section, the topic of aggression from a cultural-societal perspective and the expression of collective violence will be discussed.

Cultural-Societal Roots of Violence: Causes of and Strategies for Controlling Collective Violence

To this point, the discussion on aggression has focused on the individual. But we are living in a more violent society and a more violent world. Therefore, the discussion of aggression would be incomplete if it did not include a consideration of cultural and societal factors. In this section, you will turn your attention to the causes and control of cultural-societal violence.

Causes of Collective Violence: Contributions to a Violent World

One psychologist who is attempting to use what we know to understand the cultural-societal roots of violence, as well as its reduction, is Ervin Staub of the University of Massachusetts at Amherst. As Staub (1996) notes, throughout history, some of the worst examples of cultural-societal violence have been genocidal violence. **Genocidal violence** is conceptualized as any systematic form of mass killing with or without the expressed intent to eliminate an entire group of people. Although it is all too easy to find examples of genocidal violence throughout history, some of the most recent examples include the systematic killing of Jews during the Holocaust, "ethnic cleansing" in Bosnia, and ethnic/tribal mass killings in Africa. While it is very difficult to explain such aggression, certain cultural conditions, when present, seem to lead to such massive acts of aggression (Staub, 1989, 1996): difficult economic times, the devaluation of others, acceptance of authority, a lack of tolerance for diversity, enhanced group self-concept, and certain ideological choices.

Difficult Economic Conditions: Hard Times and Hatred

At the core of genocidal violence is difficult economic conditions. Difficult economic conditions result in an increase of self-focused concerns and a decrease in the tendency to connect with and support others (Staub, 1989). Such self-focused tendencies result in distinctions being made between groups of people. Such a division of people then makes it possible for one group of people to blame another group of people for their economic problems. Blaming their difficult economic conditions on another group provides

Ervin Staub's work on genocidal violence is extremely significant. Staub seeks to help us understand the cultural conditions that contribute to the mass killings of certain groups of people by other groups of people, along with what strategies can be developed and implemented to control such genocidal violence. What do you think can be done to reduce genocidal violence?

a very clear solution to the problem—eliminate the other group(s) of people. Thus, economic hard times seem to foster hatred.

Devaluation of Others: Reducing the Worth of Human Life

To justify this hatred fueled by difficult economic times, members of the other group are devalued. The devaluing of others typically involves portraying them in unfavorable terms, such as being lazy and stupid. When the members of the other group are perceived as relatively more successful, they tend to be devalued by being labeled as manipulative, exploitative, dishonest, and morally deficient. They are also perceived as using such characteristics to achieve their success at the expense of other members of the society. Hitler used such a devaluing process to create cultural hatred of the Jews by blaming them for the economic hard times in Germany.

Acceptance of Authority: Follow the Leader

People in those cultures or societies who are accustomed to being guided by political authorities have an especially difficult time acting on their own during hard economic times. A strong tendency to respect authority and certain cultural values (e.g., a male-dominated society) and child-rearing practices (e.g., harsh punishment and unquestioning obedience to male authority) that foster such respect to authority make accepting authority in times of difficulty much more likely (Altemeyer, 1988; Pecjak, 1993). Thus, when political leaders propose that the solution to such economic difficulties is the punishment of a certain group of people, those cultures in which there is a tradition of accepting authority will be much more likely to accept this as a solution to their problems. A good example of such a tendency is the ethnic/religious violence that has occurred in the former Yugoslavia (Pecjak, 1993; Puhar, 1993).

A Lack of Tolerance for Diversity: The Rejection of Those Who Are Different

Within any particular society, there are differences in the attitudes, values, and characteristics among people. While such diversity within a society has tremendous value, it is also difficult to maintain. The extent to which a society is able to accept and support such diversity in the media, court system, and economy will determine the extent to which differences among the groups can be worked out. Support of such cultural diversity makes it more likely that people will speak out against injustices aimed at any particular group within the society. In societies where cultural diversity is minimized or not tolerated, the tendency to be willing to direct violence against a particular group of people becomes much more likely.

Enhanced Group Self-Concept: Increases in "We-ness"

In addition to an individual's sense of his or her self-concept (e.g., your name, what you do), people also tend to define themselves by group membership (e.g., religious, ethnic, and/or social membership). In times of difficulty, people tend to turn to other group members for support. The seeking of such support tends to increase a person's sense of identification to the group. The strengthening of group identification tends to facilitate the devaluing process between groups and decrease a tolerance for cultural diversity. In turn, both of these conditions are likely to foster collective violence against other groups.

Ideological Choices: What Do You Want?

One effect of culture is to influence the ideology of the people. One very common ideology is the "better world" ideology. It goes without saying that most people, cultural groups, and societies want things to be better. However, more destructive cultural ideologies include the "superiority" ideology, which was highly characteristic of Nazi Germany, and the "ethnic cleansing" ideology, which has occurred in the former Yugoslavia. Such destructive ideologies create an increased sense of nationalism and patriotism that promote an exaggerated sense of group self-concept and a lack of tolerance for diversity, which, in turn, facilitate the devaluing process and collective violence against other groups of people.

These are some of the cultural-societal conditions that promote genocidal violence. With this information in mind, as you begin to read the newspaper, watch televised news, and/or simply observe the conditions in your own culture, you can see the extent to which such seeds of collective violence are present. Now that you know something about the seeds of cultural-societal violence, the discussion turns to what can be done about it.

Strategies for Controlling Collective Violence: Turning the Tide on Cultural-Societal Violence

To be realistic, the solutions to reducing cultural-societal violence are neither simple nor easy. But this does not mean we should simply give up. In this section, you will consider some possible solutions to curbing cultural-societal violence (Osofsky, 1995; Staub, 1996, in press). Some of these solutions include overcoming devaluation, opposing destructive group actions, improving the conditions of parents' lives, creating caring schools, limiting weapons of destruction, and acting against violence.

Overcome Devaluation: Collaborative Contact

One step toward reducing collective violence between groups is to overcome the process of devaluation by promoting the value of all cultures. This can be done through educational processes that make people more aware of the beliefs, values, and customs of different cultural groups. Beyond just educational efforts, overcoming the devaluation process involves meaningful experiential learning through direct contact with people from different cultural groups. This contact can occur through participation on athletic teams, cooperative education programs among school districts, collaboration while addressing community problems, joint-venture business projects, and intensive cultural exchange programs. The point is, the more we know about others through greater contact with them, the less likely we are to devalue them.

Oppose Destructive Group Actions: Taking a Stand

Whether it is within their society or peer group, people need to practice critical loyalty by questioning the practices of those groups to which they belong. Critical loyalty is enhanced if people believe their words and actions will make a difference. The foundation of such a sense of empowerment is laid in the home. Young children should be given responsibilities at home so that they can begin to see that their actions have consequences. At school, children should be given the opportunity to develop certain rules for the purpose of governing their own behavior and that of their peers. The extent to which children learn at a young age that they can be instrumental in their life determines the extent to which they will engage in

independent judgments as adults and avoid the surrender of their decision-making responsibilities to those in authority.

Improve the Conditions of Parents' Lives: Provide Help at Home

It is difficult for parents to teach their children to be accepting of others when they are concentrating on more day-to-day issues of economic survival. To this end, educational, community, religious, and governmental agencies will need to help people improve the quality of their everyday lives by providing educational and occupational training opportunities to those who need it and the necessary supporting resources, such as student loans, child-care services, and transportation. Parenting skills classes can help to teach parents the skills necessary to instill in their children empowerment, esteem, social skills, and a tolerance for others while avoiding the patterns of harsh discipline that tend to foster uncritical acceptance of authority.

Create Caring Schools: Teaching Tolerance

Since schools provide probably the biggest opportunity for children to interact with others from different cultural groups, it is very important that schools be involved in the process of reducing cultural-societal violence. Teachers, along with parents, can help to develop a tolerance for cultural diversity by developing educational plans that accent different cultures and societies. Teachers can develop cooperative and collaborative strategies involving children learning from and caring for each other. Social skills and conflict mediation classes should also be made part of the educational program throughout all grades.

Limit Weapons of Destruction: Get Fired Up about Firearms

Since guns are a critical aggressive cue, as well as a major source of much community and cultural violence, parents should be educated regarding the danger of firearms and their responsible use. Parents should take the responsibility for the presence of any firearms in the home. Parents and other community officials should work with local law enforcement agencies to regulate the presence of firearms in their community. Finally, adults should vote for elected

Participating in such programs as Model United Nations can help to teach children to be aware of, sensitive to, and tolerant of cultural and ethnic diversity, which can be the first steps toward reducing collective violence.

officials who have demonstrated a tendency to minimize the use of military weapons as the principal solution to cultural and political problems.

Act Against Violence: Get Involved

Collective violence is made possible by the inactivity and uninvolvement of people in the community, culture, and society. Everyone must become involved to stop violence against others—and we must do so early, when nonviolent solutions might still be effective. This includes not only working in your own community to promote the acceptance of diversity (e.g., teaching your children conflict resolution skills) but also getting involved in the search for nonviolent solutions to conflicts in other parts of the world. This can be done by joining organizations such as "Students for World Peace" on your campus, donating your time and money to national and international organizations (e.g., Amnesty International: call 1-800-266-3789) that promote world peace, and voting for elected officials who are judicious in their use of violent solutions to solve local, national, and international conflicts. You can make a difference.

This ends the discussion of the causes and strategies for controlling cultural-societal violence and aggression. If you would like to read more on this issue, consider any of these sources: *The Roots of Evil: The Origins of Genocide and Other Group Violence* (Staub, 1989); "The Origins of Caring, Helping and Nonaggression: Parental Socialization, the Family System, and Cultural Influences" (Staub, 1992); and "Chronic Community Violence: What Is Happening to Our Children?" (Osofsky, Wewers, Hann, & Fick, 1993). These three sources present insightful information on the nature, consequences, and control of violence and aggression at the community and cultural-societal level.

The discussion of aggression as an interpersonal process of personality is now complete. In addition to the Berkowitz (1993) and Baron and Richardson (1994) sources noted previously, if you would like to read more about aggression, the author recommends the following sources: *Aggression and Violence: Social Interactionist Perspectives* (Felson & Tedeschi, 1993) and *Human Aggression* (Geen, 1991). These sources provide a very thorough survey of contemporary research on aggression, including many of the topics presented in this chapter.

Chapter Summary: Reexamining the Highlights

▲ *Aggression as an Interpersonal Personality Process.* Aggression is considered an interpersonal process of personality because its expression and effect involve the interaction of people.

▲ *Aggression Defined.* Aggression is any expression of interpersonal behavior that involves the intent to do harm to another individual or group of people who are motivated to avoid it. A distinction is also made between hostile aggression and instrumental aggression.

▲ *Theoretical Perspectives on Aggression*
  —*Instinct Perspective.* The instinct perspective on aggression assumes aggression is an innate tendency. The instinct perspective on aggression includes the psychoanalytical, ethological, and sociobiology viewpoints.
  —*Biological Perspective.* The biological perspective assumes that certain biological processes within

the individual contribute to aggressive behaviors. Three of these biological processes include certain brain structures, hormonal influences, and genetic transmission.

—*The Social Learning Viewpoint.* The social learning viewpoint assumes that aggression is acquired through certain principles of learning. Two principles of learning that play an important part are reinforcement and social modeling.

▲ *Personal Determinants of Aggression.* Personal determinants of aggression are internal emotional states that increase the possibility of people engaging in aggressive behavior. Three such emotional states include heightened arousal, frustration, and intoxication.

▲ *The Application of Personality Psychology*

—*Assessing the Effect of Media Violence.* A principal effect of media violence is the modeling of aggressive behavior. Extended exposure to such media violence is associated with increases in both short-term and long-term aggressive behavior, feelings of emotional indifference to violence, and an exaggerated perception of violence in everyday life.

—*Strategies for the Prevention and Control of Aggression.* The complexity of aggressive behavior requires a variety of approaches and techniques for its prevention and control.

—*Punishment.* For punishment to be effective in the prevention and control of aggression, the individual's level of anger must be low to moderate, the aggressive behavior must not be associated with a reward, and the delivery of the punishment must be swift, severe, and certain. The limiting presence of these conditions in real life restricts the effectiveness of punishment to prevent and control aggression.

—*Catharsis.* According to the process of catharsis, aggressive behavior is believed to be reduced through the discharging of anger when engaging in nonaggressive activities. The evidence supporting the process of catharsis is mixed.

—*Cognitive Strategies.* Aggression can be controlled by adding alternative sources of information to help lessen the individual's feelings of anger. Such information can include providing explanations for behavior that might have produced feelings of anger in others and cognitive training

to help people rethink anger-provoking situations as less threatening.

—*Modeling Nonaggressiveness.* Teaching alternatives to aggressive behavior through the use of models who demonstrate nonaggressive behavior seems to be a promising approach to the prevention and control of aggression. Such an approach has proven to be successful with a variety of populations, including parents and police officers.

—*Social Skills Training.* People who frequently engage in aggressive behavior seem to lack social skills. To offset this deficiency, social skills training programs help teach such people how to deal more effectively and less aggressively with others by developing nonaggressive strategies of conflict resolution and by building empathy with and sensitivity to others.

▲ *Cultural-Societal Roots of Violence*

—*Causes of Collective Violence.* Genocidal violence is the massive killing of an entire group of people. Some causes of genocidal violence include difficult economic conditions, devaluation of others, acceptance of authority, a lack of tolerance for diversity, enhanced group self-concept, and ideological choices.

—*Strategies for Controlling Collective Violence.* Strategies for controlling cultural-societal violence include overcoming devaluation, opposing destructive group actions, improving the conditions of parents' lives, creating caring schools, limiting weapons of destruction, and acting against violence.

Glossary

aggression   Any form of behavior designed to harm another.

aggressive cue   Any object that is associated with aggression.

alcohol myopia   The tendency for an intoxicated state to restrict an individual's ability to assess alternatives.

catharsis hypothesis   The theoretical assertion that releasing anger through nonharmful methods reduces aggressive tendencies.

causal accounts   An explanation offered to others for the purpose of reducing their feelings of anger and aggressive behavior.

death instinct   A psychoanalytical concept that describes the tendency for people to seek a tension-free state.

ethology   The study of animal behavior in its natural habitat.

fighting instinct   The innate tendency for organisms to release aggressive impulses.

frustration-aggression hypothesis   The theoretical assertion that a major cause of aggression is the frustration of an individual.

genocidal violence   The mass killing of an entire group of people.

hostile aggression   Acts of aggression in response to anger and with the intention of inflicting harm.

instrumental aggression   Acts of aggression performed to achieve a specific objective.

interpersonal personality process   A dimension of personality that influences how you interact with others.

limbic system   A brain structure involved in the expression of emotion.

lobotomy   A surgical procedure that severs neurological tissue for the purpose of controlling extreme emotional behavior.

sadomasochists   People who receive sexual pleasure from having pain inflicted upon them.

social modeling   The acquisition of new behaviors by observing them being performed by others.

sociobiology   The study of the biological bases of social behavior.

testosterone   A hormone associated with a variety of masculine physical characteristics and behaviors.

XYY syndrome   The tendency for males born with an extra Y chromosome to possess certain physical, cognitive, and behavioral characteristics.

REFERENCES

Chapter 1

Allport, G. W. (1961). *Pattern and growth in personality*. New York: Holt, Rinehart & Winston.

Allport, G. W. (1937). *Personality: A psychological interpretation*. New York: Henry Holt.

American Psychological Association (1977). *Standard for providers of psychological services*. Washington, DC: Author.

American Psychological Association (1981a). Ethical principles of psychologists. *American Psychologist, 36*, 633–638.

American Psychological Association (1981b). Specialty guidelines for the delivery of services. *American Psychologist, 36*, 639–685.

American Psychological Association (1982). *Ethical principles in the conduct of research with human participants*. Washington, DC: Author.

American Psychological Association (1990). Ethical principles of psychologists (Amended June 2, 1989). *American Psychologist, 45*, 390–395.

American Psychological Association (1992a). APA continues to refine its ethics code. *The APA Monitor, 23*, 38–42.

American Psychological Association (1992b). Ethical principles of psychologists and code of conduct. *American Psychologist, 47*, 1597–1611.

Baumrind, D. (1971). Current patterns of parental authority. *Developmental Psychology Monographs, 80*, (1, Pt.2) 1–103.

Bond, R., & Smith, P. B. (1996). Culture and conformity: A meta-analysis of studies using Asch's (1952b, 1956) line judgment task. *Psychological Bulletin, 119*, 111–137.

Byrne, D., & Kelley, K. (1981). *An introduction to personality* (3rd ed.). Englewood Cliffs, NJ: Prentice Hall.

Blanck, P. D., Bellack, A. S., Rosnow, R. L., Rotheram-Borus, M. J., & Schooler, M. J. (1992). Scientific rewards and conflicts of ethical choices in human subjects research. *American Psychologist, 47*, 959–965.

Carducci, B. J., & Applegeet, C. J. (1984, March). *Personality and occupational correlates of nursing burnout*. Paper presented at the meeting of the Southeastern Psychological Association, New Orleans.

Carlson, R. (1971). Where is the person in personality research? *Psychological Bulletin, 75*, 203–219. (Mischel, 1986, 531)

Carlson, R. (1984). What's social about social psychology? Where's the person in personality research? *Journal of Personality and Social Psychology, 47*, 1304–1309.

Carsrud, A. L., Olm, K. W., & Thomas, J. B. (1984). Small business productivity: Relationship of owner's personality to organizational success. In M. Wortman (Ed.), *Proceedings of the 29th World Conference, International Council on Small Business*.

Cattell, R. B. (1950). *Personality: A systematic, theoretical, and facutal study*. New York: McGraw-Hill.

Collister, T. D., & Straatmeyer, A. J. (1983, August). *Relationship of MMPI scores to pilot error in aviation*. Paper presented at the meeting of the American Psychological Association, Anaheim, CA.

Comer, R. J. (1992). *Abnormal psychology*. New York: W. H. Freeman.

Comer, R. J. (1995). *Abnormal psychology* (2nd ed.). New York: W. H. Freeman.

Cook, T., et al. (1992). *Meta-analysis for explanation: A casebook*. New York: Russell Sage Foundation.

Coopersmith, S. (1967). *Antecedents of self-esteem*. San Francisco: Freeman.

Darbonne, A. R. (1969). Suicide and age: A suicide note analysis. *Journal of Consulting and Clinical Psychology, 33*, 46–50.

Derby, T., Cozby, P. C. (1983, August). *Predicting effective human-computer interaction using personality and cognitive variables*. Paper presented at the meeting of the American Psychological Association, Anaheim, CA.

Eagly, A. H., & Steffen, V. J. (1986). Gender and aggressive behavior: A meta-analytic review of the social psychological literature. *Psychological Bulletin, 100*, 309–330.

Elms, A. C. (1976). *Personality and politics*. New York: Harcourt Brace Jovanovich.

Elms, A. C. (1994). *Uncovering lives: The uneasy alliance of biography and psychology*. New York: Oxford University Press.

Funder, D. C., Parke, R. D., Tomlinson-Keasey, C., & Widaman, K. (Eds.). (1993). *Studying lives through time: Personality and development*. Washington, DC: American Psychological Association.

Grimm, L. G., & Yarnold, P. R. (Eds.). (1995). *Reading and understanding multivariate statistics*. Washington, DC: American Psychological Association.

Gross, R. T., & Duke, P. (1980). The effect of early versus late physical maturation on adolescent behavior. In I. Litt (Ed.), *Symposium on adolescent medicine: The pediatric clinics of North America, 27*, 71–78.

Guilford, J. P. (1959). *Personality*. New York: McGraw-Hill.

Hall, C. S., & Lindzey, G. (1978). *Theories of personality* (3rd ed.). New York: John Wiley & Sons.

Hansen, C. P. (1991). Personality characteristics of the accident-involved employee. In J. W. Jones, B. D. Steffy, & D. W. Bray (Eds.), *Applying psychology in business: The handbook for managers and human resource professionals* (pp. 801–812). Lexington, MA: Lexington Books.

Helmreich, R. L., & Spence J. T. (1978). The work and family orientation questionnaire: An objective instrument to assess components of achievement motivation and attitudes toward family and career. *JSAS: Catalog of Selected Documents in Psychology, 8*, 35. (Ms. No. 1677)

Jones, J. W. (1981). Attitudinal correlates of employee theft of drugs and hospital supplies among nursing personnel. *Nursing Research, 30*, 349–351.

Jones, J. W., & Terris, W. (1991). Personnel selection to control employee theft and counterproductivity. In J. W. Jones, B. D. Steffy, & D. W. Bray (Eds.), *Applying psychology in business: The handbook for managers and human resource professionals* (pp. 851–861). Lexington, MA: Lexington Books.

Jones, J. W., & Terris W. (1982). Predicting employees' theft in home improvement centers. *Psychological Reports, 52*, 187–201.

Jones, J. W., & Wuebker, L. (1984, April). *Development and validation of the Safety Locus of Control (SLC) Scale*. Paper presented at the American Industrial Hygiene Association Research Conference, Upper Midwest Section, Roseville, MN.

Jones, J. W., Wuebker, L., & Dubois, D. (1984). *The Safety Locus of Control SLC) Scale: A validation study*. Paper presented at the meeting of the American Industrial Hygiene Association Research Conference, Upper Midwest Section, Roseville, MN.

Jones, M. C. (1957). The later careers of boys who were early- or late-maturing. *Child Development, 28*, 113–128.

Jones, M. C. (1965). Psychological correlates of somatic development. *Child Development, 36*, 899–911.

Jones, M. C., & Bayley, N. (1950). Physical maturing among boys as related to behavior. *Journal of Education Psychology, 41*, 129–148.

Kendall, P. C., & Norton-Ford. J. D. (1982). *Clinical psychology: Scientific and professional dimensions*. New York: John Wiley & Sons.

Leenaars, A. A. (1989). *Suicide notes: Predictive clues and patterns*. New York: Human Sciences.

Levy, L. H. (1970). *Conceptions of personality*. New York: Random House.

Matthews, K. A., & Glass, D. C. (1981). Type A behavior, stressful life events, and coronary heart disease. In B. S. Dohrenwend & B. P. Dohrenwend (Eds.), *Stressful life events and their context* (pp. 167–185). New York: Prodist.

Mazlish, B. (1973). *In search of Nixon*. Baltimore: Penguin Books.

McClelland, D. C. (1951). *Personality*. New York: Dryden Press.

Mischel, W. (1986). *Introduction to personality* (4th ed.). New York: Holt, Rinehart & Winston.

Mussen, P. H., & Jones, M. C. (1957). Self-conceptions, motivations, and interpersonal attitudes of late and early maturing boys. *Child Development, 28*, 243–258.

Papalia, D. E., & Olds, S. W. (1992). *Human development* (5th ed.). New York: McGraw-Hill.

Pervin, L. A. (1990). *Handbook of personality: Theory and research*. New York: Guilford.

Pervin, L. A. (1989). *Personality: Theory and research* (5th ed.). New York: John Wiley & Sons.

Phares, E. J. (1984). *Clinical psychology: Concepts, methods, and professions* (Rev. ed.). Homewood, IL: Dorsey Press.

Rogers, R. W. (1980). *Subjects' reactions to experimental deception*. Unpublished manuscript. University of Alabama.

Rosenthal, R. (1966). *Experimenter effects in behavior research*. New York: Appleton-Century-Crofts.

Rosenthal, R. (1969). Interpersonal expectations: Effects of the experimenter's hypothesis. In R. Rosenthal & R. L. Rosnow (Eds.), *Artifacts in behavioral research* (pp. 181–277). New York: Academic Press.

Smith, S., & Richardson, D. (1983). Amelioration of deception and harm in psychological research: The important role of debriefing. *Journal of Personality and Social Psychology, 44*, 1075–1082.

Taylor, S. E. (1991). *Health psychology* (2nd. ed.). New York: McGraw-Hill.

Terris, W., & Jones, J. W. (1980). Attitudinal and personality correlates of theft among supermarket employees. *Journal of Security Administration, 3*, 65–78.

Terris, W., & Jones, J. W. (1982). *Pre-employment screening to reduce employee theft in department stores: Three separate studies*. Park Ridge, IL: London House Press.

Tuckman, J., Kleiner, R., & Lavell, M. (1959). Emotional content of suicide notes. *American Journal of Psychiatry, 116*, 59–63.

Wong, A., & Carducci, B. J. (1991). Sensation seeking and financial risk taking in everyday matters. *Journal of Business and Psychology, 5*, 525–530.

Wrightsman, L. S. (1991). *Psychology and the legal system* (2nd ed.). Pacific Grove, CA: Brooks/Cole.

Chapter 2

Adler, T. (1993, January). Separate gender norms on tests raise questions. *APA Monitor, 24*, 6.

Adorno, T. W., Frenkel-Brunswick, E. Levinson, D. J. Sanford, R. N. (1950). *The authoritarian personality*. New York: Harper & Row, 1950.

American Psychological Association (1981). Ethical principles of psychologists. *American Psychologist, 36*, 633–638.

American Psychological Association (1990). Ethical principles of psychologists (Amended June 2, 1989). *American Psychologist, 45*, 390–395.

American Psychological Association (1992). APA continues to refine its ethics code. *The APA Monitor, 23*, 38–42.

Anastasi, A. (1988). *Psychological testing* (6th ed.). New York: Macmillan.

Association of Personnel Test Publishers (1989). *Model guidelines for preemployment integrity testing programs*. Washington, DC: Author.

Bashore, T. R., & Rapp, P. E. (1993). Are there alternatives to traditional polygraph procedures? *Psychological Bulletin, 113*, 3–22.

Briggs, S. R. (1991). Personality measurement. In V. J. Derlega, B. A. Winstead, & W. H. Jones (Eds.), *Personality: Contemporary theory and research* (pp. 15–53). Chicago: Nelson-Hall.

Bronfenbrenner, U., & Ceci, S. J. (1994). Nature-nurture reconceptualized in developmental perspective: A bioecological model. *Psychological Review, 101*, 568–586.

Burns, R. C. (1987). *Kinetic-House-Tree-Person (K-H-T-P)*. New York: Brunner/Mazel.

Butcher, J. N., Dahlstrom, W. G., Graham, J. R., Tellegen, A., & Kaemmer, B. (1989). *Minnesota Multiphasic Personality Inventory-2 (MMPI-2): Manual for administration and scoring*. Minneapolis: University of Minnesota Press.

Butcher, J. N. (1990). *Assessing patients in psychotherapy: Use of the MMPI-2 for treatment planning*. New York: Oxford University Press.

Cacioppo, J. T., & Berntson, G. G. (1992). Social psychological contributions to the decade of the brain: Doctrine of multilevel analysis. *American Psychologist, 47*, 1019–1028.

Carducci, B. J., & Webber, A. W. (1979). Shyness as a determinant of interpersonal distance. *Psychological Reports, 44*, 1075–1078.

Cash, T. F., & Pruzinsky, T. (Eds.) (1991). *Body images: Development, deviance, and change*. New York: Guilford.

Comer, R. J. (1992). *Abnormal psychology*. New York: W. H. Freeman.

Cronbach, L. J., & Meehl, P. E. (1955). Construct validity in psychological tests. *Psychological Bulletin, 52*, 281–302.

Dahlstrom, W. G., & Welsh, G. S. (1960). *An MMPI handbook: A guide to use in clinical practice and research*. Minneapolis: University of Minnesota Press.

Dahlstrom, W. G., Welsh, G. S., & Dahlstrom, L. E. (1972). *An MMPI handbook: Clinical interpretation* (Vol. 1). (Rev. ed.). Minneapolis: University of Minnesota Press.

Dahlstrom, W. G., Welsh, G. S., & Dahlstrom, L. E. (1975). *An MMPI handbook: Research Applications* (Vol. 2). (Rev. ed.). Minneapolis: University of Minnesota Press.

Depue, R. A., Luciana, M., Arbisi, P., Collins, P., & Leon, A. (1994). Dopamine and the structure of personality: Relation of agonist-induced dopamine activity to positive emotionality. *Journal of Personality and Social Psychology, 67*, 485–498.

Drumheller, P. M., Eicke, F. J., Scherer, R. F. (1991). Cognitive appraisal and coping of students varying in stress level during three stages of a college examination. *Journal of Social Behavior and Personality, 6*, 237–254.

Edwards, A. L. (1954). *Manual for the Edwards Personal Preference Schedule*. New York: Psychological Corporation.

Edwards, A. L. (1959). *Edwards Personal Preference Schedule*. New York: Psychological Corporation.

Frank, L. K. (1939). Projective methods for the study of personality. *Journal of Psychology, 8*, 389–413.

Gable, M., Topol, M. T. (1991). Machiavellian managers: Do they perform better? *Journal of Business and Psychology, 5*, 355–365.

Geer, J. H. (1965). The development of a scale to measure fear. *Behavior Research and Therapy, 3*, 45–53.

Gilbert, D. G., Gilbert, B. O., Johnson, S., & McColloch, M. A. (1991). Electrocortical and electrodermal activity differences between aggressive adolescents and controls. *Journal of Social Behavior and Personality, 6*, 403–410.

Girodo, M. (1991). Personality, job stress, and mental health in undercover agents. *Journal of Social Behavior and Personality, 6*, 375–390.

Gough, H. G. (1957). *California psychological inventory*. Palo Alto, CA: Consulting Psychologists Press.

Gough, H. (1987). *California Psychological Inventory: Administrator's guide*. Palo Alto, CA: Consulting Psychologists Press.

Grahman, J. R. (1990). *MMPI-2: Assessing personality and pathology*. New York: Oxford University Press.

Groth-Marnat, G. (1990). *Handbook of psychological assessment* (2nd. ed.). New York: John Wiley & Sons.

Hansen, C. P. (1991). Personality characteristics of the accident-involved employee. In J. W. Jones, B. D. Steffy, & D. W. Bray (Eds.), *Applying psychology in business: The handbook for managers and human resource professionals* (pp. 801–812). Lexington, MA: Lexington Books.

Hathaway, S. R., & Meehl, P. E. (1951). *An atlas for the clinical use of the MMPI*. Minneapolis: University of Minnesota Press.

Hathaway, S. R., & McKinley, J. C. (1940). A multiphasic personality schedule (Minnesota): I. Construction of the schedule. *Journal of Psychology, 10*, 249–254.

Hathaway, S. R., & McKinley, J. C. (1943). *Manual for the Minnesota multiphasic personality inventory*. New York: Psychological Corporation.

Heath, A. C., Cloninger, C. R., & Martin, N. G. (1994). Testing a model for the genetic structure of personality: A comparison of the personality systems of Cloninger and Eysenck. *Journal of Personality and Social Psychology, 66*, 762–775.

Hollon, S. D., & Kendall, P. C. (1980). Cognitive self-statements in depression: Development of an Automatic Thoughts Questionnaire. *Cognitive Therapy and Research, 4*, 383–395.

Holt, R. R. (1971). *Assessing personality*. New York: Harcourt Brace Jovanovich.

Jones, J. W., Ash, P., & Solo, C. (1990). Employment privacy rights and pre-employment honesty tests. *Employee Relations, 15*, 561–575.

Jones, J. W., & Terris, W. (1983). Predicting employees' theft in home improvement centers. *Psychological Reports, 52*, 187–201

Jones, J. W., & Terris, W. (1991). Personnel selection to control employee theft and counterproductivity. In J. W. Jones, B. D. Steffy, & D. W. Bray (Eds.), *Applying psychology in business: The handbook for managers and human resource professionals* (pp. 851–861). Lexington, MA: Lexington Books.

Jones, J. W., & Wuebker, L. (1984, April). *Development and validation of the Safety Locus of Control (SLC) Scale*. Paper presented at the American Industrial Hygiene Association Research Conference, Upper Midwest Section. Roseville, Minn.

Kaplan, R. M., & Sacuzzo, D. P. (1989). *Psychological testing: Principles, applications, and issues* (2nd. ed.), Belmont, CA: Wadsworth.

Kleinmuntz, B. (1982). *Personality and psychological assessment*. New York: St. Martin's Press.

Liebert, R. M., & Spiegler, M. D. (1987). *Personality: Strategies and issues* (5th ed.) Chicago: Dorsey.

Lindzey, G. (1961). *Projective techniques and cross-cultural research*. New York: Appleton-Century-Crofts.

Martin, R. A., & Lefcourt, H. M. (1984). Situational Humor Response Questionnaire: Quantitative measure of sense of humor. *Journal of Personality and Social Psychology, 47,* 145–155.

Matarazzo, J. D. (1986). Computerized clinical psychological test interpretations: Unvalidated plus all mean and no sigma. *American Psychologist, 41,* 14–24.

Matarazzo, J. D (1990). Psychological assessment versus psychological testing: Validation from Binet to the school, clinic, and court room. *American Psychologist, 45,* 999–1017.

Matarazzo, J. D. (1992). Psychological testing and assessment in the 21st century. *American Psychologist, 47,* 1007–1018.

Mehr, J. (1983). *Abnormal psychology*. New York: Holt, Rinehart & Winston.

Messick, S. (1995). Validity of psychological assessment: Validation of inferences from persons' responses and performances as scientific inquiry into score meaning. *American Psychologist, 50,* 741–749.

Meyer, R. G. (1992). *Abnormal behavior and the criminal justice system*. New York: Lexington Books.

Morgan, C. D., & Murray, H. A. (1935). A method for investigating fantasies. The Thematic Apperception Test. *Archives of Neurology and Psychiatry, 34,* 289–306.

Murray, H. A. (Ed.). (1938). *Explorations in personality*. New York: Oxford University Press.

Murray, H. A. (1943). *Thematic apperception test*. Cambridge, MA: Harvard University Press.

Myers, D. G. (1992). *The pursuit of happiness: Who is happy—and why*. New York: William Morrow.

Phares, E. J. (1984). *Clinical psychology: Concepts, methods, and profession* (Rev. ed.). Homewood, Ill.: Dorsey.

Pilkonis, P. A. (1977). The behavioral consequences of shyness. *Journal of Personality, 45,* 596–611.

Ozer, D. J., & Reise, S. P. (1994). Personality assessment. In L .W. Porter & M. R. Rosenzweig (Eds.), *Annual review of psychology. Vol. 45* (pp. 357–388). Palo Alto, CA: Annual Reviews Inc.

Riggio, R. E. (1990). *Introduction to industrial/organizational psychology*. Glenview, IL: Scott, Foresman/Little, Brown Higher Education.

Riordan, C. A., Johnson, G. D., & Thomas, J. S. (1991). Personality and stress at sea. *Journal of Social Behavior and Personality, 6,* 391–409.

Rorschach, H. (1942). *Psychodiagnostics*. Berne, Switzerland: Huber.

Rotter, J. B., & Rafferty, J. E. (1950). *Manual for the Rotter incomplete sentences blank, college form*. New York: Psychological Corporation.

Sherman, M. (1979). *Personality: Inquiry and application*. New York: Pergamon.

Sherry, P. (1991). Person-environment fit and accident prediction. *Journal of Business and Psychology, 5,* 411–416.

Slora, K. B., Joy, D. S., & Terris, W. (1991). Personnel selection to control employee violence. *Journal of Business and Psychology, 5,* 417–426.

Szondi, L. (1944). *Schicksalsanalyse*. Basel, Switzerland: Benno, Schwabe.

Terris, W., & Jones, J. W. (1985). Psychological factors related to employees' theft in the convenience store industry. In W. Terris (Ed.), *Employee theft: Research, theory, and applications* (pp. 25–47). Park Ridge, IL: London House Press.

Wolpe, J., & Lang, P. J. (1964). A fear survey schedule for use in behavior therapy. *Behavior Research and Therapy, 2,* 27–34.

Wrightsman, L. S. (1991). *Psychology and the legal system* (2nd. ed.). Pacific Grove, CA: Brooks/Cole.

Zimbardo, P. G. (1977). *Shyness: What it is, what to do about it*. Reading, Mass.: Addison-Wesley.

Zuckerman, M. (1994). *Behavioral expression and biosocial bases of sensation seeking*. New York: Cambridge University Press.

Zuckerman, M. (1995). Good and bad humors: Biochemical bases of personality and its disorders. *Psychological Science, 6,* 325–332.

Chapter 3

Ainsworth, M. D. S. (1979). Infant-mother attachment. *American Psychologist, 34,* 932–937.

Ainsworth, M. D. S., Blehar, M. C., Walters, E., & Wall, S. (1978). *Patterns of attachment: A psychological study of the strange situation*. Hillsdale, NJ: Erlbaum.

Anastasi, A. (1988). *Psychological testing* (6th ed.). New York: Macmillan.

Anooshian, L. J., & Seibert, P. S. (1996). Conscious and unconscious retrieval in picture recognition: A framework for exploring gender differences. *Journal of Personality and Social Psychology, 70,* 637–645.

Arlow, J. A. (1995). Psychoanalysis. In R. J. Corsini & D. Wedding (Eds.), *Current psychotherapies* (5th ed.) (pp. 15–50). Itasca, IL: F. E. Peacock Publishers.

Benjamin, L. T., Jr., & Dixon, D. N. (1996). Dream analysis by mail: An American woman seeks Freud's advice. *American Psychologist, 51,* 461–468.

Bibring, E. (1954). Psychoanalysis and the dynamic psychotherapies. *Journal of the American Psychoanalytic Association, 2,* 745–770.

Blum, G. S. (1949). A study of the psychoanalytic theory of psychosexual development. *Genetic Psychology Monograph, 39,* 3–99.

Blum, G. S. (1950). *The Blackey Pictures and manual*. New York: Psychological Corporation.

Blum, G. S. (1968). Assessment of psychodynamic variables by the Blacky Pictures. In P. McReynolds (Ed.), *Advances in psychological assessment: Vol. 1,* (pp. 150–168). Palo Alto, CA: Science and Behavior Books, Inc.

Bowlby, J. (1982). Attachment and loss: Retrospect and prospect. *American Journal of Orthopsychiatry, 52*, 664–678.

Brenner, C. (1955). *An elementary textbook of psychoanalysis*. New York: International Universities Press.

Bretherton, I. (1985). Attachment theory: Retrospect and prospect. In I. Bretherton & E. Waters (Eds.), Growing points of attachment theory and research. *Monographs of the Society for Research in Child Development, 50*(1–2, Serial No. 209), 3–35.

Breuer. J. B., & Freud, S. (1955). Studies in hysteria. In *Standard edition*. Vol. 2. London: Hogarth Press. (Original work published in 1895)

Cashden, S. (1988). *Object relations theory: Using the relationship*. New York: Norton.

Crits-Christoph, P. (1992). The efficacy of brief dynamic psychotherapy: A meta-analysis. *The American Journal of Psychiatry, 149*, 151–158.

Cross, D. G., Sheehan, P. W., & Khan, J. A. (1982). Short and long term follow-up of clients receiving insight oriented therapy and behavior therapy. *Journal of Consulting and Clinical Psychology, 50*, 103–112.

DeFleur, M. L., & Petranoff, R. M. (1959). A television test of subliminal persuasion. *Public Opinion Quarterly, 23*, 170–180.

Dichter, E. (1949). A psychological view of advertising effectiveness. *Journal of Marketing, 14*, 61–66.

Dichter, E. (1960). *The strategy of desire*. Garden City, NJ: Doubleday.

Dichter, E. (1964). *Handbook of consumer motivations*. New York: McGraw-Hill.

Dixon, N. F. (1971). *Subliminal perception: The nature of a controversy*. London: McGraw-Hill.

Dixon, N. F. (1981). *Preconscious processing*. Chichester, England: Wiley.

Erdberg, P., & Exner, J. E., Jr. (1984). Rorschach assessment. In G. Goldstein & M. Hersen (Eds.), *Handbook of psychological assessment* (pp. 332–347). New York: Pergamon.

Erdelyi, M. H. (1985). *Psychoanalysis: Freud's cognitive psychology*. New York: W. H. Freeman.

Exner, J. E., Jr. (1978). *The Rorschach: A comprehensive system, Volume 2. Current research and advance interpretation*. New York: Wiley.

Exner, J. E., Jr. (1986). *The Rorschach: A comprehensive system, Volume 1. Basic foundations* (2nd ed.). New York: Wiley.

Exner, J. E., Jr., & Weiner, I. B. (1982). *The Rorschach: A comprehensive system, Volume 3. Assessment of children and adolescents*. New York: Wiley.

Eysenck, H. J. (1978). An exercise in megasilliness. *American Psychologist, 33*, 517.

Foxall, G. R., & Goldsmith, R. E. (1988). Personality and consumer research: Another look. *Journal of the Market Research Society, 30*, 111–125.

Freud, S. (1953). The interpretation of dreams. In *Standard edition*. Vols. 4 and 5. London: Hogarth Press. (Original work published in 1900)

Freud, S. (1953). Three essays on the theory of sexuality. In *Standard edition*. Vol. 7. London: Hogarth Press. (Original work published in 1905)

Freud, S. (1955). Beyond the pleasure principle. In *Standard edition*. Vol. 18. London: Hogarth Press. (Original work published in 1920)

Freud, S. (1957a). On narcissism. In *Standard edition*. Vol. 14. London: Hogarth Press. (Original work published in 1914)

Freud, S. (1957b). On the history of the psychoanalytic movement. In *Standard edition*. Vol. 14. London: Hogarth Press. (Original work published in 1914)

Freud, S. (1957). Instincts and their vicissitudes. In *Standard edition*. Vol 14. London: Hogarth Press. (Original work published in 1915)

Freud, S. (1959). Inhibitions, symptoms, and anxiety. In *Standard edition*. Vol 20. London: Hogarth Press. (Original work published in 1926)

Freud, S. (1960). Psychopathology of everyday life. In *Standard edition*. Vol. 6. London: Hogarth Press. (Original work published in 1901)

Freud, S. (1960). Jokes and their relation to the unconscious. In *Standard edition*. Vol. 8. London: Hogarth Press. (Original work published in 1905)

Freud, S. (1961). The ego and the id. In *Standard edition*. Vol. 19. London: Hogarth Press. (Original work published in 1923)

Gallo, P. S. (1978). Meta-analysis—A mixed meta-phor? *American Psychologist, 33*, 515–517.

Garchik, L. (1996, April 1). Personals: Madison Avenue is a place where dreams come true. *The Courier-Journal*, D-4.

Gray-Little, B. (1995). The assessment of psychopathology in racial and ethnic minorities. In J. N. Butcher (Ed.), *Clinical personality assessment* (pp. 140–157). New York: Oxford University Press.

Greenwald, A. G., Spangenberg, E. R., Pratkanis, A. R., & Eskenasi, J. (1991). Double-blind test of subliminal self-help audiotapes. *Psychological Science, 2*, 119–122.

Hall, C. S. (1954). *A primer of Freudian psychology*. Cleveland, OH: World Publishing Company.

Hall, C. S., & Lindzey, G. (1978). *Theories of personality* (3rd ed.). New York: John Wiley & Sons.

Heart, S. H., & McDaniel, S. W. (1982). Subliminal stimulation: Marketing applications. In J. U. McNeal & S. W. McDaniel (Eds.), *Consumer's behavior: Classical and contemporary dimensions* (pp. 165–175). Boston: Little, Brown. (Harrell's *Consumer Behavior*, 1986, p. 97)

Hedegard, S. (1969). *A molecular analysis of psychological defenses*. Unpublished doctoral dissertation, University of Michigan.

Henry, W. P., Strupp, H. H., Schacht, T. E., & Gaston, L. (1994). Psychodynamic approaches. In A. E. Bergin & S. L. Garfield (Eds.), *Handbook of psychotherapy and behavior change* (4th ed.) (pp. 467–508). New York: John Wiley & Sons.

Holmes, D. S. (1974). Investigations of repression: Differential recall of material experimentally or naturally associated with ego threat. *Psychological Bulletin, 81*, 632–653.

Jahoda, M. (1977). *Freud and the dilemmas of psychology*. London: Hogarth Press.

Jones, E. (1953, 1955, 1957). *The life and work of Sigmund Freud* (Vols. 1–3). New York: Basic Books.

Kazdin, A. E. (1982). Symptom substitution, generalization, and response covariantion: Implications for psychotherapy outcome. *Psychological Bulletin, 91*, 349–365.

Kernberg, O. (1984). *Severe personality disorder*. New Haven: Yale University Press.

Kihlstrom, J. F. (1990). The psychological unconscious. In L. A. Pervin (Ed.), *Handbook of personality: Theory and research* (pp. 445–464). New York: Guilford.

Kimeldorf, C., & Geiwitz, P. J. (1966). Smoking and the Blacky orality factors. *Journal of Projective Techniques, 30*, 167–168.

Kotler, P. , & Armstrong, G. (1994). *Principles of marketing* (6th ed.). Englewood Cliffs, NJ: Prentice Hall.

Klein, D. (1980). Psychosocial treatment of schizophrenia or psychosocial help for people with schizophrenia? *Schizophrenia Bulletin, 6*, 122–130.

Klein, M. (1937). *The psycho-analysis of children* (2nd ed.). London: Hogarth Press.

Klein, M. (1948). *Contributions to psycho-analysis, 1921–1945*. London: Hogarth Press.

Klopfer, B., & Davidson, H. H. (1962). *The Rorschach technique: An introductory manual*. New York: Harcourt, Brace & World.

Kohut, H. (1971). *The analysis of the self*. New York: International University Press.

Kohut, H. (1977). *The restoration of the self*. New York: International University Press.

Kohut, H. (1984). *How does analysis cure?* Chicago: University of Chicago Press.

Kotler, P., & Armstrong, G. (1994). *Principles of marketing* (6th ed.). Englewood Cliffs, NJ: Prentice Hall.

Kunst-Wilson, W., & Zajonc, R. (1980). Affective discrimination of stimuli that cannot be recognized. *Science, 207*, 557–558.

Luborsky, L., & Spence, D. P. (1978). Quantitative research on psychoanalytic therapy. In S. L. Garfield & A. E. Bergin (Eds), *Handbook of psychotherapy and behavior change: An empirical analysis* (2nd ed.) (pp. 331–368). New York: Wiley.

Mahler, M. S. (1968). *On human symbiosis and the vicissitudes of individuation: Infantile psychosis*. New York: International Universities.

Mahler, M., Pine, F., & Bergman, A. (1975). *The psychological birth of the human infant: Symbiosis and individuation*. New York: Basic Books.

McConnell, J. V., Cutler, R. L., & McNeil, E. B. (1958). Subliminal stimulation: An overview. *American Psychologist, 13*, 229–242.

McCullough, L., Winston, A., Farber, B. A., Porter, F., Pollack, J., Laikin, M., Vigiano, W., & Trujillo, M. (1991). The relationship of patient-therapist interaction to outcome in brief psychotherapy. *Psychotherapy, 28*, 525–533.

Moore, T. E. (1982). Subliminal advertising: What you see is what you get. *Journal of Marketing, 46*, 38–47.

Morf, C. C., & Rhodewalt, F. (1993). Narcissism and self-evaluation maintenance: Explorations in object relations. *Personality and Social Psychology Bulletin, 19*, 668–676.

Mosher, L. R., & Keith, S. J. (1979). Research on the psychosocial treatment of schizophrenia. *American Journal of Psychiatry, 136*, 623–631.

Murphy, K. R., Davidshofer, C. O. (1994). *Psychological testing: Principles and applications* (3rd ed.). Englewood Cliffs, NJ: Prentice Hall.

Packard, V. (1957). *The hidden persuaders*. New York: Pocket Books.

Perry, J. C., & Cooper, S. H. (1986). A preliminary report on defenses and conflicts associated with borderline personality disorder. *Journal of the American Psychoanalytic Association, 34*, 863–893.

Perry, J. C., & Cooper, S. H. (1989). An empirical study of defense mechanisms: I. Clinical interview and life vignette ratings. *Archives of General Psychiatry, 46*, 444–460.

Piper, W. E., Azim, F. A., Joyce, S. A., & McCallum, M. (1991). Transference interpretations, therapeutic alliance and outcome in short-term individual psychotherapy. *Archives of General Psychiatry, 48*, 946–953.

Porter, F. A. (1987). *The immediate effects of interpretation on patient response in short-term dynamic psychotherapy*. Unpublished doctoral dissertation, Columbia University, New York.

Ricks, M. H. (1985). The social transmission of parental behavior: Attachment across generations. In I. Bretherton & E. Waters (Eds.), Growing points of attachment theory and research. *Monographs of the Society for Research in Child Development, 50*(1–2, Serial No. 209), 211–227.

Rorschach, H. (1942). *Psychodiagnostics: A diagnostic test based on perception* (P. Lemkau & B. Kronenberg, Trans.). Berne, Switzerland: Huber (1st German ed. published 1921; U.S. distributor, Grune & Stratton).

Runyon, K. E. (1980). *Consumer behavior and the practice of marketing* (2nd ed.). Columbus, OH: Merrill.

Rychlak, J. F. (1981). *Introduction to personality and psychotherapy: A theory-construction approach* (2nd ed.). Boston: Houghton Mifflin.

Schiffman, L. G., & Kanuk, L. L. (1987). *Consumer behavior.* (3rd ed.). Englewood Cliffs, NJ: Prentice Hall.

Schoell, W. F., & Guiltinan, J. P. (1995). *Marketing: Contemporary concepts and practices* (6th ed.). Englewood Cliffs, NJ: Prentice Hall.

Schwartz, S. (in press). *Abnormal psychology*. Mountain View, CA: Mayfield.

Silverman, L. H. (1976). Psychoanalytic theory: "The reports of my death are greatly exaggerated." *American Psychologist, 31*, 621–637.

Silverman, L. H. (1980). A comprehensive report of studies using the subliminal psychodynamic activation method. *Psychological Research Bulletin, 20*, 1–22.

Silverman, L. H. (1982). A comment on two subliminal psychodynamic activation studies. *Journal of Abnormal Psychology, 91*, 126–130.

Silverman, L. H., Ross, D. L., Adler, J. M., & Lustig, D. A. (1978). Simple research paradigm for demonstrating subliminal psychodynamic activation: Effects of Oedipal stimuli on dart-throwing accuracy in college males. *Journal of Abnormal Psychology, 87*, 341–357.

Slone, R. B., Staples, F. R., Cristol, A. H., Yorkston, N. J., & Whipple, K. (1975). *Short-term analytically oriented psychotherapy versus behavior therapy*. Cambridge, MA: Harvard University Press.

Smith, M. L., & Glass, G. V. (1977). Meta-analysis of psychotherapy outcome studies. *American Psychologist, 32*, 752–760.

Smith, M. L., Glass, G. V., Miller, T. I. (1980). *The benefits of psychotherapy*. Baltimore: Johns Hopkins University Press.

Sroufe, L. A., & Fleeson, J. (1986). Attachment and the construction of relationships. In W. W. Hartup & Z. Rubin (Eds.), *Relationships and development* (pp. 51–71). Hillsdale, NJ: Erlbaum.

Stone, M. (1985). Shellshock and psychologists. In W. F. Bynum, R. Porter, & M. Shepherd (Eds.), *The anatomy of madness*. (Vol. 2, pp. 242–247). London: Tavistock.

Strahan, R. F. (1978). Six ways of looking at an elephant. *American Psychologist, 33,* 693.

Strupp, H. H., Fox R. E., & Lessler, K. (1969). *Patients view their psychotherapy.* Baltimore: Johns Hopkins University Press.

Svartberg, M. & Stiles, T.C. (1991). Comparative effects of short-term psychodynamic psychotherapy: A meta-analysis. *Journal of Consulting and Clinical Psychology, 59,* 704–714.

Vaillant, G. E. (1977). *Adaption to life.* Boston: Little, Brown.

Vaillant, G. E. (Ed). (1986). *Empirical studies of ego mechanisms of defense.* Washington, DC: American Psychiatric Press.

Vaillant, G. E., & Drake, R. E. (1985). Maturity of defenses in relation to DSM-III Axis II personality disorder. *Archives of General Psychiatry, 42,* 597–601.

Vivian, J. (1993). *The media of mass communication.* Boston: Allyn & Bacon.

Westen, D. (1990). Psychoanalytic approaches to personality. In L. A. Pervin (Eds.), *Handbook of personality: Theory and research* (pp. 21–65). New York: Guilford.

Westen, D. (1991). Social cognition and object relations. *Psychological Bulletin, 3,* 429–455.

Wilhelm, R. (1956). Are subliminal commercials bad? *Michigan Business Review, 8,* 26.

Zajonc, R. B. (1980). Feeling and thinking: Preferences need no inferences. *American Psychologist, 35,* 151–175.

Zeanah, C. H., & Zeanah, P. D. (1989). Intergenerational transmission of maltreatment: Insights from attachment theory and research. *Psychiatry, 52,* 177–196.

Chapter 4

Adler, A. (1956). The study of organ inferiority and its physical compensation. In H. L. Ansbacher & R. R. Ansbacher (Eds.), *The individual psychology of Alfred Adler.* New York: Harper & Row. (Original work published in 1907)

Adler, A. (1956). The psychology of hermaphroditism in life and in neurosis. In H. L. Ansbacher & R. R. Ansbacher (Eds.), *The individual psychology of Alfred Adler.* New York: Harper & Row. (Original work published in 1910)

Adler, A. (1927). *Practice and theory of individual psychology.* New York: Harcourt, Brace & World.

Adler, A. (1929a). *The science of living.* New York: Greenberg.

Adler, A. (1929b). *Problems of neurosis.* London: Kegan Paul.

Adler, A. (1930). Individual psychology. In C. Murchison (Ed.), *Psychologies of 1930* (pp. 395–405). Worcester, Mass.: Clark University Press.

Adler, A. (1931). *What life should mean to you.* Boston: Little, Brown.

Adler, A. (1935). The fundamental views of individual psychology. *International Journal of Individual Psychology, 1,* 5–8.

Adler, A. (1939). *Social interest.* New York: Putnam.

Adler, A. (1956). The meaning of life. In H. L. Ansbacher & R. R. Ansbacher (Eds.), *The individual psychology of Alfred Adler.* New York: Harper & Row. (Original work published in 1933).

Altus, N. C. (1966). Birth order and its sequelae. *Science, 151,* 44–49.

Ansbacher, H. L., & Ansbacher, R. R. (1956). *The individual psychology of Alfred Adler.* New York: Harper.

Baron, R. A. & Byrne, D. (1991). *Social psychology: Understanding human interaction* (6th ed.). Boston: Allyn & Bacon.

Belmont, L., & Marolla, F. A. (1973). Birth order, family size, and intelligence. *Science, 182,* 1096–1101.

Belsky, J., Gilstrap, B., & Rovine, M. (1984). The Pennsylvania infant and family development project, I: Stability and change in mother-infant and father-infant interaction in a family setting at one, three, and nine months. *Child Development, 55,* 692–705.

Blake, J. (1989). Number of siblings and educational attainment. *Science, 245,* 32–36.

Bonner, M. A. (1989). *The Myers-Briggs type indicator as an aid to instructional design in interior design and apparel merchandising.* Unpublished master's thesis, Indiana University, Bloomington, IN.

Boroson, W. (1973). First born—fortune's favorite? In *Readings in human development* (pp. 192–196). Guilford, CT: Dushkin Publishers.

Bottome, P. (1957). *Alfred Adler: A portrait from life* (3rd ed.). New York: Vanguard.

Breland, H. M. (1974). Birth order, family configuration, and verbal achievement. *Child Development, 45,* 1011–1019.

Cann, D. R., & Donderi, D. C. (1986). Jungian personality typology and the recall of everyday and archetypal dreams. *Journal of Personality and Social Psychology, 50,* 1021–1030.

Carlson, R. (1980). Studies of Jungian typology: II. Representations of the personal world. *Journal of Personality and Social Psychology, 38,* 801–810.

Carlson, R., & Levy, N. (1973). Studies of Jungian typology: I. Memory, social perception, and social action. *Journal of Personality, 41,* 559–576.

Carlyn, M. (1977). An assessment of the Myers-Briggs Type Indicator. *Journal of Personality Assessment, 41,* 461–473.

Corneau, H. (1980). An examination of the relationship between sex, birth order, and creativity. *Creative Child and Adult Quarterly, 5,* 251–258.

Crandall, J. E. (1975). A scale for social interest. *Journal of Individual Psychology, 31,* 187–195.

Crandall, J. E. (1980). Adler's concept of social interest: Theory, measurement, and implications for adjustment. *Journal of Personality and Social Psychology, 39,* 481–495.

Crandall, J. E. (1981). *Theory and measurement of social interest: Empirical tests of Alfred Adler's concept.* New York: Columbia University Press.

Crandall, J. E. (1984). Social interest as a moderator of life stress. *Journal of Personality and Social Psychology, 47,* 164–174.

Crandall, J. E., & Putman, E. L. (1980). Social interest and psychological well-being. *Journal of Individual Psychology, 36,* 156–168.

Darley, J. M., & Aronson, E. (1966). Self-evaluation vs. direct anxiety reduction as determinants of the fear-affiliation relationship. *Journal of Experimental Social Psychology Supplement, 1*, 66–79.

Dimond, R. E., & Munz, C. (1968). Ordinal position of birth and self-disclosure in high school students. *Psychological Reports, 21*, 829–833.

Ellenberger, H. F. (1970). *The discovery of the unconscious: The history and evolution of dynamic psychiatry.* New York: Basic Books.

Ernst, C., & Angst, J. (1983). *Birth order: Its influence on personality.* New York: Springer-Verlag.

Eysenck, H. J. (1990). Biological dimensions of personality. In L. A. Pervin (Ed.), *Handbook of personality: Theory and research* (pp. 244–276). New York: Guilford.

Eysenck, H. J., & Cookson, D. (1969). Personality in primary school children: 3. Family background. *British Journal of Educational Psychology, 40*, 117–131.

Falbo, T., & Polit, D. F. (1986). Quantitative review of the only child literature: Research evidence and theory development. *Psychological Bulletin, 100*, 176–189.

Forer, L. (1976). *The birth order factor.* New York: McKay.

Furtmuller, C. (1964). Alfred Adler: A biographical essay. In H. L. Ansbacher & R. R. Ansbacher (Eds.), *Superiority and social interest* (pp. 311–393). Evanston, IL: Northwestern University Press.

Glass, D. C., Neulinger, J., & Brim, O. G. (1974). Birth order, verbal intelligence, and educational aspiration. *Child Development, 45*, 807–811.

Hall, C. S., & Nordby, V. J. (1973). *A primer of Jungian psychology.* New York: New American Library.

Harris, I. D. (1964). *The promise seed: A complete study of eminent first and later sons.* New York: Free Press.

Helson, R. (1978). Dimensions and patterns in writings of critics. *Journal of Personality, 46*, 348–361.

Helson, R. (1982). Critics and their texts: An approach to Jung's theory of cognition and personality. *Journal of Personality and Social Psychology, 43*, 409–418.

Hetherington, E. M., & Feldman, S. E. (1964). College cheating as a function of subject and situational variables. *Journal of Educational Psychology, 55*, 212–218.

Hilton, I. (1967). Differences in the behavior of mothers toward first and later born children. *Journal of Personality and Social Psychology, 7*, 282–290.

Hoffman, L. W. (1991). The influence of the family environment on personality: Accounting for sibling differences. *Psychological Bulletin, 2*, 187–203.

Howarth, E. (1980). Birth order, family structure, and personality variables. *Journal of Personality Assessment, 44*, 299–301.

Hoyenga, K. B., & Hoyenga, K. T. (1984). *Motivational explanations of behavior.* Monterey, CA: Brooks/Cole.

Ickes, W., & Turner, M. (1983). On the social advantages of having an older, opposite-sex sibling: Birth order influences in mixed-sex dyads. *Journal of Personality and Social Psychology, 45*, 210–222.

Jung, C. G. (1973). The reaction time ratio in the association experiment. In *The collected works of C. G. Jung.* Vol. 2. Princeton: Princeton University Press. (Original work published in 1905)

Jung, C. G. (1907). On the psychological relations of the association experiment. *Journal of Abnormal Psychology, 7*, 247–255.

Jung, C. G. (1973). The psychological diagnosis of evidence. In *The collected works of C. G. Jung.* Vol. 2. Princeton: Princeton University Press. (Original work published in 1909)

Jung, C. G. (1960). The transcendent function. In *The collected works of C. G. Jung.* Vol. 8. Princeton: Princeton University Press. (Original work published in 1916)

Jung, C. G. (1969). General aspects of dream psychology. In *The collected works of C. G. Jung.* Vol. 8. Princeton: Princeton University Press. (Original work published in 1916)

Jung, C. G., (1966). Two essays on analytical psychology. In *The collected works of C. G. Jung.* Vol. 7. Princeton: Princeton University Press. (Original work published in 1917)

Jung, C. G. (1971). Psychological types. In *The collected works of C. G. Jung.* Vol. 6. Princeton: Princeton University Press. (Original work published in 1921)

Jung, C. G. (1960). The stages of life. In *The collected works of C. G. Jung.* Vol. 8. Princeton: Princeton University Press. (Original work published in 1931a)

Jung, C. G. (1971). A psychological theory of types. In *The collected works of C. G. Jung.* Vol. 6. Princeton: Princeton University Press. (Original work published in 1931b)

Jung, C. G. (1960). A review of the complex theory. In *The collected works of C. G. Jung.* Vol. 8. Princeton: Princeton University Press. (Original work published in 1934)

Jung, C. G. (1959). The archetypes and the collective unconscious. In *The collected works of C. G. Jung.* Vol. 9, Part I. Princeton: Princeton University Press. (Original work published in 1936a)

Jung, C. G. (1959). The concept of the collective unconscious. In *The collected works of C. G. Jung.* Vol. 9, Part I. Princeton: Princeton University Press. (Original work published in 1936b)

Jung, C. G. (1959). Conscious, unconscious, and individuation. In *The collected works of C. G. Jung.* Vol. 9, Part I. Princeton: Princeton University Press. (Original work published in 1939)

Jung, C. G. (1953). The psychology of the unconscious. In *The collected works of C. G. Jung.* Vol. 7. Princeton: Princeton University Press. (Original work published in 1943)

Jung, C. G. (1953). The relations between the ego and the unconscious. In *The collected works of C. G. Jung.* Vol. 7. Princeton: Princeton University Press. (Original work published in 1945)

Jung, C. G. (1959). The shadow. In *The collected works of C. G. Jung.* Vol. 9, Part II. Princeton: Princeton University Press. (Original work published in 1948a)

Jung, C. G. (1960). On psychic energy. In *The collected works of C. G. Jung.* Vol. 8. Princeton: Princeton University Press. (Original work published in 1948b)

Jung, C. J. (1959). Psychological aspects of the mother archetype. In *The collected works of C. G. Jung*. Vol. 9, Part I. Princeton: Princeton University Press. (Original work published in 1954a)

Jung, C. G. (1959). Concerning the archetypes, with special reference to the anima concept. In *The collected works of C. G. Jung*. Vol. 9, Part I. Princeton: Princeton University Press. (Original work published in 1954b)

Jung, C. G. (1961). *Memories, dreams, reflections*. New York: Random House.

Kaufmann, Y. (1989). Analytical psychotherapy. In R. J. Corsini & D. Wedding (Eds.), *Current psychotherapies* (4th ed.) (pp. 119–152). Itasca, IL: F. E. Peacock Publishers.

Maddi, S. R. (1989). *Personality theories: A comparative analysis* (5th ed.). Homewood, IL: Dorsey.

McCall, R. B. (1984). Developmental changes in mental performance: The effect of the birth of a sibling. *Child Development, 55*, 1317–1321.

Miller, N., & Maruyama, G. (1976) Ordinal position and peer popularity. *Journal of Personality and Social Psychology, 33*, 123–131.

Monte, C. F. (1987). *Beneath the mask: An introduction to theories of personality* (3rd ed.). New York: Holt, Rinehart & Winston.

Morris, L. W. (1979). *Extraversion and introversion: An interactional perspective*. New York: Hemisphere Publishing.

Mosak, H. H. (Ed.) (1973). *Alfred Adler: His influence on psychology today*. Park Ridge, NJ: Noyes Press.

Mosak, H. H. (1989). Adlerian psychotherapy. In R. J. Corsini & D. Wedding (Eds.), *Current psychotherapies* (4th ed.). Itasca, IL: F. E. Peacock Publishers.

Myers I. B. (1962). *The Myers-Briggs Type Indicator Manual*. Palo Alto, CA: Consulting Psychologists Press.

Myers, I. B. (1980). *Introduction to type*. (3rd ed.) Palo Alto, CA: Consulting Psychologists Press.

Myers, M. B., & McCaulley, M. H. (1985). *Manual: A guide to the development and use of the Myers-Briggs Type Indicator*. Palo Alto, CA: Consulting Psychologists Press.

Nisbett, R. E. (1968). Birth order and participation in dangerous sports. *Journal of Personality and Social Psychology, 8*, 351–353.

Owyang, W. N. (1971). Ordinal position, frustration, and the expression of aggression. *Dissertation Abstracts International, 31*, 6243B.

Pervin, L. A. (Ed.) (1992). Recent theoretical contributions on views of the self. *Psychological Inquiry, 3*.

Peterson, F., & Jung, C. G. (1907). Psychophysical investigations with the galvanometer and insane individuals. *Brain, 30*, 143–182.

Parrott, L. (1992). Earliest recollections and birth order: Two Adlerian exercises. *Teaching of Psychology, 19*, 40–42.

Ricksher, C., & Jung, C. G. (1908). Further investigations on the galvanic phenomenon and respiration in normal and insane individuals. *Journal of Abnormal Psychology, 2*, 189–217.

Ring, K., Lipinski, C. E., & Braginsky, D. (1965). The relationship of birth order to self-evaluation, anxiety reduction, and susceptibility to emotional contagion. *Psychological Monographs, 79* (Whole No. 603).

Rothbart, M. K. (1971). Birth order and mother-child interaction in an achievement situation. *Journal of Personality and Social Psychology, 17*, 113–120.

Rotter, J. B., & Hochreich, D. J. (1975). *Personality*. Glenview, IL: Scott, Foresman.

Rychlak, J. F. (1981). *Introduction to personality and psychotherapy* (2nd ed.). Boston: Houghton Mifflin.

Schachter, S. (1959). *The psychology of affiliation: Experimental studies of the sources of gregariousness*. Stanford, CA: Stanford University Press.

Schachter, S. (1963). Birth order, eminence, and higher education. *American Sociological Review, 28*, 757–767.

Searleman, A., Porac, C., & Coren, S. (1989). Relationship between birth order, birth stress, and lateral preferences: A critical review. *Psychological Bulletin, 105*, 397–408.

Storr, A. (1991). *Jung*. New York: Routledge.

Stricker, L. J., & Ross, J. (1964). Some correlates of a Jungian personality inventory. *Psychological Reports, 14*, 623–643.

Sulloway, F. J. (1990). *Orthodoxy and innovation in science: The influence of birth order in a multivariate context*. Paper presented at the American Association for the Advancement of Science.

Thompson, V. D. (1974). Family size: Implicit policies and assumed psychological outcomes. *Journal of Social Issues, 30*, 93–124.

Ward, C. D., Castro, A., & Wilcox, A. H. (1974). Birth-order effects in a survey of mate selection and parenthood. *Journal of Social Psychology, 94*, 57–64.

Warren, R. (1966). Birth order and social behavior. *Psychological Bulletin, 65*, 38–49.

Wilhelm, R., & Jung, C. G. (1931). *The secret world of the golden flower*. New York: Harcourt, Brace & World.

Zajonc, R. B. (1975, January). Dumber by the dozen. *Psychology Today*, 37–43.

Zajonc, R. B. (1976). Family configuration and intelligence. *Science, 192*, 227–236.

Zajonc, R. B., & Markus, G. B. (1975). Birth order and intellectual development. *Psychological Review, 82*, 74–88.

Zimbardo, P. G. (1977). *Shyness: What it is, what to do about it*. Reading, MA: Addison-Wesley Publishing.

Zimbardo, P., & Formica, R. (1963). Emotional comparison and self-esteem as determinants of affiliation. *Journal of Personality, 31*, 141–162.

Zweigenhaft, R. L. (1975). Birth order, approval-seeking, and membership in Congress. *Journal of Individual Psychology, 31*, 205–210.

Chapter 5

Bellew-Smith, M., & Korn, J. H. (1986). Merger intimacy status in adult women. *Journal of Personality and Social Psychology, 50*, 1186–1191.

Bergman, M., Akin, S. B., & Felig, P. (1990). Understanding the diabetic patient from a psychological dimension: Implications for the patient and the provider. *American Journal of Psychoanalysis, 50*, 25–33.

Carducci, B. J. (1986). Adolescent fears of being homosexual. *Medical Aspects of Human Sexuality, 20*, 15–16.

Chapman, A. N. (1976). *Harry Stack Sullivan: His life and work.* New York: Putnam.

Cocores, J. (1987). Co-addiction: A silent epidemic. *Psychiatry Letter, 5*, 5–8.

Cohen, J. B. (1967). An interpersonal orientation to the study of consumer behavior. *Journal of Marketing Research, 4*, 270–278.

Constantinople, A. (1969). An Eriksonian measure of personality development in college students. *Developmental Psychology, 1*, 357–372.

Engel, J. F., Blackwell, R. D., & Miniard, P. W. (1993). *Consumer behavior* (7th ed.). Fort Worth, TX: Dryden Press.

Erikson, E. H. (1950). *Childhood and society.* New York: Norton.

Erikson, E. H. (1963). *Childhood and society* (2nd ed.). New York: Norton.

Erikson, E. H. (1968). *Identity, youth, and crisis.* New York: Norton.

Erikson, E. H. (1969). *Gandhi's truth.* New York: Norton.

Erikson, E. H. (1970). Autobiographic notes on the identity crisis. *Daedalus, 99*, 730–759.

Erikson, E. H. (1974). *Dimensions of a new identity.* New York: Norton.

Erikson, E. H., Erikson, J. M., & Kivnick, H. Q. (1986). *Vital involvement in old age.* New York: Norton.

Evans, R. I. (1966). *Dialogue with Erich Fromm.* New York: Harper & Row.

Fromm, E. (1941). *Escape from freedom.* New York: Rinehart.

Fromm, E. (1947). *Man for himself.* Greenwich, CT: Fawcett Books.

Hamon, S. A. (1987). Some contributions of Horneyan theory to enhancement of the Type A behavior construct. *The American Journal of Psychoanalysis, 47*, 105–115.

Hartmann, H. (1958). *Ego psychology and the problem of adaptation.* New York: International Universities Press.

Hartmann, H. (1964). *Essays on ego psychology: Selected problems in psychoanalytic theory.* New York: International Universities Press.

Hopkins, J. R. (1995). Erik Homburger Erikson (1902–1994). *American Psychologist, 50*, 796–797.

Horney, K. (1937). *The neurotic personality of our time.* New York: Norton.

Horney, K. (1939). *New ways in psychoanalysis.* New York: Norton.

Horney, K. (1942). *Self-analysis.* New York: Norton.

Horney, K. (1945). *Our inner conflicts.* New York: Norton.

Horney, K. (1950). *Neurosis and human growth.* New York: Norton.

Horney, K. (1967). *Feminine psychology.* New York: Norton.

Hyffamn, J. R. (1989). Young man Johnson. *The American Journal of Psychoanalysis, 49*, 251–265.

Jabin, N. (1987). Attitudes toward disability: Horney's theory applied. *The American Journal of Psychoanalysis, 47*, 143–153.

Kassarjian, H. H. (1971). Personality and consumer behavior: A review. *Journal of Marketing Research, 8*, 409–418.

Kernan, J. B. (1971). The CAD instrument in behavioral diagnosis. *Proceeding, Second Annual Conference, Association for Consumer Research*, 307–312.

Lyon, D., & Greenberg, J. (1991). Evidence of codependency in women with an alcoholic parent: Helping out Mr. Wrong. *Journal of Personality and Social Psychology, 61*, 435–439.

McAdams, D. P., & de St. Aubin, E. (1992). A theory of generativity and its assessment through self-report, behavior acts, and narrative themes in autobiography. *Journal of Personality and Social Psychology, 62*, 1003–1015.

McAdams, D. P., de St. Aubin, E., & Logan, R. L. (1993). Generativity among young, midlife, and older adults. *Psychology and Aging, 8*, 221–230.

Munson, J. M., & Spivey, W. A. (1982). The factor validity of an inventory assessing Horney's interpersonal response traits of compliance, aggression, and detachment. *Educational and Psychological Measurement, 42*, 889–898.

Noerager, J. P. (1979). An assessment of the CAD—A personality instrument developed specifically for marketing research. *Journal of Marketing Research, 16*, 53–59.

Ochse, R., & Plug, C. (1986). Cross-cultural investigation of the validity of Erikson's theory of personality development. *Journal of Personality and Social Psychology, 50*, 1240–1252.

Paris, B. J. (Ed.). (1989). Introduction: Interdisciplinary applications of Horney. *American Journal of Psychoanalysis, 49*, 181–188.

Pride, W. P., & Ferrell, O. C. (1993). *Marketing: Concepts and strategies* (8th ed.). Boston, MA: Houghton Mifflin.

Quinn, S. (1988). *A mind of her own: The life of Karen Horney.* Reading, MA: Addison-Wesley.

Reichard, S., Livson, F., & Peterson, P. (1962). *Aging and personality: A study of 87 older men.* New York: Wiley.

Rendon, D. (1987). Understanding social roles from a Horneyan perspective. *American Journal of Psychoanalysis, 47*, 131–142.

Roemer, W. W. (1986). Leary's circle matrix: A comprehensive model for the statistical measurement of Horney's clinical concepts. *American Journal of Psychoanalysis, 46*, 249–262.

Roemer, W. W. (1987). An application of the interpersonal models developed by Karen Horney and Timothy Leary to Type A-B behavior patterns. *American Journal of Psychoanalysis, 47*, 116–130.

Rubins, J. L. (1978). *Karen Horney: Gentle rebel of psychoanalysis.* New York: Dial.

Rychlak, J. F. (1981). *Introduction to personality and psychotherapy: A theory-construction approach* (2nd ed.). Boston: Houghton Mifflin.

Schaef, A. (1986). *Codependence: Misunderstood-mistreated.* Minneapolis, MN: Winston Press.

Sullivan, H. S. (1953). *The interpersonal theory of psychiatry.* New York: Norton.

Sullivan, H. S. (1964). *The fusion of psychiatry and social science.* New York: Norton.

Walaskay, W., Whitbourne, S. K., & Nehrke, M. F. (1983–1984). Construction and validation of an ego-integrity status interview. *International Journal of Aging and Human Development, 18*, 61–72.

Wells, W. D., & Beard, A. D. (1973). Personality and consumer behavior. In S. Ward & T. S. Robertson (Eds.), *Consumer behavior: Theoretical sources* (pp. 141–199). Englewood Cliffs, NJ: Prentice Hall.

Westkott, M. (1986a). *The feminist legacy of Karen Horney*. New Haven, CT: Yale University Press.

Westkott, M. (1986b). Historical and developmental roots of female dependency. *Psychotherapy, 23,* 213–220.

Westkott, M. (1989). Female relationship and the idealized self. *American Journal of Psychoanalysis, 49,* 239–250.

Whitbourne, S. K., Zuschlag, M. K., Elliot, L. B., & Waterman, A. S. (1992). Psychosocial development in adulthood: A 22–year sequential study. *Journal of Personality and Social Psychology, 63,* 260–271.

Chapter 6

Aronson, E. (1972). *The social animal*. San Francisco: Freeman.

Aspy, D. N. (1965). *A study of three facilitative conditions and their relationship to the achievement of third grade students.* Unpublished doctoral dissertation, University of Kentucky, Lexington.

Axline, V. M. (1947). *Play therapy*. Boston: Houghton Mifflin.

Bednar, R. L., & Kaul, T. J. (1978). Experiential group research: Current perspectives. In S. L. Garfield & A. E. Bergin (Eds.), *Handbook of psychotherapy and behavior change: An empirical analysis* (2nd ed.) (pp. 769–815). New York: John Wiley & Sons.

Bem, D. J., & Allen, A. (1974). On predicting some of the people some of the time: The search for cross-situational consistencies in behavior. *Psychological Review, 81,* 506–520.

Bem, D. J., & Funder, D. C. (1978). Predicting more of the people more of the time: Assessing the personality of situations. *Psychological Review, 85,* 485–501.

Block, J. (1971). *Lives through time*. Berkeley, CA: Bancroft Books.

Bradford, L. P. (Ed.). (1976). *Human forces in teaching and learning.* La Jolla, CA: University Associates, Inc.

Brown, S. R. (1968). Bibliography on Q technique and its methodology. *Perceptual and Motor Skills, 26,* 587–613.

Butler, J. M. (1968). Self-ideal congruence in psychotherapy. *Psychotherapy: Theory, Research, and Practice, 5,* 13–17.

Butler, J. M., & Haigh, G. V. (1954). Changes in the relation between self-concepts and ideal concepts consequent upon client-centered counseling. In C. R. Rogers & R. Dymond (Eds.), *Psychotherapy and personality change: Co-ordinated research studies in the client-centered approach* (pp. 55–75). Chicago: University of Chicago Press.

Cassel, R. N. (1958). *The leadership q-sort test: A test of leadership values*. Murfreesboro, TN: Psychometric Affiliate.

Cohen, R. J., Montague, P., Nathanson, L. S., & Swerdlik, M. E. (1989). *Psychological testing: An introduction to tests and measurements*. Mountain View, CA: Mayfield.

Ellinwood, C. G., & Raskin, N. J. (1993). Client-centered/humanistic psychotherapy. In T. R. Kratochwill & R. J. Morris (Eds.), *Handbook of psychotherapy with children and adolescents* (pp. 258–287). Boston: Allyn & Bacon.

Funder, D. C., & Block, J. (1989). The role of ego-control, ego-resiliency, and IQ in delay of gratification in adolescents. *Journal of Personality and Social Psychology, 57,* 1041–1050.

Funder, D. C., Block, J. H., & Block, J. (1983). Delay of gratification: Some longitudinal personality correlates. *Journal of Personality and Social Psychology, 44,* 1198–1213.

Funder, D.C., Parke, R. D., Tomlinson-Keasey, C., & Widaman, K. (Eds.). (1993). *Studying lives through time: Personality and development*. Washington, DC: American Psychological Association.

Gibb, J. R. (1971). The effects of human relations training. In A. E. Bergin & S. L. Garfield (Eds.), *Handbook of psychotherapy and behavior change: An empirical analysis* (pp. 839–862). New York: John Wiley & Sons.

Jackson, D. N., & Messick, S. (1958). Content and style in personality assessment. *Psychological Bulletin, 55,* 243–252.

Kendall, P. C., & Norton-Ford, J. D. (1982). *Clinical psychology: Scientific and professional dimensions*. New York: John Wiley & Sons.

Lanyon, R. I., & Goodstein, L. D. (1971). *Personality assessment*. New York: John Wiley & Sons.

Lieberman, M. A., Yalom, I. D., & Miles, M. B. (1973). *Encounter groups: First facts*. New York: Basic Books.

McCrae, R. R., Costa, P. T., & Busch, C. M. (1986). Evaluating comprehensiveness in personality systems: The California Q-Set and the five-factor model. *Journal of Personality, 54,* 430–446.

McGaw, W. H., Rice, C. P., & Rogers, C. R. (1973). *The steel shutter*. La Jolla, CA: Film Center for Studies of the Person.

Meador, B. D., & Rogers, C. R. (1973). Client-centered therapy. In R. J. Corsini (Ed.), *Current psychotherapies* (pp. 119–166). Itasca, IL: Peacock.

Merluzzi, T. V., Glass, C. R., & Genest, M. (Eds.). (1981). *Cognitive assessment*. New York: Guilford.

Mischel, W. (1972). Direct versus indirect personality assessment: Evidence and implications. *Journal of Consulting and Clinical Psychology, 38,* 319–324.

Mischel, W. (1981). Metacognition and the rules of delay. In J. H. Flavell & L. Ross (Eds.), *Social cognitive development: Frontiers and possible futures* (pp. 240–271). New York: Cambridge University Press.

Mitchell, K. M., Bozarth, J. D., & Krauft, C. C. (1977). A reappraisal of the therapeutic effectiveness of accurate empathy, nonpossessive warmth, and genuineness. In A. S. Gurman & A. M. Razin (Eds.), *Effective psychotherapy: A handbook of research* (pp. 482–502). New York: Pergamon.

Morris, R. J., & Suckerman, K. R. (1974). The importance of the therapeutic relationship in systematic desensitization. *Journal of Consulting and Clinical Psychology, 42,* 148.

Mruk, C. (1995). *Self-esteem: Research, theory, and practice*. New York: Springer.

Ozer, D. J. (1993). The Q-sort method and the study of personality development. In D. C. Funder, R. D. Parke, C. Tomlinson-Keasey, & K. Widaman (Eds.), *Studying lives through time: Personality and development* (pp. 147–168). Washington, DC: American Psychological Association.

Ozer, D. J., & Gjerde, P. F. (1989). Patterns of personality consistency and change from childhood through adolescence. *Journal of Personality, 57,* 483–507.

Raskin, N. J., & Rogers, C. R. (1989). Person-centered therapy. In R. J. Corsini & D. Wedding (Eds.), *Current psychotherapies* (4th ed.) (pp. 155–194). Itasca, IL: F. E. Peacock Publishers.

Raskin, N. J., & Rogers, C. R. (1995). Person-centered therapy. In R. J. Corsini & D. Wedding (Eds.), *Current psychotherapies* (5th ed.) (pp. 128–161). Itasca, IL: F. E. Peacock Publishers.

Rogers C. R. (1939). *The clinical treatment of the problem child.* Boston: Houghton Mifflin.

Rogers, C. R. (1951). *Client-centered therapy: Its current practice, implications, and theory.* Boston: Houghton Mifflin.

Rogers, C. R. (1952). Communication: Its blocking and facilitation. *ECT: A Review of General Semantics, 9,* 83–88.

Rogers, C. R. (1957). The necessary and sufficient conditions of therapeutic personality change. *Journal of Consulting Psychology, 21,* 95–103.

Rogers, C. R. (1958). A process conception of psychotherapy. *American Psychologist, 13,* 142–149.

Rogers, C. R. (1959). A theory of therapy, personality, and interpersonal relationship, as developed in the client-centered framework. In S. Koch (Ed.), *Psychology: A study of a science: Vol. 3. Formulations of the person and the social context* (pp. 184–256). New York: McGraw-Hill.

Rogers, C. R. (1961). *On becoming a person: A therapist's view of psychotherapy.* Boston: Houghton Mifflin.

Rogers, C. R. (1964). The concept of the fully functioning person. *Psychotherapy: Theory, Research, and Practice, 1,* 17–26.

Rogers, C. R. (1967). Autobiography. In E. G. Boring & G. Lindzey (Eds.). *A history of psychology in autobiography* (Vol. 5, pp. 341–384). New York: Appleton-Century-Crofts.

Rogers, C. R. (1969). *Freedom to learn.* Columbus, OH: Merrill.

Rogers, C. R. (1970). *Carl Rogers on encounter groups.* New York: Harper & Row.

Rogers, C. R. (1972). *Becoming partners: Marriage and its alternatives.* New York: Delacorte.

Rogers, C. R. (1977). *Carl Rogers on personal power.* New York: Delacorte.

Rogers, C. R. (1980). *A way of being.* Boston: Houghton Mifflin.

Rogers, C. R. (1982, August). Nuclear war: A personal response. *American Psychological Association Monitor,* pp. 6–7.

Rogers, C. R. (1983). *Freedom to learn for the 80's.* Columbus, OH: Merrill.

Rogers, C. R. (1986). Client-centered therapy. In I. L. Kutash & A. Wolf (Eds.), *Psychotherapist's casebook: Therapy and technique in practice* (pp. 197–208). San Francisco: Jossey- Bass.

Rogers, C. R. (1987). Inside the world of the Soviet professional. *Journal of Humanistic Psychology, 27,* 277–304.

Rogers, C. R., & Dymond, R. F. (Eds.). (1954). *Psychotherapy and personality change: Co-ordinated research studies in the client-centered approach.* Chicago: University of Chicago Press.

Rogers, C. R., & Sanford, R. C. (1985). Client-centered psychotherapy. In H. I. Kaplan, B. J. Sadock, & A. M. Friedman (Eds.), *Comprehensive textbook of psychiatry* (4th ed., pp. 1374–1388).

Schmuck, R. (1963). Some relationships of peer liking patterns in the classroom to pupil attitudes and achievement. *The School Review, 71,* 337–359.

Schmuck, R. (1966). Some aspects of classroom social climate. *Psychology in the Schools, 3,* 59–65.

Schutz, W. C. (1967). *Joy: Expanding human awareness.* New York: Grove.

Stephenson, W. (1953). *The study of behavior.* Chicago: University of Chicago Press.

Stephenson, W. (1980). Newton's fifth rule and Q methodology: Application to educational psychology. *American Psychologist, 35,* 882–889.

Truax, C. B., & Mitchell, K. M. (1971). Research on certain therapist interpersonal skills in relation to process and outcome. In A. E. Bergin & S. L. Garfield (Eds.), *Handbook of psychotherapy and behavior change: An empirical analysis* (pp. 299–344). New York: John Wiley & Sons.

Tyler, L. E. (1961). Research explorations in the realm of choice. *Journal of Consulting Psychology, 8,* 195–202.

Williams, S. K., Jr. (1978). The Vocational Card Sort: A tool for vocational exploration. *Vocational Guidance Quarterly, 26,* 237–243.

Wittenborn, J. R. (1961). Contributions and current status of Q methodology. *Psychological Bulletin, 58,* 132–142.

Chapter 7

Alderfer, C. P. (1972). *Existence, relatedness, and growth.* New York: Free Press.

Alexander, C. N., Rainforth, M. V., & Gelderloos, P. (1991). Transcendental meditation, self-actualization, and psychological health: A conceptual overview and statistical meta-analysis. *Journal of Social Behavior and Personality, 6,* 189–247.

Braun, J., & Asta, P. (1968). Intercorrelations between the Personal Orientation Inventory and the Gordon Personal Inventory scores. *Psychological Reports, 23,* 1197–1198.

Buss, A. R. (1978). The structure of psychological revolutions. *Journal of the History of the Behavioral Sciences, 14,* 57–64.

Cloninger, S. C. (1993). *Theories of personality: Understanding persons.* Englewood Cliffs, NJ: Prentice Hall.

Easterby-Smith, M. (1980). How to use repertory grids in human resource development. *Journal of European Industrial Training, 4,* (1, Whole No. 2).

Eden, C., & Sims, D. (1981). Computerised vicarious experience: The future of management induction? *Personnel Review, 10,* 22–25.

Friedlander, F. (1963). Underlying sources of job satisfaction. *Journal of Applied Psychology, 47,* 246–250.

Greeley, A. M. (1975). *The sociology of the paranormal: A reconnaissance.* Beverly Hills: Sage.

Guinan, J. F., & Foulds, M. L. (1970). Marathon group: Facilitator of personal growth? *Journal of Counseling Psychology, 17,* 145–149.

Hall, C. S., & Lindzey, G. L. (1978). *Theories of personality* (3rd ed.). New York: John Wiley & Sons.

Hattie, J. (1981). A four-stage factor analytic approach to studying behavioral domains. *Applied Psychological Measurement, 5,* 77–88.

Hattie, J., Hancock, P., & Brereton, K. (1984). The relationship between two measures of self-actualization. *Journal of Personality Assessment, 48,* 17–25.

Hollon, S. D., & Beck, A. T. (1994). Cognitive and cognitive-behavioral therapies. In A. E. Bergin & S. L. Garfield (Eds.), *Handbook of psychotherapy and behavior change* (pp. 428–466). New York: John Wiley & Sons.

Hyman, R. B. (1979). Construct validity of Shostrom's Personal Orientation Inventory: A systematic summary. *Measurement and Evaluation in Guidance, 12,* 174–184.

James, W. (1958). *The varieties of religious experience.* New York: Mentor-NAL. (Original work published 1902)

Jankowicz, A. D. (1985, May). *Repertory grid techniques in performance appraisal.* Paper presented at the meeting of the Rio Grande Chapter of the Human Factors Society, El Paso, Texas.

Jankowicz, A. D. (1987). Whatever became of George Kelly?: Applications and implications. *American Psychologist, 42,* 481–487.

Jankowicz, A. D., & Cooper, K. (1982). The use of focussed repertory grids in counselling. *British Journal of Guidance and Counseling, 10,* 136–150.

Jankowicz, A. D., & Hisrich, R. (1987). Intuition in small-business lending decisions. *Journal of Small Business Management, 25,* 45–52.

Jones, A., & Crandall, R. (1986). Validation of a short index of self-actualization. *Personality and Social Psychology Bulletin, 12,* 63–73.

Jones, A. & Crandall, R. (Eds.). (1991). Handbook of self-actualization. [Special Issue]. *Journal of Social Behavior and Personality, 6.*

Kelly, G. A. (1955a). *The psychology of personal constructs. Volume 1: A theory of personality.* New York: W. W. Norton.

Kelly, G. A. (1955b). *The psychology of personal constructs. Volume 2: Clinical diagnosis and psychotherapy.* New York: W. W. Norton.

Kelly, G. A. (1969). Humanistic methodology in psychological research. In B. Maher (Ed.), *Clinical psychology and personality: The selected papers of George Kelly* (pp. 133–146). New York: Wiley.

Knapp, R. R. (1976). *Handbook for the POI.* San Diego: Educational and Industrial Testing Service.

Landfield, A. W., & Leitner, L. M. (Eds.). (1980). *Personal construct psychology: Psychotherapy and personality.* New York: Wiley.

Lawler, E. E., & Suttle, J. L. (1972). A causal correlational test of the need hierarchy concept. *Organizational Behavior and Human Performance, 7,* 265–287.

Leak, G. K. (1984). A multidimensional assessment of the validity of the Personal Orientation Inventory. *Journal of Personality Assessment, 48,* 37–41.

LeMay, M., & Damm, V. (1968). The Personal Orientation Inventory as a measure of self-actualization of underachievers. *Measurement and Evaluation in Guidance, 1,* 110–114.

Maddi, S. R. (1989). *Personality theories: A comparative analysis* (5th ed.). Homewood, IL: Dorsey.

Maher, B. (Ed.). (1969). *Clinical psychology and personality: The selected papers of George Kelly.* New York: Wiley.

Margoshes, A., & Litt, S. (1966). Vivid experiences: Peak and nadir. *Journal of Clinical Psychology, 22,* 175.

Maslow, A. H. (1943). A theory of human motivation. *Psychological Review, 50,* 370–396.

Maslow, A. H. (1954). *Motivation and personality.* New York: Harper & Row.

Maslow, A. H. (1962). *Toward a psychology of being.* Princeton, NJ: Van Nostrand.

Maslow, A. H. (1965). *Eupsychian management: A journal.* Homewood, IL: Irwin-Dorsey Press.

Maslow, A. H. (1968). *Toward a psychology of being* (2nd ed.). New York: Van Nostrand Reinhold.

Maslow, A. H. (1970a). *Religions, values, and peak-experiences.* Columbus: Ohio State University.

Maslow, A. H. (1970b). *Motivation and personality* (2nd ed.). New York: Harper & Row.

Maslow, A. H. (1971). *The farther reaches of human nature.* New York: Viking.

Matteson, M. T. (1974). Some reported thoughts on significant management literature. *Academy of Management Journal, 17,* 386–389.

McClain, E. W., & Andrews, H. B. (1969). Some personality correlates of peak experiences—a study in self-actualization. *Journal of Clinical Psychology, 25,* 36–38.

Mitchell, V. F., & Moudgill, P. (1976). Measurement of Maslow's need hierarchy. *Organizational Behavior and Human Performance, 16,* 334–349.

Monte, C. F. (1991). *Beneath the mask: An introduction to theories of personality* (4th ed.). Fort Worth, TX: Holt, Rinehart & Winston.

Muchinsky, P. M., (1983). *Psychology applied to work: An introduction to industrial and organizational psychology.* Homewood, IL: Dorsey.

Pervin, L. A. (1993). *Personality: Theory and research* (6th ed.). New York: John Wiley & Sons.

Plous. S. (1993). *The psychology of judgment and decision making.* New York: McGraw-Hill.

Polyson, J. (1985). Students' peak experiences: A written exercise. *Teaching of Psychology, 12,* 211–213.

Privette, G. (1983). Peak experience, peak performance, and flow: A comparative analysis of positive human experiences. *Journal of Personality and Social Psychology, 45,* 1361–1368.

Privette, G. (1984). *Experience Questionnaire.* Pensacola, FL: The University West Florida.

Privette, G., & Bundrick, C. M. (1991). Peak experience, peak performance, and flow: Correspondence of personal descriptions and theoretical constructs. *Journal of Social Behavior and Personality, 6,* 169–188.

Roberts, T. B. (1972). *Maslow's human motivation needs hierarchy: A bibliography.* De Kalb, IL: Northern Illinois University.

Ross, L., & Nisbett, R. E. (1991). *The person and the situation: Perspectives of social psychology.* New York: McGraw-Hill.

Rychlak, J. F. (1981). *Introduction to personality and psychotherapy: A theory-construction approach* (2nd ed.). Boston: Houghton Mifflin.

Schultz, D. (1990). *Theories of personality* (4th ed.). Pacific Grove, CA: Brooks/Cole.

Shostrom, E. (1963). *Personal Orientation Inventory (POI): A test of self-actualization.* San Diego: Educational and Industrial Testing Service.

Shostrom, E. (1964). An inventory for the measurement of self-actualization. *Educational and Psychological Measurement, 24,* 207–218.

Shostrom, E. L. (1975). *Personal Orientation Inventory*. San Diego: Educational and Industrial Testing Service.

Shostrom, E. L. (1977). *Manual for the Personal Orientation Dimensions*. San Diego: Edits.

Silverstein, A. B., & Fisher, G. (1968). Is item overlap responsible for a "built-in" factor structure? *Psychological Reports, 23,* 935–938.

Silverstein, A. B., & Fisher, G. (1972). Item overlap and the "built-in" factor structure of the Personal Orientation Inventory. *Psychological Reports, 31,* 491–494.

Stewart, R. A. C. (1968). Academic performance and components of self-actualization. *Perceptual and Motor Skills, 26,* 918.

Stewart, V., & Stewart, A. (1982). *Business applications of repertory grid*. London: McGraw-Hill.

Thomas, L. E., & Cooper, P. E. (1977). *The mystic experience: Can it be measured by structured question?* Paper presented at the American Sociological Association, Chicago.

Tosi, D. J., & Lindamood, C. A. (1975). The measurement of self-actualization: A critical review of the Personal Orientation Inventory. *Journal of Personality Assessment, 39,* 215–224.

Wahba, M. A., & Bridwell, L. G. (1976). Maslow reconsidered: A review of research on the need hierarchy theory. *Organizational Behavior and Human Performance, 15,* 212–240.

Wulff, D. M. (1991). *Psychology of religion: Classic and contemporary views*. New York: John Wiley & Sons.

Wuthnow, R. (1978). Peak experiences: Some empirical tests. *Journal of Humanistic Psychology, 18,* 59–75.

Chapter 8

Allport, G. W. (1937). *Personality: A psychological interpretation*. New York: Henry Holt.

Allport, G. W. (1954). *The nature of prejudice*. Cambridge, MA: Addison-Wesley.

Allport, G. W. (1955). *Becoming: Basic considerations for a psychology of personality*. New Haven, CT: Yale University Press.

Allport, G. W. (1958). What units shall we employ? In G. Lindzey (Ed.). *Assessment of human motives* (pp. 239–260). New York: Holt, Rinehart & Winston.

Allport, G. W. (1960). *Personality and social encounter: Selected essays*. Boston: Beacon Press.

Allport, G. W. (1961). *Pattern and growth in personality*. New York: Holt, Rinehart, & Winston.

Allport, G. W. (1965). *Letters from Jenny*. New York: Harcourt, Brace & World.

Allport, G. W. (1967). Autobiography. In E. G. Boring & G. Lindzey (Eds.), *A history of psychology in autobiography* (Vol. 5, pp. 1–25). New York: Appleton-Century-Crofts.

Allport, G. W., & Odbert, H. S. (1936). Trait-names: A psycho-lexical study. *Psychological Monographs, 47* (No. 211).

Allport, G. W., & Postman, L. (1947). *The psychology of rumor*. New York: Holt.

Allport, G. W., Vernon, P. E., & Lindzey, G. (1960). *Study of values* (3rd ed.). Boston: Houghton Mifflin.

Almagor, M., Tellegen, A., & Waller, N. G. (1995). The big-seven model: A cross-cultural replication and further exploration of the basic dimensions of natural language trait descriptors. *Journal of Personality and Social Psychology, 69,* 300–307.

Alterman, A. I. & Cacciola, J. S. (1991). The antisocial personality disorder diagnosis in substance abusers: Problems and issues. *Journal of Nervous and Mental Disease, 179,* 401–409.

Angleitner, A., & Ostendorf, F. (1989, July). *Personality factors via self and peer-ratings based on a representative sample of German trait-descriptive terms*. Paper presented at the First European Congress of Psychology, Amsterdam.

Angleitner, A., Ostendorf, F., & John, O. P. (1990). Towards a taxonomy of personality descriptors in German: A psycho-lexical study. *European Journal of Personality, 4,* 89–118.

Barnes, G. E., Malamuth, N. M., & Cheek, J. V. (1984). Personality and sexuality. *Personality and Individual Differences, 5,* 159–172.

Bem, D. J., & Allen, A. (1974). On predicting some of the people some of the time: The search for cross-situational consistencies in behavior. *Psychological Review, 81,* 506–520.

Block, J. (1989). Critique of the act frequency approach to personality. *Journal of Personality and Social Psychology, 56,* 234–245.

Bond, M. H., Nakazato, H., & Shiraishi, D. (1975). Universality and distinctiveness in dimensions of Japanese person perception. *Journal of Cross-Cultural Psychology, 6,* 346–357.

Botwin, M. D., & Buss, D. M. (1989). Structure of act-report data: Is the five-factor model of personality recaptured? *Journal of Personality and Social Psychology, 56,* 988–1001.

Bowers, K. S. (1973). Situationalism in psychology: An analysis and critique. *Psychological Review, 80,* 307–336.

Briggs, S. R. (1989). The optimal level of measurement for personality constructs. In D. M. Buss & N. Cantor (Eds.), *Personality psychology: Recent trends and emerging directions* (pp. 246–260). New York: Springer-Verlag.

Brokken, F. B. (1978). *The language of personality*. Meppel, The Netherlands: Krips.

Brooner, R. K., Schmidt, C. W., Jr., & Herbst, J. H. (1994). Personality trait characteristics of opioid abusers with and without comorbid personality disorders. In P. T. Costa, Jr. & T. A. Widiger (Eds.), *Personality disorders and the five-factor model of personality* (pp. 131–148). Washington, DC: American Psychological Association.

Brown, S. R., & Hendrick, C. (1971). Introversion, extroversion and social perception. *British Journal of Social and Clinical Psychology, 10,* 313–319.

Buss, A. H. (1989). Personality as traits. *American Psychologist, 44,* 1378–1388.

Buss, D. M. (1984). Toward a psychology of person-environment (PE) correlation: The role of spouse selection. *Journal of Personality and Social Psychology, 84,* 361–377.

Buss, D. M. (1985). The act frequency approach to the interpersonal environment. In R. Hogan & W. H. Jones (Eds.), *Personality in perspective: A research annual* (Vol. 1, pp. 173–200). Greenwich, CT: JAI.

Buss, D. M., & Cantor, N. (Eds.), (1989). *Personality psychology: Recent trends and emerging directions*. New York: Springer-Verlag.

Buss, D. M., & Craik, K. H. (1983). The act frequency approach to personality. *Psychological Review, 90,* 105–126.

Buss, D. M., & Craik, K. H. (1984). Acts, dispositions, and personality. In B. A. Maher & W. B. Maher (Eds.), *Progress in experimental personality research: Normal personality processes* (Vol. 13, pp. 241–301). New York: Academic Press.

Buss, D. M., & Craik, K. H. (1985). Why *not* measure that trait? Alternative criteria for identifying important dispositions. *Journal of Personality and Social Psychology, 48*, 934–946.

Cattell, R. B. (1943). The description of personality: Basic traits resolved into clusters. *Journal of Abnormal and Social Psychology, 38*, 476–506.

Cattell, R. B. (1945). The description of personality: Principles and findings in a factor analysis. *American Journal of Psychology, 58*, 69–90.

Cattell, R. B. (1950). *Personality: A systematic, theoretical, and factual study*. New York: McGraw-Hill.

Cattell, R. B. (1965). *The scientific analysis of personality*. Chicago: Aldine.

Cattell, R. B. (1974). Autobiography. In G. Lindzey (Ed.). *A history of psychology in autobiography* (Vol. 6, pp. 59–100). New York: Appleton-Century-Crofts.

Cattell, R. B. (1979). *Personality and learning theory*. New York: Springer.

Cattell, R. B. (1990). Advances in Cattellian personality theory. In L. A. Pervin (Ed.), *Handbook of personality: Theory and research* (pp. 101–110). New York: Guilford.

Cattell, R. B., Eber, H. W., & Tatsuoka, M., M. (1970). *Handbook for the Sixteen Personality Factor (16PF)*. Champaign, IL: Institute for Personality and Ability Testing.

Cattell, R. B. & Nesselroade, J. R. (1967). Likeness and completeness theories examined by Sixteen Personality Factor measures by stably and unstably married couples. *Journal of Personality and Social Psychology, 7*, 351–361.

Cheek, J. M. (1982). Aggregation, moderator variables, and the validity of personality tests: A peer-rating study. *Journal of Personality and Social Psychology, 43*, 1254–1269.

Church, A. T. (1994). Relating the Tellegen and five-factor models of personality structure. *Journal of Personality and Social Psychology, 67*, 898–909.

Claridge, G. S. (1983). The Eysenck Psychoticism scale. In J. P. Butcher & C. D. Spielberger (Eds.), *Advances in personality assessment* (Vol. 2, pp. 71–114). Hillsdale, NJ: Erlbaum.

Claridge, G. S., & Birchall, P. M. J. (1978). Bishop, Eysenck, Block, and psychoticism. *Journal of Abnormal Psychology, 87*, 604–668.

Claridge, G. S., & Chappa, H. J. (1973). Psychoticism: A study of its biological nature in normal subjects. *British Journal Social and Clinical Psychology, 12*, 175–187.

Clark, L. A., & Livesley, W. J. (1994). Two approaches to identifying the dimensions of personality disorders: Convergence on the five-factor model. In P. T. Costa, Jr. & T. A. Widiger (Eds.). *Personality disorders and the five-factor model of personality* (pp. 261–277). Washington, DC: American Psychological Association.

Comer, R. J. (1995). *Abnormal psychology* (2nd ed.). New York: W. H. Freeman.

Costa, P. T., Jr., & McCrae, R. R. (1985). *The NEO Personality Inventory manual*. Odessa, FL: Psychological Assessment Resources.

Costa, P. T., Jr., & McCrae, R. R. (1988). From catalog to classification: Murray's needs and the five-factor model. *Journal of Personality and Social Psychology, 55*, 258–265.

Costa, P. T., Jr., & McCrae, R. R. (1989). *The NEO-PI/ NEO-FFI manual supplement*. Odessa, FL: Psychological Assessment Resources.

Costa, P. T., Jr., & McCrae, R. R. (1994). Set like plaster? Evidence for the stability of adult personality. T. F. Heatherton & J. L. Weinberger (Eds.), *Can personality change* (pp. 21–40). Washington, DC: American Psychological Association.

Costa, P. T., Jr., & McCrae, R. R. (1995). Primary traits of Eysenck's P-E-N system: Three- and five-factor solutions. *Journal of Personality and Social Psychology, 69*, 308–317.

Costa, P. T., Jr., & Widiger, T. A. (Eds.). (1994). *Personality disorders and the five-factor model of personality*. Washington, DC: American Psychological Association.

De Raad, B., Mulder, E., Kloosterman, K., & Hofstee, W. K., (1988). Personality-descriptive verbs. *European Journal of Personality, 2*, 81–96.

Diener, E., & Larsen, R. J. (1984). Temporal stability and cross-situational consistency of affective, behavioral, and cognitive responses. *Journal of Personality and Social Psychology, 47*, 871–883.

Diener, E., Larsen, R. J., & Emmons, R. A. (1984). Person X situation interactions: Choice of situations and congruence response models. *Journal of Personality and Social Psychology, 47*, 580–592.

Digman, J. M. (1990). Personality structure: Emergence of the five-factor model. *Annual Review of Psychology, 41*, 417–440.

Drevdahl, J. E., & Cattell, R. B. (1958). Personality and creativity in artists and writers. *Journal of Clinical Psychology, 14*, 107–111.

Dudycha, G. J. (1936). An objective study of punctuality in relation to personality and achievement. *Archives of Psychology, 204*, 1–319.

Eaton, W. O. (1983). Measuring activity level with actometers: Reliability, validity, and arm length. *Child Development, 54*, 720–726.

Edwards, G., Chandler, C. & Hensman, C. (1972). Drinking in a London suburb: I. Correlates of normal drinking. *Journal of Studies in Alcohol, 33* (Suppl. No. 6), 69–93.

Ekehammer, B. (1974). Interactionism in personality from a historical perspective. *Psychological Bulletin, 81*, 1026–1048.

Ellis, C. G. (1994). Bulimia nervosa within the context of maladaptive personality traits. In P. T. Costa, Jr. & T. A. Widiger (Eds.). *Personality disorders and the five-factor model of personality* (pp. 205–209). Washington, DC: American Psychological Association.

Endler, N. S. (1973). The person versus the situation—a pseudo issue? A response to Alker. *Journal of Personality, 41*, 287–303.

Endler, N. S. (1982). Interactionism: A personality model, but not yet a theory. In M. M. Page (Ed.), *Nebraska symposium on motivation* (pp. 155–200). Lincoln: University of Nebraska Press.

Epstein, S. (1979). The stability of behavior: I. On predicting most of the people much of the time. *Journal of Personality and Social Psychology, 37*, 1097–1126.

Epstein, S. (1980). The stability of behavior: II. Implications for psychological research. *American Psychologist, 35,* 790–806.

Epstein, S. (1983). Aggregation and beyond: Some basic issues on the prediction of behavior. *Journal of Personality, 51,* 360–392.

Epstein. S., & O'Brien, E. J. (1985). The person-situation debate in historical and current perspective. *Psychological Bulletin, 98,* 513–537.

Epstein, S., & Teraspulsky, L. (1986). Perception of cross-situational consistency. *Journal of Personality and Social Psychology, 50,* 1152–1160.

Eysenck, H. J. (1947). *Dimensions of personality.* London: Routledge & Kegan Paul.

Eysenck, H. J. (1953). *The structure of personality.* New York: Wiley.

Eysenck, H. J. (1967). *The biological basis of personality.* Springfield, IL: Charles C Thomas.

Eysenck, H. J., (1970). *The structure of human personality.* (3rd. ed). London: Methuen

Eysenck, H. J. (1972). *Psychology is about people.* New York: The Library Press.

Eysenck, H. J. (1973). *The inequality of man.* London: Temple Smith.

Eysenck, H. J. (1975). *The inequality of man.* San Diego, CA: Edits.

Eysenck, H. J. (1976). *Sex and personality.* Austin, TX: University of Texas Press.

Eysenck, H. J. (1980). Autobiography. In G. Lindzey (Ed.), *A history of psychology in autobiography: Vol. 7.* San Francisco: W. H. Freeman.

Eysenck, H. J. (1982). Development of a theory. In C. D. Spielberger (Ed.), *Personality, genetics and behavior* (pp. 1–38). New York: Praeger.

Eysenck, H. J. (1990). Biological dimensions of personality. In L. A. Pervin (Ed.), *Handbook of personality: Theory and research* (pp. 244–276). New York: Guilford.

Eysenck, H. J., & Eysenck, M. W. (1985). *Personality and individual differences: A natural science approach.* New York: Plenum.

Eysenck, H. J., & Eysenck, S. B. (1975). *Manual of the Eysenck Personality Questionnaire.* San Diego, CA: Educational and Industrial Testing Service.

Eysenck, H. J., & Eysenck, S. B. G. (1976). *Psychoticism as a dimension of personality.* London: Hodder & Stroughton.

Eysenck, H. J., & Rachman, S. (1965). *The causes and cures of neurosis: An introduction to modern behavior therapy based on learning theory and the principle of conditioning.* London: Routledge & Kegan Paul.

Fiske, D. W. (1949). Consistency of the factorial structures of personality ratings from different sources. *Journal of Abnormal and Social Psychology, 44,* 329–344.

Funder, D. C. (1991). Global traits: A neo-Allportian approach to personality. *Psychological Science, 2,* 31–39.

Funder, D. G. (1995). On the accuracy of personality judgment: A realistic approach. *Psychological Review, 102,* 652–670.

Funder, D. C., & Ozer, D. J. (1983). Behaviors as a function of the situation. *Journal of Personality and Social Psychology, 44,* 107–112.

Goldberg, L. R. (1981). Language and individual differences: The search for universals in personality lexicons. In L. Wheeler (Ed.), *Review of personality and social psychology* (Vol. 2, pp. 141–165). Beverly Hills, CA: Sage.

Goldberg, L. R. (1990). An alternative "description of personality": The big-five factor structure. *Journal of Personality and Social Psychology, 59,* 1216–1229.

Goldberg, L. R. (1993). The structure of phenotypic personality traits. *American Psychologist, 48,* 26–34.

Haier, R. J., Robinson, D. L., Braden, W., & Williams, D. (1984). Evoked potential augmenting-reducing and personality differences. *Personality and Individual Differences, 5,* 293–301.

Hall, C. S., & Lindzey, G. (1978). *Theories of personality* (3rd ed.). New York: John Wiley & Son.

Harpur, T. J., Hart, S. D., & Hare, R. D. (1994). Personality and the psychopath. In P. T. Costa, Jr. & T. A. Widiger (Eds.). *Personality disorders and the five-factor model of personality* (pp. 149–173). Washington, DC: American Psychological Association.

Hartshorne, H., & May, M. A. (1928). *Studies in the nature of character: Vol. 1. Studies in deceit.* New York: Macmillan.

Harvey, F., & Hirschmann, R. (1980). The influence of extraversion and neuroticism on heart rate responses to aversive stimuli. *Personality and Individual Differences, 1,* 97–100.

Higgins, E. T. (1990). Personality, social psychology, and person-situation relations: Standards and knowledge activation as a common language. In L. A. Pervin (Ed.), *Handbook of personality: Theory and research* (pp. 301–338). New York: Guilford.

Hogan, R., DeSoto, C. B., & Solano, C. (1977). Traits, tests, and personality research. *American Psychologist, 32,* 255–264.

Holland, J. L. (1996). Exploring careers with a typology: What we have learned and some new directions. *American Psychologist, 51,* 397–406.

John, O. P. (1989). Towards a taxonomy of personality descriptors. In D. M. Buss & N. Cantor (Eds.), *Personality psychology: Recent trends and emerging directions* (pp. 261–271). New York: Springer-Verlag.

John, O. P. (1990). The "Big Five" factor taxonomy: Dimensions of personality in the natural language and in questionnaires. In L. A. Pervin (Ed.), *Handbook of personality: Theory and research* (pp. 66–100). New York: Guilford.

Karson, S., & O'Dell, J. W. (1976). *A guide to the clinical use of the 16PF.* Champaign, IL: Institute for Personality and Ability Testing.

Katigbak, M. S., Church, A. T., & Akamine, T. X. (1996). Cross-cultural generalizability of personality dimensions: Relating indigenous and imported dimensions in two cultures. *Journal of Personality and Social Psychology, 70,* 99–114.

Kelly, E. L., & Fiske, D. W. (1950). The prediction of success in the VA training program in clinical psychology. *American Psychologist, 5,* 395–406.

Kenrick, D. T., & Funder, D. C. (1988). Profiting from controversy: Lessons from the person-situation debate. *American Psychologist, 43,* 23–24.

Kenrick, D. T., & Stringfield, D. O. (1980). Personality traits and the eye of the beholder: Crossing some traditional philosophical boundaries in the search for consistency in all of the people. *Psychological Review, 87*, 88–104.

Kieren, D., Henton, J., & Marotz, R. (1975). *His and hers*. Hinsdale, IL: Dryden.

Knowles, R. T. (1966). *A pilot study of the relationship between a "creative" personality pattern and scholastic achievement*. Unpublished paper, Ball State Teacher's College, Muncie, Indiana.

Lamiell, J. T. (1987). *The psychology of personality: An epistemological inquiry*. New York: Columbia University Press.

Lamm, H., & Myers, D. G. (1978). Group-induced polarization of attitudes and behavior. In L. Berkowitz (Ed.), *Advances in experimental social psychology* (pp. 145–195). New York: Academic Press.

Lehne, G. K. (1994). The NEO-PI and the MCMI in the forensic evaluation of sex offenders. In P. T. Costa, Jr. & T. A. Widiger (Eds.). *Personality disorders and the five-factor model of personality* (pp. 175–188). Washington, DC: American Psychological Association.

Livneh, H., & Livneh, C. (1989). The five-factor model of personality: Is evidence for its cross-media premature? *Personality and Individual Differences, 10*, 75–80.

Maddi, S. R. (1989). *Personality theories: A comparative analysis* (5th ed.). Chicago: Dorsey.

Madsen, D. H., & Russell, M. T. (1982). *Marriage counseling report*. Champaign, IL: Institute for Personality and Ability Testing.

Magnusson, D., & Endler, N. S. (Eds.). (1977). *Personality at the crossroads: Current issues in interactional psychology*. Hillsdale, NJ: Erlbaum.

Maushammer, C., Ehmer, G., & Eckel, K. (1981). Pain, personality and individual differences in sensory evoked potentials. *Personality and Individual Differences, 2*, 335–336.

McCrae, R. R. (1989). Why I advocate the five-factor model: Joint factor analyses of the NEO-PI with other instruments. In D. M. Buss & N. Cantor (Eds.), *Personality psychology: Recent trends and emerging directions* (pp. 237–245). New York: Springer-Verlag.

McCrae, R. R., & Costa, P. T. (1987). Validation of the five-factor model of personality across instruments and observers. *Journal of Personality and Social Psychology, 52*, 81–90.

McCrae, R. R., Zonderman, A. B., Costa, P. T., Jr., Bond, M. H., & Paunonen, S. (1996). Evaluating replicability of factors in the revised NEO Personality Inventory: Confirmatory factor analysis versus procrustes rotation. *Journal of Personality and Social Psychology, 70*, 552–566.

Miller, T. R. (1991). The psychotherapeutic utility of the five-factor model of personality: A clinician's experience. *Journal of Personality Assessment, 57*, 415–433.

Mischel, W. (1968). *Personality and assessment*. New York: John Wiley and Sons.

Mischel, W. (1973). Toward a cognitive social learning reconceptualization of personality. *Psychological Review, 80*, 252–283.

Mischel, W. (1984). Convergences and challenges in the search for consistency. *American Psychologist, 39*, 351–364.

Mischel, W. (1985). Looking for personality. In S. Koch & D. E. Leary (Eds.), *A century of psychology as a science* (pp. 515–526). New York: McGraw-Hill.

Mischel, W. (1990). Personality dispositions revisited and revised: A view after three decades. In L. A. Pervin (Ed.), *Handbook of personality: Theory and research* (pp. 111–134). New York: Guilford.

Mischel, W., & Peake, P. K. (1982). Beyond *deja vu* in the search for cross-situational consistency. *Psychological Review, 89*, 730–755.

Moos, R. H. (1973). Conceptualizations of human environments. *American Psychologist, 28*, 652–665.

Moser, K. (1989). The act-frequency approach: A conceptual critique. *Personality and Social Psychology Bulletin, 15*, 73–83.

Moskowitz, D. S. (1982). Coherence and cross-situational generality in personality: A new analysis of an old problem. *Journal of Personality and Social Psychology, 43*, 754–768.

Moskowitz, D. S., & Schwarz, J. C. (1982). Validity comparisons of behavior counts and ratings by knowledgeable informants. *Journal of Personality and Social Psychology, 42*, 518–528.

Nimkoff, M. F., & Grigg, C. M. (1958). Values and marital adjustment of nurses. *Social Forces, 37*, 67–70.

Norman, W. T. (1967). *2,800 personality trait descriptors: Normative operating characteristics for a university population*. Ann Arbor: Department of Psychology, University of Michigan.

Ozer, D. (1986). *Consistency in personality*. New York: Springer-Verlag.

Peabody, D. (1987). Selecting representative trait adjectives. *Journal of Personality and Social Psychology, 52*, 59–71.

Peabody, D., & Goldberg, L. R. (1989). Some determinants of factor structures from personality-trait descriptors. *Journal of Personality and Social Psychology, 57*, 552–567.

Pervin, L. A. (1984). *Current controversies and issues in personality* (2nd ed.). New York: John Wiley & Sons.

Postman, L., Bruner, J. S., & McGinnies, E. (1948). Personal values as selective factors in perception. *Journal of Abnormal and Social Psychology, 43*, 142–154.

Price, R. H., & Bouffard, D. L. (1974). Behavioral appropriateness and situational constraint as dimensions of social behavior. *Journal of Personality and Social Psychology, 30*, 579–586.

Robins, R. W., John, O. P., Caspi, A., Moffitt, T. E., & Stouthhamer-Loeber, M. (1996). Resilient, overcontrolled, and undercontrolled boys: Three replicable personality types. *Journal of Personality and Social Psychology, 70*, 157–171.

Rosen, R., & Hall, E. (1984). *Sexuality*. New York: Random House.

Rushton, J. P., Brainerd, C. J., & Pressley, M. (1983). Behavioral development and construct validity: The principle of aggregation. *Psychological Bulletin, 94*, 18–38.

Russell, M. T., & Madsen, D. H. (1988). *Marriage Counseling Report User's Guide*. Champaign, IL: Institute for Personality and Ability Testing.

Sarason, I. G., Smith, R. E., & Diener, E. (1975). Personality research: Components of variance attributed to the person and the situation. *Journal of Personality and Social Psychology, 32*, 199–204.

Schooley, M. (1936). Personality resemblances among married couples. *Journal of Abnormal and Social Psychology, 31,* 340–347.

Schenk, J., & Pfrang, H. (1986). Extraversion, neuroticism, and sexual behavior: Interrelationships in a sample of young men. *Archives of Sexual Behavior, 15,* 449–455.

Seashore, H. G. (1947). Validation of the study of values for vocational groups at the college level. *Educational and Psychological Measurement, 7,* 757–763.

Shaver, P. R., & Brennan, K. A. (1992). Attachment styles and the "Big Five" Personality Traits: Their connections with each other with romantic relationship outcomes. *Personality and Social Psychology Bulletin, 18,* 536–545.

Shaw, L., & Sichel, H. (1971). *Accident proneness.* New York: Pergamon.

Spearman, C. (1910). Correlation calculated from faulty data. *British Journal of Psychology, 3,* 271–295.

Spranger, E. (1928). *Types of men: The psychology and ethics of personality.* New York: Johnson Reprint Corp.

Steinmetz, S. K., Clavan, S., & Stein, K. F. (1990). *Marriage and Family Realities: Historical and Contemporary Perspectives.* New York: Harper & Row.

Stewart, G. L., & Carson, K. P. (1995). Personality dimensions and domains of service performance: A field investigation. *Journal of Business and Psychology, 9,* 365–378.

Tellegen, A. (1993). Folk concepts and psychological concepts of personality and personality disorder. *Psychological Inquiry, 4,* 122–130.

Tellegen, A., & Waller, N. G. (1987, August). *Re-examining basic dimensions of natural language trait descriptors.* Paper presented at the 95th annual convention of the American Psychological Convention.

Tellegen, A., & Waller, N. G. (in press). Exploring personality through test construction: Development of the Multidimensional Personality Questionnaire. In S. R. Briggs & J. M. Cheek (Eds.), *Personality measures: Development and evaluation* (Vol. 1). Greenwich, CT: JAI.

Tupes, E. C., & Christal, R. C. (1961). *Recurrent personality factors based on trait ratings* (Tech. Rep. No. ASD-TR-61–97). Lackland Air Force Base, TX: U.S. Air Force.

Waller, N. G., & Ben-Porath, Y. (1987). Is it time for clinical psychology to embrace the five-factor model of personality? *American Psychologist, 42,* 887–889.

Waller, N. G., & Zavala, J. D. (1993). Evaluating the big five. *Psychological Inquiry, 4,* 131–134.

Widiger, T. A., & Trull, T. J. (1992). Personality and psychopathology: An application of the five-factor model. *Journal of Personality, 60,* 363–393.

Wiggins, J. S. (Ed.). (1996). *The five-factor model of personality.* New York: Guilford.

Wilson, G. (1978). Introversion/Extroversion. In H. London & J. E. Exner (Eds.), *Dimensions of personality.* New York: Wiley.

Wilson, G. (1990). Personality, time of day, and arousal. *Personality and Individual Differences, 11,* 153–168.

Zimbardo, P. G. (1970). The human choice: Individuation, reason, and order versus deindividuation, impulse, and chaos. In W. J. Arnold & D. Levine (Eds.), *Nebraska symposium on motivation, 1969* (p. 237–307). Lincoln: University of Nebraska Press.

Zuckerman, M., Buchsbaum, M. S., & Murphy, D. L. (1980). Seeking and its biological correlates. *Psychological Bulletin, 88,* 187–214.

Zuckerman, M., Koestner, R., DeBoy, T., Garcia, T., Maresca, B. C., & Sartoris, J. M. (1988). To predict some of the people some of the time: A reexamination of the moderator variable approach in personality theory. *Journal of Personality and Social Psychology, 54,* 1006–1019.

Chapter 9

Allport, G. W. (1937). *Personality: A psychological interpretation.* New York: Henry Holt.

Allport, G. W. (1961). *Pattern and growth in personality.* New York: Holt, Rinehart, & Winston.

Angst, J., & Maurer-Goeli, Y. A. (1974). Blutgruppen und Personlichkeit. *Archiv fur Psychiatrie und Nervenkrankheiten, 218,* 291–300.

Arvey, R. D., Bouchard, T. J., Segal, N. L., & Abraham, L. M. (1989). Job satisfaction: Environmental and genetic components. *Journal of Applied Psychology, 74,* 187–192.

Bouchard, T. J., & McGue, M. (1990). Genetic and rearing environmental influences on adult personality: An analysis of adopted twins reared apart. *Journal of Personality, 58,* 263–292.

Buss, A. H., & Plomin, R. (1975). *A temperament theory of personality development.* New York: John Wiley & Sons.

Buss, A. H., & Plomin, R. (1984). *Temperament: Early developing personality traits.* Hillsdale, NJ: Erlbaum.

Buss, D. M. (1989). Sex differences in human mate preferences: Evolutionary hypotheses tested in 37 cultures. *Behavioral and Brain Sciences, 12,* 1–49.

Buss, D. M. (1990). Toward a biologically informed psychology of personality. *Journal of Personality, 58,* 1–16.

Buss, D. M. (1994). *The evolution of desire: Strategies of human mating.* New York: Basic Books.

Buss, D. M., & Barnes, M. (1986). Preferences in human mate selection. *Journal of Personality and Social Psychology, 50,* 559–570.

Cloninger, C. R., Svrakic, D. M., & Przybeck, T. R. (1993). A psychobiological model of temperament and character. *Archives of General Psychiatry, 50,* 975–990.

Comer, R. J. (1992). *Abnormal psychology.* New York: W. H. Freeman.

Dabbs, J. M., Jr., de La Rue, D., & Williams, P. M. (1990). Testosterone and occupational choice: Actors, ministers, and other men. *Journal of Personality and Social Psychology, 59,* 1261–1265.

Daitzman, R., & Zuckerman, M. (1980). Disinhibitory sensation seeking personality and gonadal hormones. *Personality and Individual Differences, 1,* 103–110.

Daitzman, R., Zuckerman, M., Sammelwitz, P., & Ganjam, V. (1978). Sensation seeking and gonadal hormones. *Journal of Biosocial Sciences, 10*, 401–408.

Damon, A. (1955). Physique and success in military flying. *American Journal of Physical Anthropology, 13*, 217–252.

Darwin, C. (1958). *The origin of species* (6th ed.). New York: New American Library. (Original work published 1859)

Davidson, R. J. (1991). Biological approaches to the study of personality. In V. J. Derlega, B. A. Winstead, & W. H. Jones (Eds.), *Personality: Contemporary theory and research*. Chicago: Nelson-Hall.

Diamond, S. (1957). *Personality and temperament*. New York: Harper & Row.

Draper, P., & Belsky, J. (1990). Personality development in evolutionary perspective. *Journal of Personality, 58*, 141–161.

Eysenck, H. J. (1967). *The biological basis of personality.* Springfield, IL: Charles Thomas.

Eysenck, H. J. (1982a). The biological basis of cross-cultural differences in personality: Blood group antigens. *Psychological Reports, 51*, 531–540.

Eysenck, H. J. (1982b). *Personality, genetics, and behavior: Selected papers*. New York: Praeger.

Eysenck, H. J., (1983). A biometrical-genetical analysis of impulsive and sensation seeking behavior. In M. Zuckerman (Ed.), *Biological bases of sensation seeking, impulsivity, and anxiety* (pp. 1–27). Hillsdale, NJ: Erlbaum.

Eysenck, H. J. (1990a). Biological dimensions of personality. In L. A. Pervin (Ed.), *Handbook of personality: Theory and research* (pp. 244–276). New York: Guilford.

Eysenck, H. J. (1990b). Genetic and environmental contributions to individual differences: The three major dimensions of personality. *Journal of Personality, 58*, 245–261.

Eysenck, H. J., & Eysenck, M. W. (1985). *Personality and individual differences: A natural science approach*. New York: Plenum.

Feingold, A. (1990). Gender differences in effects of physical attractiveness on romantic attraction: A comparison across five research paradigms. *Journal of Personality and Social Psychology, 59*, 981–993.

Feingold, A. (1991). Sex differences in the effects of similarity and physical attractiveness on opposite-sex attraction. *Basic and Applied Social Psychology, 12*, 357–367.

Feingold, A. (1992). Gender differences in mate selection preferences: A test of the parental investment model. *Psychological Bulletin, 112*, 125–139.

Fisher, H. (1992). *Anatomy of love: The mysteries of mating, marriage, and why we stay*. New York: Fawcett Columbine.

Gale, A. (1983). Electroencephalographic studies of extraversion-introversion: A case study in the psychophysiology of individual differences. *Personality and Individual Differences, 4*, 371–380.

Gale, A., & Eysenck, M. W. (Eds.) (in press). *Handbook of individual differences: Biological perspectives*. New York: Wiley.

Gangestad, S. W. (1989). The evolutionary history of genetic variation: An emerging issue in the behavioral genetic study of personality. In D. M. Buss & N. Cantor (Eds.), *Personality psychology: Recent trends and emerging directions* (pp. 320–332). New York: Springer-Verlag.

Glueck, S., & Glueck, E. (1950). *Unraveling juvenile delinquency*. New York: Harper & Row.

Glueck, S., & Glueck, E. (1956). *Physique and delinquency*. New York: Harper & Row.

Gottesman, I. I., & Shields, J. (1982). *Schizophrenia: The epigenetic puzzle*. Cambridge, UK: Cambridge University Press.

Hastie, R., & Park, B. (1986). The relationship between memory and judgment depends on whether the judgment task is memory based or on-line. *Psychological Review, 93*, 258–268.

Hofstede, G. (1976). *Nationality and organizational stress*. Brussels: European Institute for Research in Management.

Hofstede, G. (1980). *Culture's consequences: International differences in work-related values*. London: Sage.

Kagan, J. (1994). *Galen's prophecy: Temperament in human nature*. New York: Basic Books.

Kagan, J. & Arcus, D. (1995). Temperament and craniofacial variation in the first two years. *Child Development, 66*, 1529–1540.

Kagan, J., Reznick, J. S., & Snidman, N. (1988). Biological bases of childhood shyness. *Science, 240*, 167–171.

Kenrick, D. T. (1989). A biosocial perspective on mates and traits: Reuniting personality and social psychology. In D. M. Buss & N. Cantor (Eds.), *Personality psychology: Recent trends and emerging directions* (pp. 308–319). New York: Springer-Verlag.

Kenrick, D. T., & Dengelegi, L. (1988). *Gender differences in spontaneous recall of faces: Default processing fits a reproductive fitness model*. Manuscript in preparation. Arizona State University, Tempe, AZ.

Kenrick, D. T., Montello, D. R., & MacFarlane, S. (1985). Personality: Social learning, social cognition, or sociobiology? In R. Hogan & W. H. Jones (Eds.), *Perspectives in personality: A research annual* (Vol. 1, pp. 201–234). Greenwich, CN: JAI.

Kenrick, D. T., Sadalla, E. K., Groth, G., & Trost, M. R. (1990). Evolution, traits, and the stages of human courtship: Qualifying the parental investment model. *Journal of Personality, 58*, 97–116.

Kenrick, D. T., & Trost, M. R. (1987). A bisocial theory of heterosexual relationships. In K. Kelly (Ed.), *Females, males, and sexuality: Theories and research* (pp. 59–100). Albany, NY: State University of New York Press.

Kretschmer, E. (1925). *Physique and character*. New York: Harcourt.

Loehlin, J. C. (1977). Psychological genetics from the study of human behavior. In R. B. Cattell & R. M. Dreger (Eds.), *Handbook of modern personality theory* (pp. 329–347). New York: Halsted.

Leohlin, J. C., Horn, J. M., & Willerman, L. (1990). Heredity, environment, and personality change: Evidence from the Texas Adoption Project. *Journal of Personality, 58*, 221–243.

Loehlin, J. C., & Nichols, R. C. (1976). *Heredity, environment, and personality: A study of 850 sets of twins.* Austin, TX: University of Texas Press.

Loehlin, J. C., Willerman, L., & Horn, J. M. (1982). Personality resemblances between unwed mothers and their adopted-away offspring. *Journal of Personality and Social Psychology, 42,* 1089–1099.

Loehlin, J. C., Willerman, L., & Horn, J. M. (1987). Personality resemblance in adoptive families: A 10–year follow-up. *Journal of Personality and Social Psychology, 53,* 961–969.

Lynn, R. (1981). Cross-cultural differences in neuroticism, extraversion and psychoticism. In R. Lynn (Ed.), *Dimensions of personality* (pp. 263–286). London: Pergamon.

McLaughlin, R. J., & Eysenck, H. J. (1967). Extraversion, neuroticism and paired-associate learning. *Journal of Experimental Research in Personality, 2,* 128–132.

Mazur, A. (1985). A biosocial model of status in face-to-face primate groups. *Social Forces, 64,* 377–402.

Mazur, A., Booth, A., & Dabbs, J. M., Jr. (1992). Testosterone and chess competition. *Social Psychology Quarterly, 55,* 70–77.

Neary, R. S., & Zuckerman, M. (1976). Sensation seeking trait and state anxiety and the electrodermal orienting reflex. *Psychophysiology, 13,* 205–211.

O'Connor, K. (1980). The CNV and individual differences in smoking behavior. *Personality and Individual Differences, 1,* 57–72.

O'Connor, K. (1982). Individual differences in the effect of smoking on frontal-central distribution of the CNV. Some observations on smokers' control of attentional behavior. *Personality and Individual Differences, 3,* 271–285.

Omenn, G. S. (1978). Prenatal diagnosis of genetic disorders. *Science, 200,* 952–958.

Papalia, D. E., & Olds, S. W. (1992). *Human development* (5th ed.). New York: McGraw-Hill.

Pennebaker, J. W., Rime, B., & Blankenship, V. E. (1996). Stereotypes of emotional expressiveness of Northerners and Southerners: A cross-cultural test of Montesquieu's hypotheses. *Journal of Personality and Social Psychology, 70,* 372–380.

Pervin, L. A. (1984). *Current controversies and issues in personality* (2nd ed.). New York: John Wiley & Sons.

Plomin, R. (1986). *Development, genetics, and psychology.* Hillsdale, NJ: Erlbaum.

Plomin, R., Chipuer, H. M., & Loehlin, J. C. (1990). Behavior genetics and personality. In L. A. Pervin (Ed.), *Handbook of personality: Theory and research* (pp. 225–243). New York: Guilford.

Plomin, R., DeFries, J. C., & Fulker, D. W. (1988). *Nature and nurture during infancy and early childhood.* New York: Cambridge University Press.

Plomin, R., DeFries, J. C., & McClearn, G. E. (1990). *Behavioral genetics: A primer* (2nd ed.). San Francisco: Freeman.

Plomin, R., & Nesselroade, J. R. (1990). Behavioral genetics and personality change. *Journal of Personality, 58,* 191–220.

Plomin, R., Pedersen, N. L., McClearn, G. E., Nesselroade, J. R., & Bergeman, C. S. (1988). EAS temperaments during the last half of the life span: Twins reared apart and twins reared together. *Psychology and Aging, 3,* 43–50.

Plomin, R., & Rowe, D. C. (1977). A study of temperament in young children. *Journal of Psychology, 97,* 107–113.

Purifoy, F. E., & Koopmans, L. H. (1979). Androstenedione, testosterone, and free testosterone concentration in women of various occupations. *Social Biology, 26,* 179–188.

Rathus, S. A., & Nevid, J. S. (1991). *Abnormal psychology.* Englewood Cliffs, NJ: Prentice Hall.

Rowe, D. C. (1989). Personality theory and behavioral genetics: contributions and issues. In D. M. Buss & N. Cantor (Eds.), *Personality psychology: Recent trends and emerging directions* (pp. 294–307). New York: Springer-Verlag.

Sanford, R. N., Adkins, M. M., Miller, R. B., Cobb, E. A., et al. (1943). Physique, personality, and scholarship: A cooperative study of school children. *Monographs of the Society for Research in Child Development, 8* (1, Serial No. 34).

Sadalla, E. K., Kenrick, D. T., & Vershure, B. (1987). Dominance and heterosexual attraction. *Journal of Personality and Social Psychology, 52,* 730–738.

Schindler, G. L. (1979). Testosterone concentration, personality patterns, and occupational choice in women. *Dissertation Abstracts International, 40,* 1411A. (University Microfilms No. 79–19,403).

Schooler, C., Zahn, T. P., Murphy, D. L., & Buchsbaum, M. S. (1978). Psychological correlates of monoamine oxidase in normals. *Journal of Nervous and Mental Disease, 166,* 177–186.

Scarr, S., Webber, P. L., Weinberg, R. A., & Wittig, M. A. (1981). Personality resemblance among adolescents and their parents in biologically related and adoptive families. *Journal of Personality and Social Psychology, 40,* 885–898.

Shagass, C., & Kerenyi, A. B. (1958). Neurophysiological studies of personality. *Journal of Nervous and Mental Diseases, 126,* 141–147.

Sheldon, W. H. (with the collaboration of S. S. Stevens) (1942). *The varieties of temperament: A psychology of constitutional differences.* New York: Harper & Row.

Sheldon, W. H. (with the collaboration of C. W. Dupertuis & E. McDermott) (1954). *Atlas of men: A guide for somatotyping the adult male at all ages.* New York: Harper & Row.

Sheldon, W. H., Lewis, N. D. C., & Tenney, A. M. (1969). Psychotic patterns and physical constitution: A thirty-year follow-up of thirty-eight hundred psychiatric patients in New York State. In D. V. Siva Sankar (Ed.), *Schizophrenia: Current concepts and research* (pp. 838–912). New York: PJD Publications.

Smith, B. D. (1983). Extraversion and electrodermal activity: Arousability and the inverted-U. *Personality and Individual Differences, 4,* 411–420.

Stalling, M. C., Hewitt, J. K., Cloninger, C. R., Heath, A. C., & Eaves, L. J. (1996). Genetic and environmental structure of the Tridimensional Personality Questionnaire: Three or four temperament dimensions? *Journal of Personality and Social Psychology, 70,* 127–140.

Staw, B. M., & Ross, J. (1985). Stability in the midst of change: A dispositional approach to job attitudes. *Journal of Applied Psychology, 70,* 469–480.

Stelmack, R. M. (1985). Extraversion and auditory evoked potentials: Some empirical and theoretical considerations. In D. Papakostopoulos, S. Butler, & I. Martin (Eds.), *Experimental and clinical neuropsychophysiology* (pp. 238–255). Lancaster: Medical and Technical Publications.

Stelmack, R. M. (1990). Biological bases of extraversion: psychophysiological evidence. *Journal of Personality, 58,* 293–311.

Stelmack, R. M., & Geen, R. G. (in press). The psychophysiology of extraversion. In A. Gale & M. W. Eysenck (Eds.), *Handbook of individual differences: Biological perspectives.* New York: Wiley.

Stelmack, R. M., & Wilson, K. G. (1982). Extraversion and the effects of frequency and intensity on the auditory brainstem evoked response. *Personality and Individual Differences, 3,* 373–380.

Taylor, J. R., & Carroll, J. L. (1987). Current issues in electroconvulsive therapy. *Psychological Reports, 60* (3, Pt. 1).

Tellegen, A., Lykken, D. T., Bouchard, T. J., Jr., Wilcox, K., Segal, N., & Rich, S. (1988). Personality similarity in twins reared apart and together. *Journal of Personality and Social Psychology, 54,* 1031–1039.

Thomas, A., Chess, S., Birch, H., Hertzig, M., & Korn, S. (1963). *Behavioral individuality in early childhood.* New York: New York University Press.

Triandis, H. C. (1996). The psychological measurement of cultural syndromes. *American Psychologist, 51,* 407–415.

Trivers, R. (1985). *Social evolution.* Menlo Park, CA: Benjamin-Cummings.

Wigglesworth, M. J., & Smith, B. D. (1976). Habituation and dishabituation of the electrodermal orienting reflex in relation to extraversion and neuroticism. *Journal of Research in Personality, 10,* 437–445.

Wilson, E. O. (1975). *Sociobiology.* Cambridge, MA: Harvard University Press.

Wong, A., & Carducci, B. J. (1991). Sensation seeking and financial risk taking in everyday matters. *Journal of Business and Psychology, 5,* 525–530.

Zuckerman, M. (1971). Dimensions of sensation seeking. *Journal of Consulting and Clinical Psychology, 36,* 45–52.

Zuckerman, M. (1979). *Sensation seeking: Beyond the optimal level of arousal.* Hillsdale, NJ: Erlbaum.

Zuckerman, M. (Ed.). (1983). *Biological bases of sensation seeking, impulsivity, and anxiety.* Hillsdale, NJ: Erlbaum.

Zuckerman, M. (1989). Personality in the third dimension: A psychobiological approach. *Personality and Individual Differences, 10,* 391–418.

Zuckerman, M. (1990). The psychophysiology of sensation seeking. *Journal of Personality, 58,* 313–345.

Zuckerman, M., Ballinger, J. C., & Post, R. M. (1984). The neurobiology of some dimensions of personality. *International Review of Neurobiology, 25,* 391–436.

Zuckerman, M., Buchsbaum, M. S., & Murphy, D. L. (1980). Sensation seeking and its biological correlates. *Psychological Bulletin, 88,* 187–214.

Zuckerman, M., Eysenck, S. B. G., & Eysenck, H. J. (1978). Sensation seeking in England and America: Cross-cultural, age, and sex comparisons. *Journal of Consulting and Clinical Psychology, 46,* 139–149.

Zuckerman, M., Simons, R. F., & Como, P. G. (1988). Sensation seeking and stimulus intensity as modulators of cortical, cardiovascular, and electrodermal response: A cross-modality study. *Personality and Individual Differences, 9,* 361–372.

Chapter 10

Abramson, L. Y., Metalsky, G. I., & Alloy, L. B. (1989). Hopelessness depression: A theory-based subtype of depression. *Psychological Review, 96,* 358–372.

Abramson, L. Y., Seligman, M. E. P. & Teasdale, J. D. (1978). Learned helplessness in humans: Critique and reformulation. *Journal of Abnormal Psychology, 87,* 49–74.

Ayllon, T., & Azrin, H. H. (1965). The measurement and reinforcement of behavior of psychotics. *Journal of Experimental Analysis of Behavior, 8,* 357–383.

Baer, D. M., Wolf, M. M., & Risley, T. (1968). Some current dimensions of applied behavior analysis. *Journal of Applied Behavioral Analysis, 1,* 91–97.

Bandura, A. (1969). *Principles of behavior modification.* New York: Holt, Rinehart & Winston.

Barker, L. M. (1994). *Learning and behavior: A psychobiological perspective.* New York: Macmillan College Publishing Company.

Baron, R. A., & Byrne, D. (1994). *Social psychology: Understanding human interaction* (7th ed.). Boston: Allyn & Bacon.

Basmajian, J. V. (1977). Learned control of single motor units. In G. E. Schwartz & J. Beatty (Eds.), *Biofeedback: Theory and Research* (pp. 415–431). New York: Academic Press.

Belles, D., & Bradlyn, A. S. (1987). The use of the changing criterion design in achieving controlled smoking in a heavy smoker: A controlled case study. *Journal of Behavior Therapy and Experimental Psychiatry, 18,* 77–82.

Berkowitz, L., & Knurek, D. A. (1969). Label-mediated hostility generalization. *Journal of Personality and Social Psychology, 13,* 200–206.

Birnbrauer, J. S., Wolf, M. M., Kidder, J. D., & Tague, C. E. (1965). Classroom behavior of retarded pupils with token reinforcement. *Journal of Experimental Child Psychology, 2,* 219–235.

Blanchard, E. B. (1992). Psychological treatment of benign headache disorders. *Journal of Consulting and Clinical Psychology, 60,* 537–551.

Blanchard, E. B. (1994). Behavior medicine and health psychology. In A. E. Bergin & S. L. Garfield (Eds.), *Handbook of psychotherapy and behavior change* (pp. 701–733). New York: Wiley.

Blanchard, E. B., McCoy, G. C., Musso, A., Geraridi, M. A. (1986). A controlled comparison of thermal biofeedback and relaxation training of essential hypertension: I. Short-term and long-term outcome. *Behavior therapy, 17,* 563–579.

Boudewyns, P. A., Tanna, V. L., & Fleischman, D. J. A. (1975). A modified shame aversion therapy for compulsive obscene telephone calling. *Behavior Therapy, 6,* 704–707.

Brehm, S. S. (1992). *Intimate relationships* (2nd ed.). New York: McGraw-Hill.

Budney, A. J., Higgins, S. T., Delaney, D. D., Kent, L. & Bickel, W. K. (1991). Contingent reinforcement of abstinence with individuals abusing cocaine and marijuana. *Journal of Applied Behavior Analysis, 24,* 657–665.

Buss, A. H. (1995). *Personality: Temperament, social behavior, and the self*. Boston: Allyn & Bacon.

Byrne, D. (1971). *The attraction paradigm*. New York: Academic Press.

Callahan, E. F., & Leitenberg, H. (1973). Aversion therapy for sexual deviation: Contingent shock and covert sensitization. *Journal of Abnormal Psychology*, *81*, 60–73.

Cannon, D. S., Baker, T. B., & Wehl, C. K. (1981). Emetic and electric shock alcohol aversion therapy: Six- and twelve-month follow-up. *Journal of Consulting and Clinical Psychology*, *49*, 360–368.

Carr, A. T. (1971). Compulsive neurosis: Two psychophysiological studies. *Bulletin of the British Psychological Society*, *24*, 256–257.

Catania, A. C. (1992). *Learning* (3rd ed.), Englewood Cliffs, NJ: Prentice Hall.

Cautela, J. R. (1966). Treatment of compulsive behavior by covert sensitization. *Psychological Record*, *16*, 33–34.

Cautela, J. R., & Kearney, A. J. (Eds.). (1993). *Covert conditioning casebook*. Pacific Grove, CA: Brooks/Cole.

Claeson, L. E., & Malm, U. (1973). Electro-aversion therapy of chronic alcoholism. *Behavior Research and Therapy*, *11*, 663–665.

Clore, G. L., & Byrne, D. (1974). A reinforcement-affect model of attraction. In T. L. Huston (Ed.), *Foundations of interpersonal attraction* (pp. 143–170). New York: Academic Press.

Cohen, D. (1981). *Consumer behavior*. New York: Random House.

Comer, R. J. (1992). *Abnormal psychology*. New York: W. H. Freeman.

Comer, R. J. (1995). *Abnormal psychology* (5th ed.). New York: W. H. Freeman.

Davison, G. C., & Neale, J. M. (1994). *Abnormal psychology* (6th ed.). New York: John Wiley & Sons.

Deaux, K., Dane, F. C., & Wrightsman, L. S. (1993). *Social psychology in the '90s* (6th ed.). Pacific Grove, CA: Brooks/Cole.

DeBell, C. S., & Harless, D. K. (1992). B. F. Skinner: Myth and misperception. *Teaching of Psychology*, *19*, 68–73.

Diament, C., & Wilson, G. T. (1975). An experimental investigation of the effects of covert sensitization in an analogue eating situation. *Behavior Therapy*, *6*, 499–509.

Domjan, M. (1993). *The principles of learning and behavior* (3rd ed.). Pacific Grove, CA: Brooks/Cole.

Drabman, R. S., Spitalnik, R. S., & O'Leary, K. D. (1973). Teaching self-control to disruptive children. *Journal of Abnormal Psychology*, *82*, 10–16.

Emmelkamp, P. M. G. (1994). Behavior therapy with adults. In A. E. Bergin & S. L. Garfield (Eds.), *Handbook of psychotherapy and behavior change* (4th ed.) (pp. 379–427). New York: Wiley.

Engel, J. F., Blackwell, R. D., & Miniard, P. W. (1993). *Consumer behavior* (7th ed.). Fort Worth, TX: Dryden Press.

Epstein, A. W. (1965). Fetishism. In R. Slovenko (Ed.), *Sexual behavior and the law* (pp. 515–520). Springfield, IL: Charles C Thomas.

Fernando, C. K., & Basmajian, J. V. (1978). Biofeedback in physical medicine and rehabilitation. *Biofeedback and Self-regulation*, *3*, 435–455.

Fixsen, D. L., Braukmann, C. J., Kirigin, K. A., Willner, A. G., & Schumaker, J. (1976). Achievement place: The teaching-family model. *Child Care Quarterly*, *5*, 92–103.

Freeman, H. R. (1977). Reward vs. reciprocity as related to attraction. *Journal of Applied Social Psychology*, *7*, 57–66.

Fuchs, C. Z., & Rehm, L. P. (1977). A self-control behavior therapy program for depression. *Journal of Consulting and Clinical Psychology*, *45*, 206–215.

Gauthier, J., Côté, G. & French, D. (1994). The role of home practice in the thermal biofeedback treatment of migraine headache. *Journal of Consulting and Clinical Psychology*, *62*, 180–184.

Glynn, S. M. (1990). Token economy approaches for psychiatric patients: Progress and pitfalls of chronic psychiatric illness. *Behavior Modification*, *14*, 383–407.

Gulanick, N., Woodburn, L. T., & Rimm, D. C. (1975). Weight gain through self-control procedures. *Journal of Consulting and Clinical Psychology*, *43*, 536–539.

Harver, A. (1994). Effects of feedback on the ability of asthmatics to detect increases in the flow resistance component of breathing. *Health Psychology*, *13*, 52–62.

Hawkins, D. I., Best, R. J., Coney, K. A. (1989). *Consumer behavior: Implications for marketing strategy* (4th ed.). Homewood, IL: Irwin.

Hayes, S. C., Brownell, K. D., & Barlow, D. H. (1978). The use of self-administered covert sensitization in the treatment of exhibitionism and sadism. *Behavior Therapy*, *9*, 283–289.

Hodgson, R. J., & Rachman, S. J. (1972). The effects of contamination and washing on obsessional patients. *Behaviour Research and Therapy*, *10*, 111–117.

Hovanitz, C. A., & Wander, M. R. (1990). Tension headache: Disregulation at some levels of stress. *Journal of Behavioral Medicine*, *13*, 539–560.

Ingham, R., & Bennett, P. (1990). Health psychology in community settings: Models and methods. In P. Bennett, J. Weinman, & P. Spurgeon (Eds.), *Current developments in health psychology*. London: Harwood Academic Publishers.

Johnson, S. M., & White, G. (1971). Self-observation as an agent of behavior change. *Behavior Therapy*, *2*, 488–497.

Kazdin, A. E. (1994). *Behavior modification in applied settings* (5th ed.). Pacific Grove, CA: Brooks/Cole.

Kazdin, A. E., & Wilcoxon, L. A. (1976). Systematic desensitization and nonspecific treatment effects: A methodological evaluation. *Psychological Bulletin*, *83*, 729–758.

Kendall, P. C., & Norton-Ford, J. D. (1982). *Clinical psychology: Scientific and professional dimensions*. New York: John Wiley & Sons.

Kenrick, D. T., Montello, D. R., & MacFarlane, S. (1985). Personality: Social learning, social cognition, or sociobiology. In R. Hogan & W. H. Jones (Eds.), *Perspectives in personality: A research annual* (Vol. 1) (pp. 201–234). Greenwich, CT: JAI.

Kondo, C. Y., & Canter, A. (1977). Time and false electromyographic feedback: Effect on tension headache. *Journal of Abnormal Psychology*, *86*, 93–95.

Krasner, L., & Ullmann, L. P. (1965). *Research in behavior modification*. New York: Holt, Rinehart & Winston.

Kuhlman, W. H., & Kaplan, B. J. (1979). Clinical applications of EGG feedback training. In R. J. Gatchel & K. P. Price (Eds.), *Clinical applications of biofeedback: Appraisal and status* (pp. 65–96). Elmsford, NY: Pergamon.

Lamal, P. A. (1995). College students' misconceptions about behavior analysis. *Teaching of Psychology, 22,* 177–180.

Lanyon, R. I., Barrington, C. C., & Newman, A. C. (1976). Modification of stuttering through EMG biofeedback: A preliminary study. *Behavior Therapy, 7,* 96–103.

Levine, F. M., & Fasnacht, G. (1974). Token rewards may lead to token learning. *American Psychologist, 29,* 816–820.

Lichstein, K. L. (1988). *Clinical relaxation strategies.* New York: Wiley.

Liebert, R. M., & Spiegler, M. D. (1990). *Personality: Strategies and issues* (6th ed.). Pacific Grove, CA: Brooks/Cole.

Loevinger, J. (1987). *Paradigms of personality.* New York: W. H. Freeman.

Lohr, J. M., & Staats, A. W. (1973). Attitude conditioning in Sino-Tibetan languages. *Journal of Personality and Social Psychology, 26,* 196–200.

Lott, A. J., & Lott, B. E. (1974). The role of reward in the formation of positive interpersonal attitudes. In T. Huston (Ed.), *Foundations of interpersonal attraction* (pp. 171–189). New York: Academic Press.

Lovaas, O. I., & Simmons, J. Q. (1969). Manipulation of self-destruction in three retarded children. *Journal of Applied Behavioral Analysis, 2,* 143–157.

Maier, S. F., & Seligman, M. E. P. (1976). Learned helplessness: Theory and evidence. *Journal of Experimental Psychology: General, 105,* 3–46.

Malott, R. W., Whaley, D. L., & Malott, M. E. (1993). *Elementary principles of behavior* (2nd ed.). Englewood Cliffs, NJ: Prentice Hall.

Martin, G., & Pear, J. (1992). *Behavior modification: What is it and how to do it* (4th ed.). Englewood Cliffs, NJ: Prentice Hall.

Martin, R. A., & Poland, E. Y. (1980). *Learning to change: A self-management approach to adjustment.* New York: McGraw-Hill.

Masters, J. C., Burish, T. G., Hollon, S. D., & Rimm, D. C. (1987). *Behavior therapy: Techniques and empirical findings* (3rd ed.). San Diego, CA: Harcourt Brace Jovanovich.

Mattick, R. P., & Peters, L. (1988). Treatment of severe social phobia: Effects of guided exposure with and without cognitive restructuring. *Journal of Consulting and Clinical Psychology, 56,* 251–260.

McConaghy, N. (1971). Aversive therapy of homosexuality: Measures of efficacy. *American Journal of Psychiatry, 127,* 141–144.

McGrady, A., & Gerstenmaier, L. (1990). Effect of biofeedback assisted relaxation training on blood glucose levels in a Type I insulin dependent diabetic: A case report. *Journal of Behavior Therapy and Experimental Psychiatry, 21,* 69–75.

McNally, R. J. (1986). Preparedness and phobia: A review. *Psychological Bulletin, 101,* 283–303.

Mehr, J. (1983). *Abnormal psychology.* New York: Holt, Rinehart & Winston.

Metalsky, G. I., Habertadt, L. J., & Abramson, L. Y. (1987). Vulnerability and invulnerability to depressive mood reactions: Toward a more powerful test of the diathesis-stress and causal mediation components of the reformulated theory of depression. *Journal of Personality and Social Psychology, 52,* 386–393.

Metalsky, G. I., Joiner, T. E., Jr., Hardin, T. S. & Abramson, L. Y. (1993). Depressive reactions to failure in a naturalistic setting: A test of the hopelessness and self-esteem theories of depression. *Journal of Abnormal Psychology, 102,* 101–109.

Moss, M. K., & Page, R. A. (1972). Reinforcement and helping behavior. *Journal of Applied Social Psychology, 2,* 360–371.

Motley, M. T. (1988). Taking the terror out of talk. *Psychology Today, 22,* 46–49.

O'Leary, K. D., & Drabman, R. (1971). Token reinforcement programs in the classroom. *Psychological Bulletin, 75,* 379–398.

O'Leary, K. D., & Wilson, G. T. (1975). *Behavior therapy: Application and outcome.* Englewood Cliffs, NJ: Prentice Hall.

Ollendick, T. H. (1981). Self-monitoring and self-administered overcorrection: The modification of nervous tics in children. *Behavior Modification, 5,* 75–84.

Ost, L-G, & Hugdahl, K. (1981). Acquisition of phobias and anxiety response patterns in clinical patients. *Behavior Research and Therapy, 19,* 439–447.

Overmier, J. B., & Seligman, M. E. P. (1967). Effects of inescapable shock upon subsequent escape and avoidance responding. *Journal of Comparative and Physiological Psychology, 63,* 23–33.

Paul, G. L. (1966). *Insight vs. desensitization in psychotherapy.* Palo Alto, CA: Stanford University.

Paul, G. L. (1969). Outcome of systematic desensitization II: Controlled investigations of individual treatment, technique variations, and current status. In C. M. Franks (Ed.), *Behavior therapy: Appraisal and status* (pp. 105–159). New York: McGraw-Hill.

Pavlov, I. P. (1927). *Conditioned reflexes.* London: Clarendon.

Pervin, L. A. (1989). *Personality: Theory and research* (5th ed.). New York: John Wiley & Sons.

Peter, J. P., & Olson, J. C. (1990). *Consumer behavior and marketing strategy* (2nd ed.). Homewood, IL: Irwin.

Peterson, C., Schulman, P., Castellon, C., & Seligman, M. E. P. (1991). The explanatory style scoring manual. In C. P. Smith (Ed.), *Thematic content analysis for motivation and personality research.* New York: Cambridge University Press.

Peterson, C., & Seligman, M. E. P. (1984). Causal explanations as a risk factor for depression: Theory and evidence. *Psychological Review, 91,* 347–374.

Petty, R. E., & Cacioppo, J. T. (1981). *Attitudes and persuasion: Classic and contemporary approaches.* Dubuque, IA: Wm. C. Brown.

Quick, J. C., Murphy, L. R., & Hurrell, J. J., Jr. (Eds.). (1992). *Stress and well-being at work: Assessments and interventions for occupational mental health.* Washington, DC: American Psychological Association.

Rachman, S. (1966). Sexual fetishism: An experimental analogue. *Psychological Record, 16,* 293–296.

Rajecki, D. J. (1989). *Attitudes* (2nd ed.). Sunderland, MA: Sinauer Associates.

Rathus, S. A., & Nevid, J. S. (1991). *Abnormal psychology.* Englewood Cliffs, NJ: Prentice Hall.

Rathus, S. A., & Nevid, J. S. (1992). *Adjustment and growth: The challenges of life* (5th ed.). Fort Worth, TX: Harcourt Brace Jovanovich College Publishers.

Redd, W. H., Porterfield, A. L., & Anderson, B. L. (1979). *Behavior modification: Behavioral approaches to human problems.* New York: Random House.

Rescorla, R. A. (1967). Pavlovian conditioning and its proper control procedures. *Psychological Review, 74,* 71–80.

Rescorla, R. A. (1968). Probability of shock in the presence and absence of CS in fear conditioning. *Journal of Comparative and Physiological Psychology, 66,* 1–5.

Rescorla, R. A. (1988). Pavlovian conditioning: It's not what you think. *American Psychologist, 43,* 151–160.

Rimm, D. C., & Masters, J. C. (1979). *Behavior therapy: Techniques and empirical findings* (2nd ed.). New York: Academic Press.

Rutter, D., Quine, L., & Chesham, D. J. (1993). *Social psychological approaches to health.* New York: Harvester.

Schroeder, D. A., Penner, L. A., Dovidio, J. F., & Piliavin, J. A. (1995). *The psychology of helping and altruism: Problems and puzzles.* New York: McGraw-Hill.

Schwartz, S. (in press). *Abnormal psychology.* Mountain View, CA: Mayfield.

Seligman, M. E. P. (1975). *Helplessness: On depression, development, and death.* San Francisco: Freeman.

Seligman, M. E. P., & Maier, S. F. (1967). Failure to escape traumatic shock. *Journal of Experimental Psychology, 74,* 1–9.

Shahidi, S., & Salmon, P. (1992). Contingent and noncontingent biofeedback training for Type A and B health adults: Can type As relax by competing? *Journal of Psychosomatic Research, 36,* 477–483.

Skinner, B. F. (1948). "Superstition" in the pigeon. *Journal of Experimental Psychology, 38,* 168–172.

Skinner, B. F., & Ferster, C. (1957). *Schedules of reinforcement.* New York: Appleton-Century-Crofts.

Spiegler, M. D., Guevremont, D. C. (1992). *Contemporary behavioral therapy* (2nd ed.). Pacific Grove, CA: Brooks/ Cole.

Stern, R. M., Ray, W. J., Davis, C. M. (1980). *Psychophysiological recording.* New York: Oxford University Press.

Thorndike, E. L. (1911). *Animal intelligence: Experimental studies.* New York: Macmillan.

Ullmann, L. P., & Krasner, L. (1965). *Case studies in behavior modification.* New York: Holt, Rinehart & Winston.

Ullmann, L. P., & Krasner, L. (1969). *A psychological approach to abnormal behavior.* Englewood Cliffs, NJ: Prentice Hall.

Wilson, G. T. (1989). Behavior therapy. In R. J. Corsini & D. Wedding (Eds.), *Current psychotherapies* (4th ed., pp. 241–282). Itasca, IL: F. E. Peacock Publishers.

Wilson, G. T. (1995). Behavior therapy. In R. J. Corsini & D. Wedding (Eds.), *Current psychotherapies* (5th ed., pp. 197–228). Itasca, IL: F. E. Peacock Publishers.

Wolf, S. L., Nacht, M., & Kelly, J. L. (1982). EMG feedback training during dynamic movement for low back pain patients. *Behavior Therapy, 13,* 395–406.

Wolpe, J. (1958). *Psychotherapy by reciprocal inhibition.* Stanford, CA: Stanford University Press.

Wolpe, J. (1973). *The practice of behavior therapy* (2nd ed.). New York: Pergamon.

Wolpe, J. (1981). Reciprocal inhibition and therapeutic change. *Journal of Behavior Therapy and Experimental Psychiatry, 12,* 185–188.

Wolpe, J. (1987). The promotion of scientific psychotherapy: A long voyage. In J. K. Zeig (Eds.), *The evolution of psychotherapy* (pp. 133–142). New York: Brunner/Mazel.

Wolpe, J. (1990). *The practice of behavior therapy* (4th ed.). Elmsford, NY: Pergamon.

Wolpe, J., & Lang, P. J. (1964). A fear survey schedule for use in behavior therapy. *Behaviour Research and Therapy, 2,* 27–30.

Wolpe, J., & Lazarus, A. A. (1966). *Behavior therapy techniques: A guide to the treatment of neurosis.* New York: Pergamon.

Wulbert, M., & Dries, R. (1977). The relative efficacy of methylphenidate (Ritalin) and behavior-modification techniques in the treatment of a hyperactive child. *Journal of Applied Behavior Analysis, 10,* 21–31.

Zimbardo, P. G., Ebbesen, E. B., & Maslach, C. (1977). *Influencing attitudes and changing behavior* (2nd ed.). New York: Random House.

Zimbardo, P. G., & Leippe, M. R. (1991). *The psychology of attitude change and social influence.* New York: McGraw-Hill.

Chapter 11

Abramowitz, S. I. (1973). Internal-external control and social-political activism: A test of the dimensionality of Rotter's I-E Scale. *Journal of Consulting and Clinical Psychology, 40,* 196–201.

American Psychological Association. (1981). Awards for distinguished scientific contributions: 1980. Albert Bandura. *American Psychologist, 36,* 27–34.

American Psychological Association (1983). Awards for distinguished scientific contributions: 1982. Walter Mischel. *American Psychologist, 38,* 9–14.

Anderson, C. R. (1977). Locus of control, coping behaviors and performance in a stress setting: A longitudinal study. *Journal of Applied Psychology, 62,* 446–451.

Baehr, M. E., Jones, J. W., & Nerad, A. J. (1993). Psychological correlates of business ethics orientation in executives. *Journal of Business and Psychology, 7,* 291–308.

Bandura, A. (1961). Psychotherapy as a learning process. *Psychological Bulletin, 58,* 143–159.

Bandura, A. (1968). A social learning interpretation of psychological dysfunctions. In P. London & D. Rosenhan (Eds.), *Foundations of abnormal psychology* (pp. 293–344). New York: Holt, Rinehart & Winston.

Bandura, A. (1969). *Principles of behavior modification.* New York: Holt, Rinehart & Winston.

Bandura, A. (1977a). Self-efficacy: Toward a unifying theory of behavioral change. *Psychological Review, 84,* 191–215.

Bandura, A. (1977b). *Social learning theory.* Englewood Cliffs, NJ: Prentice Hall.

Bandura, A. (1978). The self system in reciprocal determinism. *American Psychologist, 33,* 344–358.

Bandura, A. (1982). Self-efficacy mechanism in human agency. *American Psychologist, 37*, 122–147.

Bandura, A. (1986). *Social foundations of thought and action: A social cognitive theory.* Englewood Cliffs, NJ: Prentice Hall.

Bandura, A. (1988). Perceived self-efficacy: Exercise of control through self-belief. In J. P. Dauwalder, M. Perrez, & V. Hobi (Eds.), *Annual series of European research in behavior therapy* (Vol. 2, pp. 27–59). Lisse, The Netherlands: Swets & Zeitlinger.

Bandura, A. (1989a). Human agency in social cognitive theory. *American Psychologist, 44*, 1175–1184.

Bandura, A. (1989b). Regulation of cognitive processes through perceived self-efficacy. *Development Psychology, 25*, 729–735.

Bandura, A. (1990). Perceived self-efficacy in the exercise of control over AIDS infection. *Evaluation and Program Planning, 13*, 9–17.

Bandura, A. (Ed.). (1995). *Self-efficacy in changing societies.* New York: Cambridge University Press.

Bandura, A. (1991a), Social cognitive theory of moral thought and action. In W. M. Kurtiness & J. L. Gewirtz (Eds.), *Handbook of moral behavior and development: Vol. 1. Theory* (pp. 45–103). Hillsdale, NJ: Erlbaum.

Bandura, A. (1991b). Social cognitive theory of self-regulation. *Organization Behavior and Human Decision Processes, 50*, 248–287.

Bandura, A., Blanchard, E. B., & Ritter, B. (1969). Relative efficacy of desensitization and modeling approaches for inducing behavioral, affective, and attitudinal changes. *Journal of Personality and Social Psychology, 13*, 173–199.

Bandura, A., Grusec, J. E., & Menlove, F. L. (1967). Some social determinants of self-monitoring reinforcement systems. *Journal of Personality and Social Psychology, 5*, 449–455.

Bandura, A., & Walters, R. (1963). *Social learning and personality development.* New York: Holt, Rinehart & Winston.

Barker, L. M. (1994). *Learning and behavior: A psychobiological perspective.* New York: Macmillan.

Baron, R. A., & Richardson, D. R. (1994). *Human aggression* (2nd ed.). New York: Plenum.

Bar-Tal, D., & Bar-Zohar, Y. (1977). The relationship between perception of locus of control and academic achievement. *Contemporary Educational Psychology, 2*, 181–199.

Barnet, H. S. (1990). Divorce stress and adjustment model: Locus of control and demographic predictors. *Journal of Divorce, 13*, 93–109.

Beck, A. T. (1976). *Cognitive therapy and the emotional disorders.* New York: International Universities Press.

Beck A. T., & Weishaar, M. E. (1995). Cognitive therapy. In R. J. Corsini & D. Wedding (Eds.), *Current psychotherapies* (pp. 229–261). Itasca, IL: F. E. Peacock Publishers.

Berkowitz, L. (1993). *Aggression: its causes, consequences, and control.* New York: McGraw-Hill.

Bryant, J. (1985, September). *Testimony on the effects of pornography: Research findings.* Paper presented at the U.S. Justice Department Hearings, Houston.

Burger, J. M. (1991). Control. In V. J. Derlega, B. A. Winstead, & W. H. Jones (Eds). *Personality: Contemporary theory and research* (pp. 287–312). Chicago: Nelson-Hall.

Cacioppo, J. T., & Petty, R. E. (1982). The need for cognition. *Journal of Personality and Social Psychology, 42*, 116–131.

Cacioppo, J. T., Petty, R. E., & Morris, K. J. (1983). Effects of need for cognition on message evaluation, recall, and persuasion. *Journal of Personality and Social Psychology, 45*, 805–818.

Cantor, N. (1990). From thought to behavior: "Having" and "doing" in the study of personality and cognition. *American Psychologist, 45*, 735–750.

Cantor, N. (1994). Life task problem solving: Situational affordances and personal needs. *Personality and Social Psychology Bulletin, 20*, 235–243.

Cantor, N., Acker, M., & Cook-Flannagan, C. (1992). Conflict and preoccupation in the intimacy life task. *Journal of Personality and Social Psychology, 63*, 644–655.

Cantor, N., & Harlow, R. E. (1994). Social intelligence and personality: Flexible life task pursuit. In R. J. Sternberg & P. Ruzgis (Eds.), *Personality and intelligence* (pp. 137–168). New York: Cambridge University Press.

Cantor, N., & Kihlstrom, J. F. (1985). Social intelligence: The cognitive basis of personality. In P. Shaver (Ed.), *Review of personality and social behavior* (Vol. 6, pp. 15–33). Beverly Hills, CA: Sage.

Cantor, N., & Kihlstrom, J. F. (1987). *Personality and social intelligence.* Englewood Cliffs, NJ: Prentice Hall.

Cantor, N., & Malley, J. (1991). Cognition in close relationships. In G. J. O. Fletcher & F. D. Fincham (Eds.), *Cognition in close relationships* (pp. 101–125). Hillsdale, NJ: Erlbaum.

Cantor, N., Norem, J., Langston, C., Zirkel, S., Fleeson, W., & Cook-Flannagan, C. (1991). Life tasks and daily life experience. *Journal of Personality, 59*, 425–451.

Cantor, N., Norem, J. K., Niedenthal, P. M., Langston, C. A., & Brower, A. M. (1987). Life tasks, self-concept ideals, and cognitive strategies in a life transition. *Journal of Personality and Social Psychology, 53*, 1178–1191.

Cantor, N., & Zirkel, S. (1990). Personality, cognition, and purposive behavior. In L. A. Pervin (Ed.), *A handbook of personality: Theory and research* (pp. 135–164). New York: Guilford.

Cantor, N., Zirkel, S., & Norem, J. K. (1993). Human personality: Asocial and reflexive? *Psychological Inquiry, 4*, 273–277.

Chaiken, S. (1987). The heuristic model of persuasion. In M. P. Zanna, J. M. Olson, & C. P. Herman (Eds.), *Social influence: The Ontario Symposium* (Vol. 5, pp. 3–40). Hillsdale, NJ: Erlbaum.

Doherty, W. J., & Ryder, R. G. (1979). Locus of control, interpersonal trust, and assertive behavior among newlyweds. *Journal of Personality and Social Psychology, 37*, 2212–2220.

Doherty, W. J. (1980). Divorce and belief in internal versus external control of one's life: Data from a national probability sample. *Journal of Divorce, 3*, 391–401.

Doherty, W. J. (1981). Locus of control difference and marital dissatisfaction. *Journal of Marriage and the Family, 43*, 369–377.

Doherty, W. J. (1983a). Impact of divorce on locus of control orientation in adult women: A longitudinal study. *Journal of Personality and Social Psychology, 44*, 834–840.

Doherty, W. J. (1983b). Locus of control and marital interaction. In H. M. Lefcourt (Ed.), *Research with the locus of control construct: Developments and social problems* (Vol. 2, pp. 155–183). New York: Academic Press.

Donnerstein, E. (1980). Aggressive erotica and violence against women. *Journal of Personality and Social Psychology, 39,* 269–277.

Ellis, A. (1962). *Reason and emotion in psychotherapy.* New York: Lyle Stuart.

Ellis, A. (1980). Rational emotive therapy and cognitive behavior therapy: Similarities and differences. *Cognitive Therapy and Research, 4,* 325–240.

Ellis, A. (1987). The impossibility of achieving consistently good mental health. *American Psychologist, 42,* 364–375.

Ellis, A. (1989). Rational-emotive therapy. In R. J. Corsini & D. Wedding (Eds.), *Current psychotherapies* (4th ed., pp. 196–238). Itasca, IL: F. E. Peacock Publishers.

Ellis, A. (1995). Rational-emotive behavior therapy. In R. J. Corsini & D. Wedding (Eds.), *Current psychotherapies* (5th ed., pp. 162–196). Itasca, IL: F. E. Peacock Publishers.

Eron, L D. (1987). The development of aggressive behavior from the perspective of a developing behaviorism. *American Psychologist, 42,* 435–442.

Evans, R. I. (Ed.). (1976). *The making of psychology: Discussions with creative contributors.* New York: Knopf.

Evans, R. I. (1989). *Albert Bandura, the man and his ideas . . . a dialogue.* New York: Praeger.

Findley, M. J., & Cooper, H. M. (1983). Locus of control and academic achievement: A literature review. *Journal of Personality and Social Psychology, 44,* 419–427.

Fiske, S. T., & Taylor, S. E. (1991). *Social cognition* (2nd ed.). New York: McGraw-Hill.

Giles, W. F. (1977). Volunteering for job enrichment: A test of expectancy theory predictions. *Personnel Psychology, 30,* 427–435.

Gilmore, T. M., & Reid, D. W. (1978). Locus of control, prediction, and performance on university examinations. *Journal of Consulting and Clinical Psychology, 46,* 565–566.

Gilmore, T. M., & Reid, D. W. (1979). Locus of control and causal attribution for positive and negative outcomes on university examinations. *Journal of Research in Personality, 13,* 154–160.

Gore, P. M., & Rotter, J. B. (1963). A personality of social action. *Journal of Personality, 31,* 58–64.

Gurtman, M. B., & Lion, C. (1982). Interpersonal trust and perceptual vigilance for trustworthiness descriptors. *Journal of Research in Personality, 16,* 108–117.

Hamsher, J. H., Geller, J. D., & Rotter, J. B. (1968). Interpersonal trust, internal-external control, and the Warren Commission Report. *Journal of Personality and Social Psychology, 9,* 210–215.

Hollon, S. D., & Beck, A. T. (1994). Cognitive and cognitive-behavioral therapies. In A. E. Bergin & S. L. Garfield (Eds.), *Handbook of therapy and behavior change* (4th ed., pp. 428–466). New York: John Wiley & Sons.

Isen, A. M., Niedenthal, P. M., & Cantor, N. (1992). An influence of positive affect on social categorization. *Motivation and Emotion, 16,* 65–78.

Jarvis, W. B. G., & Petty, R. E. (1996). The need to evaluate. *Journal of Personality and Social Psychology, 70,* 172–194.

Josephson, W. L. (1987). Television violence and children's aggression: Testing the priming, social script, and disinhibition predictions. *Journal of Personality and Social Psychology, 53,* 882–890.

Kazdin, A. E. (1994). *Behavior modification in applied settings* (5th ed.). Pacific Grove, CA: Brooks/Cole.

Langston, C. A., & Cantor, N. (1989). Social anxiety and social constraint: When making friends is hard. *Journal of Personality and Social Psychology, 56,* 649–661.

Lassiter, G. D., Briggs, M. A., & Bowman, R. E. (1991). Need for cognition and the perception of ongoing behavior. *Personality and Social Psychology Bulletin, 17,* 156–160.

Lassiter, G. D., Briggs, M. A., & Slaw, R. D. (1991). Need for cognition, causal processing, and memory for behavior. *Personality and Social Psychology Bulletin, 17,* 694–700.

Lawler, E. E. (1971). *Pay and organizational effectiveness: A psychological view.* New York: McGraw-Hill.

Lefcourt, H. M. (1981). *Research with the locus of control construct: Assessment methods* (Vol. 1). New York: Academic Press.

Lefcourt, H. M. (1982). *Locus of control: Current trends in theory and research* (2nd ed.). Hillsdale, NJ: Erlbaum.

Lefcourt, H. M. (Ed.) (1983). *Research with the locus of control construct: Developments and social problems* (Vol. 2). New York: Academic Press.

Lefcourt, H. M. (Ed.) (1984). *Research with the locus of control construct: Extensions and limitations* (Vol. 3). Orlando, FL: Academic Press.

Lefcourt, H. M., & Davidson-Katz, K. (1991). Locus of control and health. In C. R. Snyder & D. R. Forsyth (Eds.), *Handbook of social and clinical psychology: The health perspective* (pp. 246–266). New York: Pergamon.

Leyens, J., Camino, L., Parke, R. D., & Berkowitz, L. (1975). Effects of movie violence on aggression in a field setting as a function of group dominance and cohesion. *Journal of Personality and Social Psychology, 32,* 346–360.

Liebert, R. M., & Baron, R. A. (1972). Some immediate effects of televised violence on children's behavior. *Development Psychology, 6,* 469–475.

Liebert, R. M., & Schwartzberg, N. S. (1977). Effects of mass media. *Annual Review of Psychology, 28,* 141–173.

Liebert, R. M., Sprafkin. J. N., & Davidson, E. S. (1989). *The early window: Effects of television on children and youth* (3rd ed.). New York: Pergamon.

Linz, D., Donnerstein, E., & Penrod, S. (1984). The effects of multiple exposure to filmed violence against women. *Journal of Communication, 34,* 130–137.

London House, Inc. (1980). *Personal Selection Inventory (PSI).* Park Ridge, IL: London House Press.

MacDonald, A. P. (1970). Internal-external locus of control and the practice of birth control. *Psychological Reports, 27,* 206.

Malamuth, N. M. (1984). Aggression against women: Cultural and individual causes. In N. M. Malamuth & E. Donnerstein (Eds.), *Pornography and sexual aggression* (pp. 19–52). Orlando, FL: Academic Press.

Malamuth, N. M., & Briere, J. (1986). Sexual violence in the media: Indirect effects on aggression against women. *Journal of Social Issues, 42,* 75–92.

Mann, J., Berkowitz, L., Sidman, J., Starr, S., & West, S. (1974). Satiation on the transient stimulating effect of erotic films. *Journal of Personality and Social Psychology, 30,* 729–735.

Marshall, W. L. (1985, September). *The use of pornography by sex offenders.* Paper presented at the U.S. Justice Department Hearings, Houston.

Meichenbaum, D. H. (1977). *Cognitive-behavior modification: An integrative approach*. New York: Plenum.

Meichenbaum, D. H. (1985). *Stress inoculation training*. New York: Pergamon.

Melamed, B. G., & Siegel, L. J. (1975). Reduction of anxiety in children facing hospitalization and surgery by use of filmed modeling. *Journal of Consulting and Clinical Psychology, 43*, 511–521.

Melamed, B. G., Hawes, R. R., Heiby, E., & Glick, J. (1975). The use of filmed modeling to reduce uncooperative behavior of children during dental treatment. *Journal of Dental Research, 54*, 797–801.

Miller, P. C. (1981). *The construct validation of the Marital Locus of Control Scale*. Unpublished master's thesis, University of Waterloo, Waterloo, Ontario.

Miller, P. C., Lefcourt, H. M., Holmes J. G., Ware, E. E., & Saleh, W. E. (1986). Marital locus of control and marital problem solving. *Journal of Personality and Social Psychology, 51*, 161–169.

Miller, S. M., Shoda, Y., & Hurley, K. (1996). Applying cognitive-social theory to health-protective behavior: Breast self-examination in cancer screening. *Psychological Bulletin, 119*, 70–94.

Mischel, W. (1968). *Personality and assessment*. New York: John Wiley and Sons.

Mischel, W. (1973). Toward a cognitive social learning reconceptualization of personality. *Psychological Review, 80*, 252–283.

Mischel, W. (1977). On the future of personality assessment. *American Psychologist, 32*, 246–254.

Mischel, W. (1979). On the interface of cognition and personality: Beyond the person-situation debate. *American Psychologist, 34*, 740–754.

Mischel, W. (1984). On the predictability of behavior and the structure of personality. In R. A. Zucker, J. Aronoff, & A. I. Rabin (Eds.), *Personality and the prediction of behavior* (pp. 269–305). New York: Academic Press.

Mischel, W. (1990). Personality dispositions revisited and revised: A view after three decades. In L. A. Pervin (Ed.), *Handbook of personality: Theory and research* (pp. 111–134). New York: Guilford.

Mischel, W. (1993). *Introduction to personality* (5th ed.). Fort Worth, TX: Harcourt Brace Jovanovich.

Mischel, W., & Baker, N. (1975). Cognitive appraisals and transformations in delay behavior. *Journal of Personality and Social Psychology, 31*, 254–261.

Mischel, W., & Ebbesen, E. B. (1970). Attention in delay of gratification. *Journal of Personality and Social Psychology, 16*, 329–337.

Mischel, W., Ebbesen, E. B., & Zeiss, A. R. (1972). Cognitive and attentional mechanisms in delay of gratification. *Journal of Personality and Social Psychology, 21*, 204–218.

Mischel, W., & Rodriguez, M. L. (1993). Psychological distance in self-imposed delay of gratification. In R. R. Cocking & K. A. Renninger (Eds.), *The development and meaning of psychological distance* (pp. 109–121). Hillsdale, NJ: Erlbaum.

Mischel, W., Shoda, Y., & Rodriguez, M. L. (1989). Delay of gratification. *Science, 244*, 933–937.

Mischel, W., Shoda, Y., & Rodriguez, M. L. (1992). Delay of gratification in children. In G. Loewenstein & J. Elster (Eds.), *Choice over time* (pp. 147–164). New York: Russell Sage Foundation.

Mlott, S. R., & Lira, F. T. (1977). Dogmatism, locus of control, and life goals in stable and unstable marriages. *Journal of Clinical Psychology, 33*, 142–146.

Moore, B., Mischel, W., & Zeiss, A. R. (1976). Comparative effects of the reward stimulus and its cognitive representation in voluntary delay. *Journal of Personality and Social Psychology, 34*, 419–424.

Multon, K. D., Brown, S. D., & Lent, R. W. (1991). Relation of self-efficacy beliefs to academic outcomes: A meta-analytic investigation. *Journal of Consulting Psychology, 38*, 30–38.

Murphy, K. R., & Davidshofer, C. O. (1994). *Psychological testing: Principles and applications* (3rd ed.). Englewood Cliffs, NJ: Prentice Hall.

Nietzel, M. T., Bernstein, D. A., & Milich, R. (1994). *Introduction to clinical psychology* (4th ed.). Englewood Cliffs, NJ: Prentice Hall.

Nord, W. R., Connelly, F., & Daignault, G. (1974). Locus of control and aptitude test scores as predictors of academic success in graduate school. *Journal of Educational Psychology, 66*, 956–961.

Norem, J. K. (1989). Cognitive strategies as personality: Effectiveness, specificity, flexibility, and change. In D. M. Buss & N. Cantor (Eds.), *Personality psychology: Recent trends and emerging directions* (pp. 45–60). New York: Springer-Verlag.

Norem, J. K., & Cantor, N. (1986a). Anticipatory and post hoc cushioning strategies: Optimism and defensive pessimism in "risky" situations. *Cognitive Therapy and Research, 10*, 347–362.

Norem, J. K., & Cantor, N. (1986b). Defensive pessimism: "Harnessing" anxiety as motivation. *Journal of Personality and Social Psychology, 51*, 1208–1217.

Norem, J. K., & Illingworth, K. S. S. (1993). Strategy-dependent effects of reflecting on self and tasks: Some implications of optimism and defensive pessimism. *Journal of Personality and Social Psychology, 65*, 822–835.

Osofsky, J. D. (1995). The effects of exposure to violence on young children. *American Psychologist, 50*, 782–788.

Ozer, E. M., & Bandura, A. (1990). Mechanisms governing empowerment effects: A self-efficacy analysis. *Journal of Personality and Social Psychology, 58*, 472–486.

Parke, R. D., Berkowitz, L., Leyes, J. P., West, S. G., & Sebastian, R. J. (1977). Some effects of violent and nonviolent movies on the behavior of juvenile delinquents. In L. Berkowitz (Ed.), *Advances in experimental social psychology* (Vol. 10, pp. 135–172). New York: Academic Press.

Parkes, K. R. (1984). Locus of control, cognitive appraisal and coping in stressful episodes. *Journal of Personality and Social Psychology, 46*, 655–668.

Petty, R. E., Cacioppo, J. T., & Kasmer, J. (1985. May). *Effects of need for cognition on social loafing*. Paper presented at the meeting of the Midwestern Psychological Association, Chicago.

Phares, E. J. (1968). Differential utilization of information as a function of internal-external control. *Journal of Personality, 36*, 649–662.

Phares, E. J. (1976). *Locus of control in personality*. Morristown, NJ: General Learning Press.

Phares, E. J. (1988). *Introduction to personality* (2nd ed.). Glenview, IL: Scott, Foresman.

Prociuk, T. J., & Breen, L. J. (1975). Defensive externality and academic performance. *Journal of Personality and Social Psychology, 31,* 549–556.

Rathus, S. A., & Nevid, J. S. (1991). *Abnormal psychology*. Englewood Cliffs, NJ: Prentice Hall.

Reitz, H. J., & Jewell, L. N. (1979). Sex, locus of control, and job involvement: A six-country investigation. *Academy of Management Journal, 22,* 72–80.

Riggio, R. E. (1986). Assessment of basic social skills. *Journal of Personality and Social Psychology, 51,* 649–660.

Rodriguez, M. L., Mischel, W., & Shoda, Y. (1989). Cognitive person variables in the delay of gratification of older children at risk. *Journal of Personality and Social Psychology, 57,* 358–367.

Rosenthal, T. L., & Steffek, B. D. (1991). Modeling methods. In F. H. Kanfer & A. P. Goldstein (Eds.), *Helping people change* (4th ed., pp. 70–121). New York: Pergamon.

Rotter, J. B. (1954). *Social learning and clinical psychology*. Englewood Cliffs, NJ: Prentice Hall.

Rotter, J. B. (1966). Generalized expectancies for internal versus external control of reinforcement. *Psychological Monographs, 80* (1, Whole No. 609).

Rotter, J. B. (1967). A new scale for the measurement of interpersonal trust. *Journal of Personality, 35,* 651–665.

Rotter, J. B. (1970). Some implications of a social learning theory for the practice of psychotherapy. In D. J. Levis (Ed.), *Learning approaches to therapeutic behavior change* (pp. 208–241). Chicago: Adline.

Rotter, J. B. (1971). Generalized expectancies for interpersonal trust. *American Psychologist, 26,* 443–452.

Rotter, J. B. (1978). Generalized expectancies for problem solving and psychotherapy. *Cognitive Therapy and Research, 2,* 1–10.

Rotter, J. B. (1980). Interpersonal trust, trustworthiness, and gullibility. *American Psychologist, 35,* 1–7.

Rotter, J. B. (1982). *The development and applications of social learning theory: Selected paper*. New York: Praeger.

Rotter, J. B. (1990). Internal versus external control of reinforcement: A case history of a variable. *American Psychologist, 45,* 489–493.

Rotter, J. B. (1993). Expectancies. In C. E. Walker (Ed.)., *The history of clinical psychology in autobiography: Vol. 2* (pp. 273–284). Pacific Grove, CA: Brooks/Cole.

Rotter, J. B., Chance, J. E., & Phares, E. J. (1972). *Applications of a social learning theory of personality*. New York: Holt, Rinehart & Winston.

Rotter, J. B., & Hochreich, D. J. (1975). *Personality*. Glenview, IL: Scott, Foresman.

Schmidt, G., & Sigusch, V. (1970). Sex differences in responses to psychosexual stimulation by film and slides. *Journal of Sex Research, 6,* 268–283.

Schutte, N. S., Malouff, J. M., Post-Gorden, J. C., & Rodasts, A. L. (1988). Effect of playing video games on children's aggressive and other behavior. *Journal of Applied Social Psychology, 18,* 454–460.

Seeman, M. (1963). Alienation and social learning in a reformatory. *American Journal of Sociology, 69,* 270–284.

Seeman, M., & Evans, J. (1962). Alienation and learning in a hospital setting. *American Sociological Review, 27,* 772–782.

Shoda, Y., Mischel, W., & Peake, P. K. (1990). Predicting adolescent cognitive and self-regulatory competencies from preschool delay of gratification: Identifying diagnostic conditions. *Developmental Psychology, 26,* 978–986.

Shoda, Y., Mischel, W., & Wright, J. C. (1989). Intuitive interactionism in person perception: Effects of situation-behavior relations on dispositional judgments. *Journal of Personality and Social Psychology, 56,* 41–53.

Shoda, Y., Mischel, W., & Wright, J. C. (1993). The role of situational demands and cognitive competencies in behavior organization and personality coherence. *Journal of Personality and Social Psychology, 65,* 1023–1035.

Spector, P. E. (1982). Behavior in organizations as a function of employee's locus of control. *Psychological Bulletin, 91,* 482–497.

Strickland, B. R. (1965). The prediction of social action from a dimension of internal-external control. *Journal of Social Psychology, 66,* 353–358.

Strickland, B. R. (1989). Internal-external control expectancies: From contingency to creativity. *American Psychologist, 44,* 1–12.

Strentz, T., & Auerbach, S. M. (1988). Adjustment to the stress of simulated captivity: Effects of emotion-focused versus problem-focused preparation on hostages differing in locus of control. *Journal of Personality and Social Psychology, 55,* 652–660.

Valecha, G. K. (1972). Construct validation of internal-external locus of reinforcement related to work-related variables. *Proceedings of the 80th Annual Convention of the American Psychological Association, 7,* 455–456.

Walker, C. E. (1993). *The history of clinical psychology in autobiography: Vol. 2*. Pacific Grove, CA: Brooks/Cole.

Weary, G., & Edwards, J. A. (1994). Individual differences in causal uncertainty. *Journal of Personality and Social Psychology, 67,* 308–318.

Webster-Stratton, C. (1992). Individually administered videotape parent training: "Who benefits?" *Cognitive Therapy and Research, 16,* 31–52.

Wood, W., Wong, F. Y., & Chachere, J. G. (1991). Effects of media violence on viewers' aggression in unconstrained social interaction. *Psychological Bulletin, 109,* 371–383.

Wright, J. C., & Mischel, W. (1987). A conditional analysis to dispositional constructs: The local predictability of social behavior. *Journal of Personality and Social Psychology, 53,* 1159–1177.

Wright, J. C., & Mischel, W. (1988). Conditional hedges and the intuitive psychology of traits. *Journal of Personality and Social Psychology, 55,* 454–469.

Wrightsman, L. S. (1991). Interpersonal trust and attitudes toward human nature. In J. P. Robinson, P. R. Shaver, & L. S. Wrightsman (Eds.), *Measures of personality and social psychological attitudes: Vol. 1* (pp. 373–412). San Diego, CA: Academic Press.

Zillmann. D., & Bryant, J. (1984). Effects of massive exposure to pornography. In N. M. Malamuth & E. Donnerstein (Eds.)., *Pornography and sexual aggression* (pp. 115–138). Orlando, FL: Academic Press.

Zirkel, S. (1992). Developing independence in a life transition: Investing the self in the concerns of the day. *Journal of Personality and Social Psychology, 62,* 506–521.

Zirkel, S., & Cantor, N. (1990). Personal construal of life tasks: Those who struggle for independence. *Journal of Personality and Social Psychology, 58,* 172–185.

Chapter 12

Banaji, M. R., & Prentice, D. A. (1994). The self in social context. In L. W. Porter & M. R. Rosenzweig (Eds.), *Annual review of psychology* (Vol. 45, pp. 297–332). Palo Alto, CA: Annual Reviews Inc.

Baumeister, R. F. (1986a). *Identity: Cultural change and the struggle for self.* New York: Oxford University Press.

Baumeister, R. F. (1886b). (Ed.). *Public self and private self.* New York: Oxford University Press.

Baumeister, R. F. (1987). How the self became a problem: A psychological review of historical research. *Journal of Personality and Social Psychology, 52,* 163–176.

Baumeister, R. F. (1991). Self-concept and identity. In V. J. Derlega, B. A. Winstead, & W. H. Jones (Eds.), *Personality: Contemporary theory and research* (pp. 349–380). Chicago: Nelson-Hall.

Baumeister, R. F. (1995). Self and identity: An introduction. In A. Tesser, *Advanced social psychology* (pp. 50–97). New York: McGraw-Hill.

Breakwell, G. (1986). *Coping with threatened identities.* London: Methuen.

Buss, A. H. (1980). *Self-consciousness and social anxiety.* San Francisco: Freeman.

Buss, A. H. (1995). *Personality: Temperament, social behavior, and the self.* Boston: Allyn & Bacon.

Buss, A. H., & Perry, M. (1992). The Aggression Questionnaire. *Journal of Personality and Social Psychology, 63,* 452–459.

Carver, C. S. (1975). Physical aggression as a function of objective self-awareness and attitudes toward punishment. *Journal of Experimental Social Psychology, 11,* 510–519.

Carver, C. S. (1977). Self-awareness, perception of threat, and the expression of reactance through attitude change. *Journal of Personality, 45,* 501–512.

Carver, C. S., & Scheier, M. F. (1981a). *Attention and self-regulation: A control-theory approach to human behavior.* New York: Springer-Verlag.

Carver, C. S., & Scheier, M. F. (1981b). Self-consciousness and reactance. *Journal of Research in Personality, 15,* 16–29.

Carver, C. S., & Scheier, M. F. (1992). *Perspectives on personality* (2nd ed.). Boston, MA: Allyn & Bacon.

Cheek, J. M. (1989). Identity orientations and self-interpretation. In D. M. Buss & N. Cantor (Eds.), *Personality psychology: Recent trends and emerging directions* (pp. 275–285). New York: Springer-Verlag.

Cheek, J. M., & Briggs, S. R. (1981, August). *Self-consciousness, self-monitoring, and aspects of identity.* Paper presented at the meeting of the American Psychological Association, Los Angeles.

Cheek, J. M., & Briggs, S. R. (1982). Self-consciousness and aspects of identity. *Journal of Research in Personality, 16,* 401–408.

Cheek, J. M. & Bush, C. M. (1982, April). *Self-monitoring and the inner-outer metaphor: Principled versus pragmatic self?* Paper presented at the meeting of the Eastern Psychological Association, Baltimore, MD.

Cheek, J. M., & Hogan, R. (1983). Self-concepts, self-presentations, and moral judgments. In J. Suls & A. G. Greenwald (Eds.), *Psychological perspectives on the self* (Vol. 2, pp. 249–273). Hillsdale, NJ: Erlbaum.

Cheek, J. M., Underwood, M. K., & Cutler, B. L. (1985). *The Aspects of Identity Questionnaire (III).* Unpublished manuscript. Wellesley College.

Cutler, B. L., Lennox, R. D., & Wolfe, R. N. (1984, August). *Reliability and construct validity of the Aspects of Identity Questionnaire.* Paper presented at the meeting of the American Psychological Association, Toronto, Canada.

Damon, W., & Hart, D. (1982). The development of self-understanding from infancy through adolescence. *Child Development, 53,* 841–864.

Damon, W., & Hart, D. (1988). *Self-understanding in childhood and adolescence.* Cambridge: Cambridge University Press.

Davis, M. H., & Franzoi, S. L. (1991). Self-awareness and self-consciousness. In V. J. Derlega, B. A. Winstead, & W. H. Jones (Eds.), *Personality: Contemporary theory and research* (pp. 311–347). Chicago: Nelson-Hall.

Deaux, K. (1993a). Reconstructing social identity. *Personality and Social Psychology Bulletin, 19,* 4–12.

Deaux, K. (1993b). Enhancing social identity: Maintaining stability and dealing with change. In S. Stryker (Eds.), *Self and affect in society.*

Deaux, K. (in press). Social identification. In E. T. Higgins & A. W. Kruglanski (Eds.), *Social psychology: Handbook of basic principles.* New York: Guilford.

Diener, E., Diener, M., & Diener, C. (1995). Factors predicting the subjective well-being of nations. *Journal of Personality and Social Psychology, 69,* 851–864.

Duval, S., & Wicklund, R. A. (1972). *A theory of objective self-awareness.* New York: Academic Press.

Ethier, K. A., & Deaux, K. (1990). Hispanics in ivy: Assessing identity and perceived threat. *Sex Roles, 22,* 427–440.

Ethier, K. A., & Deaux, K. (1994). Negotiating social identity when contexts change: Maintaining identification and responding to threat. *Journal of Personality and Social Psychology, 67,* 243–251.

Fenigstein, A. (1979). Self-consciousness, self-attention, and social interaction. *Journal of Personality and Social Psychology, 37,* 75–86.

Fenigstein, A. (1984). Self-consciousness and the overprotection of the self as a target. *Journal of Personality and Social Psychology, 47*, 860–870.

Fenigstein, A., Scheier, M. F., & Buss, A. H. (1975). Public and private self-consciousness: Assessment and theory. *Journal of Consulting and Clinical Psychology, 43*, 522–527.

Fenigstein, A., & Vanable, P. A. (1992). Paranoia and self-consciousness. *Journal of Personality and Social Psychology, 62*, 129–138.

Frable, D. E. S., Wortman, C., Joseph, J., Kirscht, J., & Kessler, R. (1994). *Predicting self-esteem, well-being, and distress in a cohort of gay men: The importance of cultural stigma and personal visibility.* Manuscript submitted for publication.

Froming, W. J., & Carver, C. S. (1981). Divergent influences of private and public self-consciousness in a compliance paradigm. *Journal of Research in Personality, 15*, 159–171.

Froming, W. J., Walker, G. R., & Lopyan, K. J. (1982). Public and private self-awareness: When personal attitudes conflict with societal expectations. *Journal of Experimental Social Psychology, 18*, 476–487.

Frone, M. R., & McFarlin, D. B. (1989). Chronic occupational stressors, self-focused attention, and well-being: Testing a cybernetic model of stress. *Journal of Applied Psychology, 74*, 876–833.

Gallaher, P. (1992). Individual differences in non-verbal behavior: Dimensions of style. *Journal of Personality and Social Psychology, 63*, 133–145.

Gallup, G. G. (1977). Self-recognition in primates: A comparative approach to the bidirectional properties of conscious. *American Psychologist, 32*, 329–338.

Gallup, G. G., Jr., & Suarez, S. D. (1986). Self-awareness and the emergence of mind in humans and other primates. In J. Suls & A. G. Greenwald (Eds.), *Psychological perspectives on the self* (Vol. 3). Hillsdale, NJ: Erlbaum.

Gardner, J. N., & Jewler, A. J. (1989). *College is only the beginning: A student guide to higher education* (2nd ed.). Belmont, CA; Wadsworth.

Gardner, J. N., & Jewler, A. J. (1992). *Your college experience: Strategies for success.* Belmont CA: Wadsworth.

Gergen, K. J. (1971). *The concept of the self.* New York: Holt, Rinehart & Winston.

Gibbons, F. X., Smith, T. W., Ingram, R. E., Pearce, K., Brehm, S. S., & Schroeder, D. J. (1985). Self-awareness and self-confrontation: Effects of self-focused attention on members of a clinical population. *Journal of Personality and Social Psychology, 48*, 662–675.

Greenberg, J. (1983). Self-image versus impression-management in adherence to distributive justice standards. *Journal of Personality and Social Psychology, 44*, 5–19.

Hermans, H. J. (1996). Voicing the self: From information processing to dialogical interchange. *Psychological Bulletin, 119*, 31–50.

Houghton, W. E. (1957). *The Victorian frame of mind: 1830–1870.* New Haven, CT: Yale University Press.

Hogan, R., & Cheek, J. M. (1983). Identity, authenticity, and maturity. In T. R. Sarbin & K. E. Scheibe (Eds.), *Studies in social identity* (pp. 339–357). New York: Praeger.

Hull, J. G., & Young, R. D. (1983). Self-consciousness, self-esteem, and success-failure as determinants of alcohol consumption in male social drinkers. *Journal of Personality and Social Psychology, 4*, 1097–1109.

Hull, J. G., Young, R. D., & Jouriles, E. (1986). Applications of the self-awareness model of alcohol consumption: Predicting patterns of use and abuse. *Journal of Personality and Social Psychology, 51*, 790–796.

James, W. (1890). *The principles of psychology* (Vol. 1). New York: Holt.

Jewler, A. J., Gardner, J. N., & Owens, H. F. (1993). Keys to success. In A. J. Jewler & J. N. Gardner (Eds.), *Your college experience: Strategies for success* (pp. 1–22). Belmont, CA: Wadsworth.

Jenkins, S. R. (1996). Self-definitions in thought, action, and life path choices. *Personality and Social Psychology Bulletin, 22*, 99–111.

Kagan, S., & Knight, G. P. (1979). Cooperation-competition and self-esteem: A case of cultural relativism. *Journal of Cross-Cultural Psychology, 10*, 457–467.

Kashima, Y., Yamaguchi, S., Kim, U., Choi, S., Gelfand, M. J., & Yuki, M. (1995). *Journal of Personality and Social Psychology, 69*, 925–937.

Katakis, C. D. (1984). *The three identities of the Greek family.* Athens, Greece: Kedros.

Kernis, M. H., & Reis, H. T. (1984). Self-consciousness, self-awareness, and justice in reward allocation. *Journal of Personality, 52*, 58–70.

Kitayama, S. (1992). Some thoughts on the cognitive-psychodynamic self from a cultural perspective. *Psychological Inquiry, 3*, 41–44.

Kitayama, S., Markus, H., Tummala, P., Kurokawa, M., & Kato, K. (1990). *Cultural and self-cognition.* Unpublished manuscript.

Leary, M. R., Wheeler, D. S., & Jenkins, T. B. (1986). Aspects of identity and behavioral preference: Studies of occupational and recreational choice. *Social Psychology Quarterly, 49*, 11–18.

Lewis, M., Sullivan, M. W., Stranger, C., & Weiss, M. (1989). Self-development and self-conscious emotions. *Child Development, 60*, 146–156.

Markus, H., & Cross, S. (1990). The interpersonal self. In L. A. Pervin (Ed.), *Handbook of personality: Theory and research* (pp. 576–608). New York: Guilford.

Markus, H. R., & Kitayama, S. (1991). Culture and the self: Implications for cognition, emotion, and motivation. *Psychological Review, 98*, 224–253.

Markus, H. R., Kitayama, S., & Heiman, R. J. (in press). Culture and basic psychological principles. In E. T. Higgins & A. W. Kruglanski (Eds.), *Social psychology: Handbook of basic principles.* New York: Guilford.

Markus, H., & Wurf, E. (1987). The dynamic self-concept: A social psychological perspective. In L. W. Porter & M. R. Rosenzweig (Eds.), *Annual review of psychology* (Vol. 38, pp. 299–337). Palo Alto, CA: Annual Reviews Inc.

Miller, J. G. (1984). Culture and the development of everyday social explanation. *Journal of Personality and Social Psychology, 46*, 961–978.

Miller, L. C., & Cox, C. L. (1982). For appearances' sake: Public self-consciousness and makeup use. *Personality and Social Psychology Bulletin, 8*, 748–751.

Ouchi, W. G. (1981). *Theory Z: How American business can meet the Japanese challenge.* New York: Avon Books.

Pennebaker, J. W., Rime, B., & Blankenship, V. E. (1996). Stereotypes of emotional expressiveness of northerners and southerners: A cross-cultural test of Montesquieu's hypotheses. *Journal of Personality and Social Psychology, 70*, 372–380.

Penner, L. A., & Wymer, W. E. (1983). The moderator variable approach to behavioral predictability: Some of the variables some of the time. *Journal of Research in Personality, 17*, 339–353.

Porterfield, A. L., Mayer, F. S., Dougherty, K. G., Kredich, K. G., Kronberg, M. M., Marsee, K. M., & Okazaki, Y. (1988). Private self-consciousness, canned laughter, and responses to humorous stimuli. *Journal of Research in Personality, 22*, 409–423.

Pryor, J. B., Gibbons, F. X., Wicklund, R. A., Fazio, R. H., & Hood, R. (1977). Self-focused attention and self-report validity. *Journal of Personality, 45*, 513–527.

Sampson, E. E. (1978). Personality and the location of identity. *Journal of Personality, 46*, 552–568.

Scheier, M. F. (1976). Self-awareness, self-consciousness, and angry aggression. *Journal of Personality, 44*, 627–644.

Scheier, M. F., Buss, A. H., & Buss, D. M. (1978). Self-consciousness, self-report of aggressiveness, and aggression. *Journal of Research in Personality, 12*, 133–140.

Scheier, M. F., & Carver, C. S. (1977). Self-focused attention and the experience of emotion: Attraction, repulsion, elation, and depression. *Journal of Personality and Social Psychology, 35*, 624–636.

Scheier, M. F., & Carver, C. S. (1980). Public and private self-attention, resistance to change, and dissonance reduction. *Journal of Personality and Social Psychology, 39*, 390–405.

Scheier, M. F., & Carver, C. S. (1985). The self-consciousness scale: A revised version for use with general populations. *Journal of Applied Social Psychology, 15*, 687–699.

Scheier, M. F., Carver, C. S., & Gibbons, F. X. (1979). Self-directed attention, awareness of bodily states, and suggestibility. *Journal of Personality and Social Psychology, 37*, 1576–1588.

Sennett, R. (1974). *The fall of public man.* New York: Random House.

Shikanai, K. (1978). Effects of self-esteem on attribution of success-failure. *Japanese Journal of Experimental Social Psychology, 18*, 47–55.

Smith, J. D., & Shaffer, D. R. (1986). Self-consciousness, self-reported altruism, and helping. *Social Behavior and Personality, 14*, 215–220.

Takata, T. (1987). Self-deprecative tendencies in self-evaluation through social comparison. *Japanese Journal of Experimental Social Psychology, 27*, 27–36.

Tice, D. M., Buder, J., & Baumeister, R. F. (1985). Development of self-consciousness: At what age does audience pressure disrupt performance. *Adolescence, 20*, 301–305.

Tobey, E. L., & Tunnell, G. (1981). Predicting our impressions on others: Effects of public self-consciousness and acting, a self-monitoring subscale. *Personality and Social Psychology Bulletin, 7*, 661–669.

Trafimow, D., Triandis, H. C., & Goto, S. G. (1991). Some tests of the distinction between the private self and the collective self. *Journal of Personality and Social Psychology, 60*, 649–655.

Triandis, H. C. (1989). The self and social behavior in differing cultural contexts. *Psychological Review, 96*, 506–520.

Triandis, H. C. (1995). *Individualism vs. collectivism.* Boulder, CO: Westview.

Triandis, H. C. (1996). The psychological measurement of cultural syndromes. *American Psychologist, 51*, 407–415.

Turner, R. G., Gilliland, L., & Klein, H. M. (1981). Self-consciousness, evaluation of physical characteristics, and physical attractiveness. *Journal of Research in Personality, 15*, 182–190.

Whyte, L. L. (1960). *The unconscious before Freud.* New York: Basic Books.

Chapter 13

Abramson, P. R., Goldberg, P. A., Greenberg, J. H., & Abramson, L. M. (1977). The talking platypus phenomenon: Competency ratings as a function of sex and professional status. *Psychology of Women Quarterly, 2*, 114–124.

Allgood-Merten, B., & Stockard, J. (1991). Sex role identity and self-esteem: A comparison of children and adolescents. *Sex Roles, 25*, 129–139.

Archer, J. (1988). *The behavioral biology of aggression.* Cambridge/New York: Cambridge University Press.

Ashmore, R. D. (1990). Sex, gender, and the individual. In L. A. Pervin (Ed.), *Handbook of personality: Theory and research* (pp. 486–526). New York: Guilford.

Bandura, A. (1969). Social learning theory of identificatory processes. In D. A. Goslin (Ed.), *Handbook of socialization theory and research* (pp. 213–262). Chicago: Rand McNally.

Bandura, A. (1989). Social cognitive theory. In R. Vasta (Ed.), *Annals of child development (Vol. 6).* Greenwich, CT: JAI.

Bandura, A., & Walters, R. (1963). *Social learning and personality development.* New York: Holt, Rinehart & Winston.

Bargh, J. A., & Tota, M. E. (1988). Context-dependent automatic processing in depression: Accessibility of negative constructs with regard to self but not others. *Journal of Personality and Social Psychology, 54*, 925–939.

Baron, R. A., & Richardson, D. R. (1994). *Human aggression* (2nd ed.). New York: Plenum.

Baumeister, R. F. (1991a). Self-concept and identity. In V. J. Derlega, B. A. Winstead, & W. H. Jones (Eds.), *Personality: Contemporary theory and research* (pp. 349–380). Chicago: Nelson-Hall.

Baumeister, R. F. (1991b). On the stability of variability: Retest reliability of metatraits. *Personality and Social Psychology Bulletin, 17*, 633–639.

Baumeister, R. F. (1995). Self and identity: An introduction. In A. Tesser (Ed.), *Advanced Social Psychology* (pp. 51–97). New York: McGraw-Hill.

Baumeister, R. F., Smart, L., & Boden, J. M. (1996). Relation of threatened egotism to violence and aggression: The dark side of high self-esteem. *Psychological Review, 103*, 5–33.

Beall, A. E., & Sternberg, R. J. (Eds.). (1993). *The psychology of gender*. New York: Guilford.

Bednar, R. L., Wells, M. G., Peterson, S. R. (1989). *Self-esteem: Paradoxes and innovations in clinical theory and practice.* Washington, DC: American Psychological Association.

Bem, S. L. (1974). The measurement of psychological androgyny. *Journal of Consulting and Clinical Psychology, 42*, 155–162.

Bem, S. L. (1975). Sex-role adaptability: One consequence of psychological androgyny. *Journal of Personality and Social Psychology, 31*, 634–643.

Bem, S. L. (1978). Beyond androgyny: Some presumptuous prescriptions for a liberated sexual identity. In J. Sherman & F. Denmark (Eds.), *Psychology of women: Future directions of research* (pp. 1–23). New York: Psychological Dimensions.

Bem, S. L. (1981). Gender schema theory: A cognitive account of sex typing. *Psychological Review, 88*, 354–364.

Bem, S. L. (1983). Gender schema theory and its implications for child development; Raising gender aschematic children in a gender-schematic society. *Signs: Journal of Women in Culture and society, 8*, 598–616.

Bem, S. L. (1985). Androgyny and gender schema theory: A conceptual and empirical integration. In T. B. Sonderegger (Ed.), *Nebraska Symposium on Motivation* (Vol. 32, pp. 179–226). Lincoln: University of Nebraska Press.

Bem, S. L. (1987). Gender schema theory and the romantic tradition. In P. Shaver & C. Hendrick (Eds.), *Sex and gender: Review of personality and social psychology* (Vol. 7, pp. 251–271). Beverly Hills, CA: Sage.

Bem, S. L. (1989). Genital knowledge and gender constancy in preschool children. *Child Development, 60*, 649–662.

Bem, S. L., & Lenney, E. (1976). Sex-typing and the avoidance of cross-sex behavior. *Journal of Personality and Social Psychology, 33*, 48–54.

Bem, S. L., Martyna, W., & Watson, C. (1976). Sex-typing and androgyny: Further explorations of the expressive domain. *Journal of Personality and Social Psychology, 34*, 1016–1023.

Benbow, C. P., & Stanley, J.C. (1980). Sex differences in mathematical ability: Factor artifact? *Science, 210*, 1262–1264.

Berkowitz, L. (1993). *Aggression: Its causes, consequences, and control*. New York: McGraw-Hill.

Blascovich, J., & Tomaka, J. (1991). Measure of self-esteem. In J. P. Robinson, P. R. Shaver, & L. S. Wrightsman (Eds.), *Measures of social psychological attitudes: Vol. 1. Measures of personality and social psychological attitudes* (pp. 115–160). San Diego: Academic Press.

Block, J. H. (1976). Issues, problems and pitfalls in assessing sex differences. *Merrill-Palmer Quarterly, 22*, 283–308.

Block, J., & Robins, R. W. (1993). A longitudinal study of consistency and change in self-esteem from early adolescence to early adulthood. *Child Development, 64*, 909–923.

Boldizar, J. P. (1991). Assessing sex-typing and androgyny in children: The children's sex-role inventory. *Developmental Psychology, 27*, 505–515.

Bromberger, J. T., & Matthews, K. A. (1996). A "feminine" model of vulnerability to depressive symptoms: A longitudinal investigation of middle-aged women. *Journal of Personality and Social Psychology, 70*, 591–598.

Brehm, S. S. (1992). *Intimate relationships* (2nd ed.). New York: McGraw-Hill.

Briggs, S. R., & Cheek, J. M. (1988). On the nature of self-monitoring: Problems with assessment, problems with validity. *Journal of Personality and Social Psychology, 54*, 663–678.

Briggs, S. R., Cheek, J. M., & Buss, A. H. (1980). An analysis of the self-monitoring scale. *Journal of Personality and Social Psychology, 54*, 679–686.

Brooks, J., & Lewis, M. (1974). Attachment behavior in thirteen-month-old opposite-sex twins. *Child Development, 45*, 243–247.

Brodzinsky, D. N., Messer, S. B., & Tew, J. D. (1979). Sex differences in children's expression and control of fantasy and overt aggression. *Child Development, 50*, 372–379.

Broverman, I. K., Broverman, D. M., Clarkson, F. E., Rosenkrantz, P., & Vogel, S. R. (1970). Sex-role stereotypes and clinical judgments of mental health. *Journal of Consulting and Clinical Psychology, 34*, 1–7.

Broverman, I. K., Vogel, S. R., Broverman, D. M., Clarkson, F. E., & Rosenkrantz, P. S. (1972). Sex-role stereotypes: A current appraisal. *Journal of Social Issues, 28*, 59–78.

Brown, R. (1986). *Social psychology, the second edition*. New York: Free Press.

Buss, A. H. (1995). *Personality: Temperament, social behavior, and the self*. Boston: Allyn & Bacon.

Buss, D. M. (1995). Psychological sex differences: Origins through sexual selection. *American Psychologist, 50*, 164–168.

Bussey, K., & Bandura, A. (1984). Influence on gender constancy and social power on sex-linked modeling. *Journal of Personality and Social Psychology, 47*, 1292–1302.

Buunk, B. (1982). Anticipated sexual jealousy: Its relationship to self-esteem, dependency, and reciprocity. *Personality and Social Psychology Bulletin, 8*, 310–316.

California Task Force to Promote Self-Esteem and Personal and Social Responsibility (1990). *Toward a state of self-esteem*. Sacramento, CA: California State Department of Education.

Campbell, J. D., Trapnell, P. D., Heine, S. J., Katz, I. M., Lavallee, L. F., & Lehman, D. R. (1996). Self-concept clarity: Measurement, personality correlates, and cultural boundaries. *Journal of Personality and Social Psychology, 70*, 141–156.

Carmickle, M., & Carducci, B. J. (1993, March). *Examining the internal structure of and gender differences in the Multidimensional Jealousy Scale*. Paper presented at the meeting of the Southeastern Psychological Association, Atlanta.

Chipman, S. F., & Thomas, V. G. (1985). Women's participation in mathematics: Outlining the problem. In S. F. Chipman, L. R. Brush, & D. M. Wilson (Eds.), *Women and mathematics: Balancing the equation* (pp. 1–24). Hillsdale, NJ: Erlbaum.

Collins, R. L. (1996). For better of worse: The impact of upward social comparison on self-evaluations. *Psychological Bulletin, 119*, 51–69.

Comer, R. J. (1995). *Abnormal psychology* (2nd ed.). New York: W. H. Freeman.

Coopersmith, S. (1967). *The antecedents of self-esteem*. San Francisco: W. H. Freeman.

Crane, M., & Markus, H. (1982). Gender identity: The benefits of a self-schema approach. *Journal of Personality and Social Psychology, 43*, 1195–1197.

Crutchfield, R. A. (1955). Conformity and character. *American Psychologist, 10*, 191–198.

Deaux, K. (1982, August). *Sex as a social category: Evidence for gender stereotypes*. Paper presented at the meeting of the American Psychological Association, Washington, DC.

Deaux, K., & Emswiller, T. (1974). Explanations of successful performance on sex-linked tasks: What is skill for the male is luck for the female. *Journal of Personality and Social Psychology, 29*, 80–85.

Deaux, K., Kite, M. E., & Lewis, L. L. (1985). Clustering and gender schemata: An uncertain link. *Personality and Social Psychology Bulletin, 11*, 387–397.

DeBono, K. G., & Packer, M. (1991). The effects of advertising appeal on perceptions of product quality. *Personality and Social Psychology Bulletin, 17*, 194–200.

Diener, E., Sandvik, E., & Larson, R. J. (1985). Age and sex effects for emotional intensity. *Development Psychology, 21*, 542–546.

Diamond, M. (1982). Sexual identity, monozygotic twins reared in discordant sex-roles and a BBC follow up. *Archives of Sexual Behavior, 11*, 181–186.

Dimitrovsky, L., Singer, J., & Yinon, Y. (1989). Masculine and feminine traits: Their relation to suitedness for and success in training for traditionally masculine and feminine army functions. *Journal of Personality and Social Psychology, 57*, 839–847.

Dion, K. L., & Dion, K. K. (1973). Correlates of romantic love. *Journal of Consulting and Clinical Psychology, 41*, 51–56.

Dion, K. L., & Dion, K. K. (1975). Self-esteem and romantic love. *Journal of Personality, 43*, 39–57.

Dipboye, R. L., Fromkin, H. L., & Wiback, K. (1975). Relative importance of applicant sex, attractiveness, and scholastic standing in evaluations of job applicant resumes. *Journal of Applied Psychology, 60*, 39–43.

Dorans, N. J., & Livingston, S. A. (1987). Male-female differences in SAT-verbal ability among students of high SAT-mathematical ability. *Journal of Educational Measurement, 24*, 65–71.

Dykman, B. M., Abramson, L. Y., Alloy, L. B., & Hartlage, S. (1989). Processing of ambiguous and unambiguous feedback by depressed and nondepressed college students: Schematic biases and their implications for depressive realism. *Journal of Personality and Social Psychology, 56*, 431–445.

Eagly, A. H. (1987). *Sex differences in social behavior: A social-role interpretation*. Hillsdale, NJ: Erlbaum.

Eagly, A. H. (1995). The science and politics of comparing men and women. *American Psychologist, 50*, 145–158.

Eagly, A. H., & Carli, L. L. (1981). Sex of researchers and sex-typed communications as determinants of sex differences in influenceability: A meta-analysis of social influence studies. *Psychological Bulletin, 90*, 971–981.

Eccles, J. S. (1989). Bringing young women to math and science. In M. Crawford & M. Gentry (Eds.), *Gender and thought: Psychological perspectives* (pp. 36–58). New York: Springer.

Ehrhardt, A. A., (1985). The psychobiology of gender. In A. S. Rossi (Ed.), *Gender and the life course*. New York: Aldine.

Fagot, B. I. (1977). *Sex-determined parental reinforcing contingencies in toddler children*. Paper presented at the biennial meeting of the Society for Research in Child Development, New Orleans.

Fagot, B. I., & Hagan, R. (1991). Observations of parental reactions to sex-stereotyped behaviors: Age and sex effects. *Child Development, 62*, 617–628.

Fagot, B. I., & Leinbach, M. D. (1989). The young child's gender schema: Environmental input, internal organization. *Child Development, 60*, 663–672.

Feingold, A. (1990). Gender differences in the effects of physical attractiveness on romantic attraction: A comparison across five research paradigms. *Journal of Personality and Social Psychology, 59*, 981–993.

Feingold, A. J. (1992). *Sex differences in personality: A quantitative analysis of personality inventory norms and gender stereotyping experiments*. Unpublished doctoral dissertation, Yale University, New Haven, CT.

Fiske, S. T. (1995). Social cognition. In A. Tesser (Ed.), *Advanced Social Psychology* (pp. 148–193). New York: McGraw-Hill.

Fiske, S. T., & Taylor, S. E. (1984). *Social cognition*. New York: McGraw-Hill.

Fiske, S. T., & Taylor, S. E. (1991). *Social cognition* (2nd ed.). New York: McGraw-Hill.

Festinger, L. (1954). A theory of social comparison processes. *Human Relations, 7*, 117–140.

Flaherty, J. F., & Dusek, J. B. (1980). An investigation of the relationship between psychological androgyny and components of self-concept. *Journal of Personality and Social Psychology, 38*, 984–999.

Fox, S. (1984). *The mirror makers*. New York: Morrow.

Frable, D. E. S., & Bem, S. L. (1985). If you're gender schematic, all members of the opposite sex look alike. *Journal of Personality and Social Psychology, 49*, 459–468.

Frey, K. S., & Ruble, D. N. (1985). What children say when the teacher is not around: Conflicting goals in social comparison and performance assessment in the classroom. *Journal of Personality and Social Psychology, 48*, 550–562.

Fuchs, D., & Thelen, M. H. (1988). Children's expected interpersonal consequences of communicating their affective state and reported likelihood of expression. *Child Development, 59*, 1314–1322.

Fuhrman, R. W., & Funder, D. C. (1995). Convergence between self and peer in the response-time processing of trait-relevant information. *Journal of Personality and Social Psychology, 69*, 961–974.

Garcia, L. T. (1982). Sex role orientation and stereotypes about male-female sexuality. *Sex Roles, 8*, 863–876.

Garland, H., & Price, K. H. (1977). Attitudes toward women in management and attributions for their success and failure in a managerial position. *Journal of Applied Psychology, 62*, 29–33.

Gibbons, F. X., & Gerrard, M. (1989). Effects of upward and downward social comparison on mood states. *Journal of Social and Clinical Psychology, 8*, 14–31.

Gibbons, F. X., & McCoy, S. B. (1991). Self-esteem, similarity, and reactions to active versus passive downward comparison. *Journal of Personality and Social Psychology, 60*, 414–424.

Glaude, B. A. (1991). Aggressive behavioral characteristics, hormones, and sexual orientation in men and women. *Aggressive Behavior, 17*, 313–326.

Glick, P., & Fiske, S. T. (1996). The Ambivalent Sexism Inventory: Differentiating hostile and benevolent sexism. *Journal of Personality and Social Psychology, 70*, 491–512.

Glick, P., Zion, C., & Nelson, C. (1988). What mediates sex discrimination in hiring decisions. *Journal of Personality and Social Psychology, 2*, 178–186.

Goldberg, P. A. (1968). Are women prejudiced against women? *Transaction, 5*, 28–30.

Greenwald, A. G., Bellezza, F. S., & Banaji, M. R. (1988). Is self-esteem a central ingredient of the self-concept? *Personality and Social Psychology Bulletin, 14*, 34–45.

Gruber, J. E., & Bjorn, L. (1982). Blue-collar blues: The sexual harassment of women autoworkers. *Work and Occupations, 9*, 271–298.

Halpern, D. F. (1986). *Sex differences in cognitive abilities.* Hillsdale, NJ: Erlbaum.

Hamachek, D. E. (1978). *Encounters with the self.* New York: Holt, Rinehart & Winston.

Harlow, H. F., & Suomi, S. J. (1971). Social recovery by isolated-reared monkeys. *Proceedings of the National Academy of Sciences, U.S.A., 68*, 1534–1538.

Harris, N. B. (1992). Sex, race, and experiences of aggression. *Aggressive Behavior, 18*, 201–217.

Harter, S. (1982). The Perceived Competence Scale for Children. *Child Development, 53*, 87–97.

Harter, S. (1983). Developmental perspectives on the self-system. In P. H. Mussen (Series Ed.) & E. M. Hetherington (Vol. Ed.), *Handbook of child psychology: Vol. 4. Socialization, personality, and social development* (4th ed., pp. 275–385). New York: Wiley.

Harvey, J. H., Flanary, R., & Morgan, M. (1986). Vivid memories of vivid loves gone by. *Journal of Social and Personal Relationships, 3*, 359–373.

Helgeson, V. S., & Mickelson, K. D. (1995). Motives for social comparison. *Journal of Personality and Social Psychology, 21*, 1200–1209.

Herrmann, D. J., & Crawford, M., & Holdsworth, M. (1992). Gender-linked differences in everyday memory performance. *British Journal of Psychology, 83*, 221–231.

Hetherington, E. M., & Frankie, G. (1967). Effect of parental dominance, warmth, and conflict on imitation in children. *Journal of Personality and Social Psychology, 6*, 119–125.

Heatherton, T. F., & Polivy, J. (1991). Development and validation of a scale for measuring state self-esteem. *Journal of Personality and Social Psychology, 60*, 895–910.

Huston, A. C. (1983). Sex-typing. In P. H. Mussen (Series Ed.), *Handbook of child psychology. Vol. 4. Socialization, personality, and social development* (pp. 387–467). New York: Wiley.

Hyde, J. S. (1991). *Half the human experience: The psychology of women* (4th ed.). Lexington, MA: D. C. Heath.

Hyde, J. S. (1994). *Understanding human sexuality* (5th ed.). New York: McGraw-Hill.

Hyde, J. S., & Linn, M. C. (1988). Gender differences in verbal ability: A meta-analysis. *Psychological Bulletin, 104*, 53–69.

Ickes, W., & Barnes, R. D. (1978). Boys and girls together—and alienated: On enacting stereotyped sex roles in mixed-sex dyads. *Journal of Personality and Social Psychology, 36*, 669–683.

Imperato-McGinley, J., Peterson, R. E., Gautier, T., & Sturla, E. (1979). Androgyns and the evolution of male gender identity among male pseudohermaphrodites with 5 alpha-reductase deficiency. *New England Journal of Medicine, 300*, 1233–1237

Izraeli, D. N., Izraeli, D., & Eden, D. (1985). Giving credit where credit is due: A case of no sex bias in attribution. *Journal of Applied Social Psychology, 15*, 516–530.

Jackson, L. A., Gardner, P., & Sullivan, L. (1992). Explaining gender differences in self-pay expectations: Social comparison standards and perceptions of fair play. *Journal of Applied Psychology, 77*, 651–663.

Jackson, L. A., & Grabski, S. V. (1988). Perceptions of fair play and the gender wage gap. *Journal of Applied Psychology, 18*, 606–625.

James, W. (1890). *Principles of psychology.* New York: Holt.

Jones, M. (1994). Linking dispositions and social behavior: Self-monitoring and advertising preferences. *Teaching of Psychology, 21*, 160–161.

Kaplin, M. (1983). A woman's view of DSM-III. *American Psychologist, 38*, 786–792.

Kelly, J. A. (1983). Sex role stereotypes and mental health: Conceptual models in the 1970s and issues for the 1980s. In V. Franks & E. D. Rothblum (Eds), *The stereotyping of women: Its effects on mental health* (pp. 11–29). New York: Springer.

Karoly, P. (1993). Mechanisms of self-regulation: A systems view. In L. W. Porter & M. R. Rosenzweig (Eds.), *Annual review of psychology* (pp. 23–52). Palo Alto, CA: Annual Reviews Inc.

Kashima, Y., Yamaguchi, S., Kim, U., Choi, S., Gelfand, M. J., & Yuki, M. (1995). Culture, gender, and self: A perspective from individualism-collectivism research. *Journal of Personality and Social Psychology, 69*, 925–937.

Kernis, M. H. (1993). The roles of stability and level of self-esteem in psychological functioning. In R. Baumeister (Ed.), *Self-esteem: The puzzle of low self-regard* (pp. 167–182). New York: Plenum.

LaBreche, L. (1995). Switching schools can hurt self-esteem. *Monitor, 26*, 40–41.

Lamb, M. E. (1981). *The role of the father in child development.* New York: Wiley.

Lamborn, S. D., Mounts, N. S., Steinberg, L., & Dornbush, S. M. (1991). Patterns of competence and adjustment among adolescents from authoritative, authoritarian, indulgent, and neglectful families. *Child Development, 62*, 1049–1065.

Lao, R. C., Upchurch, W. J., Corwin, B. J., & Grossnickle, W. F. (1975). Biased attitudes toward females as indicated by ratings of intelligence and likeability. *Psychological Reports, 37*, 1315–1320.

LeUnes, A. D., & Nation, J. R. (1989). *Sport psychology: An introduction.* Chicago: Nelson-Hall.

Liebert, R. M., & Sprafkin, J. (1988). *The early window: Effects of television on children and youth* (3rd ed.). New York: Pergamon.

Linn, M. C., & Petersen, A. C. (1985). Emergence and characterization of sex difference in spatial ability: A meta-analysis. *Child Development, 56*, 1479–1498.

Linn, M. C., & Petersen, A. C. (1986). A meta-analysis of gender differences in spatial ability: Implications for mathematics and science achievement. In J. S. Hyde & M. C. Linn (Eds.), *The psychology of gender: Advances through meta-analysis* (pp. 67–101). Baltimore; Johns Hopkins University Press.

Lippa, R. (1995). Do sex differences define gender-related individual differences within the sexes? Evidence from three studies. *Personality and Social Psychology Bulletin, 21,* 1995.

Lubinski, D., Tellegen, A., & Butcher, J. N. (1981). The relationship between androgyny and subjective indicators of emotional well-being. *Journal of Personality and Social Psychology, 40,* 722–730.

Maccoby, E. E., & Jacklin, C. N. (1974). *The psychology of sex differences.* Stanford, CA: Stanford University Press.

MacKinnon, C. E., Stoneman, Z., & Brody, G. H. (1984). The impact of maternal employment and family form on children's sex-role stereotypes and mothers' traditional attitudes. *Journal of Divorce, 8,* 51–60.

Major, B., Carnevale, P. J. D., & Deaux, K. (1981). A different perspective on androgyny: Evaluations of masculine and feminine personality characteristics. *Journal of Personality and Social Psychology, 41,* 988–1001.

Major, B., & Konar, E. (1984). An investigation of sex differences in pay expectations and their possible causes. *Academy of Management Journal, 27,* 777–792.

Major, B., Vanderslice, V., & McFarlin, D. B. (1985). Effects of pay expected on pay received: The confirmatory nature of initial expectations. *Journal of Applied Social Psychology, 14,* 399–412.

Markstorm-Adams, C. (1989). Androgyny and its relation to adolescent psychological well-being: A review of the literature. *Sex Roles, 21,* 325–340.

Markus, H., Crane, M., Bernstein, S., & Siladi, M. (1982). Self-schemas and gender. *Journal of Personality and Social Psychology, 42,* 38–50.

Marsh, H. W. (1989). Age and sex effects in multiple dimensions of self-concept: Preadolescence to early adulthood. *Journal of Educational Psychology, 81,* 417–430.

Marsh, H. W. (1996). Positive and negative global self-esteem: A substantively meaningful distinction or artifactors? *Journal of Personality and Social Psychology, 70,* 810–819.

Marsh, H. W., & Myers, M. (1986). Masculinity, femininity, and androgyny: A methodological and theoretical critique. *Sex Roles, 14,* 397–430.

Martin, C. L. (1987). A ratio measure of sex stereotyping. *Journal of Personality and Social Psychology, 52,* 489–499.

Martin, C. L., & Halverson, C. F., Jr. (1981). A schematic processing model of sex typing and stereotyping in children. *Child Development, 52,* 1119–1134.

Martin, C. L., & Halverson, C. F., Jr. (1983). The effects of sex-typing schemas on young children's memory. *Child Development, 54,* 563–574.

Martin, C. L., & Halverson, C. F., Jr. (1987). The roles of cognition in sex-role and sex-typing. In D. B. Carter (Ed.), *Current conceptions of sex roles and sex-typing: Theory and research* (pp. 123–137). New York: Praeger.

Maypole, D. E. (1986). Sexual harassment of social workers at work: Injustice within? *Social Work, 31,* 29–34.

McCann, C. D., & Hancock, R. D. (1983). Self-monitoring in communicative interactions: Social cognitive consequences of goal-directed message modification. *Journal of Experimental Social Psychology, 19,* 109–121.

McGhee, P. E., & Frueh, T. (1980). Television viewing and the learning of sex-role stereotypes. *Sex Roles, 6,* 179–188.

McKenzie-Mohr, D., & Zanna, M. P. (1990). Treating women as sexual objects: Look to the (gender schematic) male who has viewed pornography. *Personality and Social Psychology Bulletin, 16,* 266–308.

Mellema, A., & Bassili, J. N. (1995). On the relationship between attitudes and values: Exploring the moderating effects of self-monitoring and self-monitoring schematicity. *Personality and Social Psychology Bulletin, 9,* 885–892.

Messer, S. B., & Lewis, M. (1972). Social class and sex differences in the attachment and play behavior of the year-old infant. *Merrill-Palmer Quarterly, 18,* 295–306.

Mischel, W. (1970). Sex-typing and socialization. In P. H. Mussen (Ed.), *Carmichael's manual of child psychology* (Vol. 2, pp. 3–72). New York: Wiley.

Miles, C. C. (1935). Sex in social psychology. In C. Murchison (Ed.), *A handbook of social psychology* (Vol. 2, pp. 683–797). New York; Russell & Russell.

Money, J., & Ehrhardt, A. A. (1972). *Man and woman, boy and girl.* Baltimore: John Hopkins University Press.

Morse, S., & Gergen, K. J. (1970). Social comparison, self-consistency, and the concept of the self. *Journal of Personality and Social Psychology, 16,* 148–156.

Mruk, C. (1995). *Self-esteem: Research, theory, and practice.* New York: Springer.

Mussen, P. H., & Rutherford, E. (1963). Parent-child relations and parental personality in relation to young children's sex-role preferences. *Child Development, 34,* 589–607.

Myers, D. G. (1992). *The pursuit of happiness: Who is happy—and why.* New York: William Morrow.

Nottelmann, E. D. (1987). Competence and self-esteem during transition from childhood to adolescence. *Developmental Psychology, 23,* 441–450.

O'Connor, K., Mann, D. W., & Bardwick, J. M. (1978). Androgyny and self-esteem in the upper-middle class: A replication of Spence. *Journal of Personality and Social Psychology, 46,* 1168–1169.

O'Heron, C. A., & Orlofsky, J. L. (1990). Stereotypic and nonstereotypic sex role trait and behavior orientations, gender, identity and psychological adjustment. *Journal of Personality and Social Psychology, 58,* 134–143.

Orlofsky, J., L., & O'Heron, C. A. (1987). Stereotypic and non-stereotypic sex role trait and behavior orientations: Implications for personal adjustment. *Journal of Personality and Social Psychology, 52,* 1034–1042.

Osborne, J. W. (1995). Academics, self-esteem, and race: A look at the underlying assumptions of the disidentification hypothesis. *Personality and Social Psychology Bulletin, 21,* 449–455.

Osborne, R. E. (1996). *Self: An eclectic approach.* Boston: Allyn & Bacon.

Park, B., & Hahn. S. (1988). Sex-role identity and the perception of others. *Social Cognition, 6,* 61–87.

Pazy, A. (1992). Sex-linked bias in promotion decisions: The role of candidate's career relevance and respondent's prior experience. *Psychology of Women Quarterly, 16,* 209–228.

Pedhazur, E. J., & Tetenbaum, T. J. (1979). Bem Sex-Role Inventory: A theoretical and methodological critique. *Journal of Personality and Social Psychology, 37,* 996–1016.

Petersen, A. C. (1988). Adolescent development. *Annual Review of Psychology, 39,* 583–607.

Pomerleau, A., Bolduc, D., Malcuit, G., & Cossette, L. (1990). Pink or blue: Environmental gender stereotypes in the first two years of life. *Sex Roles, 22,* 359–367.

Prager, K. J., & Bailey, J. M. (1985). Androgyny, ego development, and psychological crisis. *Sex Roles, 13,* 525–536.

Roberts, J. E., Gotlib, I. H., & Kassel, J. D. (1996). Adult attachment security and symptoms of depression: The mediating roles of dysfunctional attitudes and low self-esteem. *Journal of Personality and Social Psychology, 70,* 310–320.

Rogers, C. R. (1951). *Client-centered therapy.* Boston: Houghton Mifflin.

Rosen, B., & Jerdee, T. H. (1974). Influence of sex role stereotypes on personnel decisions. *Journal of Applied Psychology, 59,* 9–14.

Rosen, B., & Jerdee, T. H. (1975). Effects of employee's sex and threatening versus pleading appeals on managerial evaluations of grievances. *Journal of Applied Psychology, 60,* 442–445.

Rosenberg, M. (1965). *Society and the adolescent self-image.* Princeton, NJ: Princeton University Press.

Rosenkrantz, P. S., Vogel, S. R., Bee, H., Broverman, I. K., & Broverman, D. M. (1968). Sex-role stereotypes and self-concepts in college students. *Journal of Consulting and Clinical Psychology, 32,* 287–295.

Rosenwasser, S. M., & Lingenfelter, M., & Harrington, A. F. (1989). Nontraditional gender role portrayals on television and children's gender role perceptions. *Journal of Applied Developmental Psychology, 10,* 97–105.

Rosenzweig, J. M., & Daley, D. M. (1989). Dyadic adjustment/sexual satisfaction in women and men as a function of psychological sex role self-perception. *Journal of Sex and Marital Therapy, 15,* 42–56.

Ross, A. O. (1992). *The search of self: Research and theory.* New York: Springer.

Ruble, D. N., Balaban, T., & Cooper, J. (1981). Gender constancy and the effects of sex-typed televised toy commercials. *Child Development, 52,* 667–673.

Shaffer, D. R. (1994). *Social and personality development* (3rd ed.). Pacific Grove, CA: Brooks/Cole .

Shaffer, D. R., Pegalis, L. J., & Cornell, D. P. (1991). Interactive effects of social context and sex-role identity on self-disclosure during the acquaintance process. *Sex Roles, 24,* 1–19.

Shotland, R. L., & Hunter, B. A. (1995). Women's "token resistant" and compliant sexual behaviors are related to uncertain sexual intentions and rape. *Personality and Social Psychology Bulletin, 21,* 226–236.

Simmons, R. G. (1987). Self-esteem in adolescence. In T. Honess & K. Yardly (Eds.), *Self and identity* (pp. 172–192). London: Routledge & Kegan Paul.

Simmons, R. G., Burgeson, R., Carlton-Ford, S., & Blyth, D. A. (1987). The impact of cumulative change in early adolescence. *Child Development, 58,* 1220–1234.

Sistrunk, F., & McDavid, J. W. (1971). Sex variable in conforming behavior. *Journal of Personality and Social Psychology, 17,* 200–207.

Slaby, R. G., & Frey, K. S. (1975). Development of gender constancy and selective attention to same-sex models. *Child Development, 46,* 849–856.

Snyder, M. (1974). The self-monitoring of expressive behavior. *Journal of Personality and Social Psychology, 30,* 526–537.

Snyder, M. (1987). *Public appearances/private realities: The psychology of self-monitoring.* New York: W. H. Freeman.

Snyder, M., & DeBono, K. G. (1985b). Appeals to image and claims about quality: Understanding the psychology of advertising. *Journal of Personality and Social Psychology, 49,* 586–597.

Snyder, M., Nettle, R., & DeBono, K. G. (1985). Unpublished research. University of Minnesota.

Spence, J. T. (1984). Masculinity, femininity, and gender-related traits: A conceptual analysis and critique of current research. In B. A. Maher & W. B. Maher (Eds.), *Progress in experimental personality research* (Vol. 13, pp. 1–97). New York: Academic Press.

Spence, J. T. (1983). Comment on Lubinski, Tellegen, and Butcher. *Journal of Personality and Social Psychology, 44,* 440–446.

Spence, J. T. (1991). Do the BSRI and the PAQ measure the same or different concepts? *Psychology of Women Quarterly, 15,* 141–165.

Spence, J. T., & Helmreich, R. L. (1978). *Masculinity and femininity: Their psychological dimensions, correlates, and antecedents.* Austin: University of Texas Press.

Spence, J. T., & Helmreich, R. L. (1981). Androgyny versus gender schema: A comment on Bem's gender schema theory. *Psychological Review, 88,* 365–368.

Spence, J. T., Helmreich, R. L., & Stapp, J. (1975). Ratings of self and peers on sex-role attributes and their relation to self-esteem and conceptions of masculinity and femininity. *Journal of Personality and Social Psychology, 32,* 29–39.

Sprecher, S., & Metts, S. (1989). Development of the "Romantic Beliefs Scale" and examination of the effects of gender and gender-role orientation. *Journal of Social and Personal Relationships, 6,* 387–411.

Stanley, J. C., & Benbow, C. P. (1982). Huge sex ratios at upper end. *American Psychologist, 37,* 972.

Steele, C. (1992, April). Race and the schooling of Black Americans. *The Atlantic Monthly, 269*(4), 68–78.

Sternglanz, S. H., & Serbin, L. (1974). Sex-role stereotyping in children's television programming. *Developmental Psychology, 10,* 710–715.

Tavris, C. (1992). *The mismeasure of woman.* New York: Simon & Schuster.

Tavris, C., & Wade, C. (1984). *The longest war: Sex differences in perspective.* New York: Harcourt Brace Jovanovich.

Taylor, M. C., & Hall, J. A. (1982). Psychological androgyny: A review and reformulation of theories, methods, and conclusions. *Psychological Bulletin, 92,* 347–366.

Terman, L. M., & Miles, C. C. (1936). *Sex and personality*. New York: McGraw-Hill.

Terman, L. M., & Merrill, M. A. (1937). *Measuring intelligence*. Boston: Houghton Mifflin.

Tesser, A. (1980). Self-esteem and family dynamics. *Journal of Personality and Social Psychology, 39*, 77–91.

Tesser, A. (1991). Emotions in social comparison and reflection processes. In J. Suls & T. A. Wills (Eds.), *Social comparison: Contemporary theory and research* (pp. 115–145). Hillsdale, NJ: Erlbaum.

Tolar, C. J. (1968). An investigation of parent-offspring relationships. *Dissertation Abstracts, 28*(8–B), 3465.

Top, T. J. (1991). Sex bias in the evaluation of performance in scientific, artistic, and literary professions: A review. *Sex Roles, 24*, 73–106.

Troll, L. E., Neugarten, B. L., & Kraines, R. J. (1969). Similarities in values and other personality characteristics in college students and their parents. *Merrill-Palmer Quarterly, 15*, 323–336.

Unger, R., & Crawford, M. (1992). *Women and gender: A feminist psychology*. New York: McGraw-Hill

Warren, J. (1996, March 6). Self-esteem engine, far from sputtering has picked up speed. *The Courier-Journal*, p. B4.

Waterman, A. S., & Whitbourne, S. K. (1982). Androgyny and psychosocial development among college students and adults. *Journal of Personality, 50*, 121–133.

Wattenberg, W. W., & Clifford, C. (1964). Relation of self-concept to beginning achievement in reading. *Child Development, 35*, 461–467.

Weiten, W., Lloyd, M. A., Lashley, R. L. (1991). *Psychology applied to modern life: Adjustment in the 90s* (3rd ed.). Pacific Grove, CA: Brooks/Cole.

Weitzman, L. J., Eifler, D., Hokada, E., & Ross, C. (1972). Sex-role socialization in picture books for preschool children. *American Journal of Sociology, 77*, 1125–1149.

Westoff, L. A. (1979). Women: In search of equality. *Focus, Vol. 6*. Princeton, NJ: Educational Testing Service.

White, G. L. (1981a). A model of romantic jealousy. *Motivation and Emotion, 5*, 295–310.

White, G. L. (1981b). Some correlates of romantic jealousy. *Journal of Personality, 20*, 55–64.

White, G. L., & Mullen, P. E. (1989). *Jealousy: Theory, research, and clinical strategies*. New York: Guilford.

Whiting, B., & Pope, C. (1974). Across-cultural analysis of sex differences in the behavior of children aged three to eleven. *Journal of Social Psychology, 91*, 171–188.

Whitley, B. E., Jr. (1983). Sex role orientation and self-esteem: A critical meta-analytic review. *Journal of Personality and Social Psychology, 44*, 765–778.

Whitley, B. E., Jr. (1988). Masculinity, femininity, and self-esteem: A multitrait-multimethod analysis. *Sex Roles, 18*, 419–431.

Williams, J. B. W., & Spitzer, R. L. (1983). The issue of sex bias in DSM-III. *American Psychologist, 83*, 793–803.

Wills, T. A. (1991). Similarity and self-esteem in downward social comparison. In J. Suls & T. A. Wills (Eds.), *Social comparison: Contemporary theory and research* (pp. 51–78). Hillsdale, NJ: Erlbaum.

Wylie, R. C. (1989). *Measures of self-concept*. Lincoln: University of Nebraska Press.

Yoder, J. D. (1985). An academic woman as a token: A case study. *Journal of Social Issues, 41*, 61–72.

Zanna, M. P., & Olson, J. M. (1982). Individual differences in attitudinal relations. In M. P. Zanna & E. T. Higgins, & C. P. Herman (Eds.), *Consistency in social behavior: The Ontario symposium (Vol. 2*, pp. 75–104). Hillsdale, NJ: Erlbaum.

Chapter 14

Aaker, D. A., & Myers, J. G. (9182). *Advertising management* (2nd. ed.). Englewood Cliffs, NJ: Prentice-Hall.

Brown, L. L., Tomarken, A. J., Loosen, P. T., Kalin, N. H., & Davidson, R. J. (1996). Individual differences in repressive-defensiveness predict basal salivary cortisol levels. *Journal of Personality and Social Psychology, 70*, 362–371.

Buss, A. H. (1995). *Personality: Temperament, social behavior, and the self*. Boston: Allyn & Bacon.

Baron, R. A., & Byrne, D. (1977). *Social psychology: Understanding human interaction* (2nd ed.). Boston: Allyn & Bacon.

Beck, A. T., & Emery, G. (1985). *Anxiety disorders and phobias*. New York: Basic Books.

Cannon, W. B. (1929). *Bodily changes in pain, hunger, fear, and rage*. New York: Appleton-Century-Crofts.

Carducci, B. J., & Clark, D. L. (1994, August). *The personal and situational pervasiveness of chronically shy, socially anxious individuals*. Paper presented at the meeting of the American Psychological Association, Los Angeles.

Carducci, B. J. & Clark, D. L. (1996). Manuscript submitted for publication.

Carducci, B. J., & Stein, N. D. (1988, March). *The personal and situational pervasiveness of shyness in college students: A nine-year comparison*. Paper presented at the meeting of the Southeastern Psychological Association, New Orleans.

Carducci, B. J., & Zimbardo, P. G. (1995, December). Are you shy? *Psychology Today, 28*, 34–41.

Cheek, J., M. (1989). *Conquering shyness: The battle anyone can win*. New York: Dell.

Cohen, D. (1981). *Consumer behavior*. New York: Random House.

Comer, R. J. (1995). *Abnormal psychology* (2nd ed.). New York: W. H. Freeman.

Fann, W. E., & Goshen, C. E. (1973). *The language of mental health*. St. Louis: C. V. Mosby.

Fischer, W. F. (1970). *Theories of anxiety*. New York: Harper & Row.

Fiske, S. T., Morling, B., & Stevens, L. E. (1996). Controlling self and others: A theory of anxiety, mental control, and social control. *Personality and Social Psychology Bulletin, 22*, 115–123.

Ganzer, V. J. (1968). Effects of audience presence and test anxiety on learning and retention in a serial learning situation. *Journal of Personality and Social Psychology, 8*, 194–199.

Geen, R. G. (1976). Test anxiety, observation, and range of cue utilization. *British Journal of Social and Clinical Psychology, 15*, 253–259.

Geen, R. G. (1980). Test anxiety and cue utilization. In I. G. Sarason (Ed.), *Test anxiety: Theory, research and applications* (pp. 43–61). Hillsdale, NJ: Erlbaum.

Groves, P. M., & Schlesinger, K. (1982). *Biological psychology* (2nd ed.). Dubuque, IA: William C. Brown.

Hodges, W. F., & Spielberger, C. G. (1969). Digit span: An indicant of trait or state anxiety? *Journal of Clinical and Consulting Psychology, 33,* 430–434.

Holroyd, K. A., & Appel, M. A. (1980). Test anxiety and physiological responding. In I. G. Sarason (Ed.), *Test anxiety: Theory, research, and applications* (pp. 129–151). Hillsdale, NJ: Erlbaum.

Holroyd, K., Westbrook, T., Wolf, M., & Badhorn, E. (1978). Performance, cognition, and physiological responding in test anxiety. *Journal of Abnormal Psychology, 87,* 442–451.

Hull, C. L. (1943). *Principles of behavior.* New Haven, CT.: Yale University Press.

Jones, W. H., Cheek, J. M., & Briggs, S. R. (Eds.). (1986). *Shyness: Perspectives on research and treatment.* New York: Plenum.

Kendall, P. C., Finch, A. J., Jr., Auerbach, S. M., Hooke, J. F., & Mikulka, P. J. (1976). The State-Trait Anxiety Inventory: A systematic evaluation. *Journal of Consulting and Clinical Psychology, 44,* 406–412.

Klavora, P. (1975). Application of the Spielberger trait-state anxiety theory and STAI in pre-competitive anxiety research. In D. M. Landers, D, V. Harris, & R. W. Christina (Eds.), *Psychology of sport and motor behavior II* (pp. 141–143). University Park, PA: Penn State HPER Series, No. 10.

Kotler, P., & Armstrong, G. (1994). *Principles of marketing* (6th ed.). Englewood Cliffs, NJ: Prentice Hall.

Leary, M. R., & Kowalski, R. M. (1995). *Social anxiety.* New York: Guilford.

Leventhal, H. (1970). Findings and theory in the study of fear communications. L. Berkowitz (Ed.), *Advances in experimental social psychology* (Vol. 5) (pp. 120–186). New York: Academic Press.

Mandler, G., & Sarason, S. B. (1952). A study of anxiety and learning. *Journal of Abnormal and Social Psychology, 47,* 166–173.

Mandler, G. (1972). Comments on Dr. Sarason's paper. In C. D. Spielberger (Ed.), *Anxiety: Current trends in theory and research* (Vol. 2, pp. 405–408). New York: Academic Press.

Melchior, L. A., & Cheek, J. M. (1990). Shyness and anxious self-preoccupation during dating interaction. *Journal of Social Behavior and Personality, 5,* 127–140.

Mehr, J. (1983). *Abnormal psychology.* New York: Holt, Rinehart & Winston.

Mowrer, O. H. (1950). *Learning theory and personality dynamics.* New York: Ronald Press Co.

Napoli, V., Kilbride, J. M., & Tebbs, D. E. (1988). *Adjustment growth in a changing world* (3rd ed.). St. Paul, MN: West Publishing.

Pederson, A. M. (1970). Effects of test anxiety and co-acting groups on learning and performance. *Perceptual and Motor Skills, 30,* 55–62.

Pilkonis, P. A. (1977). Shyness, public and private, and its relationship to other measures of social behavior. *Journal of Personality, 45,* 585–595.

Rathus, S. A., & Nevid, J. S. (1980). *Adjustment and growth: The challenges of life.* New York: Holt, Rinehart & Winston.

Ray, W. J., Katahn, M., & Snyder, C. R. (1971). Effects of test anxiety on acquisition, retention, and generalization of a complex task in a classroom situation. *Journal of Personality and Social Psychology, 20,* 147–154.

Roger, R. W., & Mewborn, R. (1976). Fear appeals and attitude change: Effects of a threat's noxiousness, probability of occurrence, and the efficacy of coping response. *Journal of Personality and Social Psychology, 34,* 54–61.

Sarason, I. G. (1957). The effect of anxiety and two kinds of failure on serial learning. *Journal of Personality, 25,* 282–292.

Sarason, I. G. (1972). Experimental approaches to test anxiety: Attention and the uses of information. In C. D. Spielberger (Ed.), *Anxiety: Current trends in theory and research* (Vol. 2, pp. 383–403). New York; Academic Press.

Sarason, I. G. (1973). Test anxiety and cognitive modeling. *Journal of Personality and Social Psychology, 28,* 58–61.

Sarason, I. G. (Ed.). (1980a). Introduction to the study of test anxiety. In I. G. Sarason (Ed.), *Test anxiety: Theory, research, and applications* (pp. 3–14). Hillsdale, NJ: Erlbaum.

Sarason, I. G. (1980b). *Test anxiety: Theory, research, and applications.* Hillsdale, NJ: Erlbaum.

Sarason, I. G., & Palola, E. G. (1960). The relationship of test and general anxiety, difficulty of task, and experimental instructions to performance. *Journal of Experimental Psychology, 59,* 185–191.

Sarason, I. G., & Sarason, B. R. (1990). *Test anxiety.* H. Leitenberg (Ed.), *Handbook of social and evaluation anxiety* (pp. 475–495). New York: Plenum.

Sarason, I. G., & Stoops, R. (1978). Test anxiety and the passage of time. *Journal of Consulting and Clinical Psychology, 46,* 102–109.

Smith, R. E., & Smoll, F. L. (1990). Sport performance anxiety. In H. Leitenberg (Ed.), *Handbook of social and evaluation anxiety* (pp. 417–454). New York: Plenum.

Spence, K. W. (1956). *Behavior theory and conditioning.* New Haven, CT.: Yale University Press.

Spiegler, M. D., Morris, L. W., & Liebert, R. M. (1968). Cognitive and emotional components of test anxiety: Temporal factors. *Psychological Reports, 22,* 451–456.

Spielberger, C. D. (1966). Theory and research on anxiety. In C. D. Spielberger (Ed.), *Anxiety and behavior* (pp. 3–22). New York: Academic Press.

Spielberger, C. D. (1972). Anxiety as an emotional state. In C. D. Spielberger (Ed.), *Anxiety: Current trends in theory and research* (Vol. 1, pp. 23–49). New York: Academic Press.

Spielberger, C. D., Gorsuch, R. C., & Lushene, R. E. (1970). *Manual for the State-Trait Anxiety Inventory.* Palo Alto, CA: Consulting Psychologists Press.

Taylor, J. A. (1953). A personality scale of manifest anxiety. *Journal of Abnormal and Social Psychology, 48,* 285–290.

Wheatley, J. J., & Oshikawa, S. (1970). The relationship between anxiety and positive and negative advertising appeals. *Journal of Marketing, 7,* 85–90.

Zimbardo, P. G. (1977). *Shyness: What it is, what to do about it.* Reading, MA: Addison-Wesley.

Chapter 15

Altemeyer, B. (1998). *Enemies of freedom: Understanding right-wing authoritarianism.* San Francisco: Jossey-Bass.

Baily, D. S., Leonard, K. E., Cranston, J. W., & Taylor, S. P. (1983). Effects of alcohol and self-awareness on human physical aggression. *Personality and Social Psychology Bulletin, 9,* 289–295.

Bandura, A. (1973). *Aggression: A social learning analysis.* Englewood Cliffs, NJ: Prentice Hall.

Bandura, A. (1978). Learning and behavioral theories of aggression. I. L. Kutash, S. B., Kutash, L. B. Schlesinger and and associates (Eds.), *Violence: Perspective on murder and aggression* (pp. 29–57). San Francisco: Jossey-Bass.

Bandura, A., Ross, D., Ross, S. A. (1963). Imitation of film-mediated aggressive models. *Journal of Abnormal and Social Psychology, 66,* 3–11.

Baron, R. A. (1972a). Aggression as a function of ambient temperature and prior anger arousal. *Journal of Personality and Social Psychology, 21,* 183–189.

Baron, R. A. (1972b). Reducing the influence of an aggressive model: The restraining effects of peer censure. *Journal of Experimental Social Psychology, 8,* 266–275.

Baron, R. A. (1973). Threatened retaliation from the victim as an inhibitor of physical aggression. *Journal of Research in Personality, 7,* 103–115.

Baron, R. A. (1977). *Human aggression.* New York: Plenum

Baron, R. A. (1978). Aggression and heat: The "long hot summer" revisited. In A. Baum, J. E. Singer, & S. Valins (Eds.), *Advances in environmental psychology* (Vol. I, pp. 57–84). Hillsdale, NJ: Erlbaum.

Baron, R. A., & Bell, P. A. (1975). Aggression and heat: Mediating effects of prior provocation and exposure to an aggressive model. *Journal of Personality and Social Psychology, 31,* 825–832.

Baron, R. A., & Kepner, C. R. (1970). Model's behavior and attraction toward the model as determinants of adult aggressive behavior. *Journal of Personality and Social Psychology, 14,* 335–344.

Baron, R. A., & Lawton, S. F. (1972). Environmental influences on aggression: The facilitation of modeling effects by high ambient temperatures. *Psychonomic Science, 26,* 80–83.

Baron, R. A., & Ransberger, V. M. (1978). Ambient temperature and the occurrence of collective violence: The "long hot summer" revisited. *Journal of Personality and Social Psychology, 36,* 351–360.

Baron, R. A., & Richardson, D. R. (1994). *Human aggression* (2nd ed.). New York: Plenum.

Baumeister, R. F., Smart, L., & Boden, J. M. (1996). Relation of threatened egotism to violence and aggression: The dark side of high self-esteem. *Psychological Review, 103,* 5–33.

Bell, P. A., & Baron, R. A. (1981). Ambient temperature and human violence. In P. F. Brain, & D. Benton (Eds.), *A multidisciplinary approach to aggression research* (pp. 421–430). Amsterdam: Elsevier/North-Holland Biomedical Press.

Belson, W. A. (1978). *Television violence and the adolescent boy.* Westmead, England: Saxon, House, Teakfield Ltd.

Berk, R. A., & Newton, P. J. (1985). Does arrest really deter wife battery? An effort to replicate the findings of the Minneapolis spouse abuse experiment. *American Sociological Review, 50,* 253–262.

Berkowitz, L. (1978). Whatever happen to the frustration-aggression hypothesis? *American Behavioral Scientist, 21,* 691–708.

Berkowitz, L. (1988). Frustration, appraisals, and aversively stimulated aggression. *Aggressive Behavior, 14,* 3–11.

Berkowitz, L. (1989). The frustration-aggression hypothesis: An examination and reformulation. *Psychological Bulletin, 106,* 59–73.

Berkowitz, L. (1990). On the formation and regulation of anger and aggression: A cognitive-neoassociationistic analysis. *American Psychologist, 45,* 494–503.

Berkowitz, L. (1993). *Aggression: Its causes, consequences, and control.* New York: McGraw-Hill.

Berkowitz, L., & LePage, A. (1967). Weapons as aggression-eliciting stimuli. *Journal of Personality and Social Psychology, 7,* 202–207.

Bienert, H., & Schneider, B. H. (1995). Deficit-specific social skills training with peer-nominated aggressive-disruptive and sensitive-isolated preadolescents. *Journal of Clinical Child Psychology, 24,* 287–300.

Bower, G. H., & Hilgard, E. R. (1981). *Theories of learning* (5th ed.). Englewood Cliffs, NJ: Prentice Hall.

Briddell, D. W., Rimm, D. C., Caddy, G. R., Krawitz, G., Sholis, D., & Wunderlin, R. J. (1978). Effects of alcohol and cognitive set on sexual arousal to deviant stimuli. *Journal of Abnormal Psychology, 87,* 418–430.

Bushman, B. J. (1995). Moderating role of trait aggressiveness in the effects of violent media on aggression. *Journal of Personality and Social Psychology, 69,* 950–960.

Bushman, B. J., & Cooper, H. M. (1990). Effects of alcohol on human aggression: An integrative research review. *Psychological Bulletin, 107,* 341–354.

Buss, A. H. (1961). *The psychology of aggression.* New York: Wiley.

Buss, A. H. (1971). Aggression pays. In J. L. Singer (Ed.), *The control of aggression and violence: Cognitive and physiological factors* (pp. 7–18). New York: Academic Press.

Carroll, D., & O'Callaghan, M. A. J. (1981). Psychosurgery and the control of aggression. In P. F. Brain & D. Denton (Eds.), *The biology of aggression* (pp. 457–471). Rockville, MD: Sythoff & Noordhoff.

Carlson, N. R. (1988). *Foundations of physiological psychology.* Boston: Allyn & Bacon.

Check, J., & Malamuth, N. (1984). Can there be positive effects of participation in pornography experiments? *Journal of Sex Research, 20,* 14–31.

Christiansen, K. O. (1974). The genesis of aggressive study. In J. de Wit & W. W. Hartup (Eds.), *Determinants and origins of aggressive behavior* (pp. 233–253). The Hague: Mouton.

Cline, V. B., Croft, R. G., & Courrier, S. (1973). Desensitization of children to television violence. *Journal of Personality and Social Psychology, 27,* 360–365.

Coleman, J. C., Butcher, J. N., Carson, R. C. (1984). *Abnormal psychology and modern life* (7th ed.). Scott, Foresman.

Comer, R. J. (1995). *Abnormal psychology* (2nd ed.). New York: W. H. Freeman.

Comstock, G., Chaffee, S., Katzman, N., McCombs, M., & Roberts, D. (1978). *Television and human behavior*. New York: Columbia University Press.

Cotton, J. L. (1986). Ambient temperature and violent crime. *Journal of Applied Social Psychology, 16,* 786–801.

Court-Brown, W. M. (1968). Males with an XYY sex chromosome complement. *Journal of Medical Genetics, 5,* 341–359.

Crowe, L. C., & George, W. H. (1989). Alcohol and human sexuality: Review and integration. *Psychological Bulletin, 105,* 374–386.

Dabbs, J. M., Jr., Frady, R. L., Carr, T. S., & Besch, N. F. (1987). Saliva testosterone and criminal violence in young adult prison inmates. *Psychosomatic Medicine, 49,* 174–182.

Dabbs, J. M., Jr., & Morris, R. (1990). Testosterone, social class, and antisocial behavior in a sample of 4,462 men. *Psychological Science, 1,* 209–211.

Dabbs, J. M., Jr., Ruback, R. B., Frady, R. L., Hopper, C. H., & Sgoutas, D. D. (1988). Saliva testosterone and criminal violence among women. *Personality and Individual Differences, 9,* 269–275.

Demare, D., Briere, J., & Lips, H. M. (1988). Violent pornography and self-reported likelihood of sexual aggression. *Journal of Research in Personality, 22,* 140–153.

Dollard, J., Doob, L., Miller, N. E., Mowrer, O. H., & Sears, R. R. (1939). *Frustration and aggression*. New Haven, CN: Yale University Press.

Donnerstein, E. (1980). Aggressive erotica and violence against women. *Journal of Personality and Social Psychology, 39,* 269–277.

Donnerstein, E., & Berkowitz, L. (1981). Victim reactions in aggressive erotic films as a factor in violence against women. *Journal of Personality and Social Psychology, 41,* 710–724.

Donnerstein, E., & Donnerstein, M. (1976). Research in the control of interracial aggression. In R. G. Geen & E. C. O'Neal (Eds.), *Perspectives on aggression* (pp. 133–168). New York: Academic Press.

Donnerstein, E., & Hallam, J. (1978). Faciliating effects of erotica on aggression against women. *Journal of Personality and Social Psychology, 11,* 1270–1277.

Donnerstein, E., & Wilson, D. W. (1976). Effects of noise and perceived control on ongoing and subsequent aggressive behavior. *Journal of Personality and Social Psychology, 34,* 774–781.

Drabman, R. S., & Thomas, M. H. (1974). Does media violence increase children's toleration of real-life aggression? *Developmental Psychology, 10,* 418–421.

Drabman, R. S., & Thomas, M. H. (1975). Does TV violence breed indifference? *Journal of Communication, 25,* 86–89.

Drabman, R. S., & Thomas, M. H. (1976). Does watching violence on television cause apathy? *Pediatrics, 57,* 329–331.

Ebbesen, E. B., Duncan, B., & Konecni, V. J. (1975). Effects of content of verbal aggression on future verbal aggression: A field experiment. *Journal of Experimental Social Psychology, 11,* 192–204.

Egger, M. D., & Flynn, J. P. (1963). Effect of electrical stimulation of the amygdala on hypothalamically elicited behavior in cats. *Journal of Neurophysiology, 26,* 705–720.

Eichelman, B. (1983). The limbic system and aggression in humans. *Neuroscience and Biobehavioral Reviews, 7,* 391–394.

Eron, L. D., & Huesmann, L. R. (1984). The control of aggressive behavior by changes in attitudes, values, and the conditions of learning. In R. J. Blanchard & D. C. Blanchard (Eds.), *Advances in the study of aggression* (Vol. 1, pp. 139–173). Orlando, FL: Academic Press.

Eron, L. D., & Heusmann, L. R. (1985). The role of television in the development of prosocial and antisocial behavior. In D. Olweus, D., Block, J., & M. Radke-Yarrow, (Eds.), *Development of antisocial and prosocial behavior: Research, theories, and issues* (pp. 285–314). Orlando, FL: Academic Press.

Felson, R. B., & Tedeschi, J. T. (Eds.). (1993). *Aggression and violence: Social interactionist perspectives*. Washington, DC: American Psychological Association.

Feshbach, S. (1970). Aggression. In P. H. Mussen (Ed.), *Carmichael's manual of child psychology* (Vol. 2, pp. 159–259). New York: Wiley.

Freud, S. (1959). *Beyond the pleasure principle*. New York: Bantam Books.

Freud, S. (1963). Why war? In P. Reiff (Ed.), *Freud: Character and culture* (pp. 134–147). New York: Collier Books.

Ganter, A. B., & Taylor, S. P. (1992). Human physical aggression as a function of alcohol and threat of harm. *Aggressive Behavior, 18,* 29–36.

Geen, R. G. (1976). *Personality: The skein of behavior*. St. Louis, MO: C. V. Mosby.

Geen, R. G. (1991). *Human aggression*. Pacific Grove, CA: Brooks/Cole.

Geen, R. G. (1995). *Human motivation: A social-psychological approach*. Pacific Grove, CA: Brooks/Cole.

Geen, R. G., & O'Neal, E. C. (1969). Activation of cue-elicited aggression by general arousal. *Journal of Personality and Social Psychology, 11,* 289–292.

Geen, R. G., & Stonner, D. (1971). Effects of aggressiveness habit strength on behavior in the presence of aggression-related stimuli. *Journal of Personality and Social Psychology, 17,* 149–153.

George, W. H., & Marlatt, G. A. (1986). The effects of alcohol and anger on interest in violence, erotica, and deviance. *Journal of Abnormal Psychology, 95,* 150–158.

Gerbner, G., Gross, L., Morgan, M., & Signorielli, N. (1986). Living with television: The dynamics of the cultivation process. In J. Bryant & D. Zillman (Eds.), *Perspectives on media effects* (pp. Hillsdale, NJ: Erlbaum.

Gerbner, G., Gross, L., Signorielli, N., Morgan, M., & Jackson-Beeck, M. (1979). The demonstration of power: Violence profile No. 10. *Journal of Communication, 29,* 177–196.

Gorenstein, E. E. (1990). Neuropsychology of juvenile delinquency. *Forensic Reports, 3,* 15–48.

Goumeniouk, A. D., & Clark, C. M. (1992). Prefrontal lobotomy and hypofrontality in patients with schizophrenia: An integration of the findings. *Canadian Journal of Psychiatry, 37,* 17–22.

Goy, R. W. (1970). Early hormonal influences on the development of sexual and sex-related behavior. In F. O. Schmitt (Ed.), *The neurosciences* (pp. 167–207). New York: Rockefeller University Press.

Heinrichs, R. W. (1989). Frontal cerebral lesions and violent incidents in chronic neuropsychiatric patients. *Biological Psychiatry, 25,* 174–178.

Home Office Research Study (1977). *Screen violence and film censorship* (No. 40). London: HMSO.

Huesmann, L. R., & Miller, L. S. (1994). Long-term effects of repeated exposure to media violence in childhood. In L. R. Huesmann (Ed.), *Aggressive behavior: Current perspectives* (pp. 153–186). New York: Plenum.

Hull, J. G., & Bond, C. F., Jr. (1986). Social and behavioral consequences of alcohol consumption and expectancy: A meta-analysis. *Psychological Bulletin, 99,* 347–360.

Jacobs, P. A., Brunton, M., & Melville, M. M. (1965). Aggressive behavior, mental subnormality, and the XYY male. *Nature, 208,* 1351–1352.

Jarvik, L. F., Klodin, V., & Matsuyama, S. S. (1973). Human aggression and the extra Y chromosome: Fact or fantasy? *American Psychologist, 28,* 674–682.

Jasper, H. H., & Rasmussion, T. (1958). Studies of clinical and electrical responses to deep temporal stimulation in man with some consideration of functional anatomy. *Association for Research in Nervous and Mental Diseases Proceedings, 36,* 316–334.

Jeavons, C. M., & Taylor, S. P. (1985). The control of alcohol-related aggression: Redirecting the inebriate's attention to socially appropriate conduct. *Aggressive Behavior, 11,* 93–101.

Johnson, R. N. (1972). *Aggression in man and animals.* Philadelphia: Saunders.

Julian, T., & McHenry, P. C. (1989). Relationship of testosterone to men's family functioning at mid-life: A research. *Aggressive Behavior, 15,* 281–289.

Koss, M. P., Gidycz, C. A., & Wisniewski, N. (1987). The scope of rape: Incidence and prevalence of sexual aggression and victimization in a national sample of higher education students. *Journal of Consulting and Clinical Psychology, 55,* 162–170.

Lang, A. R., Goeckner, D. J., Adesso, V. J., & Marlatt, G. A. (1975). Effects of alcohol on aggression in male social drinkers. *Journal of Abnormal Psychology, 84,* 508–518.

Lang, A. R., Searles, J., Lauerman, R., & Adesso, V. (1980). Expectancy, alcohol, and sex guilt as determinants of interest in and reaction to sexual stimuli. *Journal of Abnormal Psychology, 89,* 644–653.

Leonard, K. E. (1989). The impact of explicit aggressive and implicit nonaggressive cues on aggression in intoxicated and sober males. *Personality and Social Psychology Bulletin, 15,* 390–400.

Leyens, J. P., Camino, L., Parke, R. D., & Berkowitz, L. (1975). Effects of movie violence on aggression in a field setting as a function of group dominance and cohesion. *Journal of Personality and Social Psychology, 32,* 346–360.

Liebert, R. M., & Baron, R. A. (1972). Some immediate effects of televised violence on children's behavior. *Developmental Psychology, 6,* 469–475.

Linz, D., Donnerstein, E., & Penrod, S. (1988). Effects of long-term exposure to violent and sexually degrading depictions of women. *Journal of Personality and Social Psychology, 55,* 758–768.

Lombroso, C. (1876). *L'Uomo delinquente.* Turin, Italy: Bocca.

Lorenz, K. (1966). *On aggression.* New York: Harcourt, Brace, & World.

Lorenz, K. (1974). *Civilized man's eight deadly sins.* New York: Harcourt Brace Jovanovich.

Ludwig, A. M., Marx, A. J., Hill, P. A., & Browning, R. M. (1969). The control of violent behavior through faradic shock. *Journal of Nervous and Mental Disease, 148,* 624–637.

Malamuth, N. M., & Check, J. V. P. (1981). The effects of media exposure on acceptance of violence against women: A field experiment. *Journal of Research in Personality, 15,* 436–446.

Malamuth, N. M., & Check, J. V. P. (1984). Debriefing effectiveness following exposure to pornographic rape depictions. *Journal of Sex Research, 20,* 1–13.

Malamuth, N. M, & Donnerstein, E. (Eds.). (1984). *Pornography and sexual aggression.* Orlando, FL: Academic Press.

Malamuth, N. M., Heim, M., & Feshbach, S. (1980). Sexual responsiveness of college students to rape depictions: Inhibitory and disinhibitory effects. *Journal of Personality and Social Psychology, 38,* 399–408.

Mallick, S. K., & McCandless, B. R. (1966). A study of catharsis of aggression. *Journal of Personality and Social Psychology, 4,* 591–596.

Marine, G. (1966). I've got nothing against the colored, understand. *Ramparts, 5,* 13–18.

Mednick, S. A., Garbrielli, W. F., Jr., & Hutchings, B. (1987). Genetic factors in the etiology of criminal behavior. In S. A. Mednick, T. E. Moffitt, & S. A. Stack (Eds.), *The causes of crime: New biological approaches* (pp. 74–91). New York: Cambridge University Press.

Mednick, S. A., Pollock, V., Volavka, J., & Gabrielli, W. F. Jr. (1982). Biology and violence. In M. E. Wolfgang & N. A. Weiner (Eds.), *Criminal Violence* (pp. 21–80). Beverly Hills: Sage.

Meyer-Bahlburg, H. F. L., & Ehrhardt, A. A. (1982). Prenatal sex hormones and human aggression: A review, and new data on progestogen effects. *Aggressive Behavior, 8,* 39–62.

Miller, B. A., Downs, W. R., & Gondoli, D. M. (1989). Spousal violence among alcoholic woman as compared to a random household sample of women. *Journal of Studies on Alcohol, 50,* 533–540.

Moyer, K. E. (1976). *The psychobiology of aggression.* New York: Harper & Row.

Muehlenhard, C. L., & Linton, M. A. (1987). Date rape and sexual aggression in dating situations: Incidence and risk factors. *Journal of Counseling Psychology, 34,* 186–196.

Mullin, C. R., & Linz, D. (1995). Desensitization and resensitization to violence against women: Effects of exposure to sexually violent films on judgments of domestic violence victims. *Journal of Personality and Social Psychology, 3,* 449–459.

Murdoch, D., Phil, R. O., & Ross, D. (1990). Alcohol and crimes of violence: Present issues. *International Journal of Addictions, 25,* 1065–1081.

Murry, J. P., & Kippax, S. (1979). From the early window to the late night show: International trends in the study of television's impact on children and adults. In L. Berkowitz (Ed.), *Advances in experimental social psychology* (Vol. 12, pp. 253–320). New York: Academic Press.

Novaco, R. W. (1975). *Anger control: The development and evaluation of an experimental treatment.* Lexington, MA: Lexington Books.

Newman, J. P. (1987). Reactions to punishment in extraverts and psychopaths: Implications for the impulsive behavior of disinhibited individuals. *Journal of Research in Personality, 21,* 464–480.

Nisbet, R. E. (1993). Violence and U.S. regional culture. *American Psychologist, 4,* 441–449.

O'Callaghan, M. A. J., & Carroll, D. (1987). The role of psychosurgical studies in the control of antisocial behavior. In S. A. Mednick, T. E. Moffitt, & S. A. Stack (Eds.), *The causes of crime: New biological approaches* (pp. 312–328). Cambridge, UK: Cambridge, MA.

Olweus, D. (1986). Aggression and hormones: Behavioral relationship with testosterone and adrenaline. In D. Olweus, J. Block, & M. Radke-Yarrow (Eds.), *Development of antisocial and prosocial behavior: Research, theories, and issues* (pp. 51–72). Orlando, FL: Academic Press.

Oskamp, S. (1984). *Applied social psychology.* Englewood Cliffs, NJ: Prentice Hall.

Osofsky, J. D. (1995). The effects of exposure to violence on young children. *American Psychologist, 50,* 782–788.

Osofsky, J. D., Wewers, S., Hann, D. M., & Fick, A. C. (1993). Chronic community violence: What is happening to our children? *Psychiatry, 56,* 36–45.

Patterson, G. R., Reid, J. B., Jones, R. R., & Conger, R. E. (1975). *A social learning approach to family intervention, Vol. 1: Families with aggressive children.* Eugene, OR: Castalia.

Parke, R. D., Berkowitz, L., Leyens, J. P., West, S. G., & Sebastian, J. (1977). Some effects of violence and nonviolent movies on the behavior of juvenile delinquents. In L. Berkowitz (Ed.), *Advances in experimental social psychology* (Vol. 10, pp. 135–172). New York: Academic Press.

Patterson, G. R., Littman, R. A., & Bricker, W. A. (1967). Assertive behavior in children: A step toward a theory of aggression. *Monographs of the Society for Research in Child Development, 32,* (5, Serial No. 113).

Pecjak, A. (1993). *How it is possible?* Paper presented at the 3rd Alps-Adria Symposium of Psychology, Ljubljana, Slovinia.

Pernanen, F. (1981). Theoretical aspects of the between alcohol use and crime. In J. Collins (Ed.), *Drinking and crime* (pp. 1–69). New York: Guilford.

Peterson, J. L., & Zill, N. (1981). Television viewing in the United States and children's intellectual, social, and emotional development. *Television and Children, 2,* 21–28.

Peterson, R. D., & Bailey, W. C. (1988). Murder and capital punishment in the evolving context of the post-Furman era. *Social Forces, 66,* 774–657.

Plomin, R., DeFries, J. C., & McClearn, G. E. (1990). *Behavior genetics: A primer* (2nd ed.). New York: W. H. Freeman.

Plomin, R., Foch, T. T., & Rowe, D. C. (1981). Bobo Clown aggression in children: Environment not genes. *Journal of Research in Personality, 15,* 331–342.

Price, W. H., & Whatmore, P. B. (1967). Behavior disorders and pattern of crime among XYY males identified at a maximum security hospital. *British Medical Journal, 1,* 533–536.

Puhar, I. (1993). On childhood origins of violence in Yugoslavia: II. The Zadruga. *The Journal of Psychohistory, 21,* 171–198.

Richardson, D. (1981). The effects of alcohol on male violence toward female targets. *Motivation and Emotion, 5,* 333–344.

Richardson, D. R., & Hammock, G. S. (1991). Alcohol and acquaintance rape. In A. Parrot & L. Bechofer (Eds.), *Acquaintance rape: The hidden crime* (pp. 83–95). New York: Wiley.

Robinson, J. P. (1972). Television's impact on everyday life: Some cross-national evidence. In E. A. Rubinstein, G. A. Comstock, & J. P. Murray (Eds.). *Television and social behavior:* Vol. 4.: *Television in day-to-day life: Patterns of use* (pp. 410–431). Washington, DC: Government Printing Office.

Rogers, R. W. (1980). Expressions of aggression: Aggression-inhibiting effects of anonymity to authority and threatened retaliation. *Personality and Social Psychology Bulletin, 6,* 315–320.

Ronka, A., & Pulkkinen, L. (1995). Accumulation of problems in social functioning in young adulthood: A developmental approach. *Journal of Personality and Social Psychology, 69,* 381–391.

Rubinstein, E. A. (1978). Television and the young viewer. *American Scientist, 66,* 685–693.

Rushton, J. P., Fulker, D. W., Neale, M. C., Nias, D. K. B., & Eysenck, H. J. (1986). Altruism and aggression: The heritability of individual differences. *Journal of Personality and Social Psychology, 50,* 1192–1198.

Russell, D. E. H. (1982). *Rape in marriage.* New York: Macmillan.

Schalling, D. (1987). Personality correlates of plasma testosterone levels in young delinquents: An example of person-situation interaction? In S. A. Mednick, T. E. Moffitt, & S. A. Stack (Eds.), *The causes of crime: New biological approaches* (pp. 283–291). New York: Cambridge University Press.

Schneider, B. H. (1991). A comparison of skill-building and desensitization strategies for intervention with aggressive children. *Aggressive Behavior, 17,* 301–311.

Schneider, B. H., & Byrne, B. M. (1987). Individualizing social skills training for behaviour-disordered children. *Journal of Consulting and Clinical Psychology, 55,* 444–445.

Scully, D., & Marolla, J. (1984). Convicted rapists' vocabulary of motive: Excuses and justifications. *Social Problems, 31,* 530–544.

Segal, N. L. (1993). Twin, sibling, and adoption methods: Tests of evolutionary hypothesis. *American Psychologist, 48,* 943–956.

Shapiro, D. L., Buttner, E. H., & Barry, B. (1994). Explanations: What factors effect their perceived accuracy? *Organizational Behavior and Human Decision Processes, 58,* 346–368.

Sherman, L. W., & Berk, R. A. (1984). The Minneapolis domestic violence experiment. *Police Foundation Reports (April).* Washington, DC: Police Foundation.

Siann, G. (1985). Accounting for aggression: Perspectives on aggression and violence. Boston: Allen & Unwin.

Silver, J. M., & Yudofsky, S. C. (1987). Aggressive behavior in patients with neuropsychiatric disorders. *Psychiatric Annals, 17,* 367–370.

Singer, J. L., Singer, D. G., & Rapaczynski, W. S. (1984). Family patterns and television viewing as predictors of children's beliefs and aggression. *Journal of Communication, 34,* 73–89.

Spellacy, F. (1978). Neuropsychological discrimination between violent and non-violent men. *Journal of Clinical Psychology, 34,* 49–52.

Staub, E. (1989). *The roots of evil: The origins of genocide and other group violence.* New York: Cambridge University Press.

Staub, E. (1992). The origins of caring, helping and nonaggression: Parental socialization, the family system, schools, and cultural influences. In S. Oliner, P. Oliner, L. Baron, L. A. Blum, D. L. Krebs, & M. Z. Smolenska (Eds.), *Embracing the other: Philosophical, psychological, and historical perspectives on altruism* (pp. 390–412). New York: New York University Press.

Staub, E. (1996). Cultural-societal roots of violence: The examples of genocidal violence and of contemporary youth violence in the United States. *American Psychologist, 51,* 117–132.

Staub, E. (in press). Breaking the cycle of violence: Helping victims of genocidal violence heal. *Journal of Personal and Interpersonal Loss.*

Steele, C. M., & Josephs, R. A. (1990). Alcohol myopia: Its prized and dangerous effects. *American Psychologist, 45,* 921–933.

Stock, W. (1985, May). Women's affective responses and subjective reactions to exposure pornography. Paper presented at the meeting of the Midwestern Psychological Association, Chicago.

Straus, M. A., & Gelles, R. J. (1990). *Physical violence in American families: Risk factors and adaptations to violence in 8,145 families.* New Brunswick, NJ: Transaction.

Surgeon General's Scientific Advisory Committee on Television and Social Behavior. (1972). *Television and growing up: The impact of televised violence.* Washington, DC: U.S. Government Printing Office.

Taylor, L. (1992). Relationship between affect and memory: Motivational-based selective generation. *Journal of Personality and Social Psychology, 62,* 876–882.

Taylor, S. P. (1980). *Nonaggressive models in the prevention of collective violence.* Personal communication, Kent State University.

Taylor, S. P., & Gammon, C. B. (1976). Aggressive behavior of intoxicated subjects: The effects of third-party intervention. *Journal of Studies on Alcohol, 37,* 917–930.

Taylor, S. P., Grammon, C. B., & Capasso, D. R. (1976). Aggression as a function of the interaction of alcohol and threat. *Journal of Personality and Social Psychology, 34,* 938–941.

Taylor, S. P., & Leonard, K. E. (1983). Alcohol and human physical aggression. In R. G. & E. I. Donnerstein (Eds.), *Aggression: Theoretical and empirical reviews* (Vol. 2, pp. 77–101). New York: Academic Press.

Taylor, S. P., & Sears, J. D. (1988). The effects of alcohol and persuasive social pressure on human physical aggression. *Aggressive Behavior, 14,* 237–243.

Toch, H. (1985). *Violent men* (Rev. ed.). Cambridge, MA: Schenkman.

Ulrich, R. E., Johnston, M., Richardson, J., & Wolff, P. (1963). The operant conditioning of fighting behavior in rats. *Psychological Record, 13,* 465–470.

U.S. National Commission on the Causes and Prevention of Violence. (1970). *To establish justice, to insure domestic tranquility: The final report.* New York: Praeger.

Violent television heroines having bad effect on girls. (1996, February 6). Louisville (KY). *Courier Journal,* p. B6 .

Weiner, B., Amirkham, J., Folkes, V. S., & Verette, J. A. (1987). An attributional analysis of excuse giving: Studies of a naive theory of emotion. *Journal of Personality and Social Psychology, 52,* 316–324.

Wilson, E. O. (1975). *Sociobiology: The new synthesis.* Cambridge, MA: Belknap Press of Harvard University Press.

Wilson, E. O. (1978). *On human nature.* Cambridge, MA: Harvard University Press.

Witkin, H. A., Mednick, S. A., Schulsinger, F., Bakkestrom, E., Christiansen, K. O., Goodenough, D. R., Hirschhorn, K., Lundsteen, C., Owen, R. D., Philip, J., Rubin, D. B., & Stocking, M. (1976). Criminality in XYY and XXY men. *Science, 193,* 547–555.

Wood, W., Wong, F. Y., & Chachere, J. G. (1991). Effects of media violence on viewers' aggression in unconstrained social interaction. *Psychological Bulletin, 109,* 371–383.

Zillmann, D. (1988). Cognitive-excitation interdependencies in aggressive behavior. *Aggressive Behavior, 14,* 51–64.

Zillmann, D., Katcher, A. H., & Milavsky, B. (1972). Excitation transfer from physical exercise to subsequent aggressive behavior. *Journal of Experimental Social Psychology, 8,* 247–259.

Author Index

Subject Index

Credits

Photo Credits

TO THE OWNER OF THIS BOOK:

I hope that you have found *The Psychology of Personality: Viewpoints, Research, and Applications* useful. So that this book can be improved in a future edition, would you take the time to complete this sheet and return it? Thank you.

School and address: _____

Department: _____

Instructor's name: _____

1. What I like most about this book is: _____

_____

_____

2. What I like least about this book is: _____

_____

_____

3. My general reaction to this book is: _____

_____

4. The name of the course in which I used this book is: _____

_____

5. Were all of the chapters of the book assigned for you to read? _____

   If not, which ones weren't? _____

 6. In the space below, or on a separate sheet of paper, please write specific suggestions for improving this book and anything else you'd care to share about your experience in using the book.

_____

_____

_____

_____

_____

Optional:

Your name: _____ Date: _____

May Brooks/Cole quote you, either in promotion for *The Psychology of Personality: Viewpoints, Research, and Applications* or in future publishing ventures?

Yes: _____ No: _____

Sincerely,

Bernardo J. Carducci